CW01653259

THE ROUTLEDGE HANDB(COLLECTIVE RESPONSIBILITY

The Routledge Handbook of Collective Responsibility comprehensively addresses questions about who is responsible and how blame or praise should be attributed when human agents act together. Such questions include: Do individuals share responsibility for the outcome or are individuals responsible only for their contribution to the act? Are individuals responsible for actions done by their group even when they don't contribute to the outcome? Can a corporation or institution be held morally responsible apart from the responsibility of its members?

The *Handbook's* 35 chapters—all appearing here for the first time and written by an international team of experts—are organized into four parts:

Part I: Foundations of Collective Responsibility
Part II: Theoretical Issues in Collective Responsibility
Part III: Domains of Collective Responsibility
Part IV: Applied Issues in Collective Responsibility

Each part begins with a short introduction that provides an overview of issues and debates within that area and a brief summary of its chapters. In addition, a comprehensive index allows readers to better navigate the entirety of the volume's contents. The result is the first major work in the field that serves as an instructional aid for those in advanced undergraduate courses and graduate seminars, as well as a reference for scholars interested in learning more about collective responsibility.

Saba Bazargan-Forward is Associate Professor of Philosophy at the University of California, San Diego, USA. He works on issues in normative ethics, including complicity, defensive violence, war-ethics, and the morality of benefitting from injustice. He is currently authoring a book on individual responsibility for cooperatively committed harms.

Deborah Tollefsen is Professor of Philosophy at the University of Memphis, USA. She is the author of more than 40 articles on topics such as group agency, group epistemology, and collective responsibility, as well as the book *Groups as Agents* (2015).

Routledge Handbooks in Philosophy

Routledge Handbooks in Philosophy are state-of-the-art surveys of emerging, newly refreshed, and important fields in philosophy, providing accessible yet thorough assessments of key problems, themes, thinkers, and recent developments in research.

All chapters for each volume are specially commissioned, and written by leading scholars in the field. Carefully edited and organized, *Routledge Handbooks in Philosophy* provide indispensable reference tools for students and researchers seeking a comprehensive overview of new and exciting topics in philosophy. They are also valuable teaching resources as accompaniments to textbooks, anthologies, and research-orientated publications.

Also available:

The Routledge Handbook of Social Epistemology
Edited by Miranda Fricker, Peter J. Graham, David Henderson, and Nikolaj J.L.L. Pedersen

The Routledge Handbook of Philosophy of the City
Edited by Sharon M. Meagher, Samantha Noll, and Joseph S. Biehl

The Routledge Handbook of Panpsychism
Edited by William Seager

The Routledge Handbook of Philosophy of Relativism
Edited by Martin Kusch

The Routledge Handbook of Philosophy of Colour
Edited by Derek H. Brown and Fiona Macpherson

The Routledge Handbook of Metaphysical Grounding
Edited by Michael J. Raven

The Routledge Handbook of Collective Responsibility
Edited by Saba Bazargan-Forward and Deborah Tollefsen

For more information about this series, please visit:
https://www.routledge.com/Routledge-Handbooks-in-Philosophy/book-series/RHP

THE ROUTLEDGE HANDBOOK OF COLLECTIVE RESPONSIBILITY

Edited by
Saba Bazargan-Forward and
Deborah Tollefsen

Routledge
Taylor & Francis Group
NEW YORK AND LONDON

First published 2020
by Routledge
605 Third Avenue, New York, NY 10017

and by Routledge
2 Park Square, Milton Park, Abingdon, Oxon, OX14 4RN

First issued in paperback 2021

Routledge is an imprint of the Taylor & Francis Group, an informa business

© 2020 Taylor & Francis

The right of Saba Bazargan-Forward and Deborah Tollefsen to be identified as the authors of the editorial material, and of the authors for their individual chapters, has been asserted in accordance with sections 77 and 78 of the Copyright, Designs and Patents Act 1988.

All rights reserved. No part of this book may be reprinted or reproduced or utilised in any form or by any electronic, mechanical, or other means, now known or hereafter invented, including photocopying and recording, or in any information storage or retrieval system, without permission in writing from the publishers.

Trademark notice: Product or corporate names may be trademarks or registered trademarks, and are used only for identification and explanation without intent to infringe.

ISBN 13: 978-1-138-09224-2 (hbk)
ISBN 13: 978-1-03-223666-7 (pbk)

DOI: 10.4324/9781315107608

Library of Congress Cataloging-in-Publication Data
A catalog record for this title has been requested

ISBN: 978-1-138-09224-2 (hbk)
ISBN: 978-1-315-10760-8 (ebk)

Typeset in Bembo
by Newgen Publishing UK

CONTENTS

LIST OF CONTRIBUTORS

Caroline T. Arruda is Associate Professor of Philosophy at the University of Texas at El Paso. Her work focuses on issues at the intersection of philosophy of action and metaethics and has appeared in journals such as *Australasian Journal of Philosophy*, *Analysis*, *Mind & Language*, *The Journal of the American Philosophical Association*, among others. She has been a Visiting Researcher at the Center for the Study of Mind in Nature at the University of Oslo and an Academic Visitor at the Australian National University. She is currently at work on a monograph entitled *Enriching Practical Reason*.

Gunnar Björnsson is Professor of Practical Philosophy at Stockholm University. He works on issues in metaethics, moral responsibility, collective moral agency, and philosophy of language, with recent work appearing in, among other publications, *Mind*, *Noûs*, *Ethics*, and *Philosophy and Phenomenological Research*.

Olle Blomberg is a researcher at the Department of Philosophy, Linguistics and Theory of Science at the University of Gothenburg, Sweden. He received his PhD from the University of Edinburgh in 2013. He has published mainly on topics within philosophy of action, collective intentionality, and the philosophy of cognitive science.

Liam Kofi Bright is Assistant Professor of Philosophy, Logic, and Scientific Method at the London School of Economics and Political Science. His current research focuses on social epistemology, looking especially at how the institutional arrangement of science helps or hinders our ability to produce and disseminate knowledge.

Stephanie Collins is Senior Research Fellow at the Australian Catholic University. She has published widely on collective responsibility. Her second book, *Group Duties: Their Existence and Their Implications for Individuals*, was published in 2019. Her first book, *The Core of Care Ethics*, was published in 2015.

David Copp is Distinguished Professor of Philosophy, Emeritus, at the University of California, Davis. He is author of *Morality, Normativity, and Society* (1995) and *Morality in a Natural World*

(2007), and he has edited several anthologies, including *The Oxford Handbook of Ethical Theory* (2006). He is editor of a monograph series with Oxford University Press called "Oxford Moral Theory." He has published and lectured widely on topics in moral and political philosophy.

Michael D. Doan is Assistant Professor of Philosophy at Eastern Michigan University. His research interests are in social epistemology, social and political philosophy, and moral psychology. He is the author of "Resisting Structural Epistemic Injustice," *Feminist Philosophical Quarterly* (forthcoming), and "Epistemic Injustice and Epistemic Redlining," *Ethics and Social Welfare* (2017).

Robin Downie is Emeritus Professor of Moral Philosophy at Glasgow University. Recent books include: *The Philosophy of Palliative Care* (2006, with Fiona Randall), *Bioethics and the Humanities* (2007, with Jane Macnaughton), and *End of Life Choices* (2009, with Fiona Randall).

Wim Dubbink is Professor of Philosophy at Tilburg University in the Netherlands. His research is focused on the development of a Kantian theory of the market, which involves both a moral theory of the duties of individual market actors and a political theory of the market within liberal democracies. He is the author of *Assisting the Invisible Hand: Contested Relations Between Market, State and Civil Society* (2003) and is currently editor of *The Journal of Ethics.*

Anton Eriksson is a PhD student at the Department of Philosophy at the University of Sheffield. His thesis work focuses on climate ethics and the issue of moral responsibility for GHG emissions in global supply chains.

Peter A. French is Emeritus Professor of Philosophy at Arizona State University. He was the Lincoln Professor of Ethics and the Founding Director of the Lincoln Center for Applied Ethics and its Director at ASU. He is the author of 21 books including *War and Moral Dissonance* (2012); *The Virtues of Vengeance* (2012); *Ethics and College Sports* (2004); *Corporate Ethics* (1998); *Cowboy Metaphysics* (1997); *Responsibility Matters* (1992); *Collective and Corporate Responsibility* (1987); *Ethics in Government* (1983); and *The Scope of Morality* (1980).

Shannon Fyfe is Assistant Professor of Philosophy at George Mason University, where she is also a Faculty Fellow at the Institute for Philosophy and Public Policy. She recently published *International Criminal Tribunals: A Normative Defense* (with Larry May) in 2017.

Margaret Gilbert is Melden Chair in Moral Philosophy and Distinguished Professor of Philosophy at the University of California, Irvine. Her many books include, most recently, *Rights and Demands* (2018) and *Joint Commitment: How We Make the Social World* (2014).

Michael O. Hardimon is Professor of Philosophy at the University of California San Diego. Before teaching there he taught at Harvard University and MIT. His writings include "Role Obligations" (*Journal of Philosophy*, 1994), *Hegel's Social Philosophy: The Project of Reconciliation* (1994), and *Rethinking Race: The Case for Deflationary Realism* (2017).

Kendy M. Hess is Brake Smith Associate Professor of Social Philosophy and Ethics at the College of the Holy Cross. She has a JD from Harvard Law School and a PhD from the University of Colorado. Her research currently focuses on developing a metaphysically robust theory of group agency, which will justify ascribing moral obligations to corporations without granting them personhood. Her recent books include *Collectivity: Ontology, Ethics, and Social Justice* (2018, edited with Tracy Isaacs and Violetta Igneski) and *Nonviolence as a Way of Life: History, Theory, Practice* (2017, edited with Predrag Cicovacki).

Frank Hindriks is Professor of Ethics, Social and Political Philosophy at the Faculty of Philosophy of the University of Groningen and director of the Centre of Philosophy, Politics and Economics (PPE). He is one of the founding editors of the *Journal of Social Ontology*. He has published on topics within economic methodology, moral psychology, and social ontology.

Bryce Huebner is Provost's Distinguished Associate Professor of Philosophy at Georgetown University. He is the author of *Macrocognition: A theory of distributed minds and collective intentionality* (2015), and the editor of *The Philosophy of Daniel Dennett* (2018). His current research focuses on the role of reinforcement learning in social cognition, the relationships between individual and group agency, and the nature of emotional states.

Violetta Igneski is Associate Professor of Philosophy at McMaster University in Canada. Her primary research interests include the nature and limits of our individual and collective duties of beneficence and also their connection to human rights. She has co-edited (with Tracy Isaacs and Kendy M. Hess) *Collectivity: Ontology, Ethics, and Social Justice* (2018).

Christopher Kutz is C. William Maxeiner Distinguished Professor of Law in the Jurisprudence & Social Policy Program at Berkeley Law School, UC Berkeley. He is the author of *Complicity: Ethics and Law for a Collective Age* (2001, reissued 2007) and, most recently, *On War and Democracy* (2016). He is currently working on the ethics of climate change.

Holly Lawford-Smith is Senior Lecturer in Political Philosophy at the University of Melbourne, and a Research Associate at the Australian National University. She works mainly within social philosophy, with a focus on collective agency and responsibility.

Kirk Ludwig is Professor of Philosophy and Cognitive Science at Indiana University, Bloomington. He works in the philosophy of language, philosophy of mind and action, epistemology, and metaphysics. His most recent books are *From Individual to Plural Agency: Collective Action 1* (2016), *From Plural to Institutional Agency: Collective Action 2* (2017), and *The Routledge Handbook of Collective Intentionality* (2018, edited with Marija Jankovic).

Pekka Mäkelä is the head of discipline in Practical Philosophy and the coordinator of the Centre for Philosophy of Social Science (TINT) in the Faculty of Social Sciences at the University of Helsinki. He is an editor of *Trust: Analytic and Applied Perspectives* (2013).

Gregory Mellema is Professor of Philosophy at Calvin College. He has published in 30 different peer-reviewed journals, including *American Philosophical Quarterly*, *Canadian Journal of Philosophy*, *Philosophical Studies*, *Australasian Journal of Philosophy*, *Journal of Ethics*, *Analysis*, and *Philosophia*. His book, *The Expectations of Morality*, appeared in 2004.

Seumas Miller holds research appointments at Charles Sturt University, Delft University of Technology, and the University of Oxford. He is the author or coauthor of over 200 academic articles and 20 books, including *Social Action* (2001) and *Moral Foundations of Social Institutions* (2010).

Avia Pasternak is Associate Professor at the Department of Political Science, The School of Public Policy, University College London.

Björn Petersson is Associate Professor in Practical Philosophy, Lund University. His research focuses on collective intentions and actions ("Collectivity and Circularity", *Journal of Philosophy* 2007), and the implications of such analyses for practical rationality ("Team Reasoning and Collective Intentionality" *Review of Philosophy and Psychology* 2017) and for responsibility ("Co-responsibility and Causal Involvement" *Philosophia* 2013).

Maura Priest is Assistant Professor of Philosophy and Bioethicist at Arizona State University. She has published over 20 articles in ethics, epistemology, and collective action. She is currently working on a book for Routledge about elites and elitism.

Linda Radzik is Professor of Philosophy at Texas A&M University. The author of *Making Amends: Atonement in Morality, Law, and Politics* (2009), her research addresses moral, legal, and political issues that emerge in the aftermath of wrongdoing. She has published on topics such as forgiveness, criminal punishment, and political reconciliation. Radzik's most recent work explores bystanders' responses to wrongdoing and the ethics of social punishment.

Juha Räikkä is Professor of Philosophy and the Dean of the Faculty of Social Sciences at the University of Turku, Finland. He is the author of *Social Justice in Practice* (2014) and a co-editor of *Adaptation and Autonomy* (2013).

Abraham Sesshu Roth is Professor in the Philosophy Department at Ohio State University. He has taught at UCLA and at the University of Illinois at Chicago, and received his PhD from Princeton. He works mainly in the philosophy of action, focusing on issues concerning intentions, practical reasoning, reasons explanation, shared agency, and related issues in epistemology and moral psychology. He has published in *The Philosophical Review*, *Noûs*, *Ethics*, *Oxford Studies in Agency and Responsibility*, *Philosophy and Phenomenological Research*, *Stanford Encyclopedia of Philosophy*, and *Philosophical Studies*.

Carol Rovane is Professor of Philosophy at Columbia University. She is the author of *The Bounds of Agency: An Essay in Revisionary Metaphysics* (1998) and *The Metaphysics and Ethics of Relativism* (2013) and numerous articles on interrelated topics such as the first person, personal identity, relativism, the foundations of value, group vs. individual responsibility, and some new problems for liberal theory.

Hans Bernhard Schmid is Professor for Social and Political Philosophy at the University of Vienna. His areas of research include social and political philosophy, philosophy of the social sciences, social ontology, and phenomenology.

Anne Schwenkenbecher is Lecturer in Philosophy at Murdoch University in Western Australia. Her PhD in Philosophy is from Humboldt University of Berlin. Much of her current research revolves around the ideas of collective agency and morality of groups. Further interests include social epistemology, environmental philosophy, ethics of political violence, and activism. Her first book *Terrorism: A Philosophical Enquiry* was published in 2012. She is currently working on her second book titled *Collective Moral Obligations*. Her work has been published in journals such as *Ratio*, *Midwest Studies in Philosophy*, *The Monist*, and *Environmental Values*.

Amy J. Sepinwall is Associate Professor in the Department of Legal Studies and Business Ethics at Wharton, University of Pennsylvania, with training in law and philosophy. She writes on issues of shared responsibility, corporate personhood, and constitutional rights. Much of her work seeks to defend an account of liability to blame without fault, developed in articles addressing slavery reparations; citizen responsibility for national transgressions; complicity through material support; criminal liability for corporate executives; and parental responsibility for the crimes of their adolescent children.

Kenneth Shockley is Associate Professor at Colorado State University where he holds the Holmes Rolston III Chair in Environmental Ethics and Philosophy. His research interests are in the expression of environmental values in public policy, the ethical dimensions of climate policy, environmental justice, and collective responsibility. Currently, he is exploring the intersection of environmental ethics, climate ethics, and sustainable development. His work has appeared in such journals as *Philosophical Studies*, *Environmental Ethics*, *Environmental Values*, *Ethics, Policy, and Environment*, *Journal of Social Philosophy*, *Philosophy of the Social Sciences*, and *Philosophy and Public Policy Quarterly*.

Michael Skerker is Associate Professor in the Leadership, Ethics, and Law department at the US Naval Academy. His academic interests include professional ethics, just war theory, and moral pluralism. Publications include works on ethics and asymmetrical war, moral pluralism, intelligence ethics, and the book *An Ethics of Interrogation* (2010).

Jeffery Smith is Seattle University's Frank Shrontz Chair in Professional Ethics and Professor of Management in the Albers School of Business and Economics where he teaches ethics in the management, finance, and accounting programs. Professor Smith's research interests lie at the intersection of philosophy and business and have been published in journals such as *Business Ethics Quarterly*, *Ethical Theory and Moral Practice*, and the *Journal of Business Ethics*. He has held visiting appointments at Tilburg University in the Netherlands, the Janet Prindle Institute for Ethics and the Keck Graduate Institute.

Cassie Striblen is Associate Professor of Philosophy at West Chester University near Philadelphia, Pennsylvania. Her book, *Group Responsibility: A Narrative Account* (2014), attempts to explain shared responsibility for hate crime. Prior to academia, she taught public school and served as a US Peace Corps volunteer.

András Szigeti is Senior Lecturer in Practical Philosophy at Linköping University (Sweden) and an Associate Director and Research Fellow of the Lund Gothenburg Responsibility Project in Lund (Sweden). He serves as associate editor of the journal *Ethical Theory and Moral Practice*. He specializes in action theory, emotion theory, and the ethics and metaphysics of individual and collective responsibility. He has published among others in *Dialectica*, *Ethical Theory and Moral Practice*, the *Review of Philosophy and Psychology*, and the *Journal of Value Inquiry*.

Raimo Tuomela is Professor Emeritus of Philosophy, University of Helsinki, Finland; also permanent Visiting Professor of Philosophy, University of Munich. His recent books include *The Philosophy of Sociality* (2007) and *Social Ontology* (2013). His philosophical work was the subject of the book *Social Ontology and Collective Intentionality: Critical Essays on the Philosophy of Raimo Tuomela with His Responses* (2017, edited by Gerhard Preyer and Georg Peter).

INTRODUCTION

Deborah Tollefsen and Saba Bazargan-Forward

What is Collective Responsibility?

What "collective responsibility" means is hotly contested. There is no consensus in the literature regarding the meaning of the phrase "collective responsibility" (used interchangeably in some cases with group responsibility) and the phrase itself is unclear in at least two ways. First, the term "collective" often refers to lots of different types of groups, including committees, nation-states, corporations, aggregates such as the citizens of a state, task groups, and people unified by spatial location and context such as strangers on the beach. Second, scholars working on this topic will sometimes use the phrase "collective responsibility" to refer to the responsibility individuals have within a group for outcomes produced by their group, or for the contributions that they make to that outcome, or they use it to refer to the responsibility the group, itself, has for the outcomes of a group action. That is, some scholars will provide a theory of collective responsibility, which reduces to individual responsibility (a distributive account) whereas others will argue that in some cases the responsibility lies with the group itself and with no particular individual (a non-distributive account). The question "Who's responsible?" gets a different answer depending on different theories.

This handbook is no different in that the reader will notice the variable uses of the phrase. Although our authors have been instructed to be clear about how *they* are using the phrase, they were not instructed to use the phrase in a uniform way. The same goes for other frequently used terms such as "shared responsibility," "joint responsibility," "group responsibility," and so on.

Rather than using the phrase to identify a state of affairs in the world we think the phrase best describes an area of inquiry. Those working on collective responsibility are unified by their focus on certain types of questions. To motivate those questions, consider the following cases:

On July 8, 2017 8-year-old Stephen Ursey and his 11-year-old brother were swimming with their family in the waters of Panama Beach, Florida. A powerful riptide swept them away from their family and as their parents and several other people tried to save them, they were all overpowered and swept out into the ocean where they struggled to stay afloat and were unable to swim against the force of the tide to the shore. As they screamed for help, more people began to enter the water in an attempt to help but it became clear that tide was too strong to conquer individually. Each time an individual went out to save one person they were swept away. No one knows for sure where the idea came from or how it was initiated but people began to clasp hands at the edge of the water and they formed a human chain that extended 90 meters into the water. Seventy to eighty strangers formed the chain and did so at considerable risk to their own lives. Through their joint action more than 30 lives were saved.

The Raccoon River in central Iowa runs through one of the most intensely farmed regions of the nation. Agriculture is vital to the area's economy, but polluted runoff from farms poses an acute threat to the residents' tap water—and a daunting challenge to utilities struggling to keep the water clean. No one farmer is responsible for the pollution nor could any single farmer prevent it. But *together* those farms produce serious health risks to residents' tap water and have been linked directly to cancer and other poor health outcomes in those areas.

In 1996, Purdue Pharma (a privately held pharmaceutical company owned by members of the Sackler family) released a new prescription painkiller called OxyContin. The drug uses a controlled release mechanism to deliver large doses of a chemical closely related to heroin. Over the next two decades, Purdue aggressively pushed sales of OxyContin and the opioid addiction grew. From 1999 to 2017, almost 400,000 people[1] died from opioid overdoses.

In each of these cases, a collection of people did something, through their joint or aggregate actions, that produced a morally significant outcome. Who is responsible and how ought praise and blame be allocated? These are the central questions that unify the field of collective responsibility.

How is the Handbook Organized?

The handbook is divided into four parts. Each part begins with a short introduction that provides an overview of issues and debates within that area and a brief summary of its contents.

Part I of the handbook focuses on the metaphysical foundations of collective responsibility and theories of collective responsibility. Just as theories of individual moral responsibility begin with theories about individual action and agency, so too discussions of collective responsibility need to be informed by theories of joint action and shared or group agency. Those working within the field of collective intentionality have developed these theories over the past few decades. Within that field a central task is to explain the intentional structure of joint agency. Moral responsibility of individual human agents often rests on whether or not the individual intended to do X. So, too, shared responsibility and group responsibility is thought to rest, in part, on whether the individuals in the group intended the joint outcome or whether a group itself acted intentionally. One of the central issues uniting the contributions in this part of the handbook is whether collective agency and collective responsibility can be reduced to individual agency and responsibility or whether it requires for its analysis an anti-individualistic approach.

Part II of the handbook addresses a variety of theoretical issues within the domain of collective responsibility. One such issue asks: how can an individual bear responsibility for what the group, of which she is a part, does when that individual has limited to no control over the conduct of that group? Pinning responsibility for what the group does on any marginally contributing individual seems to violate a basic principle of ethics that says that an individual can only be morally responsible for events within her causal reach.

Another major issue concerns collective inaction or omission—the failure of a group to act. Should individuals who are capable of forming a group, but fail to do so, be responsible for the harms that that potential group could have prevented or rectified? The obligation of the bystander and the ways in which individuals might be complicit in group harms is discussed in a number of the contributions in this section. In addition, the possibility of group emotions such as guilt and their relation to collective responsibility, the concept of a commitment and its role in joint action and responsibility, collective obligation, and the possibility that groups are self-aware are all topics covered in this section.

Part III of the handbook focuses on collective responsibility in the context of politics, the sciences, law, and business ethics. The issue of collective responsibility shows up in myriad ways within each one of these several domains. Part IV of the volume focuses on specific applied issues in collective responsibility. Each topic in this part of the volume can be characterized under the heading of "collective responsibility *for.*"

What is the Goal of the Handbook?

The goal of the handbook is to serve as an instructional aid for those in advanced undergraduate courses and graduate seminars, as well as a reference for scholars interested in learning more about collective responsibility. The intended audience for the handbook includes professors, graduate students, and advanced undergraduates who want to situate themselves in the current state of the debates. This audience includes those interested in the topic of collective responsibility as such, as well as those who do not work squarely within that field but who believe that the topic of collective responsibility is relevant to their own work on other issues. Accordingly, the handbook will be of interest not only to philosophers and students working on collective responsibility and group agency, but also to those studying law, history, business ethics, and political science, as well as those working on the ethics of war, racism, sexism, climate change, and more.

Acknowledgements

We would like to thank Reese Faust for assistance in copyediting, and Emma Duncan for assistance in compiling the index.

Note

1 www.cdc.gov/drugoverdose/epidemic/index.html

PART I

Foundations of Collective Responsibility

The chapters in Part I discuss some of the central debates and theories in the area of collective responsibility including whether collective responsibility should be understood distributively, as attributions of responsibility to group members or non-distributively, as attributions to groups themselves; whether a group, such as a corporation, could meet the conditions for moral agency; and whether moral obligations are obligations of individuals only or whether they can be shared among people or had by groups themselves.

In Chapter 1, Peter French, well known for his work defending the view that corporations are moral agents, begins his contribution with a discussion of the prerequisites for membership in the moral community. According to French moral competency or reasons responsiveness is necessary for membership in the moral community and he argues that certain groups, particularly corporate organizations, may demonstrate the requisite mechanisms for reasons responsiveness. He goes on to offer a helpful taxonomy of collective-types, types of collective responsibility, and ends with a discussion of the theory of corporate responsibility he has developed over the last several decades.

In Chapter 2, Margaret Gilbert and Maura Priest provide an overview of Gilbert's contributions to debates regarding collective moral responsibility. Gilbert's *On Social Facts* (1989) is a foundational text in the area of collective intentionality and responsibility. According to Gilbert social groups and social phenomenon such as collective action can be understood in terms of a joint commitment formed by individuals to act as a body or single unit. Gilbert's work can be understood as offering an anti-individualistic account of collective responsibility. In this chapter, the authors further elucidate Gilbert's joint commitment account, the theory of collective blameworthiness that results from it, and its implications, if any, for the blameworthiness of members of the relevant collective. Further, they provide an argument for the intelligibility of a member's feeling guilt over what her group has done.

In Chapter 3, Seumas Miller begins by distinguishing three kinds of theories of collective moral responsibility. The first of these conceives of collective moral responsibility as a convenient way of referring to what is in fact simply an aggregate of individual responsibilities. He refers to this account as the atomistic account. The second holds that it is the group or collective itself that is the bearer of moral responsibility. He refers to this view as the collectivist account. The third theory is a relational account in which collective moral responsibility is a form of joint moral responsibility (JMR); this is the account developed by Miller elsewhere (Miller

2001b; Miller 2006). JMR contrasts with collectivist accounts since the only bearers of moral responsibility are individual human persons (or like creatures) and not collective entities per se. However, JMR also contrasts with atomistic accounts since on this third view collective moral responsibility is to be understood in relational terms; joint responsibility is not analyzable into a mere aggregate of individual responsibilities. Miller further develops the JMR in this chapter and shows how JMR might accommodate at least some of the central categories of collective omissions and morally significant diachronic institutional action.

In Chapter 4, Carol Rovane explores the concept of self-constitution and offers a distinction between collective agency and group agency. When an agent constitutes itself, it establishes boundaries within which it thinks and acts as a single unified subject. The boundaries of an agent, according to Rovane, are the bounds of their deliberative point of view. In setting these boundaries an agent not only sets metaphysical boundaries (determining the self) but also normative ones, setting the boundaries of responsibility. Building on her prior work, Rovane argues that although agency is often realized within the boundaries of a single human life, it can also be realized by multiple human lives. When this happens, there is a genuine individual that constitutes itself by thinking and acting from its own rational point of view. This is group agency. It is different from collective agency in which multiple humans coordinate their agency, by thinking and acting from their distinct points of view. This distinction makes a difference for issues of responsibility. Rovane argues that the human constitutions of a group agent cannot take responsibility for what the group agent does, as they do not have a first personal relation to what the group does. However, collective agency does not involve an individual agent in its own right and therefore the individual humans who comprise the collective must take responsibility for the outcomes of their shared agency.

In Chapter 5, Raimo Tuomela and Pekka Mäkelä also offer a distributed understanding of collective responsibility. On their view, the "truthmaker" of a collective attribution of moral responsibility is the moral responsibility borne by the individual members, qua members, of the group. Unlike Ludwig in the next chapter, however, Tuomela and Mäkelä acknowledge that certain groups, such as institutions, can act. Accordingly, they allow for cases in which the individual responsibility is held jointly or ascribed jointly to members of the group acting qua members of the group. The group members are together and interdependently responsible for the action.

In Chapter 6, Kirk Ludwig provides a defense of an individualistic account of collective responsibility. He motivates his view by the following claim: if there is no link between collective moral responsibility and individual moral responsibility then collective moral responsibility becomes detached from pressures to alter collective behavior. If individual members are not moved to change their behavior because they are not individually responsible, there is no normative mechanism by which holding collectives morally responsible can induce relevant change. "Attributions of collective moral responsibility will become idle." He then goes on to argue against that, because groups are not agents, they cannot be moral agents and, therefore, cannot be held morally responsible. Given that we cannot let moral responsibility become detached from a mechanism by which the behavior on the basis of which it is attributed can be changed, Ludwig presents a view he calls the factor model of collective moral responsibility: Any claim that a group is morally responsible for something must be resolved into a distribution of moral responsibility to its members, with none left over for the group per se.

In Chapter 7, David Copp argues that there is nothing metaphysically or morally problematic in the idea that institutional entities, such as corporations, are capable of intentional action, and that they can have moral obligations and bear moral responsibility. The analogy between individual human agents and institutions is strong enough to establish that institutions act. At least on one conception of the point of morality, and on the normative theory it supports, we can explain how institutional entities can have moral obligations. According to Copp, this means that facts about the obligations or responsibility of institutional entities are grounded in the same kinds of facts that ground the obligations or responsibility of relevant individuals.

In Chapter 8, Kendy M. Hess argues that theories of corporate or group agency often focus on certain aspects of it to the exclusion of others. For instance, the literature on corporate agency often focuses on the mechanism by which decisions are made in a corporation. According to Hess, a broader and richer conception of corporate agency is required and must appeal to different mechanisms and different group members. According to Hess, this also has implications for understanding the responsibility of a corporation and the responsibility of its members.

In Chapter 9, Gunnar Björnsson discusses what he calls the agency challenge. Often, no individual member of a group had control over the outcome for which they are blamed, and no individual member can make a difference as to whether the group meets its obligation. This makes it difficult to understand group attributions of obligation or responsibility in terms of individual blameworthiness and obligations. But the groups themselves often fall short of standard conditions of moral agency. They seem to lack many properties normally associated with agenthood. Finding the agency responsible is a challenge. Björnsson details some cases where it is natural to attribute obligations or blameworthiness to groups that cannot be plausibly attributed to their individual members, and discusses replies, problems, and prospects for resolving the agency challenging. According to Björnsson, the most promising replies understand group obligations and blameworthiness as grounded in demands on individual agents.

In Chapter 10, Olle Blomberg and Frank Hindriks explore the difference between acting together (which involves shared intention) and strategic cooperation (which does not involve shared intention). According to Blomberg and Hindriks, the degree to which the participants in a shared intentional wrongdoing are blameworthy is normally higher than when agents bring about the same wrong as a result of strategic interaction. This might be explained by the fact that shared intentions cause intended outcomes in a more robust manner than the intentions involved in strategic interaction. However, Blomberg and Hindriks argue that this isn't an adequate explanation. Rather, what explains the higher degree of collective blameworthiness in the case of acting together is a difference in the quality of will. When we share intentions, we are implicated in each other's will, whereas in strategic interactions we are not, and degrees of blameworthiness depend on the quality of will an agent displays in actions.

1
TYPES OF COLLECTIVES AND RESPONSIBILITY

Peter A. French

In the mid-1960s I had the privilege of studying with H.D. Lewis while he was writing *The Elusive Mind* (Lewis 1970). During a lunch chat about Vietnam War issues, Lewis expressed dismay at my insistence that the whole population of a nation could be held morally responsible for the untoward actions of the government it elected and the military fighting in its name. He referred me to a paper he had published during the Nuremburg Trials after World War II in which he maintained that the very idea of collective responsibility was barbaric (Lewis 1948).

Over a few more lunches he argued, or rather politely pressed, his position. I contended that ordinary language spoke in my favor. Exasperated with my recalcitrance, Lewis suggested the matter between us could be dropped if he acknowledged that in ordinary discourse we often ascribe responsibility to various types of human collectives and I accepted that such ascriptions to collectives are nothing more than colloquial shorthand devices that are always reducible to attributions of responsibility to individual humans, the members of those collectives, or at least some of them, without any remainder of moral responsibility residing in the collective as a whole. He pointed out that my countenancing any sort of irreducible collective moral responsibility wandered too far from the boundaries of most Western moral philosophy. None of the justly famous ethicists, Kant for example, were collectivists when it came to attributing moral responsibility. The Categorical Imperative is not collectivized in any of Kant's formulations of it, Lewis reminded me. The moral world is exclusively the domain of flesh and blood individual human beings, so he maintained. He then quoted from a poem by Rudyard Kipling, one he later used to bolster his case in a paper he contributed to the book I edited on individual and collective responsibility (Lewis 1972). The crucial lines were: "carry my word to the Sons of Men or ever ye come to die: That the sin they do by two and two they must pay for one by one!"(Kipling 1932).

Powerful stuff—Kant and Kipling! And H.D. Lewis! Still, I continued to point out that political theorists, sociologists, and ordinary people often characterize human experience in collective terms and not infrequently attribute what certainly looks like moral responsibility to groups and organizations qua collectivities—no divisibility, no reductions to specific individual humans implied or entailed. Lewis replied that our job as philosophers is to point out that only individual human beings with certain capacities populate the moral community. The subjects of all moral responsibility ascriptions necessarily are individual human beings. Morality does not recognize collectives or organizations. He insisted that the missteps of the collectivists in other fields must be corrected, as he had labored to do in his paper attacking the collectivist positions of some of the judges on the Nuremburg Tribunal. He also tossed in a reproach at me for paying too much attention to the Oxford clique of Ordinary Language Philosophers with whom I also was studying.

I replied that the bias favoring individualism blinds many philosophers in the Western ethical tradition to the crucial roles groups, collectives, organizations, and nations play in social/political/moral affairs and devolving the responsibility for what groups do on individuals may not always capture what occurred in specific cases when something goes awry, why it occurred, and who or what group, or organization ought to be blamed for it. Even when responsibility for an untoward event has been fairly distributed among the individual participants there may remain a not insubstantial amount sticking to a collective qua collective and that will have to be ignored, swept under the mental or moral rug, if moral philosophers continue to insist on individual-centric responsibility theories. Unless we want to render moral philosophy incapable of addressing many, perhaps most, social issues and events, I argued, other kinds of entities will have to be admitted into the community morality addresses and evaluates. A reductionist individualistic human bias significantly limits the scope of morality.

I agreed with Lewis that Christian theology conceives of salvation (for Kant the reward of the *summum bonum*), and damnation in individualist terms, but morality, I maintained, should not be so much concerned with afterlives, despite Kipling's warning, as about how we can manage to get along relatively successfully in this life, often in groups and very often dealing with and in organizations. He told me to read some of the latter parts of Kant's *Second Critique* where I would find Kant's argument that the immortality of the human soul is necessary if humans are to satisfy Kant's moral perfection requirement and be rewarded with true happiness. I told him that part of the *Critique* never impressed me. It seemed like a backhanded sop to the utilitarians, albeit shifting the reward of happiness for doing the right thing into a distant dim future existence of one's soul.

We agreed to disagree, and I decided to explore a different tack and approach the topic of collective responsibility from a structural and functional basis rather than focusing on arguments regarding calcified principles of responsibility championed by the ethicists that then almost unanimously favored some form of methodological individualism[1] when collectives are involved.

Two matters require a bit of clarification before sorting out collectives and when and how moral responsibility might reasonably be ascribed to at least some of them. First, membership qualifications in the community to whom responsibility ascriptions are directed should be identified, if only in a rudimentary way. Second, some distinctions need to be drawn regarding the types of moral responsibility that may come into play when collections of people are morally judged, especially when events break badly.

1.1 The Moral Community

The prerequisites for membership in the moral community are a crucial factor in any discussion of moral responsibility. If collectives cannot satisfy the basic entrance requirements, nothing further is needed to support Lewis's pronouncement that the very notion of collective moral responsibility is barbaric. It is not likely to raise too many hackles if I stipulate that to be a full-fledged member of the moral community and so susceptible to moral responsibility appraisals, a candidate must be normatively competent. Minimally that means that it must possess some internal mechanism with the functional capacity to appreciate moral reasons as relevant to its act choices, the ability to react to those reasons with intentional actions, and thereby acknowledge ownership of its actions, and the facility to participate in moral dialogue and address. Put another way, members of the moral community must be "moderate moral reasons responsive" (Fischer and Ravizza 1998). Also, it should be noted, to satisfy those criteria an entity must have more than an instantaneous existence. It cannot exist for a flash and never again. It must persist.

Adult humans are prototypical members of the moral community. For over 40 years since my lunches with Lewis, I have argued that adult humans do not uniquely possess the functional capacities required for normative competence. Two types of mechanisms can demonstrate at least a modicum of moderate moral reasons responsiveness: neuro-psychological mechanisms and some organizational mechanisms.[2] Most adult humans fall into the first category and one type of collective and many corporate organizations may demonstrate the requisite mechanisms.

To qualify as an appropriate target of moral scrutiny a candidate must to some degree be self-referential (in the collective cases that minimally includes the use of the pronoun "we"[3] when describing or discussing its actions), act from, at least, rudimentary internal mechanisms that can recognize a sufficient moral reason not to do what they are about to do, conceivably react to that reason, even if, in the circumstances, that is a rather remote possibility, and care about the moral quality of their actions, i.e., be affective.[4] Whether or not something is normatively competent is a fact about the functional and structural internal mechanisms and motivational triggers that generate an individual's or a group's decisions and actions.

1.2 Types of Moral Responsibility

Gary Watson, in a well-known paper (Watson 2004), distinguishes between the attributability aspect of responsibility, and the accountability aspect. Watson, Tim Scanlon (Scanlon 1998), and Angela Smith (Smith 2007) among others, opt for the attributability aspect, maintaining that justifiably holding an entity responsible is dependent on whether the event that occasioned the ascription is expressive of the entity's inner structure with respect to value. Angela Smith writes that to say something is morally responsible for an action or event

> is merely to say that she [or it] is connected to it in such a way that she [or it] can, in principle, serve as a basis for moral appraisal of that person [or group or organization]. What is in question here is the relation between an agent and her [its] actions, attitudes, values, etc., and the conditions under which those things can be said to reflect on her [its] morality… should they turn out to exceed or fall short of certain moral norms or expectations.
>
> *(Smith 467–468)*

Marina Oshana (Oshana 1997) defends the accountability position. She maintains that for something to be held to account by members of the moral community, it must be capable of entering into moral conversation, defend itself, make excuses, confess, justify its behavior, etc.

Although I haven't a convincing argument to support adopting one or the other of those approaches, I follow Watson and maintain that an entity (human person, group, or organization) is attributably morally responsible for an event, if the occurrence of the event discloses something positive or negative about the nature of the entity's inner functionalities, how it works or worked, decides or decided, and translates its intentions into actions. A negative responsibility ascription, blaming a human, a group or an organization for a morally bad or unacceptable action or event, makes the claim that its subject is internally morally defective in some crucial and relevant way. It is an assessment of the entity's decision mechanisms as measured against a normative standard. In the case of an individual human it says the quality of that human's will is not up to the expected par. In the case of some collectives and organizations it says there are moral flaws in the way it is organized and/or how and on what basis it makes decisions leading to its actions. Apart from and somewhat different from legal responsibility, moral responsibility is first and foremost an assessment of the workings of the internal mechanisms of its subjects, which was the occasion for raising the issue of moral responsibility or accountability in the first place.

Subjects are held morally responsible for their actions that under some true description were intended by them. In moral assessment what was intended matters more than what subsequently occurred. The consequences of an action, if not fitted into the scope of the subject's intentions in acting, are externalities to moral assessment and not directly relevant to holding the subject morally responsible for the action. Andrew Khoury writes: "In order for a given consequence to result from some action the world must cooperate in some way and this is a matter external to the agent" (Khoury 2012). If a person, a group, or an organization were held morally responsible for the consequences of an action that fall outside the scope of its intentions in acting and beyond the limits of reasonable foreseeability, sheer luck would be a dominating factor in what may be a majority of responsibility ascription cases.

The moderate reasons responsiveness condition for membership in the moral community is an internal condition that connects the motivational mechanism of the subject to an action. Moral responsibility ascriptions focus on a subject's internal decision states, including what it intended, not on events that may have a direct causal relationship to its actions though were not captured in the scope of the operations of its neuro-psychological mechanism or its decision processes.

There are two ways moral responsibility may be assessed. One holds the subject responsible or not for an action or event at the time of its occurrence (responsibility at t_1 for what was done at t_1)—call that synchronic moral responsibility. The other holds the subject responsible or not for the action committed at t_1 at a time later than t_1 (responsibility at t_1+n for what was done at t_1)—call that diachronic moral responsibility (or the diachronic ownership) of a past action.[5] In some cases they may be significantly different with respect to the degree of responsibility ascribed for what was done at t_1. In other words, moral responsibility for the same event or action may change over time. However, the truth of a synchronic moral responsibility ascription holding its subject responsible for an action or event at the time of its occurrence (t_1) is invariant over time. The degree or amount of diachronic moral responsibility ascribed to the subject for the same action or event at a later date may be more, less, or the same as the synchronic moral responsibility ascribed at t_1. Diachronic moral responsibility is not limited by the degree of synchronic moral responsibility justifiably accessed at t_1. Over the passage of time the subject may have undergone psychological or operational changes and/or had opportunities to rectify, remedy, or redress what it did at t_1 in a morally meaningful way. Diachronic responsibility ascriptions are revisitations of moral assessments of a subject's previous actions, but they are not revisions of justified synchronic responsibility assessments.[6]

If something untoward occurred at t_1, we are likely to have moral reasons to want to know if the subject that was synchronically responsible for it at t_1 is an appropriate candidate at t_1+n for punishment, blaming, or other forms of retrospectively being held to account for it. It is crucial to diachronic moral responsibility that the subject under our scrutiny at t_1+n has endured, bears the appropriate or right relationship to the synchronically responsible subject at t_1 before we increase or decrease the subject's degree of responsibility. A basic tenet of moral responsibility appears to be that a subject at t_1+n only can be held morally responsible for an action performed at t_1 if the subject at t_1+n is the same subject in all the relevant respects as the subject that performed the action at t_1. Subject sameness is crucial.

Philosophers have proposed a variety of candidates for subject sameness from soma-centricity focused on physical continuity to versions of the Lockean memory criterion and psychological continuity. In the recent philosophical literature two alternatives to straightforward numerical soma-centric identity in the case of humans have been championed. One is psychological connectedness; the other is narrative coherence. If psychological connectedness is adopted in the case of humans, diachronic responsibility/ownership for an action at t_1 is dependent on the degree to which and the way in which the subject's current psychology in its neuro-psychological mechanism is connected to the psychology of the subject at t_1 that was the spring of the subject's action at t_1.[7] Justifiable diachronic responsibility at t_2 for an action performed at t_1 is dependent on the degree to which and the way in which identified psychological states and functions of a person's current neuro-psychological mechanism, such as beliefs, values, desires, and the like, are causally connected to those that were the effective motivational springs of the subject at t_1. Only if they are psychologically connected to a reasonably high degree can the human at t_2 be held responsible for what was done at t_1. Translating this from neuro-psychological states to collective operational mechanisms, diachronic responsibility for a past act is dependent on the degree to which and the way in which the current policies and procedures of an operational mechanism are causally connected to those that were the effective springs of its actions in the past.

Benjamin Matheson writes of the narrative coherence account of sameness: "An agent is morally responsible for a past action to the extent that the action coheres with the agent's self-told narrative" (Matheson 2014). Most human lives are to some extent self-told stories in that we, the autobiographers, organize the acts we have performed, the things we have done, and what we plan to do, into intelligibly structured storylines even if we only tell those stories to ourselves during reflective interludes.[8] Briefly, the narrative coherence account of sameness required for diachronic responsibility is that a person is morally responsible for a past action to the extent that the action coheres with that person's self-told narrative, as long as that narrative is not delusional or fictional. On this account, the narrative self, not personal identity or psychological connectedness, is the locus in persons of diachronic moral responsibility. If a past action no longer coheres with the person's current self-narrative, it is not something for which the person legitimately can be held morally diachronically responsible. It is likely that among collectives only the highly organized ones can satisfy the conditions of narrative coherence. In them operational sameness is likely to be preserved over time.

I propose to use the clarifications of the previous two sections in taking a stab at sorting out types of collectives and moral responsibility.

1.3 Types of Collectivities

After my unresolved discussions with Lewis, I decided to take up the matter of collective moral responsibility by first looking at rocks. Actually I didn't just look at rocks, I purloined a geology book from a science colleague's bookshelf, adopted some basic terminology from it and published a paper (French 1975) maintaining there are at least two different categories into which human groups or collectives can be sorted for the purposes of evaluating their actions from the moral point of view: aggregates and conglomerates—like rocks.

A group of people is an aggregate collective if it is nothing more than a gathering of folks. The identity of an aggregate is just the sum of the identities of its parts. If an aggregate were formed naturally, like sand, gravel, and limestone formed by pedogenic processes, adopting the geologist's lingo, it could be called a ped. If the aggregate was formed artificially, again using the nomenclature of geology, it is a clod. Most human aggregate collectives are clods. I suppose natural family relations, if understood to be collectives, e.g. my two children and me, are peds. A change in the membership of a clod (or a ped, for that matter), substituting a new member for an old one or adding or eliminating a member, changes the identity of that particular aggregate. Clodhopping is a way of changing aggregate identities. (Throughout our daily lives most of us do rather a lot of clodhopping.) Simply, an aggregate collective is the sum of its individual members at a specific time and/or in a specific space. Generally, what is predicable of a clod is reducible to the assignment of a like predication to each of its members, allowing for the grammatical fact that certain verbs can be predicated of an aggregate collective but not of any individual member—disbanded, for example. Nonetheless, when it is true that a clod, a mob in a park for example, disbanded, it is also true that its members left the clod and took off in various directions, no longer amassed.

Katherine Ritchie distinguishes what she calls "feature social groups" from "organized social groups" (Ritchie 2018). She fails to mention unorganized aggregate groups, or what I have called clods (and peds), which, along with organized social groups, would constitute the class of what she calls "social objects." Feature social groups, for Ritchie, are "social kinds." Social kinds, on her account, have instantiation conditions such as specific identifiable types of behavior, beliefs, practices, activities, norms, and intentions. To be a member of a feature social group one must have or exhibit the specific traits (or at least a significant number of them) that define that group. For example, to be a member of the feature clod of "American White Supremacists" one must be an American that exhibits racist behaviors, spouts or holds racist beliefs, or practices racism during one's typical activities, regardless of one's location in time and space.[9] According to Ritchie, American White Supremacists are a social kind (not a natural kind!), which undoubtedly includes slave owners in the antebellum American South as well as all of the Neo-Nazi marchers in Charlottesville, Virginia in 2017. Claiming American White Supremacists are responsible for the ill treatment of African Americans, Native American Indians, Asian Americans, and other minority groups in American society in the past and present is feature social group (or clod) blaming. It lacks a specific temporal or spatial identification of its subject. The responsibility ascribed to a feature social group devolves on the individual members of the group.

Holding the Neo-Nazi group that marched in Charlottesville responsible for the death of a bystander blames what Ritchie calls a specific social object. That social object, for her, was an organized social group formed to carry out specific concerted actions. It had a rudimentary decision structure and even evidenced, qua group, a degree of normative competency. Consequently, it was not a mere aggregate, a clod, though all of its members also belonged to what Ritchie calls a feature social group: White American racists. The point being that a person can be a member of an organized social group and also a feature social group with respect to the same activity.

An accidental grouping of six people waiting on a corner for a bus clearly constitutes a clod. Each person in that clod, we will suppose, is on the corner pursuing his or her private interests, though they share the intent of boarding the bus when it arrives and many may be planning to disembark at the same bus stop on the route. The clod has no established collective decision procedure for determining how to act in unison should circumstances arise that might require their concerted actions. They are strangers, just would-be bus passengers, and might be called a "random collective," as Virginia Held (Held 1970) and David Cooper (Cooper 1968) maintained.

Clods qua clods obviously are not normatively competent, though their members, or most of them, typically are. Any responsibility for not doing something that is attributed to a clod must, as with all aggregates, devolve on its individual members. Clods are prime examples of the sort of entities about which the reductionism of methodological individualism (MI) is appropriate. Clods per se cannot bear moral responsibility. Paraphrasing Kipling, in the case of clods, what two and two do (or three and three do, etc.) morally must be paid for one by one.

Suppose a summer wind comes blowing in, scatters trash from an overstuffed barrel all over the place, and the members of the clod standing on the corner watching all the trash swirl around their shoes make no attempt to pick it up and deposit it back in the barrel. None, it turns out, are citizens with enough civic pride to make the effort. It seems reasonable to say that the clod on that corner is responsible for failing to pick up the trash, but Anne Schwenkenbecher rightly argues that a random collection, like the people on the corner, should not in itself be thought of as a moral agent (Schwenkenbecher 2018). In the case of such clods MI reductionism will entail that each member of the clod is responsible for failing to pick up the trash, or for failing to pick up some part of it, a fair share, before their bus arrives.

However, according to Held (1970) there may be something else for which those in the clod on the corner as a group may be held responsible. In cases where a group action is required to perform a task, Held maintains the individuals gathered in a clod can be held responsible for failing to form themselves into an informal association capable of some deliberation that leads to coordinated action. The clod on the corner certainly does not need to create a full-fledged organization with elected or appointed leadership and decision-making rules just to pick up the trash, but, on Held's account, they each ought to contribute to transforming their group, so they are capable of completing the task by becoming what Schwenkenbecher refers to as a goal-oriented collective, if not a group agent (Schwenkenbecher 2018). Doing so might involve little more than agreeing among themselves about which part of the trash each is going to try to corral before their bus arrives. In effect, recognizing the capabilities of a clod to perform a task seems to be sufficient on both Held's and Schwenkenbecher's accounts to hold a clod responsible, albeit retrospectively, for not forming into a goal-oriented collective and doing what they, qua clod, were capable of doing. Even if a clod formed into a goal-oriented collective, it will not be a group agent per se, so any responsibility ascriptions to it will devolve in some way on its putative members without remainder. [It may not devolve in equal portions as I argued in "Power, Control, and Group Situations: And Then There Were None" (French 1992)]. So Schwenkenbecher's goal-oriented collectives still are no more than clods.

Toni Erskine thinks that all that is morally required of the individuals in cases like the trash on the corner is to jointly act, forming "a coalition of the willing" (Erskine 2014) in which responsibility ultimately distributes between the members of the group and none resides at the group level. On her account each of the folks on the corner has an individual obligation to do what it takes to be able to collaborate in picking up the trash. Each individual needs to take steps towards getting the job done, but there is no reason from the moral point of view to aim a responsibility ascription at the clod qua group. The people on the corner ought to independently see that they are jointly capable of picking up the trash. Insofar as the clod in itself is not normatively competent, it cannot be held synchronically morally responsible for not picking up the trash and, that being the case, the clod also cannot be diachronically morally responsible for leaving the trash cluttering the corner. As each individual member of the clod may be held both synchronically and diachronically morally responsible for not cleaning up some portion of the mess on that street corner, if one of the members of the clod returns on the bus to the corner hours later and picks up and tosses some of the rubbish back in the trashcan, that returnee may minimize his or her diachronic moral responsibility to some degree.

I believe Erskine's position is more consistent with the way aggregate collectives might form and act than one that grounds collective responsibility of the aggregate on a counterfactual of the aggregate creating a minimal organization. A coalition of the willing requires no collective organization, but it also is not a moral agent and cannot be held morally responsible as a collective for what was done or not done. From the moral point of view, such a clod dissolves into individuals. It never has any moral standing. Kipling would approve.

Back to the study of rocks for the characteristics of a conglomerate—a conglomerate is a clastic, lithified sedimentary rock containing rounded clasts of various kinds of rock material cemented together in a matrix with calcite, iron oxide, silica, or clay by the action of moving water. The rounded clasts can be mineral particles or sedimentary, metamorphic or igneous fragments. A change in the identity of one or more of those clasts associated in a particular conglomerate does not necessarily change the identity of the conglomerate. A conglomerate collective is a group of people such that the identity of the collective is not exhausted by the sum of the identities of its individual members. A conglomerate collective can be composed of disparate types of people with disparate views who bind together by some sort of cementing factor and endure for some period of time. In many cases the cementing factor will be a collective agreement on a decision procedure by which courses of collective action are chosen and tasks relative to the agreed-upon actions are assigned among the membership. Becoming a member of a conglomerate collective generally involves some sort of mutual commitment or undertaking or some sort of standardized method of joining, though that need not be a complicated procedure. What conglomerate collectives have in common is that they have at least a minimal degree of normative competence. They can, in and of themselves, be targets of moral responsibility ascriptions without being susceptible to MI reductionism.

Consider the townspeople and cowboys hanging out in the Canby Saloon in Bridger's Wells in Walter Van Tilburg Clark's novel *The Ox-Bow Incident* (Clark 1940). Each is in the saloon for personal reasons. Some have just ridden into town in need of a drink to wash the dust of the trail out of their throats. At the beginning of the story the patrons of the Canby Saloon form a clod, not unlike the folks on the street corner waiting for a bus. Then they learn that a herd of cattle were rustled from a local ranch and the rustlers murdered a cowboy known to some of them. A subset of the Canby Saloon crowd, augmented by others from the town, forms into a vigilante posse committed, if they catch the rustlers, to doing justice in a rough, quick, and sure manner at the end of noosed ropes. They cannot be formally deputized because the sheriff is out of town, so the deputy who has no legal authority to do so, garbles the administering of an oath to which they all nod agreement. The clod by that process is cemented into a conglomerate of very disparate parts. They agree on rudimentary rules of operation and select an ersatz major, who may or may not have been in the Civil War, as their leader. They ride out of town to the Ox-Bow where they capture three men with a herd of cattle and no bill of sale, and, as a group, conclude they have caught the rustlers. The posse lynches the three, only to learn later that the cattle were legitimately purchased and were being driven to the ranch of the purchaser. The "murdered" cowhand also is very much alive. The conglomerate acted on gross misinformation.

1.4 Types of Collective Responsibility

A distinction between collective responsibility and types of individual-collective responsibility is important in sorting out the complications in distributing responsibility in conglomerate collective cases like that of the Ox-Bow posse. "Individual-collective responsibility"[10] is the responsibility an individual member of a conglomerate collective bears for an untoward action or event for which the collective as a whole is blamed. Consequently, the collective responsibility of the conglomerate is conceptually prior to any assignment of individual-collective responsibility to a conglomerate collective member. Jeff Farnley is a member of the Ox-Bow posse that is responsible for lynching three innocent men. Farnley is individual-collective responsible for the hangings because Farnley was a member of the posse that carried out the hangings, as are all of the members of the Ox-Bow posse members regardless of their actual specific participation in the lynchings of the innocent cowboys. Membership is the factor that matters. Call this form of individual-collective responsibility "individual-collective *membership* responsibility."

A member's affiliation in the Ox-Bow posse may have come about in a variety of ways, and, it may be argued, not all of the members of the posse should bear the full weight of individual-collective *membership* responsibility. The major's son, for example, was coerced into joining the posse and that may be adequate to assign him a lesser amount of individual-collective *membership* responsibility for the hangings than most of the other members, like Farnley. Voluntarily agreeing to join the posse and not quitting when the posse reached a collective decision to administer "rough justice" should be sufficient to secure a full measure of individual-collective *membership* responsibility for the posse's murderous activities.

Another type of individual-collective responsibility is *participatory*. The degree or amount of such responsibility a member has for the collective's deeds is a function of two factors: a member's power within the collective and the member's contribution in bringing about whatever untoward event is the focus of the responsibility ascription that targets the collective. Individual contribution sets the degree of individual-collective *participatory* responsibility, but power within a collective that itself has power to do something is also a crucial element in determining degrees of individual-collective *participatory* responsibility.

To have power in a conglomerate is to possess the dispositional property of being able, if one wants, under certain conditions, to move the conglomerate to action or inaction. When someone has power[11] with respect to a particular action or event, there is something that he or she can do at an appropriate time that will insure that the event or collective action will occur and there is something that he or she can do at that time that will prevent the event or action from occurring. The major definitely had such power with respect to the Ox-Bow posse, as did a few of the other members of the posse, but definitely not all of them. (William Golding's *Lord of the Flies* (Golding 1954) can be read as portraying how power in a conglomerate is revealed and exercised and how it can shift among the members, alter the behavior of subsets of and the entire conglomerate, and change the distribution of individual-collective *participatory* responsibility for collective actions committed by the members.)

Suppose we speculate that, besides the major, a subset of eight members of the Ox-Bow posse had the power to prevent the hanging of the three innocent cowboys. They are a critical mass with respect to the participation of the posse in the event. We might expect that the subset's power distributes in some way over its members. Although each member is essential to the identity of the subset because it is an aggregate within the conglomerate, each subset member may not be non-dispensable with regard to the power that this subgroup has to control the activities the conglomerate collective qua collective may undertake. We might say that a member of the group is dispensable with respect to a certain task, if all of the members of the group except that member wanted the task to be done, it would be done, even if that person vehemently opposed its being done. A person may be non-dispensable with regard to the task in at least two ways: (1) His or her opposition significantly would change the group's course of action. The task would not get done despite the fact that the other members of the group were willing to do it. (2) The member's skillset or position is recognized by the group as crucial to the successful completion of the task and whether or not the member harbors a positive attitude toward the doing of the task, it will be done because he or she will be forced to participate by the members who want the task done.

Suppose if Farnley had opposed the hangings and swayed the critical mass subgroup of the posse not to support the hangings, the hangings would not have occurred and if Farnley advocated for the hangings, they would occur, in either case, regardless of the opposition of even a majority of other members of the posse. That would mean that Farnley was a non-dispensable member of the crucial sub-group. He has power with respect to the hangings. Farnley wants the hangings to occur and they occur. So Farnley should bear more individual-collective *participatory* responsibility for the murders of the three innocent men than other members of the posse who pulled the nooses around their necks or started the horses on which they sat, even though Farnley cannot carry out the hangings without the participation of at least some of the other members of the posse. The major not only wanted the hangings to occur, he had an ulterior motive for ordering them: he wanted his son, whom he regarded as effeminate, to participate in the hangings to "make a man out of him." The major had considerable power within the posse and had he not wanted the hangings to occur, the suspected rustlers would have been carted back to Bridger's Wells to stand trial. He therefore bears more individual-collective *participatory* responsibility for the illicit hangings than most of the other members of the collective, including Farnley.

The Ox-Bow posse was normatively competent. The members of the posse spent much of the night after they captured the supposed rustlers debating reasons to haul them back to town or to lynch them in the morning. As a collective they recognized reasons supporting both options. As a group they certainly were capable of acting on either option and some recognized the first option as the morally better one though they choose to follow the bidding of Farnley and the major and other members of the pro-execution sub-group and carry out the hangings. Most of the members of the posse clearly cared about the moral quality of their actions. After the posse learns they made a colossal mistake, many of them display remorse and try to work out some way to compensate the widow of one of the cowboys they hanged. Two of them, the major and his son, commit suicide.

Of course, there is no way the posse can alter its synchronic moral responsibility for the hangings. After being chastised by the sheriff who encounters them as they are leaving the Ox-Bow, their feeble attempts back in town to rectify or redress what they did may slightly alter the remaining members of the posse's diachronic moral responsibility for the hangings, but barely an iota. It may be tempting to regard the suicides of the major and his son as positive modifiers of their diachronic individual-collective *participatory* responsibility for the hangings. But I doubt a convincing case can be made in that regard. There is good reason to believe that the major's suicide was more motivated by his disappointment in his son than deep regret at his having led the posse to commit the unjustified incident on the Ox-Bow. The synchronic and diachronic moral responsibility of the Ox-Bow posse for the lynchings are virtually the same, even though the posse members collect more than five hundred dollars to give to the widow. One of them comments, "It's not a bad price at that … for a husband that don't know any better than to buy cattle in the spring without a bill of sale." That sentiment and the money hardly lightens the diachronic responsibility of the posse and its members, if at all.

A further point is worth mentioning: There are likely to be cases of collective responsibility in which sorting out the individual-collective *participatory* responsibility for an event or action of a conglomerate is extremely difficult. In such cases moral evaluation will likely have to settle for individual-collective *membership* responsibility assessed on each member of the conglomerate. But in all cases of individual-collective responsibility the collective responsibility of the conglomerate takes precedence and that requires that the collective is minimally normatively competent qua collective. Otherwise, what may have appeared to be a conglomerate is nothing more than a clod.

1.5 Corporations and Corporate Responsibility

Not infrequently in the philosophical literature on collective responsibility another type of entity has been identified as a collective of the conglomerate variety: a corporation. In "The Corporation as a Moral Person" (French 1979) I offered an analysis of how formal corporate institutions can qualify as full-fledged moral persons in and of themselves. They can be as normatively competent as humans, and that does not require flesh and blood bodies. Corporations exhibit intentionality, are capable of rationality regarding their intentions, and are able to alter their intentions and behavior to respond to reasons, including moral reasons. Conglomerates may, usually minimally, exhibit those characteristics during their typically brief existences focused on specific tasks. Many corporations, however, generally sustain satisfaction of the criteria of moral community membership over time and while engaged in a variety of activities. Corporations have established internal decision structures (CID Structures) that make their concerted decisions and actions possible. By coordinating, subordinating, and synthesizing the actions and intentions of individual humans (employees) and often its machines within a formal organization, a CID Structure transforms them into corporate actions taken for corporate reasons, such as promoting corporate interests. CID Structures are basically composed of two elements: an organizational chart that delineates stations and levels within the institution; and rules that reveal how to recognize decisions that are institutional ones and not simply personal decisions of the humans who occupy positions on the chart. Those rules are typically embedded, whether explicitly or implicitly, in corporate policy. A CID Structure synthesizes the actions, judgments, and attitudes of individuals into the intentions (plans) and actions of an institution while also providing a mechanism for self-reflection essential to its responsive function and rational decision-making processes. Ordinary conglomerates have no such complex internal structures and typically have limited lifespans. Corporations, it could be said, are intricately evolved, complex, and structurally and functionally integrated conglomerates.

Corporate plans might radically diverge from those that motivate the humans who occupy corporate positions and whose bodily movements and judgments are necessary for the corporation to act. A CID Structure licenses redescribing the actions of humans as the devising and executing of institutional plans thereby revealing the institutional moral person. Gunther Teubner, along similar lines, describes a corporation (or institution) as an autopoietic system of actions that reproduces itself (Teubner 1988), and Carlos Gomez-Jara Diez maintains that (corporate-like) institutions are not made up of human beings or even human actions. They are composed of institutional decisions and actions that construct their own social realities that may be quite different from the reality constructions of the humans working in them (Gomez-Jara Diez 2008).

Some philosophers that favorably view my theory that corporate organizations are capable of intentional action, maintain that moral personhood essentially involves affectivity and such formal institutions lack that capacity qua institutions. They cannot care about the moral quality of their actions or have reactive attitudes and so cannot be full-fledged moral persons. I agree with Deborah Tollefsen that what is needed is an argument to the effect that corporate organizations do not necessarily lack affectivity (Tollefsen 2003 and 2008), though like some humans, they may not always show it. They certainly are objects of the reactive attitudes of humans, such as resentment and indignation, and Tollefsen reads human expressions of reactive attitudes towards such institutions as a demonstration that they are morally addressable, and that entails that they are presumed to have the ability to consider criticism and respond in a morally appropriate fashion. Corporate entities, however, also regularly express reactive attitudes and emotions in their communications with humans and each other. To account for institutional affectivity Tollefsen offers a vicarious emotion theory in which employees are "conduits" for institutional emotions. The idea is that an institutional employee in her role qua institutional employee may be the vicarious moral emotion expresser for the institution in its dealings with those outside of the institution. Tollefsen notes that humans can have vicarious reactive attitudes and moral emotions for others even if those others do not (cannot?) have the same attitudes about themselves. So, on Tollefsen's account, though corporations cannot directly feel moral emotions, moral emotions can be institutionalized within them.

I have maintained that corporate intentional acts are typically human bodily movements under an institutional redescription, CID Structures providing epistemically transparent bases for that descriptive transformation. A similar redescription account might be applied to expose corporate affectivity rather than depending on a vicarious emotion theory. A CID Structure may contain conversion rules for descriptions of certain types of utterances by appropriate humans into descriptions of the expression of corporate reactive attitudes.

No one claims that corporations experience "pangs" of regret or remorse or sorrow as humans might when they express reactive attitudes with regard to the behavior of others or themselves, but the ability phenomenologically to feel emotions may not be a necessary element of moral personhood. Expressions of reactive attitudes generally are performative, ritualistic, conventional. Perhaps the expression in accord with rules is all that is required to attribute affectivity. We might, of course, regard mere ritualistic expressions as insincere if they are not "backed" by a certain sort of feeling, however, even in human affairs, an apology is not void should the apologizer not feel sorrow, regret, or remorse. If the CEO of an oil company expresses the corporation's regret for an oil spill, it seems reasonable to take as prima facie true the sentence "The oil company regrets the spill," though we typically test the sincerity of such regret by monitoring subsequent corporate behavior. Something similar seems usually to occur in the case of human expressions of emotions. Where sincerity is the issue, subsequent behavior trumps appeals to feelings.

If the expression of institutional reactive attitudes and other forms of affectivity can be functionally engineered by the inclusion of rules and policies in a CID Structure so that when an occupant of a certain corporate role expresses regret, sorrow, or some other emotion, that just is the corporation expressing the emotion or making the apology or regretting what it has done, then, regardless of whether or not humans in the corporation, individually, collectively or vicariously, have the appropriate emotion, corporations would seem to meet the standard conditions of moral personhood and be normatively competent; their behavior is subject to moral assessment qua corporations and not merely as conglomerate collectives like the Ox-Bow posse and they certainly are not in any way akin to aggregate collectives.

1.6 Conclusion

My thinking about collectives travelled a far piece from my discussions with H.D. Lewis and my poring over a stolen geology book. Admittedly, I learned a few things about and from rocks—how they form, disintegrate, bond, and shatter. Certain sorts of rocks, aggregates and conglomerates, evoked for me basic structural and functional aspects that distinguish distinctly different types of human collectives and organizations.

Most humans populate, are members of, a spectrum of collectives throughout their lives. As Shakespeare said, in our time we play many parts or, as I would add, become parts of many different clods, peds, conglomerates, and corporations. We are organizational animals, associative, tribal, and often accidental elements of clods and inadvertent clodhoppers in planes, trains, buses, classes, street corners, etc. Hardly any human's life is hermetical. Aristotle told those who listened to him that we are social animals. As far as we know, he didn't expound upon how, consequently, morality should not only synchronically and diachronically assess our intentional behavior as individual joiners, but evaluate our concerted activities qua collectives—the actions of the organizations, clusters, assemblies, crowds, bands, alliances, consortia, and cliques in which we function as voluntary and involuntary members and that, in large measure, shape our thoughts, provoke our actions, form our communities, and define our identities—the companies we keep. What we do within the numerous social configurations into which we intentionally fit ourselves or are thrust by forces beyond our control for brief moments or even as long as lifetimes, more often than not, are focal occasions in which deciding justifiable moral responsibility attributions matters with respect to how we as individuals and collectives endure.

Justifiably affixing blame and awarding credit or praise with respect to collective activity is seldom a simple or a tidy task. Collective responsibility, often ignored in the history of ethics where the focus generally was on the single atomic particle and not the clod or the conglomerate or the corporation, is essential to an effective ethics that relates to the complexities of human life far more, I came to believe, than plotting ways for an individual to nurture a good will and achieve a personal *summum bonum*. Put simply, despite its messiness, collective responsibility matters and requires considerable serious attention in the field of philosophy in which criteria of moral assessment of human conduct and events is of primary concern.

A few years before he died in 1992, H.D. Lewis informed me that although he was impressed with my work on collective and corporate responsibility, he would remain steadfast in insisting that moral responsibility could only be ascribed to individual humans. He suggested that collective and corporate responsibility may well be a kind of responsibility, perhaps in the way we also talk of legal responsibility, but they are not moral. He also reminded me of his book *Clarity is Not Enough* (Lewis 1963) that was the text of his course I attended back in the 1960s. He didn't explain the relevance of that reference. I guess he figured he didn't have to.

Notes

1 Methodological Individualism (MI) is the theory that social phenomena, collective actions, can only be explained as resulting from and reducible to the motivations and actions of individual persons.
2 I have offered arguments for this position in a number of articles and books, most recently in French 2017.
3 See Silver 2002.
4 See French 2008.
5 This distinction is owed to Andrew Khoury (Khoury 2013).
6 Of course, synchronic responsibility ascriptions should be modified if at a later date it is learned they were false, biased, based on insufficient information, etc. Such modifications are not diachronic responsibility ascriptions as I am using the term. They were simply false or unjustified responsibility ascriptions when made and morally require alteration. Diachronic responsibility ascriptions do not alter synchronic responsibility ascriptions.
7 For more on psychological connectedness see Khoury (2013).
8 Think of Ortega y Gasset's comment: "Man is the novelist of himself" (Ortega y Gasset 1939).
9 I have no idea how many of the traits of a racist one must have in order to be a racist. I suspect people could argue for hours on end about whether someone is a racist if they hold racist beliefs but do not express them in public or overtly act on them. In general, I think a person does not actually believe things that make no difference in the person's life, the way the person lives his or her life. But, people have told me that a person can be a latent racist (a closet racist), though racism never overtly surfaces during the person's life. I will make no attempt here to pursue the issue, but that idea brings to mind the Red Queen believing as many as six impossible things before breakfast.

10 The term is owed to Andrew Khoury.
11 My account of power in a group is based on Alvin Goldman's discussion (Goldman 1972).

References

Clark, W. Van Tilberg (1940) *The Ox-Bow Incident*, New York: Signet.
Cooper, D. (1968) "Collective Responsibility," *Philosophy* 43, 165.
Erskine, T. (2014) "Coalitions of the Willing and Responsibilities to Protect: Informal Associations, Enhanced Capacities, and Shared Moral Burdens," *Ethics and International Affairs* 28, 1, 115–145.
Fischer, J.M. and Ravizza, M. (1998) *Responsibility and Control*, Cambridge: Cambridge University Press, Ch. 3.
French, P.A. (1975) "Types of Collectivities and Blame," *Personalist* 56, 160–169.
French, P.A. (1979) "The Corporation as a Moral Person," *American Philosophical Quarterly* 16, 3, 207–215.
French, P.A. (1992) *Responsibility Matters*, Lawrence: University Press of Kansas, Ch. 6.
French, P.A. (2008) "Responsibility with No Alternatives, Loss of Innocence, and Collective Affectivity," in S. Scalet and C. Griffin (eds.) *APA Newsletter on Philosophy and Law*, 7.
French, P.A. (2017) "The Diachronic Moral Responsibility of Firms," in E. Orts and C. Smith (eds.) *The Moral Responsibility of Firms*, Oxford: Oxford University Press.
Golding, W. (1954) *Lord of the Flies*, London: Faber and Faber.
Goldman, A. (1972) "Toward a Theory of Social Power," *Philosophical Studies* 23, 221–268.
Gomez-Jara Diez, C. (2008) "Corporations as Victims of Mismanagement: Beyond the Shareholders vs. Managers Debate," *Pace University Law Review* 28, 101–120.
Held, V. (1970) "Can a Random Collection of Individuals Be Morally Responsible," *Journal of Philosophy* LXVII, 14.
Khoury, A. (2012) "Responsibility, Tracing, and Consequences," *The Canadian Journal of Philosophy* 42, 187–208.
Khoury, A. (2013) "Synchronic and Diachronic Responsibility," *Philosophical Studies* 165, 735–752.
Kipling, R. (1932) "Tomlinson," *The One Volume Kipling*, New York: Doubleday, Doran & Company, 28.
Lewis, H.D. (1948) "Collective Responsibility," *Philosophy* 23, 84, 3–18.
Lewis, H.D. (1963) *Clarity is Not Enough*, London: Routledge & Kegan Paul.
Lewis, H.D. (1970) *The Elusive Mind*, London: Allen & Unwin.
Lewis, H.D. (1972) "The Non-Moral Notion of Collective Responsibility," in P.A. French (ed.) *Individual and Collective Responsibility*, Cambridge: Schenkman Publishing, 119–144.
Matheson, B. (2014) "Compatibilism and Personal Identity," *Philosophical Studies* 170, 317–334.
Ortega y Gasset, J. (1939) *Meditacion de la Tecnica*, Madrid: Espasa Calpe. [Trans. As "Man as Project" by S.P. Moody available online at http://philosophy.lander.edu/intro/articles/ortega-a.pdf, 9.]
Oshana, M. (1997) "Ascriptions of Responsibility," *American Philosophical Quarterly* 34, 1, 71–83.
Ritchie, K. (2018) "Social Creationism and Social Groups," in K. Hess, V. Igneski, and T. Isaacs (eds) *Collectivity*, London: Rowman & Littlefield, Ch. 1.
Scanlon, T.M. (1998) *What We Owe To Each Other*, Cambridge, MA: Harvard University Press.
Schwenkenbecher, A. (2018) "Making Sense of Collective Moral Obligations: A Comparison of Existing Approaches," in K. Hess, V. Igneski, and T. Isaacs (eds) *Collectivity*, London: Rowman & Littlefield, Ch. 5.
Silver, D. (2002) "Collective Responsibility and the Ownership of Actions," *Public Affairs Quarterly*, 16, 3, 287–304.
Smith, A.M. (2007) "On Being Responsible and Holding Responsible," *The Journal of Ethics*, 11, 465–484.
Teubner, G. (1988) "Enterprise Corporatism: New Industrial Policy and the 'Essence' of the Legal Person," *American Journal of Comparative Law*, 36, 1, 130–155.
Tollefsen, D. (2003) "Participant Reactive Attitudes and Collective Responsibility," *Philosophical Explorations*, 6, 3, 218–234.
Tollefsen, D. (2008) "Affectivity, Moral Agency, and Corporate-Human Relations," in S. Scalet and C. Griffin (eds.) *APA Newsletter on Philosophy and Law*, 7, 2, 9–14.
Watson, G. (2004) "Two Faces of Responsibility," in *Agency and Answerability*, Oxford: Oxford University Press.

2

COLLECTIVE MORAL RESPONSIBILITY AND WHAT FOLLOWS FOR GROUP MEMBERS

Margaret Gilbert and Maura Priest

2.1 Introduction

People tend to be comfortable praising or blaming both individuals and groups for their actions. The case of groups, however, has occasioned a number of special concerns. For instance, if a group is to blame for its bad action, does that mean all of its members are at least to some extent personally to blame? Or are its individual members somehow relieved of any blameworthiness in the matter? Neither of these options seems right. Surely all members *need not* be blameworthy? Some, for instance, may have tried their best to prevent the action in question. Surely, at the same time, all members *may* be blameworthy?

What are the implications for group members of the praise- or blameworthiness of a group's action? More succinctly: what are the implications for group members of collective moral responsibility?

Margaret Gilbert has discussed this question in several places, beginning with her book *On Social Facts* (Gilbert 1989: esp. 425–427).[1] She has also focused on related questions having to do with the emotions that may be prompted by a group's praise- or blameworthy action.

One of these questions is this. If my group acted badly, but I myself did nothing wrong, does it make sense for me to feel guilt over the group's action?[2] Another question is: What exactly do we mean when we ascribe such emotions as guilt, remorse, and pride to groups? For example, what do we mean when we say "The committee is proud of what it did"?[3]

This chapter offers an overview of Gilbert's work on collective moral responsibility and related topics. We start by setting out a working account of moral responsibility. We then outline Gilbert's account of acting together and related notions and set out a corresponding account of collective moral responsibility. Given this account, we consider the implications for group members of the praise- or blameworthiness of a group's action, focusing on the latter. We then review Gilbert's answers to the questions about emotions noted above. At some points in our discussion, and in the concluding section, we respond to concerns that have been or might be expressed in relation to Gilbert's work in this area. This is a fair amount to cover, and we should emphasize at the outset that many of the topics in question deserve a longer treatment.

2.2 Moral Responsibility

Moral responsibility of the kind at issue here is backward-looking: it has to do with the moral assessment of actions which have occurred or are in progress. It concerns in particular whether the action in question is worthy of moral praise or blame. Following the practice of much of the literature, we focus here on blame. Similar things can be said of its more positive counterpart.

For present purposes we shall not attempt to argue for a nuanced account of moral blameworthiness as such, regarding which there are important controversies in a large literature. Rather, drawing on some relatively clear judgments on examples involving individuals as opposed to groups, we shall adopt a rough working account of moral blameworthiness as such that has some intuitive appeal.[4]

Suppose that Jane has stolen a watch from a store, and that stealing a watch from a store is morally wrong, all else being equal. We might initially blame Jane for stealing the watch. After all, she did something that is morally wrong, all else being equal. Most likely we would cease to blame her for doing so, given some kinds of further information.

Suppose, for instance, that Jane stole the watch because someone threatened to kill her unless she did so. We might then say that she cannot be blamed for stealing the watch. We might feel, indeed, that in the circumstances her stealing the watch was not morally wrong, all things considered.

One way to avoid blame for an action that *is* morally wrong, all things considered, is to be non-culpably ignorant of its having this character. Thus suppose Jane was brought up in isolation to think it morally praiseworthy to steal things without getting caught, at least in the circumstances in question. We might say that Jane cannot be blamed for stealing the watch, though her doing so was morally wrong in the circumstances.

In light of such considerations, we shall adopt the following rough account of moral blameworthiness for present purposes. One who performs an action is morally to blame for doing so if and only if the following three conditions are met: the action was morally wrong, all else being equal; all else was equal: in particular, one was not coerced into performing the action, and one knew, or was at least in a position to know that the first two conditions were fulfilled.

In this formulation of the account we intend the pronoun "one" to be neutral with respect to the different kinds of entities for whom moral responsibility is possible. More precisely, it allows for the possibility of both individual and collective moral responsibility.

2.3 We Did It

Our question is: What are the implications of collective moral responsibility for group members? In order for a group to be worthy of blame for what it did, it must indeed have done something. So it is reasonable to begin answering the question by asking what precisely it is for a group—as opposed to an individual—to do something.

There are, of course, many kinds of groups. Some are small and some large, some lack any particular organization and some are highly organized, and so on. That said, one way to start the process of inquiry into what it is for a group to do something is to ask what it is for two people to do something together, assuming that any two people constitute a group of sorts by virtue of their joint activity.[5] What is it, for instance, for Jill and Jane to rob a bank together? In what way does this differ from the situation in which each of them is robbing the bank at the same time that, coincidentally, the other is pursuing the same aim?[6]

A central part of Gilbert's account of acting together (Gilbert 1989, 1990, and elsewhere) is an account of a group or collective goal: a goal that the participants can properly refer to as "our" goal—where this is not seen as elliptical for "the goal that each one of us espouses."[7] In developing this account Gilbert's primary aim has been to explain how people understand such everyday statements as "Our goal is to rob the bank" or "Our family wants only to live in peace with its neighbors."

On Gilbert's account, Jill and Jane can properly refer to the goal of robbing a bank as non-distributively "ours" if and only if they are *jointly committed* to espouse as a body that goal. Clearly, to understand this one needs first to know what Gilbert means by saying that two or more people are jointly committed in some way. She has written at length about this in several places.[8] Our aim here is to offer a rough account of it that will suffice for present purposes.

Gilbertian joint commitment involves both a particular process and a particular product. The process is broadly speaking psychological; the product is normative.[9]

When we say the process of joint commitment is psychological, we mean that it involves psychological states of the people in question, states which must be sincerely expressed to one another in order to complete the process. When we say the product is normative, we mean that to be jointly committed is to be in a particular normative situation, now there is something that they, collectively, *ought* to do, all else being equal. In other terms, there is something that they, collectively, *have reason* to do.[10]

We now say more about both the process and the product of joint commitment, starting with the latter.

We said that when two or more parties are jointly committed, there is something that they, collectively, ought to do, all else being equal. Another way of putting this is to say that they are normatively committed *as one* or *co-committed*. Either all are normatively constrained in the relevant way, or none are. Accordingly, if the constraint is removed from one, it is removed from all.[11]

What are the normative implications of this collective normative constraint for the individuals involved? All else being equal, any one of the co-committed persons will act in error in failing to comply with the commitment, that is, in failing to act as it requires, given what the others are doing. One's personal desires and inclinations do not change matters. In short, the normative constraint in this case is to that extent *peremptory*. Gilbert has argued that once the parties have co-committed them all, each of them has the standing to demand of any other that he comply with their joint commitment.[12] This standing is present even when, as in the case of the bank robbers, the content of the joint commitment is morally dubious. One can have the *standing* to demand an action, without being justified, all things considered, in exercising that standing.

Absent special background understandings of the parties, no one party can unilaterally do away with or rescind a joint commitment. Of course, any one party can fail to conform, at will, but, in and of itself, that does not mean that the joint commitment goes away. It is perhaps worth emphasizing that Gilbert takes the joint rescission condition on joint commitment to reflect the way those who act together understand their situation.[13]

With regard to the process of joint commitment, Gilbert distinguishes between *basic* and *non-basic* cases, both of which are of great practical importance.[14] We shall explain this distinction by reference to a joint commitment of Jane and Jill to espouse as a body the goal to rob the Philosophers' Bank.

If this is a basic case, the parties will have jointly committed themselves to espouse as a body the goal in question by openly expressing to one another their readiness to do precisely that. More fully: Jane and Jill's joint commitment will have been established by open expressions of readiness on the part of both Jane and Jill to espouse as a body the goal of robbing the Philosophers' Bank. For instance, Jill may have said, "Let's go rob that bank!" after which Jane said, "Indeed! Let's do it!"

Although a joint commitment may be made using verbal expressions, a given party's readiness for a particular joint commitment need not be expressed in words. Indeed, it may be expressed through a series of relatively subtle indications over time.[15]

As to what it is for the parties to "espouse a particular goal as a body," Gilbert has in mind roughly this. By virtue of their several actions and utterances, coordinated appropriately, they are to act as would the representatives of a single possessor of the goal in question, in relevant contexts. Accordingly if a given party to the joint commitment wants to express a conflicting or, for that matter, corresponding personal goal, that party must make that clear. For instance, some time after Jill and Jane have established their joint commitment, Jill might reflect that "Personally, I'm against robbing the bank." Note that Jill's being personally against robbing the bank and expressing this position does not remove or alter the joint commitment in question.

Once a basic joint commitment has been created, someone who was not one of its original co-creators may be able, in effect, to "sign on" to it, given appropriate expressions of readiness from the other parties. So if Maria discovers that Jill and Jane are going to rob the Philosophers' Bank that evening, says "May I join you?", and receives an affirmative nod from the other two, the original joint commitment of the two is thereby replaced by or, perhaps better, transmuted into a joint commitment of the three. Now Maria, Jill, and Jane are jointly committed to endorse as a body the goal of robbing the Philosophers' Bank. In some groups, particularly those that are large and long-standing, there may be agreed-upon entry and exit rules and procedures allowing people to enter and leave a group without involving all of the parties.

If Jane and Jill's joint commitment to espouse as a body the goal of robbing the Philosophers' Bank is a non-basic commitment, it will have been established in something like the following way. Jill and Jane are discussing what to do that afternoon. Jane says to Jill, "You decide!" and Jane responds, "Okay." Jill and Jane have now established a basic joint commitment to accept as a body that Jane is in a position to determine what they will do that afternoon. If Jane now says, "This is what we're going to do! We're going to rob the Philosophers' Bank!" that will be enough jointly to commit them to espouse as a body the goal of robbing the bank.

What if Jill thinks Jane's decision is completely unreasonable? In some such cases it may be possible to argue that implicit conditions on the authorization have not been met, and that, therefore, the decision in question has created no new joint commitment for the parties. For instance, if Jane and Jill were already jointly committed to espouse as a body the goal of following the law, Jill might argue in light of this that Jane had not been authorized to commit them to robbing a bank, or to doing anything else illegal.

Jane and Jill's joint commitment to espouse as a body the goal of robbing the Philosophers' Bank could have been formed in a single stage by open expressions of readiness to espouse as a body the goal of robbing that bank, making it a basic case of joint commitment. Alternatively it could have been formed in two stages, starting with an initial basic joint commitment authorizing one of them—or some other person or body of persons—to determine the content of one or more further joint commitments of theirs, and concluding with the person or body in question determining its content. Then it would be a non-basic joint commitment.

Of course it is somewhat risky for people to authorize others to determine the content of their joint commitments. On the other hand, non-basic commitments can be of immense practical value, allowing for the members of both small and large populations to be jointly committed in appropriate ways by well-informed and benevolent authorities.

For present purposes an important aspect of non-basic joint commitments as opposed to basic commitments is this. Someone who is subject to a non-basic joint commitment may not be aware of its content. The person or body of persons authorized to determine its content may not have informed all of those subject to it of that content. This could be so temporarily or indefinitely. Thus the authorities may jointly commit the members of a given population to endorse as a body the prosecution of a certain war, may prosecute the war with the aid of relatively few members of the population, and do all of this in such a way that most members of the population are unaware of what is happening.

There are several reasons for invoking joint commitment in an account of acting together as this is understood in everyday life. The order in which we now briefly review two of these reasons is not supposed to prioritize one over the other.

The first concerns the standing or authority to make demands on other people, and begins with an observation of Gilbert's. When people understand themselves to be doing something together, they take themselves to have the standing or authority to demand appropriate action of one another, along with the standing to rebuke one another for inappropriate action.[16] So if Maria is robbing the bank with Jill and Jane and suddenly sits down on a bench and starts reading a novel, one of the others may well demand that she stop doing so, and all will take her to have the standing to do so.

According to Gilbert, as discussed above, a constitutive joint commitment will explain this observation. She has argued, further, that, most likely, only Gilbertian joint commitment or something very like it suffices to give one person the standing to demand an action of another.[17]

If these points about the standing to demand acts of others are correct, it is reasonable to suppose that those who act together understand at some level that they are jointly committed to espouse as a body the relevant goal.

A second reason for invoking joint commitment in an account of acting together relates to the thought that those who act together are in some way unified. There are at least two ways in which this thought may be spelled out.

First, theorists often characterize social groups of a certain central kind as unified or as constituting a unity.[18] Further, it is natural to think of those acting together as constituting a social group of the relevant kind.[19] If such social groups—including those constituted by people acting together—are constituted by one or more joint commitments, this would help to explain the thought that they are indeed unified or are unities.[20]

Second, it has been held that any agent, as such, is necessarily unified, or is a unity. This is necessary in order that the act in question can be seen as an act *of* that agent.[21] Assuming that this is correct, one might think it means that only individual people, such as Jane, on the one hand, or Jill, on the other, can be agents. It is not clear, however, that this must be the case. If, for instance, Jill and Jane rob a bank while acting in light of their joint commitment to espouse as a body the goal of robbing that bank, it does seem to be appropriate for either one to say "*We* did it," referring to the two of them *as one*, unified by their joint commitment. Of course, this is compatible with each one's personally having participated in the robbery and being morally responsible for her participation. Whether she is so responsible depends on the case.

Given the evident appropriateness of using the collective "we" in order to refer to situations of joint commitment, Gilbert has used the phrase "plural subject" to refer to any set of jointly committed persons. Her use of the phrase "plural subject" is not intended to imply that plural subjects have their own subjective states in the sense of conscious experiences, or that they have minds of their own, where to have a mind is understood to involve at least in part having conscious experiences.

For Gilbert, to say that Jane and Jill constitute the plural subject of a goal is to say that they are jointly committed to espouse as a body the goal in question, and to imply that it is appropriate for them to use the collective "we" in referring to "our goal." To say that Jane and Jill constitute a plural subject, period, is to say that they are jointly committed in some way.

Gilbertian joint commitments can take a variety of contents. To generalize, a given joint commitment can always be described as a joint commitment to phi as a body, where substitutions for "phi" are broadly speaking psychological predicates, as is "espouse goal G as a body."

Those who are jointly committed in one way may, and most likely will, at the same time be jointly committed in other ways. Jane and Jill may, for instance, be jointly committed to espouse as a body the goal of robbing the bank, and also jointly committed to believe as a body that this will not take long, where the latter joint commitment is understood along the lines we have sketched for the former.

In this section we have explained Gilbert's account of what it is for two or more people to do something together, or collectively. Central to that account is a joint commitment of the parties, a joint commitment to espouse as a body a particular goal. The action will be complete when the goal is achieved by virtue of appropriate, conforming actions of relevant parties.

In discussing non-basic cases, we noted that after jointly committing the members of a given population to endorse as a body the prosecution of a certain war, the authorities may prosecute the war with the aid of relatively few members of the population and in such a way that most members of the population are unaware of what is happening. On Gilbert's account, then, it can be appropriate to say that we, collectively, did something, even though some of us—perhaps many of us—did not directly contribute to the action.

Many wars are of this kind. They are fought by a country's army, navy, and air-force, at the direction of its rulers, while millions stay home, going to work as usual, tending their gardens, and so on, possibly ignorant of what is going on. Nonetheless, a joint commitment of the people authorizing the rulers to decide whether and when to instigate a war would make intelligible such thoughts as "We are at war" on the part of each one. In principle there can be such a joint commitment even in very large populations.[22]

We just proposed that it "can be appropriate" to say that we, collectively, did something, even though many of us did not directly contribute to the action. There are many related questions to be discussed.

For instance—taking up again the war example, and mentioning just a few cases—what about those who actively protested the war? Or those who did not vote for the politician who—now in power—authorized it? The short answer is this. A given protestor, or one who did not vote for X as ruler, may yet be jointly committed with the other members of the population to support and uphold as a body the rules according to which X was elected ruler, with the power to start a war "in our name." This would be enough to make appropriate saying "We are at war," as opposed to "They are at war." [23]

2.4 Collective Moral Responsibility

We now consider whether and if so when it makes sense to talk of collective moral responsibility. Recall our rough working account of moral responsibility as such, with a focus on blame: one is morally to blame for performing an action if and only if it was morally wrong, all else being equal; there were no mitigating circumstances—in particular, one was not coerced into performing it, and one knew, or was in a position to know, that these things were so.

We assume that two or more people can collectively perform an action, understanding this along Gilbertian lines. In what follows we refer to actions collectively performed as *collective* actions, and those who perform them as constituting *collectives*.[24]

We have yet to consider the following questions. First, can collective actions, as such, be morally wrong? Second, is there such a thing as a coerced collective action, so that the requirement that a culpable action be at least voluntary in the sense of "not coerced" has some teeth in the context of collective as well as individual human action? Third, can we collectively know that what we were doing was wrong, so that it makes sense to say, at least, that we were in a position to know that it was wrong?

As to the first question, people talk easily of the wrongness of actions people perform together. For example, someone might say "Jill and Jane should not have robbed the bank", intending the "should" in question to apply to Jill and Jane, considered as one, rather than to Jane, on the one hand, and Jill, on the other. Further, there seems to be no reason to deny that a moral requirement can fall on two or more people as one. Certainly, if we allow that Gilbertian joint commitments are possible, we should be comfortable with the idea that normative constraints generally can fall on two or more people as one. In the case of a Gilbertian joint commitment, the constraint is the result of the parties appropriately exercising their wills. We need not think of moral requirements in this way. For present purposes it suffices to allow that whatever the source or sources of moral requirements generally, such requirements can fall on two or more people as one, as when it is morally required of Jane and Jill, as one, not collectively to rob a bank.[25]

We turn now to the question of voluntary versus coerced collective action. Are there conditions under which one can appropriately say that the action of a collective, as such, was coerced? It seems that there are.[26] Here we describe a situation in which one might say that Jill and Jane, collectively, were coerced into robbing a bank.

Suppose that one day Jack, an acquaintance of Jill's, confronts Jane and Jill and threatens to harm their parents unless they rob a bank and give him the money. Jill says they will talk it over, and when they are alone she asks Jill "What shall we do? We swore we'd not rob any more banks, but Jack means what he says. The last thing we want is to have him hurt our parents!" They discuss the matter back and forth and finally agree to rob the Philosophers' Bank. Shortly after, they carry out the robbery. It seems reasonable to say that their robbing of the bank—an action ascribable to them, collectively—was performed under duress. In that case their robbing the bank would not count as blameworthy given our general conditions on blameworthiness.

Clearly, in many cases of collective action there will be no antecedents that will allow the parties to say "We had no choice." To that extent, then, they—collectively—acted freely.[27]

We come, finally, to the question whether we, collectively, can know or be in a position to know that what we are doing together is morally wrong. We shall assume, with Gilbert, that the core of an account of collective knowledge generally will be an account of collective belief.[28]

On Gilbert's account, for us collectively to believe that it is morally wrong to rob banks, for instance, is for us to be jointly committed to espouse as a body the belief that it is morally wrong to rob banks. This formulation is to be understood as indicated earlier. We shall not try fully to explore the conditions under which people who collectively believe some proposition collectively know that it is true. One relevant consideration, though, is this. People can collectively believe a proposition on the basis of good reasons, and this can happen with moral beliefs also, as in the following dialogue. Jane to Jill, who has proposed that they rob a bank: "It's wrong to rob banks!" Jill, in reply: "Why? We need the money!" Jane, "Yes, but it's someone else's money!" Jill, "True." Some such discussion may suffice for us properly to ascribe to Jill and Jane, collectively, the knowledge that robbing banks is morally wrong.[29]

From Gilbert's plural subject perspective, then, it is possible for collectives as such to fulfill the conditions necessary for them to be morally responsible for what they do, though in some cases a given collective may not be so responsible. For instance, its moral perspective may be warped, or it may have no such perspective, or it may have been coerced into doing what it did.

2.5 Implications of Collective Moral Responsibility for Group Members: (1) A Radical Disjunction Between Our Responsibility and Mine

Suppose that we—collectively—did something wrong, were not coerced into doing so, and knew, or should have known, that it was wrong, and that one can infer from this that we are to blame for doing what we did. As we shall explain, given Gilbert's understanding of the relevant terms, it is possible that I am not personally blameworthy in any way in connection with our action. It is also possible that I *am* personally blameworthy in connection with it. Finally, it is possible that insofar as I am blameworthy, I am either more or less blameworthy than many others: *our* blameworthiness does not imply an equality of personal blameworthiness for all, even when all are personally blameworthy to some degree. You may have wholeheartedly instigated our action; I may have made some effort not to participate, though I did not do as much in that regard as could reasonably have been expected of me. And so on.

There are several ways of disjoining collective blameworthiness from that of a given member, given Gilbert's understanding of the relevant terms. Some of these ways apply given other such understandings, but we focus on the implications of Gilbert's perspective here. In our discussion the unqualified "we" and cognate terms refer to the people in question, considered collectively, and "I" refers to any given member.

Under at least the following three conditions my culpability may be non-existent, or minimal, in relation to our performance of some action for which we may be blamed, perhaps strongly.

First, I may be non-culpably ignorant of what we are doing or how we are doing it. Such ignorance is particularly likely in cases of larger groups where an action was ordered by authorities and carried out by members other than myself in ways that I cannot have been expected to notice. It is also possible in smaller groups, particularly with respect to the means by which our goal is carried out.

Second, though I knew what was happening, I may have done all I could reasonably be expected to do to stop the action or minimize its effects. Perhaps I organized a large protest march, or hid potential victims, at considerable risk to myself.

Third, I may have had no real choice with respect to participation. For instance, my life or that of a family member or members may have been threatened. In some cases less than that would be enough. A threat to fire me from my job, say, might suffice to excuse me for participating. As Gilbert has argued I can be genuinely ready to co-commit myself with others in such circumstances.[30] There is a further factor that is always apt to mitigate my culpability in the context of our blameworthiness. The very existence of our collective goal put a considerable amount of pressure upon me to participate in the relevant collective action, for at least the following reasons.

Any joint commitment normatively constrains the parties to act accordingly, irrespective of their personal desires and inclinations. Thus there is always some reason to participate, though this may be overridden, and massively overridden, by other considerations.

Further, joint commitment is a primary, if not the primary context for trust, on the one hand, and betrayal, on the other (Gilbert 2006b: 149–52). A given party may be reluctant to do something that his fellows may well count as a betrayal.

Joint commitment is also a primary site of accountability: the members are answerable to one another for their conformity or otherwise, as the parties will understand (Gilbert 2006b: 253). So, if Jill suddenly stops acting in ways to promote their bank robbery, and Jane calls her to account—asking her why she is so acting, implying that she needs an excuse—Jill cannot appropriately respond "That's none of your business." Knowing this, Jill may want to avoid being called to account by Jane.

Relatedly, Jane has standing to rebuke Jill for stopping, and to demand that she get a move on. In other terms, Jane has a right to Jill's conformity to the commitment, and Jill an equivalent obligation to Jane to comply. A given party may be reluctant to violate the others' rights and default on his own obligations to her, or at least not want to be rebuked for non-conformity or subjected to relevant demands which may be expressed publicly in front of other members, and potentially by physical means.

A further consideration offering some mitigation of a member's personal blame in the context of a group's wrongdoing is this. Collective goals will often be associated with supportive collective moral beliefs. Let us assume that the goal was morally untenable, and that the supportive collective moral beliefs are false. Whether or not the existence of these beliefs absolves *us* from blame, they put further pressure on *me* to participate in our action.

As said, the pressures on an individual from within the system of collective goals, beliefs, and so on within which he is embedded may be quite strong, and mitigate his culpability for participating in a blameworthy collective action. That is not to say that in certain circumstances he will not at the end of the day be more or less blameworthy for his participation: everything depends on the details of the case.

Someone may think that my being a member of a blameworthy group—being and continuing to be party to the relevant joint commitments—suffices to lay some blame on me. Here again, everything depends on the details of the case.

It is possible to be party to a joint commitment while having no real choice in the matter.[31] One must have been ready to do so, but the kind of readiness at issue can exist when there are no feasible alternatives. In that case my being party to the relevant joint commitment may not be culpable.

Further, since I cannot unilaterally rescind our joint commitment, absent special background understandings, my failure to rescind it cannot be blamed. I may, of course, be blameworthy for conforming to it, or for failing to urge others to join in its rescinding,

2.6 Implications for Group Members (2): The Intelligibility of Feeling Guilt Over What One's Group Has Done

Suppose that I am blameless in connection with an extremely bad action of ours. Could it still make sense for me to feel guilt over our action? Karl Jaspers raised this question in the wake of the Second World War. He was clearly torn: he had the feeling in question—but could not see how it could make sense.[32]

Gilbert has argued that given her account of collective action and related concepts, it does make sense—given some important distinctions and assumptions (Gilbert 1996a; 1997a).

First, we allow that someone can only bear *personal guilt* for an action of his own. More fully, it is only someone's *personal wrongdoing* that allows for an ascription of moral guilt to that person—to Jill, on the one hand, or to Jane, on the other. We allow, further, that it makes sense for someone who bears personal guilt to feel it, that is, to feel guilt over what he has done. This feeling will be expressible by such words as "I am guilty." Call it *a feeling of personal guilt.*

Finally, we allow that if an action is ours, collectively, in the sense articulated by Gilbert, and that action is morally blameworthy, it makes sense for any one of us to feel guilt *in our capacity as one of us*. In other words, what I can intelligibly feel guilt over is *what we—collectively—did*. This is so by virtue of my participation in the joint commitment or commitments that lie at the foundation of the action in question.

To be clear, what I feel guilt over in this case is *what we collectively did*. It is not guilt over my participation in the joint commitment. That might well not have been culpable, after all.

Gilbert has labeled the feeling just described *a feeling of membership guilt*. It will be expressible in such words as "We are guilty" where the collective "we" is at issue. Importantly, no personal guilt is implied.

According to Gilbert, then, what she calls a feeling of membership guilt is intelligible, even when I am personally blameless with respect to our action, or minimally blameworthy. It makes sense for me to feel membership guilt in this case, because *the target of this feeling is not me, or my action, but us, and our action*.

As Gilbert understands it, then, I may intelligibly feel membership guilt even when it is not appropriate for me to feel personal guilt. For "We—collectively—are guilty" does not imply "I—personally—am guilty."

In a particular case it may of course be reasonable for me to feel guilt both over our collective action and over my part in it, or something that I did or did not do in connection with it, such as making no effort to stop it. Whether or not this is so, my feeling of membership guilt is directed *at the plural subject we form*, not at *me personally* or *in some particular guise*. It is, rather, a feeling that is apt for members of a guilty plural subject to have.

To say that qua members: people, *share in* a collective's guilt, as Gilbert sometimes does, misleads as to her intent if it suggests otherwise. Indeed, when writing of members "sharing in" their group's guilt (Gilbert 1997a) she makes it clear that that she does not mean that each party has his own piece of it, contrary to what some commentators have suggested.[33]

2.7 Moral Responsibility-Based Collective Emotions

Allowing that *I* can intelligibly feel guilt over our action, provided this feeling is understood as just discussed, can *we collectively* feel guilt or, for that matter, pride over our action? This raises the more general question of collective emotions, a topic on which Gilbert has written at length.[34]

She approaches this topic from the same angle that she approaches the topics of collective goals, beliefs, and so on, with an interest in understanding the ascriptions of emotions to "us" that people make every day, as in "We feel remorse over what we did" and "The team is jubilant after its win."

Here is Gilbert's positive proposal regarding the case of collective remorse. According to Gilbert, we collectively feel remorse over our doing A if and only if we are jointly committed to feel remorse as a body over our doing A. The technical terms here—"jointly committed" and "feel remorse *as a body*"—are to be understood in the usual way, and the implications for the participants in a case of collective remorse are as usual. Importantly, everyone is obligated to everyone else to act in ways expressive of remorse over our doing A in relevant contexts.

Some have claimed that emotions, whether of a group or of an individual human being, must involve what Gilbert has called "feeling-sensations," distinctive conscious states such as pangs of regret. This claim may stem from an implicit assumption that collective emotions must be understood along the same lines as the emotions of individual humans, coupled with the assumption that emotions necessarily involve feeling-sensations. The second assumption is denied by some of the emotion theorists who focus on the individual case. The first seems to beg the question with respect to everyday collective emotion ascriptions.[35]

Whether or not one thinks that Gilbert has successfully characterized the referents of everyday collective emotion ascriptions, or a class of emotions according to a given account of emotions, the presence of collective remorse and other emotions understood along the lines she has sketched is liable to have significant consequences in the aftermath of collective wrongdoing.[36] For instance, if we have harmed you, and we are known to be remorseful, on Gilbert's account, you are more likely to forgive us, and peace to be restored between us.

Note that our collective belief that we did wrong is less likely to have precisely that effect. It seems that we could believe this while appearing not to care about it.[37]

2.8 Responses To Some Comments

The working account of moral responsibility with which we began this chapter is just that. A Gilbertian approach to collective action, and so on, allows for the possibility of collective moral responsibility given at least some accounts that posit a different set of conditions. This is so in at least some cases where the theorist offering an account supposes that, given the conditions in question, there can be no such thing as collective moral responsibility.

Thus Marion Smiley (Smiley 2010: 183) suggests that in order to be morally responsible one must have a mind.[38] She does not say that only individual human beings (or other animals) have minds, or offer necessary and sufficient conditions for mindedness. She does, however, emphasize the unitary nature of any being that is minded in the relevant way, so we shall focus here on Smiley's claim that moral responsibility can only be ascribed to something properly conceived of as a unity.

As we have discussed, on Gilbert's joint commitment account of collective goals, and so on, these are attributable to the jointly committed persons as one. So Smiley's unity condition does not rule out the moral responsibility of a plural subject in Gilbert's sense.

Referring to Gilbert's work as being unhelpful in this connection, Smiley characterizes her as invoking "shared" commitments (Smiley 2010: 182–3). If Smiley has in mind a set of personal commitments of individual human beings, however, that is not the same as a joint commitment in Gilbert's sense.

Here we understand *personal* commitments as Gilbert does. An example of the formation of a personal commitment is the formation of a personal intention or the making of a personal decision, such as Jane's decision to steal a watch. One with a personal commitment so formed is subject to a normative constraint of the type to which those who are jointly committed are subject, but makes, and can rescind, the commitment unilaterally.[39] Shared in the sense of *identical personal commitments* may not unify the parties but a single *joint* commitment surely does.

It may be worth emphasizing that Gilbert does not take a joint commitment to be constituted by a set of personal commitments, since she often introduces the concept of a joint commitment by starting with personal commitments, thinking that doing so will be helpful to readers.

In another discussion that doubts the possibility of collective moral responsibility, Michael McKenna (McKenna 2006: 20) prefers not to talk in terms of "irreducible collective agents (or plural subjects)," and doubts the plausibility of understanding "allegedly irreducible" collective agents as potentially morally responsible ones (McKenna 2006: 17). He doubts this in part because he assumes that the only agents that can be morally responsible are those whose actions exhibit a rich and stable pattern of responses to reasons.

This assumption may be overly strong. Suppose we accept it for the sake of argument. Collectives understood along Gilbertian lines can exhibit a rich and stable pattern of responses to reasons. For instance, in discussion of actions proposed for their organization members may regularly appeal to its moral code "We can't do that—it conflicts with our moral code!" and "Our moral code demands that we do it!"

We have argued so far that Gilbert's approach to collective actions and so on allows for collective moral responsibility given a variety of different conditions on moral responsibility in general, contrary to what the theorists in question suppose. We now turn to a different kind of concern with her approach.

Tracy Isaacs (Isaacs 2006) sees Gilbert's account of collective actions as having important merits. She mentions in particular that "it makes sense to think about plural subjects as operating on a different [i.e. collective] level of agency" (Isaacs 2006: 71).[40] That said, she does not adopt Gilbert's account because of something she finds troubling: that someone who is a member of a plural subject intent on genocide, for instance, "is obligated to participate unless the others grant him permission to get out" (71–2).

This claim would indeed be troubling if the obligation in question is understood as a matter of all-things-considered moral requirement. As Gilbert understands it, however, the obligation in question is a directed obligation grounded in a joint commitment, an obligation each party has to each party that is equivalent to the other party's standing to demand that he conform to the commitment. Importantly, such obligations are not a matter of moral requirement, let alone all-things-considered moral requirement.

Gilbert can easily agree, therefore, that if we are collectively perpetrating a genocide, I am *not* morally required to participate. Indeed, I may be *morally required to thwart our action* as best I can. The same applies to many less horrendous group goals.

That said, an account of collective action that includes directed obligations of the parties to one another accords with observations on the behavior of those engaged in joint action who take themselves and others to have the standing to demand behavior appropriate to the collective action at issue. The fact that I am not morally required to participate in our genocidal project does not mean that you don't have the standing to demand that I participate. To say that you have that standing, however, is not to say that you would be morally justified in exercising it.

In sum, instead of the obligations of joint commitment speaking against Gilbert's account of collective action and responsibility, that account squares well with a number of considerations, including moral considerations, that may otherwise be unexplained.

We now briefly mention one further concern, which affords us the opportunity to emphasize a central point about Gilbert's approach to collective moral responsibility. Gilbert argues that a collective's moral blameworthiness, as such, implies nothing about the personal blameworthiness of its members—implying nothing, either, about their innocence. This means that even when a collective's blameworthiness is established, a proposed punishment of the collective for its wrongdoing may not be morally justified overall, in that it may adversely affect the innocent, perhaps to disastrous effect.[41]

It may then be proposed that it is pointless to be concerned with collective blameworthiness, since it is never appropriate just to go ahead and punish the collective. One must always be concerned, in the final analysis, with the blameworthiness or otherwise of the individual members of the collective.[42]

The charge of pointlessness should be resisted for several reasons of which we mention just one here. There are ways of punishing groups that may not affect their members adversely and may even strongly enhance their lives. For instance, a group may have developed a set of rules and practices that are highly undesirable from the point of view of individual members. Were the group to be disbanded, as punishment for its actions, the individual members may well benefit rather than suffer.

2.9 Concluding Note

The topic of collective moral responsibility is a rich and important one. It is important from both a theoretical and practical point of view. In this chapter we have outlined Margaret Gilbert's approach to collective moral responsibility and some closely related topics, and responded to some of the comments on her work in this area. In several cases we discussed a theme very briefly rather than failing to mention it at all. Clearly there is much more to be said.[43]

Notes

1 Later discussions include Gilbert (1997a; 2002a; 2002b; 2006a; 2011).
2 Gilbert (1997a).
3 Gilbert (2000b—on collective remorse); Gilbert (2002a—on collective guilt feelings), and Gilbert (2014b—on collective emotions in general).
4 Cf. Gilbert (2006a: 96–8).
5 For discussion of this assumption see Gilbert (1989: ch. 4; 1990).
6 There has been significant debate as to how to answer this question. In addition to Gilbert's proposals, to be discussed in the text, central sources include Searle (1990) and Bratman e.g. (1993). Gilbert critically discusses the work of Searle and Bratman respectively in Gilbert (2007) and e.g. (1997b).
7 This was originally and is now Gilbert's preferred approach; in some writings, following other theorists, she invoked a collective or shared intention as opposed to a collective goal, understanding collective or shared intention along the same lines as she understands a collective goal. It is not necessary to adjudicate between these options here. For present purposes the outcome is the same. Gilbert focuses specifically on shared intention in several places including Gilbert (1997b) and Gilbert (2009).
8 For some of Gilbert's more extended discussions see e.g. Gilbert (2006b: ch. 7); Gilbert (2014: Introduction and ch. 2); Gilbert (2018: ch. 8). See also Gilbert (2015).
9 Gilbert (2014a: 6–7).
10 Gilbert prefers not to talk about reasons, with an "s," in this context. See e.g. Gilbert (2006b: 27–30). As to the "ought," here, she does not see it as the *moral* "ought." In other terms, it can properly be characterized without invoking the qualifier "moral."
11 Given the points made in this paragraph it is wrong to say that the parties to a joint commitment "simply share commitments," if this means that each of them has a personal commitment with the same content. (The quoted words are from Smiley (2010: 182–3) to whom we respond here.)
12 See, most recently, Gilbert (2018: ch. 8).
13 The condition has been questioned by various authors from what seems to be a moral perspective. For further discussion of the joint rescission condition see Gilbert (2006b: ch. 7).
14 She sometimes uses the term "derived" instead of "non-basic."
15 See e.g. Gilbert (2006b: 140).
16 See e.g. Gilbert (1990).
17 See Gilbert (2018: esp. chs. 8, 11, and 12).
18 Cf. Hobbes (1982/1651: 227): a commonwealth is a "real Unity of them all."
19 See Gilbert (1990), citing Georg Simmel.
20 Cf. Hobbes (1982/1651): the creation of a commonwealth is a matter of people "reducing all their Wills ... unto one Will." This is what makes "a real Unity of them all." It is easy to think of the process of joint commitment as a matter of reducing or, perhaps, combining two or more wills into one will, at least for a limited purpose.
21 Cf. Korsgaard (2014: esp. 207f).
22 See Gilbert (2006b: ch. 8).
23 Of course one who allows that "We are at war" may personally object to the war and engage in related public protests.
24 We assume that collectives can have multiple psychological properties, similarly construed, and that if we, collectively, believe that p, for instance, then we constitute a collective even if we are not engaging in any action. In short, two or more people constitute a collective, in the present sense, if some psychological property is ascribable to them, as one.
25 See Gilbert (2018: ch. 8, sec. 6.1).
26 See e.g. Gilbert (2000a: ch. 8).
27 For further discussion see Gilbert (2006a: 108–9).
28 Gilbert (2006a: 106). Gilbert has written copiously on collective belief as this is understood in everyday life. See e.g. Gilbert (1989 ch. 5) and essays in Gilbert (1996b, 2000a, and 2014a).

29 Someone may think that moral culpability depends not on the possession or accessibility of moral knowledge, strictly speaking, but rather on having morally appropriate attitudes or emotions, such as valuing the right actions. This would not rule out understanding collective moral culpability along Gilbertian lines. See section 2.6 on her joint commitment approach to collective attitudes and emotions.
30 See e.g. Gilbert (1993).
31 See e.g. Gilbert (1997a).
32 Jaspers (1947) writes (as translated) of feeling "co-responsible" with other Germans for the actions of Nazi Germany. Gilbert (1997a) attempts to answer Jaspers' question in the affirmative. His lectures are an excellent starting point for anyone interested in collective moral responsibility.
33 See e.g. Miller and Mäkelä (2005); Tollefsen (2006). Mäkelä (2000) is more cautious.
34 See Gilbert (2000a) on collective remorse, (2002a) on collective guilt feelings, (2014b) on collective emotions generally.
35 On the first assumption see Gilbert and Pilchman (2014) focusing on the case of belief. Contrary to what some critics have implied, in developing her account of everyday collective emotion ascriptions Gilbert has not relied on the truth of accounts of emotion that do not stipulate the involvement of feeling-sensations.
36 Cf. Gilbert (2000b).
37 This note responds to remarks in Isaacs (2011: 91).
38 Cf. van den Beld (2002: 188) in a related context.
39 See e.g. Gilbert (2006b: ch. 7) on commitments of the will generally and personal commitments in particular).
40 Referencing Gilbert, Giubilini and Levy (2018: 214) usefully emphasize the distinction between *collective* and *corporate* agents, where only the former's identity is "essentially 'plural'."
41 Cf. Gilbert (2000b).
42 Cf. McMahan (2010).
43 We thank Matthew Dean for help in preparation of the manuscript.

References

Bratman, M. (1993) "Shared Intention," *Ethics* 104: 97–113.

Gilbert, M. (1989) *On Social Facts*, Princeton: Princeton University Press.

Gilbert, M. (1990) "Walking Together," in P. A. French, T. E. Uehling, and H. K. Wettstein (eds.) *Midwest Studies in Philosophy* 15: 1–14.

Gilbert, M. (1993) "Agreements, Coercion, and Obligation," *Ethics* 103: 679–706.

Gilbert, M. (1996a) "On Feeling Guilt for What One's Group Has Done", in Gilbert, M. (1996b).

Gilbert, M. (1996b) *Living Together: Rationality, Sociality, and Obligation*, Lanham: MD, Rowman & Littlefield.

Gilbert, M. (1997a) "Group Wrongs and Guilt Feelings," *Journal of Ethics* 1: 65–84.

Gilbert, M. (1997b) "What Is It For *Us* to Intend?" in G. Holmstrom-Hintikka and R. Tuomela (eds.) *Contemporary Action Theory*, vol. 2, Dordrecht: D. Reidel, 65–85. Repr. in Gilbert, M. (2000a).

Gilbert, M. (2000a) *Sociality and Responsibility: New Essays in Plural Subject Theory*, Lanham, MA: Rowman & Littlefield.

Gilbert, M. (2000b) "Collective Remorse" in Gilbert, M. (2000a).

Gilbert, M. (2002a) "Collective Guilt and Collective Guilt Feelings," in *Journal of Ethics* 6: 115–43. Repr. in Gilbert, M. (2014a).

Gilbert, M. (2002b) "Collective Wrongdoing; Moral and Legal Responses," *Social Theory and Practice* 28: 167–87.

Gilbert, M. (2006a) "Who's to Blame? Collective Moral Responsibility and Its Implications for Group Members," in Peter French (ed.) *Midwest Studies in Philosophy* 30: 91–114. Repr. in M. Gilbert (2014a).

Gilbert, M. (2006b) *A Theory of Political Obligation: Membership, Commitment, and the Bonds of Society*, Oxford: Oxford University Press.

Gilbert, M. (2007) "Searle on Collective Intentions," in Savas L. Tsohatsidis (ed.) *Intentional Acts and Institutional Facts: Essays on John Searle's Social Ontology*, Dordrecht: Springer.

Gilbert, M. (2009) "Shared Intention and Personal Intentions," *Philosophical Studies* 1444: 167–87.

Gilbert, M. (2011) "Foundations and Consequences of Collective Moral Responsibility," *Teoria e Critica della Regolazione Sociale*, Quaderno 1: 1–20.

Gilbert, M. (2014a) *Joint Commitment: How We Make the Social World*, New York: Oxford University Press.

Gilbert, M. (2014b) "How We Feel: Understanding Collective Emotion Ascription," in C. von Sheve and M. Salmela (eds.) *Collective Emotions: Perspectives from Psychology, Philosophy, and Sociology*, Oxford: Oxford University Press.

Gilbert, M. (2015) "Joint Commitment: What It Is and Why It Matters," *Phenomenology and Mind* 9: 17–26.

Gilbert, M. (2018) *Rights and Demands: A Foundational Inquiry*, Oxford: Oxford University Press.

Gilbert, M. and D. Pilchman (2014) in J. Lackey (ed.), *Essays in Collective Epistemology*, Oxford: Oxford University Press.

Giubilini, A. and Levy, N. (2018) "What in the World is Collective Responsibility?" *Dialectica* 72(2): 191–217.

Hobbes, T. (1982/1651) *Leviathan*, London: Penguin Books.

Isaacs, T. (2006) "Collective Moral Responsibility and Collective Intention," in P. French and H. Wettstein (eds.) *Shared Intentions and Collective Responsibility*, *Midwest Studies in Philosophy*, 30: 59–73.

Isaacs, T. (2011) *Moral Responsibility in Collective Contexts*, Oxford: Oxford University Press.

Jaspers, K. (1947) *The Question of German Guilt*, tr. E. B. Ashton. New York: Capricorn.

Korsgaard, C. (2014) "The Normative Constitution of Agency," in Manuel Vargas and Gideon Yaffee (eds.) *Rational and Social Agency*, New York: Oxford University Press.

Mäkelä, P. (2000) "Collective Moral Responsibility: a Collective as an Independent Moral Agent?" *Australasian Journal of Professional and Applied Ethics* 2(2): 86–101.

McKenna, M. (2006) "Collective Responsibility and an Agent Meaning Theory," *Midwest Studies in Philosophy* 30(1): 16–34.

McMahan, J. (2010) "Torture and Collective Shame," in A. Leist and P. Singer (eds.) *J.M. Coetzee and Ethics: Philosophical Perspectives on Literature*, New York: Columbia University Press.

Miller, S. and Mäkelä, P. (2005) "The Collectivist Approach to Collective Moral Responsibility," *Metaphilosophy* 36(5): 634–51.

Searle, J. (1990) "Collective Intentions and Actions" in P.R. Cohen, J. Morgan and M.E. Pollack (eds.) *Intentions in Communication*, Cambridge, MA: Harvard University Press, 401–415.

Smiley, M. (2010) "From Moral Agency to Collective Wrongs: Re-Thinking Collective Moral Responsibility," *Journal of Law and Policy* 1: 171–202.

Tollefsen, D. (2006) "The Rationality of Collective Guilt," in P. French and H. Wettstein (eds.) *Shared Intentions and Collective Responsibility*, *Midwest Studies in Philosophy* 30: 222–39.

van den Beld, A. (2002) "Can Collective Responsibility for Perpetrated Evil Persist Over Generations?" *Ethical Theory and Moral Practice* 5(2): 181–200.

Further Reading

Jansen, L. (2014) "A Plural Subject Approach to the Responsibilities of Groups and Institutions," *Midwest Studies in Philosophy* 38: 91–102. (Applies a Gilbertian perspective to forward-looking collective moral responsibility.)

3

COLLECTIVE MORAL RESPONSIBILITY AS JOINT MORAL RESPONSIBILITY

Seumas Miller

Collective moral responsibility is a species of moral responsibility and contrasts, in particular, with individual moral responsibility. However, the notion of moral responsibility, whether individual or collective, contrasts with a number of other notions.

First, we need to distinguish moral responsibility (including collective moral responsibility) from causal responsibility. A person or persons can inadvertently cause a bad outcome without necessarily being morally responsible for so doing. For example, a careful and competent driver who is obeying all the rules of the road might, nevertheless, accidently and unavoidably hit and maim a child who suddenly and unpredictably runs onto the road and in front of the moving vehicle.

Second, we can distinguish moral responsibility from what can be referred to as natural responsibility. Moral responsibility typically requires not only causal responsibility but also an intention to cause good or evil (or at least the knowledge that one's action will or may well cause good or evil) and an intention that is itself under one's control (and connects in the right way with one's action (Davidson 1963)). On the other hand, one is not necessarily *morally* responsible for one's actions under one's control since such action might not have any moral significance. If I get myself a cup of coffee then I am normally responsible for this since the action is entirely under my control; however, arguably, I am not *morally* responsible for doing so, given the action has no moral significance. At any rate, I assume in this chapter that there is a distinction along these lines to be made between moral responsibility and natural responsibility. I also note that natural responsibility is not the same thing as causal responsibility, since I can unknowingly cause some outcome without intending to do so, or even knowing that I have done so, e.g. when I accidentally spill my coffee.

Third, we need to distinguish moral responsibility from institutional responsibility, e.g. legal responsibility. I might be morally responsible for breaking my promise to meet my friend for lunch without being legally responsible for so doing.

Fourth, I distinguish between moral responsibility and blameworthiness and praiseworthiness (albeit, this is controversial – see Strawson (1962)). If I keep my promise to meet my friend for lunch and doing so is easily done then, although I am morally responsible for keeping my promise, I am neither blameworthy nor praiseworthy. I am not blameworthy since I kept my promise, but nor am I praiseworthy since I was under an obligation to keep it and doing so entailed minimal, if any, cost to myself.

Finally, we need to distinguish prospective or forward-looking from retrospective or backward-looking responsibility. Suppose a thief is morally responsible for his past crimes; this is retrospective responsibility. Now suppose a police officer is morally (and, for that matter, institutionally) responsible for arresting the thief if and when he comes across him; this is prospective responsibility.

As is the case with individual responsibility we can distinguish between collective moral responsibility, on the one hand, and collective causal, collective natural and collective institutional responsibility, on the other hand. (Here I assume that there is some, at least notional, distinction to be made between aggregate causal responsibility and collective causal responsibility, e.g. by virtue of the causal power of the collective per se being greater than the sum of the causal power of each of the contributing agents.) Moreover, we can distinguish between collective retrospective and collective prospective moral responsibility.

Collective moral responsibility is the moral responsibility that attaches to structured and unstructured groups of human persons for their morally significant actions and omissions. Thus, an *organised* gang of thieves who carry out a million-dollar bank heist are collectively morally – and, for that matter, collectively causally and legally – (retrospectively) responsible for the theft. Again, a number of bystanders – an unstructured group – who act jointly to save a child trapped in a burning house are collectively morally responsible for saving the child's life. Notice that sometimes it is the members of a group that are said to be collectively responsible and sometimes it is the group or other collective entity per se, e.g. the Mafia might be said to be collectively morally responsible for a crime wave in southern Italy.

There are three prominent kinds of theories of collective moral responsibility. The first of these conceives of collective moral responsibility as a convenient way of referring to what is in fact simply an aggregate of individual responsibilities. I refer to it as the atomistic account. The second holds that it is the group or collective itself which is the bearer of moral responsibility. I refer to this view as the collectivist account (albeit there are different versions of this account). The third theory is a relational account; collective moral responsibility as joint moral responsibility (JMR) (Miller 2001b; Miller 2006). JMR contrasts with collectivist accounts since the only bearers of moral responsibility are individual human persons (or like creatures) and not collective entities per se. However, JMR also contrasts with atomistic accounts since on this third view collective moral responsibility is to be understood in relational terms; joint responsibility is not analyzable into a mere aggregate of individual responsibilities.

In this chapter, I first situate JMR in relation to atomism and collectivism (section 3.1). In section 3.2 I elaborate JMR. I then go on to show how JMR might accommodate at least some of the central categories of collective omissions (section 3.3) and morally significant diachronic institutional action – what I refer to as chains of moral responsibility (section 3.4).

3.1 Atomism, Collectivism, and Joint Moral Responsibility

Advocates of atomism with respect to collective moral responsibility include H. D. Lewis (Lewis 1948), R. S. Downie (Downie 1969), Stephen Sverdlik (Sverdlik 1987), Jan Narveson (Narveson 2002), and András Szigeti (Szigeti 2014). (For criticisms see Copp (2006).) The strength of atomism is that it does not postulate supra-human collective entities as the mysterious bearers of moral responsibility and of the psychological states (e.g. beliefs and intentions) necessary for moral responsibility. Moreover, since it ascribes moral responsibility only to individual human beings, it has no tendency to let the members of collective entities, such as criminal organizations or negligent corporations, off the hook by relocating moral responsibility at the supra-human level. The weakness of atomism is that it does not seem to be able to accommodate the full range of cases in which we pre-theoretically ascribe collective moral responsibility. For example, in our above million-dollar bank heist example, robber A might be individually responsible for planning the heist, robber B for driving the getaway car, C for blowing the safe, D for taking one hundred thousand dollars, E for taking a second hundred thousand and so on. However, arguably none of the robbers was individually causally responsible – and, therefore, individually morally responsible – for stealing one million dollars. Again, we pre-theoretically hold BP morally responsible for the massively environmentally damaging oil spill in the Gulf of Mexico in 2009. But here we seem to be doing something above and beyond simply ascribing individual moral responsibility to each of BP personnel who did something wrong, and aggregating these. BP's moral responsibility seems to be more than the aggregate of individual responsibilities.

On collectivist accounts "collective responsibility" should be understood as attaching to the collective entity per se. Paradoxically, therefore, collective moral responsibility turns out to be a species of individual responsibility, albeit the "individual" is a collective entity. At any rate, on this collectivist view whether the members of a collective – that is, the individual human persons who constitute the collective in question – are each individually responsible is a separate question and, in any case, not directly a question of collective responsibility. In David Copp's terminology the collectivist claim is equivalent to the claim that a collective can be an independent moral agent (Copp 2006) (for criticisms of Copp see Miller (2007)). An important corollary of the collectivist view is that collectives are capable of bearing moral responsibility for outcomes, even when none of their members is in any degree *individually* morally responsible for those outcomes. Other prominent representatives of the collectivist approach include Peter French (French 1984) (for criticisms of French see Velasquez (1983)), Margaret Gilbert (Gilbert 2002) (for criticisms of Gilbert see Miller and Mäkelä (2005)), and Christian List and Philip Pettit (List and Pettit 2011) (for criticisms of List and Pettit see Szigeti (2014)).

Perhaps unsurprisingly, collectivism tends to be regarded as being able to accommodate many of the problems that beset atomism but, nevertheless, to lack the virtues of atomism (Mäkelä 2007). Thus, to return to our examples, collectivism will ascribe moral responsibility to (respectively) the gang of robbers as a collective entity and to BP per se (and not merely to some individual BP personnel for their individual moral failings). However, in so doing it admits supra-human collective entities (the gang, BP), which (somewhat mysteriously) bear moral responsibility (and, therefore, the associated psychological states (but see List and Pettit (2011) and for the rejoinder Szigeti (2014)) and which have the potential to get (respectively) the individual gang members and BP personnel off the moral hook. Potentially at least, BP is morally responsible but none of its managers, employees etc. have any moral responsibility; and the same goes for the individual gang members, at least as far as the theft of the million dollars is concerned (as opposed to, say, driving the getaway car or stealing one hundred thousand dollars). At any rate, on the collectivist account difficult questions arise concerning the relation between the moral responsibility of the collective entity per se and the moral responsibility of each of the members of the collective.

Having situated JMR in relation to atomistic and collectivist accounts of collective moral responsibility, I turn in the next section to its elaboration. Before doing so, I should make it clear that one might hold either a monistic or a pluralist view of collectivist moral responsibility and that this has implications for the theoretical reach of JMR. On the monistic view, JMR provides an analysis of the one and only concept of collective moral responsibility; therefore, its theoretical reach is comprehensive. On the pluralist view, JMR provides an analysis of one of a number of central concepts of collective moral responsibility; therefore, its theoretical reach while still considerable, is not comprehensive. Moreover, on the monistic view, JMR, atomism and collectivism are competing theories of collective responsibility. However, on the pluralist view, JMR might be consistent with collectivism (and perhaps atomism, assuming atomism were to abandon its reductionist claim); they are simply different theories because they are theories of different species of collective moral responsibility. In this chapter I take a neutral stance on this issue. I provide an elaboration of JMR as an analysis of one central concept of collective responsibility while leaving it open whether there are other concepts of collective responsibility. However, I note that JMR is well-positioned to avoid some of the main problems besetting atomism or besetting collectivism. Thus, JMR does not postulate supra-human collective entities as the mysterious bearers of moral responsibility, and has no tendency to let the members of collective entities off the moral hook by relocating moral responsibility at the supra-human level. Moreover JMR, being relational in character, seem better equipped than atomistic accounts to provide a plausible account of the ascription of moral responsibility to groups. For instance, in the heist example, while each is individually responsible for his contributory action (e.g. C for blowing the safe), each is also responsible, jointly with the others, for stealing the million dollars. Let us, then, consider JMR in more detail.

3.2 Collective Moral Responsibility as Joint Moral Responsibility

JMR takes *joint* actions as its starting point (Miller 1992; Miller 2001b; Miller 2006; see also Mellema (1988) and May (1992)). According to JMR, at least one of the central senses of collective responsibility is responsibility arising from joint actions (and joint omissions). Roughly speaking, a joint action can be understood thus: two or more individuals perform a joint action if each of them intentionally performs an individual action but does so with the (true) belief that in so doing each will do their part and they will jointly realise an end which each of them has and which each has interdependently with the others (a collective end, in my parlance (Miller 1992)). (For related theories of joint action see Tuomela and Miller (1988) and Bratman (2014).) On this view of collective responsibility as joint responsibility, collective responsibility is ascribed to individuals. Each member of the group is individually morally responsible for his or her own contributory action, and (at least in the case of most small-scale joint action – see below) each is also individually (fully or partially – see below) responsible for the aimed-at outcome, i.e. the realised collective end, of the joint action. (I note that an outcome of a joint action might not be aimed at and, if so, it is not a constitutive element of a successful joint action, i.e. it is not the realised collective end of the joint action.) However, each is individually responsible for the realised collective end, *jointly with the others*; hence the conception is relational in character. Thus, in our million-dollar bank heist example, each member of the gang is responsible jointly with the others for the theft of the million dollars because each performed his contributory action in the service of that collective end (the theft of the million dollars). I note that if the joint action has no moral significance then the participants have joint *natural* responsibility for their action but not joint, i.e. collective, *moral* responsibility for it. Since theft is a morally significant action, our bank robbers are jointly (collectively) morally responsible for stealing the million dollars.

I note that on JMR it is possible that while each participant in a morally significant joint action makes a causal contribution to the aimed-at outcome of the joint action, none of these contributing actions considered on its own is either necessary or sufficient for this outcome (Miller 2006). Consider the following example of a murder. Six men simultaneously (deliberately and without moral justification) stab a seventh (innocent) man, and each does so having as an end to kill their victim. However, each knows that his one act of stabbing will only wound the victim, and that four stab wounds are necessary and sufficient to kill the victim. I further note that on JMR it is possible that in such scenarios – scenarios in which each participant makes a causal contribution which is neither necessary nor sufficient for the outcome – each participant is *fully* morally responsible (jointly with the others) for the outcome (Miller 2006). Consider, for instance, our stabbing scenario. First, each of the six men is individually fully morally responsible for the stab wound he inflicted. Second, the six men are jointly morally responsible for killing the man, i.e. they are jointly responsible for murder. Significantly, in relation to this joint responsibility, each of the six is *fully* morally responsible (jointly with the other five) for the murder (and, assuming there was sufficient evidence, each would in all likelihood be held criminally responsible for murder).

What of large-scale morally significant joint actions and omissions, such as the BP oil spill disaster mentioned above? These introduce a range of issues that are often not present in small-scale, morally significant joint actions and omissions. For one thing, large-scale cases often involve hierarchical organisations and hence the potential for those in subordinate positions having diminished moral responsibility. For another thing, the extent of the contribution to the outcome of a joint action or omission can vary greatly from one participant to another. Indeed, some of those who make a causal contribution to a joint action – and especially to large-scale joint actions – might, nevertheless, not be genuine participants in that joint action because in performing their contributory action they were not aiming at the outcome constitutive of the joint action; they did not have its collective end as their end. On a relational view such as JMR, BP can be ascribed collective moral responsibility for the Gulf oil spill to the extent that BP personnel jointly acted – or, more likely, jointly (and culpably) failed to act (see section 3.4) – in ways that led to the disaster. Here the network of joint actions and omissions could be quite wide and complex without involving (either causally or in terms of their intentions, ends or responsibilities) all, or even most, BP personnel. Moreover, some joint actions or omissions are likely to be of greater moral significance than others, and some individual contributions, e.g. those of the BP managers, of greater importance than others, e.g. those of lower echelon employees (Zimmerman 1985).

It is important to note here that not only is each agent individually (naturally) responsible for performing his contributory action, each is responsible by virtue of the fact that he intentionally performs this action (and his intention is under his control and connects to his action in the right way), and the action is not intentionally performed by anyone else. Of course, the other agents (or agent) *believe* that he is performing, or is going to perform, the contributory action in question. But mere possession of such a belief is not sufficient for the ascription of responsibility to *the believer* for performing the individual action in question. So, what are the agents *collectively* (naturally) responsible for? As already mentioned, the agents are collectively (naturally) responsible for the realisation of the (collective) *end* that results from their contributory actions. Consider 10 men jointly pushing a car up a hill. Each is individually (naturally) responsible for his own pushing action, and the 10 men are collectively (naturally) responsible for intentionally bringing it about that the car is at the top of the hill, given that each performed an action which made a significant causal contribution. Perhaps the pushing action of each of the men is necessary if the car is to be pushed up the hill. However, if we assume that the pushing actions of nine of the men would have been sufficient, then although each pushing action made a causal contribution, no single pushing action was causally necessary (or, obviously, sufficient) to realise the collective end. Evidently, as already noted above, in joint actions (as opposed to joint omissions – see section 3.3), while each single constitutive individual action needs to make a causal contribution, none needs to be causally necessary to realise the relevant collective end.

This theoretical point has an important implication for the ascription of collective (i.e. joint) moral responsibility to participants in morally significant, large-scale joint actions, in particular, since typically in large-scale joint actions no contribution of a single participant taken on its own is necessary in order to realise the collective end of the joint action. Specifically, it is now possible, at least in principle, to ascribe collective, i.e. joint, moral responsibility to participants in morally significant, large-scale joint actions. The fact that in a large-scale joint action the action of each participant taken on its own is not necessary to realise the collective end of the joint action is not, given this theoretical point, a barrier to the ascription of moral responsibility to each participant (jointly with the others) for the realisation of this collective end. Note that it does not follow from this that each participant in a large-scale joint action is *fully* morally responsible (jointly with the others) for the realisation of the collective end of the joint action. Indeed, this is unlikely given that the causal contribution of each in large-scale joint actions is often very small and the commitment of each to the collective end correspondingly very weak. Rather in such cases each might only have *partial* moral responsibility (jointly with the others), or perhaps a *share* in the moral responsibility, for the realisation of the collective end (Miller 2011).

Notice that by analogy with individual natural responsibility for a single action, in the case of collective natural responsibility for a joint action, the collective end is under the joint control of the participating agents and this end connects in the right way with its outcome. Thus, agents would not be naturally responsible for a joint action if the collective end was under the control of some third party or if the collective end caused its outcome by way of some deviant causal chain (Davidson 1963). In relation to the control condition, consider a slave-owner who coerces his slaves to perform a joint action of painting his house. The slave-owner's coercive efforts are in part directed at ensuring that each has as an end that the house be painted – and has this end interdependently with the others having it. So the forming of the collective end is not something under the control of the slaves but rather of the slave-owner (as, of course, are the individual actions performed by each to realise that collective end). In relation to the condition outlawing deviant causal chains, consider the following example. The collective end of two car drivers going in opposite directions on a road in Australia is to avoid a collision and do so by each steering his car onto the left-hand side of the road (this being the convention in Australia). However, as it happens both drivers have recently arrived from the USA for a holiday in Australia and each is unused to driving on the left. Moreover, neither is wide-awake after their respective long flights and, as they approach one another around a bend but outside one another's field of vision, each is simultaneously startled by the sudden realisation that he is intentionally driving on the left. The act of being startled by this realisation of the unfamiliar intentional act of driving on the left automatically triggers the involuntary action of switching to driving on the right. The consequence of this is that each is now driving his car on the right-hand side of the road as he goes around the bend, thereby realising the collective end of averting a collision. So there is a collective end to avoid a collision and each has an initial intention to drive on the left in the correct belief that if each drives on the left a collision will be avoided (it being Australia). Moreover, the intentional action of driving on the left – which was itself caused by the prior intention to drive on the left – did cause the realisation of the collective end, i.e. the averting of the collision. However, it did so indirectly via the involuntary action of driving on the right and this was not the intended means to the collective end. Evidently, therefore, the agents were not (naturally or, for that matter, morally) responsible for averting the collision.

In section 3.1 we distinguished between natural, moral and institutional responsibility, and in section 3.2 we have been discussing collective natural responsibility and collective moral responsibility. What of collective institutional responsibility? For our purposes here an institution can be understood as an organisation or system of organisations constituted at least in part by a structure of roles and by some collective end(s) served by that structure of roles (Miller 2010; Ludwig 2017). For instance, a business organisation in the construction industry might consist of managers, architects, engineers, carpenters, labourers, salespeople, and so on, and have as a collective end to construct high rise buildings. Notice that the joint actions performed by the occupants of such organisations often consist of *layered structures of joint actions* (Miller 1992; Miller 2010). For instance, the organisation's team of architects, structural engineers etc. might design a given high rise building (joint action j1); its team of concrete-layers, crane-drivers etc. might construct the shell of the building according to the designers' specifications (joint action j2); its team of carpenters, labourers etc. might construct and place the internal walls, windows, doors, etc. (j3). Let us refer to the large-scale, complex joint action that consists in building this high rise as J. J consists of the actions of all the above, i.e. architects, structural engineers, concrete-layers, carpenters etc. Moreover, J consists in the subsidiary joint actions, j1, j2 and j3, and the collective ends of each of these subsidiary joint actions, e.g. to construct the shell of the high rise, ultimately serves the collective end of J, i.e. to build the high rise. Other things being equal, we can now say that all or most of the members of the above teams have, at least in principle, collective responsibility, i.e. joint natural responsibility, for building the high rise by way of their participation in a layered structure of joint actions. Of course, things might not be equal if, for instance and as mentioned above, many of these persons did not perform their actions having as at least one of their ends the construction of the high rise building.

However, institutional role occupants have more than simply natural responsibility (individual or joint) for their actions and omissions. Institutional role occupants are governed by sanction-backed regulations and laws that both constrain and enable the actions that they (institutionally, e.g. legally) ought, and ought not, to perform qua institutional role occupants. If the occupants of institutional roles have institutional responsibilities with respect to their performance of joint actions (or joint omissions) then these responsibilities are collective institutional responsibilities. Note that in some cases these collective institutional responsibilities will be prospective, such as in cases where there is a *joint* institutional duty to realise the collective end of some joint action. Here the individual duty of each to perform his or her contributory action is interdependent with the individual duty of each of the others to perform theirs. On the other hand, as was mentioned above, collective institutional responsibility can also be retrospective, such as in cases where the institutional actors have failed to do their joint duty. Note also that while institutional responsibilities are often congruent with moral responsibilities, this is not necessarily the case. In apartheid South Africa police were legally, i.e. institutionally, required to enforce morally repugnant laws, such as those banning sex across the colour bar.

There is an important sense of institutional responsibility attaching to those in authority. Suppose the members of the relevant government committee collectively decide to exercise their institutionally determined right to introduce an anti-corruption measure, e.g. mandatory reporting of corrupt and criminally negligent actions. The committee members are then collectively responsible for this policy, and potentially for the untoward consequences of its implementation, e.g. vexatious reporting.

There are a couple of things to keep in mind here. First, the notion of responsibility in question is, at least in the first instance, institutional – as opposed to moral – responsibility. Second, the "decisions" of committees, as opposed to the individual decisions of the members of committees, need to be analysed in terms of the notion of a joint institutional mechanism (introduced and analysed in detail elsewhere (Miller 1992; Miller 2006; Miller 2018)). So, the "decision" of the committee, can be analysed as follows: At one level each member of the committee voted for or against the policy of mandatory reporting. Let us assume some voted in the affirmative and others in the negative. But at another level, each member of the committee agreed, let us assume, to abide by the outcome of the vote; each voted having as a collective end that the outcome with a majority of the votes in its favour would be realised. Accordingly, the members of the government committee were jointly institutionally responsible for the policy change; that is, the committee were collectively institutionally responsible for the change.

What, then, of collective *moral* responsibility? According to JMR, collective moral responsibility is a species of joint responsibility (Miller 2001b; Miller 2006; Miller 2007). Accordingly, other things being equal (see section 3.3 for more complex cases), each agent is individually morally responsible, but this is conditional, based on the others being likewise individually morally responsible. There is interdependence in respect of moral responsibility. This account of collective moral responsibility arises naturally out of the account of joint actions. Roughly speaking, according to JMR, if agents are jointly naturally, and/or jointly institutionally, responsible for a joint action (or the realisation of a foreseen or reasonably foreseeable outcome of that action), and if the joint action or the outcome is morally significant, then – other things being equal – the agents are collectively morally responsible for that action or outcome. Moreover, other things being equal, the agents ought to attract moral praise or blame, and (possibly) punishment or reward for realising the collective end of the joint action or for bringing about the outcome.

I note that an action might be morally significant in a number of ways. For instance, the action might be inherently morally right or wrong, or the intention in performing it or its outcome morally good or bad. Note also that the "other things being equal" clauses provide for the possibilities that the agents in question either lack the requisite moral capacities – and so cannot be held morally responsible – or are possessed of moral capacities, but in the circumstances in question have an excuse or justification for their joint actions or for their outcomes. Finally, I note that this account provides a sufficient, but not a necessary, condition for collective moral responsibility. Accordingly, it leaves the way open for other notions of collective moral responsibility.

3.3 Collective Moral Responsibility for Omissions

JMR looks to be generalisable to, at least, some central categories of collective moral responsibility for omissions and, in particular, morally significant joint omissions.[1]

Assume that there are multiple persons, A1, A2, A3 etc., whose lives are at high risk, but that there are multiple bystanders, B1, B2, and B3 etc., who could, if they performed a salient joint action, J, save these lives without significant cost to themselves. So, the bystanders can perform J, and if J was performed it would, in fact, save the lives of A1 etc. (Miller 2001a; Miller 2006; Clarke 2014: 125–32). Here I am assuming that all this is a matter of mutual true belief among the bystanders, e.g. B1 truly believes that performing J would save the lives of A1 etc., B2 truly believes that performing J would save the lives of A1 etc., B1 truly believes that B2 truly believes that performing J would save the lives of A1 etc. (Smith 1982). The bystanders in such scenarios have a collective, or joint, moral responsibility to save those at risk by virtue of the (aggregate) positive rights of the latter. Moreover, this collective moral responsibility is (under some more or less adequate description, e.g. the notion of a joint responsibility or a positive right might not be fully understood) also a matter of mutual true belief among the bystanders. Accordingly, each bystander has an individually possessed moral obligation to perform his individual action as a contribution to the joint action, and thus to the realisation of the collective end of saving the multiple lives at high risk. However, this obligation is possessed interdependently with the others; it is a joint moral obligation. So joint moral obligations can be derived from collective moral responsibilities to realise morally required collective ends. Roughly speaking, the realisation of such a collective end calls for the performance of some salient joint action. The determination of this joint action, in turn, enables the specification of the contributory individual actions, and thereby the generation of the individual moral obligations of the participants. Each participant has a moral obligation to perform a contributory action. However, just as the action of each participant is performed interdependently with the actions of the others, so are the corresponding individual moral obligations interdependent. This is because each individual action is only part of the means to realise the collective end, and its performance would have no point if the others refrained from performing their contributory actions. Accordingly, the moral obligation of each to perform his contributory action would lapse if the others did not perform theirs; hence these moral obligations are joint moral obligations. At any rate, in cases of this kind, if the agents omit to perform the joint action then – other things being equal – they have failed to discharge their joint obligation and, therefore, they are collectively morally responsible for their omission. This is so whether or not each intended *not* to perform his or her contributory action or merely failed to form an intention to do so. I note that even if each failed to form an intention to perform his contributory action, each did believe that he ought to perform his contributory action (supposing the others performed theirs). Moreover, the performance of his contributory action is something that "comes to mind" to each; at the very least, it occurs to each that he could perform his contributory action (Clarke 2014: 35–87).

Notice that there can be cases where the morally significant collective end of a joint action is realised, yet one individual (or a minority) fails to successfully perform his contributory individual action, and cases where the morally significant collective end of a joint action is not realised because most fail to perform their contributory actions, yet one individual (or a minority) successfully performs his contributory individual action. What are we to say about collective moral responsibility in such cases?

Consider the cases in which one individual (or a minority) fails to successfully perform his contributory action. (Note that the arguments below are also valid in the case of minorities, as opposed to individuals. However, to reduce verbal clutter, I won't refer to minorities on every occasion.) Assuming the individual (or minority) had the collective end in question (and, therefore, tried, albeit unsuccessfully, to perform his individual contributory action), the individual shares in the collective moral responsibility for the realisation of the collective end, notwithstanding his individual failure to perform his contributory action. For, as was the case with the other agents, the individual had the collective end in question. Moreover, as was also the case with the other agents, the individual *indirectly* causally contributed to the realisation of the collective end, notwithstanding his failure to perform his contributory action. He made an indirect causal contribution since the other individuals acted in part on the basis of their beliefs that the individual in question would perform his contributory action. Nevertheless, the failure of such an individual to perform his individual contributory action reduces his share of the collective moral responsibility for the realisation of the collective end.

The following question might now be asked of a would-be participant in a joint action who tried but failed to perform his contributory action.[2] What if the other individuals did not for some reason act even in part on the basis of their belief that the individual in question would perform his contributory action. If so, then the individual would not even have indirectly causally contributed to the collective end. In such cases it seems that the individual does not share in the collective moral responsibility for the realisation of the collective end. For, on the one hand, the individual did not make any actual causal contribution to the realisation of the collective end; but only attempted to do so. On the other hand, while he presumably believed that his end was an integral element of the collective end; it was not. The others possessed and successfully pursued the collective end independently of his possession and pursuit of that end.

Now consider cases in which the morally significant collective end is not realised due to the fact that most fail to perform contributory actions, yet one individual (or a minority) performs his. Once again, assuming all the individuals had the collective end in question (and, therefore, tried, albeit unsuccessfully, to perform their contributory actions), then the individual shares in the collective moral responsibility for the failure to realise the collective end, notwithstanding his individual success in performing his contributory action. For, as was the case with the other agents, the individual had the collective end in question, and that end was not realised; in short, each agent, including the individual in question, failed to realise an end each had (the collective end), and each failed to make a causal contribution to that end. Nevertheless, the success of such an individual in performing his own individual contributory action reduces his share of the collective moral responsibility for the failure to realise the collective end, at least in cases in which each would not have been *fully* morally responsible (albeit jointly with the others) for the realisation of the collective end supposing it had been realised (and it is not clear that there are cases of collective, i.e. joint, morally responsibility for omissions to perform a joint action in which each would have been *fully* responsible for the realisation of the collective end of the joint action, supposing it had been realised). In response to this it might be argued that the individual cannot have a share in the collective *moral* responsibility for the failure because, after all, he had the collective end in question and performed his contributory action; he did all that he could reasonably have been expected to do. Certainly, he is not morally culpable or blameworthy, but then neither are the others morally culpable or blameworthy, given they tried to perform their own contributory actions. The theoretical conclusion to be drawn at this point is twofold: (1) moral responsibility, including collective moral responsibility, should not be equated with culpability/non-culpability or blameworthiness/praiseworthiness (Miller 2007); and (2) agents can be (individually or collectively) morally responsible for failing to realise an outcome, even if they did all that can be reasonably expected of them; responsibility is not simply a matter of possession of the relevant subjective states, such as intentions and ends.

It is consistent with this that if an individual (or minority) *culpably* failed to realise his or her individual end yet knew that the collective end would nevertheless be realised, then that individual does *not* share in the collective moral responsibility for the successful outcome, since, for one thing, the individual did not, in fact, have the collective end. It is also consistent with the above that if an individual (or minority) *culpably* failed to realise his or her individual end in the knowledge that, as a consequence of this culpable failure, the collective end would not be realised, then the individual (a) does not have the collective end, and (b) is individually morally responsible for the collective failure (of the others) to realise the collective end. So, there is no collective moral responsibility, let alone collective moral culpability, for the failure.

3.4 Chains of Moral Responsibility

Let us now consider whether JMR can generalise to, at least, some central categories of morally significant diachronic institutional action.[3] Here I note that while JMR relies on a theory of joint action, some theories of joint action are not serviceable in this role. In particular, theories of joint action, such as Bratman's (Bratman 2014), that hold that participants in a joint action *intend* one another's contributory actions – rather than merely believe that they have performed, are performing or will perform these actions – are not serviceable. The reason for this is that in such diachronic joint actions it is often the case that a later participant is not a participant at the time when some earlier participants made their contributions. (See Miller (1995) on this point.) Consider the construction of the Sydney Harbour Bridge. This complex joint action, indeed layered structure of joint actions (Miller 1992 and 2018), was performed over a number of years. Now assume that Jones was involved in building the foundations of the bridge that were laid on the shores on either side of the harbour, but retired and then died before the arch of the bridge was started. Caranti, on the other hand, migrated to Australia from Italy after the foundations were completed, and he was involved in working on the arch of the bridge (but not the foundations). However, Caranti had not even heard of the Sydney Harbour Bridge project before arriving in Australia. Accordingly, he had no intentions with respect to the work of those, including Jones, who worked on the foundations, since they were completed before he arrived in Australia and intentions, unlike beliefs, are necessarily forward-looking; one can have beliefs in the present about the past, but one cannot intend in the present what has already happened in the past.

Let us now turn to the application of JMR to morally significant diachronic institutional action. Consider a team of detectives investigating a major crime. Let us assume that the team is engaging in a joint institutional action, namely, that of determining the identity of the Yorkshire Ripper. So, members of the team gather physical evidence, interview witnesses and, in particular, the main suspect, Peter Sutcliffe. Moreover, they do so having as a collective end to determine the *factual* guilt or innocence of this and other suspects. At some point the detectives complete this process and provide a brief of evidence to the prosecutors according to which, and based on all the evidence, Sutcliffe is the Yorkshire Ripper. So far so good, but the criminal justice processes do not terminate in the work of the detectives. For there is now the matter of the trial; that is, the determining by the members of a jury of the legal guilt or innocence of Sutcliffe. Let us assume that the members of the jury perform the joint (epistemic) action (Miller 2018) of deliberating on the *legal* guilt or innocence of Sutcliffe, and jointly reach the verdict of guilty (as in fact happened). The question that now arises concerns the institutional relationship between the joint institutional action of the detectives and the joint institutional action of the members of the jury. It is here that the notion of a chain of institutional responsibility is illuminating (Miller 2014).

Let us assume in what follows that the collective end of the criminal justice process comprised of both the investigating detectives *and* the members of the jury (as well as others, but here I simplify), is that the factually guilty be found legally guilty (and the factually innocent not be found legally guilty). Note that from the perspective of this larger institutional process the collective end of the detectives (that of determining the factual guilt or innocence of a suspect) is merely *proximate* whereas that of the members of the jury is *ultimate.* (It is, of course, only penultimate from the perspective of the criminal justice system more broadly conceived, given the need for sentencing and incarceration.)

Moreover, in all this there is an institutional division of labour and segregation of roles which involves each type of institutional actor, e.g. investigator, prosecutor, judge, jury etc. making a contribution to the further (collective) end of identifying and appropriately punishing the guilty and exonerating the innocent. However, unlike many institutional arrangements, the criminal justice process is predicated on strict adherence on the part of institutional actors to the segregation of roles on pain of compromising this further end. I emphasise that this segregation of roles is consistent with all of these actors, each with their own different and segregated role, having a common further aim; agents can have a common aim and yet it be a requirement that each is to make a different and distinct contribution to that aim, and not perform the tasks assigned to the others, and do all this in the service of that common aim.

In respect of this segregation of roles, the relationship between the institutional actors, including investigators, in the criminal justice process is *unlike* that which holds between (say) a manager, a waiter and a barman in a small pub. There is no reason why, for example, the manager and the waiter might not assist the barman in doing his job of pouring beers during a rush period or even stand in his place when he is called away. But there is good reason why the prosecutor should not also be the judge or the investigator the jury; in an adversarial system any such conflation of roles would constitute a structural conflict of interest and, as such, would be likely to undermine the administration of justice.

Institutional arrangements, such as this, in which there is a segregation of roles (and associated responsibilities) but, nevertheless, a common further end involve a chain of institutional responsibility. In chains of institutional responsibility all the participants aim (or should be aiming) at the further end in addition to undertaking their own roles (and, therefore, aiming at the end definitive of their own particular role). (Naturally, there are institutional arrangements consisting of role structures in which this is not the case; these do not consist of chains of institutional responsibility in my sense.) Moreover, all the participants (at least, in principle) share in the *collective responsibility* for achieving that further end (or for failing to do so). Let us work with our example of Peter Sutcliffe, the Yorkshire Ripper, who was ultimately convicted of 13 counts of murder (the victims being prostitutes working in Yorkshire in the UK).

The detectives involved were (collectively in the sense of jointly) institutionally responsible for gathering and analysing the evidence that identified Peter Sutcliffe as the Yorkshire Ripper; they acquired the required knowledge of Sutcliffe's *factual* guilt and, thereby, realised the collective end of their institutional role as detectives. On the other hand, members of the court and, in particular, the members of the jury were (collectively) institutionally responsible for finding Sutcliffe *legally* guilty and, thereby, realised the (collective) end of their institutional roles as jury members. So far so good, but what was the ultimate end that was realised by the detectives *and* the members of the jury (as well as the other actors involved in the institutional process, e.g. the judge)?

Presumably the end in question is for the factually guilty to be found legally guilty (and the factually innocent not to be found legally guilty) and this is an end (a collective end) that is realised by the detectives working jointly with the members of the jury (and the other relevant institutional actors). It is not an end that the detectives could achieve on their own; they can only arrive at knowledge of factual guilt. But equally it is not an end that the members of the jury could realise on their own; for they rely on the knowledge provided by the detectives. (Chains of institutional and moral responsibility consist of a process in which the completion of one stage institutionally triggers the commencement of the next stage, e.g. arrest is followed either by the suspect being charged or released within a specified time-frame.) Moreover, it is a morally significant end. Accordingly, other things being equal, the members of the detective team and the members of the jury are collectively (i.e. jointly) morally responsible for the realisation of this end (the factually guilty being found legally guilty and the factually innocent not being found legally guilty).

3.5 Conclusion

In this chapter, I have elaborated the theory of collective moral responsibility as joint moral responsibility (JMR). Roughly speaking, other things being equal, participants in a morally significant joint action are collectively morally responsible for that action, i.e. they are jointly morally responsible for it. Moreover, I have extended the reach of JMR beyond morally significant small-scale joint actions to large-scale ones, to some central categories of morally significant *omissions* to perform joint actions, and also to some central categories of morally significant institutional actions involving chains of institutional responsibility, i.e. to *chains of moral responsibility*.

Notes

1 An earlier version of the material in this section appeared in Miller (2001a).
2 Thanks to the editors for thinking of this possibility.
3 An earlier version of the material in this section appeared in Miller (2014).

References

Bratman, Michael (2014) *Shared Agency*, Oxford: Oxford University Press.

Clarke, Randolph (2014) *Omissions: Agency, Metaphysics and Responsibility*, Oxford: Oxford University Press.

Copp, David (2006) "On the Agency of Certain Collective Entities," *Midwest Studies in Philosophy* XXX: 194–220.

Davidson, Donald (1963) "Actions, Reasons and Causes," *Journal of Philosophy* 60(23): 685–700.

Downie, R. S. (1969) "Collective Responsibility," *Philosophy* 44: 66–69.

French, Peter (1984) *Collective and Corporate Responsibility*, New York: Columbia University Press.

Gilbert, Margaret (2002) "Collective Guilt and Collective Guilt Feelings," *Journal of Ethics* 6(2): 115–143.

Lewis, H. D. (1948) "Collective Responsibility," *Philosophy* 24: 3–18.

List, Christian and Pettit, Philip (2011) *Group Agency*, Oxford: Oxford University Press.

Ludwig, Kirk (2017) *From Plural to Institutional Agency*, Oxford: Oxford University Press.

Mäkelä, Pekka (2007) "Collective Agents and Moral Responsibility," *Journal of Social Philosophy* XXXVIII(3): 456–469.

May, Larry (1992) *Sharing Responsibility*, Chicago: University of Chicago Press.

Mellema, Gregory (1988) *Individuals, Groups and Shared Moral Responsibility*, New York: Peter Lang.

Miller, Seumas (1992) "Joint Action," *Philosophical Papers* 21(3): 275–297.

Miller, Seumas (1995) "Intentions, Ends and Joint Action," *Philosophical Papers* XXIV(1): 51–67.

Miller, Seumas (2001a) "Collective Responsibility and Omissions," *Business and Professional Ethics Journal* 20(1): 5–24.

Miller, Seumas (2001b) "Collective Responsibility," *Public Affairs Quarterly* 15(1): 65–82.

Miller, Seumas (2006) "Collective Moral Responsibility: An Individualist Account," *Midwest Studies in Philosophy* XXX: 176–193.

Miller, Seumas (2007) "Against the Moral Autonomy Thesis," *Journal of Social Philosophy* 38(3): 389–409.

Miller, Seumas (2010) *The Moral Foundations of Social Institutions: A Study in Applied Philosophy*, New York: Cambridge University Press.

Miller, Seumas (2011) "Collective Responsibility, Epistemic Action and Climate Change," in N. Vincent, I. van de Poel and J. van den Hoven (eds.) *Moral Responsibility: Beyond Free Will and Determinism*, Heidelberg: Springer: 219–246.

Miller, Seumas (2014) "Police Detectives, Criminal Investigations and Collective Moral Responsibility," *Criminal Justice Ethics* 33(1): 21–39.

Miller, Seumas (2018) "Joint Epistemic Action: Some Applications," *Journal of Applied Philosophy* 35(2): 300–318.

Miller, Seumas and Mäkelä Pekka (2005) "Collectivist Approach to Collective Moral Responsibility," *Metaphilosophy* 36(5): 634–651.

Narveson, Jan (2002) "Collective Responsibility," *Journal of Ethics* 6: 179–198.

Smith, N. (ed.) (1982) *Mutual Knowledge*, London: Academic Press.

Strawson, P. F. (1962) "Freedom and Resentment," *Proceedings of the British Academy* 48: 1–25.

Sverdlik, Stephen (1987) "Collective Responsibility," *Philosophical Studies* 51: 61–76.

Szigeti, András (2014) "Are Individualist Accounts of Collective Moral Responsibility Morally Deficient?" in A. Konzelman Zif and H. Bernhard Schmid (eds.) *Institutions, Emotions and Social Groups*, Dordrecht: Springer: 343–354.

Tuomela, Raimo and Miller, Kaarlo (1988) "We-intentions," *Philosophical Studies* 53: 115–137.

Velasquez, Manuel G. (1983) "Why Corporations are Not Morally Responsible for Anything They Do," *Business and Professional Ethics* 2(3): 1–18.

Zimmerman, Michael, J. (1985) "Sharing Responsibility," *American Philosophical Quarterly* 22(22): 115–122.

4

WHAT SETS THE BOUNDARIES OF OUR RESPONSIBILITY?

Lessons from a Reductionist Account of Individual Agency

Carol Rovane

In this chapter, I will be concerned to address the question of my title by taking on three somewhat more specific questions:

(1) In what sense is it correct to say that individual agents set the boundaries of their own responsibility?
(2) How does the issue of responsibility sort out when a group of human beings qualifies as an individual agent in its own right?
(3) To what extent, and why, are individual agents responsible for the outcomes of collective endeavours to which they contribute, but which do not lie within their power to bring about on their own?

Before proceeding to answer these questions, I want to register a preliminary point about responsibility. For various reasons, we are predisposed to focus on *backward looking* responsibility – on holding someone to account for something already done. Locke famously argued that it is a necessary condition for backward looking responsibility that the responsible agent be *conscious* of whatever it did. What such consciousness secures is a first personal relation to that action, as what *I* did. Such a first personal relation to one's past actions couldn't *be* first personal, unless it registered the first personal relation that one had to those actions at the time of acting. I infer that the sort of personal consciousness of one's past actions to which Locke was referring must include a memory of how, at the time of acting, one regarded the action as something that lay within one's *power* to do, where this power was a power to perform the action *intentionally*. To approach the world in this agential way – by reflecting on what lies within one's power to do, and then considering whether to do it – is to *take* responsibility for some bit of what will actually happen in the world, *by acting*.[1] This is *forward looking* responsibility. It would not be coherent to hold agents responsible in the backward looking sense – to hold them to account for their past actions – if they themselves had not already been in a position to take responsibility in the forward looking sense, by acting to begin with. This is why holding someone accountable is a form of *engagement* – because those whom we hold to account are agents who have already *taken* responsibility by acting; and this is why there can be uptake on their part when we hold them responsible. In this chapter, I shall be as much concerned with forward looking responsibility as with backward looking responsibility.

With these preliminary points about responsibility in hand, I can now outline the answers that I will be developing in this chapter to my three questions:

(1) The sense in which it is correct to say that individual agents set the boundaries of their own responsibility is supplied by a reductionist account of individual agency, according to which agents are *self-constituting* in a quite literal sense. When an individual agent constitutes itself, it sets boundaries within which it thinks and acts *as one*. These boundaries are at once the boundaries of the rational point of view from which it thinks and acts, and the boundaries that mark it off from other agents. In setting these boundaries, the agent not only sets the boundaries of its own thought and action, but also, the boundaries of its own responsibility. According to the reductionist account, these boundaries of individual agency need not coincide with the boundaries that mark one human life off from another. Thus, while the condition of individual agency can be realized within the boundaries of a single human life, it can also be realized within a group of human lives, and within different parts of a single human life. In other words, there can be group agents and multiple agents as well as agents of human size.

(2) When the condition of individual agency is realized within a group of human lives, this is not a case of collective agency in which many distinct agents of human size exercise their agency together, by thinking and acting from their distinct points of view. It is a case of genuinely *individual* agency. The group agent constitutes itself, by thinking and acting *as one*, from its own rational point of view. In so constituting itself, it sets the boundaries within which it thinks and acts; and these are boundaries within which the group agent can and should *take* responsibility for what *it* does. Furthermore, the human constituents of a group agent do not individually bear a first personal relation to what the group agent does – only the group agent itself bears that relation to what it does. This means that the human constituents of a group agent cannot, strictly speaking, take responsibility for what the group agent does.

(3) In contrast, collective agency is a social phenomenon in which many distinct individual agents bring about shared ends by acting together. Individual agents do this by thinking and acting from their own separate rational points of view, even as they coordinate their thoughts and actions in order to realize a collective outcome together. This means that the collective does *not* qualify as an individual agent in its own right, for *it* does not think and act *as one*, and indeed *it* does not think and act at all. Therefore, the collective itself cannot *take* responsibility for the outcomes of the collective endeavour; *only* the individual agents who comprise the collective can do that.

Before going on, a side note about terminology. For many philosophical purposes, and indeed, in many real life settings (personal, moral, legal, political), it makes sense to equate the concept of a person with the concept of an individual agent. But there are also many purposes and settings in which the custom is to equate the concept of a person with the concept of a human being. It should already be apparent from what I have said so far that if we accept the former equation then we cannot accept the latter equation – because we will have to accept that there can be group persons and multiple persons as well as persons of human size. Elsewhere I have argued that there is good reason to accept all of this, and to regard the reductionist account of agency as an account of the condition of personal identity (Rovane 1998). But since this is a controversial, and indeed revisionist, recommendation, I will refrain from the language of personhood in this chapter, and simply speak of agency.

The reductionist account of personal identity bears a significant resemblance to Parfit's psychological reductionist account of personal identity, which claims that the existence of a person consists in *nothing but* the existence of certain sorts of events standing in certain sorts of relations – in other words, it doesn't consist in any *further fact* such as a Cartesian ego (Parfit 1984). Yet it could fairly be objected that Parfit's reduction left out of account the fact that persons are *agents*.[2] For on his description, the events that make up a person's life *just happen* in more or less the same sense that the events that make up the rest of the course of nature – events from which agency is entirely missing – *just happen*. I propose to rectify this shortcoming by characterizing the reductive base of the reductionist account of individual agency in fully *agential* terms.[3] The events that I claim make up the life of an agent are not mere happenings, but *intentional activities* of a certain kind, in the form of both *thinkings* and *doings*; and the relations in which such thinkings and doings must stand in order to constitute the existence and identity of an individual agent are normative relations; through these relations a certain kind of unity is achieved, which defines individual rationality. All of these terms of the reductionist account of agency – intentional activities, normative relations, rational unity – are *irreducibly normative* in the sense that they cannot be reduced to the terms in which the natural sciences describe nature.[4] Yet the account is nevertheless reductionist in the following sense: it reduces the identity of any particular agent to the various *intentional activities* – the thinkings and doings – that constitute its life, and does not equate it with any further fact such as a Cartesian ego, or any other metaphysical condition that is allegedly distinct from the various intentional activities in which the life of an agent consists.[5]

Now that I have clarified the sense in which the reductionist account of individual agency is reductionist, I want to clarify next why it entails the possibility that the conditions of individual agency can be realized at the level of a whole group of human beings. We shall see that the reductionist account takes this case of group agency as a good model on which to understand *all* cases of individual agency, no matter how they fall with respect to human lives.

Consider a philosophy department that wants to review and revise its requirements for the PhD in philosophy. We would normally describe such a department as constituted by its human 'members', and so, to start with, I shall use this terminology. But we will soon see that the terminology can be misleading, precisely because when we refer to the human 'members' of a group agent such as a philosophy department, we normally presume that they must necessarily function as individual agents in their own right, who then constitute the group agent through social activities – in other words, the presumption is that group agency is a special case of collective agency. Once I have shown how and why this presumption is mistaken, I will no longer use the terminology of 'members', and refer instead to the human *constituents* of group agents, or more simply, to human *beings*. It will be important to bear in mind that whenever I employ this other terminology, of 'human constituents' and 'human beings', I myself do *not* presume that human beings always necessarily qualify as individual agents in their own right. But let me start by referring to the human 'members' of a department, while leaving the presumption to the side for the moment, without further comment.

Suppose that the 'members' of the department come to believe that they ought not to argue and vote on the requirements for the PhD, because they recognize that, then, if students were to ask about why they must satisfy certain degree requirements, the only available response would be, *Well that's the way the vote cut*. Thus, the 'members' of the department recognize that what a *responsible* department should want to do instead is to work out what set of degree requirements would be *best*, all things considered. But in order to do that, the department must identify *the things-to-be-considered*. This set of *things-to-be-considered* cannot be confined to thoughts that figure in the biological life of one or another human 'member' of the department, because that would have the effect of making that human 'member' dictator of the department's decisions concerning the requirements for the PhD. In order to avoid such a dictatorship, the set of *things-to-be-considered* must include various thoughts of the department's human 'members' insofar as they bear on the deliberative question before it. These thoughts, which are scattered across distinct human lives, would then constitute the proper basis of the *department's* deliberation. The aim of this *group* deliberation is to work out the joint normative significance of *all* of these thoughts, for the question what would it be best for the *department* to do in the light of them. In working this out, the department forges a group point of view, from which there are real answers to the question, when it is addressed to the department as a whole, *Why did you impose the requirements that you did?* The answers will not reflect the deliberations of any one human 'member' of the department, but rather the deliberations of the department as a whole. In this way, the department itself can *take* responsibility for what it has done, and therefore be *held* responsible as well.

When this kind of departmental deliberation takes place, each of the human 'members' is a site of intentional activities – thinkings and doings – that are carried out from the departmental point of view. I want to emphasize that this point of view is necessarily *distinct* from the points of view of its human 'members' – whom we ordinarily think of as individual human beings, who are also faculty members. In order to bring this feature of the case, concerning the *distinctness* of the department's point of view from the points of view of its 'members', into better relief, it may be helpful if I admit that it is a real case and not a manufactured example. *I* am a faculty member of a philosophy department in which I persuaded my colleagues that we should not argue about and then vote on the requirements for the PhD, but rather, the department should deliberate about them as a single body, working out the all-things-considered significance of everything that all of the faculty members might 'bring to the table' for consideration. As it happens, my own *personal* view was that the only requirement that the department should impose for the PhD in philosophy is a completed and successfully defended dissertation, and that everything else should be viewed as mere preparation for this one requirement, and furthermore, whatever additional preparation any given student should be required to make should be dictated by the nature of their particular philosophical interests and projects, and previous training. So *I* advocated individual programmes of study, rather than uniform requirements such as distribution requirements, logic requirements, foreign language requirements, comprehensive and qualifying examinations, third year essays, etc. But, predictably, all of those other requirements, and various reasons for and against them, were also put on the table for consideration. This would ordinarily be an occasion for arguments among the 'members' of the department, in which each would try to persuade the others of their own personal view. But instead of launching into such arguments, what my department actually did in this case was consider all of the possible requirements that had been put on the table for consideration, and the various reasons for and against them, and then work towards a *deliberated conclusion* about which combination of them would best serve our PhD students and why. The conclusion that the department actually arrived at imposed many more requirements than a completed and successfully defended dissertation, and so it clearly was *not* a conclusion that followed from my personal point of view – that is, the *department's* conclusion did not follow from what *I* believed about what would be best for our students. The conclusion followed from a set of considerations that included beliefs that *I* didn't happen to share, but which were definitely on the table for consideration by the department. And the same held for each and every 'member' of the department: the conclusion that the *department* arrived at did not strictly follow from what they individually believed from their own personal point of view, but rather from a larger set of considerations that had been put on the table for consideration by the department, which constituted the *department's* point of view.

I'm now ready to clarify why the reductionist account of individual agency takes the case of group agency as a model for all cases of individual agency. Insofar as the department deliberated in the way I just described – aiming to work out what would be best for *it* to do, by taking into account all of the thoughts that figure in *its* point of view – it aimed to realize a *rational ideal* that *defines* what it is for an *individual* agent to be fully, or ideally, rational. The ideal is to achieve *overall rational unity* within oneself by arriving at and acting upon all-things-considered judgements about what it would be best to do, that take into account all and only one's *own* thoughts about what is true and good. It is because the department aimed to meet this ideal of *individual* rationality that it makes sense to say that it thought and acted *as one*, and thereby qualified as an individual agent in its own right, who can be engaged and held responsible by others. The reductionist account of individual agency moves from this insight about group agency to a general claim about all cases of individual agency: *whenever* and *wherever* there is a commitment to realizing the ideal of overall rational unity, by arriving at and acting upon all-things-considered judgements, there is an individual agent that thinks and acts *as one*, in the sense that it deliberates and acts from its own point of view, in accord with the requirements of individual rationality. And here is why this general claim qualifies as *reductionist*: The existence and life of the philosophy department, qua group agent, consists in *nothing but* the intentional activities through which it thinks and acts *as one*, by striving for the kind of overall rational unity among them that is characteristic of individual rationality; and so it is with all individual agents, that their existence and life consists in *nothing but* such intentional activities, through which the kind of unity that is characteristic of individual rationality is achieved.[6]

The reductionist account allows that the basic agential capacities through which rational unity is achieved belong by nature to human beings. But there is no necessity that such unity must be achieved within the *whole* of a human life, for it can also be achieved within different parts of a human life, thereby giving rise to *multiple agents* within it. This is perhaps the most controversial implication of the reductionist account.[7] And yet, we often come close to recognizing it in ordinary life. For example, we are all aware that the considerations from which we deliberate for the purposes of our work life may be quite separate from the considerations from which we deliberate for the purposes of our home life. Similarly, it is almost a cliché that someone whom we regard as our close friend may suddenly seem like 'another person' when we encounter them in their role of loan officer at the bank, because of the way in which, in that context, everything they say and do reflects bank policy rather than their attachment to *us* – and so we say that the 'bureaucrat' we encounter at the bank is not recognizably the same person as our friend at all. It may seem an unnecessary exaggeration to construe these cases as ones in which a human being is actually host to multiple *agents*, as opposed to multiple *projects*. And it is important that the reductionist account can distinguish cases in which there are *many distinct agents* within a single human life from cases where there is *one agent* within that life, with *many distinct projects*. It does so in terms of whether there is an overarching commitment to overall rational unity within that life. It should not be surprising that such an overarching commitment to unity within the whole of a human life tends to be present in most of the cases of individual agency that we know. After all, we agents of human size tend to teach one another, and urge one another, to approach life in a unified way, by asking *What are you going to do with your life?* and by declaring the worth of so-called *life projects* that generally do take up the whole of a human life, such as marriages and careers. But we should not overlook the ways in which our social conditions may sometimes actually promote multiplicity over unity within a single human life. Consider, for example, the social conditions of many immigrant children in New York City who come from highly traditional immigrant homes, and who must also navigate the social space of an elite public high school. In order to navigate each of these spaces effectively, it may well be that a 'switch' is required as they go back and forth between home and school, between the mind-set and values that would enable harmonious and dutiful life in a traditional home, and the mind-set and values that would afford a suitably ambitious and autonomous response to the educational opportunities afforded by the culture of liberal individualism.[8]

I am not arguing that the *best* human life would be one that was marked by the kind of division, or rational fragmentation, that would go together with the existence of multiple agents within it. Perhaps the *best* use of a human life would be to achieve the kind of overall unity within it that would go together with the existence of a roughly human-sized agent. But if that *were* so, then it would still be important to acknowledge the difference that it makes when we regard such overall unity within a human life as an *option* that is *worthy* of our pursuit, rather than as our metaphysically given condition. Correlatively, it is important to acknowledge that such overall rational unity within a whole human life is not a rational requirement any more than it is a metaphysically given condition. All there is here, is the following *constitutive truth*: any rational agent will be committed to achieving overall rationality within *itself*, because that is *what it is* to be a rational agent. It might be tempting to construe this commitment as a rational response to a categorical imperative to be rational. I myself am not so tempted – I think rational beings might find reasons to cease to be rational, even if acting on those reasons amounted to a kind of suicide. But in any case, even if we *were* tempted to think that there is a categorical imperative to be rational, it could be obeyed by any rational agent, no matter what its size – it could be obeyed equally by multiple agents, by agents of human size, and by group agents too. And there is an important corollary point, which is that according to the reductionist account of individual agency such an imperative, that simply said *Be rational!* would inevitably be *incomplete*: it cannot be followed until the boundaries are set, within which the demand for rational unity is to be realized!

And so the question arises: How do such boundaries get set? The answer supplied by the reductionist account is: Through a commitment to a *unifying project* that cannot be pursued without arriving at and acting upon all-things-considered judgements within particular boundaries. In my chapter so far, I've referred to various such unifying projects: a philosophy department's project of setting requirements for the PhD degree in philosophy, which mandates thinking and acting *as one* at the level of the whole department; life projects, such as marriages and careers, that mandate thinking and acting *as one* within a whole human life; smaller projects that mandate thinking and acting *as one* within one or another of many different social spheres that a single human being might move among.

I said at the outset that, according to the reductionist account, individual agents are *self-constituting*. Let me now add that part of what I mean is that they are not constituted by anything else. In particular, an individual agent is not constituted by any metaphysically given facts, such as the existence of a given human body and consciousness – for it comes to be only with and through the intentional activities, the thinkings and doings that constitute its agential life. An agent is not constituted by other agents either – for to repeat, it comes to be only through *its own* intentional activities. If an individual agent comes to be only through its *own* intentional activities, and if its existence consists in *nothing else besides* these intentional activities, then it follows that it is literally *self*-constituting.

I also said at the outset that when an individual agent constitutes itself it sets boundaries within which it thinks and acts *as one*. And then I added: these boundaries are the boundaries of the point of view from which the agent thinks and acts; and they are the boundaries that mark the agent off from other agents; and they are the boundaries of the agent's own responsibility.

Let me elaborate what I meant by these further claims by returning to the example about the philosophy department.

In my descriptions so far, I have taken care to emphasize that the *department's* point of view is distinct from *my* point of view, because the department deliberates from considerations that *I* don't embrace from *my* point of view. But what I have not yet emphasized is that *I* emerge to be an individual agent of somewhat *smaller* than human size, in a way that is very much like what I described above in connection with multiple agents. That is, the human life that is the site of my existence is also a site of rational fragmentation in the following sense: some of the intentional activities that go on within that human life proceed from the point of view of the department, while other intentional activities that go on within the same human life proceed from *my* point of view. This is what I had in mind when I said at the outset that the boundaries of an agent's rational point of view are also boundaries that mark its life off from the lives of other agents. Although it may seem a strange way to put it, the department's unifying project, of setting the requirements for the PhD in philosophy, set boundaries within which the department deliberated and acted *as one*, supplied the reasons for setting those boundaries in such a way that thoughts and actions spanning many different human lives figured in, and constituted, the life of the department rather than its members.

So let me turn now, finally, to the issue of responsibility. As I've just explained, when the department thinks and acts *as one*, the thinkings and doings through which it constitutes itself belong to *it* and to no one else – including even *me*, and even in the case of its thinkings and doings which are located in the same human organism that my thinkings and doings are located in. It follows that I stand in an *interpersonal relation* to my department. It also follows that *I* do not bear any personal responsibility for what the department does – such responsibility lies squarely with the department. This makes for a profound difference between a group agent's responsibility and what we ordinarily think of as *collective* responsibility.

Collective agency is the agency of *many*, not one. It is a *social* phenomenon, in which many distinct individual agents exercise their agency together in order to do something that does not lie within the agents' power to do all on their own. There is an important ambiguity here, about what does and does not lie within the power of the individual agents who together comprise a collective. Although it is true by definition that a collective action, which is intended and undertaken by many individual agents, does not lie within the power of any one of them to do on their own, it is sometimes the case that one or another of them has the power to bring about the same *outcome* on their own. Consider a gruesome case in which many individual agents of human size intentionally exercise their agency together in order to kill a human being, by each inflicting just one of a thousand cuts. It may be that any one of those agents has the power to bring about that human being's *death* on their own. But all the same, it does *not* lie within their individual power to bring about the death in the way that it is actually intended in the collective case, which is that it be brought about by each member of the collective inflicting only one of a thousand cuts. When I refer to collective ends from here on, I will be referring to them in this way that takes due account of the description under which they are intended, as *collectively achieved* ends. And I repeat that *by definition*, such collective ends do not lie within the power of any one individual agent to bring about on their own. The puzzle about collective responsibility, then, is *who* is in a position to take responsibility for such a collective end. It is in the nature of the case that the collective itself has no point of view *of its own* from which *it* thinks and acts *as one*. It is by hypothesis and definition, the agency of *many* agents who each act from their own individual points of view. One natural *first* thought is that these individual agents can only take responsibility for what lies within their power to do individually, and so the extent of their responsibility is confined to just their own contribution to the collective end. Thus in my gruesome example, each individual would be responsible for just one cut. A natural *second* thought, though, is that this is a completely unacceptable conclusion, because each individual agent intends their cut *as a contribution to a death by a thousand cuts*, and so each is really trying to take responsibility for the intended *collective end* as well as their own individual contribution to it.[9] Whichever one of these thoughts we find more plausible, I take it we need to embrace one or other of them when we seek to locate responsibility for collectively achieved ends – for there simply is no other *agent* available to hold responsible for them, if what we mean by an *agent* is someone who can be *held* responsible for what they do in the engaged way that presupposes that the agent can keep up their end of the engagement by *taking* responsibility for what they do.[10]

I have argued that the situation is entirely different when we find that the conditions of individual agency are realized at the level of a group of human beings. Then there *is* someone besides the human 'members' of the group to hold responsible, namely, the group agent itself. I have also argued that when we embrace the reductionist account of individual agency, not only is it the case that groups of human beings can be sites of individual agency, but also, the human 'members' of such groups may not qualify as individual agents of human size, because those human lives will be marked by rational fragmentation, owing to the ways in which some of the intentional activities within those lives both constitute, and proceed from, the group agent's point of view and *not* from any *other* points of view – they are the thinkings and doings of the group agent and no one else. And for this reason, insofar as the human 'members' appear to be sites of agents of human size, the truth is that they are agents who are somewhat smaller than human size, whose lives are constituted by the *other* intentional activities that proceed from their own smaller points of view, which exclude those of the group agent.

Most philosophers who are prepared to allow that a group of human beings may qualify as an individual agent in its own right would not agree with these latter claims, because they view the human 'members' of such group agents as *natural* agents, who must necessarily remain the individual agents that they are, even when they combine their efforts so as to forge a group point of view from which thought and action proceed, and which can be engaged and held responsible.[11] To take this view is to reject the reductionist account of agency – it is to say that individual agents are *not* self-constituting, via the thinkings and doings through which they live their lives as the individual agents they are, but rather, they are human beings, and as such their lives are metaphysically given with the biological facts of human life. When we suppose that the human 'members' of a group agent are natural agents, we will conceive the group agent not as natural but as *artificial* – as brought into being by the individual efforts of its human 'members'; and then group agency will emerge as a special case of collective agency, in which the human 'members' of the collective must necessarily always be thinking and acting from their individual, human-sized, points of view – which are *also* metaphysically given with their biological existence. As I've made clear, one primary reason why I am convinced that the reductionist account of agency is correct is that I am convinced that there can be thinkings and doings on the part of a group agent that proceed from a point of view that is *distinct* from any such human-sized points of view.

I realize that matters may not *appear* this way to the 'members' of a group agent – even in a case like my own philosophy department, in which the 'members' had become convinced that it would be better if the department arrived at a *reasoned conclusion* about what PhD requirements to set, by thinking and acting *as one*, rather than having a social process of debate and argument followed by a vote. The problem was not that the 'members' of the department did not appreciate that there is a real difference between a process of deliberation that would proceed from a single set of pooled considerations that comprise the department's point of view, and a social process of debate and argument that would be carried out from the many different points of view of the department's 'members'. The problem was that they found it hard to reconceive both the boundaries of their own agency and responsibility, and their relation to the department, as these things would emerge to be if the former condition were realized.

One reason why this reconception is so difficult derives from the fact that the method by which a group agent like a philosophy department achieves the sort of rational unity that is characteristic of individual agency involves speech and communication, which we take to be social phenomena, and therefore very unlike individual deliberation. Thus, when the 'members' of my department filed into their meeting, the way in which the considerations that constituted the department's point of view were pooled together involved each of the 'members' making 'utterances' that probably felt to them as though they were being made from their own points of view. And if they felt that way, then perhaps that is what they were – utterances that expressed the individual viewpoints of the 'members' of the department. But they were also acts of communication, through which the *department* came to be aware of the many considerations that *it* ought to take into account as it deliberated. And insofar as those deliberations involved certain utterances that issued from the mouths of different 'members' of the department, they counted as steps in *the department's deliberations* because they articulated steps in reasoning that was aimed at working out the joint normative significance of all of the pooled considerations that constituted the point of view from which the department was deliberating. Insofar as such utterances *did* articulate steps in such reasoning, they *did not* express the separate views of the separate 'members' of the department, but rather the view of the department itself. This is compatible with such an utterance giving voice to a point of *agreement* between a given faculty member and the department. But all the same, insofar as a step in reasoning really was taken, which aimed to work out what that utterance entailed, when considered together with the other considerations that constituted the department's point of view, it was a step in the department's deliberations, as opposed to the deliberations of one or another of its 'members'.

Thus, when 'I' initially put on the table, for the department's consideration, the proposal that there be no requirements for the PhD besides a completed and successfully defended dissertation, it is *not* correct to say that 'I' was making a causal contribution to a collective outcome that I was jointly pursuing with other 'members' of the department. It was not like laying one brick alongside other bricks in the joint activity of building a house together. Once I had put my consideration on the table, I had 'conveyed' it to an active process that took on a life of its own, of working its way to conclusions from a deliberative base, which is to say, a point of view, that was *not mine*. Of course, if I were to build a house together with others by laying down some bricks, neither the bricks nor the house would strictly speaking be mine either, and nor would the collective process through which the house that got built. But building a house with others is a collective effort in which my intentional efforts combine with those of others; and what makes it a *collective* process is not the fact that many distinct *human beings* are involved, but the fact that the process is carried out from *many different rational points of view*. And this is *not* going on in the case where the department comes to function as an individual agent. When a department does this, it comes to function as an individual agent *in its own right*, and then whatever its 'members' do in relation to it is not a contribution to a shared collective process, but an interpersonal effort to influence another individual agent, which is the department itself. Surely, some of the utterances that come out of the mouths of the department's 'members' during departmental deliberations will have this *social* character or function, of trying to *influence* another agent, which is the department. But for the most part, this will not be so in the sort of case I am describing, in which the department is deliberating and acting *as one* from a departmental point of view. For the most part, such utterances either articulate, or *are*, steps in deliberations that are being carried out by the department. This is why they are *not* properly thought of as contributions made by department's 'members' to a 'collective' process – for such contributions would have to be made from separate points of view, whereas these steps proceed from the department's point of view.

What follows about responsibility for a group agent's actions? I take it to follow that the human constituents of a group agent are no *more* responsible for what a group agent thinks and does, and *also*, no *less* responsible for what a group agent thinks and does, than *any* individual agent is ever responsible for what *another* individual agent thinks and does. We might suppose that one agent *may* and *should* take responsibility for another agent's attitudes – by, say, sharing information with them about what is really true and good. We may suppose that one agent *may* and *should* take responsibility for another agent's actions – by, say, using any means available to get the other agent to do good things, and to prevent the agent from doing bad things. But if we believe in individual autonomy, then we may be consigned to leave others to think and act as they judge best, once we have done due diligence by informing them of what *we* think. And if this belief in individual autonomy is coherent, then there is room for carrying it over to our relations to group agents, and this is true even in those cases where the human lives that are the sites of our own existence are also sites of intentional activities that constitute the life of a group agent. Thus, I may leave my department to think and do what it judges to be best, even though if it were up to me, the department would not be imposing all of the requirements that it currently does impose for the PhD in philosophy; and I do not bear any kind of *personal* responsibility for what the department does, of the sort that I would bear in cases of *collective* agency, where there was no group agent acting from *its own* point of view.

I have found that when I share these claims with others, many of them may follow me a good part of the way to my own conclusions, but then they stop short of following me all the way. Here are some of the points along the way that they might be willing to accept: A human being does not begin life already able to exercise its agential capacities. Rather, a human being begins life as a creature that is buffeted about by its perceptions and desires, and it isn't able to take responsibility by acting in a truly considered way until fairly well on in its development. At some point, there is a stepping back from desires, and an evaluation of them in the light of what is really good and what is really better than what; and at some point, there is a recognition of more complicated and interesting projects that would require significant coordination of thought and effort over time; it is when such unifying projects are embraced that there is a real need to deliberate before acting – to consider what would be best in the light of many considerations taken together.[12] Here is what the reductionist account makes of these undeniable facts of human life: It is *only* when such unifying projects are embraced, which actually *require* coordinated thought and effort, that the human being becomes the site of agency in the full sense, which involves *forging* a point of view from which deliberation and action proceed, by arriving at and acting upon all-things-considered judgements. It is only once such a *deliberative* point of view has been forged that there is an agent whom others can hold fully responsible, as an agent who is taking charge of its own priorities, choices, and actions. Of course, long before a human being develops sufficiently to have such a deliberative point of view, it has a point of view in other senses. It has a *bodily* point of view from which it perceives and moves, and it also has a *phenomenological* point of view from which there is something it is like for it to experience and feel. Points of view in these latter two senses are both *biologically given* with the existence of a normally functioning human organism – and for this reason, I count them as *metaphysically* given, as opposed to products of effort and will. What is also biologically given are basic agential capacities.[13] But according to the reductionist account of agency, what is metaphysically given in this way with human life does not suffice to make the individual human being an individual agent. What is both necessary and sufficient for individual agency is that certain thinkings and doings actually occur, in a way that is directed at achieving the kind of rational unity that is characteristic of individual agency, by arriving at and acting upon all-things-considered judgements. According to the reductionist account, what an individual agent *ought* to take into account in such judgements are *all of its own* thoughts, both about what it *can* do, and also about what it would be *best* to do in the light of its thoughts about what is good and true. Thus it equates the scope of an agent's *all* in all-things-considered judgements with the boundaries of that agent's deliberative point of view – whatever falls within the one falls within the other. And these boundaries that circumscribe the agent's own deliberative point of view are not set by the boundaries of its body or its consciousness. Possessing the kind of bodily point of view from which an animal perceives and moves, and possessing the kind of phenomenological point of view from which a subject is directly aware of its own subjective states in consciousness, is neither necessary nor sufficient for possessing a deliberative point of view from which to deliberate and act – what I have elsewhere called a *rational* point of view. We generally assume that these things *all coincide* in human life – that is, we assume that deliberation is a *conscious process*, which is directed at options that are metaphysically given to us by virtue of possessing a *body* over which we have *direct intentional control*. But according to the reductionist account of individual agency this assumption is mistaken twice over: firstly, by overlooking how group agents do not require a single, unified consciousness in order to reason *as one* or a single human body through which to act *as one*; and secondly, by overlooking how a single unified consciousness housed within a single human body does not suffice for such reasoning and acting as one, owing to the possibility that there can be multiple agents within a single human life.

As I've said, many philosophers will follow me a good part of the way towards the conclusions of the reductionist account, but then they persist anyway in viewing human beings as natural agents. Their view seems to be that even if it requires effort and will to become an individual agent each human life must necessarily become the site of just one such agent. Sometimes it is claimed in support of this view that a human agent can do *only one thing*. This claim is patently false, for right now I am typing these words on my laptop while stroking my dog with my foot. But what is more important here is this: even if it were true that actions involving the human body can occur only one at a time, this would not suffice to undermine my claim that a human being can be the site of non-pathological rational fragmentation. This claim does not turn on whether only one thing can be done at a time through any one human body (which as I've said I deny anyway); it turns on whether a human being must be the site of a single deliberative point of view at any given time, or whether it can be the site of two (or more) co-existing deliberative points of view. I am claiming that the test of whether this is so is not how many things are being *done* at once, but whether the point of view from which such things are done must be a point of view of human size, or one of several points of view within the same human being. Take speech as such a test. Let me assume for the sake of argument that words cannot come out of a given human being's mouth in such a way that they simultaneously express two such co-existing points of view. This assumption does not rule out the possibility that some of the words that come of that human being's mouth can express a smaller-than-human-size point of view while others express the departmental point of view, and that both points of view exist simultaneously. And so it is with all actions that might be performed with or through that human being's body.

I think the better way to object to the reductionist account of individual agency is not to try to argue for the false claim that there is a *practical necessity* of overall rational unity within a whole human life, as there would be if human beings were natural agents. The better way would be to try to argue from the true claim that there is at least a *practical possibility* of such overall rational unity within a whole human life, and to try to make the case that this possibility has important implications concerning who is ultimately responsible for the actions of a group agent. For such an argument would be proceeding from a premise that the reductionist account acknowledges to be true, which is that it is not only *possible*, but often close to *actual*, that a human life is the site of overall rational unity within it. The argument might begin by suggesting that, in any case I would describe as a case of rational fragmentation, in which a smaller-than-human-size agent co-exists within the same human life as intentional activities that figure in the life of a group agent, it is always *possible* for that smaller-than-human-size agent to exert intentional control over *all* of the intentional activities within that human life; and then the objection would proceed by suggesting that the mere fact that this is *possible* renders that smaller-than-human-size agent *personally responsible* for all that goes on within the human life in question, including the intentional activities that belong to the group agent. To put it another way, the argument would be that the smaller-than-human-size agent would have *ceded control* over certain parts of that human life to the group agent, and that the smaller-than-human-size agent could always *regain* such control, and that this would be a morally important thing to do in cases where the smaller agent finds that the group agent reasons and acts in ways they do not approve of.

The problem with this line of objection is that it fails to reckon with the true nature of intentional control. There is no *thing – the agent* – that stands apart from the intentional activities through which it exists, that is standing ready to take control, and therewith, responsibility, for everything that falls within its own metaphysically given sphere of intentional control. Such intentional control as exists, enters the world through intentional activities themselves. So if the kind of rational unity that is characteristic of individual agency ever comes to be, it is because there are intentional activities that include a recognition of ends (unifying projects) for the sake of which it is worth achieving such unity, along with efforts to achieve such ends via such unity. When such efforts are directed at achieving unity within a philosophy department, those efforts do not somehow intrude upon 'my' metaphysically given sphere of intentional control and personal responsibility. They are just what they are, efforts directed at ends, and it is in part through those efforts that a departmental point of view gets formed. They do not belong to *me*, the philosopher writing this chapter. What *I* do is constitute *myself*. And that is what the philosophy department does too, insofar as it comes to function as an individual agent in its own right. Each of us is setting the boundaries within which we are taking responsibility for what happens, by exercising our agency in the unified way that is characteristic of individual agency. But this just means that the efforts through which we come to be are directed at achieving unity within those different boundaries. Each of us takes *personal* responsibility for our own thoughts and actions. Each of us might bear some limited *interpersonal* responsibility for what the other does, insofar as we have opportunities to influence each other for the better, or even to promote or hinder the other's actions. But the situation is very unlike the situation of collective agency, in which many distinct agents act together, but from their own points of view, for the sake of a collective end, which is then brought about by *them* – and not by any further agent who is distinct from them.

I think it is correct to say that in the collective case, the individual agents who make up the collective each aim to *extend* the reach of their personal responsibility, by aiming to help bring about the collective end to which they are contributing. And one of the important things for such individual agents will be to assess whether and why they should contribute vs. refuse to contribute – this would be, as we like to say, a matter of individual conscience. Because what these individual agents are working out is what *they* should do, by exercising *their own individual agency*. And my argument in this chapter is that this is not the right model on which to understand cases in which a group agent emerges, who functions as an individual agent in its own right. Individual agents are never *made by*, or *made up of*, smaller agents, as we see pictures in the great frontispiece to Hobbes's *Leviathan*. This is the truth about self-constitution, as it emerges via the reductionist account of individual agency.[14]

Notes

1 This assertion may not answer everyone's idea of what it means to take responsibility for what happens. Some may construe the idea more narrowly, perhaps in connection with undertaking *obligations* of one kind or another. But what I am getting at here is that agents are not by-standers when it comes to their own actions, waiting to see what happens, because they aim to bring it about that something or other happens. In such cases, what happens is *their* doing – that is why we *hold* them responsible – and if it is *their* doing then they have *already* taken a kind of responsibility for what happens, because they are not merely standing by, but acting.

2 This is an objection that Christine Korsgaard raised early on in response to Parfit. See her 'Personal Identity and Unity: A Kantian Response to Parfit', *Philosophy and Public Affairs*. 18, no. 2: 101–132.

3 For a fuller elaboration of the reductionist account see *Bounds of Agency*, Princeton University Press (Princeton, NJ: 1998), and for further discussion of what it means to say that agents are *literally* self-constituting, see 'Reductionism, Self-Constitution and The Moral Significance of Personal Identity' in *Reading Parfit*, Andrea Sauchelli, ed. (Routledge, forthcoming).

4 I have deliberately left out of my description of the reductive base a term that has figured centrally in all of my other discussions of the reductionist account of agency, namely, 'commitment'. I use that term mainly to refer to intentional attitudes, insofar as they are conceived entirely in terms of their contents – thus I would describe a belief that P as a commitment to the truth of P, and I would describe an evaluative attitude that registers the value of Q as a commitment to goodness of Q. Commitments so conceived are irreducibly normative in the following sense: they are not dispositions to reason and act in accord with them. What they register is the agent's own recognition that it *ought* to reason and act in accord with them. But it is possible to recognize an *ought* without necessarily conforming to it – so long as one views failures to conform to it as grounds for self-criticism. So, according to the reductionist account of individual agency, the life of an agent consists in undertakings of commitments (intentional attitudes), and efforts to live up to those commitments by reasoning and acting in accord with them. This is what I am referring to in the text above, when I refer to the *intentional activities* – the *thinkings* and *doings* – in which the life of the agent consists.

5 Of course, it may be wondered, doesn't there have to be a further fact – *the agent* – who is carrying out all of the intentional activities that I am claiming constitute the agent's life. My answer is *no* – see the work cited in note 3 for further discussion of why.

6 Here I mean to be speaking, specifically, of the existence and life of the philosophy department *qua group agent*. Most philosophy departments do *not* qualify as individual agents in this sense. Yet even when they do not, they do *exist* nevertheless, as *some* kind of thing – a thing that has a certain life and function within the institutional setting of a university, and in the academic world at large. I thank an anonymous reviewer for inviting this clarification.

7 This is a crucial point of disagreement with Korsgaard, which I press in Rovane, op. cit.

8 For further elucidation of the possibility of multiple agents within a single human life, see my works cited in note 3. See also, 'A Nonnaturalist Account of Personal Identity', in *Perspectives on Naturalism*, ed. M. deCaro, Harvard University Press (Cambridge, MA: 2004).

9 This line is convincingly pushed by Kirk Ludwig. See his contribution to this volume, 'From Individual to Collective Responsibility'.

10 As an aside, I will confess that I myself feel the pull of both of the natural thoughts about the extent of an individual agent's responsibility for collective ends, on which it is either confined to individual contributions or extended to the intended collective end. On the one hand, I'm inclined to think that an individual agent who inflicts one of a thousand cuts while aiming to contribute to a death should bear full responsibility for that death. But, on the other hand, when individuals make small contributions to an extremely large fund that will pay for something like ending extreme poverty, I'm not so sure they should get much credit for anything beyond their own individual contribution – *especially* in cases where they can afford to give much more than they do. This makes me wonder if there is any *general* truth about the extent of individual agents' responsibility for the collective ends to which they contribute, or whether it might be a matter of context.

11 The most influential account of group agency along these lines is Christian List and Philip Pettit, *Group Agency: The Possibility, Design and Status of Corporate Agents* (Oxford University Press, 2011).

12 This transition from being an animal that is merely pushed around by its desires, to an agent that can step back from its desires and evaluate them is one that Christine Korsgaard makes much of in her account of self-constitution. But she makes many claims that I do not accept. She claims, for example, that the fundamental act is one of laying down a law for oneself, whereas I claim it is undertaking commitments of various kinds – beliefs, evaluative attitudes, unifying projects, all-things-considered judgements. She also claims that anything with agential capacities will necessarily regard itself as bound by categorical imperatives, first to be rational by laying down laws for oneself, and then by respecting a Kantian style universalizability constraint, whereas I do not think there are any categorical imperatives to be rational or moral. She claims that the human organism cannot be the site of multiple agents within it, whereas I claim it can be. See her *Self-Constitution, Agency, Identity, and Integrity* (Oxford University Press, 2009).

13 I do not think we should equate these basic agential capacities of human beings either with motor capacities or with powers to perform basic actions in Arthur Danto's sense. They go beyond mere motor control, because they include whatever capacities make it possible for a human being to develop full intentionality and rationality; and they fall short of powers to perform basic actions, because basic actions are fully intentional actions that require self-conscious knowledge of one's power to perform them, and it is clear that human beings are not born with such self-known powers. (For a classic statement of Danto's conception, see his 'Basic Actions', *American Philosophical Quarterly*, 2, no. 2, April 1965.)

14 I would like to thank many colleagues, students, and friends for their help as I thought through and wrote up this chapter, and to especially mention: Akeel Bilgrami, Michael Della Rocca, Francey Russell, the editors of this volume, and an anonymous reviewer.

References

Danto, A. (1965) "Basic Actions", *American Philosophical Quarterly* 2, no. 2: 141–148.

Korsgaard, C. (1989) "Personal Identity and Unity: A Kantian Response to Parfit", *Philosophy and Public Affairs* 18, no. 2: 101–132.

Korsgaard, C. (1996) *The Sources of Normativity*, Cambridge University Press.

Korsgaard, C. (2009) *Self-Constitution: Agency, Identity, and Integrity*, Oxford University Press.

List, C. and Pettit, P. (2011) *Group Agency: The Possibility, Design and Status of Corporate Agents*, Oxford University Press.

Parfit, D. (1984) *Reasons and Persons*, Oxford University Press.

Rovane, C. (1998) *Bounds of Agency: An Essay in Revisionary Metaphysics*, Princeton University Press.

Rovane, C. (2003) "A Nonnaturalist Account of Personal Identity", in *Perspectives on Naturalism*, ed. M. de Caro, Harvard University Press.

Rovane, C. (2017) "Is Group Agency a Social Phenomenon?" *Synthese* DOI 10.1007/s11229-017-1384-1.

Rovane, C. (forthcoming) "Reductionism, Self-Constitution and The Moral Significance of Personal Identity" in *Derek Parfit's Reasons and Persons: An Introduction and Critical Inquiry*, ed. Andrea Sauchelli, Routledge Press.

5

A WE-MODE ACCOUNT OF GROUP ACTION AND GROUP RESPONSIBILITY

Raimo Tuomela and Pekka Mäkelä

5.1 Introduction

We commonly attribute actions to social collectives and especially to proper social groups. *Social collectives can be practically any kind of groups, organized or not and their members need not be psychologically connected. Proper social groups on the other hand require that the group members share goals and beliefs and possibly other propositional attitudes, etc.*

Thus, we use locutions like "Apple produces smartphones," "Russia attacked Ukraine," "the board dismissed Smith," "the soccer team scored," and so on. Not only do we attribute actions to groups but we ascribe responsibility to social groups for (their) actions as well. Locutions like the following are quite common. "The Exxon Corporation was responsible for the worst oil spill in American history when the Exxon Valdez ran aground in Alaska," or "Germany was responsible for the Second World War," or "The club as a whole is to blame for being relegated." On the basis of examples like these it seems reasonable to accept this common-sense view at least in part and to think that true statements of the above kind can be made.

We will do so here and investigate some central philosophical and conceptual problems related to actions performed by groups and responsibility for such actions. Our main interest is in the (retrospective) moral responsibility for actions performed by groups. Roughly, when we hold a group retrospectively morally responsible for some action we take the members of the group, qua members of the group, to be praiseworthy or blameworthy for what the group has done in light of some normative standard. Thus, in our view, the "truthmaker" of a collective attribution of moral responsibility is the moral responsibility borne by the individual members, qua members, of the group. Moral standard is of course the paradigm but an action can also be appraised from other evaluative perspectives, e.g. from the point of view of legal norms, etiquette, or rational long-term interests. In this chapter we only consider cases of moral blameworthiness. To begin with, a group is blameworthy for performing X only if there is an acceptable normative standard which prohibits X. Due to the fact that praiseworthiness and blameworthiness are not completely symmetrical our analyses may need some tinkering when praiseworthiness is at stake.

It is fair to hold an individual agent responsible for some action only if the agent has certain capacities (e.g. rationality, capability of intentional action) and the agent freely exercised these capacities in acting. Thus, there are both internal and external factors to be taken into account here when deciding whether the action was "up to the agent" in the right way.

In this chapter we will look for precise criteria for group action and, especially, for the group's moral responsibility for such action. We will focus on the following questions: a) When is an action attributable to a group as its action? b) Under what conditions do the actions by the members of the group generate action attributable to the group? c) What does it mean that a group bears responsibility for its action? d) Under what conditions is it justified to hold the group responsible for the actions performed by the members of the group? Questions a) and b) will be answered in terms of the account given in Tuomela (2013), chapter 3, and our discussion will mainly summarize that account. As to c) and d), we will have new things to say, and in part our answer to a) and b) will be used to generate answers to the latter two questions.

We claim that the strongest case for group responsibility is the responsibility in the following case concerned with a voluntary group. The responsibility concerns an internally and externally free group action, or the outcome of such action, as evaluated on the basis of a "relevant" normative standard (viz. evaluative perspective) that the group was aware of and accepted as its standard or at least in some sense ought to have accepted as its standard. The group action we are speaking about here is action that the group performed as an agent and that therefore binds the group members. When this group action is viewed from the perspective of the group members' action that constituted it we can require that the latter action be we-mode action. By "we-mode" we, roughly, mean thinking and acting as a group member which consists in we-thinking and we-acting with a collective commitment (see Tuomela 2007, 2013). To we-act means acting together as group members, indeed as a group. To we-think means to think in terms of "we": the group members believe something or intend to act together (viz. as a group), on the basis of their we-attitudes, according to their group plan (viz. the ethos of the group), etc. We-mode thinking and acting are based on the fulfillment of the three criteria of a group reason, a collectivity principle, and collective commitment (see e.g. Tuomela, 2013, chapter 2 for discussion).

In our view group responsibility for an action performed by the group can be accounted for in terms of responsibility ascribed jointly to (individual) members of the group acting qua members of the group, that is, the group members are together and interdependently responsible for the action. Group responsibility understood along these lines is a central notion of collective responsibility if not *the* notion of collective responsibility.

"Internally free" group action depends on such action performed by the members of the group g that none of the members of g was forced or coerced by other members of the group to agree with the group decision, or to act in accordance with it. A group action was "externally free" if there was no external pressure on the members of the group to adopt the goal, to make the plan and to perform the action. By external pressure we mean pressure exerted on the group by other groups or agents outside the group. If the action performed by the group was both internally and externally free we can say, in somewhat metaphorical terms, that the group acted out of its own free "group-will."

In our account the central criteria for a legitimate ascription of group responsibility to a member qua a member of the group are collective commitment and collective acceptance of the action (acceptance, belief, intention or what have you) in question. Individual members of a group, in the case of a we-mode action, bear moral responsibility together and interdependently, the moral responsibility satisfies the collectivity principle, in part due to collective commitment and acceptance, that if one member is responsible, then every member is. That is what group responsibility in our view means. Collective commitment and collective acceptance are entailed by the proper we-mode. Our notion of we-mode action captures the core of group agency, or at least so we claim. More precisely the we-mode is primarily meant to concern attitudes and derivatively actions ensuing from attitudes held in the we-mode.

Social groups will here be assumed to be collectives capable of action possessing an authoritative decision-making mechanism (see Tuomela 2013: chapter 3). Group membership here need not involve more than that an agent regards himself as a member of the group and that the other members of the group tend to regard him as a member of the group. Thus, legitimate ascription of group responsibility is not based on or justified by mere formal membership.

In our view group responsibility, qua joint responsibility as explained above, is, or can be, legitimately ascribed to both *operative* and *non-operative* members of the group. Operative members are the actively acting members in virtue of whose action the group's action comes about (cf. Tuomela 2013: chapter 3). Here we take it for granted that the notion of group responsibility admits degrees pretty much the same way as the notion of moral responsibility does. A non-operative member who learned only afterwards of the action performed by his group and accepted it retrospectively may bear less joint responsibility than an agent who acted as an operative member. The strength of the group responsibility borne by non-operative members depends on their awareness of what the group is doing, their possibility to control or influence the group's action, and so on.

Our primary focus will be on voluntary and internally authorized groups. By voluntary groups we mean groups the membership of which is up to the members, that is, in the paradigm case both entry and exit are voluntary. We presuppose that the agents have had a choice whether to become a member of the group in question or not, as opposed to nations for instance where citizenship typically is not a result of the agent's choice. Non-voluntary groups are obviously more problematic from the point of view of the collective responsibility of the non-operative members. Internally authorized groups as opposed to externally authorized groups are groups in which operative agents, either operative members or representatives, get their authority to act on behalf of the group from the members of the group in question. (For more on authorization see Tuomela 2013: ch 3.)

5.2 Group Action

In this section we will give an account of the conceptual nature of actions performed by social groups and do it primarily by investigating under which conditions attributions of actions to social groups can correctly be made.

One of the central theses below will be that the actions performed by social groups are "made up" of, or "constituted" by, joint actions of persons. This thesis will be discussed and made precise below. Here is a simplified formulation of this thesis: If a group (with the agents $A_1,\ldots,A_n$ as its members) does something X then at least some of its members, say $A_1,\ldots,A_m$ ($m \leq n$) must, in the right circumstances, do something $X_1,\ldots,X_m$, as their parts of a joint action X (or of a joint action generating X); and in normal circumstances these parts serve to generate or "make up" X. Here, $X_1,\ldots,X_m$ will be parts of a joint action of $A_1,\ldots,A_m$, which need not be of the type X but which still generates or brings about a token of X. In the case of intentional group action, intentional joint action and therefore shared "we-intentions" by the agents will be involved (see Tuomela 2013: ch. 3). Roughly speaking, we-intentions are intentions of an individual with the collective content "we intend to do X" accompanied with the true belief that there are other agents similarly intending to contribute to the joint action, and thus the success conditions of the joint action are satisfied. From the we-intention the individual infers to his or her part action; we-intend to do X thus I will do X_i. A we-intention is a collective intention with "we" as its agent. A single group member can have a we-intention as one of the members of a collection or group of we-intenders. Consider: "We intend to do X together."

I as a member of "us" we-intend to take part in our action of performing X, and the same for the other participating members (see Tuomela 2013: 79 and 89).

Consider an example, say, a hockey team's scoring. Some player, or perhaps players, did the scoring. We may say that it was the operative members of the team who did it and define that the operative members in the group relative to an action, X, are those in virtue of whose acting the performance of action X can be attributed to the group in this situation. We can also say in our example case that the team's scoring was constituted by these operative members' actions. When a hockey team scores we are dealing with the whole team of players being the group agent jointly causing the goal to come about. Although only one player ultimately caused the puck to move to the goal for scoring, the whole team of players was involved. They jointly intended, or so we suppose, to score. Joint intention means here the players intending together (jointly) to score. This kind of joint intending involves that the individual players are supposed to we-intend to contribute to scoring. So joint intending involves shared we-intention, where the sharing is of the strong kind involved in the members' joint action with the same main goal, viz. to score and ultimately to win the match (see Tuomela 2013: 88).

More generally, it is a common situation in the case of groups with normatively specified positions that some of those positions and their holders are related to action in the analogous way and that the position holders thus designated as operative members are indeed operative members for a large range of actions, perhaps all the actions that the group in question is capable of undertaking. In such cases we need not always speak of specific actions in the context of group action, but may speak of operative members for all the activities or for some broad subclass such as decision making (or plan formation) and for carrying out decisions and plans.

As actions by groups will, in the core case, be analyzed in terms of joint actions, some (additional) comments on them may start our discussion. An intentionally performed joint action must come about because of a joint intention (jointly had we-intentions). Joint actions in our sense will include joint task-performances, task performance is satisfying an obligation, e.g. the obligation to (try to) score, based on (at least believed) explicit or implicit agreement or joint plan. Thus typically these qualify: carrying a table jointly, playing tennis, satisfying a (many-person) contract, and sometimes, questioning-answering and conversing.

Actions by groups are connected closely (and in a precise sense) to joint actions by the members of the group performed qua members of the group (see section 5.3). The basic content of our general thesis on the nature of actions by groups is this: a group's intentional action requires (ultimately on conceptual grounds) that at least some of its members suitably act and that as a consequence the group will have acted. Indeed, a joint action appropriately performed in the we-mode in the right social and normative circumstances by the operative members of the collective will be redescribable as a group action. Accordingly, if a group can be taken to be responsible for its actions, by way of this analysis we can speak of the members of the group being jointly responsible for such group actions.

This thesis analyzes *intentional* actions performed by social groups. Such actions are obviously as central in the case of groups as they are in the case of single individuals. Thus, for instance, a group can be regarded as legally and morally responsible for its intentional action.

The concept of joint action that our thesis on group action relies on requires some further remarks. First, as an important special case we technically allow actions performed by one individual, in order to have unified terminology (cf. the President representing the country). Furthermore, we accept the following liberal usage: in the present context we need not be able to say that the operative agents jointly do X (even in the above wide technical sense) but only that they jointly (in the indicated technical sense) do something which will bring about X and is believed by them to bring it about. What they thus perform could be a joint action Y, non-identical with X. To see the reason for this consider a case of a state's entering a treaty where the operative agents jointly ratified the treaty and did whatever was needed; but of course they did not jointly enter the pact even if they jointly brought about that the state entered the pact. Our view of group action implicitly contains the idea that the non-operative members minimally tacitly accept or at least ought to accept the fact that the operative members perform X. Tacit acceptance here means not only acceptance as true but – what is central here – acceptance in the sense of not very seriously disagreeing with what the operative members do.

The present requirement applies to all cases with internal authorization, that is, authorization via the members' commitment to the group-internal decision-making procedure, thus also to e.g. societies, which are collectives with involuntary group membership. On the other hand, in the case of teams, for instance, we need to require more of them in either all the members are operative members or the non-operative members stand "in reserve" in the strong sense that they may be called in at any moment and could equally well in principle have been selected as operative ones. In this kind of strong case we must require, it seems, that all group members accept or at least ought to accept the we-intentions and group beliefs needed for group action.

Given the above, there will be a shared we-intention to perform X (in our schematic case), and that involves the idea that the members of the group are collectively committed to bringing about X (see Tuomela and Mäkelä 2016: ch. 3). But in the general case this does not require that all the members strongly "participate" in the satisfaction of the group will in question. Thus, in the case of non-operative members this involves not a commitment to doing one's part of X but the commitment to supporting passively – or at least not overtly opposing – what the operative members are doing when carrying out their commitments, given, of course, that the non-operative members are adequately informed about what the operative members are doing. Those non-operative members who also endorse "We will do X" are, however, committed to contributing, actually or potentially, to X.

We can now spell out our preliminary thesis in a more precise, although stylized form and arrive at the following formulation, assuming that – on conceptual grounds – acting for the group is a task rather than only a right of the operative members (we draw on Tuomela 2013: 163):

> (IGA) A group g *brought about an action or a state X intentionally* (or alternatively, saw to it that X was the case) as a group in the social and normative circumstances C if and only if in C there were specific (internally or externally) authorized operative agents $A_1,\ldots,A_m$ for action in g such that
>
> (1) $A_1,\ldots,A_m$, when acting qua group members intentionally together brought about X (i.e., there was an action Y such that these operative agents intentionally together brought about Y and this performance of Y generated X, and was correctly believed and purported by the operative members to generate X), or, respectively these operative agents saw to it that X;
>
> (2) because of (1), the (full-fledged and adequately informed) nonoperative members of g, as members of g, tacitly accepted the operative agents' intentional bringing about (or seeing to it that) X – or at least ought to have accepted it;
>
> (3) there was a mutual belief in g to the effect that there was at least a chance that (1) prior to action and to the effect that (2).

Accordingly, given the right C, we claim that (*IGA*) is acceptable as an account of intentional group action. It also analyzes the sense in which individuals can bring about a group action and also the sense in which group actions can be said to be constituted by the we-mode actions (essentially: proper actions qua a group member) by their members and authorized representatives (for a longer discussion, see Tuomela 2013: ch. 3).

What we have been analyzing above in (*IGA*) is group action in a sense involving the group as a whole. The exercise of the decision making system was claimed to involve the whole group. Especially, in (*IGA*) the non-operative members are assumed to have the obligation to (tacitly) accept what the operative ones did. In our view, proper group action requires at least implicit agreement or plan about relevant goals and views.

5.3 We-mode and Acting Qua Group Member

As already mentioned, in our account of group responsibility we avail ourselves of the closely related notions of we-mode and acting qua group member.

For the purposes of the present chapter it suffices to say that the group members act in the we-mode only if they act as group members and are collectively committed to the group action in question. In the more general case we can speak of the group's constitutive goals, norms, and standards instead of group action. Those constitutive goals etc. can be called the "ethos" of the group.

Given this it remains to be said what acting qua group member amounts to. For our present purposes we can say the following. We assume that the group in consideration is concerned with certain specific topics in its activities. Let us speak of the group's realm of concern. Obviously the topics its ethos is about must at least belong to this realm, if not exhaust it.

Considering the general case of a structured group, we can classify the types of actions within the group's realm of concern as follows: (1) positional actions related to a group position, which include (i) actions (tasks) that the position holder in question *ought to* perform in certain circumstances and (ii) actions that he *may* perform in some circumstances; (2) actions which the ethos of the group requires or allows; (3) actions which are based on agreement making which have not been codified by the group but which still are consistent with actions in (1) and (2); (4) freely chosen activities which include actions and activities not within classes (1)–(3) but which, although not incompatible with them, still are actions within the realm of concern of g and rationally (understood broadly to amount to *reasonably*) collectively accepted by, or acceptable to, the members of g as such actions.

Basically, acting as a group member is to intentionally act within the group's realm of concern. It can be either successful action or an unsuccessful action. What is required is that the group member in question will intentionally attempt to act in a way related to what he takes to be the group's realm of concern such that he does not violate what he takes to be the group's ethos. Thus full success will not be required. There may thus be failures due to false beliefs about the group's norms and standards, due to lack of skill, or due to environmental obstacles. Thus *acting as a group member* in the positional case, viz. in a structured group, is equivalent to acting intentionally in one of the senses (1)–(4) or attempting so to act. Below this notion will be meant when we speak of acting or functioning qua group member. Note especially that one can act within the realm of the group's concern but intentionally fail to obey the norms and standards of the group. Then the group may not be responsible for this group member's action, except perhaps when it has promised – or has otherwise obligated itself – to see to it that its members do not violate its ethos.

Considering the group's E, which here means the ethos of the group, roughly its basic constitutive goals, beliefs, practices, and other similar features, we assume that the group members have collectively accepted it and are collectively committed to it. We can say that E is internal to the group as it depends on the group members' collective acceptance and commitment. Note that E can be in contradiction with the normative standard, N, in light of which the praiseworthiness or blameworthiness of the group's action is to be judged. N is assumed to be external to the group in the sense that it is not, at least not solely, dependent on the collective acceptance and commitment of the members of the group, the action of which is to be appraised. N offers an external yardstick against which the group's action is measured. We may say that E should, and of course could, be compatible with N but is not necessarily so (e.g. criminal groups can be proper groups).

Actions in (1) are of course typical positional actions that accordingly qualify as acting qua member of g in one's position. Subclass (ii) of (1) thus consists of actions that the holder of a position may choose from. However, classes (2)–(4) also can occur at least in the positional case. Note that in the case of unstructured groups, class (1) is empty.

5.4 Group Responsibility

In this section we will discuss responsibility for group action. To recapitulate, we claim that the strongest case for group responsibility is the responsibility of a voluntary group for an internally and externally free group action, or the outcome of such action, performed in the we-mode, given that the action, or the outcome, is relevant with respect to some normative standard. In our view group responsibility is to be understood in the sense of responsibility ascribed jointly to members of the group qua members of the group for an action performed by the group, that is by at least some of the members of the group intentionally acting qua members of the group in the we-mode.

A we-mode group is a group that can act and does act as a group on the basis of its members' group-based we-thinking and we-reasoning, or, briefly put, we-mode thinking (see Tuomela 2007 and Tuomela 2013: 27, for the notions). A we-mode group makes the members strongly interconnected – the group is supposed to function as a whole that consists of the individual members' performing their parts of the group's action.

A we-mode group is based on the group members' we-mode we-thinking and we-reasoning with the result that all their we-mode attitudes and actions must (at least ideally) satisfy the three criterial elements of the we-mode viz. the *group reason*, *collectivity*, and *collective commitment* conditions (for these see Tuomela 2007: ch. 2 and Tuomela 2013: ch. 2). The group reason element concerns the reasons "given" by the group to the members for their participation in its activities. The collectivity condition here refers to a kind of "being in the same boat" condition concerning the members, and collective commitment ties them to the group, especially its ethos, and the mutual commitment to the fellow members concerning the promotion of the group's ethos (involving its constitutive goals) and other goals.

A we-mode group, as treated in Tuomela (2007 and 2013), is generally viewed as an autonomous egalitarian group where the only normative structural group connections, if any, between the members are based on group-internally constructed operative-nonoperative member-level normative connections. (For non-autonomous we-mode groups involving external power, see Appendix 1 of chapter 2 of Tuomela 2013.)

When a paradigmatic we-mode group acts, there are operative members acting for the group as ethos-respecting group members (in some cases all the members might be operatives). The operatives are in standard cases identified and collectively accepted by the group members for specific tasks. To put the matter in terms of joint action, the basic idea is that the members share a (we-mode) we-intention expressible by "We will do Y together" and, when the intention is satisfied, the joint action expression "We did Y together" applies. The intentional agent of the intention is "we" (namely, the group members forming a non-distributive "we"), and its content is the members' jointly intentionally performed joint action.

Group responsibility is often taken to rely on the members' attitudes and actions as group members. In the case of a we-mode group the group members are extrinsically involved in the group's responsibility through the actions they perform qua group members. Extrinsic versus intrinsic means here roughly the following. A mental state of a person is intrinsic if it is an ingrained property, e.g. genetically determined property, of that person. It is extrinsic if it is externally attributed to him by others (see Tuomela 2013). Yet it may be emphasized that if the members of a group act together or jointly in a strong sense so that we can speak of them acting *as a group* and as their being responsible as a group, it thus seems plausible to regard their group as being fit for responsibility.

A we-mode group that is not dominated by another group and that can itself determine its ethos is not literally an agent, but it can yet be regarded as a group agent on the basis of its capacity to act as a group (as a unit). As it is not a full-blown agent with a biological constitution it is not an intrinsically intentional agent (i.e. does not have mental states and phenomenal features comparable to what their individual members on biological and psychological grounds have). As a group it can only have extrinsically intentional attitudes and mental states, viz. states that have been attributed to it, typically by its members, while its members qua private persons normally are capable of intrinsic intentionality. Analogously, we argue that a group qua group cannot, so to speak, be "intrinsically" responsible (in the sense individuals are when acting as private persons) for its activities. The group members are capable of having intrinsically intentional mental states, but when functioning as group members they, strictly speaking, only operate on the basis of their extrinsic mental states deriving from the group's "mental" states that are comparable with role states in a theater play. However, the group's mental states are efficacious only via the intrinsic intentionality of the individual members. Note that the extrinsic mental states are attributed to the group by the members – via those of their proposals that are collectively accepted by the members as the group's states. The members can have intentional *joint* mental states (e.g. intentions) but those states often involve compromises and the like. The compromises concern a group attitude based on the (partly) inconsistent proposals by the members. Those proposals concern the group attitudes, typically extrinsically intentional ones, on which the members' functioning in their roles in the group are to be based. These "role attitudes" are typically extrinsically intentional – and not intrinsically created by their bearers. This situation arises because we are here dealing with the members' proposals for group attitudes. Note that putting together the members' attitude proposals may create consistency problems in addition to those that compromises involve. The collective acceptance of such proposals for the purpose of creating unique group attitudes does not always go smoothly (cf. List and Pettit 2011: ch. 2).

Assuming that the above is about right, suppose now that the group members have collectively accepted and thus created the group's extrinsic "mental" states and have also themselves "internalized" them. Given this, we can see an analogy between the present kind of group and the case involving intrinsic attitudes and regard an autonomous we-mode group (and other similar groups appropriately organized for action) as morally responsible for its intentional actions in an approximately intrinsic sense. As is the case with a group's mental states and actions, also the group's actually taking responsibility for its actions is analyzed through its members' mental states and activities, their acting jointly as a group.

If a we-mode group with external and internal autonomy is normatively responsible for an action or outcome X, then in general no one of its members is *solely* normatively responsible for X as a group member. This claim is about *moral responsibility as a group member* but bypasses the question of his purely *personal (or "private") moral responsibility*. To take an example of an internally non-autonomous hierarchical group with a dictator, for example, an army unit closely simulates this case. The members cannot voluntarily leave the group (or can only do it on pain of heavy sanctions). The dictator's power can be enforced by means of strong punishment, in special cases even death, if the order is disobeyed. In such a group, to speak of an idealized case, the dictator will normally alone be fully responsible for X as a group member, as the other members do not act freely and as they obey the dictator's orders being coerced to do what they do as group members.

In a we-mode group the holistic idea of the members being to an extent morally responsible for the others' undertakings qua group members holds true. All the group members acting appropriately as group members are, or at least ought to be, collectively committed to the group's action, and they accordingly collectively bear moral responsibility for what the group did, and this includes mistaken actions and dissidents' actions. In all, in a we-mode group (with or without an internally agreed operative-nonoperative division) the members are responsible for the group's action both as group members and to an extent as private persons – the first because of the holistic, interconnected nature of the we-mode group and the second centrally because intentional group action requires the participation of group members as group members – when they function as sentient and morally sensitive human beings.

Note, however, that a member of an autonomous we-mode group (one capable of forming its ethos and, in principle, of acting freely) can at least partly escape attribution of responsibility to her qua group member in a case where the group is responsible for a blameworthy action X if she was not involved directly in the actual causal production of X and if in addition she publicly disassociates herself from the production of X (e.g., by explicitly publicly speaking against the production of X before its occurrence and perhaps even by disclaiming her membership in the group).

Consider now the responsibility of groups for their actions. "*Actus reus*" and "*mens rea*" are classical principles and requirements for intentional responsibility as well as blame and punishment. *Actus reus* is the requirement of the presence of the responsible agent's own action, and *mens rea* is the requirement that the action was performed intentionally by the agent in question. These two principles have been discussed in the case of the responsibility of individual agents, for which case they seem largely appropriate. Manuel Velasquez puts together the classical *actus reus* and *mens rea* principles as follows (Velasquez 1983: 114):

> Moral responsibility is the kind of responsibility that is attributed to an agent only for those actions that *originate* in the agent, in so far as the action [is] derived from the agent's intentions (the *mens rea* requirement) and from the same agent's bodily movements (the *actus reus* requirement).

The requirement of the presence of bodily movements is clearly too strict in general, but otherwise the account is acceptable as an ideal. Yet, we argue that it goes against the common view that groups are often responsible for what they do and cause.

In the strict classical account under discussion, moral responsibility for an act or outcome can be attributed only to the agent who originated the act in his own body, in cases of bodily action in the relevant activities of his brain and body parts over which he has direct control. This requirement cannot be literally satisfied in the case of a group or a corporation (a corporate agent), for it does not have a body that it could move. Collectivities like corporations act only through their members' actions, but those actions strictly speaking are not the corporation's actions. A corporation's actions are constituted or brought about by the members' (bodily) actions that are not in its direct control but at best under its indirect control. (But the members have direct control of their participatory actions.) Thus a corporation is not fit for responsibility in the strict classical sense (that relies on *actus reus* and *mens rea*).

Corporations and "tightly connected" groups such as we-mode groups can yet be responsible for their actions in a slightly different sense through their members' participatory actions: Assume that the members on the basis of their joint intention realize their intention and act *jointly as a group* (rather than in a weaker sense of sharedness or of interaction). This can normally be taken to entail that the *group acts intentionally as "one agent"* and is thus (extrinsically) *responsible* for its action.

Of course, the members' joint action does not quite amount to the group's action in full analogy with an individual agent's intentional action, as the biological and psychological unity between the intention and ensuing action in the individual agent's case is clearly different, as seen. But if we can realistically assume that a group's action here is what the members do as a unit or as one agent, we seem to get close to the case of an individual agent's case and other cases satisfying the *actus reus – mens rea* unity requirement. Yet full unity cannot be obtained on conceptual and metaphysical grounds: the group members' mental states and actions in general cannot be aggregated or otherwise combined to become, respectively, the mental states and actions of a group agent (cf. Tuomela 2013: ch. 5). Accordingly, the *actus reus – mens rea* requirement does not in general apply to the group case.

Even if groups (such as we-mode groups and corporations) cannot be responsible in the sense individual agents can be, the present view holding groups fit for responsibility in suitable cases still is intuitive. In contrast, the strict classical idea (that assumes *actus reus* and *mens rea* in unison) fits individual responsibility in the case of standard individual action, but it does not apply to the group agent case. It was not originally created to apply either and, it goes counter to common intuitions concerning group responsibility.

In the present account, then, there are the aforementioned two conceptually involved elements – group members and the group – as central elements of group responsibility, and we can speak of the group level (the group viewed as a group agent), the collective or jointness level (viz. the members viewed collectively or jointly), and the purely individual level (individuals viewed as separate individual group members or as private persons).

Our analysis of group responsibility engages each of these three levels. When the group is responsible as a group, at least some of the members generally, except for some special cases, are collectively responsible for what the group does intentionally, and, as a default, every member is to an extent responsible for a we-mode group's actions and indeed for every other group member's participatory actions.

The above idea of the responsibility of a group and also of its members for one and the same outcome has been disputed in the literature. The core of the criticism is that this kind of dual responsibility idea is redundant as only individual members' responsibility really counts in attributions of responsibility: If the individuals are collectively causally responsible for an outcome, the group cannot at the same time be causally responsible for it. The alleged causal group responsibility is taken by the critics to be redundant and hence it suffices to deal with the individual group members' causal responsibility and control.

Group responsibility typically connects to the members' responsibility by entailing their responsibility qua group members, or, as we may say, it entails that the members qua members are jointly responsible for the item that the group is responsible for. The members' responsibility need not always be responsibility qua group members, but might be their responsibility qua private persons in the case of a group with loosely connected members (e.g. consider an organized tourist trip to Paris by some people, or think of an I-mode group). An I-mode group is a social group consisting of members who typically think and act individualistically. In all cases the members are also privately morally responsible for their own actions.

Our general view of a group's attitudes is that they are irreducible to the members' attitudes (see Tuomela 2013: chapters 3 and 5, and Tuomela and Mäkelä 2016 for discussion), and it can accordingly be suggested that the same also holds for the case of group responsibility.

Basically, the group's (or group agent's) control can be taken to amount to the group's filtering for what is in accordance with the group's ethos (i.e. group's constitutive goals, beliefs etc.) and excludes other possibilities. Here "filtering" can be taken to mean group members' jointly seeing to it that the group acts in accordance with its ethos, this can take place by way of members assisting, supporting, and monitoring one another.

This kind of filtering approach involves a kind of concrete plan making by the group for what its members should bring about by their actions as group members. Such bringing about a planned and intended outcome by the group in many cases requires additional planning and decision making by the group, e.g. concerning what is to be done, when, where, and how, etc. In all, the group members here do what they do based on the background platform that the group, so to speak, here represents when viewed as an (extrinsically) intentional agent. The group not only plans and initiates its action, but also monitors and controls that the group members carry it out when the circumstances are feasible. Loosely speaking, at least in simple cases, the group is constituted by its members and its main principles (ethos), and the members not only plan and reason but also realize the plans through their actions with the idea that the group is constituted by "us-together" and its ethos. If the group disintegrates after its intentionally performing, say, a blameworthy action (that perhaps originally was meant to be a praiseworthy action in accordance with the group's ethos but was not performed with the care it should have been performed) the members are generally collectively responsible for it. Here the blameworthy result occurred because they had not acted properly as group members in accordance with the group's plan. The fact that the ethos of the group in question is fully shared (or so we presently assume) and mutually known by the group members to be shared can be taken to play the role of filtering the actions and leaving out only the unfeasible ones, and leaving the group perhaps only with a single action normatively required by the ethos or possibly by the group leader and assigned to the group to act on.

The group is typically an occurrent active cause of the outcome in question – through its members' functioning in the right way as ethos-furthering group members – in some cases based on a leader's instructions or orders. However, a group can sometimes be a mere dispositional passive cause as well.

Assuming that the members of a (we-mode) group identify with the group and thus are disposed to act in accordance with its ethos, the group necessarily figures in the group members' minds and actions and, we can say, motivates the members' thinking and acting in the direction required or triggered by the ethos. The central idea here is that the group serves to initiate and maintain the members' action through the mentioned psychological mechanism. The group, through its ethos suitably internalized by its members and through their accordingly motivated actions, can be said to intermediately cause the group's relevant action (the "occurrent" or "active case") or at least be a standing cause (the "dispositional" or "passive case") for it – such a standing cause may become manifest in appropriate circumstances. As a result the group will be responsible both for its praiseworthy and its blameworthy actions and their outcomes, which take place through the members' actions. As the group's actions are constituted by its members' actions, the group will be responsible also for its members' participatory actions (and lack of them in other cases). This kind of group responsibility involves that the members of a we-mode group are responsible for their own participatory actions as well as typically to an extent responsible also for the other members' participatory actions (e.g. in situations in which some of them require help). We suggest that the members may be regarded as responsible for what the group has intentionally done even in cases where the group disintegrates after the action has been performed and where the members had valid excuses for non-participation in the case of a blameworthy group action or group-induced outcome.

5.5 Conclusion

In this chapter we have discussed group responsibility. According to our account the paradigm of group responsibility is the responsibility of a voluntary group for an internally and externally free group action performed in the we-mode, given that the action is relevant to some normative standard, say N. We have defended collective acceptance and collective commitment as the core elements of group agency, or central analytic notions of group agency if you like. According to our view a group can legitimately be held responsible as a group for some action or outcome only if at least some members of the group performed some action in the we-mode.

It does not follow from our analyses that a group is always responsible for actions performed by its members. For instance, there may be an intentional dissident in the group who intentionally deviates from the group's ethos or acts on purpose against what has been collectively accepted in the group, and thus does not act in the we-mode. In a case like this, according to our account, the dissident primarily bears individual responsibility for such an action and other members of the group qua members of the group are not to blame. However, if there is collective commitment to satisfy and/or uphold the ethos, as indeed we have claimed, then the group members are responsible for "correcting" dissidents' behavior. How "far" they should go in this correction is a moot point depending e.g. on the normative and factual cohesion of the group.

References

List, C. and Pettit, P. (2011) *Group Agents*, New York: Oxford University Press.

Preyer, G. and Peter, G. (2017) *Social Ontology and Collective Intentionality: Critical Essays on the Philosophy of Raimo Tuomela with His Responses*, New York City: Springer.

Tuomela, R. (1995) *The Importance of Us: A Philosophical Study of Basic Social Notions*, Stanford: Stanford University Press.

Tuomela, R. (2002) *The Philosophy of Social Practices: A Collective Acceptance View*, Cambridge: Cambridge University Press.

Tuomela, R. (2007) *The Philosophy of Sociality: The Shared Point of View*, New York: Oxford University Press.

Tuomela, R. (2013) *Social Ontology: Collective Intentionality and Group Agents*, New York: Oxford University Press (slightly improved paperback ed. 2016).

Velasquez, M. (1983) "Why Corporations Are Not Morally Responsible for Anything They Do," *Business and Professional Ethics Journal* 1:1–18.

Further Reading

Copp, D. (2007) "The Collective Moral Autonomy Thesis," *Journal of Social Philosophy* 38: 369–388.
Kutz, C. (2000) *Complicity: Ethics and Law for a Collective Age*, Cambridge University Press.
Ludwig, K. (2007) "The Argument from Normative Autonomy for Collective Agents," *Journal of Social Philosophy* 38: 410–427.
May, L. and Hoffman, S. (eds.) (1991) *Collective Responsibility: Five Decades of Debate in Theoretical and Applied Ethics*, Savage, MD: Rowman & Littlefield.
Miller, S. (2007) "Against the Collective Moral Autonomy Thesis," *Journal of Social Philosophy* 38: 389–409.
Pettit, P. (2007) "Responsibility Incorporated," *Ethics* 117: 171–201.
Tollefsen, D. P. (2015) *Groups as Agents*, Cambridge: Polity Press.
Tuomela, R. and Mäkelä, P. (2016) "Group Agents and Their Responsibility," *Journal of Ethics* 20: 299–316.

6
FROM INDIVIDUAL TO COLLECTIVE RESPONSIBILITY
There and Back Again

Kirk Ludwig

6.1 Introduction

None of us *individually* is causally responsible for anthropogenic global warming. None of us can do anything alone to slow it or to stop it. It is only *collectively* that we are causally responsible for global warming. It is only collectively that we can reverse the processes contributing to it or ameliorate the harm it brings. Since we are only collectively and not individually causally responsible—and none of us can do anything about it alone—there is a strong prima facie case for saying that it is, in the first instance, we together who are *collectively morally responsible* for global warming. And it is we who are together collectively morally responsible for reducing greenhouse gas emissions and ameliorating the effects of greenhouse gases already released. Anthropogenic climate change is a salient real-world example in which a *group* or *collection* of individual agents seems to be, in the first instance, the locus of both causal and moral responsibility. Other examples are stonings, riots, whisper campaigns, racketeering, acid rain, human trafficking, corporate crime and negligence, and the ocean plastic pollution crisis.

When we hold the group or collective responsible in the first instance, what does this entail about individual responsibilities? What degree of blame does each member of the group share when we hold the group collectively responsible for a harm? What obligations do members of the group have? It is not obvious that collective responsibility entails anything about individual responsibility. If the result is massively overdetermined, why should I be blamed for contributing to a harm or be required to stop? If there is nothing that I can do alone, then why should I have any obligation?[1] Yet if there is no route back from collective moral responsibility to individual moral responsibility, collective moral responsibility becomes detached from pressure to alter collective behavior. If its members are not morally required to change their individual behaviors in response to a finding that a collective is morally responsible for something, there is no normative mechanism by which holding collectives morally responsible can induce relevant change. Attributions of collective moral responsibility become idle.[2] We are led to the idea of collective moral responsibility by harms of agency that cannot be attributed solely to any one individual. But we must find our way back to individual moral responsibility if holding a collective morally responsible is to have any moral force in changing its behavior.

Some theorists argue that collectives are, in some cases, to some degree, morally autonomous from the individuals who constitute them, in the sense that they may be blamed or be responsible for things they do, though none of their realizers are, at least in the same way or to the same degree (Copp 2006; 2007; 2012; French 1979; 1984; 1995; List and Pettit 2011; Pettit 2007; 2009). I call this the AUTONOMY THESIS.

> AUTONOMY THESIS: Groups may be morally responsible for harms (or benefits) without their members being morally responsible, either at all, or in the same way or to the same degree as the group.

Beyond this, many who write about collective responsibility think that it requires a group-level agent to be the bearer of the responsibility that attaches to the outcome that none of the members could bring about alone.

I reject this picture. Collective action and collective moral responsibility should be understood in terms of individual agency, on the one hand, and individual moral responsibility in the context of group action, on the other. I argue that all collective action is a matter of individual agents contributing to bringing about some event or state. I have criticized arguments for AUTONOMY THESIS. I will not repeat those arguments here (Ludwig 2007; 2016; 2017). If I am right, we have no need for group agents in our understanding of ordinary discourse about collective actions, either in the case of informal groups or in the case of organizations. If groups, in the contexts in which we attribute moral responsibility to them, are not themselves agents, they cannot be moral agents. If they are not moral agents, they cannot be the ultimate locus of moral responsibility. Given this, and that we cannot let moral responsibility become detached from a mechanism by which the behavior on the basis of which it is attributed can be changed, I advocate the FACTOR MODEL of collective moral responsibility (Ludwig 2007).[3]

> FACTOR MODEL: Any claim that a group is morally responsible for something must be resolved into a distribution of moral responsibility to its members, with none left over for the group per se.

This leaves us with the question of the distribution of moral responsibility to members of a group judged to be collectively morally responsible for something.

> DISTRIBUTION QUESTION: How is the collective moral responsibility of a group for a harm (or benefit) to be distributed across its members?

My focus in this chapter will be on the DISTRIBUTION QUESTION. My brief direct argument for the FACTOR MODEL was that otherwise moral responsibility of collectives becomes detached from any normative mechanism for changing its behavior. My indirect argument consists in showing how to distribute moral responsibility in a range of cases based on principles we apply to individuals and our understanding of the structure of collective action and shared intention.

The account that follows is incomplete in two respects (due to limitations of space). First, I focus on backwards-looking moral responsibility, specifically for harm, rather than forward-looking moral responsibility. Second, despite its importance, I cannot explore the significance of institutional structures, role responsibilities, authority, organizational hierarchies, and task delegation in assigning responsibility to individuals acting in organizations.[4] Nonetheless, we will reach some conclusions which seem both surprising and ineluctable, when the principles upon which they are based are followed to their logical conclusions.

A natural view is that the degree of moral responsibility in collective action is proportional to one's causal contribution to a harm or benefit. This is the DILUTION PRINCIPLE.

> DILUTION PRINCIPLE: The moral responsibility of a member of a group that is collectively morally responsible for the harms (or benefits) it brings about is proportional to the causal contribution of that member to the harms (or benefits).

If the DILUTION PRINCIPLE were true, however, then in the case of harms whose etiology involves millions of people, very little moral responsibility would attach to any individual—so little, in fact, that it would have no weight against other responsibilities that each of us has. The responsibility gets diluted when it is distributed down to individuals, until there is hardly anything of significance left. In fact, in cases in which the harm is overdetermined, one might plausibly argue that since nothing one could do alone would make any difference, no responsibility attaches to any individual at all. This leads to an additional principle, which I will call the ABSOLUTION PRINCIPLE:

> ABSOLUTION PRINCIPLE: A member of a group is not responsible to any degree for the harm (or benefit) for which the group is collectively responsible if that member's contribution is not necessary to bring it about.

It is clear what the relevance of the DILUTION PRINCIPLE and the ABSOLUTION PRINCIPLE are to climate change and many other examples of harms brought about by large-scale collective activity. If we are collective morally responsible, but the causal contribution that each of us makes is insignificant, and even unnecessary, then these principles would have the consequence that none of us was individually to any significant extent morally responsible for human induced climate change or morally responsible for doing something about it. This, I argue, is an important and perilous mistake.

Here is the program for the chapter. In section 6.2, I sketch the theory of collective action that I work with. In section 6.3, I sketch the corresponding theory of shared intention. In section 6.4, I argue against the DILUTION PRINCIPLE and the ABSOLUTION PRINCIPLE in the case of collective action intentionally directed at harm. In section 6.5, I extend the argument to collective action in which a harm is foreseen but not intended. Section 6.6 summarizes. The method is to work through a series of cases, starting with a case that challenges the DILUTION PRINCIPLE, and explain why responsibility for the collective harm is in that case not diluted at all. Then I argue from that case, using the NO RELEVANT DIFFERENCE PRINCIPLE, that other similar cases likewise do not involve dilution, and then that overdetermination cannot make a difference.

> NO RELEVANT DIFFERENCE PRINCIPLE: If in two cases we can identify no relevant differences, and in one of them a certain distribution of responsibility to members of a group which is collectively responsible for something is called for, the same distribution is called for in the other case.[5]

This leads to the view that when we are collectively morally responsible for a harm or for doing something about a potential harm, each of us is morally responsible to the degree that he would be if he were the sole agent concerned.

6.2 Collective Action

I summarize a view about the general structure of collective action and shared intention that I have developed elsewhere (Ludwig 2016; 2017). However, the main conclusions reached will not depend on the details that separate it from other individualistic accounts of collective action and shared intention.

I distinguish between plural and institutional action. In plural action discourse, we use plural noun phrases as grammatical subjects of action verbs: *we* lifted the bench, *they* danced the tango, *the girls* teased *the boys*, and so on. In institutional action discourse, we use grammatically singular noun phrases designating institutions as grammatical subjects of action verbs: *The Supreme Court* ruled in *Plessy v. Ferguson* that segregation is constitutional, *The Congress* passed the War Powers Act in 1974, *The British Eighth Army* defeated *The Panzer Army Afrika* at the Second Battle of El Alamein. Since the subject positions are occupied by terms that refer to groups, there is a prima facie case for our conceptualizing the groups themselves as agents. I argue elsewhere that this is a mistake for both plural and institutional action. I have argued instead for the MULTIPLE AGENTS ACCOUNT of collective action.

> MULTIPLE AGENTS ACCOUNT: Collective action is a matter of all the members of a group (and only them) contributing (in the right way) to bringing about some event or state.

Consider a simple plural action sentence such as [1].

> [1] We lifted a bench.

This is ambiguous between a distributive reading on which we each lifted a bench and a collective reading on which we lifted a bench together. On the distributive reading, it is clear that we are saying that there is something that each one of us did individually, namely, grasp parts of the bench and exerted upward force, that led to the bench rising. What goes on when the collective reading is true? There is still just one event of the bench rising, but now there are multiple contributions to its going up. On the distributive reading, each of us individually does something that causes a bench to go up; on the collective reading, a bench goes up as a result of contributions from all of us (and no one else). It follows from the MULTIPLE AGENTS ACCOUNT that collective action is not essentially intentional because while to do something individually always involves an intention to do something, we might fail to share an intention to do something together though individually intending to do something separately. For example, we may each intend to lift an end of the bench not knowing the other is going to lift the other end, and so lift the bench together without intending to do so.

Institutional action sentences also turn out to be about what (the then-) members of the institution do. The agency of all members (at the time) is implicated in what the group does, though sometimes *very* indirectly, especially when the group employs proxy agents institutionally authorized to act in the name of the organization.[6] We get a sense of how the basic account can be extended in noticing that [2] exhibits the same distributive/collective ambiguity as [1].

> [2] The Supreme Court went to lunch after the morning's session.

They could have gone individually or together. On the collective reading, it is a matter of each of them contributing to their lunching together. The same idea extends to the Supreme Court exercising its essentially collective constitutional duties. For example, [3]

> [3] The Supreme Court ruled in *Brown v. Board of Education* that segregation is unconstitutional.

just says that each justice (and no one else) contributed in their roles as justices to bringing about a ruling in *Brown v. Board of Education* that segregation is unconstitutional—by each voting in a decision procedure that results in a ruling.

6.3 Shared Intention

If the MULTIPLE AGENTS ACCOUNT of collective action is right, then for a group to do something is just for its members (or some of its members) to all make contributions to something's coming about. What then is it for a group to *intend* to do something together and to do it *intentionally*? We can say that when a group intends to do something, they share an intention. A shared intention is attributed using a sentence like [4].

> [4] We intend to lift the bench.

[4] has a distributive and a collective reading. On the distributive reading, it just means that each of us herself intended to lift the bench. On the collective reading, it means we intend to lift the bench together. Since we have no need for a group to be the agent of a group action, we have no need for the group per se to intend anything. Instead, when we say that a group intends to do something, we mean each of them has an intention directed toward their doing something together. In the case of [4], we mean that each of us intends for us to lift the bench together. Thus, it is just a matter of each of us having an appropriate intention directed toward our acting together. We can call the individual intentions directed toward joint action that make up a shared intention *we-intentions* (Tuomela and Miller 1988). A group shares an intention when they all have we-intentions directed toward doing something together. They do something together intentionally when their we-intentions are carried out successfully.

However, it is not enough for us to share an intention that we each intend that we do something together. If we each intend to trick each other into our lifting the bench together, we do not share an intention. What's special about we-intentions can be located in a special mode of intending (Gilbert 2009; Searle 1990) or in the content (Bratman 1992; 2014; Miller 2001; Tuomela 2005; 2013). I favor an account in terms of the content (Ludwig 2016: chs. 12–14), which I call the SHARED PLAN ACCOUNT.

> SHARED PLAN ACCOUNT: x we-intends that we J if x intends that x contribute (in accordance with a plan x has at the time of acting) to there being a plan in accordance with which each of us makes our contribution to our J-ing (at the time of acting).

If this intention is carried out, then when we act together in J-ing, we each have the same joint action plan in mind (in the sense that we can locate the plan that is the same for all and know our part). To put it informally: we all intend to be on the same page about what we are doing together when we act. Since we each intend this, *we each intend something that will result in our*

J-ing if successful. This feature is shared by most individualistic accounts of shared intention and will be what we rely on in analyzing collective responsibility in the next section.

6.4 Collective Responsibility When Harm is Intended

With this as background we can turn to the question of collection responsibility. I focus on cases of backwards-looking collective responsibility for a harm. In this case, (a) a group has done something that results in a harm; and (b) it is the group that is the causal locus of the harm in the sense that the group is causally responsible; but (c) while all of its members make contributions, none of them are individually causally responsible for the harm. We have rejected the view that the group is an autonomous agent. Our primary question, then, is the DISTRIBUTION QUESTION—that is, what the implications are of the attribution of collective responsibility to the group for the individual responsibilities of its members. I develop a response to this question by taking up the challenges presented by the DILUTION PRINCIPLE and the ABSOLUTION PRINCIPLE. I argue from examples that neither can be correct and explain why not in terms of the logic of responsibility and the structure of collective action.

I begin with cases of a group sharing an intention to cause harm that provide grounds for rejecting the DILUTION PRINCIPLE.

> EQUAL BLOWS: A 10-man gang intentionally beats another man to death. They share an intention to do so and they kill him intentionally as a result of executing their shared intention. They each land an equal number of equally powerful blows on their victim, which contribute equally to his death. The contributions of each are necessary and jointly sufficient.

The gang is collectively morally responsible for the victim's death, but none alone is causally responsible for it. What is the extent of the blame for each? The DILUTION PRINCIPLE divides the responsibility evenly among them. Suppose that we can make sense of being morally responsible for $1/10^{th}$ of a death. According to the DILUTION PRINCIPLE, each of them is morally responsible only for the equivalent of $1/10^{th}$ of a death. This is an unacceptable result. First, they all have the intention to kill. But it is not the weight of a death that any of them would be responsible for. The object of their intentions, which is realized, has disappeared from the moral calculus, and no one is morally responsible for an intended death brought about intentionally. Second, it would have the consequence that they could make themselves less and less to blame simply by making the group that shared the intention larger. If a million people contribute, then no individual bears any significant moral blame at all. We should in fact hold each of them *fully* responsible for the death. The degree to which each of them is blamable for participating is not reduced by adding more people to the gang. If two people each want to kill the same person, they do not become less responsible individually by joining forces.

To say that they are each fully responsible for the death is one thing; to explain it is another. Here are two possible explanations.

> PRAGMATIC NEED: There is no deep explanation for this grounded in the structure of agency or the logic of responsibility; it is just that if we let people off for this reason it would be a license for collective murder and mayhem. So as a practical matter we don't dilute responsibility.

However, if there is no ground for it in the logic of responsibility and the structure of shared agency, then none of them is in fact fully responsible. This fails to explain how we can *legitimately* hold each of them fully responsible.

> INDIVISIBLE HARM: The harm, the death, is indivisible. There is no group agent per se to blame. Therefore, on pain of it being assigned to no one, it must be assigned to all equally.

There is something to the idea that the harm is indivisible. How can the death be apportioned among them? The death is not the *sum* of their individual contributions, like contributing grains of sand to a heap. Even so, why isn't it an injustice to assign the whole harm to each, so that what we have is instead simply a moral paradox? Moreover, it is not clear that we would reach a different verdict in a case in which the harm is divisible as in MONEY HEIST.

> MONEY HEIST: Suppose that 10 thieves working together steal $100,000,000 from the Denver mint, each contributing equally to the theft, which they carry out intentionally.

Do we want to say that each is responsible for only a tenth of the theft? If so, then if we increase the number of thieves, eventually none of them will be guilty of more than the moral equivalent of a misdemeanor. Do they all get a slap on the wrist for stealing 100 million dollars? The fact that they are working together in carrying out the theft is morally significant.

We have been thinking about harms caused, causal contributions, and numbers of agents. We have not been thinking about the structure of their intentions when they act. It becomes clear why we should hold each of them equally responsible when we consider the structure of their intentions. Thus, we arrive at an explanation in terms of logic of responsibility and the structure of shared agency

On the SHARED PLAN ACCOUNT, to share an intention to kill their victim, each gang member must have a we-intention of the form:

> I intend to bring it about (in accordance with a plan I have at the time of acting) that there is a plan in accordance with which we bring it about that X dies.

Each has an intention whose successful execution requires that X die. Thus, their intentions are not relevantly different from someone whose intention is of the form:

> I intend to bring it about (in accordance with a plan I have at the time of acting) that X dies.

The difference lies only in what the content of the plan is. In the first case, it goes by way of our several contributions. In the second case, it may but need not involve cooperation with others. One intends to do something that leads to another's death either way. Consequently, each individual in EQUAL BLOWS is just as liable for blame as he would be if he were the sole agent of the death.[7]

This explanation works for any account of shared intention which resolves it into an intention (or commitment) of an individual to contribute to a group doing something. This includes all of the major individualistic accounts of shared intention: Searle (1990), Miller (2001), Gilbert (2013), Tuomela (2013), and Bratman (2014). So it is not an explanation that is sensitive to the details of the account of we-intentions.

One might object: when one intends oneself to kill someone, one thinks it is in one's power alone. But when cooperating with others, one does not typically think it lies in one's power alone. If it does not lie in one's power alone to do it, the case of individual intentions and we-intentions is not parallel.[8]

Everything we do requires the cooperation of the world. If I shoot someone, I rely on the operation of the gun, the absence of obstacles intervening at the last second, enough sunlight to see by, and so on. As Davidson wrote, "We never do more than move our bodies: the rest is up to nature" (2001: 59). Sometimes the conditions required for our contributions to bring about the end involve others acting in certain ways. This can be so even for an assassination attempt: I rely on my victim's regular habits while I lie in wait. In the case of joint intentional action involving the cooperation of others, their contributions are, relative to my intention, parts of what I expect to happen, given my contribution, which sets the stage for the victim's death. So there is not after all any relevant difference between the case of killing someone with others or by oneself.

The explanation extends straightforwardly to variations on EQUAL BLOWS in which the contributions of the members differ causally, but are all still insufficient by themselves to bring about the harm for which the group is responsible, as in UNEQUAL BLOWS.

> UNEQUAL BLOWS: As for EQUAL BLOWS except that the blows are not all equal. Some contribute more or harder blows than others, so that the distribution of causal responsibility is not equal. The contribution of each of them is necessary but none alone is sufficient.

When we keep in mind what it is that each intends we can see that the blows being unequal does not make a difference. Each intends what the others do to be part of the background against which what they do is seen as contributing to the death. Thus, it is still not relevantly different from forming and executing an individual intention to kill someone. A consequence is that one is still equally to blame for the death even if one's contribution is small relative to the contributions of others.

This shows that the DILUTION PRINCIPLE is false for joint intentional action directed at bringing about a harm. But in the cases considered so far, the contributions of each is at least necessary for the harm. What if the contributions overdetermine the result as in OVERDETERMINED BLOWS?

> OVERDETERMINED BLOWS: A gang of 10 men intentionally beat another man to death. They share an intention to do so. They kill him intentionally as a result of executing their shared intention. They each land an equal number of equally powerful blows on their victim. The blows of any nine of them are sufficient to bring about the victim's death.

In OVERDETERMINED BLOWS, none of the contributions of individual gang members is either necessary or sufficient. The ABSOLUTION PRINCIPLE says that none of them is responsible to any degree.

This can't be right. It would let all of them off. Nobody would be responsible for the death, when if they had done less violence, they would all be equally responsible. But the death would have occurred even if any one of them had not contributed. How can I be responsible for something that would have happened anyway?[9]

One might suggest that one intends to make one's contribution even if one of the others drops out: so one both makes a contribution and is willing that it be a necessary contribution.

This can't be the explanation, because we wouldn't let everyone off if each intended to make his contribution only if it weren't necessary.

There are three justifications one might consider. First, when *n* many people intentionally contribute to a harm, where any $m < n$ contributing would have been sufficient, each is a necessary part of some sufficient condition for the death. If one's contribution is a necessary part of *some* (even if not every) sufficient condition for the death one intends, then one is to blame as if one did it alone. These are INUS conditions in Mackie's sense (1974), Insufficient Necessary parts of Unnecessary but Sufficient conditions, which Mackie identified as causes. So, in Mackie's terms, being an intentional cause of the death suffices for full responsibility.

> NECESSARY PART OF A SUFFICIENT CONDITION: If one participates in a joint action A intentionally to bring about harm H, then one is liable to full blame for H if one's contribution is a necessary part of some sufficient condition for H.

Second, one's intention represents one as doing something that brings about something sufficient for the death, namely, the whole group's doing something more than sufficient for the death. Compare this with the case of TWO-GUN PETE.

> TWO-GUN PETE: Two-Gun Pete wears a holster on either hip. When he decides to kill someone, he draws both guns and shoots the victim through each eye simultaneously.

Two-Gun Pete intends something more than sufficient to bring about his victim's death. But we do not let him off on that account: since the content of the we-intention in OVERDETERMINED BLOWS is that we all make our contributions so as to bring about the death, we each intend to contribute to a more than sufficient condition for the death. There is no relevant difference from the individual case. Two-Gun Pete intends to do something more than sufficient for the death of his victim. Hence, he intends to do something sufficient. Thus, one's contribution might not be causally necessary in the sense that counterfactually holding the contributions of others fixed and removing yours, the victim would still have been killed, but since one intended to bring about a sufficient condition, one is liable for the blame just as if one had done it alone.

> INTENDING SOMETHING SUFFICIENT: If one intends to bring about something sufficient for a harm H in acting with others intentionally, then even if one's contribution is not counterfactually necessary, one is fully to blame for H.

Third, one's contribution was a necessary part of the actual cause of the death. A 10-man firing squad shoots their victim through the heart, and any shot, if the others' guns jammed at that moment, would have been sufficient to kill the victim.[10] Nonetheless, the actual cause was the totality of the forces exerted on his body by the impact of 10 bullets. In any counterfactual scenario in which one or more of the guns failed to fire, the cause of his death would have been different. Alternatively suppose 10 men decide to suffocate their victim by standing on his chest so that he cannot take a breath. Any four of them would have been sufficient, in the sense that the force exerted by four of them standing on his chest would be sufficient to prevent him from drawing a breath. Nonetheless, the total force is the force exerted by the 10 of them. So they each make necessary contributions to the actual cause of his death, which was a force 2.5 times that needed to suffocate him.

> NECESSARY PART OF THE ACTUAL CAUSE: If one's contribution to a harm H that a group brings about jointly intentionally is a necessary part of the actual cause of H, then one is fully to blame for H.

If any of these justifications is sufficient, the ABSOLUTION PRINCIPLE is false in application to joint intentional action. But it is not merely that one does not get off scot-free. No matter how large the group, no matter how overdetermined counterfactually, no matter whether one's contribution is large or small, one is as responsible for the harm as if one had done it by oneself.

6.5 Collective Responsibility When Harm is a Foreseen Side-Effect of Collective Action

Many harmful effects of aggregate human activity are not intended. If these results bear on responsibility for climate change, ocean plastic pollution, and so on, they must extend to foreseen as well as intended harm. I look first at a group doing one thing intentionally while recognizing it has a harmful side effect. Then I consider cases in which a group is not acting together intentionally but its members foresee that what they do together unintentionally will have a harmful side effect. I do not consider overdetermination, because the reasoning of the previous section can be repeated once we reach the conclusion that, in cases in which there is no overdetermination, there is undiluted distribution of responsibility to members of a group collectively responsible for something.

Intentional collective action with a foreseen harmful side effect is illustrated in FILLING THE TANK.

> FILLING THE TANK: Ten men are hired to fill a tank at the aquarium by dipping buckets in a salt water pool and then pouring the water into the tank. They get a bonus if they fill the tank by noon. They notice that a toddler has fallen into the tank. They do not intend to harm him, but they foresee that when they fill the tank he will drown. The boy drowns.

In FILLING THE TANK, the 10 men are collectively responsible for a toddler's death. What are their individual responsibilities? From the moral standpoint there is no relevant difference between this case and cases in which the group intends to bring about the harm. Why is there no relevant difference?

First, we can apply the NO RELEVANT DIFFERENCE principle by way of analogy. Consider a single person first who intends to drown the toddler by filling the tank. He is fully morally responsible for the death. Now suppose that he merely intends to fill the tank and foresees that the toddler will drown. He is equally morally responsible. There is no morally relevant difference. This is an act evaluation rather than an agent evaluation. Intending harm may reveal a more vicious character than indifference. However, our concern is the relation of the agent to an outcome *for* which he can be held morally responsible. It is with respect to the latter that there is no morally relevant difference. By parity of reasoning, if members of a group who jointly intend to bring about a harm and do so are each fully responsible, so are members of a group who each foresee a harm as a side effect of something they do together intentionally and then do it.[11]

Second, we can explain why there is no morally relevant difference. One has a duty not to harm others (extenuating circumstances aside). This is why it is wrong to aim intentionally at harming someone and why you are to blame if you do. The duty not to harm others is not a duty merely not to harm others *intentionally*, but a duty not to harm others *period*, whether intentionally or not. We derive from the duty not to cause harm that it is wrong to intentionally do so—not the other way around. So there can be no relevant moral difference between the case of intended and foreseen harm.

Next, what if we foresee harm as a result of our doing something together that is not intentional under any description, like causing global warming? First, we consider harms brought about by unintentional group action in which the total harm is not simply the aggregate of individual harms foreseen but brought about unintentionally by members of the group. Second, we consider harms that are aggregative in the sense that the total harm is simply the sum of the individual harms.

The case of non-aggregative harms is illustrated by UNINTENDED TANK FILLING.

> UNINTENDED TANK FILLING: The aquarium pays $1 for every bucket of water someone puts in the tank until it is full. Ten men independently carry buckets of water to the tank noticing the others doing the same thing. They are not working together but realize that they will together fill the tank. Each sees a toddler has fallen into the tank. None of them intends the toddler harm, but each realizes that when they have filled the tank through their independent actions, the toddler will drown. They fill the tank. The toddler drowns.

Is this relevantly morally different from FILLING THE TANK? No. In this case, they are jointly morally responsible for drowning the toddler, and the distribution of blame is exactly the same as in the previous case. UNINTENDED FILLING THE TANK differs from FILLING THE TANK in there not being an intentional joint action that the men are undertaking. But it does not differ in their epistemic position with respect to what they are doing together (filling the tank) or with respect to their individual knowledge of what side effects they bring about by what they do jointly. The moral principle is not to do anything to harm another. It is immaterial that the background conditions for one's making a contribution to a sufficient condition for the harm is a state of nature or of society, and it is immaterial when background conditions involve the actions of others whether those contributions are jointly intended or not. Other aspects of this case can be brought out by the contrast with aggregative harms.

The case of aggregative harms is illustrated by ARMORED CAR.

> ARMORED CAR: An armored car turns over on the road, the back doors pop open, a sack of money spills out. Twenty bystanders each take $1000 in a stack of twenties. The total loss is $20,000. Each sees the others taking a single stack and that the total loss will be $20,000.

Is each responsible for the full amount? No. Why not? The main difference is the relation of the harm to what each does individually. In UNINTENDED TANK FILLING, the harm was not the sum of the harm that each of them does. While there may be harms that each contributes as a sole agent, the death is not the sum of individual harms but a harm brought about only by all of them together. There is no separable portion of the death as such to be assigned to each. There may be differences in their causal contributions, but this doesn't isolate a portion of the death to assign to each. None do anything sufficient and what each does is not an incremental contribution to the death (as if it were the sum of a lot of smallish harms) as opposed to a partial cause of it. There is then no way to assign to each independently just a bit of the harm. ARMORED CAR differs in this respect: there is for each a harm for which he or she is solely responsible. When these have been taken into account, the total harm has been accounted for. In this case, the group is not in the first instance the locus of responsibility but instead the individual members of the group. Thus, the case of foreseen but unintended aggregative harms does not engage the mechanism by which I argued that each member of a group is equally and fully responsible for what the group did. This contrast is illustrated in Figure 6.1.

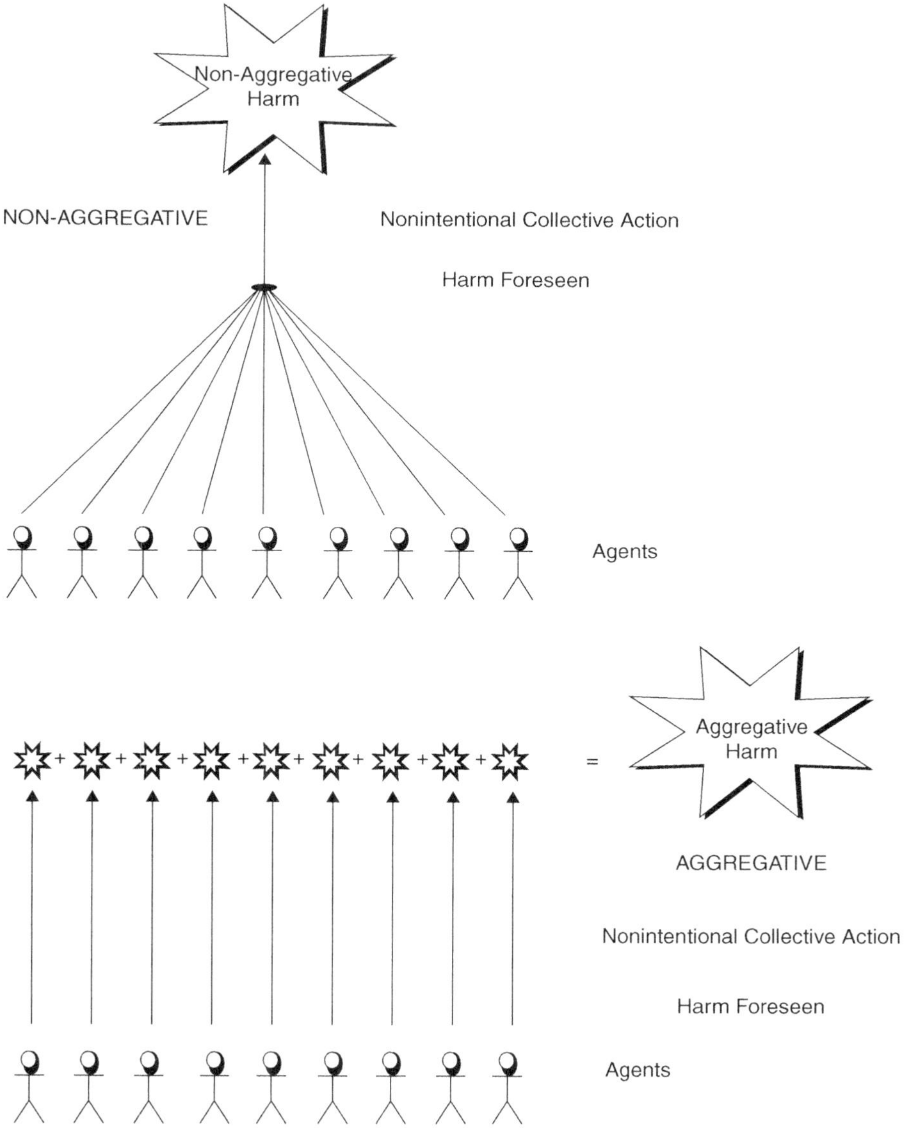

Figure 6.1 Non-Aggregative vs Aggregative Harms. In the top image, the contributions of the individual agents combine to produce a harm that is not just the sum of their causing individual harms. In the bottom image, the contributions of each leads to a discrete harm and the total harm is the sum of the individual harms.

Why is it different with aggregative harms that are intended or foreseen side effects of intended action? For *intended* harm the individual members conceptualize what they are doing as contributing to bringing about the total harm. When successful they do it. They take on the responsibility for doing what they intended. In the case of foreseen harm that results from something one intends to do with a group, the foreseen harm is also seen as a consequence of something intended. Thus, members conceptualize it as a consequence of something they are doing. They take on the responsibility for foreseen harms that are the result of what they bring about intentionally.

6.6 Conclusion

The view we have been led to is summarized in Figure 6.2. An arrow with a "Yes" beside it indicates the condition in the box from which it originates is met. An arrow with a "No" beside it indicates the condition in the box is not met. A box with rounded corners contains conditions. Square boxes contain conclusions about collective and individual responsibility. A path through a series of conditions indicates the conjunction of their being met or not met.

We ascribe collective backwards-looking moral responsibility to a group, in the first instance, for something that has been done when

(a) all (or, perhaps in institutional cases, some) members of the group, and no one else, made contributions (of a relevant sort) to bringing it about;
(b) it was a moral harm;

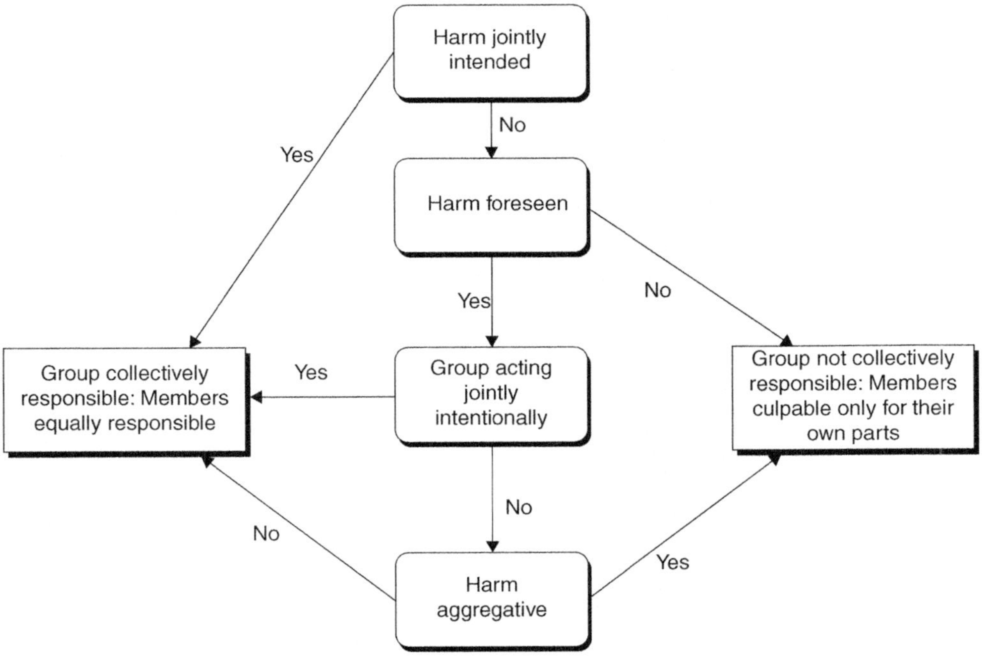

Figure 6.2 Conditions and Consequences of Collective Responsibility.

(c) its having been done by a single individual, knowingly or under conditions under which she should have known what she was doing, would ground the claim that she was morally responsible for it;
AND
(d) (i) they intended to do it;
OR
(ii) they foresaw (or should have foreseen) it as a side effect of something they intended to do;
OR
(iii) it was non-aggregative and they foresaw (or should have foreseen) it as a side effect of something they were doing nonintentionally.

Responsibility distributes to members of the group on the basis of degree of culpability. In the case of *collective* backwards-looking moral responsibility for a harm, each member of the group is culpable to the degree he would be if acting alone regardless of the size of the causal contribution and regardless of whether it was overdetermined. Thus, the surprising result of this study is that the rejection of the DILUTION PRINCIPLE and the ABSOLUTION PRINCIPLE for collective responsibility leads directly to the view that the degree of responsibility in genuine cases of collective responsibility is indivisible. It passes undiminished to the individual members of the group, no matter how large it is.

This result may seem incredible. Is each of us in affluent or industrialized societies who contributes to global warming really fully to blame for its consequences and called on to act in light of the magnitude of the full harm? And what exactly are we called upon to do? If we can't do anything to stop it, are we really called upon to do something? The answer is complicated in this case for at least two reasons. First, there is not only one moral demand or other demand on us. We have many obligations to others both in particular and in general, and many others that are connected with collective action, on-going or potential, together with our life projects. We are called on to balance all of them as best we can, with limited informational and computational resources. Second, we must consider what are the most effective means to the end of reducing the accumulations of greenhouse gases and addressing other conditions that cause harm that are the side-effects of massive unintentional collective activity. Effective response requires collectivizing. Yet there is already a vehicle for collectivizing action for the public good, namely, governmental action. Thus, the single most effective thing that individuals can do is to try to influence governmental policy to respond effectively to anthropogenic climate change. A primary and minimal duty then is to contribute to effective governmental and intergovernmental policy to address especially unintended harmful side-effects of human activity. This is something that it is in everyone's power to do in a democracy by voting for representatives who will advocate for policy changes that address recognized harmful side-effects of human activity. If everyone did their minimal duty, we would respond effectively. Anyone who does not therefore cannot be relieved of responsibility for the consequences.

Acknowledgments

I would like to thank my colleagues Kate Abramson and Allen Wood, and the editors of this volume, Saba Bazargan-Forward and Deborah Tollefsen, for helpful discussion and comments, as well as the audiences at presentations of the ideas in this chapter at the University of California, Merced, March 13, 2017; the College of Charleston, March 23, 2017; and Indiana University, September 14, 2018.

Notes

1 See Sinnott-Armstrong 2005 for some of the puzzles in the case of climate change.
2 There is a conceptual tie between moral responsibility and moral reasons for action, and hence between holding morally responsible and the possibility of change of behavior. Darwall expresses the general idea: "In a slogan: the moral sense of 'responsible for' is conceptually tied to 'responsible to' (whether to individuals or to one another as members of a moral community)" (Darwall 2008: 68). Being responsible to others implies an obligation and so gives one moral reasons for action in response to being found responsible for something. This connects being responsible to the possibility of change of behavior in agents who are responsive to moral reasons.
3 For some responses to the claim that corporations per se are suitable subjects for ascription of moral responsibility, see Ashman and Winstanley 2007; Hasnas 2012; Garrett 1989; Rönnegard 2015; Velasquez 1983; 2003.
4 Many organizations delegate authority to individuals or subgroups to act for, or in the name of, the group. The role occupiers are the locus of moral responsibility for those organizational actions over which they exercise control. Sometimes moral responsibility rests wholly with the person or subgroup. In this case, their failing their role responsibilities screens off the other members of the group from moral responsibility. Sometimes others bear moral responsibility, e.g., those who execute decisions they recognize as harmful, careless, negligent, etc., those who fail oversight responsibilities, or those who assign roles irresponsibly.
5 While the principle as stated is trivial, it serves as a schema we can apply on the basis of more substantive considerations in particular cases.
6 Ultimately it is not important whether the agency of everyone in an organization is involved when we say it acts. What is important here is that the basis for saying the organization acts is that all *or* some of its members have acted in their roles in the organization—see Tollefsen 2015 and Tuomela 1995: ch. 5.
7 When I hire an assassin to kill someone, he and I are both equally and fully responsible for the death. But in this case my plan does involve other agents contributing, and in more direct ways than I do. The same goes if I hire a team of assassins. I am still equally and fully responsible.
8 One objection to we-intending being directed at what the group does is that it requires us to think we will make others cooperate, so that joint action becomes mutual coercion (Stoutland 1997; Velleman 1997). All it requires, however, is that one think that what one does, given what else one expects will most likely happen, will bring about what one aims at (Bratman 1999; Ludwig 2016: ch. 14.1).
9 One reason might be that someone else would have done it if I had not, though if I do it, no one else contributes. In this case I would be fully responsible even though it would have occurred anyway. But in the present case it is not that counterfactually another cause would have taken my place, but just that my contribution could be subtracted without replacement and it would still have happened.
10 Sometimes a gun with a blank or wax bullet, a "conscience round," is distributed randomly to one member of the firing squad with the intention of diffusing responsibility or at least allowing each member of the firing squad to think that he is not responsible for the death. Does this relieve the person who fires the conscience round (or any of the others) of moral responsibility for the death? No. Each member of the firing squad shares an intention with the others to kill the victim, and intends to make a contribution to their doing so, the same contribution—firing a gun aimed at the victim which has a 1/10 (e.g.) chance of having the conscience round—and so to contribute to a sufficient condition for the death of the victim. My thanks to Allen Wood for raising this case.
11 What about the doctrine of double effect? The doctrine of double effect only applies to foreseen but unintended harm resulting from *intending something morally good that outweighs the harm*. The workmen are not intending to do something morally good but morally neutral; and whatever good outcomes there might be do not outweigh the harm.

References

Ashman, I., and Winstanley, D. (2007) "For or Against Corporate Identity? Personification and the Problem of Moral Agency," *Journal of Business Ethics* 76(1): 83–95.
Bratman, M. (1992) "Shared Cooperative Activity," *The Philosophical Review* 101(2): 327–41.
Bratman, M. (1999) *Faces of Intention: Selected Essays on Intention and Agency*, Cambridge: Cambridge University Press.
Bratman, M. (2014) *Shared Agency: A Planning Theory of Acting Together*, Oxford: Oxford University Press.

Copp, D. (2006) "On the Agency of Certain Collective Entities: An Argument from Normative Autonomy," *Midwest Studies in Philosophy: Shared Intentions and Collective Responsibility* XXX: 194–212.
Copp, D. (2007) "The Collective Moral Autonomy Thesis," *Journal of Social Philosophy* 38(3): 369–88.
Copp, D. (2012) "The Collective Moral Autonomy Thesis: Reply to Ludwig and Miller," *Journal of Social Philosophy* 43(1): 78–95.
Darwall, S. (2008) *The Second Person Standpoint*, Cambridge: Harvard University Press.
Davidson, D. (2001) *Essays on Actions and Events* (2nd edn), Oxford: Clarendon Press.
French, P.A. (1979) "The Corporation as a Moral Person," *American Philosophical Quarterly* 16(3): 207–15.
French, P.A. (1984) *Collective and Corporate Responsibility*, New York: Columbia University Press.
French, P.A. (1995) *Corporate Ethics*, Fort Worth: Harcourt Brace College Publishers.
Garrett, J.E. (1989) "Unredistributable Corporate Moral Responsibility," *Journal of Business Ethics* 8(7): 535–45.
Gilbert, M. (2009) "Shared Intention and Personal Intentions," *Philosophical Studies: An International Journal for Philosophy in the Analytic Tradition* 144(1): 167–87.
Gilbert, M. (2013) *Joint Commitment: How We Make the Social World*, New York: Oxford University Press.
Hasnas, J. (2012) "Reflections on Corporate Moral Responsibility and the Problem Solving Technique of Alexander the Great," *Journal of Business Ethics* 107(2): 183–95.
Johnson, B.L. (2003) "Ethical Obligations in a Tragedy of the Commons," *Environmental Values* 12(3): 271–87.
List, C., and Pettit, P. (2011) *Group Agency: The Possibility, Design, and Status of Corporate Agents*, Oxford: Oxford University Press.
Ludwig, K. (2007) "The Argument from Normative Autonomy for Collective Agents," *Journal of Social Philosophy, Special Issue: Collective Responsibility*, 38(3): 410–27.
Ludwig, K. (2016) *From Individual to Plural Agency: Collective Action 1*, Oxford: Oxford University Press.
Ludwig, K. (2017) *From Plural to Institutional Agency: Collective Action 2*, Oxford: Oxford University Press.
Mackie, J.L. (1974) *The Cement of the Universe: A Study of Causation*, Oxford: Clarendon Press.
Miller, S. (2001) *Social Action: A Teleological Account*, Cambridge: Cambridge University Press.
Pettit, P. (2007) "Responsibility Incorporated," *Ethics* 117(2): 171–201.
Pettit, P. (2009) "Corporate Responsibility Revisited," *Netherlands Journal of Legal Philosophy* 2: 159–76.
Rönnegard, D. (2015) *The Fallacy of Corporate Moral Agency*, Netherlands: Springer.
Searle, J. (1990) "Collective Intentions and Actions," in P.R. Cohen, J. Morgan, and M.E. Pollack (eds), *Intentions in Communication*, Cambridge: MIT Press, 410–15.
Sinnott-Armstrong, W. (2005) "It's Not My Fault: Global Warming and Individual Moral Obligations," in W. Sinnott-Armstrong and R. Howarth (eds), *Perspectives on Climate Change*, Elsevier, 221–53.
Stoutland, F. (1997) "Why are Philosophers of Action so Anti-Social?" in L. Alanen, S. Heinamaa, and T. Wallgreen (eds), *Commonality and Particularity in Ethics*, New York: St. Martin's Press, 45–74.
Tollefsen, D. (2015) *Groups as Agents*, Malden, MA: Polity Press.
Tuomela, R. (1995) *The Importance of Us: A Philosophical Study of Basic Social Notions*, Stanford: Stanford University Press.
Tuomela, R. (2005) "We-Intentions Revisited," *Philosophical Studies* 125: 327–69.
Tuomela, R. (2013) *Social Ontology: Collective Intentionality and Group Agents*, New York: Oxford University Press.
Tuomela, R. and Miller, K. (1988) "We-intentions," *Philosophical Studies* 53: 367–89.
Velasquez, M. (1983) "Why Corporations Are Not Morally Responsible for Anything They Do," *Business and Professional Ethics Journal* 2(3): 1–18.
Velasquez, M. (2003) "Debunking Corporate Moral Responsibility," *Business Ethics Quarterly* 13(4): 531–62.
Velleman, D. (1997) "How to Share an Intention," *Philosophy and Phenomenological Research* 57(1): 29–49.

7
COLLECTIVE OBLIGATIONS AND THE POINT OF MORALITY

David Copp

7.1 Introduction

History reveals many examples of the doings of institutional entities, such as states and corporations. For instance, I take it to be uncontroversial that, in 1989, the United States removed Manuel Noriega from the Presidency of Panama, and that, in 1991, the U.S. and a coalition of other countries waged war against Iraq. Further, in waging war against Iraq, the apparent intention of the U.S. was to end Iraq's occupation of Kuwait, although some contend that the intention was instead to secure access to Kuwait's oil. I also take it to be uncontroversial that Saudi Arabia has intervened in the civil war in Yemen. These are merely examples.

These claims about what the U.S. and Saudi Arabia did might be false. Yet I take it that no-one would seriously argue against them on a priori metaphysical grounds, such as on the basis of the view that states cannot do anything at all, much less wage war. If these claims are false, they are false for the prosaic reason that they are not borne out by the history of what actually happened in Panama, Kuwait, or Yemen.

We might nevertheless debate how to interpret the claims, or we might debate their truth conditions. It *appears* that they are straightforwardly claims about *intentional actions* performed by *states* – a kind of *institutional entity* – for which these states might well be *blameworthy*, depending on whether they violated their moral *obligations* in so acting. So, depending on what actually happened, Saudi Arabia might have been in violation of its moral obligations in carrying out air-strikes in Yemen, and it might be morally blameworthy for the resulting deaths of civilians. But perhaps a different interpretation of these claims can be defended. There is, indeed, a philosophical debate as to whether institutional entities, "as such," are capable of intentional action "in their own right" and as to whether they, "as such," can have moral obligations or bear moral responsibility.

Institutional entities are a kind of collective entity. They have individual natural persons as members.[1] States, corporations, and organized criminal gangs are examples. Entities of this kind are distinguished from unorganized groups, such as the group of all brown-haired men, and the mob that stormed the Bastille, in virtue of having an organizational structure and a collective decision procedure, grounded in laws, regulations, institutional practices, norms, or the like.

I shall not discuss views that deny that collective entities exist. Such a view could have a variety of motivations. There is, first, the metaphysical thesis that only the ontologically most fundamental entities exist. On this view, collectives do not exist, but neither do persons. I will use the term "existence" more expansively to allow that things can truly be said to "exist" even if they are not ontologically fundamental (see Rosen 2010; Baker 2006). There is also, second, "Occam's Razor," the idea that, other things being equal, we should give more credence to ontologically more parsimonious theories than to less parsimonious ones. I would deny that it is ontologically profligate to think that institutional entities and other collectives exist, for they are constituted by their members, given the laws, regulations, norms, and the like that are in place. It is no more profligate to think that collectives exist than to think there are dining room suites, bee colonies, and tractor-trailer units. But I cannot discuss these metaphysical issues, and I will assume that collective entities exist.

The philosophical debate I mentioned is between those who deny, and those who affirm, that institutional entities "as such" are capable of intentional action. Call people who deny this, "agency individualists." There is the closely related debate between those who deny, and those who affirm, that institutional entities "as such" can have moral obligations or bear moral responsibility. Call people who deny these things, "moral individualists." To be charitable, I shall not construe individualists of either kind as doing a priori history – as claiming on a priori metaphysical grounds that the U.S. did not in fact wage war against Iraq, or did not do this intentionally, and that Saudi Arabia did not in fact wrongly carry out air-strikes in Yemen. Instead, to be charitable, I shall construe individualists as aiming to accept the common-sense historical claims as true, and perhaps also the moral claims, while offering an individualist reading of them.

It will be helpful to distinguish between different forms of individualism about agency. An "extreme agency individualist," or an "extremist," holds that institutional entities are not capable of acting, or are not capable of acting intentionally. A "moderate agency individualist," or a "moderate," allows that institutional entities are capable of intentional action, yet contends that their actions are "reducible," "without remainder," to the actions of individual (natural) persons, so that institutional entities *as such* are not capable of intentional action. The U.S. waged war against Iraq. The extremist denies that this waging of war was *an action of the U.S.* The moderate admits that it was an action of the U.S. but holds that it was not an action of the U.S. *as such* since it was reducible to the actions of individual persons.

The extremist seems to be committed to denying that an institutional entity could have any moral obligations or bear moral responsibility for anything it has done. For, arguably, obligations are obligations to *act* in one way or another and responsibility of the relevant kind is responsibility for *action*. By way of contrast, a moderate *might* allow that institutional entities can have moral obligations and bear moral responsibility. But given that the moderate thinks that the actions of institutional entities are reducible without remainder to the actions of individual persons, she might be tempted to argue on this basis that their obligations and responsibilities are likewise reducible without remainder to the obligations and responsibilities of individual persons. Any obligations of the U.S. boil down to obligations of individual persons, and, similarly, if the U.S. is ever responsible for something it does, this also boils down to the responsibility of individual persons. I reject this kind of "moral individualism."

I do nevertheless agree to a point with the moderate agency individualist. Indeed, I take it to be uncontroversial that the actions of collective entities are in some appropriate sense "constituted" by the actions of relevant persons (Copp 1976; 1979).[2] The U.S. action in invading Kuwait was constituted by relevant actions of relevant persons, including the President. To capture this idea, I will say that collective entities are not "independent agents." But I do not want to say on this basis that collective entities "as such" are not capable of acting. I do not know what this would mean, unless it is simply another way of saying that collective entities are not independent agents. Perhaps, then, the debate between me and the moderate agency individualist is simply about details. Is the relation between collective institutional action and individual action as tidy as the moderate individualists contend? Can there be untidy "remainders"?

I do not agree with moral individualists. Of course I agree that if the U.S. invasion of Kuwait was wrong, this was a reason for the relevant persons not to do what they did. If the U.S. was blameworthy for what it did, then, other things being equal, some relevant person was blameworthy (Copp 2007a; 2012). As I have argued in other places, however, there can be cases in which an institutional entity has an all-things-considered moral obligation to do something, but where no person has an all-things-considered moral obligation to do what she would have to do in order for the institutional entity to meet its obligation (Copp 1976; 2006; 2007a; 2012). So I do not agree with the individualist who thinks that the obligations and responsibilities of collective entities are reducible without remainder to the obligations and responsibilities of individual persons.

My goal in this chapter is to combat the idea that there is something metaphysically or morally objectionable or problematic in the idea that institutional entities are capable of intentional action, properly so-called, and that, strictly speaking, they can have moral obligations and bear moral responsibility. I will argue that, at least on one conception of the point of morality, and on the normative theory supported by this account, we can explain how it might be that institutional entities have moral obligations. I have sketched the basic idea before (Copp 2012). Here I will go into more detail. I will argue that the account I favor can provide a satisfying explanation of the reason there is for individual persons to do what they need to do in order that collective entities they belong to meet their moral duties. I contend that similar arguments can be offered from other theoretical perspectives. In the middle sections of the chapter, I will argue that, even though institutional entities are not independent agents, they can be involved in events in the way that the U.S. was involved in the bombing of Hiroshima. I will argue that such "institutional actional events" qualify as actions. In the final substantive section of the chapter, I will reject reductionist views that are sometimes offered in support of extreme agency individualism or moral individualism. The upshot, I contend, is that facts about the obligations or responsibility of collective entities plausibly are grounded in the same kinds of facts about the content of morality as ground the obligations or responsibility of relevant individuals.

7.2 The Point of Morality and Society-Centered Moral Theory

In this section, I sketch an account of the nature and point of morality. In the next section, I argue that this account is congenial to the idea that institutional entities have moral obligations and can bear moral responsibility, such as being blameworthy. In section 7.4, I contend that various other normative moral theories can also make room for this idea.

In my view, the point of morality is to enable people to cope with what I call the "problem of sociality." Human beings obviously are not self-sufficient. They have needs of various kinds, and cannot generally meet these needs except by cooperating with, and, at times, relying on other people. They also generally cannot achieve, protect, or realize the things they value except by cooperating with other people. Unfortunately people have conflicting interests, limited resources, and limited sympathy as well as a tendency to pursue their own advantage, and because of this, cooperation might break down or fail to develop. The problem of sociality is the problem that although people need to live together cooperatively, and would fare well to do so, there is a significant potential for conflict among them, given conflicts of interest and the like.

It seems obvious that this problem can be ameliorated if the members of society subscribe to a suitable system of norms calling for a willingness to cooperate with others, for non-interference with others, and so on. Different moral codes, were they to serve as the moral culture of a society, or were they to be generally subscribed to,[3] would do more or less to enable people to do this. Further, with functional kinds, a good instance of the kind is one that best fulfills the relevant function. So, I think, the justified or authoritative moral code – the "ideal" moral code – is the one the currency of which would do more to enable society to cope with the problem of sociality than would the currency of any other code (see Copp 1995; 2007b; 2009).[4]

This, of course, is only a sketch of the theory. I have elsewhere called it the society-centered theory.[5] It is a kind of rule consequentialism (Copp forthcoming). Let me fill in the details a bit more fully.

We can think of a moral code as a system of standards, rules, or norms, where a standard is a content expressible by an imperative. There are purely arbitrary standards as well as standards that seem to correspond to moral truths, such as the standard that prohibits torture. The society-centered theory says that a "pure and basic" moral proposition is true if and only if (roughly) a corresponding moral standard is included in, or implied by, the ideal moral code for the society.[6,7] For example, torture is morally wrong, if and only if (roughly) a standard that prohibits torture is included in or derivable from the ideal moral code.

A moral code has "currency" in a society, or forms the moral culture, just when the members of the society by and large "subscribe" to its standards or have "internalized" them. That is, they by and large are disposed to comply with the standards, to have negative attitudes toward themselves if they fail to do so, to have negative attitudes toward others who fail to do so, and so on. In subscribing to a moral code, a person comes to have corresponding general intentions or moral policies. For example, if the moral code someone has internalized includes the rule, "Be honest," she will have a policy of being honest. Because of this, the currency of a moral code would significantly affect the motivations of the members of a society. This explains why the currency of a moral code can help a society to deal with the problem of sociality provided that it calls on people to behave in appropriate ways or to have appropriate traits of character.

It is important that the ideal moral code on this view is the code the currency of which in society – that is, its serving as the moral culture of society – *would* do most to mitigate the problem of sociality *holding constant* human psychology and the basic facts of our social lives. The ideal code is a kind of tool that could actually be used by people to address the problem of sociality by, *inter alia*, teaching the code to their children. Facts about human psychology and about our social lives affect and constrain how people teach new generations about morality and how people learn about moral matters. Limitations in human intelligence likewise affect and constrain the content of the ideal code since this is to be a code that realistically could by and large be subscribed to and internalized by the members of society. The ideal code is one that it is realistically possible for people by and large to internalize.

7.3 Institutional Entities and Moral Obligation

On the society-centered theory, the question whether institutional entities have moral obligations is the question whether the ideal moral code would include principles "directly regulating" the actions of such entities. Of course, an extreme agency individualist would object. She might think that there could not be standards that regulate the actions of institutional entities – or perhaps that no such standard would be coherent – since there is no such thing as an action of an institutional entity. I will return to this worry.

I assume everyone agrees that the United States dropped an atomic bomb on Hiroshima. Agency individualists and the rest of us agree that this event was constituted in some appropriate sense by actions of individuals.[8] What extremists deny is that this event was *an action* of *the U.S.*

and that the U.S. is an *agent*. In general, they deny that true statements that appear to ascribe actions to institutional entities actually do so. They presumably would agree, however, that such statements refer to complex events that in some way involve the institutional entity and that also involve relevant actions of individual persons. Call complex events of this kind "institutional actional events." And call an institutional entity that is involved in an actional event, in the way that the U.S. was involved in the bombing of Hiroshima, a "doer." One question we have is whether actional events involving institutional doers are, properly speaking, *actions* of those entities – whether institutional entities are *agents* capable of performing actions *properly speaking*. I will return to this question.

To investigate whether institutional entities have moral obligations, according to the society-centered theory, I ask whether the ideal moral code plausibly would include principles or standards directly regulating institutional actional events. Standards regulating actions of individual persons might *indirectly* regulate such events, of course, by requiring individual persons to do their part in bringing about certain institutional actional events. But the ideal moral code might also or instead include or imply standards that *directly* regulate institutional actional events in one of two ways. First, a standard might quantify over collective entities and actional events involving them and require or prohibit institutional actional events of certain kinds. For instance, a code might include the standard "No state is ever to attack a civilian population." Second, a standard might quantify over agents and doers alike, and actions and actional events alike, and require or prohibit actions or institutional actional events of certain kinds. For instance, a code might include the standard, "In war, do not ever attack a civilian population." If the ideal code included or implied such standards then corresponding moral propositions would be true. It might be true that it is morally wrong for any agent or doer to attack a civilian population in war.

To make the issue more vivid, it might help to think as social engineers who are designing the ideal moral code. The issue is whether we would be well-advised to design the code to include standards that directly regulate institutional actional events or whether we would do better to include only standards that directly regulate actions of individual persons. Suppose we aim to design a code such that people who subscribe to it will be inhibited from supporting or engaging in actional events that involve their state in attacking civilian populations. On the "individualist approach," we might include in the code a standard such as, "No person who is in a position to support her state's attacking a civilian population is ever to do so, and no person who is in an official position in a state is ever to perform an action that would be partly constitutive of her state's attacking a civilian population." On the "collectivist approach," we might include the simpler standard, "No state is ever to attack a civilian population," or even the standard, "Do not ever attack a civilian population." On this approach, for reasons I will explain, we would also want to include in the ideal code a "transitional standard" to the effect that "If a collective entity is required to do something, then its members, and any relevant officers in the collective, are to do their part in bringing it about that the collective acts as required." In this way, the ideal code would underwrite the existence of a "transitional duty." The issue is whether to take the collectivist or the individualist approach.

This is a complex empirical problem. As social engineers, we would aim to encourage some kinds of institutional actional events and to discourage other kinds. On the individualist approach, the ideal code might accordingly include a large number of standards such as, "No person who is in a position to support a corporation's polluting a waterway is ever to do so and no person who is in an official position in a corporation is ever to perform an action that would be partly constitutive of the corporation's polluting a waterway." The collectivist approach would seem to provide a simpler strategy. For, given that the ideal code would include the transitional standard, it could include a range of simpler standards directly governing institutional actional events of certain kinds, such as "No corporation is ever to pollute a waterway," or, more simply, "Do not ever pollute a waterway." The collectivist approach seems to allow for a simpler moral code, a code that would be less difficult to internalize and to have as the moral culture.

Consider, for example, the principles of just war theory. The familiar principles in the morality of war speak both to the actions of individuals and to institutional actional events involving the state or its armed forces. For example, a state's armed forces are obligated not to directly target noncombatants. On a collectivist approach, we can read such principles as directed both to the relevant institutions and to the relevant persons. On an individualist approach, we presumably would need principles speaking to individuals when acting in their own right as well as when acting in ways that will contribute to an institutional actional event. So we would need a principle saying that no person is to directly target noncombatants as well as a principle saying that no person who is in an official position in a state or a state's armed forces is ever to perform an action that would be partly constitutive of that entity's directly targeting noncombatants.

The greater simplicity of the collectivist approach seems to argue in its favor. As I explained, the ideal code must be designed in a way that takes into account human psychology, including our cognitive limitations. It would seem less difficult and costly to internalize and teach a moral code designed in accord with the collectivist strategy than to internalize and teach one designed in accord with the individualist strategy. This suggests that the ideal code would be designed in accord with the collectivist strategy. If this is right, I take it, then the ideal code would include standards directly governing institutional actional events. Its rules would regulate institutional actional events in the way that they regulate actions of individual persons.

It is important, as I said before, that if the ideal code includes standards that directly regulate institutional actional events, it plausibly would also include the transitional rule. The transitional rule would say, roughly, "If a collective is required to do something, then its members, and any relevant officers in the collective, are to do their part in bringing it about that the collective acts as required." The reason for including this rule is not hard to see. Collective entities are not independent agents. They do things only if relevant individual persons perform actions that constitute their doings. This means that standards that directly regulate institutional actional events will not motivate action unless they motivate the relevant individual persons, ideally by providing them with a reason to act.[9] Inclusion of a transitional standard in the ideal code would address this worry. It would ensure that the relevant people have at least a pro tanto duty to do the things that would constitute the collective's doing what the ideal code requires.

It is not clear, however, whether the fact that the ideal code would be designed in accord with the collectivist strategy means that, according to the society-centered theory, institutional entities have moral obligations. One might object that moral obligations are requirements governing *actions*. So even if some of the ideal rules directly concern institutional actional events, it does not follow that these events are actions, properly speaking, so it does not follow that any institutional entities have moral obligations.

We will return to this objection in a later section. As a first response, however, let me note that the objection is based on the twin assumptions that only actions in the proper or privileged sense can be governed by obligations, and that institutional actional events do not qualify as actions in that sense. These assumptions need defense.

7.4 Normative Theories and Institutional Obligations and Rights

For now, let me set aside the worry that institutional actional events are not actions in the proper or privileged sense. And let me also set aside for now the society-centered theory. In this section,

I will first contend, briefly, that, if institutional actional events *are* actions, strictly speaking, then many familiar normative moral theories make room for the idea that institutional entities have moral obligations and can bear moral responsibility. I will then turn, second, to the worry that, on the assumption that institutional entities have moral obligations and can bear moral responsibility, it follows, implausibly, that they have moral rights and must be treated with respect, as moral agents.[10]

First, as far as I can tell, if institutional entities are capable of intentional action, then any moral theory can allow that they have moral obligations. The only exceptions I can think of would be theories that postulate only a restricted range of obligations governing actions of kinds that institutional entities clearly would be incapable of performing, such as riding a bicycle or eating a cake. We can safely set aside such theories to focus on more familiar ones.

Society-centered theory is a form of rule consequentialism (Copp forthcoming), and I think that other forms of rule consequentialism can also allow for the idea that institutional entities have moral obligations. Elsewhere, I have argued that act consequentialism allows for institutional obligations (Copp 2007a; Copp 2012). Consider now the Kantian view that an agent is to act only on a maxim that it can at the same time will to be a universal law. If institutional entities are capable of acting on maxims in some relevant sense, and if they are capable of "willing" – as I will argue in what follows – then, arguably, again, institutional entities are agents in the scope of the theory. There is also the Kantian idea that our fundamental moral obligation is to respect persons as ends in themselves. If institutional entities are capable of showing respect for persons, or of treating persons as ends in themselves, this theory should apply to them.

Second, let me turn to the worry I mentioned. I think it simply is not true that, if institutional entities are agents that can have moral obligations and bear moral responsibility, it follows that they have rights, and that we are obligated to show respect for them, as ends-in-themselves. We are not forced to view institutional entities as having the same sort of moral value, or the same rights, as persons do, simply in virtue of viewing them as agents. According to the society-centered theory, it is an empirical issue whether institutional entities of one kind or another have any rights or any moral value. The issue is what kinds of rules the ideal moral code would include. It is not likely that it would include rules requiring agents to respect institutional entities of every kind, including criminal gangs. Furthermore, note that we are not viewing institutional entities as *persons*. We are instead, in this section, assuming that they are *agents* capable of acting intentionally. Even if there is an obligation to respect *persons* as ends in themselves, nothing follows about our obligations toward institutional entities.

One important point that distinguishes institutional entities morally from persons is that institutional entities are not *independent agents*. I believe that they do act, as I will explain in what follows, but they do not act *on their own*, pursuing values that they have *in their own right*. Instead, their actions are constituted by actions of relevant individual persons (Copp 1976; 1979), and their having the values they do have is constituted by the attitudes, values, and dispositions of relevant individual persons (Copp 1979; 1995). The Kantian intuition that persons must be treated with respect, as ends-in-themselves, is best understood, for my purposes here, as the idea that rational agents who have set ends for themselves – ends that they have in their own right – must be treated with respect as ends-in-themselves. Institutional entities are not in the scope of this demand because they are not independent agents and their values exist only, roughly, as a function of the states of mind of their members. They have not set their own ends in the relevant sense. This point needs further discussion, but I cannot pursue it here.

We could say more about the features that distinguish institutional entities morally from persons. They do not have conscious experiential states. So they do not experience pain and they do not experience emotional states in the way that human beings do. They do not form emotional attachments. These matters are important, but for present purposes I set them aside.

Of course, we have not agreed at this point that institutional entities are agents capable of intentional action. We have agreed only that institutional entities are capable of being involved as doers in institutional actional events. The interesting question we are left with is whether this is enough to support the idea that they are capable of having obligations, or whether it must be shown that institutional entities are agents, properly so-called, capable of performing actions, properly so-called. I now turn to this question.

7.5 Agents and Doers, Actions and Actional Events

To this point, we have left it open whether institutional actional events are actions, properly so-called, and whether institutional doers are agents, properly so-called. Further, we have not had a serious discussion of the issue whether or not it is only the actions, properly so-called, of agents, properly so-called, that can be governed by obligations. Suppose it turns out that, given some privileged concepts of *action* and *agent*, institutional actional events are *not* actions and institutional doers are *not* agents. Before concluding that institutional entities have no moral obligations, we need an argument to show that, in order to have an obligation (under the privileged concept of obligation), an entity must qualify as an agent (under the privileged concept) capable of doing what qualify as actions (under the privileged concept).

The society-centered theory gives us a way to think about this question. For suppose that the ideal code would include both standards that directly regulate institutional actional events and the transitional rule. In that case, it does not matter whether institutional actional events qualify as actions and whether institutional doers qualify as agents. For according to the theory, the point of morality is to help ameliorate the problem of sociality. On our supposition, the ideal code would impose requirements on institutional doers, requirements encoded in the standards that directly regulate institutional actional events. It does not matter whether these requirements qualify as obligations under some privileged concept of obligation.

Indeed, if the point of morality is to help ameliorate the problem of sociality, and if a moral code that included standards that directly regulate institutional actional events would be better designed (other things being equal) to ameliorate the problem than a code that included no such standards, then, I think, the *ideal* concept of obligation would classify moral requirements that are incumbent on institutional entities as moral obligations. What does this mean? It means, I propose, that whatever concept we actually express with the term "moral obligation," ideally we would express a concept such that requirements imposed by the ideal code would count as moral obligations, so understood. Given such a concept, requirements imposed by the ideal code on institutional entities could correctly be classified as obligations.

I do not want to rest my case on the plausibility of the society-centered moral theory, however. To give my argument a wider reach, I need to address two of the questions I raised before: whether institutional actional events are actions, properly so-called; and whether institutional doers are agents, properly so-called. The other question I raised before – the question whether it is only actions, properly so-called, of agents, properly so-called, that can be governed by obligations, properly so-called – will be of little interest if it turns out that institutional actional events *are* actions and that institutional doers *are* agents. It is of course obvious that institutional doers differ in many ways from individual agents. They have *members* whereas individual agents do not. They are organized under *constitutive rules* of various kinds[11] – laws, regulations, institutional practices or norms, or the like – and their existence depends on this being so, whereas this is not the case for an individual agent. Further, institutional actional events differ in many ways from standard examples of actions performed by individual agents. An institutional actional event is *constituted* by actions performed by individual agents. It would not occur *but for* actions performed by individual agents who are of course distinct from the institution and whose role in bringing about the event is, in typical cases, determined by the constitutive rules of the institutional entity. This is not the case where typical actions of individual agents are concerned (Copp 1979).[12] The question, however, is whether any of these differences are conceptually critical such that they entail, given the nature of the privileged concepts, that institutional doers are not agents and that institutional actional events are not actions.

7.6 Agency

In this section, I explore arguments based on views about agency against both the thesis that institutional actional events qualify as actions, and the thesis that institutional entities can have moral obligations and bear moral responsibility. There is an enormous literature on agency and I could not begin to explore this literature in any detail here. I need to sidestep most of the difficult metaphysical issues. Instead I will begin with a minimal characterization of what is involved in agency.

In the most familiar cases, an action is or is constituted by an event that is under the intentional control of a person and, in virtue of this, the person has the property of doing A, for some action-type A. For example, the event of my writing this sentence is under my intentional control and, in virtue of this, I have the property of writing this sentence, where writing is a type of action. For my purposes, in generalizing from the familiar cases, I need to leave it open whether every action must be constituted by an event that is under the control of a *person*. So I will say that an action is or is constituted by an event that is under the intentional control of some entity, and, in virtue of this, the entity has the property of doing A, for some action-type A.[13,14]

Given even this minimal characterization, there are two ways that one might contest the thesis that institutional actional events are actions. First, one might deny that institutional entities have intentions, and second, one might deny that institutional entities can control events even if they have intentions.

On the above characterization, in order to act, an entity must exercise intentional control over some event, and, I assume, this requires having an intention. One worry is that intentions are states of mind. Given this, entities that lack minds, such as collective entities, also lack intentions. A second worry, due to John Searle, is that intentions are "in principle accessible to consciousness" (Searle 1990: 586).[15] If so, then since collective entities are not capable of consciousness, they also lack intentions. But if collective entities are not capable of having intentions, it follows that they are not capable of acting intentionally.

I take it to be common ground that collective entities do not have minds and are not capable of having conscious phenomenal states of any kind. I am willing to concede that it follows from this that, if collective entities have intentions, their intentions do not have all the properties that the intentions of persons possess. The important point, however, is whether collective entities can be in states that have the key action-relevant properties that are possessed by intentions. Such states would make institutional entities capable of exercising intentional control over an event. And for this, the key factor arguably is whether institutional entities are capable of having plans such that having the plan has an effect on events, or makes a difference to what happens, in the characteristic way.[16] What is this characteristic way?

As Donald Davidson (2001) taught us, a person's intention can have an effect on events, or make a difference to what happens, even if the person lacks intentional control over these events. For example, a novice skier might form the intention to ski down Headwall Face, but this intention might make her so nervous that she loses control and falls. Her intention made a difference, but not in the way characteristic of intentions. Even if the intention led to her skiing down Headwall Face in accord with her plan, it might not have done this in the characteristic way. Perhaps her intention made her so nervous that she slipped and was forced to ski before she intended to do so. She skied as she intended to, but not when and how she intended. Her skiing was caused by her intention, but not in the way that is characteristic in intentional action.

Unfortunately, it has proven exceedingly difficult to say what this characteristic way is without using the concept of an intention. Fortunately, we can set this aside. Our question is whether an institutional entity can have a plan that has a characteristic kind of effect on actional events involving that entity.

Characteristically, a person with a plan can refer to her plan in deliberation and reasoning, and she can draw on her plan in setting priorities and making decisions about how to go about achieving the goals set by her plan. Further, a person will standardly have non-inferential knowledge of her plans. Her intentions or plans are standardly "non-inferentially accessible."[17] Indeed, it is arguable that an agent *must* be capable of having non-inferentially accessible intentions and beliefs. Suppose that a person intends to ski down Headwall Face. The function of her intention is to bring it about that she skis down Headwall Face. It is to do this by being combined with her beliefs about the circumstances such that, if she comes to believe that the circumstances are right, her intention leads her to intend to ski right then, and, as a result, to start skiing. The ability to bring beliefs and intentions together in deliberation in the way illustrated by the example, and in more complex ways as well, is needed in order for intentions to play their characteristic functional role. This arguably requires an agent's intentions to be non-inferentially accessible, for otherwise, an agent would not be able to deliberate without making inferences to figure out what she intends. The premises of some such inferences would have to be immediately accessible, on pain of regress (see Ludwig 2007: 424–426).

The non-inferential accessibility of an intention is not the same, however, as its being conscious or potentially conscious. There is not a recognizable way that having an intention or a plan feels to the person with the intention or the plan, not even when one brings one's intention "to mind" in order to think about how to carry it out. The skier might decide to take the Headwall chairlift, in light of her intention to ski Headwall Face, without being conscious of her intention. Even though her intention plays its characteristic role in her decision, and does so without her having to infer that she has the intention, she needn't be conscious of it at the time of her decision. And at the top of Headwall, she might know she intends to ski the run, and start skiing in light of her intention, without being conscious of her intention.

I believe, furthermore, that institutional entities are capable of having non-inferentially accessible intentional states. The U.S. knew it was aiming to get Iraq out of Kuwait, and it had this knowledge in an immediately usable way, such that it could monitor what the armed forces were doing to ensure that they were acting efficiently to achieve its goals. If so, it had non-inferentially accessible intentions. In my view, then, institutional entities are capable of having intentions and beliefs to which they have the kind of access needed for reasoning and deliberation.

My reasoning in this section assumes, but also supports, a kind of "functionalism" about intentional states. I think functionalism gives the most plausible account of the nature of such states.[18] As I suggested, the key question for our purposes is whether institutional entities are capable of being in states – having intentions or plans – that make them capable of exercising control of a characteristic kind over actional events involving them, where their being in such states can have an effect on events or make a difference to what happens, in the characteristic way. This is a functional characterization of a kind of state. Even if the intentions of persons have non-functional properties that the intentions of institutional entities do not have, the issue is control of a characteristic kind over actional events, and this is a functional matter.[19]

Of course, I have not said anything about what the intentions of institutional entities consist in – or about what grounds them. I have proposed that the *actions* of institutional entities (or actional events involving them) are constituted by the actions of individual persons. Similarly, I think, the *intentions* or *plans* of an institutional entity exist in virtue of the actions, intentions and beliefs of relevant individual persons, given the organizational structure and collective decision procedure of the institutional entity in question. We can see what is involved by reflecting on examples, such as the intention the United States had in 1991 to get Iraq out of Kuwait. In addition to examples of clear cases, it can be useful to consider cases where an institutional entity is conflicted, such as the case of Great Britain and Brexit. There is room to work on examples in order to arrive at a detailed understanding of the variety of cases. But for my purposes here, it suffices to say that the intentions of institutional entities exist in virtue of actions, intentions, and beliefs of relevant individual persons given relevant laws, institutional practices, and the like.

One might object to my minimal characterization of agency on the grounds that agents, at least in paradigm cases, are responsive to *reasons*, and they decide what to do based on their understanding of the reasons bearing on their choice. And moral agents are responsive to *moral* reasons (Wolf 1990; Fischer and Ravizza 1999; Hindriks 2018). *This* is the kind of control characteristic of agency. I agree with this, so I need to address the issue of whether, and if so how, institutional entities respond to reasons, including moral reasons.

There is no puzzle here. A case study would help to make this clear.[20] We can imagine the members of the British cabinet, during World War II, deciding not to permit the Royal Air Force to bomb a city for the reason that it is morally wrong to target civilians. Their decision would constitute the cabinet's deciding against doing something for moral reasons, and presumably it would also constitute Britain deciding this. The example reveals that, just as the people who serve in relevant roles in an institutional entity typically do things that constitute actions of that entity when they act in accord with its collective decision procedure, so they can make decisions about the goals of the entity, or about its values, or about what its moral duties are in a given situation, or about whether to comply with its duties. And when they do so in accord with relevant laws and institutional practices, their decisions typically will constitute decisions of the entity in question (see Björnsson and Hess 2017; Hindriks 2018). This is how it can be that institutional entities respond to reasons of various kinds, including moral ones.

One might now ask what moral reason the people who serve in relevant roles in an institutional entity would have to pay attention to the moral obligations of the collective. I have already addressed this issue. On the collectivist approach to understanding the moral status of institutional entities, the relevant people have a transitional duty to do their part in ensuring that relevant institutional entities act morally. In virtue of this, they have a moral reason to do so.

One might now object that institutional entities do not have the kind of autonomy that is required for full agency, including moral agency. After all, they are not independent agents.[21] The issue is whether this fact entails that the actions (or actional events) of institutional entities lack the freedom or autonomy characteristic of the actions of individual persons. There is of course an important controversy as to whether individual persons have the kind of freedom that would be required for it to make sense to hold them morally responsible for their actions. According to the view I take to be the most plausible one, people have the relevant kind of freedom or autonomy just in virtue of being *responsive to reasons* (Wolf 1990; Fischer and Ravizza 1999). I have already explained how it is that institutional entities respond to reasons, so, on this view,

I have already shown how it is that they can have the kind of freedom required for full agency and moral responsibility.

One might think that the fact that institutional entities are not independent agents makes for an additional problem. For, at a fundamental level, an institutional entity has no control over whether individual persons do what would need to be done in order for the institutional entity to comply with its moral duties. So it fundamentally has no control over whether it complies with its moral duties.

This worry does not take seriously enough the point that the actions of individual persons constitute actions of collective entities under relevant conditions. Exercising control is a kind of action. Institutional and other collective entities exercise control in virtue of the actions of persons that constitute their exercising control. For example, a government can threaten with legal sanctions any person who does not do her part in bringing about what the government has decided to do. This example reveals how an institutional entity can exercise control over what people do and thereby exercise control over what it does.

A variety of additional worries could be raised at this point about my thesis that institutional actional events qualify as actions. But I hope that the strategy for responding to them is now clear.

Given the considerations I have discussed in this section, I conclude that there is no conceptual barrier to holding that institutional doers are moral agents and that institutional actional events are actions, properly and strictly speaking. I therefore reject extreme agency individualism. In the next section, however, I consider one last argument for the extreme view. Assuming that we reject the extreme view, I draw the further conclusion that there is no conceptual barrier to holding that institutional entities can have moral obligations and can bear moral responsibility. For if institutional entities are moral agents and can perform actions, then they are relevantly like individual persons in that they are in the scope of obligations. And, like persons, if they fail to act accordingly, they can be responsible for this failing. In the next section, I consider arguments against this further conclusion.

7.7 Reduction and Individualism

As I have said, I take it to be common ground that an institutional actional event is *constituted* by actions performed by individual agents. There are different ways to understand this. First, we might understand it as the metaphysical thesis that facts about the actions of institutional entities are *grounded* in facts about the actions of individual persons (Rosen 2010). As Gideon Rosen (2018) explains, grounding facts *explain* the facts they ground, so the grounded fact is a *further* fact. Nothing explains itself. On the grounding view, the fact that the U.S. removed Noriega from the Presidency of Panama is grounded in facts about what was done by individuals in the Bush administration and the U.S. armed forces. So the U.S. action was over and above what these individuals did. Yet, Rosen insists (2018), there is a sense in which the grounded fact is not a *significant* addition to reality over and above the grounding fact.

I want to remain neutral about the grounding view, but agency individualists would reject it on the basis that, they hold, actions of institutional and other collective entities are *not* "over and above" the actions of relevant individuals. Accordingly, they offer a different interpretation of the thesis that collective entities are not independent agents. They understand it as a claim about *reduction* – a conceptual or semantic thesis to the effect that our concepts, or the meanings of our terms, ensure that, necessarily, any proposition about an action of a collective entity has exactly the same truth conditions as some corresponding proposition about actions of relevant individuals – where the latter does not contain any term referring to or quantifying over an action of a collective. Call this the "reductionist thesis."[22] The *extreme* individualist takes the reductionist thesis to be a basis for denying that collective entities are agents. The *moderate* individualist allows that at least some collective entities are agents, but she insists that their actions are *reducible, without remainder,* to the actions of individual persons.

Kirk Ludwig is an example of an extreme agency individualist, and he has defended the reductionist thesis in detail (2016 and 2017). He says, "all collective action is a matter of individual agents contributing to bringing about some event or state." And he seems to conclude on this basis that "we have no need for group agents in our understanding of ordinary discourse about collective actions, either in the case of informal groups or in the case of organizations" (Ludwig 2020: 79). But even if the reductionist thesis is correct, it does not follow that collective entities do not act and are not agents. Facts about bachelors can be reduced to facts about unmarried adult males. It would be a mistake to conclude from this that no person has ever been a bachelor. Reduction is not the same as elimination.

I believe that the thesis that institutional entities are capable of intentional action *follows* from the reductionist thesis when it is properly understood. The reductionist thesis provides non-mysterious truth conditions for propositions about collective action. It implies that, necessarily, propositions about the actions of institutional entities have the same truth conditions as corresponding propositions about the actions of relevant individuals. There is no reason to think that the truth conditions of the latter propositions cannot be satisfied. Individual persons can do things in their capacities as members of collective entities to bring about institutional actional events. When they do, it follows from the reductionist thesis that these collective entities act.

Ludwig claims that, given the reductionist thesis, "we have no need for group agents" (Ludwig 2020: 79). He might here be supposing that, given the reductionist thesis, it would be ontologically profligate to suppose there are collective agents. But, by way of analogy, it is not ontologically profligate to suppose there are bachelors. I am assuming we have groups and institutions in our ontology, and we have actions and agency. We also have obligations and other moral properties and relations. There is no loss of *ontological parsimony* in supposing that institutional entities are among the entities that have action properties and moral properties.

Furthermore, as I have argued before, we can often best understand the moral situation of a person – the requirements she faces and her responsibility or lack of it for things that have happened – by reference to the moral situation of a collective entity she belongs to (Copp 2007a; Copp 2010; Copp 2012; see Lyons 2004; Wringe 2014a). In particular, the transitional duty can explain why a person who is a member of a collective entity has a moral obligation. The transitional duty is the requirement, if a collective entity is required to do something, that its members, and any relevant officers, do their part in bringing it about that the collective acts as required. It presupposes that collective entities do have moral obligations, which means that it presupposes that collective entities can be agents and can perform actions. On Ludwig's view, the transitional duty is empty, since no collective entity is an agent. So on his view there is a puzzle. Why is it that people have duties in their roles as members or officers of collectives? What is it about their roles that gives them obligations if not that they are obligated to do their parts in bringing it about that the collective acts as required?

The moderate agency individualist agrees with me that the reductionist thesis does not entail or imply the extreme view that institutional and other collective entities are incapable of action. Let me now, then, turn from the issue whether institutional entities are agents, to the issue whether they can have moral obligations or bear moral responsibility. As I argued in the preceding section of this chapter, if institutional entities are agents properly so-called, then they are moral agents. They are capable of having moral obligations and bearing moral responsibility for their actions. Moral individualists deny this.

Seumas Miller is a clear case of a moral individualist.[23] He contends that in any case where it seems that an institutional entity has an obligation or bears responsibility, an "individualist analysis" can be given according to which no collective has a moral property that is not possessed by its individual members. He further suggests that the availability of individualist analyses shows that, "properly speaking, no collective [is] possessed of any moral properties" at all (Miller 2007: 390).

One problem with Miller's view is that, if we had an individualist analysis of the truth conditions of sentences of the form, "Collective C has a moral obligation," this analysis would show the circumstances under which a collective C would have a moral obligation. It would not show that, properly speaking, no collective has any moral obligations. As I mentioned before, there is an analysis of facts about bachelors in terms of facts about unmarried adult males. It would be a mistake to conclude from the availability of this analysis that, properly speaking, no person has ever been a bachelor.

On Miller's thesis that "no collective [is] possessed of any moral properties" at all, we could not use the transitional duty to explain why a person has a moral obligation. On Miller's view, no collective has any duties, so we might wonder why people have duties in their roles as members or officers of collectives. What is it about their role that gives them obligations if not that they are obligated to do their part in bringing it about that the collective acts as required?

Ludwig also advocates a kind of moral individualism. He argues for what he calls the "Factor Model" of collective responsibility according to which "any claim that a group is morally responsible for something must be resolved into a distribution of moral responsibility to its members, with none left over for the group per se" (Ludwig 2020: 79; Ludwig 2007). It seems that he would also advocate a factor model of collective obligations. His argument for the Factor Model has two main parts. First, he argues, collective entities are not agents, and, given this, they cannot bear moral responsibility or have moral obligations (Ludwig 2020: 79). Second, he argues, if collective entities could bear moral responsibility and have moral obligations, and if their responsibility and obligations could not be reduced to the responsibility and obligations of individual persons, their responsibility and obligations would have no practical import. For example, it could be that some collective has a moral obligation, but no agent has a moral reason to alter her behavior. But in this case, attributions of responsibility and obligations to collective entities would be "idle" (Ludwig 2020: 78).

I have already discussed Ludwig's argument that collective entities are not agents, so let me here consider his argument from the "idleness worry." This is not a good argument. The most it shows is that if a collective is responsible for something, some relevant persons must have moral reason to alter their behavior. It does not follow that there is no responsibility "left over for the group per se." Moreover, the argument is compatible with the collectivist model I proposed earlier in this chapter. The collectivist model postulates the transitional duty, which guarantees that relevant people have a pro tanto duty or reason to do the things that would constitute a collective's doing what it is morally required to do.

In earlier work, I argued for a version of the "Collective Moral Autonomy Thesis" or "CMA thesis" (Copp 2007a; Copp 2012). On the version I defended, it is conceptually possible for a collective to bear all-things-considered moral responsibility, or to have an all-things-considered moral obligation, without any relevant member being all-things-considered morally responsible in the matter, or having a relevantly related all-things-considered moral obligation. Ludwig and Miller both reject this thesis (Ludwig 2007; Ludwig 2020: 79; Miller 2007).

One of my arguments for my version of the CMA thesis is an argument from moral complexity. To illustrate the point, I gave an example in which a government has an all-things-considered moral obligation to do something. The Prime Minister is the person charged with carrying out the government's obligation. Unfortunately, she has a significant conflicting personal duty to her daughter, and in the circumstances, it outweighs her transitional duty to do what she would have to do in order for the government to fulfill its obligation. Hence the Prime Minister does not have an all-things-considered moral obligation to do what she would have to do in order for the government to fulfill its obligation. In the example, no-one else does either (Copp 1976; Copp 2007a; Copp 2012).

Ludwig has several responses to the example, and I have responded to them elsewhere (Copp 2012). It is perhaps worth mentioning that one of his responses turns on the "idleness worry" (Ludwig 2007: 424–426). If the Prime Minister does not have an all-things-considered moral obligation to bring it about that the government fulfills its duty, then, Ludwig says, she has no moral reason to do this, and it is idle to hold that the government has the all-things-considered obligation in question. But given the transitional duty, the Prime Minister has a pro tanto obligation to bring it about that the government fulfills its duty, which entails that she has a *reason* to do this. In the example, this reason is outweighed, but it still exists. It is a reason for her to regret what she does, even though she does what she is morally obligated all-things-considered to do. This is the moral residue of the transitional duty. The government's all-things-considered obligation also has significance. The fact that it was not fulfilled can mean that the government is obligated to make amends.

Miller claims that, in my example, the Prime Minister must have a relevant duty "qua Prime Minister" to do what she would have to do in order for the government to fulfill its obligation (Miller 2007: 400; Miller 2010). I agree. Given that there is the transitional duty, and given her role in the government, the Prime Minister does have a pro tanto duty to do what she would have to do in order for the government to fulfill its obligation. Miller claims that this is what she is morally obligated all-things-considered to do *qua Prime Minister* (Miller 2007: 400; see also Miller 2010; Forrester 2010). The point, however, is that, to decide what to do, the Prime Minister must balance the transitional duty she has, qua Prime Minister, with the duty she has to her daughter, qua mother, in order to arrive at a conclusion as to what she (the person) is morally obligated to do *simpliciter*, all-things-considered. We each have a variety of roles. In deciding what to do, we need to take into account the duties we have in these roles. But, as moral persons, we need to reach a decision about the balance among these duties. In the example, the person who is Prime Minister is not morally obligated all-things-considered to do what she would have to do in order for the government to fulfill its all-things-considered obligation.

I believe that the example of the Prime Minister and her daughter shows that my version of the CMA thesis is true. This means that we should reject the strong reductionist thesis according to which our concepts, or the meanings of our terms, ensure that, necessarily, propositions about the all-things-considered obligations or responsibility of collective entities have the same truth conditions as corresponding propositions about the all-things-considered obligations or responsibility of relevant individuals. Despite this, of course, one might think that facts about the obligations or responsibility of collective entities are *grounded* in facts about the obligations or responsibility of relevant individuals (Björnsson 2020: 128, 134; see Wringe 2014a). I cannot pursue this idea here, but I doubt it is right. I think it is too simple.

7.8 Conclusion

I began this chapter by introducing a view about the point of morality and a normative theory that this view supports. On this theory – the society-centered theory – the issue whether institutional entities have moral obligations or bear moral responsibility is the issue whether the ideal moral code contains rules that directly regulate the actions of institutional entities, if there are any such actions. Extreme agency individualists would deny that there are any such actions, but, to be charitable to them, I assume they would not deny that there are institutional actional events – events that involve institutional entities in the way that, for example, the U.S. was involved in Noriega's removal from office. On the society-centered theory, it is an empirical issue whether the ideal moral code contains rules that directly regulate institutional actional events.

In the middle section of the chapter, I argued that institutional actional events are actions, properly so-called, and that institutional doers are agents, properly so-called. I offered a minimal characterization of agency, which I then adjusted in order to accommodate a variety of claims about moral agents. In each case, I tried to explain how it can be that an institutional entity meets the conditions required for agency, especially moral agency. I concluded that there is no conceptual barrier to the view that institutional doers are moral agents and that institutional actional events are actions, properly and strictly speaking. I further concluded that there is no conceptual barrier to the thesis that institutional entities can have moral obligations and can bear moral responsibility. For if institutional entities are moral agents and can perform actions, then they are relevantly like individual persons in that they are in the scope of obligations, such as the obligation not to torture anyone. And, like persons, if they fail to act accordingly, they can be responsible for this failing.

I hope that these arguments eliminate the worry that attributions of blameworthiness and obligations to groups are "metaphysically or ethically suspect" (Björnsson 2020: 127). In my view, as I have attempted to explain, facts about the obligations or responsibility of collective entities obtain in virtue of the same kinds of facts about the content of the ideal moral code as do the obligations or responsibility of relevant individuals.

The actions of collective entities are constituted by the actions of individual persons. Because of this, a fully satisfying theory of collective moral obligation and responsibility must explain how the obligations and responsibility of collective entities give relevant individual persons moral reason to act appropriately – reason to bring it about that collectives fulfill their obligations and respond appropriately to their responsibility (Ludwig 2020: 78). The society-centered theory provides an explanation of this reason. For it is plausible that the ideal moral code contains a transitional rule according to which, roughly, agents are required to do their part to bring it about that collectives they belong to, or to which they are otherwise relevantly related, fulfill their obligations and respond appropriately to their responsibility. Beyond this, I doubt that there is an exceptionless formula that takes us from the obligations and responsibility of collective entities to the obligations and responsibility of individual persons.

This chapter has focused on institutional entities, a kind of collective that has an organizational structure and a collective decision procedure grounded in laws, regulations, institutional practices, norms, or the like. Entities of this kind are distinguished from groups that lack an organizational structure and collective decision procedure, but these groups can be organized to various degrees. Some unorganized and even "random" groups seem to be capable of a relevant kind of involvement in actional events. Suppose, for example, that a group of people on a beach fail to rescue some drowning children when they easily could have done this (Held 1970; Björnsson 2020). In some such cases, it seems to me, a group of this kind meets the conditions required of agents. If so, the account I have given applies to them as well.

Acknowledgments

For helpful comments and suggestions, I am grateful to Saba Barzagan-Forward, Frank Hindriks, Deborah Tollefsen, and members of the Davis Ethics Discussion Group: Rohan French, Justin Morton, Hermes Rocha, Tina Rulli, Ramiel Tamras, Khang That Vinh Ton, and Jacob Velasquez.

Notes

1 People can stand in a variety of relevant relations to institutional entities. They can be shareholders, citizens, officers, employees, directors, members, and so on. I use the term "member" as a generic term to refer to relations of these kinds.

2 I use the term "constituted" here without meaning to commit myself to the precise nature of the relation in question. Perhaps the relation is that of metaphysical grounding (see Rosen 2010; 2018). Baker (2006) proposes a technical notion of constitution. See also Hindriks 2013. I return to this issue.

3 The moral culture of a society is the moral code that has been internalized by the bulk of the society's members or that is subscribed to by them. I explain this more fully in what follows.

4 In another essay (Copp forthcoming), I provide a model of what I have in mind, roughly as follows. (I assume something like Stalnaker's (1968) and Lewis's (1973) approach to counter-factuals.) Construct a set of possible worlds "accessible" from the actual world, holding constant human psychology and the basic facts of our social lives. These worlds are like the actual one in most ways, including how people would learn about morality, how people would teach new generations about morality, and the various ways in which human intelligence is limited. These "stage-one" worlds differ from the actual world in that people in these worlds have no "external preferences" and no moral beliefs or attitudes. My hypothesis is that the currency of an appropriate moral code in such worlds *would* mitigate the problem of sociality. (This is the "point" of morality.) Now select the stage-one world W that is "closest" to or most similar to the actual world. For each moral code M that is under consideration, pair W with a "stage-two" world W* (1) that is accessible both from the actual world and from W, (2) that is just like W except that M serves in W* as the moral culture, thereby affecting people's actions and attitudes in various ways, and (3) that, of all worlds meeting the first two conditions, is closest to or most similar to the actual world. Finally, rank the moral codes that are under consideration on the basis of, for each, the expected degree to which the problem of sociality is less serious in the stage-two world where it forms the moral culture than it is in W. In ranking a code M, take into account the expected social cost and degree of difficulty of sustaining over the long-run the fact that M forms the moral culture as well as the expected degree to which its forming the moral culture would mitigate the problem of sociality. The highest ranking code is the "ideal" code. It is the code that (in the relevant sense) *would do most* to mitigate the problem of sociality in the actual world *if it formed the moral culture*.

5 I have stated the theory in different ways in different places. The version presented here is closest to that found in Copp 2009. Different formulations can be found in Copp 2007b and Copp 1995. The theory raises a number of questions that are addressed elsewhere (See Copp 1995: 124–128, 192–197, 198–200, 218–223; Copp 2007b: 16–26).

6 If several codes are tied as best, then society-centered theory says that the truth conditions of a moral claim depend on the content of all the codes tied as best. For instance, torture is morally wrong if and only if, roughly, it is permitted by none of the moral codes tied as best. On ties, see Copp 1995, 198–199.

7 Here I follow Copp 2007b, 14–18. A "pure" moral proposition has no non-moral entailments or presuppositions (other than those given by the standard-based theory itself). A "basic" moral proposition ascribes a moral property to something. The proposition that theft is wrong is both pure and basic. There are complications I cannot address here.

8 Recall my caveat, in note 2, about my use of the term "constituted."

9 For a similar argument, see Ludwig 2020: 78.

10 For this worry, see Hindriks 2014, Wringe 2014b.

11 For a useful overview and discussion of the distinction between constitutive and regulative rules, see Hindriks 2009.

12 I ignore "secondary actions," actions that are attributed to an individual in virtue of an action performed by someone to whom she has given relevant authorization, such as an attorney or a trustee (Copp 1979). Everything done by an institutional doer is constituted by actions performed by individual

agents. Note that there can be cases where a trustee acts on behalf of someone else, in a way that constitutes an action of hers, without having been authorized *by her* (Copp 1979).

13 One might object that this characterization makes no room for *unintentional* actions. But I am assuming that an unintentional action is constituted by some action over which the agent had intentional control. For example, if I unintentionally frighten someone, and if this was an action, it was constituted by some event over which I did exercise intentional control, such as flipping a switch. Nothing in what follows turns on this assumption.

14 Recall my caveat, in note 2, about my use of the term "constitute." My formulation blurs the differences between Alvin Goldman's theory of action (Goldman 1970) and Donald Davidson's (Davidson 2001).

15 John Searle contends that intentional states "can be brought to consciousness" in that they are "capable of causing subjective conscious thoughts" (Searle 1990: 588). This is his "connection principle" (Searle 1990). Elsewhere I have argued against this principle (Copp 2006).

16 Michael Bratman contends that intentions are planning states (Bratman 1987).

17 Perhaps this point lies behind Searle's (1990) idea that "intentions are accessible to consciousness," at least in principle.

18 See Pettit 1993, ch. 1, esp. pp. 43–52. There are complications that I do not have the space to discuss.

19 For more detailed discussion of this idea, see Björnsson 2020; Björnsson and Hess 2017; Hindriks 2014; Hindriks 2018.

20 For a case study, see Björnsson and Hess 2017.

21 Ludwig says that collectives are not "autonomous agents," using "autonomous" here where I use "independent" (Ludwig 2020: 83). My usage allows us to distinguish conceptually between the thesis that "actions" of institutional entities are constituted by actions of individual persons and the thesis that the "actions" of institutional entities lack the autonomy characteristic of the actions of individual persons.

22 If the reductionist thesis is correct, it will be rather complex. The actions of institutional entities are not reducible to the *actions* of individual persons just as such. Actions of individual persons constitute an action of an institutional entity only in virtue of its organizational structure and collective decision procedure. An institution's collective decision procedure and organizational structure are grounded in laws, regulations, institutional practices, norms, and the like. To be sure, facts about the organizational structures and collective decision procedures of institutional entities are grounded in facts about individual persons and about the circumstances and institutional environment. But they are not grounded exclusively in facts about *the actions* of persons. Other properties of persons as well as facts about circumstances and the institutional environment are presumably aspects of the grounding.

23 Gunnar Björnsson seems to accept a kind of moral individualism, at least regarding unorganized groups (Björnsson 2020). He suggests that what looks like an attribution of an obligation to a group "is in fact" an attribution of relevantly corresponding obligations to members of the group (Björnsson 2020: 134). In characterizing his position, however, Björnsson says that, on the account he recommends, the obligations of groups are *grounded* in the obligations of their members (Björnsson 2020: 128, 134). And as we have seen, when one fact grounds another, the grounded fact is a *further* fact (Rosen 2018). So Björnsson is not committed to moral individualism. See also Björnsson 2014.

References

Baker, Lynne Rudder. 2006. "Everyday Concepts as a Guide to Reality," *The Monist* 89: 313–333.

Björnsson, Gunnar. 2014. "Essentially Shared Obligations," *Midwest Studies in Philosophy* 38: 103–120.

Björnsson, Gunnar. 2020. "Collective Responsibility and Collective Obligations without Collective Moral Agents." In Deborah Tollefsen and Saba Barzagan-Forward, eds., *Routledge Handbook of Collective Responsibility*. London: Routledge.

Björnsson, Gunnar and Hess, Kendy. 2017. "Corporate Crocodile Tears? On the Reactive Attitudes of Corporate Agents." *Philosophy and Phenomenological Research* 94: 273–298.

Bratman, Michael. 1987. *Intention, Plans, and Practical Reason*. Stanford: Center for the Study of Language and Information.

Copp, David. 1976. *Individuals, Collectives and Moral Agency*, unpublished Ph.D. dissertation, Cornell University.

Copp, David. 1979. "Collective Actions and Secondary Actions," *American Philosophical Quarterly* 16: 177–186.

Copp, David. 1980. "Hobbes on Artificial Persons and Collective Actions," *The Philosophical Review* 89: 579–606.
Copp, David. 1984. "What Collectives Are: Agency, Individualism and Legal Theory," *Dialogue* 23: 49–269.
Copp, David. 1995. *Morality, Normativity, and Society*. New York: Oxford University Press.
Copp, David. 2006. "On the Agency of Certain Collective Entities: An Argument from 'Normative Autonomy'," *Midwest Studies in Philosophy* 30: 194–221.
Copp, David. 2007a. "The Collective Moral Autonomy Thesis," *Journal of Social Philosophy* 38: 369–388.
Copp, David. 2007b. *Morality in a Natural World*. Cambridge: Cambridge University Press.
Copp, David. 2009. "Toward a Pluralist and Teleological Theory of Normativity," *Philosophical Issues* 19: 21–37.
Copp, David. 2010. "Corrective Justice as a Duty of the Political Community: David Lyons on the Moral Legacy of Slavery and Jim Crow," *Boston University Law Review* 90: 1731–1754.
Copp, David. 2012. "The Collective Moral Autonomy Thesis: Reply to Ludwig and Miller," *Journal of Social Philosophy* 43: 78–95.
Copp, David. Forthcoming. "The Rule Worship and Idealization Objections Revisited and Resisted." In Mark Timmons, ed., *Oxford Studies in Normative Ethics*. New York, NY: Oxford University Press.
Davidson, Donald. 2001. *Essays on Actions and Events* (2nd edn). Oxford: Clarendon Press.
Fischer, John Martin and Ravizza, Mark. 1999. *Responsibility and Control: A Theory of Moral Responsibility*. Cambridge: Cambridge University Press.
Forrester, Alexa. 2010. Review of Seumas Miller, *The Moral Foundations of Social Institutions*. *Notre Dame Philosophical Reviews*. Accessed at https://ndpr.nd.edu/news/the-moral-foundations-of-social-institutions/.
Goldman, Alvin I. 1970. *A Theory of Human Action*. Englewood Cliffs, NJ: Prentice-Hall.
Held, Virginia. 1970. "Can a Random Collection of Individuals Be Morally Responsible?" *The Journal of Philosophy*, 67: 471–481.
Hindriks, Frank. 2009. "Constitutive Rules, Language, and Ontology," *Erkenntnis* 71: 253–275.
Hindriks, Frank. 2013. "The Location Problem in Social Ontology," *Synthese*, 190: 413–437.
Hindriks, Frank. 2014. "How Autonomous Are Collective Agents? Corporate Rights and Normative Individualism," *Erkenntnis* 79, Supp, 9: 1565–1585.
Hindriks, Frank. 2018. "Collective Agency: Moral and Amoral," *Dialectica* 72: 3–23.
Lewis, David K. 1973. *Counterfactuals*. Cambridge, MA: Harvard University Press.
Ludwig, Kirk. 2007. "The Argument from Normative Autonomy for Collective Agents," *Journal of Social Philosophy* 38: 410–427.
Ludwig, Kirk. 2016. *From Individual to Plural Agency: Collective Action 1*. Oxford: Oxford University Press.
Ludwig, Kirk. 2017. *From Plural to Institutional Agency: Collective Action 2*. Oxford: Oxford University Press.
Ludwig, Kirk. 2020. "From Individual to Collective Responsibility: There and Back Again." In Deborah Tollefsen and Saba Barzagan-Forward, eds., *Routledge Handbook of Collective Responsibility*. London: Routledge.
Lyons, David. 2004. "Corrective Justice, Equal Opportunity, and the Legacy of Slavery and Jim Crow," *Boston University Law Review* 84: 1375–1404.
Miller, Seumas. 2007. "Against the Collective Moral Autonomy Thesis," *Journal of Social Philosophy* 38: 389–409.
Miller, Seumas. 2010. *The Moral Foundations of Social Institutions*. Cambridge: Cambridge University Press.
Pettit, Philip. 1993. *The Common Mind: An Essay on Psychology, Society, and Politics*. New York: Oxford University Press.
Rosen, Gideon. 2010. "Metaphysical Dependence: Grounding and Reduction." In Bob Hale and Aviv Hoffmann, eds., *Modality*. Oxford: Oxford University Press.
Rosen, Gideon. 2018. "Metaphysical Relations in Metaethics." In Tristram MacPherson and David Plunkett, eds., *Routledge Companion to Metaethics*. New York: Routledge.
Searle, John. 1990. "Consciousness, Explanatory Inversion, and Cognitive Science," *Behavioral and Brain Sciences* 13: 585–596.
Stalnaker, Robert C. 1968. "A Theory of Conditionals." In *Studies in Logical Theory*, Nicholas Rescher, ed., Oxford: Basil Blackwell, 98–112.
Wolf, Susan. 1990. *Freedom within Reason*. New York: Oxford University Press.
Wringe, Bill. 2014a. "Collective Obligations: Their Existence, Their Explanatory Power, and Their Supervenience on the Obligations of Individuals," *European Journal of Philosophy* 24: 472–497.
Wringe, Bill. 2014b. "May I Treat a Collective as a Mere Means?" *American Philosophical Quarterly* 51: 1–12.

8

ASSEMBLING THE ELEPHANT

Attending to the Metaphysics of Corporate Agents

Kendy M. Hess

> *A group of blind men heard that a strange animal called an elephant had been brought to the town. Curious, they sought it out and attempted to know it by touch, each reporting what he had discovered. The first man, whose hand landed on the trunk, said "The elephant is like a thick snake." The next, whose hand reached its ear, said, "No, the elephant is like a kind of fan." The man whose hand was upon its tail disagreed, saying "The elephant is a rope." The last man felt its tusk, and said, "You are all mistaken, as the elephant is hard and smooth like a spear."*[1]

Western analytic explorations of human agency and moral agency have been overwhelmingly focused on rational autonomy. Kant is the classic source, but Aristotle also singled out "the rational soul" and Aquinas focused on "man's rational nature"; even Mill, basing his entire theory on the intrinsic value of pleasure, gave it no role to play in the enactment of moral agency. None of the traditions that have grown from these and other philosophers deny that there are other aspects of the human agent. They simply do not, as a rule, include those aspects in their treatments of agency. The collective result is a literature in which the central figure is a caricature of a human agent reduced to a single mechanism: a robotic calculator who gathers data (empirical, intellectual, or intuitive), processes, and – ideally – executes; other aspects or inputs that might shape behavior are generally treated as impediments to "proper" agential or moral function (Blum 1982, Held 1990). In short, the collective result is a literature about human agency which lacks a recognizable human agent, one in which a wide range of human behaviors are ignored, read as flawed, or rejected as not truly "actions" (or not fully "human"). Philosophers working in this field have begun to flesh out the caricature, drawing on findings from cognitive science, psychology, and neglected aspects of traditional philosophical accounts to incorporate some of the aspects of human agents excluded from the traditional treatments.[2] This process has generated illuminating theories that address the whole human agent, and thus provide a much richer conception of her agency.

The literature on corporate agency has – perhaps unsurprisingly – followed a similar path, with dominant accounts from Peter French (1979, 1984, 1995) and Christian List and Philip Pettit (2011) each presenting a single (rational) mechanism by which corporate agents can exercise their agency. While none have explicitly denied the possibility of other mechanisms, or of other significant aspects of the corporate agent, neither they nor the scholars working with their accounts have done anything to develop or even acknowledge the possibility of other factors and inputs *as* factors or inputs. These accounts have been treated as essentially complete (and mutually exclusive) accounts of corporate agency. The collective result is a literature in which the central figure is a caricature of a corporate agent reduced to a single mechanism: a vaguely assumed group of people with only one acknowledged form of interaction among the members, either following procedures or voting (and in an idealized form at that). Other aspects, inputs, or forms of engagement that might shape corporate behavior are generally treated as impediments to "proper" corporate agential function. In short, the collective result is a literature about corporate agency which lacks a recognizable corporate agent, one in which a wide range of familiar corporate behaviors are ignored, read as flawed, or dismissed as not truly "actions" (or at least, not "corporate" ones). I suggest that this has left us with a sadly impoverished conception of corporate agency – one that inhibits our ability to account for actual events, or to assign responsibility for them.

As outlined in section 8.1, French, List and Pettit (L&P), and the scholars working with their accounts have done an excellent job of detailing some of the mechanisms by which corporate agents exercise their agency. However, like the philosophers who treated rational autonomy as the whole of human moral agency – and the blind men who took the trunk or the tail as the whole of the elephant – they have not searched beyond their chosen mechanism to place it in the context of the whole of the corporate agent, or its agency. In response, section 8.2 presents an account of the whole *agent*, of the single metaphysically robust entity that bears the capacity of agency. Once we recognize the whole of agent *as* a whole, we can see that the behavior of this whole is not adequately captured by French's or L&P's accounts (as they themselves acknowledge, in different ways). Rather than rejecting these "non-captured" behaviors as failures of agency, however, this approach allows us to recognize them as arising from other, unrecognized aspects of the agent and its agency – from a multiplicity of mechanisms, many of which draw on different sources and involve different members than those picked out by French and L&P (FLiP). As discussed in section 8.3, this broader, richer understanding of corporate agents and their agency has significant implications for how we understand the moral responsibility of the corporate agent itself, and of the members who constitute it.

8.1 Theories of Corporate *Agency*

French, L&P, and the scholars working with their accounts have focused almost entirely on *the agency* of corporate agents – primarily on the function underlying their intentionality (the generation of commitments by various mechanisms) and more rarely on the function underlying the actions that flow from those commitments. In doing so they have made passing mention of "the corporation," "the group," or "the members," but have given little consideration to any other characteristics of the collective loosely picked out by such references.

To see their mechanisms in context – and to distinguish between the corporate agent itself and the larger context in which *it* operates – we need a way to identify *the agent*, the whole that bears the capacity of agency. The existence of such an agent is assumed, or even entailed, by FLiP's accounts. Barring a pretty radical metaphysical dualism, capacities like intentionality, rationality, and agency cannot be free-floating, so there must be a bearer, and here it seems clear that it will have something to do with "the members" (whoever they are, exactly). But the corporate agency literature has remained generally silent about the *res* that bears the capacity of agency – about the basic metaphysical questions of its existence, unity, limits, identity, and persistence conditions, among other things. It is well beyond the scope of this chapter to address those issues here (but see Hess 2018c), but we can at least look for the *res* – for the reasonably unified, cohesive, and well-defined entity that provides an adequate subvenient base for the intentionality that FLiP have claimed for it. Having identified it, we can then ask whether FLiP's theories account for its behavior.

8.1.1 French

French argues that "corporations"[3] are capable of "intentionality" – and hence agency – because they can make decisions and act on them. They are able to do this because they have corporate internal decision structures ("CID Structures"), which have two elements:

> (1) an organizational or responsibility flow chart that delineates stations and levels within the corporate power structure and (2) corporate decision recognition rule(s) (usually embedded in something called "corporation policy"). The CID Structure is the personnel organization for the exercise of the corporation's power with respect to is ventures.
>
> *(French 1979: 212, also 1984: 41–42, 1995: 25)*

CID Structures establish the rules about how corporate decisions should be made with respect to established corporate ends, and thus set the standard for what counts as a corporate decision and a corporate action. This implies that decisions and actions that come about by other mechanisms are not corporate decisions or actions – an implication which French affirms (French 1984: 53, 1995: 31). In doing so, he acknowledges that the whole does act on other bases, and that his account simply doesn't address such actions.

Of course no corporation ever follows its own official rules perfectly, and French acknowledges the occasional need for "less formal decision lines ... [which] although they may not have the baptismal blessing of the organization's directors, ... function in important ways in decision-making" (1984: 49). He acknowledges that "in practice, corporate policies are rather more flexible than my earlier comments may have suggested. Often they are no more than partial plans that will be revised, modified, extended, and reconsidered as the corporation confronts unanticipated situations and opportunities" (1995: 33). It is thus possible for the official CID Structure to be amended around the edges, and French even considers the possibility of a "phantom, i.e. unpublished, network" that would run counter to the published network; the phantom would be the real structure – apparently replacing the published CID Structure rather than supplementing or amending it – as long as "everyone who matters in the corporate decision structure is well aware of [it]" (1984: 51). The CID Structure that forms the basis for corporate intentionality is thus looser and less formal than French's critics have often allowed.

Despite this slight softening, however, French's CID Structures are still quite limited, encompassing only the publicly identified and acknowledged policies and procedures that shape corporate behavior – the ones that are "epistemically transparent" (1995: 25–26) and "relatively easy to detect, even from outside the corporation" (1995: 33). These elements are "stable and transparent ... and not couched in the kind of language that would be appropriate to individual purposes" (1995: 30). It is essential to his later claims about the superior moral potential of corporations (1995: chapter 14) that the policies and procedures of the CID Structure be obvious to outsiders (and, apparently, "couched in language"). Further, these policies

> seem to be inviolate. Certainly the basic ones are – indeed, they must be. In that respect they are unlike policies adopted by individual humans. You could adopt a policy of honesty but you may occasionally violate that policy by lying. Yet, when you

> lie, it is still you lying. If employees act in ways that violate [the adopted] corporate policy [of honesty], their acts are no longer corporate.
>
> *(1995: 32, see also 1984: 58–59)*

French's CID Structures thus include only those policies and practices that enable corporations to do what they're supposed to do, pursuing acknowledged ends by acknowledged means.

This theoretical commitment has significant practical and normative implications. Seemingly "corporate" behaviors – collective action by members using corporate resources and relationships from their positions within the corporation – which deviate from acknowledged policies are not captured by the account, and are in fact actively rejected as not truly "corporate." The awkward result is that the members can violate official corporate policy, but the corporation itself literally cannot. Corporate intentionality (and agency) is thus an oddly constrained sort of thing on this account, able to pursue legitimate ends by legitimate means and constitutionally incapable of anything else. It is unsurprising that French finds it necessary to develop a distinct moral system specifically for his corporations (1995: chapters 7–12, 14).

Setting that difficulty aside, what does this account tell us about the agent itself – about the thing that *has* this CID Structure and bears the intentionality that it facilitates? French does not address the matter, but there must be some kind of material bearer of the capacity – a subvenient base adequate to the supervenient properties French has claimed.[4] Given the breadth of the CID Structure – which includes the official "stations and levels within the corporate power structure … for the exercise of the corporation's power with respect to is ventures" (1979: 212) – it seems plausible that the base will include at least most of the apparent membership of the corporation, though probably not all of it. It will have to, in order to meet the requirements for supervenience, where every change in the upper-level property ("planning that X" or "acting on plan X") has a correlating change in a lower-level property within the base (presumably, some configuration of the membership).

This is a good start, but leaves at least four "loose ends" regarding the metaphysics. First, does the agent include just the human members, or does it include things like artifacts (production machinery, communication technologies), recorded data (memos, programs), or infrastructure (buildings, property)? All of this becomes more significant in an age of increasing automation, and French does acknowledge the possibility of a fully automated corporation with no human members (1995: 35). The answer to this question will have implications for continuity, identity, and location, all of which will be relevant to action and (thus) to responsibility.[5]

Second, more importantly, does the agent defined by the CID Structure *include* all of the apparent members? French's CID Structure will certainly capture a broad swath of the apparent membership, but it is unclear whether this will include (e.g.) support staff and custodial staff. The fact that such people are perhaps necessary for the existence or function of the corporation is not relevant to the question of whether they are a mereological part of the entity: my own existence and function are dependent on a number of external factors that are nonetheless *external*, not part of me, so dependence can't entail integration. This may seem like quibbling but the question of membership carries significant implications for responsibility. If X is *not* a member then X's actions cannot be corporate actions, not something that the corporate agent did or is responsible for; if X *is* a member then they may be. Further, if individual responsibility turns on membership (rather than, e.g. causal contributions) then this has implications for individual moral responsibility as well.

Third, is the agent *limited* to the apparent membership, or does it include external contributors like consultants, attorneys, and subcontractors? If membership is a function of a contract, or influence, or a continuing relationship then such apparently external players will be included; in terms of influence, in fact, they would be included while many intuitively "internal" contributors would not. It's important that the subvenient base be sufficient for the supervenient capacity, but also desirable that it not extend infinitely (as on theories of global supervenience), and it well may if we're tracking causal chains of influence.

Fourth and finally, whatever is included in the agent, what *unifies* all those pieces into a single entity? What holds them together, welding them into an entity that is robust enough to bear sophisticated capacities like intentionality, rationality, and action?

French's account puts us in a place to ask such questions about the agent, but (in itself) lacks the resources to answer them.

8.1.2 List and Pettit

French's account generally dominated the literature until L&P's *Group Agency: The Possibility, Design, and Status of Group Agents* (2011). On French's account, corporate intentionality and agency are enacted via a complex – if limited – heterogeneous structure comprising epistemically transparent policies and procedures. On L&P's account, corporate intentionality is enacted exclusively via voting procedures; they do not discuss mechanisms for the implementation of agency. L&P acknowledge the possibility of alternative mechanisms for intentionality, that group agents might act in ways not captured by their account: "Let a collection of individuals form and act on a single, robustly rational body of attitudes, whether by dint of a joint intention or on some other basis, and it will be an agent" (75). Their own account, however, is explicitly limited to a much smaller subclass of entities, i.e. those group agents which are "jointly intentional" and adhere to a specific decision procedure.

A group agent is "jointly intentional" (possesses the capacity of intentionality) when its members "each intend that they together act so as to form and enact a single system of belief and desire, at least within a clearly defined scope ... [and] all of this is a matter of common awareness" (34). L&P differ from collectivists like Margaret Gilbert and Seumas Miller in acknowledging that "some, or even many, group members may not participate in any joint intention at all. Generally, all we require for a group agent to count as 'jointly intentional' is that the group's performance involve joint intentions on the part of some of its members" (35). The membership is thus not defined by this joint intention; instead, the relevant group consists of those members who *do* share the joint intention, those who "authorize" the group agent by "accepting its claim to speak and act for the group," and those who act "in full awareness for the pursuit of the group's ends" (35).

Even within the sub-class of group agents captured by this definition, however, L&P's account of group agency is explicitly limited to groups that (1) form exclusively binary commitments, (2) on the basis of communication, or more narrowly still, on the basis of various forms of voting (formal and informal). The former limits the account to groups with "on-off" commitments to propositions rather than "attitudes that come in degrees of strength"[6]; the latter limits the account to groups that form these attitudes – and thus to attitudes formed – via "communication," which includes deliberation, voting, and dictatorship (in which one member's attitudes are simply imposed on the group) (37). L&P present a variety of scenarios in which members consider a proposition (X), and then "aggregate" their individual attitudes towards X in various ways to yield a group attitude towards X. These group attitudes "supervene holistically" on the attitudes of the members (or at least, presumably, on the attitudes of the members who participated in the process, since they are the only ones who expressed attitudes towards X).[7] L&P acknowledge the logical possibility of group attitudes that "are not dependent on individual attitudes on the relevant propositions," but reject this as "not very realistic"; they thus – again – restrict themselves to "cases where the members' attitudes play this role" (66). Despite their title and the way their work has been received, then, L&P have not attempted to address the broad phenomenon of group agency at all. They have instead presented a highly developed account of one very specialized – and somewhat exotic – mechanism for the enactment of group *intentionality*, and explicitly so.

So again, what does this account tell us about the agent itself – about the thing that *has* these voting procedures and bears the intentionality that it facilitates? There must be some kind of material bearer of the capacity – a subvenient base that is adequate to the "holistically supervenient group attitudes" L&P have claimed, and (presumably) for the enactment thereof.

For one thing, L&P's assumed agent will presumably involve "the membership," and unlike French, L&P have carefully defined the group: within the intuitive "whole" of an organization, the membership of the group agent will include only those members who are jointly committed to the shared enactment of group agency, act "in full awareness for the pursuit of the groups ends," and/or have authorized the group agent to "speak on their behalf." This is actually a rather high bar, and it requires that each member have far more conscious, intentional engagement with the broader structure, function, and guidance of the group than is often acknowledged. This is a much smaller group within the organization than French's, and seems unlikely to extend very far beyond management in most cases.

This raises a difficulty, as it is not clear that the membership L&P identify would form an adequate subvenient base for the full agency they have claimed. Agency requires both intentionality and action – an agent constitutionally incapable of acting on its beliefs is a bit of an oxymoron – and while this group would probably provide an adequate subvenient base for the group intentionality L&P have claimed, it's not clear that it provides an adequate subvenient base for enactment. To form an adequate subvenient base for action, the membership must include the people involved in implementing the group actions that follow from the group intentionality, as well as the people involved in the voting processes that generate the group intentional states, but it is not clear that the people in this (much) larger group would meet the requirements of acting "in full awareness" or authorizing the group agent to "speak on their behalf." So many people in large organizations are just "doing their jobs" without the kind of engagement or attention that L&P require for membership. This is an empirical question, of course, and the answer will vary from group to group, but it seems unlikely that the line workers at (say) Exxon are acting in full awareness of Exxon's agency or have authorized Exxon to speak on their behalf.[8]

For another thing, L&P explicitly acknowledge the legitimacy of mechanisms other than their voting procedures (unlike French, who denies the legitimacy of mechanisms beyond the "epistemically transparent" practices and policies of his CID Structure). This is unsurprising, given their explicit commitment to functionalism (21), but again raises questions. While L&P accept the possibility of *alternate* mechanisms, it is unclear how they would accommodate *multiple* mechanisms, and it seems likely that their assumed agent would have them. Given a group that generates *some* commitments by voting and meets all of their other criteria (thus falling within the scope of their account), how would they incorporate commitments generated by those other mechanisms *within the same agent*? French's proceduralist approach avoids this difficulty – any commitments, patterns, or behaviors arising via other mechanisms simply don't count, no matter how reliable or effective they may be – but L&P already rejected this constraint. L&P's assumed agent thus seems likely to include a multiplicity of mechanisms, but their account gives us no way to address the resulting complexity.

Finally, L&P's account leaves many of the same metaphysical loose ends as French's: it doesn't tell us whether "the agent" is limited to the members or includes artifacts, or how to understand the relationship between the group agent and the people who are members of the organization – and perhaps necessary for enactment – but not members of the group agent.

This is a more pressing concern here, as the scope of L&P's agent (membership) is far more restricted than French's. Certainly support and custodial staff are unlikely to clear the high bar established here, and it seems unlikely that line workers or people in entry level positions will qualify (though it does seem to exclude apparently external players like consultants). And finally, again, there's no discussion of what unifies these pieces into a single entity – of what (all) holds them together, welding them into an entity that is robust enough to bear sophisticated capacities like intentionality, rationality, and action.

In each case, then, we have developed accounts of corporate agency that focus exclusively on a single mechanism and pass silently over the matter of the agent – the metaphysically robust *res* that bears the sophisticated capacities claimed for it. This has led critics to conclude, in effect, that there is no agent – that corporate agency involves some kind of "ghostly," "mysterious," "incorporeal," "bizarre", and "hovering entity."[9] Given the collective silence about the agent itself, this is not an unreasonable interpretation, but nor is it a particularly charitable one. Again, FLiP's claims of corporate agency entail the existence of a corporate agent, and their regular, general references to members give a general sense of where to look for it. The critics are correct, though, that neither FLiP nor the theorists working with their accounts have told us much about it.

8.2 A Theory of Corporate *Agents*

With our myopic focus on these limited mechanisms, and our willingness to ignore all of the other aspects of the agent – even the basic metaphysical questions of its existence and extent – we have collectively implied that nothing beyond that one mechanism is relevant to its agency. We have implied that we can understand the elephant from its tail, or its tusk. Things look different if we begin with the whole of the agent, defining the thing (*res*) that *is* an agent, among other things, and only then turning to the question of how it goes about exercising its agency. This is the whole that is assumed by FLiP (or any theorist of group agency), which should form the adequate subvenient base for the intentionality they recognize and the larger phenomenon of agency that they are taken to address.

On my account, a corporate agent is (1) a collective that is (2) unified by a structure that (3) embodies a rational point of view. The corporate agent is not defined exclusively by its intentionality or its agency, or by any single mechanism or decision procedure. Rather, it is defined by the deep social structure which unifies the membership, transforming a disparate mass of agents into a coherent social whole; it is this whole that is then capable of bearing the sophisticated capacities of intentionality, rationality, normative competence, and action (among others) that are typically claimed for a corporate agent. I will briefly outline my account, then close by noting some of the ways it differs from FLiP's.

Again, on my account corporate agents are collectives unified by a "structure" that embodies a "rational point of view" (RPV). As developed by Carol Rovane (1997), an RPV is a logically integrated set of beliefs and desires that forms the basis for rational action. It is "a point of view from which [practical] deliberation proceeds" – deliberation which is, among other things, "necessarily directed toward the goal of achieving overall rational unity" within the set (23) – and it sets the standard against which that agent's actions can be judged as instrumentally rational. Rovane distinguishes the RPV from the more Cartesian phenomenological point of view (25–26) and argues both that the two need not coincide, and that the RPV need not be associated with any particular "animal body" (32–33). This RPV is "rational" in that its contents are (ideally) mutually coherent, justified, and true; in that there is an imperative to organize them rationally; and in that it sets the standard by which an agent's choices can be judged instrumentally rational (or not). It is not "rational" because it was produced by rational processes.

(To the contrary, the RPVs of most human and corporate agents will include a number of commitments that arose by nonrational or even irrational means; these commitments are the primary targets of the imperative to rationalize.)

As discussed at length by FLiP and other scholars, organized collectives are capable of generating commitments about fact and value – about how the world is and what matters in it – that diverge from those of the members that generate them. While there will be inconsistencies among these commitments (as there are for any agent), there is an enormous amount of pressure to rationalize them so that the corporate agent is not pursuing contradictory goals or acting on the basis of contradictory commitments about "how the world is." To the extent that these corporate commitments have been integrated into a logically coherent set, providing a basis from which practical deliberation can proceed and against which corporate actions can be judged instrumentally rational or irrational, they form a corporate RPV.

While FLiP's accounts effectively involve an RPV (though not labeled as such), if we adopt their accounts then the (recognized) content of that RPV will be limited to the commitments that are "properly" generated, via either "epistemically transparent" processes or voting. On my account, the RPV will include any corporate commitment that meets the criteria for a belief, desire, or intention, however generated; I have argued elsewhere (Hess 2014b) that corporate commitments generated by a variety of non-transparent, non-voting mechanisms qualify as beliefs, desires, and intentions on standard philosophical accounts. While the causal history and supporting mechanisms for those commitments extend (all the way) down into the membership, the content, integration, and effectiveness of the commitments reside at the corporate level. Looking at the same corporate agent, then, my account will recognize a different set of commitments in its RPV than either French's or L&P's accounts, and thus a different set of corporate behaviors that qualify as "corporation actions" for which moral responsibility is appropriate. The possession of an effective RPV of its own marks the corporate entity – the social whole defined by the structure – as an agent in its own right.

This RPV is embodied in the "structure" of the corporate agent – in a network of social relationships internal to the corporate agent, which imposes certain constraints on the actions of the members.[10] The structure establishes templates of interaction that favor certain forms of action and coordination, and it encourages the adoption of these templates by making certain kinds of things available to the members – concepts, resources, social relationships, and power. The elements of the structure include the kinds of formalized procedures described by L&P and the "widely recognized" incentive schemes and demands of French's CID Structure (albeit only as these are socially enforced), but the structure also includes the tacit incentive schemes bound up in culture and peer expectation, the tacit demands embodied in office politics and unpublished actual practices, and (often) familiar biases and prejudices that will privilege the contributions of some members over those of others. Some of these structuring elements may have been intentionally designed, and some may be described or recorded in written documents, but this kind of transparency or "official" status is irrelevant to their causal efficacy and thus to their standing (on my account). The structure is pervasive, likely to inflect every interaction among members regardless of whether or how those interactions relate to official business. As Haslanger notes, such structures organize the very thought and communication of the members while they are acting in their roles as members, essentially "structuring the possibility space for [their] agency" (127).

Three points about these corporate structures: First, they differ significantly from French's CID Structure in being distinctively social. According to French, a CID Structure would not be "appreciably altered" by the loss of all of the human members (1995: 35), but the structure that defines my corporate agents is generated by the social interactions of the members and would be completely destroyed by their loss. The content of the RPV could in theory be transferred or "re-embodied" in a different social structure, and it would remain an RPV (and the same RPV) to the extent that it guided the actions of the new agent defined by that social structure. It is not clear that it would be the same agent, however, and even less clear that it would remain the same agent in the absence of the idiosyncratic member contributions that form an integral part of corporate function on my account. This brings us into direct contact with mind-body dilemmas familiar from philosophy of mind and I will not pursue the matter further.

Second, these structures are *immensely* complex, extending well beyond "recognized practices" and voting procedures. Comprising both recognized and unrecognized policies and practices, explicit and tacit expectations, always multiply (though not indefinitely) interpretable, the corporate structure at a time is the culmination of the actions and decisions of dozens (or hundreds, or thousands, or hundreds of thousands) of people over the entire length of the corporate agent's existence.

Third and most importantly, these structures evolve over time. Most elements can be strategically, officially amended in the ways envisioned by FLiP, etc. (though some elements can be remarkably resistant to amendment in ways these formalist accounts have difficulty capturing[11]). This structure can also, however, evolve in the absence of strategic member behavior, nudged along according to its own logic due to unintended results and implications or by larger (but unacknowledged) shifts in member behavior at all levels of the organization.[12] Too much rapid disruption of the structure will destroy the agent, and it will dissolve into its component members and resources; gradual evolution, on the other hand, is inevitable and appropriate, and members can adapt to changing structures without even consciously realizing that they have done so. These evolved processes are not flaws or failures that interfere with agency. They are features, as integral to corporate agency as the more transparent, designed, and intended components that FLiP recognize, but our mechanism-focused literature has generally failed to leave room for either these processes or the commitments that arise from them.

So on this approach a corporate agent is a collective unified by a social structure that embodies an RPV. The social structure includes elements that enable the agent to generate commitments that diverge from those of its members, and elements that allow it to act effectively on the basis of those (divergent) commitments, but the structure is not limited to even that multiplicity of elements. Like the physical body and socially shaped personality that unifies the human agent and her agency, the corporate collective and structure are likely to incorporate elements that actively undermine its capacities for intentional rational action – templates of action, concepts, practices, alliances, and biases that gum up the works, generating irrational outcomes and akratic behavior (pace French, who argues that corporations cannot act akratically; 1995: 46–48). However irrational or unintended these elements may be, they are nonetheless part of the agent and shape its intentionality and agency; any account that fails to address these elements risks idealizing corporate agency to the point of irrelevance.

In contrast to FLiP's accounts, the agent here – the subvenient base – is defined by reference to the social structure, and the RPV that it embodies, rather than by reference to any one means of contributing to it; as such, it is necessarily adequate to both the intentionality and the action of the agent. Moreover, this account addresses three of the four "metaphysical loose ends" that FLiP's accounts leave open. First, this account does not, in itself, answer the question of whether artifacts are part of the corporate agent. Haslanger explicitly includes objects and artifacts in the account of social structures that I have relied on here (128), which suggests that they would be, and I refer the interested reader to her work to see what this would look like for corporate agents. Here, as elsewhere, I leave this question for a later date. Second, the corporate agent generally will include the apparent membership, though this will be a matter of social interaction rather than title, contract, or legal status. It will certainly include support and custodial staff, as well as employees at every level. Third, the corporate agent generally will not include external contributors such as consultants and outside counsel. Such players can become embedded in the social structure, if they work in-house for long enough (these relationships can last for years), but this will again be a matter of social engagement with the other members rather than contract or influence. Outside players are often quite powerful, and can exercise significant influence over the commitments embodied in the RPV, but they do so from outside in much the same way that an advisor, mentor, or friend can exercise significant influence over the RPV of a human agent "from the outside" (see Hess 2014a, 2018d for further discussion).

Fourth and finally, of course, this account addresses the question of what unifies all those pieces – whether the "pieces" are all agents, or whether those pieces include artifacts – into a single entity robust enough to bear sophisticated capacities like intentionality, rationality, and action. Defining the corporate agent by reference to the social structure gives us a base that is far more deeply integrated and enduring than anything in FLiP's accounts. The breadth and pervasiveness of this structure enables a much deeper and more robust integration of the members, and hence of the social entity, than is available on FLiP's accounts. Participating in this kind of structure is not just a matter of engaging in discourse, casting the occasional vote, or fulfilling a job description. Participation in social structures is immersive, and as Haslanger notes in reference to other situations: once internalized, the constraints of a social structure affect not only the member's beliefs and desires but also her perception, attention, cognitive associations, and other sub-personal processes. Sustained participation in these kinds of structures creates lasting changes in the members (Haslanger 127).[13] It is this deep, pervasive integration of the members into the structure that establishes the powerful cohesion of the corporate agent. In fact, so defined, the corporate agent arguably qualifies as a material object on traditional accounts (see Hess 2018c); it is this robust ontological status that answers the critics' concerns about "ghostliness." Recognizing the agent as a material object (and drawing on the resources of the related metaphysical literatures) has the added benefit of providing an outer limit to the subvenient base: support staff who are embedded in the social structure are members, e.g., while outside consultants are not, however essential and effective their influence may be.

I'd like to emphasize again that this approach does not invalidate or undermine FLiP's accounts, as far as they go, or the literature that has grown from them. FLiP and the scholars working with their accounts *have* picked out real things about corporate agency – ears, tails, and tusks – and any account of the whole that could not incorporate their insights would be deeply problematic. So this account does not exclude their accounts; it encompasses them. The corporate RPV described here would include all the commitments they recognize (and, for that matter, Michael Bratman's shared intentions, Margaret Gilbert's joint obligations, and Seumas Miller's collective ends), and the practices encouraged by the structure would include the acknowledged practices of French's CID Structures, the voting practices from L&P, and the mechanisms underlying the collectivists' accounts. It simply extends beyond them to include entirely tacit mechanisms (like the cultural biases that can give a distinctive cast to corporate actions), and provides a base within which we can begin the work of incorporating *all* of these varied mechanisms. This approach allows us to see that the whole of corporate agency – and of the corporate agent – is far more complex, autonomous, and deeply anchored in its base than suggested by earlier accounts, and it allows us to incorporate all of those details into our analyses and prescriptions.

8.3 Implications for Responsibility

There are a number of benefits to an account grounded in the agent in this way. As a minor point, it answers reasonable critical concerns about free-floating intentionality, and it forces us to articulate some of the unacknowledged (and untested) assumptions in the FLiP-dominated literatures. More importantly, it is more true to life, both in recognizing the complexity of the underlying mechanisms and in recognizing the presence of all the "unofficial" factors that so regularly, reliably influence corporate intentionality and agency. This shows corporate agency to be more closely analogous to human agency than is allowed by the dominant accounts, and allows (requires) us to account for the fact that corporate agency can be dogged by the same kinds of unintentional, unarticulated, *unhelpful* – and yet frustratingly patterned and predictable – irrationalities and confusions as human agency. This deeper similarity between human and corporate agency opens up the possibility of drawing far more heavily on traditional theories of mind, agency, and morality than has generally been acknowledged. It also opens up the possibility of exploring questions about the agent that go beyond its agency: basic metaphysical questions about boundaries and "fastenation" (Markosian 1998), identity over time (relevant to moral responsibility), the possibility of corporate racism or sexism that is present in action despite being utterly absent from "transparent" policies and votes, and even the fascinating question of whether corporate agents are or can be gendered. Beyond those possibilities, it shows that there is no need to follow French in constructing a morality specific to corporate agents.[14]

Most of all, though, this approach forces us to confront the true complexity of corporate agents and corporate agency in a way that has important practical and moral implications for responsibility.

First, the presence of multiple mechanisms undermines assumptions about the degree of control executives and managers (the primary players in FLiP's accounts) actually exercise over corporate intentionality and action. With commitments arising from multiple mechanisms, some of which bypass the upper levels of the hierarchy completely, the effective control of the upper-level players is shown to be more tenuous than is often acknowledged. With so many different mechanisms feeding into the RPV, the resulting complex of corporate beliefs and desires is far less sensitive to the input of any one person or small group of persons than is suggested by the single-mechanism accounts. Further, simply following proper procedures is not sufficient to create a new commitment here. To be part of the RPV, the proposed commitment (however properly voted on) must actually shape the actions of the corporate agent, and this requires substantial, effective participation by the broader membership. This account reflects that reality, and reveals that the commitments of the RPV are not as easily adjusted by executive or high-ranking members as has been assumed by the literature. Corporate intentionality and agency thus become much more autonomous vis-à-vis any particular member or group of members than is typically realized – especially vis-à-vis the ranking executives who figure so prominently in the work with FLiP's accounts. Understood in this way, corporate agents can survive criticisms based on autonomy that trouble other approaches (see, e.g. Albertzart 2017, Altman 2007), and are thus stronger candidates for bearing moral responsibility in their own right.

Second, the lesser control exercised by higher-ranking members and the more significant roles available to lower-ranking members have implications for individual/member moral responsibility as well. It suggests that, in some cases, the higher-ranking members may bear less responsibility than is commonly assumed, and it suggests that the lower-level players – almost entirely absent from the traditional accounts – may bear more. This will depend in part on how we move from corporate responsibility to member responsibility. Critics have suggested that recognizing the robust moral responsibility of the corporate agent absolves the members of any moral responsibility at all (see e.g. Ranken 1987, Hasnas 2012), but this need not follow (see Hess 2018d). I'm not aware of any strong commitments about member responsibility directly from French or L&P, but it seems that member responsibility must turn on either membership or contribution; on either approach, this account will recognize a different set of individuals than either French's or L&P's.

If responsibility is distributed purely on the basis of membership, then – as described above – this account will pick out a much larger and more diverse set of members than FLiP's accounts (and a more clearly delineated group than French's). If responsibility attaches on the basis of causal contribution, then the plethora of practices acknowledged by this approach become significant. Attending to the multiplicity of mechanisms shows us that almost every member of the corporate agent – every agent embedded in the social structure – is in a position to shape the content of the RPV, in addition to implementing it. This remains true regardless of whether their ability to do so is officially recognized by others and regardless of whether they engage in discourse and voting (however informal). This is not to say that every member has an equal ability to influence the development of the RPV – far from it. The structuring elements will almost always include a strict hierarchy, and massive inequalities in power and authority as well as strict constraints on access to information and other resources. But no contribution (and no member) is automatically excluded from the account. Practically speaking, this emphasizes the need to take lower-level contributions more seriously during the planning and implementation of corporate policies. Morally speaking, this reminds us to look beyond the executive levels – albeit carefully – and to look to the full membership with respect to moral obligation and responsibility.[15] Unlike membership, causal contributions come in degrees, and that makes this approach sensitive to the situatedness of individual members in a way that pure membership-based allocations are not.[16]

8.4 Conclusion

As should be clear, the account sketched above does not compete with those put forward by French, List and Pettit, and the rest. It incorporates them, providing a foundation that allows us to assemble all of the sophisticated, insightful work done to date into an even broader and more encompassing understanding of corporate agents and their agency.

In the old Hindu parable, each of the blind men inspecting the elephant insists that he knows what elephants are like: they are like the part that he happens to be inspecting. Each treats the part he is attending to as if it captures the whole of what an elephant is, and is thus led sadly astray in his theorizing about what an elephant looks like, how it functions, and how it is likely to behave. Similarly, to date we have treated accounts of specific mechanisms – CID Structures, vote aggregation, even joint intentions, etc. – as if they captured the whole of corporate agency, and thus of corporate agents.

Recognizing the broader, deeper social structure that unifies the membership into a (material) whole lets us move past this. It lets us answer critical concerns about "ghostly," "bizarre," "hovering entities," and allows us to recognize the existing accounts as complements rather than competitors. More importantly, it reveals corporate intentionality and agency as a vastly richer and more complex process than previously acknowledged: more deeply rooted in the full membership *and* more independent of any individual member than the current accounts allow. In short, it lets us assemble the elephant, and see her for the magnificent, independent beast she really is.

Notes

1 Hindu parable, adapted from Wikipedia contributors. (2018, October 29). Blind men and an elephant. In *Wikipedia, The Free Encyclopedia*. Retrieved 21:29, December 30, 2018, from https://en.wikipedia.org/w/index.php?title=Blind_men_and_an_elephant&oldid=866284758

2 For philosophical work regarding the importance of incorporating the emotions and other aspects of the relational self, see Baier 1986, Held 1990, Wallace 1993, and Kleingeld 2014. For scientific work on the role of the emotions in moral agency, see Greene et al. 2001, Young and Koenigs 2007 (but see McAuliffe 2018). Regarding the relevance in an organizational context, see Mumby and Putnam 1992. For philosophical work regarding the importance of incorporating the body, see Damasio 1994; in an organizational context, see Naqvi et al. 2006, Bisel and Adame 2018.

3 While French typically refers to his entities as "corporations," legal status plays no apparent role in his account and I will assume that his account extends beyond legally incorporated entities.

4 French has not (to my knowledge) addressed the metaphysical relationship between the commitments generated by his CID Structures and the membership that enacts them, but others working with his account (and similar ones) have generally assumed supervenience. See e.g. (McMahon 1995, Forge 2002). Supervenience is the least demanding of the available options, so I have assumed it as well.

5 Hindriks 2008, 2013 explicitly incorporates artifacts.

6 They acknowledge the possibility that things might be otherwise, but treat it as a very special case (37).

7 L&P acknowledge the possibility of "perhaps other contributions" (61), but do not develop the possibility or give it any role to play in their own account.

8 In fact, I suspect that you would need to go pretty high up into management to find the discoursing, committing, fully knowing, and authorizing that L&P have proposed. I leave that question to the empiricists.

9 In order: Velasquez 2003, Miller and Mäkelä 2005, Rönnegard 2015, Rönnegard and Velasquez 2017, and Ludwig 2017.

10 This account is drawn directly from (Haslanger 2016), who builds on Stuart Shapiro's (1997) account of a "system" as "a collection of objects with certain relationships" and a structure as "the abstract form of a system highlighting the interrelationships among the objects, and ignoring any features of them that do not affect how they relate to other objects in the system" (118, quoting Shapiro 1997: 73).

11 See Ritchie 2018 for an interesting discussion of the comparative difficulties in amending feature groups versus organized groups (i.e. corporate agents).

12 See Hess 2014a, Bjornsson and Hess 2017, Hess 2018a, and Hess 2018d for discussion of the mechanisms that allow lower-level members to shape corporate intentionality in addition to inflecting corporate actions.

13 See Hess 2018b for further discussion about social-psychological implications of participating in the kind of social structure that defines a corporate agent. Rovane 2014 addresses related concerns.

14 See Hess 2014b, 2018b for further argument along these lines.

15 For detailed examples, see Bjornsson and Hess 2017, Hess 2018b, 2018d.

16 See Hess 2018d for a more fully developed application of this approach.

References

Albertzart, M. (2017) "Monsters and their Makers: Group Agency without Moral Agency." In Zachary J. Goldberg (ed.), *Reflections on Ethics and Responsibility: Essays in Honor of Peter French*, Springer International Publishing, 21–35.

Altman, M. (2007) "The Decomposition of the Corporate Body: What Kant Cannot Contribute to Business Ethics," *Journal of Business Ethics*, 74(3), 253–266.

Baier, A. (1986) "Trust and Antitrust," *Ethics*, 96(2), 231–260.

Bisel, R. and Adame, E. (2018) "Encouraging Upward Ethical Dissent in Organizations: The Role of Deference to Embodied Expertise," *Management Communication Quarterly*, DOI: 10.1177/0893318918811949

Björnsson, G. and Hess, K (2017). "Corporate Crocodile Tears?: The Reactive Attitudes of Corporate Agents," *Philosophy and Phenomenological Research*, 94(2), 273–298.

Blum, L. (1982) "Kant's and Hegel's moral rationalism: A feminist perspective," *Canadian Journal of Philosophy*, 12(2), 287–302.

Damasio, A. (1994) *Descartes' Error*, Random House.

Forge, J. (2002) "Corporate Responsibility Revisited," *International Journal of Applied Philosophy*, 16(1), 13–32.
French, P. (1979) "The Corporation as a Moral Person," *American Philosophical Quarterly*, 16(3), 207–215.
French, P. (1984) *Collective and Corporate Responsibility*, Columbia University Press.
French, P. (1995) *Corporate Ethics*, Harcourt Brace.
Greene, J. et al. (2001) "An fMRI Investigation of Emotional Engagement in Moral Judgment," *Science*, 293, 2105–2108.
Haslanger, S. (2016) "What is a (Social) Structural Explanation?" *Philosophical Studies*, 173(1), 113–130.
Hasnas, J. (2012) "Reflections on Corporate Moral Responsibility and the Problem Solving Technique of Alexander the Great," *Journal of Business Ethics*, 107, 183–195.
Held, V. (1990) "Feminist Transformations of Moral Theory," *Philosophy and Phenomenological Research*, 50, 321–344.
Hess, K. (2014a) "The Free Will of Corporations (and Other Collectives)," *Philosophical Studies*, 168(1), 241–260.
Hess, K. (2014b) "Because They Can: The Basis for the Moral Obligations of (Certain) Collectives," *Midwest Studies in Philosophy*, 38, 203–221.
Hess, K. (2018a) "Does the Machine Require a Ghost? The Role of Phenomenal Consciousness in Kantian Moral Agency," *Journal of the American Philosophical Association*, 4(1), 67–86.
Hess, K. (2018b) "Fractured Wholes: Corporate Agents and their Members." In P. Ivanhoe, O. Flanagan and V. Harrison (eds), *The Oneness Hypothesis: Beyond the Bounds of the Self*, Columbia University Press, 192–211.
Hess, K. (2018c) "The Peculiar Unity of Corporate Agents." In K. Hess, T. Isaacs, and V. Igneski (eds), *Collectivity: Ontology, Ethics, and Social Justice*, Rowman & Littlefield, 35–59.
Hess, K. (2018d) "Who's Responsible? (It's Complicated.) Assigning Blame in the Wake of the Financial Crisis," *Midwest Studies in Philosophy*, 42, 133–155.
Hindriks, F. (2008) "The Status Account of Corporate Agents," *Concepts of Sharedness: Essays on Collective Intentionality*, 119–144.
Hindriks, F. (2013) "The Location Problem in Social Ontology," *Synthese*, 190(3), 413–437.
Kleingeld, P. (2014) "Debunking Confabulation: Emotions and the Significance of Empirical Psychology for Kantian Ethics." In A. Cohen (ed.), *Kant on Emotion and Value*, Palgrave Macmillan, 146–165.
List, C. and Pettit, P. (2011) *Group Agency: The Possibility, Design, and Status of Corporate Agents*, Oxford University Press.
Ludwig, K. (2017) "Do Corporations have Minds of their Own?" *Philosophical Psychology*, 30(3), 265–297.
Markosian, N. (1998) "Brutal Composition," *Philosophical Studies*, 92(3), 211–249.
McAuliffe, W. (2018) "Do Emotions Play an Essential Role in Moral Judgements?" *Thinking & Reasoning*, DOI: 10.1080/13546783.2018.1499552.
McMahon, C. (1995) "The Ontological and Moral Status of Organizations," *Business Ethics Quarterly*, 5(3), 541–554.
Miller, S. and Mäkelä, P. (2005) "The Collectivist Approach to Collective Moral Responsibility," *Metaphilosophy*, 36(5), 634–651.
Mumby, D. and Putnam, L. (1992) "The Politics of Emotion: A Feminist Reading of Bounded Rationality," *Academy of Management Review*, 17(3), 465–486.
Naqvi, N., Shiv, B., and Bechara, A. (2006) "The Role of Emotion in Decision Making: A Cognitive Neuroscience Perspective," *Current Directions in Psychological Science*, 15(5), 260–264.
Ranken, N.L. (1987) "Corporations as Persons: Objections to Goodpaster's 'Principle of Moral Projection,'" *Journal of Business Ethics*, 6 (8), 633–637.
Ritchie, K. (2018) "Social Creationism and Social Groups." In K. Hess, T. Isaacs, and V. Igneski (eds), *Collectivity: Ontology, Ethics, and Social Justice*, Rowman & Littlefield, 13–34.
Rönnegard, D. (2015) *The Fallacy of Corporate Moral Agency*. 44 Vol. Springer.
Rönnegard, D. and Velasquez, M. (2017) "On (Not) Attributing Moral Responsibility to Organizations." In M. Smith and E. Orts (eds), *The Moral Responsibility of Firms*, Oxford University Press, 123.
Rovane, C. (1997) *The Bounds of Agency: An Essay in Revisionary Metaphysics*, Princeton University Press.
Rovane, C. (2014) "Group Agency and Individualism," *Erkenntnis*, 79(9), 1663–1684.
Shapiro, S. (1997) *Philosophy of Mathematics: Structure and Ontology*, Oxford University Press.
Velasquez, M. (2003) "Debunking Corporate Moral Responsibility," *Business Ethics Quarterly*, 13(4), 531–562.
Wallace, K. (1993) "Reconstructing Judgment: Emotion and Moral Judgment," *Hypatia*, 8(3), 61–83.
Young, L. and Koenigs, M. (2007) "Investigating Emotion in Moral Cognition: A Review of Evidence from Functional Neuroimaging and Neuropsychology," *British Medical Bulletin*, 84, 69–79.

9

COLLECTIVE RESPONSIBILITY AND COLLECTIVE OBLIGATIONS WITHOUT COLLECTIVE MORAL AGENTS

Gunnar Björnsson

Sometimes, bad things are the aggregate result of actions and omissions of more than one agent. In such cases, we often blame that group of agents for the result. Some blame their divorced parents for not preserving a reasonable relationship. Others blame voters for electing corrupt leaders. Others yet blame the growing threat of climate catastrophe on people who have known about the risks of greenhouse gas emissions without taking appropriate measures.

As it is with blame, so it is with obligations. We often think that groups of agents have obligations that no individual could discharge on their own. The parents had an obligation to preserve their relationship, we might think, while the voters had an obligation not to elect corrupt leaders, and people aware of climate risks an obligation to significantly reduce those.

Attributions of blameworthiness to groups are not mere theoretical exercises. They direct our indignation over what has happened and indicate who should compensate those harmed or bear the burdens involved in preventing further negative consequences. Likewise, attributions of group obligations often seem relevant for what actions group members should take; for whether the group can be justly coerced to behave in a certain way; and for distributions of blame and compensatory or reparative burdens should the group shirk its duties.

Though common and seemingly important, attributions of group blameworthiness and group obligations can also seem metaphysically or ethically suspect. Often, no individual member of the group had control over the outcome for which they are blamed, and no individual member can make a difference as to whether the group discharges its obligation. This makes it difficult to understand group attributions in terms of attributions of corresponding individual blameworthiness and obligations. Moreover, the groups themselves often fall short of standard conditions of moral agency. They seem to lack many properties normally associated with agenthood, including beliefs about their circumstances, and they lack the sort of stable inner organization that might make it clear what capacities they have and what demands can be properly directed at them, other than those directed at their members.

In response to this agency challenge, philosophers who want to defend attributions of collective obligations to groups of these kinds have either (i) argued that the groups in question have the requisite capabilities to have obligations of their own or (ii) suggested ways in which the existence of related individual obligations can make it true that these groups have obligations.

Philosophers who have defended attributions of collective responsibility and blameworthiness have suggested that members of the relevant collectives can *share* responsibility for an outcome in virtue of being causally or socially connected to that outcome.

This chapter details some cases where it is natural to attribute obligations or blameworthiness to groups that cannot be plausibly attributed to their individual members, and discusses the agency challenge mentioned above, as well as proposed replies and problems and prospects for these. The most promising replies, I will argue, understand these groups' obligations and blameworthiness as grounded in demands on individual agents.

9.1 Attributable to the Group, But Not to Any Individual

Consider:

> *Offshore Wind*: Like on most summer days, a large group of children are enjoying the beach, playing on their air mattresses close to land. This particular day, there are fifteen of them: three came with a parent, the other twelve live nearby. Without warning, the weak onshore wind quickly turns strongly offshore, and the children begin drifting out, beyond the range of their swimming capabilities. They need to be rescued. In response, each of the three adults can swim out and catch one child before the wind has carried it too far, provided that she starts swimming now. But there is also a lifeboat that could be dragged a few yards to the sea if at least two adults joined forces; with it, two of them could row out and pick up all the children. Each of the adults quickly realizes all this. (This case, like many discussed in the literature, is modeled on cases in Held 1970.)

About this situation, it is very natural to think that:

> THREE'S OBLIGATION: The three adults have an obligation to save all the children.

If the group lacks any weighty reasons not to save all the children, the obligation is naturally understood as an *all-things-considered* rather than a mere *pro tanto* obligation. (In what follows, when I talk about obligations, I will have the former kind in mind unless otherwise stated.)

Clearly, to attribute this obligation is not to attribute to each of the three adults an obligation to save all the children, as none of them can do this on her own: the relevant reading of THREE'S OBLIGATION is not straightforwardly *distributive*. Instead, one might be tempted to understand it as saying that each individual has an obligation to *help* save all the children: to participate or do her part in or contribute to a joint action resulting in the saving of all the children. But whereas THREE'S OBLIGATION is independent of the three adults' willingness to help, their individual obligations to help save all are not. Consider:

> *Plenitude*: Each of the three adults is willing and ready to help save all the children. Because of this, if one of them didn't help, the other two would join forces and save all. (None has stronger normative reasons to help than the others.)
>
> *Helplessness*: Each of the three adults is a closet racist. Because the other twelve children are of what she considers the wrong color, she is unwilling to help save all the children and would refuse if prompted.
>
> *Scarcity*: One adult is ready to help save all the children and would do so together with whoever would be willing to help her. But the other two are closet racists, unwilling to help, and would refuse to help if prompted.

In *Plenitude*, no individual adult has an obligation to help save all, because the other two will gladly do what is required. In *Helplessness*, no individual has an obligation to help save all, because the reluctance of the others makes it impossible for her to do so. Here, the individual might have an obligation to quickly try to get the others to join her in saving all, say, before turning attention to her own child. But because she *cannot* help save all, she has no more of an individual obligation to do so than the adult in:

> *Solitary Helplessness*: Like *Helplessness*, but there is only one adult on the beach when the wind turns, and she can save only one child.

In *Scarcity*, finally, the willing individual has no obligation to help save all the children, because the unwillingness of the two racists makes it impossible for her to do so. By contrast, each of the racists can help save all the children (thanks to the willing individual) and her help is needed (because of the unwillingness of the other racist). Each of the racists thus seems to have an individual obligation to contribute.

The plausibility of THREE'S OBLIGATION seems independent of these variations in the willingness of the members of the group and their resulting individual obligations. They have an obligation to save all, regardless of whether more or fewer individuals than needed are willing to help.

In light of this, one might be tempted to interpret THREE'S OBLIGATION as saying that each individual has a *conditional* obligation to help: an obligation to help *if that would make a difference*. Each adult in each of *Plenitude*, *Helplessness*, and *Scarcity* plausibly has such an obligation. But the same seems true about the lonely adult in *Solitary Helplessness*, and we don't want to conclude that she has an obligation to save all the children. Moreover, even when individual conditional obligations coincide with a corresponding group obligation, the proposal gets things wrong. Consider *Helplessness*: since no individual adult could have made a difference as to whether all children were saved, none of the conditional obligations is violated when each proceeds to save only their own child. But the obligation of THREE'S OBLIGATION is most definitely violated.

Although THREE'S OBLIGATION is independent of the willingness of members to help, it clearly does depend on the group's ability to save all children, which in turn requires that there are things that the individuals can do that, together, result in the saving of all the children. Because the group's obligation is independent of directly corresponding individual obligations, but is dependent of what the individuals can do together, it is natural to say that it is their *collective* obligation. And the same reasoning seems applicable to the other cases of group obligations mentioned earlier: the obligation of the parents to uphold a reasonable relationship, the obligation of eligible voters not to elect corrupt leaders, and the obligation of people aware of the risk of climate catastrophe to significantly reduce it. They all seem to be collective obligations. (For related arguments, see, e.g., Aas 2015; Björnsson 2014; Forthcoming; Dietz 2016; Schwenkenbecher 2014; Wringe 2016; cf. Copp 2007, though he focuses mainly on institutional groups.)

Offshore Wind can also illustrate the phenomenon of collective responsibility and collective blameworthiness. (For simplicity, I will focus on blameworthiness rather than responsibility more generally.) Specifically, consider the *Helplessness* version, where each of the three adults swims out to save her own child. Here, it seems that the adults are responsible for not saving all the children, and deserve blame for not doing so. After all, they could easily have done so by joining forces in some constellation or other, and they didn't because of their lack of regard for the lives of the twelve. Corresponding to THREE'S OBLIGATION, we thus have:

> THREE'S BLAMEWORTHINESS: The three adults deserve blame for not saving all the children.

But it is also clear that we cannot blame them individually for the failure to save all, or the failure to help save all. Given the racism of the other two, no one individual was the reason that not all the children were saved, and no individual could have helped save them all. The three seem to be to blame for the outcome collectively, not individually.

As with collective obligations, then, collective responsibility and blameworthiness seem independent of corresponding individual blameworthiness. The other cases mentioned above could illustrate the same phenomena. The failure of the two divorced parents to preserve a reasonable relationship could not be pinned individually on either of them if the recalcitrance of each would have foiled any attempt on the part of the other; the failure would still seem to be *their* fault, due to *their* recalcitrance. Likewise, but on grander scales, for the election of corrupt leaders and the failure to significantly reduce the risk of global climate catastrophe: No one who voted for the leadership can be individually blamed for the outcome. And no one—at least no ordinary citizen—who understood the risk for climate catastrophe but failed to take significant measures can be blamed for the current grave risk. But together they can be. (See e.g., Björnsson 2011; Held 1970; Kutz 2000; May 1992; Miller 2006; Sadler 2006; Sartorio 2004; Sverdlik 1987.)

Or so it seems. In the remainder of the chapter, we look at how these natural attributions of collective obligations and collective blameworthiness give rise to philosophical puzzles, and at various attempts to solve these puzzles.

9.2 Collective Obligations: Agency Worries

The central problem with the idea of collective obligations is that groups of the sort we have looked at rarely qualify as *moral agents* in any strict sense. This is a problem if we assume that:

> AGENCY REQUIREMENT: Only moral agents have obligations.

For an individual to be subject to moral obligations, it seems, it needs to have some amount of self-control—including some control over its goals and some basic capacity for moral cognition—and to be guided by its beliefs towards achieving its goals. Many think that some suitably organized groups—such as institutional groups, corporations, and states—satisfy this requirement (see, e.g., Björnsson and Hess 2017; Copp 2007; French 1984; Hess 2014; List and Pettit 2011; cf. Tollefsen 2015). But the trio of adults on the beach, the divorced couple, the group of eligible voters, and the group of people aware of the risk of climate catastrophe seem to lack the relevant sort of organization. Though their members have beliefs, goals, self-control, and capacities for moral cognition, it is not clear how the groups themselves can be said to have any of these. (For an early statement of this problem, see Benjamin 1976; see also Collins 2013; Isaacs 2011; Lawford-Smith 2015.)

It is true, of course, that the groups that we have looked at are capable of the relevant states, or at least capable of acting together. Their members are moral agents who can act together with other agents in ways that involve shared goals, perspectives, and decision procedures, all possibly informed by the moral cognition of the members. For example, if the three adults in *Offshore Wind* want to, they will quickly organize to save all the children based on coordinated assumptions about the situation and a shared plan. For some groups, such as the group of people alive today and currently aware of the risk of climate catastrophe, such organization might seem farfetched. In principle, however, each member of that group could operate on the assumption that other members take the risk to be real and morally very significant, take ways of mitigating the risk to carry substantial weight in deliberation, and act on this while seeing themselves as part of a global effort to minimize that risk, even if that effort would be widely distributed.

That groups have these capacities suggests two possible ways of responding to the AGENCY REQUIREMENT, each represented in the literature. The first argues that the capacity is enough to make a group subject to moral obligations. The second instead understands collective obligations to φ as grounded in members' individual obligations, obligations the discharging of which would (likely) lead the group to φ. I discuss these responses in turn.

9.3 The Capacity Response to Agency Worries

The first suggestion, pursued by Bill Wringe (2010), is that the AGENCY REQUIREMENT is too strong and that one can be the subject of moral obligations merely by having the capacity for the sorts of properties associated with moral agency (cf. Shockley (2007) and Aas (2015), though Aas takes demands on groups to be entirely dependent on moral demands on members (2015: 18); Shockley 2007). This *capacity response* has some initial plausibility. Central requirements for moral agency, such as self-control and reasons-responsiveness, are themselves at least in part capacity requirements, and so is the most obvious precondition for the existence of an all-things-considered obligation: that the bearer of the obligation is able to discharge it. But the suggestion faces difficult problems.

The general problem is to explain why properties that are usually taken to be necessary for moral agency and moral obligations are not in fact necessary.

On certain views about the source of moral obligations, the problem is particularly stark. Consider contractualism: on standard contractualist views, agents are subject to moral norms in virtue of being parties of a hypothetical social contract. But the group of adults who happen to be on the same beach is not itself plausibly such a party in addition to its three members. Or take versions of constitutivism according to which duties have their source in constitutive aims of moral agents: the aim of rational self-determination, say. It is not obvious how the kinds of groups that we have looked at could have constitutive aims of that sort.

Of course, some will reject both contractualism and constitutivism. But the problem is raised directly by a more uncontroversial requirement on moral agency: that of self-control. It is unclear how unstructured groups can exert such control when they lack anything corresponding to a controlling self, as these are commonly understood in the literature: a practical self-conception, or a set of values, principles, or higher-order plans or preferences. The problem is also raised by standard epistemic requirements on particular obligations. Generally speaking, an agent has no obligation to respond to morally relevant factors when, for no fault of her own, she lacks any beliefs about these factors. If the sort of unstructured groups that we have looked at lack beliefs of their own, it is thus unclear how they can have any obligations. It is true, of course, that each of the three adults in *Offshore Wind* has beliefs about how all the children could be saved. But because, apparently for no fault of its own, the group is not yet organized such that individual beliefs are tied to the group's decision making in any systematic way, it is unclear how these individual beliefs can be beliefs of the group.

9.4 Grounding Collective Obligations in Demands on Individuals

The problems for the capacity response all suggest that it is the moral agency of the *members* of non-agential groups that make it seem plausible that such groups have obligations. It is because each of the three adults is a bona fide moral agent and knows what is going on in *Offshore Wind* that the trio has an obligation to save all the children. This in turn suggests that group obligations depend on or should be understood in terms of moral demands directed at the members, in some way or other. To further see this dependence, contrast *Offshore Wind* with:

> *Uncertain Success*: Like *Offshore Wind*, but the boat looks leaky and difficult to handle and the adults are unsure whether an attempt to use it to save all would be successful. If they tried, they could find themselves struggling with a useless sinking boat, having wasted their chance to save their own children while they were within swimming distance. (In fact, a joint attempt to save all would have been difficult but ultimately successful.)

Assume that the *pro tanto* agent-relative duty of each parent to save her own child outweighs the possibility of saving all, such that a parent's participation in a joint attempt would at most be permissible, not required. Unlike in *Offshore Wind*, it now seems false that the group has an obligation to save all the children. Based on this contrast, it seems that if it cannot be morally demanded of the members of the group that they react and act in ways that would result in a group's action, then that action cannot be demanded of the group.[1] Moreover, it is not clear how the agent-relative duties of the *parents* can provide the group, understood as an independent duty bearer, with reasons outweighing the prospect of saving many more of the children. This suggests that THREE'S OBLIGATION is grounded in individual obligations, which are in turn grounded in the moral issue at hand and the group's capacity to handle that issue through some combination of individual actions.

This grounding suggestion conflicts with Wringe's (2016) claim that, phenomenologically, individual obligations in cases like *Offshore Wind* depend on the collective obligation. But it allows that concrete individual obligations to contribute to a collective outcome are dependent on various collective matters. In *Offshore Wind*, for example, individual obligations to act and react in various ways in light of what others do depend on the fact that (a) it is important that two or more adults team up to save the child, which in turn depends on the fact that (b) if two or more adults wanted to save all the children, they would. In other cases, individual obligations depend on such things as members' implication in a collective harm or the importance of a joint promise being kept. It is not clear that phenomenology requires more dependence than this.

If a group's obligation to φ is grounded in obligations of individuals, we need answers to these two questions:

(1) What are the relevant individual obligations?
(2) How must they be related to the group's φ-ing?

Regarding the latter, one might think that if the individuals discharge their obligations, this should make it *sufficiently likely* that they φ (Aas 2015; Collins 2013). Alternatively, one might think that in order for the group to have an obligation to φ rather than merely an obligation to *try* to φ, the satisfaction of their individual obligations must *ensure*, under the circumstances, that they φ (Björnsson 2014; Forthcoming; cf. Pinkert 2014).

But most work has been focused on the former question, regarding what individual obligations ground group obligations. Since, as we saw in section 9.1, individual obligations to actually participate in or help bring about φ-ing are dependent on what other members will do, the relevant individual obligations will have to be farther removed from contributions to actual φ-ing. It has thus been suggested that a group's obligation to φ is grounded in the fact that the group would φ, or would be sufficiently likely to φ, if members discharged their individual obligations to:

> *take steps to collectivize*: to transform the group into a group agent that has as its own obligation to φ (Collins 2013; cf. Hindricks 2019; Isaacs 2011: 144–54 on "putative obligations");[2]
>
> *we-reason*: to identify φ-ing as the optimal solution to a problem that group members cannot solve individually and to deduce their own individual actions based on this (Schwenkenbecher 2018; 2019);[3]
>
> *be* prepared to do their part in φ-ing should they be sufficiently certain that others would as well (Aas 2015)[4]; or
>
> *care* to the right extent about what is morally at stake, in the sense of being disposed to (i) pick up information about what reactions and actions tend to promote what is morally important and (ii) be moved by such information when opportunity arises (Björnsson 2014; Forthcoming).[5]

Though these proposals all violate the AGENCY REQUIREMENT, they suggest a principled way of explaining why collective obligations are not subject to this requirement while individual obligations are: it is specifically *basic* obligations—obligations to we-reason or care, say—that require rich forms of agency. Moreover, each proposal seems to get cases like *Offshore Wind* right. At least at a first glance, it seems plausible that each of the three adults has an obligation to care about the predicament of the children, to be prepared to collaborate with the others, to think about how they can together best solve the problem at hand, and, assuming that the others discharge these obligations, to take steps to come together with the others in some constellation or other in a coordinated effort to save all children based on a shared understanding of the situation. And it seems likely that if they all discharged these duties, they would indeed save all the children. Each proposal also seems to capture the fact that what concrete actions can be demanded of the individuals will depend on what the others do, as well as the fact that the obligation to save all disappears in *Uncertain Success*.

As we shall see, however, the first three of these proposals fail to account for at least two kinds of intuitively compelling cases of group obligations. In the first, members of a group are obviously uninterested in helping, rendering futile any individual attempt to bring about a collective effort as well as any preparedness for or deliberation about such an effort. Consider a version of *Helplessness* where:

> *Visible Helplessness*: It is true of each adult that were she to consider ways of saving all the children, she would immediately see that the other two would not be interested in a joint effort and that any sufficient effort to convince them would risk her own child.

The additional features of *Visible Helplessness* seem to do nothing to undermine THREE'S OBLIGATION: together they can save all, and they would if they all wanted to. This is in line with the *caring* proposal, as it seems plausible that the individuals can be required to care about survival of all the children in the relevant dispositional sense, and that this would ensure that they saved all. But contrary to the collectivization, we-reasoning, and preparedness proposals, the individuals have no obligations to we-reason, take steps to collectivize, or be prepared to act with the others should they be willing to contribute.

In the second kind of problem case, the discharging of a collective obligation requires no collaborative coordination in relation to a joint goal. In discharging paradigmatic individual duties—such as duties not to steal, lie, or kill—we rarely have this as a goal around which we coordinate our actions: for most of us, the idea of stealing, lying, or killing never comes up.

The same seems true about various group obligations. The divorced parents might discharge their obligation to preserve a reasonable relationship by being sensible and respectful without even considering the possibility that their relationship would turn sour. Similarly for:

> *Ferry Ride*: A small ferry would capsize if many of its passengers moved laterally in sync. On this ride, as on most, almost all passengers are sitting quietly after a hard day's work.

Even if the possibility is too remote to consider, they could easily capsize the ferry if they wanted to. In light of this, it is plausibly their obligation not to. This is very much in line with the *caring* proposal, as it seems both (i) that it can be demanded of the passengers that they care about what is bad about capsizing, and (ii) that if the passengers do care, this would ensure that they don't capsize the ferry (cf. Björnsson 2014; Forthcoming). But the group's obligation not to capsize the ferry conflicts with the *preparedness*, *we-reasoning*, and *collectivization* proposals. Absent any present danger, the passengers have no obligations to try to form a group agent with all the other passengers, or to think about how the group is best to avoid capsizing the ferry, or even to be prepared to join the others to prevent it from capsizing.

In light of *Visible Helplessness* and *Ferry Ride*, it thus seems that any understanding of a collective obligation to φ as grounded in individual obligations would require us to understand the latter as concerned with dispositions of some sort to contribute towards φ-ing, rather than as some overt action, mental activity, or even active state of preparedness.

9.5 What Makes These Things *Obligations*?

Even if an account of this sort captures our intuitive attributions of group obligations, it leaves the question of why the fact that a group would φ if members cared appropriately would constitute an *obligation* on the part of the group to φ. This question is particularly pressing as this account, like all the proposals in this family, seem to suggest that what looks like a straightforward attribution of *an obligation to φ to a group* is in fact something quite different and much more complex, such as an attribution of *individual obligations to members of the group to have a certain disposition such that if all members had that disposition they would φ*.

Elsewhere, I have suggested that the relation postulated in the *caring* proposal constitutes obligation, because it is the very same relation that constitutes individual obligation, i.e., an obligation of a group of only one individual. If this is correct, there are no hidden structural differences other than the number of obligation bearers. To give a sense of this sort of reply, I will briefly recount the proposal in question and explain how it applies to the individual case, and why the relation constitutes obligation. This is the proposal:

> OBLIGATION: A group has a moral obligation to φ if and only if the group's φ-ing (i) is morally important and (ii) would be ensured, in a normal way, if members cared as can be morally demanded of them (Björnsson 2014; Forthcoming; cf. Björnsson and Brülde 2017).

As before, the concern here is with all-things-considered, not *pro tanto* obligations. The *moral importance* of the group's φ-ing can be instrumental or non-instrumental. On some views, the only relevant moral importance is the importance of not acting on certain kinds of motives, but most acknowledge the moral importance of bringing about or not preventing certain kinds of actions and outcomes, regardless of specific motives. Substantive accounts of obligations can differ with respect to what is morally important and what makes it so, but also with respect to what it can be *morally demanded* that people care about, and to what extent. On some narrow Kantian views, morality only requires that we care about acting from maxims that can be willed as universal law, and on some narrow utilitarian views, it only requires that we care about the surplus of pleasure over pain. But most will acknowledge demands to care about a variety of values, including staples of both deontological and consequentialist moral theories: telling the truth, keeping promises, not using others as mere means, human flourishing, happiness, relationships, knowledge, and so forth. Because OBLIGATION leaves open what can be morally demanded of members of groups, it is compatible with a variety of normative views, and because it leaves open what ultimately grounds such demands, it is also compatible with a variety of views about their nature and ultimate sources, including intuitionism, rationalism, contractualism, and constitutivism.[6]

Implicitly, OBLIGATION accounts for the common idea that an obligation to φ presupposes an *ability* to φ: if all members of the group care about what makes φ-ing bad, this would ensure, in a normal way, that they would φ.[7] What, though, is it for sufficient caring to *ensure* an outcome, and to ensure it in a *normal* way?

For X to *ensure* Y is for X to rule out all relevant possibilities alternative to Y, not necessarily for X to cause Y. The lock on the door might ensure that no one enters even if no one tries to enter, and if the passengers on the ferry care about staying afloat, this might ensure that they don't capsize the ferry even if the reason that the ferry remains steady is they are all sitting down to rest after a hard day's work. For obligations that can only be discharged through coordinated action, sufficient caring will often ensure such action by prompting intentions to join forces if others are similarly prepared, and act on the perception of such preparedness among other members. Even here, though, individuals might participate out of habit, group conformity, or economic interest, and morally required caring kick in only if the joint endeavor is threatened.[8]

As noted, OBLIGATION requires that the way in which appropriate caring ensures the group's φ-ing is relevantly *normal*: a matter of skill or ability rather than mere luck. This might require that members' appropriate caring would block at least some relevant threats to the group's φ-ing by at least marginally *coordinated* behavior, rather than by individual behavior completely insensitive to that of other members. It also rules out cases where group actions would ensure φ-ing only in ways deviating significantly from the intended:

> *Serendipity*: The adults' only chance of saving all the drowning children is by using a lifeboat mounted on a support structure. But an arm holding the boat in place is rusted stuck and it seems that the only way of releasing it is by hitting that arm with an iron rod lying nearby. Unfortunately, as it happens, doing so would fail to release the lifeboat. Fortunately, it would make a loud sound that would alert a coastguard boat that is anchored behind a rock and would come and rescue the children.

Suppose that it is the group's duty to try to save the child, and to try to get the lifeboat unstuck using the iron rod, and that these are the group's duties because of the importance of the child's survival. Still, if the only way that they would bring about the child's survival would be by accident, they do not plausibly have an obligation to save the child in this case. By contrast, if they had known about the nearby coastguard boat and would have employed the iron rod to catch their attention, it would have been their obligation to save the child by doing so.

A final aspect of OBLIGATION worth mentioning is the connection between obligations and blameworthiness. If a group fails to discharge an obligation, it must be because one or more members' caring fell short at some point. But if something morally bad happens as a result of people not caring about the values at stake as can be demanded of them, they are plausibly morally to blame for it: at least that seemed to be the case in *Helplessness*. (We return to the issue of collective blameworthiness in the next section.)

The claim now is that OBLIGATION is an equally plausible account of obligations of individuals, understood as "groups" of one agent. The demands on caring are the same, and what is of moral importance is the same. What is different is merely that it is the appropriate caring of a single agent that ensures the φ-ing of that one agent. Moreover, the account applies as straightforwardly to the case where one agent can either save her own child or use a lifeboat to save all children, to individual obligations to φ that are discharged without the aim of φ-ing, and to a one-person version of *Serendipity*. But if OBLIGATION is an adequate account of both individual and group obligations, it is clear why group obligations to φ are *obligations*: they are constituted by the very same relation between the obligation bearer and the φ-ing as are individual obligations.

9.6 Collective Responsibility: Agency Worries

Turn now from the issue of collective obligation to that of collective responsibility or blameworthiness. THREE'S BLAMEWORTHINESS—the idea that the three adults are to blame for not saving all the children in *Helplessness*—can seem problematic in much the same way as did THREE'S OBLIGATION.

On the one hand, we cannot plausibly understand THREE'S BLAMEWORTHINESS distributively, as attributing individual blameworthiness for not saving all the children to each of the three adults. No individual in *Helplessness* can be individually blamed for not saving all the children, or for the fact that the trio did not save all the children: the individual had no say in that matter given that the other two individuals were unwilling to participate. (This is not to deny that they might be individually to blame for other things, such as lack of concern for the other children, or failure to think about how all might be saved.)

On the other hand, the group itself seems to lack the sort of properties that are required for individual responsibility and blameworthiness. If an entity cannot be blameworthy without violating an obligation, and if only moral agents can be subject to obligations, it follows immediately that non-agential groups cannot be blameworthy. Things would be a little less straightforward if one could be to blame even without strictly speaking violating any obligations. (An example might be not giving up one's seat on the bus to someone more in need of it. For discussion, see Driver 1992.) Still, the underlying worries from section 9.2 would remain, as blameworthiness is standardly assumed to require both some degree of self-control and beliefs about morally relevant features of the situation. As already noted, the group seems to lack anything corresponding to the self that can exert relevant control over its actions as well as anything corresponding to beliefs. Furthermore, neither the group nor its members can plausibly be blamed for that lack of a self or lack of belief: prior to the unexpected offshore wind, there was no reason to form a collective agent.

9.7 Collective Blameworthiness as Shared Blameworthiness

Our discussion of collective obligations suggested that these are grounded in demands on individuals. Likewise, collective blameworthiness seems to depend on criticizable input from group members. As in the case of obligations, we can contrast *Helplessness* with *Uncertain Success*. In the former case, where the group of adults seems to deserve blame for not saving all the children, the failure to save all the children was due to the adults' callous, racist attitudes. In the latter, where the group does not seem to blame for the failure to save all, the outcome was not due to any criticizable attitude on their part, as evidence suggested to each of them that the prospects for saving all children were bleak. Here, even a morally conscientious individual could be expected to save their own child instead.

If group blameworthiness is grounded in the moral shortcomings of members, that could straightforwardly explain why the group does not have to satisfy standard requirements on blameworthiness for individual agents, again in line with what we said about collective obligations. It can also explain why individuals that are part of blameworthy non-agential groups are individually *implicated* in the collective blameworthiness. When the group is blamed for their failure to save all the children in *Helplessness*, an individual racist cannot plausibly reply, "Sure, many of the kids died because *we* didn't want to save them, but what does that have to do with *me*?" And at least partly because group blame seems to implicate members and relate intimately to individual moral shortcomings of this sort, it is natural to think, as many have, that there is such a thing as *shared* or *joint* responsibility for group actions and outcomes (e.g., Björnsson 2011; Kutz 2000; May 1992; Miller 2006; Sadler 2006; Sartorio 2004; Sverdlik 1987).

In virtue of what, though, do individuals in a group share responsibility for some action or omission of the group, or something that it has brought about or let happen? On some influential suggestions, one can share responsibility for a harm (a) in virtue of intentional or knowing participation in group activity that stands in some relevant causal relation to that harm even if one does not stand in that relation oneself (Kutz 2000; Miller 2006; Sadler 2006; Sverdlik 1987), (b) in virtue of participation in a culture or way of life giving rise to the harm (Kutz 2000; Silver 2002), or (c) in virtue of endorsing the sorts of actions or omission that directly explained the outcome (May 1992). Suggestions like these seem to make sense of some central cases of collective responsibility, explaining how participation in or endorsement of the machinery of an unjust war might make one partly responsible for its resulting atrocities, even though one could have done nothing to prevent them. But as illustrated by *Helplessness*, it seems that a group of individuals can be to blame, together, without intentional or knowing participation in anything meaningfully called a group activity, and without the harm being the upshot of a culture or way of life. Moreover, since no action or omission by any one agent directly explained or caused the outcome, other agents cannot be responsible for that outcome in virtue of endorsing or engaging in actions or omissions of the type as that which explained it. It is clear, then, that even if these suggestions identify relations in virtue of which one might share blameworthiness, they fail to provide completely general accounts of collective responsibility (Björnsson 2011).

To capture the cases that are left unaccounted for, it is natural to generalize: perhaps one can share blameworthiness for something by being to blame for part of a cause of it, regardless of relations to other agents. In *Helplessness*, for example, it might seem that each adult is to blame for part of the fact that not enough able adults were willing to save all children and looking to see if the others were too. Similarly, each person voting for the corrupt leadership might be to blame for part of the voting result that brought them to power, and each of the divorced parents might be to blame for part of the lack of cooperativeness that caused the deterioration of their relationship (cf. Sartorio 2004).

But mere blameworthiness for part of a cause does not seem sufficient. Consider:

> *Partly Excused Helplessness*: Like *Helplessness*, but only one of the adults is racist; the other two are unwilling to help because each thinks, based on very convincing but misleading evidence, that the boat is leaky and difficult to handle and that an attempt to rescue all would risk the life of their own child, who is among those farthest from the beach.

Here, like in *Helplessness*, the group fails to save all children because not enough adults are willing to attempt the rescue. Moreover, the racist seems as much to blame for her part in this fact as she was in *Helplessness*. However, we cannot here blame the trio for the failure to save all: two of them have perfectly good excuses for being unwilling to try. And although we can criticize the racist for not caring enough about some of the children and blame her for not trying to get the others to help, we cannot blame her for the failure to help save all, as she would have been unable to get the others to join. Judging from the contrast between this case and *Helplessness*, then, the way in which she is implicated in the outcome in *Helplessness* is *irreducibly collective*, as part of a blameworthy group, not just as responsible for part of a cause of the failure to save all (Björnsson 2011: 185–6).

9.8 How is Shared Blameworthiness Possible?

The conclusion of the previous section was that group blameworthiness is irreducibly collective, but not in a way that requires substantive social relations. Even if this is correct, it remains unclear *why* the involvement of other blameworthy agents in an outcome should matter for how the individual is implicated. The racist has no more control over the outcome in *Helplessness* than in *Partly Excused Helplessness*, and though it might be tempting to say that *the group* has more control in the former case because all members have access to correct information about the situation, the group seems to lack the agential properties, including self-control and beliefs about its surroundings, that we standardly take to be necessary for responsibility.

My own explanation for this lies in the nature of blameworthiness, whether individual or collective. According to an influential understanding, often employed in the collective responsibility literature (e.g., Feinberg 1968; May 1992), blameworthiness for something bad does not require that one was in full control of it, but rather that it happened partly because of some of one's *faults*. Faults are often understood as blameworthy or shameful actions or omissions, but a tradition from P.F. Strawson (1962) understands basic faults as instances of substandard responsiveness to values, or substandard caring. In line with this, I have defended the following account of the blameworthiness of both groups and individuals:

> BLAMEWORTHINESS: For a group to be morally to blame for Y is for Y to (i) be morally bad and (ii) be explained in a normal way by the group's members' not caring as can be morally demanded of them (Björnsson 2011; 2017).

Like any account that takes collective blameworthiness to be grounded in demands on individual moral agents, BLAMEWORTHINESS explains why groups can be to blame even if they do not themselves satisfy standard requirements on moral agency.

But BLAMEWORTHINESS has a number of more specific explanatory virtues: it straightforwardly explains THREE'S BLAMEWORTHINESS in *Helplessness*, as well as the trio's lack of blameworthiness for not saving all the children in *Uncertain Success* and the racists' lack of blameworthiness for the outcome in *Partly Excused Helplessness*—only in *Helplessness* was the failure to save all due to the substandard caring of the members of the group.

Importantly, the claim that the failure was due to *their* substandard caring is not distributive: it does not imply that it is true about each (or any one) of them that the failure was due to *her* substandard caring. The latter might seem implausible given that her substandard caring made no difference to the outcome. Nevertheless, BLAMEWORTHINESS explains how members are implicated in collective blameworthiness for something: the individual member's substandard caring *is part of* why that thing happened. And it explains why failures to discharge obligations, understood in line with OBLIGATION, imply that at least some agent is thus implicated in blameworthiness for this failure: because obligations are morally important things that are ensured by appropriate caring, failures to discharge an obligation must be both morally bad and due to one or more instances of substandard caring.

In addition to this, BLAMEWORTHINESS is not designed specifically to handle collective blameworthiness: it applies equally to cases of individual blameworthiness, where bad things have happened because one agent failed to care enough on one or more occasions. Because it takes individual and collective blameworthiness to consist in the very same relation, it offers the same kind of benefit as OBLIGATIONS: it explains why collective blameworthiness is *blameworthiness*.

9.9 Concluding Remarks

Attributions of collective obligations and collective responsibility or blameworthiness to non-agential groups form an important part of moral cognition. But they raise difficult problems of interpretation. What I have hoped to do in this chapter is to make clear what the central problems are, outline some of the phenomena that need to be accounted for, and point to problems and prospects for some existing proposals. In my view, the most promising accounts understand collective obligations and blameworthiness as involving the very same relations as their individual counterparts and ground both in demands on individual agents to care about morally important matters. But whether or not such accounts are ultimately successful, I hope that they help to further clarify both the phenomena and the problems they raise.

Acknowledgments

The chapter has greatly benefited from comments on earlier versions at the Moral and Practical Philosophy Seminar at UCSD, the Seminar in Practical Philosophy and Political Theory at the University of Gothenburg, and the Higher Seminar in Practical Philosophy at Stockholm University, as well as from comments by Dick Arneson, Bill Wringe, Anne Schwenkenbecher, Benjamin Matheson, Stephanie Collins, Frank Hindriks, Niels de Haan, David Copp, Olle Blomberg, Saba Bazargan-Forward, and Deborah Tollefsen.

Notes

1 This claim might seem problematic for what we might call "institutional" groups, such as committees or task forces created to fill a particular role in an organization or in society (cf. Copp 2007). But insofar as it is plausible that these are under moral obligations proper rather than merely subject to morally grounded institutional norms, I take this to be because they come close to satisfying standard requirements of moral agency.

2 I'm ignoring a complication of Collins' view here. Though she suggests that people can be charitably interpreted as conveying the sort of fact listed here when they attribute obligations to non-agential groups, she also denies that the group is, strictly speaking, an obligation bearer.

3 Strictly speaking, Schwenkenbecher talks of non-overridden reasons to we-reason, rather than obligations to do so, and restricts her account to cases where the problem cannot be solved by a single individual.

4 In a footnote, Aas (2015: 6, n. 13) says that the preparedness might come to nothing more than good character. So understood, the individual obligations he appeals to strongly resemble the caring proposal of Björnsson 2014. But in other places (pp. 13; 16; 19; 21), Aas spells out the preparedness in terms of conditional intentions. Moreover, it is central to his argument that if each individual is prepared to do their part in φ-ing if others do theirs, this counts as the group's *trying* to φ (p. 16), and this looks very implausible on a merely dispositional understanding of "preparedness."

5 Strictly speaking, the proposal is that group obligations as well as individual obligations are grounded in moral demands that individuals care. Whether these demands are best thought of as obligations is a further question.

6 While allowing for a variety of normative views, the concept captured by OBLIGATION is not the only one that we might be concerned with. It is not a concept of objective, information-independent obligations of the sort that concern at least some normative theorists, but rather a concept of what we are required to do in light of available evidence. More generally, it makes agents' morally substandard caring the only thing that can prevent them from discharging their obligations, and is thus not the one we have in mind when thinking that a failure to discharge an obligation is morally innocent, due to excusing factors. I focus on this particular concept because I take it to be both central to everyday thinking about obligations and relatively simple. For its relation to some other notions of obligation, see Björnsson Forthcoming.

7 Aas (2015: 17–19) provides a structurally similar account, but in terms of the group's "trying" to discharge its obligation, without any normality requirement, and only requiring that such trying should make the outcome sufficiently likely. Lawford-Smith 2015 and Hindriks 2019 deny that non-agential groups can have abilities required for irreducible group obligations, but they don't consider the sort of proposal offered here. For another discussion of group abilities, see Pinkert 2014.

8 Just as circumstances might be such that the appropriate caring of all three adults ensures that all children are saved, they can be such that *the appropriate caring of all moral agents in the world* ensures the outcome, because it ensures that the three adults on the beach care. But, intuitively, the group of every moral agent in the world does not plausibly have an obligation to save all the children. Why is that? According to OBLIGATION, something can be a group's obligation only if it is something that the group would do if caring appropriately. In this case, saving the children is not something that the group of every moral agent in the world would have done if all had cared appropriately. Only the people on the beach would have been involved.

What constrains attributions of φ-ing to groups? A rough rule seems to be that acceptable attributions pick out groups whose members would be relevantly involved in producing or allowing for the activity or outcome constitutive of φ-ing if they all cared appropriately. (Doing actual work might not be required if one is relevantly intentionally related to the φ-ing: in *Plenitude*, it might make sense to say that the adults saved all the children even if one of them stands by, letting the other two do the actual work. This is not to deny that differences in kind or degree of participation can matter. It will make sense to say of the two adults who did the actual work that they saved the children, but would be at least misleading to say of a pair consisting of one of those two and the adult standing by that they did.) Moreover, attributions might be more coarse-grained if a precise identification of this group is inconvenient. For example, if the saving effort involved a large number of people on the beach, it might be natural to say that "the people on the beach" saved those adrift even if a few individuals on the beach did not participate due to bad motives or lack of capacity.

It often makes sense to attribute obligations to groups that include only some of those that would be involved if everyone cared appropriately. In a version of *Offshore Wind* where one of the adults refuses to help save all, it might make good sense to say not only that the three adults have an obligation to save all, but also that the two willing adults have such an obligation: they would do so if they cared appropriately. For *Plenitude*, such a restriction would at least be misleading, as one of the two might end up standing idly by while the other does all the work together with the third adult. (I thank Saba Bazargan-Forward and Deborah Tollefsen for pressing me on these issues.)

References

Aas, S. (2015) "Distributing Collective Obligation," *Journal of Ethics and Social Philosophy*, 9(3): 1–23.

Benjamin, M. (1976) "Can Moral Responsibility Be Collective and Nondistributive?," *Social Theory and Practice*, 4(1): 93–106.

Björnsson, G. (2011) "Joint Responsibility without Individual Control: Applying the Explanation Hypothesis," in N.A. Vincent, I. van de Poel, and J. van den Hoven (eds) *Moral Responsibility: Beyond Free Will and Determinism*, Dordrecht: Springer, 181–99.

Björnsson, G. (2014) "Essentially Shared Obligations," *Midwest Studies in Philosophy*, 38(1): 103–20.

Björnsson, G. (2017) "Explaining (Away) the Epistemic Condition on Moral Responsibility," in P. Robichaud and J.W. Wieland (eds) *Responsibility: The Epistemic Condition*, New York: Oxford University Press, 146–62.

Björnsson, G. (Forthcoming) "Individual and Shared Obligations: In Defense of the Activist's Perspective," in M. Budolfson, T. McPherson, and T. Plunkett (eds) *Philosophy and Climate Change*, Oxford: Oxford University Press.

Björnsson, G. and Brülde, B. (2017) "Normative Responsibilities: Structure and Sources," in K. Hens, D. Cutas and D. Horstkötter (eds) *Parental Responsibility in the Context of Neuroscience and Genetics*, Cham: Springer International Publishing, 13–33.
Björnsson, G. and Hess, K. (2017) "Corporate Crocodile Tears? On the Reactive Attitudes of Corporate Agents," *Philosophy and Phenomenological Research*, 94(2): 273–98.
Collins, S. (2013) "Collectives' Duties and Collectivization Duties," *Australasian Journal of Philosophy*, 91(2): 231–48.
Copp, D. (2007) "The Collective Moral Autonomy Thesis," *Journal of Social Philosophy*, 38(3): 369–88.
Dietz, A. (2016) "What We Together Ought to Do," *Ethics*, 126: 955–82.
Driver, J. (1992) "The Suberogatory," *Australasian Journal of Philosophy*, 70: 286–95.
Feinberg, J. (1968) "Collective Responsibility," *The Journal of Philosophy*, 65: 674–88.
French, P.A. (1984) *Collective and Corporate Responsibility*, New York: Columbia University Press.
Held, V. (1970) "Can a Random Collection of Individuals Be Morally Responsible?," *The Journal of Philosophy*, 67: 471–81.
Hess, K.M. (2014) "The Free Will of Corporations (and Other Collectives)," *Philosophical Studies*, 168(1): 241–60.
Hindriks, Frank (2019) "The Duty to Join Forces: When Individuals Lack Control," *The Monist*, 102: 204-20.
Isaacs, T. (2011) *Moral Responsibility in Collective Contexts*, Oxford: Oxford University Press.
Kutz, C. (2000) *Complicity*, Cambridge: Cambridge University Press.
Lawford-Smith, H. (2015) "What 'We'?," *Journal of Social Ontology*, 1(2): 225–49.
List, C. and Pettit, P. (2011) *Group Agency: The Possibility, Design, and Status of Corporate Agents*, Oxford: Oxford University Press.
May, L. (1992) *Sharing Responsibility*, Chicago: University of Chicago Press.
Miller, S. (2006) "Collective Moral Responsibility: An Individualist Account," *Midwest Studies in Philosophy*, 30(1): 176–93.
Pinkert, F. (2014) "What We Together Can (Be Required to) Do," *Midwest Studies in Philosophy*, 38(1): 187–202.
Sadler, B.J. (2006) "Shared Intentions and Shared Responsibility," *Midwest Studies in Philosophy*, 30(1): 115–44.
Sartorio, C. (2004) "How to Be Responsible for Something without Causing It," *Philosophical Perspectives*, 18(1): 315–36.
Schwenkenbecher, A. (2014) "Joint Moral Duties," *Midwest Studies in Philosophy*, 38(1): 58–74.
Schwenkenbecher, A. (2018) "Making Sense of Collective Moral Obligations: A Comparison of Existing Approaches," in K. Hess, V. Igneski, and T. Isaacs (eds) *Collectivity: Ontology, Ethics, and Social Justice*, London: Rowman & Littlefield, 109–32.
Schwenkenbecher, A. (2019) "Collective Moral Obligations: 'We-Reasoning' and the Perspective of the Deliberating Agent," *The Monist*, 102(2).
Shockley, K. (2007) "Programming Collective Control," *Journal of Social Philosophy*, 38(3): 442–55.
Silver, D. (2002) "Collective Responsibility and the Ownership of Actions," *Public Affairs Quarterly*, 16(3): 287–304.
Strawson, P.F. (1962) "Freedom and Resentment," *Proceedings of the British Academy*, 48: 187–211.
Sverdlik, S. (1987) "Collective Responsibility," *Philosophical Studies*, 51(1): 61–76.
Tollefsen, D.P. (2015) *Groups as Agents*, Cambridge, UK: John Wiley & Sons.
Wringe, B. (2010) "Global Obligations and the Agency Objection," *Ratio*, 23(2): 217–31.
Wringe, B. (2016) "Collective Obligations: Their Existence, Their Explanatory Power, and Their Supervenience on the Obligations of Individuals," *European Journal of Philosophy*, 24(2): 472–97.

10

COLLECTIVE RESPONSIBILITY AND ACTING TOGETHER

Olle Blomberg and Frank Hindriks

10.1 Introduction

When several agents act together, they do not just act in parallel. Consider two friends who are walking together. What they do is qualitatively different from what two strangers do who merely walk alongside each other. This is true even if the latter are strategically responsive to each other, trying to avoid bumping into each other, and so on (Gilbert 1990: 2–3). In the former case, there is one (shared) intentional action with several participants, each of whom is performing actions that are components of the larger whole. Each participant treats the other as a partner or a co-participant. The strangers, on the other hand, treat each other merely as agents to be kept at an appropriate distance. They perform distinct intentional actions. They are engaged in strategic interaction.

There are several carefully crafted accounts of this kind of small-scale acting together, or shared intentional action, each of which is meant to capture the intuitive difference between contrast cases of this type (for similar contrast cases, see e.g. Kutz 2000: 78; Bratman 2014: 9–10). Typically, these are presented as accounts of "shared intention," where a shared intention is whatever it is that glues the participants' contributions together and distinguishes what they do from acting in parallel.[1] Just like individuals who act alone or in parallel, people who act together are responsible for what they do. But what does this mean? And what, if any, is the moral significance of the contrast between acting together and strategic interaction?

In order to answer these questions, we investigate the connection between shared intention and collective moral responsibility and collective blameworthiness.[2] In the next section, we set out how we use some key terms and briefly rebut some skeptical arguments against the very idea of collective moral responsibility. In section 10.3, we sketch Michael Bratman's influential account of shared intention and illustrate the distinction between shared action and strategic interaction with two cases. Here, we demonstrate that collective responsibility for outcomes is not uniquely tied to shared intentional action. In section 10.4, we then go on to argue that, other things being equal, the degree to which the participants in a shared intentional wrong-doing are blameworthy is greater than when agents bring about the same wrong as a result of strategic interaction.

Our point of departure is the Strawsonian idea that the degree to which one or more agents are blameworthy depends on the quality of will they display in their actions (Strawson [1962]

2013). We observe that those who form a shared intention are more intimately involved in what they do and its consequences. More specifically, they are implicated in each other's will in a distinct way, which is in turn normally reflected in their quality of will. In cases of shared intentional wrongdoing, we show that this will typically be reflected in a greater degree of blameworthiness. Although we focus on wrongdoings, our conclusion generalizes to praiseworthiness for doing the right thing together.

10.2 The Very Idea of Collective Moral Responsibility

We focus on backward-looking moral responsibility, rather than forward-looking moral responsibilities (obligations).[3] From now on, "responsibility" refers to backward-looking moral responsibility unless otherwise stated. An agent is responsible not only for doing the wrong thing or for the bad outcomes that she brings about, but also for actions or outcomes that are morally neutral, right or good.[4] Furthermore, she can be responsible for a bad action or outcome even if she is fully excused or justified and therefore not blameworthy. We will assume, as philosophers often do, that being responsible is a threshold property, so that an agent is either responsible or not for an action or outcome.[5]

As we use it, the term "collective moral responsibility" applies whenever several agents bear moral responsibility for one and the same action or outcome.[6] We restrict ourselves to collectives that are not group agents. Even so, some philosophers regard the very idea that responsibility can be collective as suspect or incoherent.

According to Elazar Weinryb, "[o]ur idea of responsibility requires that it should be uniquely ascribed [to a single agent]" (1980: 9). If there were such a unique agent requirement, then the idea of collective responsibility would be incoherent. One motivation for the requirement regarding collective responsibility *for an action* could be a Davidsonian action ontology according to which all actions are primitive actions that can be described in various ways, for example in terms of the outcomes they are intended to bring about (Davidson [1971] 2001). An agent's primitive actions are those that she can perform directly, without intending to do anything else by means of which the primitive action is performed. Davidson takes these to be restricted to a repertoire of movements of the agent's own biological body. On this view, several agents cannot share direct responsibility for an action (Sverdlik 1987: 64–66).

Another motivation for a unique agent requirement is the claim that "only agents can act," where this is taken to imply not only that "only an agent can do any component of an action," but also that "only an agent can do any action as a whole" (Collins 2013: 235). This means that, if cooperating individuals do not form a group agent, then they cannot perform an action and, *a fortiori*, cannot bear collective responsibility for an action. If they do form a group agent on the other hand, then it is the group agent that is responsible for the action, not the group members.

However, it is incontrovertible that *an outcome or event* can nevertheless be brought about by several agents, each of whom is morally responsible for it (Zimmerman 1985: 118; Sverdlik 1987: 66–67). Each could also be blameworthy for that outcome or event. Furthermore, if one accepts, as we do, that there is such a thing as acting together, where several agents perform different components of one and the same action, then there is no reason to deny that several agents can also in principle be collectively responsible and blameworthy for shared actions.

10.3 Responsibility for Shared and Parallel Action

To discuss the moral significance of the contrast between shared intentional action and strategic interaction, we need a provisional grasp of what characterizes the former. To this end, we briefly sketch Michael Bratman's account of shared intention. This account arguably captures important core features of at least many cases of shared intentional action and we will rely on it in the rest of the chapter (for overviews of other accounts, see Alonso 2018; Tuomela 2018).

According to Bratman, several agents' shared intention plays a role in their shared activity *J* that is analogous to the role that a single agent's intention plays in her individual activity. The shared intention coordinates the participants' planning and acting in pursuit of their *J*-ing, and it structures their deliberation and bargaining concerning how to *J*. On Bratman's account, what plays this role is simply an interpersonal pattern of ordinary intentions and other individual attitudes. There is no need to posit a group agent or an intention that literally belongs to the group as such. In this sense, the account is reductive.

The core of Bratman's account is what he calls the *Intention condition*. When we have a shared intention to *J*—say, to rob a bank—then "[w]e each have intentions that we *J*; and we each intend that we *J* by way of each of our intentions that we *J* [and] by way of sub-plans that mesh" (Bratman 2014: 103). Each thus intends that the bank robbery is brought about by way of each of our intentions that we do this and by way of co-realizable sub-plans for our robbing the bank. When satisfied, this condition ensures that we treat each other as partners or co-participants. Since each of us *intends* not only that our own intention is effective, but also that the other's intention is effective, we cannot rationally also intend to bring about the intended end by way of brute coercion that bypasses the other's agency (say, I cannot intend to handcuff you to the bank's entrance door against your will, in order to delay the police). Since each of us intends our subplans to be co-realizable, we also cannot rationally intend to circumvent the execution of the other's subplan by deception (say, I cannot rationally intend that we rob the bank by my threatening the bank tellers with a handgun if I know that you intend that we rob the bank non-violently, without the use of weapons). Furthermore, if the *Intention condition* is fulfilled, then each of us will to some extent be disposed to help and support the other in doing their bit to bring about the common end if it becomes necessary (see Bratman 2014: 56–57). When the *Intention condition* is met, our individual intentions interlock.

Bratman's account of shared intention also specifies that certain supporting beliefs and facts about interdependence be in place, and that the parties have common knowledge that the *Intention condition* and the other conditions are met. If the shared intention appropriately causes and coordinates the action that is performed together, then it is a "shared intentional activity" according to Bratman, which is a particularly robust form of shared intentional action.

Bratman only claims that his conditions are jointly sufficient for shared intention, but the *Intention condition* should arguably be taken as a proposed necessary condition. It is this condition that ensures that shared intentional activity is a minimal form of intentional cooperation with respect to the participants' common end.[7]

Now, consider the case of us robbing the bank and its customers together and a contrast case where we bring about the same outcome as a result of strategic interaction:

> *Shared robbery*: You and I form a shared intention to rob a bank and its customers. Acting on our shared intention, I point a gun at the bank tellers and force them to hand over the money. You point a gun at the customers in the waiting area forcing them to hand over their jewelry and smartphones. As a result, we jointly intentionally rob the bank and the customers.

> *Parallel robberies*: You and I are two independent robbers who each stake out the same bank. I plan to get the money from behind the counter, while you plan to rob the customers. However, neither of us proceeds because of the risks we each run on our own. The customers are likely to overpower me when I threaten the bank tellers, and

> the bank employees are likely to warn the police when you threaten the customers. Our chances of success would therefore be significantly higher if we acted simultaneously. As it happens, we each notice the other staking out the bank and we each realize what the other's plan is (suppose each has earlier overheard the other talking about the possibility of robbing the bank/customers). Expecting the other to follow suit, I form an intention to rob the bank and you form an intention to rob the customers. Acting on my intention, I enter the bank and start to threaten the bank tellers. Acting on your intention, you follow suit and start to threaten the customers. As a result, I rob the bank intentionally and you rob the customers intentionally. Because of the interdependence between our actions, my robbery of the bank and your robbery of the customers are both collective effects of our combined actions.

In *Shared robbery*, that we rob the bank and the customers—"that we *J*," in Bratman's account—is a common end that we are tracking together in virtue of our shared intention. In *Parallel robberies*, only I have the end that the bank is robbed as a combined result of our actions, while only you have the end that the customers are robbed as the combined result of those same actions. Of course, if we had the opportunity to communicate in *Parallel robberies*, it is likely that we would acquire or form a shared intention to rob the bank and the customers, making our actions part of one shared intentional robbery. But suppose we do not.

A moment's reflection on these cases shows that in both cases you and I are collectively responsible for the outcome. In both *Shared robbery* and *Parallel robberies* each of us is clearly morally responsible and blameworthy for the bank and the customers being robbed. Because of our awareness of the interdependence of choices and actions in *Parallel robberies*, each of us knowingly brings about—has control over—not merely our own intended end, but also the other's distinct intended end. If knowingly bringing about an outcome is sufficient to intentionally bring it about, then each also intentionally brings it about that both the bank and the customers are robbed in *Parallel robberies*. In *Shared robbery*, we each have a similar kind of awareness of and control over the total outcome, but in addition each intends that the total outcome is brought about. It follows that shared intentional action, while sufficient for collective responsibility, is not necessary for it.

According to Bratman, a shared intention can play a "linking role" that "may make us each in some way responsible for the shared activity that ensues, and not just each individually responsible for our specific contribution [...]" (1997: 32). What *Parallel robberies* shows is that a very similar linking role can be played by our awareness of the situation and our strategic intentions. A shared intention is not necessary for agents to be collectively responsible for the collective effect of their combined actions.

Contrary to what some philosophers have assumed then, there is no essential or necessary connection between shared intentional action and collective responsibility for outcomes. Seumas Miller is mistaken when he submits that what we call collective responsibility "presupposes, and is heavily reliant on, the notion of joint [intentional] action" (2001: 234). Similarly, in light of examples of what seems to be shared intentional wrongdoing, Steven Sverdlik first correctly submits that "each is responsible for the result precisely *because* each is responsible for an action aiming at this result" (1987: 67). But he then goes on to mistakenly claim that "it is *only* when more than one person intends the result that responsibility for it is collective" (1987: 67).[8]

It is telling that the few accounts of "shared intention" that have been explicitly developed to make sense of collective responsibility—and not to understand shared agency as such—in fact do *not* require the parties to each intend the result for which they may end up being collectively responsible. For example, Brook Sadler's account of shared intention allows for cases where the participants "do not see their respective actions as contributing toward a common goal or activity" (2006: 126). Similarly, on Christopher Kutz's account, "a set of individuals can jointly intentionally G even though some, and perhaps all, [...] do not even intend to contribute to G, but only know their actions are likely to contribute to its occurrence" (2000: 103; for discussion, see Blomberg 2016b: section 3).

However, the fact that we are collectively responsible for the outcome in both *Shared robbery* and *Parallel robberies* does not imply that our blameworthiness for bringing about the outcome is the same. In the next section, we consider two possible arguments for the idea that—other things being equal—agents are more blameworthy for shared intentional wrongdoing than for intentional wrongdoing that is the result of parallel action.[9]

10.4 Collective Blameworthiness and Shared Intentional Action

So far, we have argued that agents can be collectively responsible for an action or an outcome. We have also shown that they can be collectively responsible for an outcome even if it is not the result of their shared intentional action. The question remains, however, whether there is anything distinctive about collective blameworthiness in cases where the agents act together rather than in parallel. Corresponding to our use of the term "collective moral responsibility," several agents are collectively blameworthy for an action or outcome when each is blameworthy for that action or outcome.

It is sometimes assumed that an outcome or action is associated with a fixed amount of blameworthiness such that it would have to be divided and distributed in cases of collective blameworthiness (see e.g. Cohen 1981: 73). However, there is good reason to reject such a "pie model" of collective blameworthiness. If doing arithmetic with different agents' blameworthiness makes any sense, then the blameworthiness should be multiplied rather than divided in cases of collective blameworthiness. In other words, the involvement of others' agency in bringing about a bad outcome does not itself decrease or dilute—nor increase or concentrate—an agent's blameworthiness for bringing about that outcome.[10] Consider a case where I intentionally bring about a bad outcome together with other agents. Now, replace those other agents with non-agential contributing causal factors (say, advanced robotic devices), but keep my intention and contribution fixed. There seems to be no reason why I would be any less or more blameworthy in the former case than in the latter just because some of the contributing causal factors happen to be other intentional agents rather than advanced robotic devices (for this argumentative strategy, see Mellema 1985: 182–183; Zimmerman 1985: 116–117; Sverdlik 1987: 72).

So, the fact that other agents are causally involved does not in itself diminish or increase an agent's blameworthiness. It could still be, however, that the fact that individuals act on a shared intention to do wrong is significant for their degree of blameworthiness. Doing the wrong thing together rather than in parallel somehow seems to make it worse. At the same time, however, this intuition is not very strong. Some people we have presented our contrast cases to share our intuition that you and I are more blameworthy in *Shared robbery* than in *Parallel robberies*. Others, however, have had no such intuition. Furthermore, even if there were a clear uncontroversial intuitive difference in blameworthiness between these particular contrast cases, theoretical arguments would still be needed for showing that a shared intention contributes to a greater blameworthiness for wrongdoing in other contrast cases.

There are at least two ways in which one might try to support the intuition. The first focuses on a causal difference between shared and parallel action, the second on a volitional difference. The causal difference is that, due to the fact that individual intentions interlock, shared intentions cause actions in a less sensitive (that is, more robust) manner. We argue, however, that this in itself is not significant, because moral blameworthiness always implicates the will: the degree to which an agent is blameworthy depends on the quality of will she displays in her actions, and the quality of the agent's will is partly reflected in the intentions that an agent forms, retains and acts on. We therefore go on to consider the idea that the fact that agents have formed a shared intention to do something wrong normally reveals something distinctive about the quality of their wills. The idea is that there is also a volitional difference between shared and parallel action: in the case of shared actions the agents are mutually implicated in each other's will in a distinct way. We argue that, other things being equal, this typically makes them more blameworthy for the wrong they do.

Before considering the two arguments in the sub-sections that follow, a potential methodological worry should be addressed. One might think that it is possible to eliminate any proposed blameworthiness-relevant difference between cases such as *Shared robbery* and *Parallel robberies* by removing ingredients from the former case or by adding ingredients to the latter case. It is not obvious that such manipulation would undermine the contrast between shared intentional wrongdoing and bringing about the same result by strategic interaction. For example, our robbery in *Shared robbery* could arguably be jointly intentional even if we lacked common knowledge that we had the intentions required by Bratman's *Intention condition* (see Blomberg 2016a). As we have noted, Bratman's conditions are presented as jointly sufficient conditions, not also as individually necessary. Or we might add to the *Parallel robberies* case that each of us has a general disposition to be helpful to other robbers, say. Or add that each intends that the other's intention be effective, but retain the feature that there is no common end. This will be possible given any reductive account such as Bratman's, which is constructed out of multiple components (a common end, interlocking intentions, common knowledge that there is the common end and the interlocking intentions, etc.). The worry then is how we in the end will know that the blameworthy-relevant feature that we focus on is one that is always present in cases of shared intentional wrongdoing but never in cases of parallel wrongdoing.

The argument that we put forward in section 10.4.2, however, turns on Bratman's *Intention condition*, which, as we have noted, is arguably a necessary condition in Bratman's set of jointly sufficient conditions. It may be true though, that acting together is not a unified phenomenon, so perhaps our argument only applies to a certain kind of shared intentional wrongdoing.[11] Furthermore, it is possible that shared intentional wrongdoing of this particular kind is multiply realizable (Bratman 2014: 36). Hence, we cannot rule out that some ingredients could be changed or added to *Parallel robberies* to transform it into a case of shared intentional wrongdoing of this kind even if Bratman's *Intention condition* were not satisfied. But if this were done, then it is reasonable to expect that these ingredients would be such that they could also support the argument we put forward.

10.4.1 Shared Intention, Insensitive Causation and Predictive Significance

Suppose that, in one case, an innocent person is shot and killed by a skilled sniper, whereas, in another case, the shooter is a clumsy and unskilled marksman who hits and kills the target anyway. We can imagine the marksman appropriately saying "But I didn't think I'd succeed!" when blamed—an excuse that would be unavailable to the sniper. Now, one difference between the two cases is that the sensitivity of the causal pathway between the marksman's intention to shoot and kill the victim and the intended outcome is much higher than that of the causal pathway between the sniper's corresponding intention and the intended outcome. C_1 causes E_1 less sensitively—or more insensitively/robustly—than C_2 causes E_2 if the range of nearby counterfactual circumstances in which C_1 would cause E_1 is wider than that in which C_2 would cause E_2 (Lewis 1986; Woodward 2006). So, one might think that less sensitive causation generally increases blameworthiness. Arguably this idea has some intuitive pull at first glance.

This intuition can be bolstered by considering the fact that, compared to the marksman's intention, that of the sniper has higher "predictive significance" with respect to the intended outcome (Scanlon 2008: 13; see also Foot [1967] 1978: 23–24). One might think that this makes the sniper's action more wrongful than the marksman's, thus indirectly increasing the former's blameworthiness (Scanlon 2008: 31–32, 41–43). Suppose you are in a position to hire either the sniper or the marksman to indirectly kill the target. While both options are morally wrong, it may intuitively seem like hiring the sniper is morally worse, precisely because you know that it will lead to the bad outcome under a wider range of possible circumstances (and you are unaware of exactly what the actual circumstances are or will be). If the victim is killed, you would then be more blameworthy if the shooter were the sniper than if he were the marksman.

Chiara Lepora and Robert Goodin embrace a similar idea when they argue that a higher degree of prospectively known causal insensitivity between a secondary agent's act of complicity and the wrongdoing coming about increases his blameworthiness for the complicit act (2013: 66–68, 102–112).[12] They take such causal insensitivity to be an independent factor that increases blameworthiness directly, not a factor that indirectly increases blameworthiness by making the act of complicity more wrongful. Other things being equal, the wider the range of counterfactual circumstances in which the secondary agent knows that his contribution would make a difference to whether the wrongdoing comes about or not, the more blameworthy the secondary agent is.[13] Thus, it is the insensitivity that the secondary agent was prospectively aware of that matters: "[Morality] evaluates our action retrospectively only in light of what could and should have been expected to occur, at the time we had to act" (Lepora & Goodin 2013: 68). Hence, according to Lepora and Goodin, the predictive significance of an agent's intentions or actions is directly relevant to blameworthiness. While they explicitly restrict this proposal to the blameworthiness of secondary agents in cases of complicity, there is no reason why it wouldn't also apply to the blameworthiness of "co-principals" in shared intentional wrongdoing.

Other things being equal, a shared intentional action will cause the (jointly) intended result in a more insensitive manner than a parallel activity will cause the (severally) intended result. For example, the causal pathway from our shared intention to the robbery of the bank and the customers in *Shared robbery* is less sensitive to changes in circumstances than that from the strategic intentions to the robbery of the bank and the customers in *Parallel robberies*. Suppose that one of the bank tellers has a panic attack and as a result it takes her a long time to get hold of the money. If this happens in *Parallel robberies*, then you might collect all the jewelry and smartphones and leave the scene before the bank tellers have managed to hand over the money, leaving the customers to attack and overpower me. Since you don't really care about whether my robbery succeeds as such—as long as the bank tellers are prevented from warning the police—you have no reason to help me keep the customers at a safe distance once you are done robbing them. By contrast, in *Shared robbery* we both intend that we succeed in robbing the bank and in robbing the customers. If each intends that we do this by way of both our own and the other's intention, then each will also be disposed to help the other in bringing about the intended result in a wider range of nearby counterfactual circumstances.

On Bratman's account, we have common knowledge of our intentions when we have a shared intention. Hence, we will prospectively be aware in *Shared robbery* that the probability that we succeed is relatively high. We are aware that, if we succeed, then the robbery will have been brought about with a relatively high degree of insensitivity. Our shared intention in *Shared robbery* will have higher predictive significance than our strategic intentions in *Parallel robberies*.

Hence, if the bank tellers and the customers were to discover in advance what our intentions were, then they would think their situation worse in the shared case than in the parallel case.[14]

On the proposal under consideration, our shared intention not only makes the jointly produced outcome worse from the victims' point of view, each of us is also more blameworthy in *Shared robbery* than in *Parallel robberies*, both for the robbery of the bank and for the robbery of the customers. In particular, each is more blameworthy even for the outcome that we individually intended to bring about in *Parallel robberies*. This is because we would know that our shared intention in *Shared robbery* would cause that outcome under a range of nearby counterfactual circumstances that is wider than that under which our strategic intentions would cause that outcome in *Parallel robberies*.

Thus far, the claim has been that what is doing the work is the known insensitivity of the causal relation. It is far from obvious, however, that this is the case. Moral responsibility and blameworthiness are distinct from causal responsibility in that they implicate the will. As it turns out, the intuitions at issue can be better explained in terms of motives rather than causes. Consider first the case where you hire either a skilled sniper or a clumsy marksman to assassinate an innocent person. Arguably, it seems morally worse to hire the sniper because this would normally reflect a worse quality of will than in hiring the marksman. In other words, an insensitive causal pathway between intention and outcome will typically be (defeasible) evidence for a worse quality of will. To illustrate, you would normally have to pay a higher cost for the services of the sniper, which would suggest stronger determination on your part. If his services were offered at the same price, then hiring the marksman would suggest some ambivalence on your part, as if part of you wanted the shot to miss. Such a quality of will explanation undermines the motivation for thinking that the known insensitivity of causation is itself relevant to wrongfulness or blameworthiness.

Now, focus only on the role of the sniper/marksman and the victim. If the sniper's and the marksman's desire and intent to hit and kill the target are the same, then the insensitivity of the causal pathway to the victim's being killed arguably does not itself make a difference to blameworthiness.[15] The clumsy marksman's "But I didn't think I'd succeed!" would not function as an excuse if it were merely a comment about his own view of his probability of success. To be taken as an excuse, it would have to be pragmatically interpreted as a claim that he didn't actually want or intend to hit and kill (that is, a claim directly relevant to what the quality of his will was). Indeed, this seems to be the commonsense view. Results from experimental philosophy suggest that ordinary people's judgments about blameworthiness are not sensitive to the skill level of a shooter who intentionally kills an innocent victim (see Sousa & Holbrook 2010; Sousa et al. 2015).

All this also applies in cases of shared intentional wrongdoing. We are not more blameworthy for the bad outcome in *Shared robbery* than in *Parallel robberies* in virtue of the fact that the causal pathway from our intentions to the outcome is more insensitive in the former case than in the latter. Nor are we more blameworthy in virtue of our prospective awareness of this causal insensitivity. Upon being blamed by a third person for robbing the bank in *Parallel robberies*, I wouldn't be giving a valid (partial) excuse if I pointed out that I might not have succeeded if you had collected the jewelry and smartphones quickly and left early.

One might argue that it is different with respect to the foreseen but unintended side-effect that I bring about in *Parallel robberies*. If I am blamed for bringing it about that you robbed the customers, then I might be giving a valid partial excuse if I pointed out that you might not have succeeded in robbing them if I had been really quick in robbing the bank. But again, this is because (and only insofar as) it is evidence of a quality of will that manifested itself in my behavior. There is such a difference: Other things being equal, one manifests a worse quality of will if one acts on an intention to bring about an outcome that one knows to be bad than if one merely acts with the awareness that the bad outcome is likely to be brought about as an unintended side-effect of what one intends to do. Of course, if other aspects of my will varied between the cases, then this might not be true (for example, suppose that I strongly desire that you successfully rob the customers in *Parallel robberies* but not in *Shared robbery*).

This does not mean that insensitivity of causation is completely irrelevant to whether agents are collectively blameworthy for a bad outcome. Plausibly, for the bad quality of the agents' wills to be relevant to their collective blameworthiness for the outcome, the quality of these wills has to be such that it plays a role in normally explaining why such bad outcomes come about (see e.g. Björnsson & Persson 2012). It is plausible that this requires that some threshold of insensitivity of causation is passed. However, this does not mean that the difference in the sensitivity of the causal process in contrast cases such as *Shared robbery* and *Parallel robberies* explains a difference in degree of collective blameworthiness.

10.4.2 Shared Intention and Quality of Will

As we have noted, the intentions that an agent is acting on at least reflects the quality of her will. As Bratman points out, the fact that action is carried out as part of some larger plan "might constitute or indicate a *deeper level of commitment* to the action," and this at least partly explains the concern with premeditation in criminal law (1997: 31–32). The fact that a person commits to and plans to bring about an outcome is in most circumstances at least strong evidence that she cares about and desires that this outcome be brought about. Thus, when a morally bad outcome is intentionally brought about, then the fact that the agent had a prior intention to bring it about normally indicates something about her quality of will which makes her more blameworthy than if she did not have the intention. This explains why, in *Parallel robberies*, I would normally be somewhat more blameworthy than you for the robbery of the bank while you would be somewhat more blameworthy than I for the robbery of the customers.

However, forming an intention to do something wrong may not merely reflect a deeper underlying commitment to wrongdoing, the forming of the intention can also constitute an additional wrongdoing. Consider the case of a single agent who performs a morally bad action. She can perform it spontaneously in a way that is isolated from any prior activity or plan. She might immediately and spontaneously reveal an intimate secret about an acquaintance to others out of spite, for example. Alternatively, the telling of the secret might be the result of prior commitment and planning. Suppose the spiteful person committed and planned ahead of time exactly when, to whom and how to reveal the secret. Here, the spiteful pre-committed planner has arguably made herself complicit in her own wrongdoing. She not only intends to perform an action that is morally bad, but she also formed and retained an intention that her future self's intention appropriately brings about and coordinates this morally bad action. Normally, this would make her more blameworthy for revealing the secret. She will be blameworthy for it both in virtue of intentionally performing the action and more blameworthy for it in virtue of earlier forming the intention to perform it and retaining that intention. Now, this is not invariably the case, since forming an intention to do something bad might involve ruling out an alternative course of action that is even worse. Furthermore, sometimes intentions are passively acquired and immediately executed rather than formed prior to the time of action (Mele & Moser 1994: 45). But in most contexts where the agent formed an intention to do something bad, this makes her more blameworthy than she would be if she did the bad thing without having formed the prior intention.

A natural thought is that what is special about shared intentional wrongdoing is that, by analogy, there is a shared will in which all the participants are mutually implicated, normally leading to a greater degree of blameworthiness than in otherwise similar cases of parallel wrongdoing.[16] First, that I go out of my way to form a shared intention with you in a case such as *Shared robbery* would normally reflect a deeper concern for the banks and customers being robbed or a stronger desire for us to succeed than I would have in a case such as *Parallel robberies*. Hence, the presence of a shared intention normally reflects underlying desires, concerns or value judgments that are relevant for blameworthiness in cases of wrongdoing. Each of us would thus normally be more deeply committed to the intentional achievement of the morally bad outcome in *Shared robbery* than in *Parallel robberies*, where this includes both the outcome that the bank is robbed and the outcome that the customers are robbed. Second, recall that the intentions of participants are bound together in shared intentional wrongdoing in a special way. It is not only that their intentions converge on a morally bad common end. On Bratman's account, each also intends that both their own and the others' intentions to bring about that common end are effective.

Due to the way the participants' intentions are interlocked, each is implicated in the wrongdoing not only due to the fact that their own intention is aimed at the bad outcome, but also due to the fact that they formed intentions aimed at the satisfaction of the other participants' intentions to bring about the bad outcome. When these interlocking intentions are formed, retained and successfully executed, each will be complicit in the other's wrongdoing as well as responsible for their own contribution to their own intended wrongdoing. Each of the participants in shared intentional wrongdoing not only brings about the intended bad outcome, each also brings it about that their own and the others' intentions to bring about this bad outcome are formed, retained and successfully executed. When we each do our part of jointly intentionally robbing the bank and the customers in *Shared robbery*, each does this in the awareness that we are supporting and satisfying the other's intention that our own intention effectively brings about the morally bad common end. In addition, we are each indirectly supporting our own intention that the other's intention effectively brings about that same end. Crucially, each of us formed intentions that *two* intentions rather than merely one intention be directed toward the morally bad outcome and successfully executed. Each is furthermore arguably aware that the morally bad outcome is such that the intention of each of us is directed to it (Blomberg 2016b). In *Parallel robberies*, each merely intends that one intention, our own, successfully brings about our own intended bad outcome. As in the individual case, this normally (but not invariably) reflects a worse quality of will, which in most circumstances will make participants more blameworthy than they would be in a contrast case where they bring about the same bad outcome as a result of strategic interaction.

There is one final question we need to address. Thus far, we have focused on Bratman's reductive account of acting together. But does our argument generalize to non-reductive accounts? While we cannot discuss this in depth here, it seems plausible that it is compatible with accounts of shared intention such as Margaret Gilbert's (1990, 2008) and Raimo Tuomela's (2007). On their accounts, shared intention involves an irreducibly joint or collective commitment that glues group members together with respect to some joint action. As Gilbert puts it, when several agents have a shared intention to bring about some goal, then there is "a pool of wills which is dedicated, as one, to that goal" (1990: 7).

If there is a joint or collective commitment to do something morally bad then this is normally an important fact that reveals something about the quality of the wills of the parties to this joint or collective commitment. Furthermore, insofar as the joint or collective commitment is formed by parties rather than passively acquired, forming it constitutes a further wrongdoing in virtue of which the parties become complicit in the morally bad action that ensues. Arguably, the parties will then normally be blameworthy not only due to their individual commitments to do their parts, but also to the way they pooled or united their individual commitments in a joint or collective commitment. Thus, our argument generalizes from Bratman's reductive account to non-reductive accounts of shared intentions.

10.5 Conclusions

With shared action comes collective responsibility. And blameworthiness for shared intentional wrongdoing is normally greater than that of people who do the same wrong as a result of strategic interaction. The reason for this is that, when several agents form, retain, and successfully execute a shared intention to do wrong, their ill wills become mutually implicated in each other in a distinct way. Each is implicated in the wrongdoing not only because his intention is directed at the bad outcome, but also because his intention is directed at the other participants' intentions being effective. Our reactive attitudes and judgments of blameworthiness should be sensitive to this distinct kind of mutual implication of ill wills. Hence, other things being equal, agents who have a shared intention to do wrong are normally more blameworthy than agents who intentionally bring about the same wrong as the result of acting in parallel on merely strategic intentions.

Acknowledgments

We are grateful for questions and comments from Saba Bazargan-Forward, Gunnar Björnsson, Stephanie Collins, Mattias Gunnemyr, Niels de Haan, Marta Johansson, Benjamin Kiesewetter, Björn Petersson, Wlodek Rabinowicz, Paul Russell, Thomas Schmidt, András Szigeti, Matthew Talbert, Deborah Tollefsen, Caroline Touborg, and the participants at the workshop on collective responsibility that was held in Jyväskylä, Finland, December 4–5, 2015. Olle Blomberg's research was funded by project grant 421–2014–1025 from Vetenskapsrådet (the Swedish Research Council).

Notes

1 Sometimes the label used is "joint intention" or "collective intention" and, correspondingly, "joint intentional action" or "collective intentional action."
2 Surprisingly little has been written about the connection between shared intention and collective moral responsibility and collective blameworthiness. The most relevant references are: Bratman (1997), Kutz (2000: chapters 4–5), Miller (2001: chapter 8), Sadler (2006), Tuomela (2007: chapter 10), Isaacs (2006, 2011: chapter 4), and Giubilini and Levy (2018).
3 On forward-looking collective moral responsibility, see e.g. Björnsson (2014) and Hindriks (2019).
4 Talk of *moral* responsibility for a morally neutral action such as raising one's arm (in a context where this has no effect on any other agent) may sound odd and unusual. This is because, in everyday life, the issue of whether someone is responsible for an action will typically only arise when blame or praise is actually in the offing. Moral responsibility for morally neutral actions is not mere causal responsibility, as it requires that the agent is psychologically related to the action in the right way.
5 Why assume that being responsible is a threshold property? The primary question is whether or not an agent is a candidate for some kind of response, say, an appropriate target of our reactive attitudes. A vague or gradable property would not be of much help here. However, this does not exclude that components of moral responsibility such as voluntariness or reason-responsiveness can come in degrees. The degree to which these components are present can furthermore help determine an agent's degree of blameworthiness once thresholds for moral responsibility have been passed.
6 This is one of Joel Feinberg's (1968) uses of the term "collective responsibility" in his seminal paper on the topic. See also Steven Sverdlik (1987). Another term that is sometimes used is "shared responsibility" (Mellema 1985; Zimmerman 1985).

7 Kirk Ludwig's (2016) reductive account of shared intention includes a necessary condition that is similar to Bratman's *Intention condition*. According to Ludwig, each party to a shared intention must, roughly, intend to bring about that they are all agents of an event that they bring about in accordance with a shared plan.

8 Sverdlik later modifies the claim that it is only when a result is intended by several agents that responsibility for it is collective. This is because there can be collective responsibility due to collective negligence, such as when "a team of surgeons negligently leaves a sponge in a patient" (Sverdlik 1987: 69). However, note that this is nevertheless plausibly interpreted as a case where several agents perform a shared intentional action. The other cases that Sverdlik discusses are similar in this respect.

9 Tracy Isaacs (2011) argues that a reductive account of shared intention cannot make sense of the blameworthiness of shared intentional wrongdoing such as that in *Shared robbery*. A key premise of her argument is that participants can only intend their own contribution; only a group agent can intend the shared action ("that we *J*") (Isaacs 2011: 39–40). Given that full blameworthiness of an agent for an action requires that the agent intended to perform the action, and that no participant can intend the shared action, "the collective act is not adequately accounted for by individual assessments of moral responsibility [blameworthiness]" (Isaacs 2011: 57). Since we think that individual intentions "that we *J*" are possible as well as commonplace (see Bratman 2014: 60–64; Ludwig 2016: 207–210), we do not accept this argument.

10 Larry May (1992: 112–114) defends a kind of "dilutionism" concerning blameworthiness in the context of collective omissions by appealing to the socio-psychological phenomenon of the Bystander Effect (see Fischer et al. 2011). However, this is not a defense of the view that the mere fact that other agents are involved itself leads to a dilution of blameworthiness.

11 The argument we put forward in section 10.4.2 relies on shared intention involving interlocking second-order intentions, or perhaps irreducibly joint or collective commitments. Not all accounts of shared intention involve or entail such elements though. Accounts lacking both these elements are given, for example, by Kutz (2000), Miller (2001), and Pacherie (2013).

12 Lepora and Goodin (2013) put the idea in terms of "counterfactual individual difference-making" and "centrality" rather than in terms of the insensitivity of the causal pathway.

13 Without endorsing it, Gregory Mellema characterizes what might be a similar idea according to which, "when the actions of the participants in a scheme of wrongdoing are well integrated, then they are more likely to contribute more effectively to an outcome and the participants deserve more blame" (2016: 114). To what extent it is similar depends on what Mellema means by "more effectively" here.

14 As Abraham Sesshu Roth (2016) remarks regarding an imagined paranoid conspiracy theorist: "[H]e does get right that it certainly would be awful, for example, if everyone were out to get him and were working together to do so. After all, the stability and impact of agency that's shared can be expected to be more serious than the effects of a mere collection of individual acts."

15 This is not to deny that the insensitivity of causation must be above some minimal threshold in order for an agent's causing death to amount to *killing* (see Lewis 1986).

16 As we mentioned in section 10.3, Bratman argues that shared intention can play a "linking role" that makes each responsible for the shared intentional action and not only his own contribution to it. He takes this to be analogous to the way in which a larger plan can link a single agent's past, present, and future conduct. What we argue is that there is a further analogy between the individual and the shared case. For other discussions that draw on similar analogies between individual and shared cases, see Mellema (2016: chapter 9) and Scanlon (2008: 41–43).

References

Alonso, F. M. (2018) "Reductive Views of Shared Intention," in M. Jankovic and K. Ludwig (eds.), *The Routledge Handbook of Collective Intentionality*, Routledge: 34–44.

Björnsson, G. (2014) "Essentially Shared Obligations," *Midwest Studies in Philosophy* 38 (1): 103–120.

Björnsson, G. & Persson, K. (2012) "The Explanatory Component of Moral Responsibility," *Nous* 46 (2): 326–354.

Blomberg, O. (2016a) "Common Knowledge and Reductionism about Shared Agency," *Australasian Journal of Philosophy* 94 (2): 315–326.

Blomberg, O. (2016b) "Shared Intention and the Doxastic Single End Condition," *Philosophical Studies* 173 (2): 351–372.

Bratman, M. E. (1997) "Responsibility and Planning," *The Journal of Ethics* 1 (1): 27–43.

Bratman, M. E. (2014) *Shared Agency: A Planning Theory of Acting Together*. Oxford University Press.
Cohen, L. J. (1981) "Who is starving whom?," *Theoria* 47 (2): 65–81.
Collins, S. (2013) "Collectives' Duties and Collectivization Duties," *Australasian Journal of Philosophy* 91 (2): 231–248.
Davidson, D. ([1971] 2001) "Agency," in *Essays on Actions and Events* (2nd ed.), New York: Clarendon Press: 43–62. Originally published in Ausonio Marras, R. N. Bronaugh & Robert W. Binkley (eds.), *Agent, Action, and Reason*. University of Toronto Press: 1–37 (1971).
Feinberg, J. (1968) "Collective Responsibility," *Journal of Philosophy* 65 (21): 674–688.
Fischer, P., Krueger, J. I., Greitemeyer, T., Vogrincic, C., Kastenmüller, A., Frey, D., et al. (2011). "The Bystander-Effect: A Meta-Analytic Review on Bystander Intervention in Dangerous and Non-Dangerous Emergencies," *Psychological Bulletin* 137 (4): 517–537.
Foot, P. ([1967] 1978) "The Problem of Abortion and the Doctrine of the Double Effect," in *Virtues and Vices and Other Essays in Moral Philosophy*. Berkeley: University of California Press, 1978: 19–32. Originally published in *Oxford Review* 5: 5–15 (1967).
Gilbert, M. (1990) "Walking Together: A Paradigmatic Social Phenomenon," *Midwest Studies in Philosophy* 15 (1): 1–14.
Gilbert, M. (2008) "Two Approaches to Shared Intention: An Essay in the Philosophy of Social Phenomena," *Analyse & Kritik* 30 (2): 483–514.
Giubilini, A. & Levy, N. (2018) "What in the World is Collective Responsibility?" *Dialectica* 72 (2): 191–217.
Hindriks, F. (2019) "The Duty to Join Forces: When Individuals Lack Control," *Monist* 102 (2): 204–220.
Isaacs, T. (2006) "Collective Moral Responsibility and Collective Intention," *Midwest Studies in Philosophy* 30 (1): 59–73.
Isaacs, T. (2011) *Moral Responsibility in Collective Contexts*. Oxford University Press.
Kutz, C. (2000) *Complicity: Ethics and Law for a Collective Age*. Cambridge University Press.
Lepora, C. & Goodin, R. (2013) *On Complicity and Compromise*. Oxford University Press.
Lewis, D. (1986) "Postscript C to 'Causation': (Insensitive Causation)," in *Philosophical Papers: Volume 2*. Oxford University Press: 184–188.
Ludwig, K. (2016) *From Individual to Plural Agency: Collectve Action (vol. 1)*. Oxford University Press.
May, L. (1992) *Sharing Responsibility*. University of Chicago Press.
Mele, A. R. & Moser, P. K. (1994) "Intentional Action," *Nous* 28 (1): 39–68.
Mellema, G. (1985) "Shared Responsibility and Ethical Dilutionism," *Australasian Journal of Philosophy* 63 (2): 177–187.
Mellema, G. (2016) *Complicity and Moral Accountability*. University of Notre Dame Press.
Miller, S. (2001) *Social Action: A Teleological Account*. Cambridge University Press.
Pacherie, E. (2013) "Intentional Joint Agency: Shared Intention Lite," *Synthese* 190 (10): 1817–1839.
Roth, A. S. (2016) "Shared Agency," in Edward N. Zalta (ed.), *The Stanford Encyclopedia of Philosophy (Winter 2016 Edition)*, https://plato.stanford.edu/archives/win2016/entries/shared-agency/.
Sadler, B. J. (2006) "Shared Intentions and Shared Responsibility," *Midwest Studies in Philosophy* 30 (1): 115–144.
Scanlon, T. M. (2008) *Moral Dimensions: Permissibility, Meaning, Blame*. Harvard University Press.
Sousa, P. & Holbrook, C. (2010) "Folk Concepts of Intentional Action in the Contexts of Amoral and Immoral Luck," *Review of Philosophy and Psychology* 1 (3): 351–370.
Sousa, P., Holbrook, C. & Swiney, L. (2015) "Moral Asymmetries in Judgments of Agency Withstand Ludicrous Causal Deviance," *Frontiers in Psychology* 6 (1380): 1–11.
Strawson, P. F. ([1962] 2013) "Freedom and Resentment," in P. Russell and O. Deery (eds.), *The Philosophy of Free Will: Essential Readings from the Contemporary Debates*. Oxford University Press: 63–83. Originally published *Proceedings of the British Academy* 48: 1–25 (1962).
Sverdlik, S. (1987) "Collective Responsibility," *Philosophical Studies* 51 (1): 61–76.
Tuomela, R. (2007) *The Philosophy of Sociality: The Shared Point of View*. Oxford University Press.
Tuomela, R. (2018) "Non-Reductive Views of Shared Intention," M. Jankovic and K. Ludwig (eds.), *The Routledge Handbook of Collective Intentionality*, Routledge: 25–33.
Weinryb, E. (1980) "Omissions and Responsibility," *The Philosophical Quarterly* 30 (118): 1–18.
Woodward, J. (2006) "Sensitive and Insensitive Causation," *The Philosophical Review* 115 (1): 1–50.
Zimmerman, M. J. (1985) "Sharing Responsibility," *American Philosophical Quarterly* 22 (2): 115–112.

PART II

Theoretical Issues in Collective Responsibility

The articles in Part II delve deeper into a variety of theoretical issues within the domain of collective responsibility. One such issue concerns collective inaction or omission—the failure of a group to act. Should individuals who are capable of forming a group but fail to do so be responsible for the harms that that potential group could have prevented or rectified? Are bystanders responsible for not acting to prevent harms committed by a group?

Another important issue discussed in Part II is that of complicity. Are group members complicit in the actions of the group to which they belong? How can an individual bear responsibility for what the group of which she is a part does when she has limited to no control over the conduct of that group? Pinning responsibility for what the group does on any marginally contributing individual seems to violate a basic principle of ethics that says that an individual can only be morally responsible for events within her causal reach.

Other topics covered in Part II include: the possibility of group emotions such as guilt and their relation to collective responsibility, the concept of a commitment and its role in joint action and responsibility, collective obligation, and the possibility that groups are self-aware.

In Chapter 11, Gregory Mellema assumes that collectives are capable of being the bearer of moral responsibility and asks who are the moral agents that constitute such collectives and whether such individuals are complicit in the actions of the collective and actions of individuals within the collective. Although complicity and collective responsibility often intersect, they need not. Mellema argues that exploring the differences between the anatomy of a collective and the anatomy of a group of accomplices can reveal important insights about the nature of collective responsibility and the nature of complicity.

In Chapter 12, Hans Bernhard Schmid takes up the Sartrean idea of radical responsibility. Radical responsibility is the idea that as agents, we are what we decide to do, and we are therefore—in a rather radical sense of the word—responsible for who we are. Schmid argues that radical responsibility should be understood as self-determination through pre-reflective self-awareness and that such radical responsibility applies to us jointly as well as individually. It is not just the case that *each of us* is radically responsible for who he or she is; rather, we, together, are collectively responsible for what we are *jointly*, as the teams, groups, or societies we are. Radical collective responsibility, according to Schmid, is our plural self-determination through plural pre-reflective self-awareness.

In Chapter 13, Caroline Arruda explores the concept of commitment. Various accounts of shared agency appeal to commitments, either individual commitments to aid others or joint commitments to do some action. Arruda aims to identify the explicit and implicit role of commitments in shared agency and explores the ways that commitments might inform collective responsibility, highlighting the relationship between moral and non-moral commitments and forward and backward-looking responsibility.

Michael Doan, in Chapter 14, questions the use of thought experiments in discussions of collective responsibility. Beginning with an example of collective responsibility drawn from the last episode of the *Seinfeld* show, Doan considers the costs of focusing on certain cases rather than others. He asks: What questions about collective responsibility cannot be asked when the focus of inquiry is narrowed to cases fitting the mold? He argues that the use of fictional thought experiments in analyses of collective responsibility unhelpfully constrains our thinking. Focusing on the issue of responsibility for collective inaction, Doan proposes a different methodology and motivates it by exploring a concrete case of what he calls, collective brilliance.

In Chapter 15, Shannon Fyfe offers a revised version of Larry May's account of shared responsibility for wrongdoing (1987, 1992) and she argues that it can help us address important problems in the domain of collective inaction: namely, failures to prevent further harm. After setting up May's account of shared responsibility, focusing on the features that are most relevant for the issue of shared responsibility for collective inaction, she explores the most compelling criticisms of May's view and suggests that his view should be more focused on forward rather than backward-looking responsibility. She uses this revised version of May's view to sketch a way to think about responsibility for collective inaction, where no specific individual or entity has the positive obligation to act.

In Chapter 16, Björn Petersson discusses Christopher Kutz's assumption (2001) that moral responsibility presupposes the capacity for guilt feelings. Such an assumption seems to undermine arguments for the view that groups, themselves, can be held morally responsible. Petersson explores current defenses of the possibility of collective guilt and places them within two categories, positions that preserve intuitions about the phenomenology of guilt feelings by analyzing collective guilt feelings in terms of individual experiences, and views that reject the idea that guilt feelings require a phenomenological component and attribute guilt feelings to groups themselves. Petersson argues for an approach of the first kind, which builds upon the we-mode approach to collective intentionality. He concludes that Kutz is correct in that groups cannot feel guilty, but the guilt felt by individual group members has a collective character, such that the feeling is an appropriate response to assignments of collective responsibility.

Abraham Sesshu Roth argues, in Chapter 17, that if we take collective responsibility seriously it has implications for the idea of acting for a reason. According to Roth, cases of collective responsibility help us to make sense of how it is that an individual member can be *entitled* to *collective reasons* for action, i.e. entitled to a reason had by the collective rather than by the individual alone. This entitlement makes it possible for the collective reason to be a reason for which one acts, even if one's individual contribution makes little or no difference in the collective effort.

In Chapter 18, Ann Schwenkenbecher argues that in addition to having moral obligations as individuals to do and not do things, we have *collective* moral obligations. Schwenkenbecher defines collective moral obligations as those obligations we share or have in common with group members. They are moral obligations that attach to two or more agents where neither has that obligation on their own. According to Schwenkenbecher collective moral obligations can fill a conceptual gap left by cases where no individual member is obligated to do something but where collective action is obviously needed.

Michael Skerker develops, in Chapter 19, standards for assessing individual moral responsibility to group members for collective action. In some cases, these standards will result in individual member responsibility beyond what they would be responsible for if they performed the same physical behavior as a non-member. Skerker argues that structural differences between two types of groups—organizations and goal-oriented collectives—determine the baseline moral responsibility of group members for the group's collective action. The same physical behavior can make a member of a goal-oriented collective responsible for the outcome of collective action to an equal degree with her fellow group members, whereas the typical organizational member is only responsible for her contribution to the action.

In Chapter 20, Cassie Striblen reminds us that a central concept in debates regarding the responsibility of groups is the concept of an individual. Those that deny groups can be morally responsible and those that argue that they meet the standards for moral responsibility agree on the following assumption: if groups are to be morally responsible, they must mimic individuals in particular ways. Striblen argues that a narrative understanding of individuals is particularly helpful for understanding collective moral responsibility. A narrative understanding of groups provides justification for ascriptions of certain kinds of collective responsibility, particularly for shared responsibility among members of large social groups.

András Szigeti offers, in Chapter 21, a critical overview of arguments for non-distributive collective responsibility—responsibility that is had by groups rather than their members—based on the discursive dilemma. The discursive dilemma looms large in the literature on group agency and is used by many to establish a divergence between group states and individual states. Szigeti tracks the various ways the discursive dilemma is used in debates regarding collective responsibility and presents possible rejoinders to these arguments by individualists who deny the possibility of non-distributive collective responsibility.

In Chapter 22, Linda Radzik discusses the moral responsibilities of bystanders. In particular, she focuses on the ways in which witnesses to wrongs can share responsibility with others. She distinguishes between (a) shared responsibility for wrongs and harms; (b) shared responsibility to provide aid; and (c) shared responsibility to enforce moral norms. According to Radzik, bystanders are not *mere* witnesses. Rather, they are agents with choices and ought to be held morally responsible in some cases.

References

Kutz, C. (2001) *Complicity*, Cambridge: Cambridge University Press.

May, L. (1987) *The Morality of Groups: Collective Responsibility, Group-Based Harm, and Corporate Rights*, Notre Dame, IN: University of Notre Dame Press.

May, L. (1992) *Sharing Responsibility*, Chicago: University of Chicago Press.

11
COMPLICITY AND COLLECTIVE RESPONSIBILITY

Gregory Mellema

By the term "collective responsibility," I will understand a collective consisting of two or more human moral agents that bears moral responsibility for an outcome that consists of a state of affairs. Many have raised doubts about whether a collective can bear moral responsibility for what happens, and many have flat-out rejected the possibility of collective or group responsibility. I have discussed elsewhere the arguments of those raising these doubts at considerable length, and in this chapter, I will simply assume that collectives are capable of bearing moral responsibility (although I will refer to some of these arguments in passing).

In this chapter, I will focus upon the anatomy of collectives that are morally responsible for what happens. Who exactly are the individual moral agents that constitute collectives capable of bearing moral responsibility? Additionally, I will raise the parallel question concerning complicity: who exactly are the individual moral agents who are complicit in the actions of another? In some instances, a group of individual moral agents can both constitute a collective responsible for an outcome and have its members be complicit in the actions of a principal actor. In other instances, this will not be the case. Either the individuals that constitute a collective responsible for an outcome fail to qualify as accomplices, or the accomplices in the actions of another fail to constitute a collective responsible for an outcome. This is hardly a surprising conclusion in and of itself, but I believe that examining the differences between the anatomy of a collective and the anatomy of a group of accomplices can shed light both on the nature of collective responsibility and the nature of complicity.

In the first section, I present some background material relating to the topic of complicity. Section 11.2 analyzes the relationship between complicity and moral responsibility. Section 11.3 presents Kwame Anthony Appiah's notion of "moral taint," and its significance relative to a theoretical understanding of complicity. Section 11.4 lays out some basic features of the concept of collective responsibility. Finally, section 11.5 describes the intersection of complicity and collective responsibility: under what conditions are moral agents who are complicit in another's actions also collectively responsibility for the outcome of these actions?

11.1 Complicity

Suppose that agent A performs wrongful act W in order to bring about outcome O. Then a person is complicit in A's performance of O just in case the person performs an act (which might be an intentional omission) in an effort to contribute to O in the sense of making it more likely to occur.[1] In every instance of complicity, there exists a principal actor, and in some cases, there is more than one principal actor. In every instance of complicity, the principal actor performs an action (or omits to perform an action) that produces an outcome. For the purposes of this discussion, I will assume that this outcome is in some sense harmful, or at least unwanted.

The accomplices are moral agents that perform actions that contribute to this outcome. Throughout this chapter, I will refer to these actions as "contributing actions," with the understanding that they might take the form of omissions. Here it is essential to note that the accomplices are contributing to the outcome. They are not contributing to the relevant actions of the principal actor; indeed, in many cases, an accomplice's contributing actions occurs after the principal actor has performed his or her action. It is also essential to note that the contributing action of an accomplice need not causally contribute to the outcome; in cases where an accomplice's contributing action consists of an omission, it will surely fall short of constituting a causal contribution.[2]

Typically, the principal actor initiates a chain of events producing an outcome, and one or more accomplices perform an action contributing to the outcome. But occasionally, an accomplice initiates a chain of events leading to the production of an outcome by a principle actor. This can take place when someone commands a second person to produce a harmful outcome, and that person subsequently does so. The person who produces the outcome as the result of being commanded to do so is the principal actor, and the person who commanded him or her to do so is an accomplice. Normally, a principal actor bears more moral blame for the outcome than an accomplice, but in a situation where an accomplice commands the principal actor to produce a harmful outcome, it might well be that the accomplice bears more blame for the outcome than the principal actor.

Thomas Aquinas has enumerated nine ways in which a person can be an accomplice in the Treatise on Justice from the *Summa Theologiae* (II-II. Q62. A7.). First, someone can be an accomplice by way of commanding another to do something. Second, someone can be an accomplice by way of counseling someone in how to do something. Third, someone can be an accomplice by way of consenting or offering permission to undertake a course of action. Fourth, someone can be an accomplice by way of offering flattery or encouragement to another. Fifth, someone can be an accomplice by way of "receiving" or covering for another after the fact. Sixth, someone can be an accomplice by way of participating in a project of another. Seventh, someone can be an accomplice by way of remaining silent about the wrongdoing of another. Eighth, someone can be an accomplice by way of failing to prevent the wrongdoing of another. Ninth, someone can be an accomplice by way of failing to denounce the wrongdoing of another.

Several words of explanation are in order. First, the ninth way is a special case of the seventh: the failure to denounce is one manner in which a person can remain silent about the wrongdoing of another. Second, Aquinas attaches a condition to the eighth and ninth ways of being complicit, and that is the condition that one must be bound or obligated to prevent or denounce the wrongdoing. If I confront a person about to commit a wrongdoing, then, if I fail to prevent or denounce, I am an accomplice only if I have a moral obligation to prevent or denounce. This seems to be a reasonable stipulation. If I stand by and watch a child point a firearm at a younger child, I am an accomplice for failing to prevent the subsequent shooting. But if I stand by and do nothing while a terrorist fires shots at people in a public place, then, depending upon the details of the situation, I am not an accomplice. This is because I presumably have a moral obligation to act in the example of the child with a firearm, and I do not have a moral obligation (because it is too dangerous) to attempt to disarm the terrorist.

It is important to note that moral complicity is not the same as legal complicity, and I shall now point out several differences. One difference can be seen in an alternative scheme for distinguishing ways of being complicit proposed by legal scholar Sanford Kadish. His taxonomy consists of ten categories: advising, persuading, commanding, encouraging, inducing, procuring, investigating, provoking, soliciting, and assisting (1985). From a moral point of view, his list seems incomplete, because the failure to act seems capable of rendering one complicit in the wrongdoing of another (consider the example of the child with the firearm). American criminal law does not acknowledge omitting to act as capable of rendering one complicit in the wrongdoing of another (Smith 1991: 35), and this is the reason Kadish's list does not include it. If someone knows that her neighbor is providing sanctuary to a wanted fugitive and makes no effort to contact law enforcement authorities, she is at most guilty of a misdemeanor, i.e., misprision of felony.

Another way in which moral complicity differs from legal complicity involves acting after someone has committed a wrongdoing. In American criminal law, someone can be prosecuted for being an accessory after the fact, but such activity is not regarded as complicity in wrongdoing. (And the difference is more than terminological, for a person who is morally complicit by way of covering for another after the fact need not be guilty of anything that qualifies as being an accessory after the fact.)

A third way in which moral complicity differs from legal complicity concerns situations where the wrongdoer acts differently than what was understood or agreed upon by the accomplices. There is general consensus in the law that if the wrongdoing is quite different than what was agreed upon, and if the wrongdoing is not reasonably foreseeable, then the would-be accomplice is not an accomplice after all.[3] In the moral realm, by contrast, someone can be an accomplice if he or she is perfectly willing to assist the principal actor in a wrongful course of action that was not foreseeable. Perhaps the accomplice is happy to assist in causing mayhem, whatever form that might take.

A fourth and final way in which moral and legal complicity differ concerns persons who unintentionally aid another in wrongdoing. Someone can be legally complicit in another's wrongdoing when his or her actions are reckless or negligent, even though no intent to contribute to the other's wrongdoing is present. Some persons who have allowed others to drive their vehicles have been found complicit in accidents that have resulted, even though their role was totally unintentional (Smith 1991: 40). This has happened particularly in cases where they entrusted their vehicles to intoxicated or underage persons (this is actually a contentious issue in law). Someone might not necessarily be morally complicit in situations such as these if, for example, the would-be driver produced a forged document stating that he was not underage.[4]

11.2 Complicity and Responsibility

As a first step toward tying the discussion of complicity to the topic of collective responsibility, I turn to consider the conditions under which accomplices bear individual responsibility for the outcomes toward which their actions contribute. When one contemplates the taxonomy of Aquinas, it becomes evident that the nine ways of becoming complicit are not equally serious from a moral perspective. The most serious might be commanding another to commit a wrongdoing and participating in a wrongful scheme initiated by another. These modes of behavior almost certainly cause an accomplice to bear moral responsibility for the outcome, and normally in these situations the principal actor and the accomplice are each morally responsible for the outcome (though they need not be equally responsible for it).

Of the other ways of being complicit, counseling someone to wrongdoing, or consenting to the wrongdoing of another, places one within the boundaries of qualifying as morally responsible for the outcome in question. This is partly due to the fact that complicit moral agents are enabling harm,[5] or at least facilitating it.[6] Normally, a person bears moral responsibility for the harm produced by a principal actor's wrongful behavior when the person has counseled him or her to this behavior, or consented to his or her engaging in this behavior (assuming consent is something the principal actor believes necessary).

The other five ways of becoming complicit in the scheme of Aquinas involve a less active role for the complicit agent, and for this reason there tends to be less likelihood of this agent's incurring moral responsibility for the outcome in question. Flattery (encouraging) and receiving (covering for) require action on the part of the accomplice, but except for extreme cases such as providing refuge for an escaped convict, these activities are ordinarily sufficiently benign that one does not incur moral responsibility for the outcome (of course, one nevertheless incurs moral responsibility for one's actions of encouragement or covering for someone else).

The three remaining ways of becoming complicit—silence, the failure to prevent, and the failure to denounce—require little or no action on the part of the accomplice. In certain cases, failures such as these can cause one to become morally responsible for the outcome in question. If a nurse observes another nurse administering the wrong medication to a patient and does nothing, that nurse presumably bears responsibility for the resulting harm to the patient (recall that Aquinas stipulates that the failure to prevent qualifies as complicity when one has a moral obligation to prevent what happens). In typical situations, however, complicity that takes the form of failing to act does not involve one's bearing moral responsibility for the outcome, even when the omission is intentional. If I observe a total stranger parking in a no-parking zone and say nothing, that does not make me responsible for the presence of her automobile in that location.

11.3 Moral Taint

The discussion of the last section revealed that an accomplice does not always bear moral responsibility for the outcome for which the principal actor bears responsibility. In this section, it will be my contention that, when the accomplice fails to bear responsibility for such an outcome, the accomplice can still be tainted by the wrongful actions of the principal actor.

The basic idea is that a moral agent who commits a wrongdoing sometimes taints those to whom he or she is closely connected. An entire family, for example, can be tainted by the criminal actions of a son or daughter. Not only are their reputations damaged, but on a deeper level, their moral integrity is affected.

Anthony Appiah, the first to introduce this notion in the philosophical literature, believes that moral taint is produced when the wrongful actions of another produces harm, and the contagion of this wrongdoing is transferred to someone with no involvement. Consider the events of the Holocaust. Ordinary German citizens bore no responsibility for these events, but Appiah believes they were nevertheless tainted by the actions of Nazi officials. This means that they experienced a loss of moral integrity. Someone's own moral integrity, according to Appiah, is affected when someone else produces harm and some connection exists between these two persons (Appiah, 1991). Moral taint is a phenomenon that involves one's links to others in the community.

Appiah's primary example of moral taint is the issue of divesting shares of stock in firms doing business in South Africa in the 1980s. Someone holding shares in these companies bore no responsibility for the harm produced by apartheid, but he or she was nevertheless tainted by the persons who practiced apartheid. Those purchasing shares in these companies experienced a diminishing of moral integrity, and, according to Appiah, it was appropriate for them to experience shame. Those who are tainted by the actions of others need not feel guilt. Feeling guilt is not appropriate for an individual who has no personal involvement in what happens or for one who incurs no moral responsibility for the outcome.[7]

It might be objected that the notion of moral taint is flimsy, that it is hard to see how it impugns one's integrity, and that there is no reason to care if one is tainted by the misdeeds of another. I believe Appiah would be happy to concede that it is flimsy, at least compared to the notion of moral responsibility, and that it impugns one's integrity to a degree that is perhaps vanishingly small. But from this it does not follow that there is no reason to care whether or not one is tainted. Suppose that in the 1980s, I was shocked to learn that I was a stockholder in a company that did business in South Africa, and I immediately sold the stock because I was conscientious about doing the right thing. Thus, I had a reason to care about the fact that I was tainted, because I believed that my own integrity was somewhat impugned. Even if Appiah is mistaken in thinking that one's integrity is affected whenever one is tainted, one can still have a good reason to care.

I suggest that moral taint can shed light on situations where an accomplice falls short of bearing moral responsibility for the harm produced by the principal actor. When the complicity of a moral agent takes the form of commanding, counseling, consenting, and participating, he or she normally bears responsibility for the resulting harm. But when the complicity takes one of the other five forms, a person's contribution to the sequence of events might be limited enough that he or she falls short of bearing responsibility for the outcome. On occasions when this happens, one may be tempted to suppose that one has done nothing wrong and that nothing has happened to affect one's moral integrity. But one of the lessons to be learned from Appiah's account of moral taint is that an accomplice can be tainted by the wrongful actions of a principal actor, and the moral integrity of the accomplice can as a result be affected. To prevent being tainted in situations such as these, one can attempt to distance oneself from the principal actor and his or her wrongful actions.[8]

11.4 Collective Responsibility

The debate between those who favor collective responsibility and those who oppose it often can be described as follows. The opponents—Benjamin (1976), Lewis (1948), Miller (2006), Narveson (2002), Sverdlik (1987), and many others—emphasize that the only bearers of moral responsibility are individual moral agents and that it is unfair to judge that someone is responsible for a state of affairs that is due, in whole or in part, to the actions of others. A moral agent bears responsibility only for what can be correctly attributed to his or her own actions or omissions, regardless of whether what happened can be attributed as well to the actions or omissions of other moral agents. The proponents—Cooper (1968), French (1984), Held (1976), May (1992), and many others—contend that not all instances of moral responsibility can be neatly reduced to ascriptions of responsibility to individual moral agents. People must sometimes be held accountable for harmful outcomes that go beyond what can be identified as the result of particular persons performing particular actions.

Those committed to an individualist approach sometimes acknowledge that several persons can bear moral responsibility for the same outcome, a circumstance in which we can say that they share responsibility (Lewis (1948; 1972) does not make this concession, but cf. Sverdlik 1987). Those committed to collective responsibility sometimes concede that individualist principles frequently suffice to make accurate ascriptions of moral responsibility (French 1984; Held 1976).

Here I propose an approach that aims to strike a balance between the "individualists" and the "collectivists," as I will call them. The collectivists believe that not all instances of moral responsibility are reducible to the responsibility incurred by the various individuals who are involved, and this strikes me as correct. In some situations, members of a collective responsible for an outcome are not all responsible for the outcome as individuals (an example of this phenomenon will be given shortly). Nevertheless, I side with the individualists in asserting that a moral agent must do something (or omit to do something) that warrants membership in the collective; otherwise, that moral agent is not a member. This might include such things as perceiving oneself as a member of the collective, or intending to act with the members of the collective. In this way, membership in collectives is not determined in such a way as to resemble a contagious disease.

I do not claim to have a knock-down refutation of either the individualists or the collectivists, but I will attempt to show that certain excesses of each view are corrected by the approach I describe in this section. It encourages the individualists to acknowledge the contributions of moral agents who fall short of incurring moral responsibility (as individuals) for the relevant outcome. In addition, it forces collectivists to exclude from membership in collectives those who have not made at least some minimal contribution to the relevant outcome.

A qualifying act, let us say, is an act that qualifies a person for membership in a collective responsible for an outcome, with the stipulation that it might be an act of omission.[9] My proposal is that one does not qualify as a member of such a collective unless one has performed a qualifying act. The essential thought is that one must at a bare minimum contribute to the outcome in some suitably weak sense; otherwise, he or she does not qualify for membership. One must make a minimal contribution to the outcome through either action or inaction, thereby (through his/her actual or intended contribution) raising the antecedent probability of its occurrence.

It is not necessary for one to contribute causally to such an outcome for one's actions to count as a qualifying act. Suppose a number of teenagers are throwing stones at the windows of an abandoned building, and one teenager, despite trying, does not break any of the windows. Even though this teenager does not actually break any windows, her actions of throwing stones raise the antecedent probability to a degree greater than zero that windows will be broken. This suffices to qualify her for membership in the collective that is responsible for breaking the windows. She does not bear individual responsibility for breaking any windows (because she does not break any), but by virtue of performing qualifying acts, she attains membership in the collective responsible for breaking the windows.

How will the individualist and the collectivist react to my proposal? Let us begin with the individualist. When the actions of several persons produce harm, the individualist's first impulse is to determine which of the persons are responsible for the harm, and this normally takes the form of determining which of them have contributed causally to the harm. I suggest that a more enlightened approach is to determine which of them have contributed to the harm, not just causally, but in any manner of contribution. Not all of them performing qualifying acts incur responsibility for the harm as individuals. But certainly, they bear responsibility for their qualifying acts as individuals. And certainly, they contribute to the outcome by performing their qualifying acts. To judge that they are not in any manner accountable for the harm strikes me as implausible.

More could be said to persuade the individualist that the approach I am suggesting is sensible, and a fleshed-out response can be found in the Appendix.

How will my account strike the collectivist? First, it will be found acceptable by collectivists who are sympathetic to the concept of qualifying acts which serve to determine membership in collectives. But unfortunately, there are collectivists who are drawn to theories of collective responsibility whose membership are far more expansive than what can be captured by the concept of qualifying actions.

One example is Karl Jaspers, who writes the following.

> There exists a solidarity among men as human beings that makes each co-responsible for every wrong and every injustice in the world, especially for crimes in his presence or with his knowledge. If I fail to do whatever I can to prevent them, I too am guilty.
> *(1961: 36)*

Although his term "co-responsible" may not capture exactly the same meaning as moral responsibility, Jaspers appears to be articulating an account of responsibility whose scope is universal. According to Larry May, Jaspers comes "dangerously close" in this passage to saying that all members of the human race share responsibility for all of the world's harms (1992: 148). Jerzy Jedlicki is another ethicist who espouses an expansive account of collective responsibility: according to him, human moral agents often bear responsibility for their ancestors' wrongdoing (1990: 53ff).

Presented with such extravagant ascriptions of responsibility, the individualist's worst fears about collective responsibility are realized. However, I believe that turning one's attention to the concept of moral taint can help address these fears, because moral taint supplies us with the resources for describing the moral status of persons connected to others who are guilty of wrongdoing. Recall that Appiah finds that one's moral integrity is affected whenever one is tainted by the wrongdoing of others, and this is especially the case when one can distance oneself from whoever is committing the wrongdoing.

Moral taint is a weaker notion than moral responsibility, and, as such, it has the potential for enabling one to describe the moral status of persons who have no involvement whatsoever in the wrongdoing of others. And this particularly includes others who have committed wrongdoing in the distant past. Someone might be tainted by the wrongful actions of an ancestor, but he or she is not morally responsible for the wrongdoing.

Collectivists sometimes label harms that occur in the world as instances of moral responsibility, when they can more properly be identified as situations in which someone is tainted by the wrongful actions of others. Someone can be tainted by the crimes of his or her father, and someone can be tainted by the genocidal acts of persons holding positions of political authority. But it is dubious that such a person qualifies as a member of a collective that is responsible for the results of these crimes (depending upon the circumstances, of course). I contend that if a person fails to contribute personally in a suitably weak sense to an outcome, the person is not a member of a collective responsible for the outcome. In other words, the person must perform a qualifying act.

Escaping moral taint, of course, is an entirely separate matter. A moral agent contributing nothing to the occurrence of an outcome can still be tainted by the contributions of others. Earlier it was noted that persons tainted by the actions of others need not feel guilt for what they have done. But it is appropriate for them to feel a sense of shame if they are closely connected to the wrongdoers. People commonly feel shame in situations of this type, and there is nothing nonsensical in having such feelings. A sufficient condition for escaping moral taint is taking active steps to dissociate oneself from the wrongdoer. If I have severed the relationship between myself and my brother, I am no longer closely connected to him, and by Appiah's criteria I am no longer in a position to be tainted by his criminal activities.

Individualists commonly charge that extravagant judgments of collective responsibility stretch the concept of responsibility to the point that it becomes nearly meaningless. Thus, H.D. Lewis (1972), in an article about the My Lai Massacre in the days of the Viet Nam War, commented that some found it easy to slide from acknowledging the individual responsibility of Lt. Calley, to talking about the collective responsibility of all Americans. But once we slide into this "tribal" mode of thinking, according to Lewis, we are well down the road to the position that collective responsibility is not real, or at least we are well down the road to finding it easy to ignore (*Id.* at 130ff). Saying that we as Americans are collectively responsible for the atrocities in Viet Nam, Lewis says, is to ascribe responsibility in such a way that is easy to shrug off or treat lightly.

This type of argument is undercut by my suggestion to limit membership in collectives that are responsible for states of affairs to persons performing qualifying acts. One cannot easily ignore or shrug off a qualifying act, because the individual performing it has made a real, though perhaps minimal, contribution to the outcome. There is no sliding down the slippery slope to the universal ascriptions of collective responsibility that Lewis fears when membership in the collectives is denied to those who fail to perform qualifying acts. The responsibility for the horrible racial situation in America, according to Stanley Bates, is not borne by all Americans: he believes that his infant white daughter is not in any manner responsible (1971: 342–49). In making such a claim, Bates is effectively giving assurance to individualists that one can be a collectivist, and at the same time, be sensible enough to place restrictions upon the membership of collectives that bear responsibility for the outcomes in question.

In this section of the chapter, it has been my suggestion that restrictions be placed upon the membership of collectives. Only those performing a qualifying act, those making at least some contribution to the outcome, should be judged members of the collective. Whether this contribution consists in offering words of encouragement, or deliberately refraining from an opportunity to prevent an outcome from occurring, a contribution has been made, and the agent making the contribution qualifies for membership in the collective in question. Collectivists are fond of blaming individualists for their insistence that the only bearers of moral responsibility are individual moral agents, and this blame is reasonable. Individualists are fond of blaming collectivists for ascribing responsibility to collectives that are universal or extravagant in scope, and this blame is also reasonable. When the excesses of each side have been clearly pointed out, the type of compromise I have described might strike one as appealing. Courts of law analyze what a defendant has done, or refrained from doing, while acting in the company of other persons, and I have suggested that it is reasonable to focus on parallel issues bearing upon questions concerning collective responsibility.

11.5 Where Complicity and Collective Responsibility Intersect

Having surveyed the issues of complicity and of collective responsibility, it is time to examine whether and under what conditions a group of moral agents can be complicit in the wrongdoing of others, and simultaneously qualify as a collective responsible for the outcome produced (at least in part) by the wrongdoing.

Let A be an individual moral agent who commits a wrongdoing, and let B be a group of moral agents. Four possibilities can be distinguished as follows:

(1) The agents comprising B are not complicit in A's wrongdoing, and they are not collectively responsible for the outcome O produced by A's wrongdoing (or for the failure to prevent O).

(2) The agents comprising B are not complicit in A's wrongdoing, but they are collectively responsible for the outcome O produced by A's wrongdoing (or for the failure to prevent O).
(3) The agents comprising B are complicit in A's wrongdoing, but they are not collectively responsible for the outcome O produced by A's wrongdoing (or for the failure to prevent O).
(4) The agents comprising B are complicit in A's wrongdoing, and they are also collectively responsible for the outcome O produced by A's wrongdoing (or for the failure to prevent O).[10]

Examples of each possibility will now be examined.

Suppose that A is a Nazi official in a concentration camp, and A issues an order that a group of prisoners be executed. The agents comprising B are residents of a nearby town who have no knowledge of the events taking place in the concentration camp. Clearly, these residents are not complicit in A's issuing the order, and clearly, they are not collectively responsible for the resulting executions. Thus, this is an example of possibility (1).

Suppose that A fires a revolver at another person in a public building and leaves the room where the shooting occurred. A few minutes later, a group of persons enter the room and notice that someone has been shot. They decide to do nothing: they leave the room, and a short time later, the person dies of the gunshot. To say that they are complicit in A's wrongdoing does not seem correct. In particular, there is no sense in which they are covering for A after the fact, for they have no knowledge of A's identity. But they are collectively responsible for not doing anything on behalf of the shooting victim, and hence they are collectively responsible for the failure to prevent the victim's death. If so, this is an example of possibility (2).

Suppose that A and two friends, at A's instigation, plan a bank robbery. The plan calls for A to enter a bank with a loaded revolver and demand cash from a teller, while one friend stands watch and the other friend drives the getaway car. When A demands cash from a teller, a security guard appears out of nowhere. In a panic, A fires at the security guard and leaves the premises, whereupon all three leave the area in the getaway car. The friends, let us assume, have no opportunity to either assist in or prevent the shooting of the security guard.

Here, it is reasonable to judge that A is the principal actor in a scheme to rob a bank and A's two friends are accomplices. They never actually succeed in robbing the bank, but nevertheless the two friends are complicit in the attempted robbery of the bank. Now consider the injury of the security guard, the outcome of A's wrongdoing. Surely, the two friends have nothing to do with this state of affairs (though they might well be tainted by it), and hence it would be mistaken to judge that they are collectively responsible for it. I believe this situation is an example of possibility (3).

An adaptation of the previous example produces an instance of possibility (4): as before, A initiates a plan to rob a bank, and two friends agree to serve as the lookout and the getaway driver, respectively. This time the robbery is successful, and the outcome consists in acquiring $3,000 in cash, which they split in equal shares. I contend that the two friends are complicit in the bank robbery, and in addition, they form a collective that is responsible for the outcome (together with A, they might *also* form such a collective).

As a basis for my contention, I offer the following: both friends perform contributing actions toward the bank robbery by assisting in A's plan to make the robbery successful. Their intent is to support the efforts of A, and they are complicit in A's wrongdoing. In addition, both friends are acting with the intent to acquire cash. Their overall motivation is the successful robbery of the bank, and for this reason their actions to contribute to the robbery (including the intent itself) are qualifying actions. Because they perform acts that contribute to the successful robbery—that is, acts that increase the antecedent probability that the robbery will be successful—they belong to a collective that bears responsibility for the robbery.

Appendix

Perhaps the individualist will grant that those contributing to the outcome are accountable for it in some sense, but reject judging that they form a collective that bears responsibility for it. Possibly, the individualist fears the concept of an abstract object, such as a collective, bearing moral responsibility. If this captures the individualist's position, the situation could be described in the following fashion.

First, let A(x,y) denote a relation of accountability that represents the manner in which the individualist is agreeable with the claim that person x is morally accountable (in some sense) with outcome y. Second, let R(x,y) denote the relation of moral responsibility, such that R(x,y) is true if and only if x is morally responsible for outcome y. The individualist described in the previous paragraph will presumably say that, in the example of the abandoned building, the teenagers throwing stones all bear relation A to the outcome (broken windows), while only a subset of them bear R to it.

Now let Q(x,y) pick out the relation person x stands to outcome y when and only when x performs a qualifying act with respect to y. Let R*(x,y) pick out the relation person x stands to person y when and only when x belongs to a collective that is responsible for y. The individualist will emphatically maintain that R* is an empty relation, for the simple reason that the only bearers of moral responsibility are individual moral agents. What I am proposing, on the other hand, is that

(1) Necessarily, Q(x,y) if and only if R*(x,y).

Now it is beyond controversy that

(2) It is possible that A(x,y) if and only if Q(x,y).

Then it follows by the rules of modal logic that

(3) It is possible that A(x,y) if and only if R*(x,y).

What this shows is that the relation of accountability that is acknowledged by the enlightened individualist may designate the same moral agents as accountable for an outcome as collectivism (the version defended above) finds to have membership in the collective responsible for the same outcome. In other words, the accountability relation accepted by the enlightened individualist may shadow the relation of being collectively responsible for an outcome. While this is not a point of earth-shaking significance, it does strike me as a point worth making, one that, to the best of my knowledge, has not been made in the literature.

Notes

1 On this definition, the accomplice is morally responsible for performing this contributing act, but not necessarily for O. On some contemporary accounts of complicity, the accomplice is always morally responsible for O, but my account follows the medieval tradition of embracing a wider notion of what

it means to be an accomplice. For purposes of simplicity, I here ignore complications introduced by proxy agency.

2 Suppose the principal actor is about to commit a crime. A friend of the principal actor is about to prevent him from committing the crime and then changes his mind. The friend's omitting to prevent the crime is not a causal contribution to the crime, but it is a contribution. The sense of contribution I have in mind is this: he contributes to the outcome by intentionally deciding not to prevent it.

3 The word "quite" implies that specificity in the description of the foreseeable wrongdoing is part of what is at issue. Moral complicity does not seem to require as much specificity as does the law.

4 Reckless moral complicity is possible, of course. The point here is that instances where legal complicity takes place need not be cases where moral complicity is present.

5 To say that a moral agent enables a principal actor to produce harm is to say that the actions of the principal actor would not produce harm in the absence of the agent's involvement and that the agent is aware that his or her actions have this effect.

6 Suppose that a principal actor is performing an action as a means of bringing about a particular harm. To say that an agent facilitates this harm is to say that the agent increases the antecedent likelihood that either the principal actor's action is successfully performed or that the harm is brought about by this action, and doing so in a manner that is morally blameworthy.

7 Paul Ricoeur (1967) uses the term "defilement" to describe this type of phenomenon. In his words it is a "symbolic stain." If a person is defiled by the stain that attaches to her criminal brother, the defilement that attaches to her is symbolic of the stain. I believe that what Ricoeur describes as stain captures at least roughly what Appiah describes as "taint."

8 Authors whose recent work appeals to the concept of moral taint include Hud Hudson (1993), Christopher Kutz (2000), Patricia Marino (2001), and Linda Radzik (2001).

9 The notion of a "qualifying act" is introduced in my book *Collective Responsibility*.

10 A's wrongdoing might produce multiple outcomes, but here I am focusing on the main or most significant outcome. Offering a criterion for what counts as the main or most significant outcome lies beyond the scope of this chapter.

References

Appiah, K.A. (1991) "Racism and Moral Pollution," in L. May and S. Hoffman (eds), *Collective Responsibility*, Lanham, MD: Rowman & Littlefield, 219–38.

Aquinas, T. (1894) *Summa Theologica*, Torino: P. Marietti.

Bates, S. (1971) "The Responsibility of 'Random Collectives'," *Ethics* 81: 343–49.

Benjamin, M. (1976) "Can Moral Responsibility Be Collective and Non-Distributive?" *Social Theory and Practice* 4: 93–106.

Cooper, D.E. (1968) "Collective Responsibility," *Philosophy* 43: 258–68.

French, P. (1984) *Collective and Corporate Responsibility*, New York: Columbia University Press.

Held, V. (1976) "Corporations, Persons, and Responsibility," in H. Cutler (ed), *Shame, Responsibility, and the Corporation*, New York: Haven Publications, 161–81.

Hudson, H. (1993) "Collective Responsibility and Moral Vegetarianism," *Journal of Social Philosophy* 24: 89–104.

Jaspers, K. (1961) *The Question of German Guilt*, A.B. Ashton (trans), New York: Capricorn Books.

Jedlicki, J. (1990) "Heritage and Collective Responsibility," in I. Maclean, A. Montefiore, and P. Winch (eds), *The Political Responsibility of Intellectuals*, Cambridge: Cambridge University Press, 53–76.

Kadish, S.H. (1985) "Complicity, Cause, and Blame: A Study in the Interpretation of Doctrine," *California Law Review* 73: 323–410.

Kutz, C. (2000) *Complicity: Ethics and Law for a Collective Age*, Cambridge: Cambridge University Press.

Lewis, H.D. (1948) "Collective Responsibility," *Philosophy* 23: 3–18.

Lewis, H.D. (1972) "The Non-Moral Notion of Collective Responsibility," in P. French (ed.), *Individual and Collective Responsibility*, Cambridge, MA: Schocken Publishing, 116–44.

Marino, P. (2001) "Moral Dilemmas Collective Responsibility, and Moral Progress," *Philosophical Studies* 104: 203–25.

May, L. (1992) *Sharing Responsibility*, Chicago: University of Chicago Press.

Mellema, G. (1994) *Collective Responsibility*, Amsterdam: Rodopi.

Mellema, G. (2006) "Collective Responsibility and Qualifying Actions," *Midwest Studies in Philosophy: Shared Intentions and Collective Responsibility* XXX: 168–75.
Miller, S. (2006) "Collective Responsibility: An Individualist Account," *Midwest Studies in Philosophy: Shared Intentions and Collective Responsibility* XXX: 176–93.
Narveson, J. (2002) "Collective Responsibility," *Journal of Ethics* 6: 179–98.
Radzik, L. (2001) "Collective Responsibility and Duties to Respond," *Social Theory and Practice* 27: 455–71.
Ricoeur, P. (1967) *The Symbolism of Evil*, New York: Harper and Row.
Smith, K.J.M. (1991) *A Modern Treatise on the Law of Criminal Complicity*, New York: Oxford University Press.
Sverdlik, S. (1987) "Collective Responsibility," *Philosophical Studies* 51: 61–76.

12
RADICAL COLLECTIVE RESPONSIBILITY AND PLURAL SELF-AWARENESS

Hans Bernhard Schmid

Radical responsibility is the idea that as agents, we are what we decide to do, and we are therefore – in a rather radical sense of the word – responsible for who we are. This chapter argues that radical responsibility should not be understood as arbitrary self-choice through detached reflection, as it is often seen in the literature. Rather, it should be understood as self-determination through pre-reflective self-awareness. It is further argued that radical responsibility applies to us jointly as well as severally. It is not just the case that *each of us* is radically responsible for who they are; rather, we, together, are collectively responsible for what we are *jointly*, as the teams, groups, or societies we are. Radical collective responsibility is our plural self-determination through plural pre-reflective self-awareness.

12.1 Radical Responsibility

Radical responsibility is the early Sartrean idea that as agents, we exist as freedom without essence. Who we are is up to our choice, we are free to choose, and we are therefore responsible for who we are (Sartre 2007 [1945], 20). We are responsible for our thoughts and actions as well as for our emotions, dispositions, commitments, and character traits. Radical responsibility differs from what one might call regular responsibility in that it does not presuppose duty. Radical responsibility is not for living up – or failing to live up – to predetermined standards of who we should be, but rather extends to those standards themselves. As self-determined creatures, we are responsible for the values we accept, and our – or anybody else's – values cannot exculpate us from the responsibility for the choice we make. There is thus nothing on which to base our choice. Choice is fundamental, and our choices are who we are. There is no excuse because nothing else made us be who we are, and there are no standards that determine whether what we made ourselves to be is "right." "Us" is where the buck stops. We are who we are because that's whom we have chosen to be. We are radically responsible in virtue of our being radically free (Sartre 1978 [1943], 553ff.).

The Sartrean idea of responsibility as radical self-determination continues to be discussed, though in the more recent hegemonial philosophical discourse, it is not always seen favorably. It is rejected simply as a "mistake" (Velleman 1989, 168) or as outright "incoherent" (e.g. Raz 1988, 155). Others refer rather positively to it, but find it necessary to amend the Sartrean proposal in important ways. Thus even its sympathetic readers find Sartre's version either possible in theory, but overly "heroic" in practice (e.g. Korsgaard 2008, 62), or tragically self-defeating (Taylor 1988, 290). A look into the spectrum of interpretations might help us to see a bit closer what's so outrageous about Sartre's claim, and perhaps proceed to an understanding of just what a plausible version thereof might look like.

Most straightforwardly, it has been claimed that radical self-determination is an "incoherent dream" because our biological and social nature partially settles who we are, and it is only against the background of those features that a self-determined agent can "develop and flourish" (Raz 1988, 155). It thus seems that some of our essence must precede our existence after all for us to be the autonomous persons we aspire to be. Not all of our aims and goals are subject to self-choice. Some are constitutive of who we are before self-choice can kick in. In defense of the Sartrean view against this allegation, it has been argued that the radical existentialist need not claim that our autonomy can develop and flourish in any direction we might choose; the existentialist claim is one about autonomy, not the development and flourishing thereof (Mendus 1989, 96ff.). Deciding against the goals and purposes that are necessary for the development of one's autonomy might be bad, but still a choice.

The point in large parts of the more recent controversy is self-detachment, the idea that Sartrean self-choice is *ex nihilo*, as it were, rather than from the concerns and reasons which already make one the sort of agent one is (rather than having chosen them), and which are necessary as the starting point of any substantive self-scrutiny in which self-choice may become an issue. Such radical detachment is not entirely without defenders (it is sometimes recommended as the suitable theory of the self for Rawlsian liberalism [see Cohen 2008]). But most voices are critical. It is argued that "the feeling of radical freedom" is a "false sense" and a "mere pretense," because however we look reflectively at our motivation and make it the object of our detached consideration, there's always some motivation escaping our reflective gaze – our motivation to reflect (Velleman 1989, 168). Meaningful, non-delusional, "genuine" self-inquiry and self-scrutiny should be aware of this fact (ibid. 169), and even authors who claim to be more sympathetic to the existentialist venture argued that existentialist self-choice is fishy. Thus, it is sometimes claimed that while it might be conceivable for us to "heroically" choose our concerns out of nowhere, this would not be self-constitution of the truly autonomous sort (Korsgaard 2008). Proper self-constitution is self-identification with reason. In the literature on "responsibility for self," it is argued that any such responsibility should not be conceived of in terms of some Sartrean "miraculous self-choosing" (Wallner 1993, 45), but rather as the sort of self-scrutiny into which agents with evaluative higher-order attitudes can engage, but which presuppose rather than ground the reflecting agent's concerns (Taylor 1988). We do not "choose" our concerns "just like that"; rather, our concerns determine who we are. In cases of conflict, we do not choose from nowhere, but rather from the perspective in which the cares and commitments reflected in these attitudes are ours, and it is only in this way – based on conflicting cares and commitments which are one's own – that self-choice comes in.

Against the last line of criticism, it has been argued that it presupposes that there is a "substantial self" prior to the act of choice, and that this is a claim that Sartre would deny. Sartrean self-choice is not a self's act of determining who it is to be. "On his view, the self *is* its choices" (Cohen 2008, 94). For self-choice, there is no self to start with; selfhood is the choice itself. But so far, this is only stating the "mystery" of self-creation that the critics of the idea have identified. Is there any way to make sound sense of it?

"We are taking the word 'responsibility' in its ordinary sense as 'consciousness (of) being the incontestable author of an event or of an object'" (Sartre 1978 [1943], 553), Sartre claims in the famous passage on Freedom and Responsibility in his *Being and Nothingness*. One might deny that this sense of the word "responsibility" is quite as ordinary as Sartre thinks (see Flynn 1984, 15), but it is worth looking at some of the details of Sartre's definition, the most salient of which is the bracketed "of." The "consciousness (of) being the incontestable author of an event or of an object" is not an attitude in which we, "the self," have some consciousness of ourselves in the way in which we are conscious of some object when we are aware of it. The consciousness is not "of" ourselves in terms of its object. Rather, the consciousness in question is of whatever it is we are doing as far as we are doing it self-consciously, or, if you wish, self-knowingly (cf. Sartre 1948). By doing consciously what we are doing, we know – without making ourselves the object of our thought – that it is "us" who are doing it, we know it without engaging in some meta-level thinking – and we know it in the incontestably authoritative way that Sartre mentions: We cannot be mistaken here. This incontestable identity and first-person authority is all there is to selfhood, in Sartre's view. Sartrean radical responsibility is simply the first-personal self-consciousness in which we are aware of our doing as ours.

Before spelling this out further, it is worth noting that if this reading is correct, the criticisms (and perhaps even parts of the rare defenses) of Sartrean self-choice in the recent literature are wrong-headed insofar as they are predicated on self-reflection rather than pre-reflective self-awareness. Sartrean self-choice, thus reconstructed, is not about distancing oneself from the motives one happens to have, and treating them as objects of potential choice. It is not about self-evaluation in the sense of a second order stance, as some believe in the recent literature (see Taylor 1988; Velleman 1989). And neither is it about adopting the point of view of reason and distancing oneself from the inclinations one happens to have, as Kantian existentialists have it (see Korsgaard 2008). Sartrean self-choice is not about meta-level self-management of any sort. Rather, it explains the very basic sense in which at whatever level our attitudes happen to be, and whatever it is we are doing, our attitudes and actions are ours in terms of the special, first-personal way of our being conscious of them as ours by consciously having and doing them.

This responsibility, however, is more radical than any higher-level self-management view has it, for it does not allow for the cheap excuse of "disowning" a deviant desire one has and thereby exculpating oneself from having it by taking a firm volitional stance against it – as it appears in Frankfurt's conception, where deviant desires that are not in line with one's volitional second-order stance appear as "one's own" only in "a formal sense" and not "strictly" (Frankfurt 1998, 64). And similarly for Korsgaard's conception, where one disowns one's inclinations by reflectively setting one's will against them (Korsgaard 2008, 59). From a Sartrean perspective, thus reconstructed, this seems entirely beside the point – and perhaps just as another attempt to find an excuse. Of course, our lowly inclinations and disruptive emotions, which we happen to dislike, are fully ours, too, and the proof is in the way we "know" them – however much we might strive to disown them. We are thus fully responsible for them, too, and can't say that they are not "really" but only "formally" our own. Also, there seems to be no reason to assume that radical responsibility, thus reconstructed, should be at odds with the facts about our biological and social backgrounds. It is not the view that we can be whatever we like, irrespective of our biology and society.

Radical responsibility, thus reconstructed, is, at the basic level, simply the incontestable identity and first-person authority that comes with self-awareness. But how is it connected to choice in a way that makes talk of responsibility meaningful? After all, being pre-reflectively aware of one's attitudes as one's own seems far from choosing (or having chosen) them. We do not, it seems, choose the attitudes of which we are self-aware. Rather, they "occur" to us, as we say – a phrase that puts us in a rather passive position with regard to the question of consciousness. Just saying that our attitudes are ours in virtue of their being conscious does not seem to put us in a particularly obvious position of being responsible for them, or so it seems – though conversely, there is a volitional element in our ability of "paying attention" on what it is we are doing – e.g., we seem to have the option of doing consciously what otherwise would be routine action "beneath the radar" of consciousness.

Sartrean radical responsibility cannot plausibly be responsibility for being attentive. In order to make sense, Sartrean responsibility has to be of a different kind. In order to find out what it is, it is instructive to look at its opposite: Sartrean radical irresponsibility. Though Sartre could easily have chosen a case that concerns our alleged "biological nature," it is our alleged "social nature" that provides him with the example in which he discusses the structure of radical irresponsibility (or "bad faith," as he calls it). It is the famous example of a waiter who fully identifies with his social role (Sartre 1978 [1943], 59). The waiter is not inattentive; however, he attends to what it is he is doing *in the wrong way*, as it were. He fails to take the question of who he is to be up to himself. Rather, he takes his identity to be determined by the structure of generalized normative expectations of others that constitute his status. What makes Sartre's waiter radically irresponsible is that he, by identifying fully with his social role, does not take the question of what he should be doing to be determined by what he himself wants; rather, he takes it to be settled by the social structure of commitments and entitlements that make up his role status. From his own perspective, he does not act in the way he acts simply because that's what he chooses to do. Rather, he acts in this way because that's what he thinks a waiter does, or should be doing.

The practical reasoning of Sartre's waiter thus conforms exactly to the model Robert Brandom notoriously advertises as the right way of thinking about practical reason in social contexts. Brandom's example is a bank accountant thinking about what clothes to wear at work. Brandom argues that he immediately proceeds from the belief that he is a bank accountant to the conclusion that he should wear a tie – without there being a question of whether or not he wants to stick to the rules, or some such (see Brandom 2001, 90f., where Brandom argues that special pro-attitudes from the side of the agent do not figure in such practical reasoning). Brandom argues that this is how practical reasoning is done, and Sartre, with the example of his waiter in mind, agrees – though the two part ways rather decidedly where Brandom argues that this is all there is to practical commitment, while Sartre says that while this is how people reason in everyday life, it is a radically irresponsible way of reasoning, because thinking in this way, people forget that if they let themselves be committed by social roles ("it is not about whether I want to do it, it is simply my duty or what is expected from me in my social role"), this is something they themselves choose to do and they have reason to choose to do so only if this is what they want. Letting oneself be committed by one's social role is something one is fully responsible for – it is, after all, not the role that plays the role player, but the other way around.

Beyond commitment and identity, the problem with everyday irresponsibility also extends to authority. Sartre's waiter, just as Brandom's bank accountant, does not see himself as the "incontestable authority" of what he does. He is blind, as it were, for his first-personal authority, and thinks of authority only in societal terms. When he engages in his role, he does not think that what he does is something that is what it is in virtue of what he himself wants or intends. Rather, he thinks of it as something that is what it is in virtue of social roles and institutions and what society authorizes role occupants to do. He sees himself as a social role occupant through and through. Rather than knowingly *playing* his role, he – mistakenly, Sartre thinks – takes himself to *be* his role. This is what he is responsible for, in a *sort* of culpable way: he takes himself to be externally determined in a way that hides a continuous series of personal choices behind a role structure. He thus misconceives of his role as what he is rather than something he just plays at being. But how is such role identification at odds with pre-reflective self-awareness? Can't we be fully self-aware, and totally identify with our roles at the same time? How is full role-identification a failure of, or a compromised form of self-awareness?

Here are three ways in which pre-reflective self-awareness conflicts with the sort of awareness of one's roles that we have when we fully identify with our roles.

First, self-awareness identifies, from the first-personal view, in an incontestable way. When we consciously intend and act, we might occasionally be mistaken about what it is we want to do or what we are doing, but we cannot be mistaken about the attitude's being ours. Attitudes self-identify the subject. Role-awareness is not of this sort. The identity of the waiter at the *Café de Flore* is not established by the role occupant's self-awareness. Rather, it is a matter of social identification, and occasionally, we might simply be mistaken about our role identities.

Second, self-consciousness differs from role consciousness with regard to the sort of commitments it involves. It has repeatedly been pointed out in the literature that we simply cannot estrange or distance ourselves from our own attitudes (see – with special reference to Sartre – Moran 2001). We cannot not care at all about what we think and want. And it is in virtue of our self-awareness of our thoughts and intentions that our attitudes are our commitments. "I believe that p, but -p" is a conflict of commitments, and though sometimes, such cases of weakness of judgment may perhaps occur (Coliva 2015), it is not the normal case. Self-consciously judging that "-p" is believing that -p, and though contradictory beliefs might persist somewhere in our cognitive system, becoming first-personally aware of a contradiction sorts the matter out. One can have contradictory beliefs, but not in a self-aware or occurrent way. And *mutatis mutandis* for the case of "I intend to phi, but it is utterly bad/undesirable." Similarly, self-awareness is the reason why we do not need a second-order desire to fulfill our desires for desires to motivate us, or a second-order intention to do what we intend in order to be committed to act. It is in virtue of self-awareness that our attitudes *are* our commitments. This is different with role consciousness on both accounts. As a role occupant, I might occasionally find myself being committed, in my role identity, to views that personally, I do not hold to be true, and to intentions that personally, I hold to be utterly bad or undesirable. Luckily under such circumstances, however, the attitudes I am committed to in virtue of my role identity are not self-committing; thinking that what my role requires me to accept is neither true nor good puts me in an awkward position, but does not constitute a paradox. I might know what duties my social role of a waiter entails, but there is still, it seems, a meaningful question of whether or not I should actually play it. I need, it seems, a reason of my own in order to act (most plausibly, my wanting to play my role). For the commitments that come with a social role (ultimately, other people's generalized normative expectations) are not of the self-committing sort that comes with the conscious having of an attitude.

Third, and beyond self-identification and self-commitment, self-awareness is self-authorization – what is discussed under the label of first-person authority. In virtue of my being conscious of what I want, I am in a uniquely authoritative position to know what it is I am doing. Occasionally, others might have better evidence and correct me, but our lives would be very different indeed if this were the normal case. First-person authority has a special role in practice. I might be ignorant about what it is I want in many ways, but what I am doing has its meaning in virtue of what it is I want to do, and this is up to me. Not quite so in the context of social roles. What it means if I raise my hand as a policeperson on the crossroad does not depend on what it is I meant to do, but rather on what it says about a policeperson's raising his or her hand on the crossroad in the traffic code – and similarly for other role performances such as, e.g., speaking a language: what it is I am saying depends on the public meaning of the words I use rather than on what I want them to mean. In my role, I am, it seems, far from being the incontestable author of what it is I am doing. What I am doing is not under my own authority. Rather, I am authorized by the society that assigns my role. What it is I am doing is not up to me. I am, in this sense, not self-determined, but rather determined by social norms in terms of the generalized normative expectations of others.

12.2 Self-Determination and Joint Action

Radical responsibility and radical choice, thus reconstructed, is not the illusion of being able to choose to be whoever one would like to be, at the level of some meta-volition or second order attitude, irrespective of biology or the social world. It is not some capacity to take a distanced evaluative view on oneself and shape oneself according to that view. Rather, it is one's being self-identified, self-committed, and self-authorized – or, for short, one's being self-determined not in the sense that there is a substantial self that has self-awareness as its property, but in the sense that the way in which one's attitudes are one's own determines who one is. Radical responsibility is not a call to some sort of meta-level self-management or self-improvement. Rather, it is a call not to mistake oneself for something that is identified, committed, and authorized through anything but oneself.

Another way of putting this is in terms of the subject/object distinction – a distinction that features centrally in the early existentialist account, but that has gone out of fashion in the current discourse. An object is determined by its features; it has the features it has in the way that they make it what it is. A subject, by contrast, does not have its features in that way. It has the features it has in virtue of itself. As agents, we are subjects rather than objects. What characterizes us as agents is what we think, want, and decide to do. And whatever beliefs and desires, dispositions and character traits we might have (and whatever the biological and social background thereof might be), they are ours only through self-determination, that is, in virtue of our being self-identified, self-committed, and self-authorized in our having them.

Radical responsibility is best understood through its opposite, radical irresponsibility, which is the tendency to ignore that we are subjects rather than objects by ignoring that whatever role we play, refuse to play, or fail to play is ultimately a matter of our own self-determination. This reconstruction of radical responsibility does not imply that we could be doing otherwise. But it does have a connection to the idea of choice, and of the possibility of change. When we irresponsibly take our identity, commitment, and authority to be settled by society, we thereby fail to see the space for changing ourselves that there might be. It is only through taking one's life to be one's own that one is open to the alternatives one might have. Thus, radical responsibility is not directly about some ability for radical change, but about taking the perspective from which one's opportunities for change become visible, and that perspective is: taking oneself to be self-determined rather than determined by something else.

There is, however, something fishy about the way in which early Sartre depicts the relation between responsibility (in terms of self-awareness) and irresponsibility (in terms of role identification). True as it may be *in some cases* that taking oneself to *be* one's role rather than playing it is a mistake that comes with a lacking sense of self-determination, it is certainly not the case that this is the case for *all* of our social roles (see Schmid 2017a). The Sartrean analysis might seem plausible in the case of mere *jobs* such as that of Sartre's famous waiter (or merely ascriptive roles with which one has no reason to self-identify, such as the role of a slave). But what about the role of a true friend or an engaged citizen? These are not roles of the sort one *just plays* without *being* them. In fact, whoever has an extra reason of his or her own for taking on the commitments implied in the role of a good friend is not *really* a good friend, but just *plays* at being a good friend: he or she has one reason too many (and similarly for whoever engages in political issues for other reasons than her care for the issues at hand *as a citizen*, but acts for some private preference of hers). Some roles we have to *be* in order to play them well, or perhaps even in order to play them at all. And it seems utterly wrong to say that we are irresponsible by doing so, and suffering from a lack of sense of self-determination.

Sartre (and, *mutatis mutandis*, Heidegger) has no tools to distinguish these cases. What is the difference that makes a difference? I submit it is this: The roles one should play without mistaking oneself to *be* them are participations in a social activity in which one is not a full partner in the setting up of the role structure. The roles one cannot play without being them are participations in a joint intentional activity wherein one is a full partner in the setting up of the role structure. Thus, extending the notion of radical responsibility to certain types of social engagements requires of us to think about partnership in social activity, and the way in which role structures are set up.

The early Sartre's problem is that he thinks of action – and, consequently, freedom and responsibility – only in singularist terms. Only individuals are proper agents, and what they do is their own action. There is no such thing as basic joint activity, wherein individuals engage only based on a sense of the activity being theirs, collectively. This leads to a conception in which social engagement in general comes with the air of irresponsibility, and quite explicitly so in his conception of the "we" in *Being and Nothingness*. "I," that is (primarily) a subject that becomes objectified in interaction. "We," by contrast, is not a subject. Rather, it is an object that is quite literally third-personally constructed (in the famous "gaze of the Third" (see Sartre 1978 [1943], 413ff.). Sarte's early denial of the idea of a plural subject (a thought with which he struggled throughout his later work; see Flynn 1984, ch. 9) leaves a gaping lacuna in his conception of responsibility, and it is particularly obvious in the section on Freedom and Responsibility in *Being and Nothingness*, where he discusses responsibility for joint activity on the example of joining a war (the French resistance against occupant Nazi Germany serves as the paradigm of joint action in much of Sartre's thought on the matter; see Flynn 1984, 173ff.). The war, Sartre argues here, "is my war [...] and I deserve it [...] because I could always get out of it by desertion or suicide," and he continues:

> If therefore I have preferred war to death or dishonor, everything takes place as if I bore the entire responsibility for this war. Of course others have declared it, and one might be tempted perhaps to consider me as a simple accomplice. But this notion of complicity has only a juridical sense, and it does not hold here. For it depended on me that for me and by me this war should not exist, and I have decided that it does exist.
> *(Sartre 1978 [1943], 554)*

For lack of a plural subject, Sartre here ends with an overblown concept of individual responsibility and a sort of solipsistic idealism. For except perhaps from the perspective of an all-powerful leader, no war is "my" war; only my own participation therein is. The first-personal perspective that is radical responsibility for the war is not mine, but *ours* – the French Resistance's, if this is the case, or perhaps the "true" French nation's. I self-determinedly participated in the war, but the war itself is not a case of individual self-determination. If anything, going to war is plural self-determination – a concept that Sartre comes closest to endorsing in his late (and unfortunately rather hastily written and badly redacted) *Critique of Dialectical Reason* (Sartre 1991 [1960]). If joint activities are choices, they instantiate collective freedom, and radical *collective* responsibility. The lacuna becomes obvious if we consider the connection between radical responsibility and the possibility of change pointed out above. As a simple individual – one that is not authorized by the resistance army, or its exile government, as the army's leader – one can either participate in or refrain from participating in the war, but the war itself is not one's own action, which one could have done otherwise (perhaps by choosing a different strategy).

Thus, Sartrean radical singular responsibility is not the point of view from which the action in question is self-determined. Sartrean radical singular responsibility for joint action has lost its connection to self-determination.

Who is the subject of the intention in the context of such large-scale actions – subject in the sense of something that is what it is in virtue of itself, rather than in virtue of something else? One might think that the French Resistance's leader, Charles de Gaulle, might have a better claim to saying "this war is my war" than Sartre's simple pedestrian individual. But Charles de Gaulle is fighting the war against occupant Nazi Germany in a role, too. He is not the subject of the activity of fighting Nazi Germany out of singular self-determination in which he is self-identified, self-committed, and self-authorized in his "consciousness (of) being the incontestable author of the action." As the leader, he is identified through appointment or tacit recognition, he is committed by his role, and he is authorized by the organization. The candidate for self-determination in this case is the collective that came to adopt the intention of fighting Nazi Germany, and to doing so by self-organizing as the French Resistance with Charles de Gaulle as its leader. Surely, the development of the French Resistance is a process that involves people deciding to join and choosing to play their role, and thus assuming their role-identity. This is abdicating their individual self-determination insofar as they are now being determined by something that is not (just) themselves. At the same time, however, they are not thereby turning themselves into a mere object. Rather, they join the plural subject of the intentional activity of fighting occupant Nazi Germany together. Their role engagement is not simply of the sort that they are letting themselves be identified, committed, and authorized by others; rather, their engagement involves the sense that who they are is determined by their joint intention, which is their joint commitment, of which there is first-person plural authority.

But is this really radical collective responsibility? Are there really plural subjects, and even if there are, can't we engage and fully participate in joint intentional action just as a plurality of singular subjects?

12.3 Plural Subjects

A good point of departure to tackle this question is the recent debate on joint intentional action. Joint action is where people act together – cooperatively, or sometimes competitively. Where people act together, and do so consciously and willingly – intentionally, that is – it does not seem adequate to individuate the ensuing activity according to the individual participants alone. A joint action is not any aggregate of qualitatively similar – or suitably different – individual actions of a certain type. A joint action is one token action performed by a plurality of agents, and it is parts to that whole that the participants intentionally perform.

The difference at stake here is particularly obvious in small-scale examples of cooperatively neutral action types: It makes a difference whether each of us walks alone – perhaps coincidentally alongside each other – or whether we walk together. The difference might be visible in the behavior – e.g., through our mutual adaptation of pace in the case of walking together – but what's making the difference seems to be a matter of the way individual and joint actions are intended. Individual actions – parallel or not – are individually intended, joint actions are jointly (or collectively) intended, or so it is claimed in the rapidly growing literature (for an overview see Jankovic/Ludwig [eds.] 2018). Joint intention is not just an aggregate of individual practical commitments to individual goals. It is not sufficient for action to be intentionally joint that I intend to do my thing expecting that you intend to do your thing, with higher-order beliefs and an expected accumulative effect of our individual doings that I somehow desire.

Joint actions, where they are intended, are collectively intended. The target phenomenon of an adequate analysis has to be attitude of the form "We intend to J," where J is a token joint action.

While many current philosophers accept the idea of joint or collective intention of the sort that is not easily reducible to an aggregate or a summation of individual intentions, the disagreement is over what about intention that's joint or collective. Using the widely accepted analysis of intentional attitudes in terms of subject (in our case, "we"), mode (the kind of attitude in question, in our case: "intend"), and content (in our case, the intended joint action J), philosophers of collective intentionality disagree rather fiercely over the question of whether it is *just* the content that is collective about collective intentionality (as content accounts of collective intentionality claim), or whether the jointness or collectivity affects the subject and mode, too (these are the views endorsed by subject or mode-accounts of collective intentionality, respectively). I submit that the subject account emerges victorious from this controversy, and the following is why.

Content accounts of collective intentionality have the advantage of being more parsimonious than their competitors – more parsimonious that is, coming from a default understanding of intentionality as individual intentionality. All we need to add to the usual singularist picture of intentionality is collective content. According to this type of account, if we intend to J (where J is a joint action), each of us, for him- or herself, has basically the intention to J. The subject is "us," but not in the collective (or joint), but in the distributive (or several) sense. It is not about "us, together," as some sort of unit, but "each of us, for him- or herself," as an aggregate. There is nothing we need to "be" together in order for us to intend to act together. This content account is most prominently argued for in a current account of shared intention in terms of individual intentions "that we J" (plus a structure of meshing subplans and common knowledge; see Bratman 1999). This propositional way of putting the content of intention has the advantage to avoiding a problem of the more straightforward way of putting it. Saying that each of us intends, for him- or herself, to J sounds as if each intended the joint action as if it were his or her own, thus ignoring that the act is supposed to be a plurality of agents. To say that each intends "that we J" avoids this problem. However, this account is haunted by the fact that in order for intention to play the role of a commitment in practical reasoning, it has to be action-referential rather than propositional. And one can intend one's own action only. In this sense, to intend "that we J" is to intend to make it the case that we J. But intending to make it the case that an action happens is not equivalent to intending to act. And our J-ing is not my action, but *ours*, and for it to be ours we have to intend to do it intentionally, rather than just to make it the case that the act happens.

If intention is action-referential, it is therefore action self-referential. The subject of the intention and the subject of the intended action are one and the same. Thus, the subject view suggests itself as the straightforward solution to the problem of content accounts. If it is not the case that when we intend to J, each of us intends to J, because none of us can intend to J – who, then, can intend to J? Given the action self-referentiality of intention, the obvious answer is: us, jointly (or collectively) rather than severally (or distributively). This is the subject view of collective intentionality. We as the plural subject of intention intend our joint action: It is our collective act that we intend, and we intend it collectively, as a plural subject.

In spite of its simplicity, this view has found remarkably few proponents in the recent debate. And from the beginnings of the debate right up to recent contributions, the reason for shying away from the subject account is one and the same: "The We" is spooky. It smacks of mysterious collectivist emergentism and obscurantist collectivist political ideology. Once "the we" is assumed as a proper subject of intention, the "spirit of the people," the "class in and for itself," and other ghosts from the past seem to be right around the corner waiting to come back in. Even the one and only prominent proponent of a subject view in the recent debate thus hastened to assure that plural subjects are basically just voluntary associations, that they are created by the participant individuals, and that they are really just "emulations" of the unity of a subject anyway (Gilbert 2014).

The worry about the idea of the plural subject that has haunted the recent debate can be spelled out in metaphysical terms. If the two of us are walking together, it is just the two of us out there, and it is not that there is a third subject walking along with us, or pulling the strings over and above our heads.

This worry has driven most recent and current philosophers of collective intentionality to search for a third way between the content account that gives too little by way of jointness or collectivity, and the subject account, that seems to give too much. According to the position of the intentional mode between the intentional subject and the intentional content, the mode suggests itself as the place to slot in the missing element of jointness or collectivity. In the case of "we intend to J" – where "we" stands for the intentional subject, "J" for the content, and "intend" for the mode, the subject is distributive, but it is in a special, collective "mode" that each of us intends when we intend to J according to the mode accounts. In this view (which in its varieties seems to receive the most support in the recent debate), the attitude of the form "we intend to J" is really this: "We *we-intend* to J," where the first "we" is distributive and thus nothing spooky, while it is collective in the "we-intend" (and thus certainly in need of some clarification). Understandable though this move might seem as a way of solving the shortcomings of content accounts while avoiding the perceived excess of jointness or collectivity of the plural subject, it is rather mysterious what kind of "mode" the alleged "we-mode" is supposed to be. Modes are "kinds" of intentional attitudes. Received theories of intentionality simply describe intentional modes as the feature that distinguishes a case of, say, belief, from a case of, say, desire. More often than not, simple lists of examples are provided to illustrate the intentional mode. The we/I-distinction, however, does not add to the list of intentional modes. Rather, it cuts across the different modes. If it is a mode at all, it is a fundamentally different mode of mode. What kind of mode, then, is it?

The most plausible theories of intentional modes in the literature account for modes in terms of formal objects (see the references in Schmid 2017b). A belief is what it is in virtue of the (apparent) truth of its target proposition (or "material object"). A desire captures its target as good or desirable, and so on for other modes (in the case of fear, danger is the formal object). What the intentional mode modifies according to the best theories is thus the content, and it does so in a way that rationalizes, or makes intelligible, the attitude as being of the kind it is. Perceiving a dog as dangerous rationalizes being afraid of it. The I/we-mode distinction, however, does nothing of this sort. It modifies the subject; but how could it rationalize an attitude as being of the kind it is if it were true that the subject could never be collective? Properly understood, the mode account collapses into a subject account (see Schmid 2017b).

This result should not be taken as bad news, for the fear of the big spooky "We" is due to a misconception of subjectivity which in the individual case, we have long overcome. It is true that if the two of us go for a walk together, it is just the two of us out there, and no third subject over and above our heads. But this does not prove that there are no plural subjects any more than the fact that if I go for a walk alone, it is just me out there, and no second subject, "the I," within me (or over and above my head, for that matter). The lesson which we have learned about the singular subject, "the I," should be applied to the plural case. We need not avoid a spooky plural substance over and above our heads by postulating a new (and altogether mysterious) kind of mode. If we intend to J, it is neither that we we-intend to J, nor that some singular collective subject over and above our heads intends to J. Rather, we collectively intend to J – in the case of our walk, it is just you and I – but *together*. The subject is plural rather than either a spooky collective singular, or just a distribution of individual subjects. The whole idea of the "mode" in the we-mode accounts of collective intentionality is just an unfortunate way of capturing the adverbial nature of intentional subjectivity – and it is unfortunate because it confuses the adverbial nature of subjectivity with an intentional mode (Schmid 2018).

The fact that content accounts of collective intentionality fail, and that mode accounts, understood correctly, collapse into subject accounts, however, does not tell us much about plural subjectivity and whether and how it really exists. Are we, together, the subject of we-attitudes in the same general way we, severally or distributively, are the subjects of I-attitudes? Are there real plural subjects, or just, as some have argued, emulations or fictions thereof?

To answer this question, we have to remember what exactly is at stake here. Above, I characterized subjectivity in contradistinction to being an object. I claimed that subjectivity is self-determination, and that this is the sort of radical responsibility a suitable reconstruction of Sartrean self-choice must mean. I claimed further that this is self-determination, and that it is in the way consciously intending self-identifies, self-commits, and self-authorizes. Are we, the ones sharing attitudes, really of that sort? Is the couple of people who go for a walk or dance a tango together, the team that volunteers to clean up the park, the group that performs a play, or perhaps even a nation that decides on an issue by taking a vote inexplicable and radically responsible in that way? Are we – collectively – the author of what we do and what we are in the same way we are individually self-constituted?

The most straightforward way of accounting for plural subjectivity is to show that in the way singular subjectivity is individual self-awareness, plural subjecthood is collective self-awareness, that is, our pre-reflective awareness of an attitude as ours. The claim is a threefold one (for more on the following see Schmid 2018):

(1) The conscious sharing of a collective attitude self-identifies us, collectively, in the same general way the conscious having of an individual attitude self-identifies me. Though I might be mistaken in having some pre-intentional "sense of us," where there is really no "we," the point is that plural subjectivity is not my or anyone's pre-intentional "sense of us," but rather ours. The self-awareness in question is plural, and it self-identifies the subject. It is the sense in which there is an expressive rather than demonstrative use of "we" (see Schmid 2014).
(2) "I believe that p, but -p" is logically sound and possibly true, but it is a contradiction nevertheless, and it is a contradiction in virtue of the fact that "-p" first-personally expresses one's belief that -p, which contradicts one's stated belief that p. "We believe that p, but -p," expressed by a single member, is not a straightforward contradiction of this sort, but it is still a tension in commitments – I, as that member, should work it out with my group. Our collective expression of "We believe that p, but -p," however, is the same conflict of commitments as in the singular case. It is the fact that we know of what we think and intend in a first-personal rather than a third-personal way that our attitudes are under the guise of truth and the good, and thus commit us without further reasons.
(3) The sharing of a collective attitude self-authorizes us as those who are in the position of making up our collective mind the same general way in which my conscious having of an attitude self-authorizes me. As the authority in question is of the plural rather than the singular kind, it should not be surprising that under non-dictatorial conditions, we find no singular autocrat in the collective making up of our mind. What we, together, think or intend is not just up to me, or just up to you, unless I fully authorize you to settle these issues for us.

Our cooperative making up of our mind, however, is no structure of mutual authorization, but rather plural self-authorization, in which each of us appears as the co-author of what's on our collective mind. We are in the best position to know what's on our mind because we, together, made it up.

12.4 Conclusion

Qua collective self-determination, radical collective responsibility is not the idea that we, together, could be just anything we arbitrarily choose to be. Rather, it is the sort of plural pre-reflective self-awareness in which who we are and what we intend, as the teams, groups, and larger collectives we are, is determined by the attitudes we share, and not determined by anything else. In this sense, who we are is up to us – and though this does not support the illusion that we could be just anything, regardless of any facts about the world, knowing ourselves to be self-determined prevents us from making some mistakes about ourselves that cover up ways in which we could actually change. For example, a popular conception of group agency in the current literature holds that group agents consist of a plurality of people and an aggregation procedure through which they transform a plurality of individual views into a group view (e.g., List/Pettit 2011). Where there is no such organization, it is claimed, there is no collective or group agency. This view is accepted even where it is recognized that lack of organization does not prevent us from being collectively responsible, resulting in the claim that there can be collective responsibility without a collective agent (e.g., Chant 2015).

From the perspective of the radical collective responsibility of plural subjects, as reconstructed above, any such view is easily recognizable as an expression of "collective bad faith," as it were – a collective version of the cheap excuse of which Sartre was so weary. "We," as plural subjects, are not constituted by our organization. Our organization does not determine who we, together, are and what we, together, want. Rather, *we organize ourselves*, and where we fail to organize appropriately, we are collectively responsible for that failure, as its subject, or as the agency who failed to put its act together by self-organizing appropriately. The way in which we organize what we are doing together (and that is, first and foremost, living together by sharing, to some extent, our lives) is by setting up norms, procedures and institutions; an infrastructure in which we – each of us – find our individual roles. Identifying with our individual roles is irresponsible only under certain circumstances. It is irresponsible where we cannot fully participate in constituting the role structure. The constitution of the role structure is the process through which we, as the collective we are, organize ourselves in the way that assigns us, severally, our individual roles. Where we cannot participate in the process of what makes us who we are, in our roles, we, together, are collectively irresponsible, for in this case, we let the question of who we are and how we live together be determined by other factors than ourselves, jointly.

Radical singular responsibility of the early existentialist kind is thus not the answer to collective irresponsibility. As individuals, we can only stick to the norms or depart from them – go along, deviate, or kill ourselves (the exit option on which Sartre insists so much). It is only as the plural subject we are that we can actually *change* our norms, procedures, and institutions and adapt them so as to fit our shared goal of living well together. This, however, presupposes first that we be aware of ourselves, jointly, in the right pre-reflective first-person plural way. Collective self-determination is no guarantee that it is being used well. But it is radically irresponsible not to take the question of who we are collectively as being up to us, as the random collections, groups, and societies we are. It is radically irresponsible to take the question of who we are to be determined by culture, power systems, organization, institutional design, etc.

rather than by us ourselves. For culture, power systems, organizations, institutional designs etc. are features of our living together for which we, jointly or collectively, are radically responsible.

References

Brandom, Robert B. (2001) *Articulating Reasons. An Introduction to Inferentialism*. Cambridge, MA, Harvard University Press.

Bratman, Michael E. (1999) *Faces of Intention*. Cambridge, Cambridge University Press.

Chant, Sara R. (2015) "Collective Responsibility in a Hollywood Standoff." *Thought* 4, pp. 83–92.

Cohen, Andrew J. (2008) "Existentialist Voluntarism as a Source of Normativity." *Philosophical Papers* 37, pp. 89–129.

Coliva, Annalisa (2015) "How to Commit Moore's Paradox." *Journal of Philosophy* 112/4, pp. 169–192.

Flynn, Thomas R. (1984) *Sartre and Marxist Existentialism. The Test Case of Collective Responsibility*. Chicago, University of Chicago Press.

Frankfurt, Harry (1998) *The Importance of What We Care About*. Cambridge, Cambridge University Press.

Gilbert, Margaret (2014) *Joint Commitment. How We Make the Social World*. Oxford, Oxford University Press.

Jankovic, Marija/Ludwig, Kirk (eds.) (2018) *The Routledge Handbook of Collective Intentionality*. London, Routledge.

Korsgaard, Christine M. (2008) *The Constitution of Agency*. Oxford, Oxford University Press.

List, Christian/Pettit, Philip (2011) *Group Agency*. Oxford, Oxford University Press.

Mendus, Susan (1989) *Liberalism and the Limits of Toleration*. Basingstoke, MacMillan.

Moran, Richard (2001) *Authority and Estrangement. An Essay on Self-Knowledge*. Princeton, Princeton University Press.

Raz, Joseph (1988) *The Morality of Freedom*. Oxford, Oxford University Press.

Sartre, Jean-Paul (1948) "Conscience de soi et connaissance de soi." *Bulletin de la Société Française de Philosophie* 42, pp. 49–91.

Sartre, Jean-Paul (1978 [1943]) *Being and Nothingness. A Phenomenological Essay on Ontology*. New York, Simon & Schuster.

Sartre, Jean-Paul (1991 [1960]) *Critique of Dialectical Reason*. Two vols., London, Verso.

Sartre, Jean-Paul (2007 [1945]) *Existentialism is a Humanism*. New Haven, Yale University Press.

Schmid, Hans B. (2014) "Expressing Group Attitudes. On First-Person Plural Authority." *Erkenntnis* 79, Suppl. 9, pp. 1685–1701.

Schmid, Hans B. (2017a) "Authentic Role Play. A Political Solution to an Existential Paradox." In: H.B. Schmid/G. Thonhauser (eds.), *From Conventionalism to Social Authenticity*. Cham, Springer, pp. 261–274.

Schmid, Hans B. (2017b) "What Kind of Mode is the We-Mode?" In: G. Preyer/G. Peter (eds.): *Social Ontology and Collective Intentionality*. Cham, Springer, pp. 79–94.

Schmid, Hans B. (2018) "The Subject of 'We Intend'." *Phenomenology & the Cognitive Sciences* 17, pp. 231–243.

Taylor, Charles (1988) "Responsibility for Self." In A. Oksenberg-Rorty (ed.), *The Identity of Persons*. Berkeley, University of California Press, pp. 281–299.

Velleman, J. David (1989) *Practical Reflections*. Princeton, Princeton University Press.

Waller, Bruce N. (1993) "Responsibility and the Self-Made Self." *Analysis* 53, No. 1, pp. 45–51.

13

COMMITMENTS AND COLLECTIVE RESPONSIBILITY[1]

Caroline T. Arruda

The debate about shared agency and its relationship to collective responsibility has focused on two related questions: (1) Is collective responsibility non-distributive or distributive—that is, should it be attributed to the group[2] as such or to its individual members?; and (2) If groups can be held collectively responsible, is this attribution explained by reference to the actions of the group or its individual members?

Answering these questions is often, although not uniformly,[3] taken to depend on whether groups are genuine agents in much the same way individual persons are. There are many views developed in the service of this end, but I will focus on one underappreciated aspect of this debate—namely, the role of commitments in explaining aspects of shared agency.

Notwithstanding the fact that commitments have received comparatively less attention than other, more central aspects of shared agency (such as what a shared intention is), they do not play a marginal role in the literature. Most notably, Margaret Gilbert (1989: 183; 2000: 23–4; 2002; 2006a: 101; 2006b; 2013; 2014; 2018) uses what she calls "joint commitments" to explain "the plural subject account of shared intention" (2014: 119).[4] More recently, she has suggested that "a plural subject *is* ... a set of jointly committed persons" (2018: 180). Commitments play a central, albeit different, role in other accounts (e.g., Bratman 2014; Heim 2015; Roth 2004; Tuomela 2006; Westlund 2009; cf. Alonso 2009). Like Gilbert, Michael Bratman (2014) regards commitments as an important feature of shared agency. Unlike Gilbert, however, he takes them to play a role in shared deliberation rather than being necessary or sufficient for shared agency itself.

Although commitments are not typically used to explain collective responsibility, their putative role in shared agency underscores the value of exploring the connection between the two. This task is complicated by the fact that there is no settled view of commitments, let alone the role that they play in shared agency. I thus have two aims in this chapter: (1) to identify the explicit and implicit roles that commitments play in accounts of shared agency, where "shared agency" is a catchall term that includes joint action, shared intention, collective intentionality, and other related phenomena;[5] and (2) to determine how these accounts of commitments do (or could) inform collective responsibility.

I begin with a discussion of commitments (§13.1). I formulate a case to highlight commitments' defining characteristics, with a special focus on how they might be fruitfully used to understand both individual and collective responsibility. In §13.2, I summarize the role of commitments in the literature on shared agency, with a particular focus on Gilbert's and

Bratman's respective accounts. I then turn to the relationship between (moral and non-moral) commitments and backward-looking collective responsibility (§13.3).

13.1 Commitments: An Overview

There are (at least) three general types of commitments:

(1) individual commitments to ourselves (e.g., my commitment to go running each morning)
(2) individual, interpersonal commitments (e.g., my commitment to call my best friend on a weekly basis)[6]
(3) fully shared commitments, where the commitments in question are those that we take on together (e.g., the commitment between two romantic partners)

The relevant question to consider in what follows is which type(s) of commitments play a role in the context of joint action and shared agency more broadly.

To do so, however, we first need to determine what a "commitment" is. Although the concept of a commitment figures prominently in a wide variety of philosophical debates, there has been comparatively little *direct* philosophical inquiry about them. There are exceptions to this generalization (e.g., Arruda ms; Bratman 2004; 2014; Brewer 2003; Chang 2009; 2013; Chartier 2017; Dorsey 2016; Elster 1985; 2000; Gilbert 2013; 2014; 2018; Helm 2017; Hieronymi 2006; 2009; Hinchman 2010; Holton 2009; Killmister 2017; Liberman and Schroeder 2016; Marušić 2015; Michael and Pacherie 2015; Ross 2012; Roth 2004; Schroeder 2013; Sen 1977; 2005; Shpall 2014; Townsend 2017). Yet even in cases where commitments are the focus, the contexts within which they are used also vary widely, from theories of intention, resolution, autonomy, and rationality, among others.

Given that this variety makes it difficult to identify *explicit* competing views about commitments, I suggest that it is most fruitful to begin from a guiding case. Doing so will help to determine the prospects of using commitments (and potential implicit views about them) to understand shared agency and collective responsibility.[7]

> *SMARTPHONES*: Imagine two close friends, Angela and Jane. They meet monthly for dinner, given that their respective jobs make it difficult to make last-minute plans to see one another. Jane notices that Angela often keeps her cell phone on the table while they are talking and is often distracted by what Angela acknowledges are unimportant text messages from other friends. Jane has told Angela that she would prefer it if Angela were to limit her phone use during their monthly dinners, given that Jane feels that it takes time away from the little time they have together. Angela agrees with Jane's assessment, and makes a commitment to be a better friend by avoiding using her cellphone during their monthly dinners.

Although this is an example of an individual, interpersonal commitment rather than a shared or joint commitment, it provides a useful model for answering the following questions:

(1) The Agency Question: What does *SMARTPHONES* show about commitments more generally such that they are helpful for understanding shared agency?
(2) The Responsibility Question: What, if anything, does *SMARTPHONES* show about the relationship between commitments and (moral) responsibility, both in the individual and collective senses?

13.1.1 The Agency Question

SMARTPHONES points to three characteristics of individual, interpersonal commitments. These characteristics will hold, *mutatis mutandis*, for commitments present in joint action, and they underscore why philosophers think commitments are important for understanding shared agency more broadly.[8]

First, under normal circumstances, commitments are attitudes that represent what we self-reflectively aim to do in light of the fact that we take this aim to have some import or value. In *SMARTPHONES*, Angela makes the commitment to Jane to limit her smartphone use during their monthly dinners *in order to* capture both that she has self-reflectively adopted this aim and that she takes this aim to have volitional significance for her future practical deliberation. This may seem like an obvious point, but there is not universal consensus on this matter. Shpall (2014: 148, 153), for example, denies that what he takes to be the philosophically compelling kinds of commitments have a "volitional" component; rather, the types of commitments that matter are those that establish normative relations between a mental state or action and its object (another mental state or action).[9] Sen (1977; 2005) denies that commitments are attitudes, and instead takes *actions* to be committed when they are undertaken for the pursuit of others' goals rather than for the sake of our own welfare. We do not, on Sen's view, *make* commitments; rather, we *engage in* committed actions. For others, such as Marušić (2015: esp. 122, 175), commitments are aspirations or resolutions to do what we have very little evidence we are likely to do.

Yet for commitments to play a substantive role in shared agency, they should have what Chang (2013) and Shpall (notwithstanding his claim that this feature is not present in the philosophically interesting cases of commitments) characterize as a "volitional" component. That is, they should be the kinds of attitudes or dispositions that figure prominently in our relationship with our own actions or the actions we undertake with others. At the same time, as I discuss in the next section, their role in shared agency is not fully explained by this characteristic.

SMARTPHONES suggests, second, that commitments are future-directed: (1) minimally, they represent what we aim to do rather than what we have done; and (2), in so doing, they add to the strength and the stability of our intentions, thereby putting rational pressure on us to follow through on them.[10] Here again, there is little consensus in the literature about whether commitments are future-directed in this second, more robust sense (Bratman 2004; 2014; 2018; Hinchman 2014; Holton 2009; Marušić 2015; Morton 2013; Morton and Paul, 2019).[11] Nonetheless, this feature of commitments is significant for shared agency. One puzzle for theories of shared agency is to explain how and why we should count on one another to follow through on our plans to act together. One way to solve this puzzle is to point to the kind of stability that either intentions or, as I suggest above, commitments provide. As will become apparent in §13.2, both Gilbert's and Bratman's respective uses of commitments will depend on the idea that they provide stability of this more robust kind.

SMARTPHONES highlights, third, that commitments have normative force. They establish backward-looking reasons, either other things being equal or all things considered, to follow through on the commitment. At Angela and Jane's next dinner, Angela can appeal to her commitment as the *source of* her reasons to, other things being equal, refrain from checking her messages. In this regard, commitments share some features with promises in that both are the source of backward-looking reasons, and the sense in which they are such a source depends on whether they were voluntarily made.

Worries about bootstrapping naturally arise here (Bratman 1987; Chang 2013; Ferrero 2006: 103; 2010; Holton 2009; Marušić 2015).[12] In the individual case, the problem of bootstrapping arises because the fact that one made a commitment to φ is potentially the *wrong kind of reason* to justify φ-ing.[13] The fact that someone makes a commitment to, say, be a jerk—or, to invoke an example from Rawls (1971: 432), to count blades of grass—does not provide an independent reason to do so. In fact, one might think that there are overriding reasons *not* to be a jerk even when one has made a commitment to do so. In the grass-counting case, there are no overriding reasons not to fulfill one's commitment to grass-counting, but one might wonder whether the fact that one has made a commitment to count blades of grass is sufficient reason to do so. Granting that commitments provide sufficient reasons in either instance is to suggest that we can bootstrap into existence reasons (that do not hold otherwise) simply by what amounts to an act of will. Even if one is willing to grant that we can do this in some circumstances, as Chang (2013) argues in the case of loving relationships, there is a genuine question about whether commitments can generally do so without falling prey to a bootstrapping problem.

Yet it is unclear whether these same worries arise in the case of shared agency. The backward-looking reasons that commitments plausibly involve in the context of shared activities are not reasons to φ; rather, they are reasons to uphold the commitment that one has made to (and with) others, where the end goal of doing so is that they φ together.[14] If this is correct, then, interestingly enough, the problem of bootstrapping is only (or largely) a problem for the case of individual (whether inter- or intra-personal) commitments.[15]

Another aspect of commitments' normative force worth emphasizing—particularly for their import in debates about shared agency—is that their normativity is not necessarily moral in nature. That is, they may always have action-guiding force, but not in virtue of their inherently moral nature. In *SMARTPHONES*, on the assumption that it is not morally wrong to multi-task while spending time with friends, Angela's commitment is normative only in the sense that it is action-guiding for her future decision-making. If commitments have any particular moral force, it is in virtue of their content—that is, the moral worth of the action that is their object. Even if one wants to grant that the commitment in *SMARTPHONES* is moral because it involves Angela's respect for Jane, it is nonetheless the *content* of the commitment—rather than the fact that Angela has made a commitment—that gives it moral force. To see why, simply compare *SMARTPHONES* with a case where Angela makes a commitment to avoid using her smartphone around Jane, but only for the sake of cultivating her ability to focus on one task rather than out of concern for Jane.

13.1.2 The Responsibility Question

SMARTPHONES suggests a number of important ways in which commitments are relevant for understanding (moral)[16] responsibility. As will become apparent, however, there are important disanalogies between their role in the individual and collective contexts.

First, *SMARTPHONES* shows that Angela has forward-looking responsibility[17] to follow through on her commitment to Jane. As Gilbert (2014: 58) notes, we are responsible in a backward-looking sense when we have caused some state of affairs for which responsibility judgments are fitting. By contrast, we are responsible in the forward-looking sense when we have obligations to fulfill.[18] *SMARTPHONES* shows that commitments, much like promises, set up obligations to the commitment's addressee (and the addressee's expectation that the commitment will be fulfilled) and thus are the grounds for forward-looking responsibility. The source of the obligation is twofold: (1) Angela has voluntarily made the commitment such that she has made herself answerable to Jane; and (2) Jane has a claim on Angela to fulfill the commitment given that Jane is the addressee of the commitment.

There are not, however, analogues to (1) and (2) in the collective case. Regarding (1), for at least some views of the role of commitments in shared agency such as Gilbert's, the obligations associated with commitments may hold simply in virtue of one's membership in a group or one's participation in a joint activity rather than solely in terms of whether one explicitly makes a commitment. There is also no clear analogue to (2) in the collective case. Although *SMARTPHONES* involves an interpersonal commitment, it is not mutual. Angela has made a commitment to Jane (and thus has an obligation to her to follow through on it), whereas Jane does not have a comparable commitment (and concomitant obligation) to Angela. By contrast, if commitments are relevant for understanding *collective* responsibility, the paradigmatic type of commitments will be mutual (or even fully shared) rather than interpersonal.

Notwithstanding this disanalogy, let's return to *SMARTPHONES* to consider what else it tells us about the relationship between commitments and responsibility. *SMARTPHONES* highlights the conditions under which Angela can be released from her commitment. Since the commitment is interpersonal, one might be tempted to think that only Jane can release Angela. There are, however, two reasons to doubt that Jane and only Jane can release Angela from her commitment: (1) this would require categorizing commitments as a special form of promises; and (2) there is an intrapersonal dimension to commitments that captures Angela's initial willingness to take on the commitment and what it requires. Regarding (1), commitments may share some features with promises. Yet we use them in different contexts and thus we should be able to explain them in ways that reflect these differences. The obligations commitments create must, in at least some cases, be jointly rescinded, whereas promises are typically rescinded only by the promisee. What about (2)? Even if Jane releases Angela from the latter's commitment to avoid using her phone during dinner, Angela may not want to give up her commitment and may still judge that she has reasons to uphold it.

As was the case above, this feature of individual, interpersonal commitments again stands in contrast to mutual (or even fully shared) commitments in the context of shared agency. As I discuss in §13.2, these commitments cannot be rescinded by one participant; rather, they must be rescinded either by all participants individually or, even, by all participants as a group. Whether there is an intrapersonal dimension to these commitments will vary among the different views of shared agency in which commitments play a role.

Thus far, I have used *SMARTPHONES* to understand the relationship between commitments and forward-looking responsibility (in both the individual and collective senses). Yet the more familiar kind of responsibility is backward-looking. *SMARTPHONES* shows that there is an important disanalogy between commitments and individual backward-looking responsibility, on the one hand, and commitments and collective backward-looking responsibility on the other. In the individual case, we will likely need a robust theory of (moral) responsibility to explain how commitments are connected in any interesting and informative way to states of affairs for which backward-looking responsibility attributions are appropriate.[19] In the collective case, by contrast, they often secure important aspects of shared agency, as I briefly outlined in the previous section and as I show in more detail in §13.2. In this regard, commitments will turn out to be directly relevant for the question of collective backward-looking responsibility even if they do not fully settle the question of whether and when it is appropriate to assign it.

Finally, there is one issue that is unique to the question of collective responsibility and for which commitments will be useful, but for which there is no analogue in the individual case. This is the question, to which I return in §13.3, of whether collective responsibility is distributive or non-distributive.

13.2 Commitments and Shared Agency

Let's now consider Gilbert's and Bratman's respective accounts of commitments and shared agency. The characteristics gleaned from *SMARTPHONES* in answer to The Agency Question suggest the following guiding questions around which to organize this discussion:[20, 21]

(1) Are joint or shared commitments propositional attitudes, dispositions or some other kind of mental state?
(2) Are joint or shared commitments distinct from or reducible to individual commitments?[22]
(3) What is joint or shared commitments' normative status?

13.2.1 Gilbert's Account of Commitments

Gilbert's (1989: 183; 2000: 23–4; 2002; 2006a: 101; 2006b; 2013; 2014; 2018) extensive treatment of the role of commitments deserves special attention.[23] Before considering Gilbert's view of what she calls joint commitment, let's briefly consider the role they play in her account of shared agency. Gilbert writes, "Persons X and Y *share an intention* to do A if and only if X and Y are jointly committed to intend as a body to do A" (2014: 114). So given the background condition of common knowledge, being jointly committed to intend as a body to φ is necessary and sufficient for sharing an intention φ.[24] What ensures that individuals *act together*, however, is that they each continue to contribute to and to maintain the joint commitment in question (Gilbert 2014: 119).

So what is a joint commitment, according to Gilbert? To answer this question, let's first consider joint commitments' origin. Two individuals have created a joint commitment if they meet the following sufficient conditions: "If it is common knowledge in a population, P, that *everyone in P has expressed his readiness to be jointly committed in a certain way*, this suffices to create the relevant joint commitment" (Gilbert 2006a: 101). The members of, say, a community garden have a joint commitment to, for short, tend to their garden's plants when it is common knowledge among the members that each and every one of them has expressed her readiness to be jointly committed to tending their garden.

Let's consider this account in greater detail. First, what constitutes "readiness"? Gilbert (2006b: 139; 2014: 27, 30) suggests that an agent expresses "readiness" when she agrees to undertake an activity with someone else or even when she simply displays her readiness to participate with others by pursuing actions with them for which such willingness is a prerequisite. Here Gilbert focuses on how readiness is expressed, but it is useful to speculate on what readiness means for each individual participating agent. Gilbert provides the following answer:

> It is not clear that there is any helpful way of breaking down the notion of expressing one's readiness to be jointly committed. It could be said that one makes it clear that *all is in order as far as one's own will is concerned* for the creation of the relevant joint commitment.
>
> *(2013: 48)*

With this point in mind, let's speculate a bit more about what readiness involves. To do so, let's consider what readiness means for individual agents. I take Gilbert's view to require something akin to the following picture of readiness *in the individual case*: I express my readiness to, say, learn Italian if I am prepared to form an intention to do so and I have no conflicting plans (e.g., that I also intend not to learn it). Here, "conflict" need not only mean "logically inconsistent";

rather, it can be read more weakly, where any conflicting attitudes or plans would indicate that I am less than wholehearted, to invoke a phrase of Frankfurt's (1998), with regard to the course of action. For Frankfurt (1998: 164–5), agents are wholehearted with regard to what they aim to do when they meet the following conditions: first, they are internally coherent insofar as their aims correspond to what they want themselves *to want*; and second, they have second-order volitions regarding what they want themselves *to will*.

Although this picture of readiness seems to apply to individual commitments, it can also be applied, *mutatis mutandis*, to Gilbert's account of joint commitments. Gilbert's (2014: 44–5) view does not require that agents have these *explicit* second-order attitudes toward a future joint commitment nor does it require that they hold concomitant individual commitments. In fact, if anything like the Frankfurtian picture of wholeheartedness helps to explain Gilbertian readiness, it is only with regard to an individual's readiness *to be party to a joint commitment* regardless of whether she herself is individually committed to the same activity.[25] Still, understanding readiness is important because it is supposed to explain how each agent is in a position to form, for Gilbert (2014: 9, 124, 126), a plural subject.[26] To see why, consider again the community garden case. Recall that it is common knowledge among the volunteers that each one has expressed her readiness to be jointly committed to tending their garden. In doing so, each is willing to adopt the goal of tending the garden *with other members of the group*, rather than merely individually contributing to such activity. By adopting this goal, she must also have no conflicting aims *with regard to what she undertakes with other members of the group*, and the same must be true of all other members.[27] As a result, they together count as being jointly committed to tending the garden. Note, however, that Gilbert denies that joint commitments must be explicit or the product of an explicit agreement such as a promise or a vow.[28] This means we may be party to joint commitments in many more contexts than our intuitive picture suggests.

Given this description of readiness, it would seem that Gilbertian commitments are what, in §13.1, I called volitional. Yet Gilbert (2014: 6) emphasizes that while "the process [of forming joint commitments] is psychological, the product is normative."[29] This suggests that joint commitments are not, themselves, reducible to the individual attitude of being committed to φ-ing nor are they, themselves, jointly-held attitudes toward φ-ing; rather, they are states of affairs that supervene on or are constituted by the conditions for agents to be jointly committed to φ-ing outlined above.[30] This suggests that Gilbert would answer question (1) in the negative.

This picture of joint commitments suggests that they are not reducible to individual commitments, thereby giving us an answer to (2) above (Gilbert 2014: 38, 40–3). What makes joint commitments irreducible is their distinctive aim—namely, to secure the foundations for agents to act together such that they "emulate" a single body (Gilbert 2014: 118–19). Here "emulate" captures the sense in which individuals' joint commitments are aimed at bringing about the state of affairs where they constitute (and maintain) a "*non*-collective body" (Gilbert 2014: 119, 41). In the case of the members of the community garden who are jointly committed to tending their plants, they aim to constitute a non-collective body insofar as each intends to bring it about that *they* tend the garden.[31] But what does it mean that "they" tend the garden? That is, they aim to act together such that they act *as though* they were a single agent by way of the actions of each participant. This has the twofold result of explaining how commitments unify individuals' actions while avoiding the need to point to a wholly distinct collective agent (Gilbert 2014: 41, 117).

Thus far, I have focused on the descriptive aspects of Gilbert's view. To understand its import for collective responsibility, let's consider its normative features. Gilbert (2014: 49–50) suggests that insofar as we are party to a joint commitment, we have obligations to follow through on it. But what sort of obligation? They create, Gilbert (2006b; 2014: 50, 276–7, 305; 2018) thinks, *directed* obligations to the other parties to the commitment, such that they are rights-bearers who can demand that it be fulfilled.[32,33] Since each party to the joint commitment is in this position and the commitment is jointly held, it follows that all parties are "answerable" to one another for violations of the joint commitment (Gilbert 2014: 40). Moreover, individual members cannot justifiably rescind the commitment (or even reject the sense in which it holds sway over each of them); rather, joint commitments must be jointly rescinded (Gilbert 2014: 40).[34] Returning to the community garden case, each member is answerable if they fail to tend the garden. If, however, the goal of tending the garden is merely one member's *aspiration* and she simply hopes that occasional visitors to the community plot will be moved to tend the garden, none of the members is answerable for the dead plants.

So in what sense are Gilbertian joint commitments normative? They are normative insofar as they establish the obligations (and concomitant answerability) outlined above. Notably, however, this normativity is non-moral. I take it that Gilbert means that the obligation to follow through on one's joint commitment to, say, go for a walk with a friend is not grounded in moral principles, such as those that say that we ought to keep our promises. The normativity in question is particular to commitments in that, like promises, they have the power to create obligations and, thereby, reasons to follow through on them.[35]

13.2.2 Bratman's Account of Commitment

Bratman's (1987; 1999a; b; 2007a; b; c; 2014; 2015) account of shared agency stands at odds with much of Gilbert's view, and his account of what he calls shared commitment is no exception (2014: 132). While he takes shared commitments to play a role in cases where agents already share an intention to engage in a joint activity, they are neither necessary nor sufficient for shared intention itself.

Consider one of his more recent formulations of the sufficient conditions for shared intention:[36]

> We are thereby led to the following somewhat compressed sufficient conditions for our shared intention to *J*: **A.** *Intention condition*: We each have intentions that we *J*; and we each intend that we *J* by way of each of our intentions that we *J* (so there is interlocking and reflexivity) and by way of relevant mutual responsiveness in sub-plan and action, and so by way of sub-plans that mesh. **B.** *Belief condition:* We each believe that if the intentions of each in favor of our *J*-ing persist, we will *J* by way of those intentions and relevant mutual responsiveness in sub-plan and action; and we each believe that there is interdependence in persistence of those intentions of each in favor of our *J*-ing. **C.** *Interdependence condition*: There is interdependence in persistence of the intentions of each in favor of our J-ing. **D.** *Common knowledge condition*: It is common knowledge that A-D.
>
> *(Bratman 2014: 103)*

Take the case of two people dancing the tango. The tango dancers share an intention to dance the tango under the following sufficient conditions. Each dancer intends that they dance the tango (that "we *J*"). Each intends to dance the tango by way of the intentions of each other agent that they act jointly (that we *J*). Each correctly believes that they will dance the tango by way of these intentions and their meshing sub-plans (e.g., the particular dance moves required to successfully dance the tango). Finally, each of these aspects of their dancing the tango are common knowledge among them.

In outlining his view of the sufficient conditions for shared intention, Bratman makes no explicit reference to, nor does his view require, joint or individual commitment. In fact, he rejects Gilbert's use of joint commitment to *ground* (even partially) shared agency. He does so for two reasons. First, he regards joint commitments as what he describes as "shared-intention-loaded concepts of shared activity" (2014: 46–7). Here the idea is that it is circular to draw on concepts that already contain reference to shared intentions (or similar shared attitudes). Instead, we ought to focus on individual intentions directed toward what he calls "shared-intention-neutral joint activity" (*Id.*), as in the case of two friends intentionally walking down the street with one another. Arguably, joint commitments are not fully neutral in this sense. Second, while Bratman (2014: 114–15, 155) acknowledges that there may be interpersonal obligations that arise in particular instances of joint activity, these obligations are neither necessary conditions for, nor are they entailed by, joint activity. Since Gilbert regards joint commitments, in the context of their role in shared intention, as entailing directed obligations, this is a second reason that Bratman does not adopt them.

Still, even if they are not necessary to explain what Bratman (2014: 3) dubs "modest sociality," Bratman suggests that they figure in its more complex expressions (2014: 132–50; 2006).[37] To see their promise, consider Bratman's (2004: 336–7) account of individual commitment. Individual commitments involve higher-order (e.g., second-order) forms of endorsement of first-order, volitionally significant attitudes (e.g., desires). These endorsements reflect, minimally, what we take to be reasons in favor of acting on the volitionally significant attitudes or, more demandingly, in light of overall policies for self-government.[38] This more demanding type[39] of individual commitment provides a starting point for understanding Bratman's (2014: 132) account of what he calls "shared" commitments. The relevant kind of commitments that figure in some instances of modest sociality are those that, first, are shared and, second, play a role in the group's shared deliberation.

Let's consider each of these claims. First, these commitments must be shared because, Bratman (2014: 132) argues, they are made possible only by other, pre-existing shared intentions. Notice that this does not mean that commitments cannot be individually held; rather, Bratman thinks that the kinds of commitments that matter for shared agency in general and modest sociality in particular are those that piggyback upon shared intentions. Second, shared commitments represent a group's policies regarding the weight they should give to reasons, matters of concern or values in shared deliberation (Bratman 2014: 132–50). They thus serve two functions: they organize and rank considerations, goals, side constraints, and values; they rule out some considerations as weighting considerations in shared deliberation (Bratman 2014: 132–3).

But why are shared commitments essential for understanding shared deliberation? For deliberation to be genuinely shared, individuals must begin from some type of common ground. Neither common knowledge, nor individual policies for deliberation, nor even "public consensus" about values[40] will be sufficient, Bratman (2014: 132, 136) contends. By contrast, shared commitments explain how individuals can move from "more or less articulated relative weights" about matters of shared deliberative concern to genuinely shared conclusions (Bratman 2014: 133). Given this role, commitments' *direct* objects are the weights or policies we want to govern our shared deliberation. So, in the example of the community garden, Bratman would likely say that the members of the group have a shared commitment to weighting the end of tending the garden more heavily than, say, socializing with one another at their weekly gardening sessions.

With Bratman's account in view, let's consider how a proponent of a view like his would answer the questions outlined at the beginning of §13.2. Given the role that Bratman contends shared commitments play in shared deliberation, it seems clear that he would answer (1) in the affirmative. Shared commitments are at least partially constituted by individual group members' attitudes regarding what they intend to do jointly with others and how they should deliberate as a group.

In a departure from Gilbert's view, Bratman (2014: 8–9) would likely answer (2)—are joint or shared commitments distinct from or reducible to individual commitments?—by noting that shared commitments are an extension of commitments' role in individual planning agency.[41, 42] In this regard, we should understand them in terms of the commitments that each individual member of the group has with regard to how they should deliberate *as a group*. Since they piggyback on already shared intentions, however, the fact that they are distributive in this way does not entail that they are simply an *aggregation of* individual commitments.

This answer sheds light on how a Bratmanian would answer (3)—viz., what is commitments' normative status? Given shared commitments' role in shared deliberation, they have normative import, but not in Gilbert's sense. While Gilbert takes joint commitments to be normative in that they entail directed obligations, Bratman's view suggests that their normativity arises from the way in which they establish positive and negative constraints on deliberation that the group has voluntarily adopted.[43] This type of normativity, if indeed it is correctly characterized as such, is akin to the normativity of the requirements of rationality.[44]

In light of these answers to the central questions about commitments, there is significant disagreement between Gilbert and Bratman about how to understand (individual, joint or shared) commitments themselves (Gilbert 2014: 122–6; Bratman 2014: 107–20, 134–6).[45] As we will see in the next section, their views also provide competing pictures of commitments' role in collective responsibility.[46]

13.3 Commitments and Collective Responsibility

Few accounts of commitments link them directly with collective responsibility.[47] Still, commitments' roles in accounts of shared agency suggest that they should inform this debate. Recall that, in §13.1, I suggested that both individual and joint (or shared) commitments establish forward-looking responsibility by virtue of establishing participants' obligations to do their part in a shared activity. This is an uncontroversial idea,[48] given the way that many philosophers, such as Gilbert (2014: 7; 2018: 163, 171–2, v–vi), take commitments to establish what Westlund (2009: 14) describes as the mutual accountability agents have to one another.[49, 50]

By contrast, the case of *SMARTPHONES* revealed very little about the role of commitments in cases of *individual* backward-looking responsibility. Still, as I suggested in §13.1, commitments may play a significant, if underappreciated, role in *collective* backward-looking responsibility. I made this suggestion on the basis of their import for views such as Gilbert's, where commitments are necessary or sufficient conditions for shared agency. In what follows, I expand upon this suggestion. I then consider a second, more ecumenical way of using commitments to (partially) explain backward-looking collective responsibility—namely, by linking it to failures to meet the obligations that commitments create.

13.3.1 Commitments, Shared Agency, and Backward-Looking Responsibility

If joint commitments are necessary and sufficient for collectively intending an action,[51] they are, by extension, at least necessary for assigning backwards-looking collective responsibility for states of affairs that, in Gilbert's language, the plural subject has caused through its intentional actions.[52] I say "at least necessary" because whether a group collectively intends an action is not alone necessary and sufficient for holding the group collectively responsible. Other conditions might need to obtain—for example, they need not only intend an action, but also successfully, intentionally bring it about. Notice that this point suggests that it is not commitments' particular content—say, we are jointly committed to being unkind—that informs the judgment that we are responsible in a backward-looking sense for being unkind; rather, it is that this joint commitment, regardless of its content, secures our capacity for shared intentional action (which happens to be an instance of acting unkindly). Naturally, commitments' content makes some difference for backward-looking responsibility attributions—the sense in which it matters is just whether it represents a course of action that is morally wrong.

Bratman's account of commitments provides an alternative way of linking commitments with backward-looking responsibility. Although Bratman denies that what he calls shared commitments are necessary or sufficient for sharing an intention or for shared agency more broadly, he contends that they play a substantive role in how shared agency is exercised. This is because commitments organize shared deliberation. In this regard, if commitments are necessary conditions for shared deliberation, then they are also relevant for the way in which groups bring about states of affairs for which they could be collectively responsible in a backward-looking sense. Recall the community garden case. Imagine that the group members deliberate about whether to dispose of their unused weed killer in the city's drains, they know that doing so will pollute the water supply, and they decide to do so in light of a commitment they have to promote their garden's beauty above all else. In this case, it is their commitment that plays a necessary role in their causing the water to be polluted. Insofar as deliberation is a condition for responsibility attribution (Yaffe 2009: 10; cf. Guerrero 2015: 83–4) and commitments play an essential role in shared deliberation, then it is plausible to think that they might be the source of backward-looking collective responsibility attributions.

With commitments' two possible roles in backward-looking collective responsibility in mind, let's consider whether commitments also help us to determine whether it is distributive or non-distributive. On first glance, it would seem that backward-looking responsibility in this context is non-distributive. Assume we adopt a robust view of commitments such as Gilbert's, according to which commitments secure a group's capacity to engage in shared intentional action such as maintaining the community garden. If we think that commitments play a role in unifying the participants such that they are able to act together, then the commitments are essential for explaining the way in which the community garden's plants died. Since these commitments are jointly held, the backward-looking responsibility for failing to uphold them should, in principle, be non-distributive. But this is not necessarily the case. The *specific* conditions under which such failures occur will determine whether, in any particular instance, it is distributive or non-distributive. Imagine that part of the group's plan for tending the garden involves applying compost. Some of the new volunteers fail to learn how to apply it correctly, and those who know how to apply it do not teach the new members. In this case, there is non-distributive collective responsibility for the group's failure to adhere to their plan and also distributive responsibility for the particular ways in which each of the individual members' actions as group members contributed to the plants' demise.

This discussion shows that it is natural, but ultimately wrong, to think that commitments' role in securing shared agency entails that, insofar as they are jointly held, the kind of backward-looking collective responsibility that commitments help to explain must be fundamentally and exclusively non-distributive. First, whether it is non-distributive will depend on how the failures to uphold the commitment occurred and whether they attach to the group as such. Second, commitments might be used to explain how a group member is *also* distributively responsible, even after we have determined that she is part of a group to which we ascribe non-distributive responsibility. This is because commitments, even when they are jointly held, are *also held or at least maintained by* individual agents.

13.3.2 *Commitments, Obligations, and Backward-Looking Responsibility*

What if one does not want to grant that commitments play such a significant and fundamental role in shared agency as that outlined in the previous section? Is there a way to link commitments with backward-looking responsibility while remaining neutral regarding their role as one of the building blocks of shared intention, shared intentional action, and the like?

One option is to return to their role in establishing the grounds of forward-looking responsibility.[53] Here the idea is that if joint commitments entail obligations to follow through on them, some failures to do so will be those for which groups are collectively responsible in the backward-looking sense. I say "some" rather than "all" failures because the way by which such a failure occurs will affect whether it is appropriate to attribute collective responsibility of any form.

Before considering this approach, four caveats are in order. First, this approach may seem inconsistent with the idea that backward- and forward-looking responsibility are different in kind (Isaacs 2014: 43–4; Rovane 2014: 12; Smiley 2014; cf. Mathiesen 2006: 254). In fact, however, this approach does not deny that they are different in kind. Instead, it is focused on the kinds of backward-responsibility we assign when people fail to meet their (moral) obligations; it is mute with regard to whether forward-looking responsibility more generally (should) focus(es) on what Rovane (2014: 12) describes as "*taking* responsibility for what will happen in the future." A more robust way of reading this approach is to interpret it as showing that while Rovane, Isaacs, Smiley, and others may be correct that these two forms of responsibility typically come apart, the role of commitments in shared agency suggest that there is one important domain where they are intimately interconnected.

Second, it may seem that this approach inverts the typical way of understanding the relationship between backward- and forward-looking responsibility. Usually, one *begins from* a backward-looking responsibility attribution—say, Jane's intentionally lighting the match and knowingly throwing it on the dry leaves caused the small forest fire—and *then moves to* the judgment that Jane has a forward-looking responsibility to correct the harm by, say, replanting the trees. My approach in this section does not rule out this type of explanation; rather, I suggest that, in contexts where we have created obligations to follow through on certain actions by virtue of our commitments to do so, the explanation of backward-looking responsibility for failing to meet these obligations is dependent upon first establishing the grounds for the relevant forward-looking responsibility.[54]

Third, this approach is not inconsistent with the standard way of understanding backward-looking responsibility attributions as those for which one has *caused* a harm. In fact, this approach takes the idea that antecedent forward-looking responsibility attributions, which are based on the duties we have to others, *identify* the context within which to determine the causal route by which we failed to meet those commitments. It is only after so doing that we can determine the propriety of attributing backward-looking responsibility.

Finally, Gilbert's view would seem to best illustrate the approach under consideration in this section. Yet I initially characterized the approach in this section as neutral regarding whether commitments are necessary or sufficient for shared agency. Gilbert's view is not neutral on this front. Although I treat Gilbert's view as the paradigm in what follows, I limit my discussion to her account of the relationship between commitments and obligations. In this regard, one could easily adopt her view about this relationship while rejecting her view about the role of commitments in shared agency more broadly.

With these caveats in mind, let's return to the original case of the community garden members. Here, joint commitments entail, first, *individual* backward-looking responsibility for any members of the group who fail to follow through on them. There may also be distributive, collective responsibility.[55] What does the latter depend on? Consider two modified versions of the case. In the first version, one member of the community garden misses his shift for weeding the vegetable plot, thereby causing an overgrowth of weeds in what the group had wanted to be a well-tended garden. This member is individually responsible for his part in failing to uphold the joint commitment to tend the garden, but there is no clear sense in which there is any collective responsibility. For the sake of comparison, imagine a second version of the case where the members are jointly committed to having a tended garden but they make no plan for how such tending will take place, thereby allowing the garden to be consumed by weeds. In this version, the group is collectively responsible in the distributive sense because each individual member, by virtue of their group membership and their failure as a group to make a plan for their garden's care, failed to uphold their joint commitment.

What about the possibility of classifying the group as (also) non-distributively collectively responsible for failing to follow through on their joint commitments? This responsibility is non-distributive only if the responsibility for failing to follow through on the commitment to tend the garden attaches to the group as such. Can such responsibility attach to the group as such? If the failure to uphold the commitment is a product of the group failing to follow through—as in the case of the community garden members failing to make a plan to beautify their garden but nonetheless being committed to doing so—then the responsibility for failing to follow through on the commitment (and for the dead plants) is the group's.

13.4 Conclusion

Commitments, perhaps surprisingly, play a wide range of roles in debates about shared agency in general and collective responsibility in particular. Commitments are often taken to be normatively and volitionally fundamental for individual agents. If what I have argued here is correct, they are just as important for understanding how we act together and the conditions under which it is appropriate to hold us collectively responsible for doing so.

Notes

1 I thank Margaret Gilbert, Deborah Tollefsen, and Saba Bazargan-Forward for comments on early drafts of this chapter.

2 I use the term "group" ecumenically, given the wide variety of views considered in this chapter. Here, I treat it as a neutral catch-all descriptor for non-agential collectives or aggregates as well as for collective or group agents. Where philosophers have specific views about this debate, I flag how the term "group" should be understood in their respective views.

3 See, e.g., Bernstein 2017; Björnsson 2014; Chant 2015; Copp 1979: 185; 2007; Feinberg 1968: 677-ff; May 1992; Mellema 1988: 48; Wringe 2010; 2014. Cf. Arruda 2017.

4 See Gilbert (2014:118–19) for a discussion of why the phrase "plural subject" has been overinterpreted. She suggests that the agents who compose it do not share a "set of *subjective* experiences that exist *apart from* any such streams or sequences associated with the individual human members of the plural subject" (2018: fn 45).

5 I cast a wide net because philosophers disagree about what (if anything) is shared and whether groups as such or the individuals who constitute them genuinely share any attitudes. This diversity of views suggests a similarly wide variety of roles for commitments to play therein.

6 It might seem that this is a case of a jointly-held commitment given that it involves my explicit commitment to another person. One might even contend that all commitments that involve others are jointly held in some literal sense. Nonetheless, as I discuss in §13.1, there is at least a putative difference between interpersonal commitments where each participant makes their respective individual commitments to one another and fully shared commitments that are taken on by us together. The relevant question to consider when invoking commitments in the context of joint action is whether there is such a difference and, if so, which type of commitments plays a fundamental role in understanding shared agency more broadly.

7 I use an example of an interpersonal commitment since the self-directed (or intrapersonal) type does not seem to be the relevant individual analogue for commitments' role in shared agency.

8 One might contend that there is no *prima facie* reason to grant that commitments' role in shared agency is analogous to their role in individual, interpersonal contexts. While this is correct, nothing about the account I provide above relies on this presumption; rather, it relies on the presumption that the characteristic *features* of commitments will largely hold between the two contexts. More important, the purpose of the account I provide above is to explain how commitments are used in the available accounts of shared agency, and this presumption is in the background of many of the accounts discussed in this chapter (notwithstanding the fact that I [Arruda ms] argue that commitments lack many of the features that these accounts take them to have).

9 See also Liberman and Schroeder (2016) and Ross (2012). Compare with Chang (2013).

10 So commitments are not reducible to intentions nor are they special, "extra strong" intentions.

11 I challenge the idea that commitments are future-directed in these more robust senses in Arruda (ms).

12 This issue is related to the question of whether one takes rational requirements to be wide- or narrow-scope.

13 See Holton (2009) and Marušić (2015), among others, for ways around this problem.

14 There may be bootstrapping worries regarding the reasons we have to follow through on the commitment itself.

15 For a related discussion of how this relates to scope of rational requirements, see Gilbert (2018: 42–6).

16 "Moral" is parenthetical here, given the question raised in the previous section regarding commitments' normative status.

17 Whether this is *moral* responsibility will depend on whether one takes the content of Angela's commitment to be moral in nature, as I argue in the previous section.

18 Compare with Rovane (2014).

19 To name one possibility, commitments might complement quality of will accounts of moral responsibility.

20 Cf. Michael and Pacherie (2015: 91–3).

21 Compare with List's (2014) distinction between different types of collective attitudes. Since part of what is at issue is *whether* and *in what sense* commitments are collective attitudes, I take this more neutral set of questions as a starting point.

22 In §13.2.2, I address whether the commitments in question are better described as "joint" or "shared".

23 For overviews, see Shockley (2004) and Wilkins (2002).

24 See Michael and Pacherie (2015: 95-ff) for a discussion of the differences among treating commitments as necessary, as sufficient or as important (but neither necessary nor sufficient conditions) for shared agency.

25 Gilbert notes that it is possible for individuals to be what she describes (in written communication) as "reluctantly ready." This suggests that using a Frankfurtian conception of wholeheartedness in this context should not be taken to entail that individuals' readiness involves throwing their full weight behind the action. Instead, as I see it, the Frankfurtian picture helps to explain what is involved in their readiness to be party to the joint commitment itself.

26 Or "a plurality of persons" (Gilbert 2014: 9).

27 I thank Margaret Gilbert for noting that agents may have conflicting personal aims.

28 Gilbert (2014: 50) argues that agreements are *constituted by*, rather than necessary or sufficient *conditions for*, joint commitments. See, e.g., Gilbert (2014: essays 12 & 13) for her account of promises.

29 I thank Margaret Gilbert for emphasizing this point.

30 Whether it is more accurate to describe the relationship as one of supervenience or constitution is outside the purview of this chapter.

31 As Gilbert has emphasized in written communication, she acknowledges the possibility that individual participants can have what she calls "subversive personal intentions."

32 For the sake of clarity, I focus on the normative implications of Gilbert's view for small groups even though she applies her view to large groups and, even, to organized society as such (see 2006b).
33 For challenges to Gilbert's account of directed obligations, see Shockley (2004: esp. 557) and Brewer (2003). For Gilbert's reply, see (2018, esp. ch. 8).
34 Individuals may be justified in failing to adhere to the commitment, as Margaret Gilbert has suggested to me.
35 But compare with the issue of bootstrapping in §13.1.
36 Compare with (1999b: 143).
37 See Smith (2015: 57) for a discussion of the advantages of making joint commitment a necessary condition for shared agency. See Bratman (2015: 75–6) for a reply.
38 See Cullity and Gerrans (2004) for a challenge to Bratman's view. The quotation above is taken from Bratman's response.
39 Bratman (2004) thinks there are three forms of what he calls "agential commitment."
40 See Bratman (2006: 7).
41 See Bratman (2014: 55) for a comparison of his view with Gilbert's.
42 See Bratman's (2014: 3–9) "continuity thesis."
43 Bratman (2014: 112–13) denies that there is a necessary connection between shared intention and "mutual obligation." Normative principles about interpersonal obligation can explain when and how such obligations hold, Bratman claims.
44 Compare with Gilbert (2018: 162).
45 Notwithstanding this point, Bratman (2014: 115, 154–5) takes his "basic thesis" to be consistent with many of Gilbert's conclusions.
46 For more on this issue, see Smith (2015) as well as Michael and Pacherie (2015: esp. section 3). See Kopec and Miller (2018) on Gilbert's view.
47 Cf. Heim (2015).
48 Whether this responsibility is distributive or non-distributive is naturally a more complicated matter, but I leave this matter aside due to space constraints.
49 Gilbert (2018: 163, 171, v–vi) echoes this idea when she argues that commitments' peremptory character partially explains their role in grounding demand-rights, or the standing and authority to demand a particular action from another agent.
50 A further question is whether these obligations are conditional or unconditional (Gilbert 2014; Shockley 2004: fn. 28; Westlund 2009: fn. 17 & 26).
51 See Gilbert (2014: 89) for an explanation of the relationship between collective intention and action.
52 For a related point, see Gilbert's (2014: esp. 79) discussion of the warrant for statements such as "We are to blame."
53 See Smiley (2014: 3).
54 Jansen (2014: 94) argues that the very idea of a "plural subject," and, in particular, one that is founded upon commitments, has forward-looking responsibility built into it.
55 Compare with Heim's (2015: 77) distinction between failures that attach to the group and failures that attach to individuals *qua* group members.

References

Alonso, F. (2009) "Shared Intention, Reliance, and Interpersonal Obligations," *Ethics* 119: 444–75.

Arruda, C. (2017) "How I Learned to Worry about the Spaghetti Western: Collective Responsibility and Collective Agency," *Analysis* 77(2): 249–59.

Arruda, C. (manuscript) *Enriching Practical Reason.*

Bernstein, S. (2017) "Causal Proportions and Moral Responsibility," in D. Shoemaker (ed), *Oxford Studies in Agency and Responsibility*, Oxford: Oxford University Press.

Björnsson, G. (2014) "Essentially Shared Obligations," *Midwest Studies in Philosophy* 38: 103–20.

Bratman, M. (1987) *Intention, Plans, and Practical Reason*. Center for the Study of Language and Information.

Bratman, M. (1999a) "Shared Intention," reprinted in *Faces of Intention: Selected Essays on Intention and Agency*, New York: Cambridge University Press, 109–29.

Bratman, M. (1999b) "I Intend that We *J*," reprinted in *Faces of Intention: Selected Essays on Intention and Agency*, New York: Cambridge University Press, 142–61.

Bratman, M. (2004) "Three Forms of Agential Commitment: Reply to Cullity and Gerrans," *Proceedings of the Aristotelian Society* 104: 329–37.

Bratman, M. (2007a) "Introduction," *Structures of Agency: Essays*, Oxford: Oxford University Press.

Bratman, M. (2007b) "Planning Agency, Autonomous Agency," in *Structures of Agency*, Oxford: Oxford University Press, 197–232.

Bratman, M. (2007c) *Structures of Agency*. Oxford: Oxford University Press.

Bratman, M. (2014) *Shared Agency: A Planning Theory of Acting Together*. Oxford: Oxford University Press.

Bratman, M. (2015) "Shared Agency: Replies to Ludwig, Pacherie, Petersson, Roth, and Smith," *Journal of Social Ontology* 1(1): 59–76.

Bratman, M. (2018) *Planning, Time, and Self-Governance: Essays in Practical Rationality*. Oxford: Oxford University Press.

Brewer, T. (2003) "Two Kinds of Commitments (and Two Kinds of Social Groups)," *Philosophy and Phenomenological Research* 66(3): 554–83.

Chang, R. (2009) "Voluntarist Reasons and the Sources of Normativity," in D. Sobel and S. Wall (eds), *Reasons for Action*, New York: Cambridge University Press.

Chang, R. (2013) "Commitments, Reasons, and the Will," in R. Shafer-Landau (ed), *Oxford Studies in Metaethics*, Vol. 8, Oxford: Oxford University Press.

Chant, S.R. (2015) "Collective Responsibility in a Hollywood Standoff," *Thought: A Journal of Philosophy* 4(2): 83–92.

Chartier, G. (2017) *The Logic of Commitment*. New York: Routledge.

Copp, D. (1979) "Collective Actions and Secondary Actions," *American Philosophical Quarterly* 16: 177–86.

Copp, D. (2007) "The Collective Moral Autonomy Thesis," *Journal of Social Philosophy* 38(3): 369–88.

Copp, D. (2012) "The Collective Moral Autonomy Thesis: Reply to Ludwig and Miller," *Journal of Social Philosophy* 43(1): 78–95.

Cullity, G. and Gerrans, P. (2004) "Agency and Policy," *Proceedings of the Aristotelian Society* 104: 317–27.

Dorsey, D. (2016) *The Limits of Moral Authority*. Oxford: Oxford University Press.

Elster, J. (1985 [1979]) *Ulysses and the Sirens: Studies in Rationality and Irrationality* (revised ed). Cambridge: Cambridge University Press.

Elster, J. (2000) *Ulysses Unbound: Studies in Rationality, Precommitment, and Constraints*. Cambridge, New York: Cambridge University Press.

Feinberg, J. (1968) "Collective Responsibility," *Journal of Philosophy* 65(21): 674–88.

Ferrero, L. (2006) "Three Ways of Spilling Ink Tomorrow," in E. Baccarini & S. Prijic-Samarzija (eds), *Rationality in Belief and Action*, Rijeka: 95–127.

Ferrero, L. (2010) "Decisions, Diachronic Autonomy, and the Division of Deliberative Labor," *Philosophers' Imprint* 10(2): 1–23.

Frankfurt, H. (1998) *Necessity, Volition, and Love*. Cambridge: Cambridge University Press.

Gilbert, M. (1989) *On Social Facts*. Routledge: New York.

Gilbert, M. (2000) *Sociality and Responsibility: New Essays in Plural Subject Theory*. Lanham: Rowman & Littlefield Publishers.

Gilbert, M. (2002) "Collective Guilt and Collective Guilt Feelings," *The Journal of Ethics* 6(2): 115–43.

Gilbert, M. (2006a) "Who's to Blame? Collective Moral Responsibility and Its Implications for Group Members," *Midwest Studies in Philosophy* 30(1): 94–114.

Gilbert, M. (2006b) *A Theory of Political Obligation: Membership, Commitment, and the Bonds of Society*. Oxford: Oxford University Press.

Gilbert, M. (2013) "Commitment," in H. LaFollette (ed.), *The International Encyclopedia of Ethics*, Blackwell Publishing, 899–905.

Gilbert, M. (2014) *Joint Commitment: How We Make the Social World*. Oxford: Oxford University Press.

Gilbert, M. (2018) *Rights and Demands: A Foundational Inquiry*. New York, NY: Oxford University Press.

Guerrero, A. (2015) "Deliberation, Responsibility, and Excusing Mistakes of Law," *Jurisprudence* 6(1): 81–94.

Heim, J. (2015) "Commitments in Groups and Commitments of Groups," *Phenomenology and Mind* 9: 74–82.

Held, V. (1970) "Can a Random Collection of Individuals Be Morally Responsible?," *The Journal of Philosophy* 67(14): 471–81.

Held, V. (2002) "Group Responsibility for Ethnic Conflict," *The Journal of Ethics* 6(2): 157–78.

Helm, B.W. (2017) *Communities of Respect: Grounding Responsibility, Authority, & Dignity*. Oxford: Oxford University Press.

Hieronymi, P. (2006) "Controlling Attitudes," *Pacific Philosophical Quarterly* 87(1): 45–74.

Hieronymi, P. (2009) "Two Kinds of Agency," in L. O'Brien and M. Soterieu (eds), *Mental Action*, Oxford: Oxford University Press, 138–62.

Hinchman, E. (2010) "Conspiracy, Commitment, and the Self," *Ethics* 180: 526–56.

Hinchman, E. (2014) "Narrative and the Stability of Intention," *European Journal of Philosophy* 23(1): 111–40.

Holton, R. (2009) *Willing, Wanting, Waiting*. Oxford: Oxford University Press.

Isaacs, T. (2014) "Collective Responsibility and Collective Obligation," *Midwest Studies in Philosophy* 38(1): 40–57.

Jansen, L. (2014) "A Plural Subject Approach to the Responsibilities of Groups and Institutions," *Midwest Studies in Philosophy* 38(1): 91–102.

Killmister, S. (2017) *Taking the Measure of Autonomy: Self-Definition, Self-Realisation, and Self-Unification*. New York: Routledge.

Kopec, M. and Miller, S. (2018) "Shared Intention is Not Joint Commitment," *Journal of Ethics and Social Philosophy* 13: 179–89.

Liberman, A. and Schroeder, M. (2016) "Commitment: Worth the Weight," in E. Lord and B. Macguire (eds), *Weighing Reasons*, New York: Oxford University Press.

List, C. (2014) "Three Kinds of Collective Attitudes," *Erkenntnis* 79(9): 1601–22.

List, C. and Pettit, P. (2011) *Group Agency: The Possibility, Design, and Status of Corporate Agents*. Cambridge: Cambridge University Press.

Marušić, B. (2015) *Evidence and Agency Norms of Belief for Promising and Resolving*. Oxford: Oxford University Press.

Mathiesen, K. (2006) "We're All in This Together: Responsibility of Collective Agents and Their Members," *Midwest Studies in Philosophy* 30: 240–55.

May, L. (1992) *Sharing Responsibility*. Chicago: The University of Chicago Press.

Mellema, G. (1988) "Causation, Foresight and Collective Responsibility," *Analysis* 48: 44–50.

Mellema, G. (2006) "Collective Responsibility and Qualifying Actions," *Midwest Studies in Philosophy* 30: 168–75.

Michael, J. and Pacherie, E. (2015) "On Commitments and Other Uncertainty Reduction Tools in Joint Action," *Journal of Social Ontology* 1(1): 89–120.

Morton, J. (2013) "Deliberating for Our Far Future Selves," *Ethical Theory and Moral Practice* 16(4): 809–28.

Morton, J. and Paul, S. (2019) "Grit," *Ethics* 129 (2): 175–203.

Peter, F. and Schmid, H.B. (eds) (2008) *Rationality and Commitment*. New York: Oxford University Press.

Pinkert, F. (2014) "What We Together Can (Be Required to) Do," *Midwest Studies in Philosophy* 38(1): 187–202.

Rawls, J. (1971) *A Theory of Justice*. Cambridge: Harvard University Press.

Ross, J. (2012) "Rationality, Normativity, and Commitment," in R. Shafer-Landau (ed.), *Oxford Studies in Metaethics*, Oxford: Oxford University Press.

Roth, A.S. (2004) "Shared Agency and Contralateral Commitments," *The Philosophical Review* 113(3): 359–410.

Roth, A.S. (2015) "Practical Intersubjectivity and Normative Guidance: Bratman on Shared Agency," *Journal of Social Ontology* 1(1): 39–48.

Rovane, C. (2014) "Forward-Looking Collective Responsibility: A Metaphysical Reframing of the Issue," *Midwest Studies in Philosophy* 38(1): 12–25.

Schmid, H.B. (2014) "Expressing Group Attitudes: On First Personal Plural Authority," *Erkenntnis* 79: 1685–701.

Schroeder, M. (2013) "Scope for Rational Autonomy," *Philosophical Issues* 23: 297–310.

Schweikard, D. and Schmid, H.B. (2013) "Collective Intentionality," in E.N. Zalta (ed.), *The Stanford Encyclopedia of Philosophy* (Summer 2013 Edition) [online] Available at: https://plato.stanford.edu/archives/sum2013/entries/collective-intentionality/ (Accessed: 23 March 2019).

Sen, A.K. (1977) "Rational Fools: A Critique of the Behavioral Foundations of Economic Theory," *Philosophy & Public Affairs* 6(4): 317–44.

Sen, A.K. (2005) "Why Exactly Is Commitment Important for Rationality?," *Economics and Philosophy* 21(1): 5–14.

Shockley, K. (2004) "The Conundrum of Collective Commitment," *Social Theory and Practice* 30(4): 535–57.

Shpall, S. (2014) "Moral and Rational Commitment," *Philosophy and Phenomenological Research* 88(1): 146–72.

Smiley, M. (2014) "Future-Looking Collective Responsibility: A Preliminary Analysis," *Midwest Studies in Philosophy* 38(1): 1–11.

Smith, T.H. (2015) "*Shared Agency*: On Gilbert and Deep Continuity," *Journal of Social Ontology* 1(1): 49–57.

Townsend, L. (2015) "Joint Commitment and Collective Belief." *Phenomenology and Mind* 9(9): 46–53.

Townsend, L. (2017) *Believing Groups: Essays on the Doxastic and Discursive Capacities of Collective Agents.* Doctoral Dissertation. University of Oslo.
Tuomela, R. (2006) "Joint Intention, We-Mode and I-Mode," *Midwest Studies in Philosophy* 30: 35–58.
Westlund, A. (2009) "Deciding Together," *Philosophers' Imprint* 9(10): 1–17.
Wilkins, B. (2002) "Joint Commitments," *The Journal of Ethics* 6(2): 145–55.
Wringe, B. (2010) "Global Obligations and the Agency Objection," *Ratio* 23(2): 217–31.
Wringe, B. (2014) "Collective Obligations: Their Existence, Their Explanatory Power, and Their Supervenience on the Obligations of Individuals," *European Journal of Philosophy* 21(4): 472–97.
Yaffe, G. (2009) "Excusing Mistakes of Law," *Philosophers' Imprint* 9(2): 1–22.

14

COLLECTIVE INACTION AND COLLECTIVE EPISTEMIC AGENCY

Michael D. Doan

14.1 Responsibility for Collective Inaction: The *Seinfeld* Paradigm

> Why would we want to help somebody? That's what nuns and Red Cross workers are for!
>
> *George Costanza ("The Finale" 1998)*

Twenty years after it aired to an audience of 76 million, the final episode of *Seinfeld* still looms large in the popular imagination. For philosophers interested in the idea of collective responsibility, it was also among the most memorable thought experiments in television history. While it seems unlikely that Larry David was cribbing philosophical perspectives on responsibility for collective inaction when he wrote the script for "The Finale," the episode does employ a particularly influential insight of Virginia Held's. According to Held, even a "random collection" of individuals[1] can sometimes be held morally responsible for not acting collectively, or else for not organizing themselves into a group capable of so doing (Held 1970). Considered as a thought experiment, "The Finale" invites us to imagine: *What would happen if Held's insight were codified into law? How would a judge hold us accountable for failing to join forces and act together when nothing less would have sufficed to prevent harm?*

Here is how the thought experiment unfolds: the scene of the crime is Latham, Massachusetts (Jerry, the New Yorker, calls it "Sticksville"). Jerry and friends are hanging out on a street corner—joking around about nothing, as usual. Across the street, and in full view and hearing of the four, a carjacker pulls an overweight man named Howie out of his car, robs him at gunpoint, and flees the scene in his vehicle. Kramer stands by, filming the entire incident on his camcorder. Meanwhile, Jerry, Elaine, and George crack sarcastic, fat-shaming jokes at Howie's expense. Howie, who could see that the four did nothing whatsoever to come to his aid, relays his plight to Matt Vogel, the reporting police officer. Vogel immediately puts the four under arrest, citing Article 223-7 of the Latham County Penal Code. Elaine protests, "What? No, no—*we didn't do anything!*" Vogel replies, "That's exactly right. The law requires you to help or assist anyone in danger so long as it's reasonable to do so." George complains, "I've never heard of that." Responds Vogel, "It's new—it's called the Good Samaritan Law" ("The Finale" 1998).

In fact, several European countries and ten U.S. states had similar laws on the books by the time the curtains closed on *Seinfeld* in 1998. These laws tend to include criteria similar to those proposed by Held, who holds that a random collection can only be held responsible for their inaction "when the action called for in a given situation is obvious to the reasonable person and when the expected outcome of the action is clearly favorable" (Held 1970: 476). According to what in the U.S. are called "duty to rescue" or "Good Samaritan" laws, the penalties for failing to come to another's aid are typically minor. In "The Finale," though, they are much stiffer: the local law calls for a maximum fine of $85,000 and as much as five years in prison. As the episode unfolds, the defendants in the controversial "Good Samaritan Trial" (the aptly named "New York Four") are ultimately found guilty of criminal indifference and sentenced to a year in prison. The upshot of the thought experiment is clear: *pace* Jackie Chiles, defense lawyer extraordinaire, there surely *is* such a thing as a "guilty bystander," and such bystanders can and will be made to pay for their crimes of omission ("The Finale" 1998).

I'm struck by how frequently "The Finale" comes up in discussions of responsibility for collective inaction. Incidentally, most philosophers working on the topic make use of a handful of thought experiments that conform to what I have come to call "the *Seinfeld* paradigm." In these relatively simple "coordinated bystander cases" (Isaacs 2011: 143), a particular harm (say, a carjacking) cannot be prevented through the isolated, uncoordinated actions of individuals, but only through a collective action undertaken by an as of yet unformed organized group (say, by Jerry, Elaine, George, and Kramer joining forces to scare off a gunman). Next to Held's bystanders to a strangling case (Held 1970), there is Larry May's bystanders to a drowning child case (May 1990); David Copp's bystanders to homelessness case (Copp 1991); Torbjörn Tännsjö's bystanders to pushing a car up a hill case (Tännsjö 2007); and Tracy Isaacs' bystanders to a river rafting disaster case (Isaacs 2011), to name a few of the most memorable variations (see also Petersson 2008). These cases share the following key features: first, the victims are always depicted as totally helpless, while the protagonists are cast as completely innocent "bystanders"—that is, they are not directly implicated in or affected by the problem prior to their alleged failure to intervene. Second, the problems can always be solved by a single collective action, even when several collective action solutions are available. Third, the risks of taking the required course of action are always minor, whereas success is assured. Since the problems have no systemic dimensions, the prospect of solving them never threatens the statuses, identities, or ways of life of anyone involved. Indeed, most of these cases have been designed to be even more clear cut than that of the New York Four, whose reluctance to confront a gunman is at least understandable.

Following Held's lead, each of the above-mentioned philosophers makes use of similarly-structured thought experiments in the course of arguing that a random collection can sometimes be blamed for failing to act collectively. However, Isaacs (2011) has recently broadened the focus of conversation by asking: what do these accounts suggest are our *present* responsibilities with respect to some of the most urgent and complex problems of our time, such as climate change, ecological degradation, and global poverty? Although there has been some disagreement about when it makes sense to say that a random collection could have done otherwise, and over how responsibility ought to be distributed when such a group has failed to act, there has also been considerable agreement both methodologically and substantively. Each philosopher agrees that we ought to employ some version of the reasonable person standard[2] when determining whether a group has failed to act or has an obligation to act now. And although each stops short of drawing out the legal implications of their views, they generally agree that blame is a morally appropriate response in many instances of collective inaction, even those involving merely "putative" or "loosely structured groups" (May 1990: 270).

In this chapter I consider the costs of this striking convergence in methodology. I wonder: What questions about collective responsibility cannot be asked when the focus of inquiry is narrowed to cases fitting the *Seinfeld* mold? I argue that the use of fictional thought experiments in philosophical analyses of collective responsibility unhelpfully constrains our thinking, precisely in those places where it needs to be at its most generative. While there are many possible avenues of criticism here,[3] I focus on how the received way of thinking about responsibility for collective inaction ignores and renders irrelevant the epistemic agency and creativity of ordinary people,[4] while excluding from consideration a range of problems that clearly call for coordinated responses, yet have no obvious, readymade solutions. What is needed, I propose, is not a different, more nuanced set of thought experiments, but an altogether different approach to thinking about responsibility for collective inaction. In the course of exploring a concrete case of collective brilliance in action, I suggest that the production of new questions, ideas, and knowledge in and through collective struggle ought to be at the very center of future inquiry.[5]

The remainder of this chapter proceeds in two parts. First, I offer a critique of the received way of thinking about responsibility for collective inaction. Second, I propose an alternative approach that takes as its point of departure the epistemic agency exhibited by people navigating impossible situations together. One such situation is becoming increasingly common in the context of climate change, particularly in coastal regions: so-called "natural" disasters, such as hurricanes and superstorms, wreaking havoc on communities—flooding homes, collapsing infrastructures, and straining the capacities of existing organizations to safeguard lives and livelihoods. What happens when philosophical reflection begins *here*—in places where the institutions and practices that have emerged over the last century seem incapable of addressing the problems communities face now,[6] and where people find themselves turning to one another for the sake of their own survival?

14.2 Breaking Free of the *Seinfeld* Paradigm

Why should philosophers break free of what I have called "the *Seinfeld* paradigm"? In this section, I explore the pitfalls of basing our accounts of collective responsibility on analyses of cases fitting the *Seinfeld* mold. I begin with a brief review of Held's influential account of responsibility for collective inaction. Next, I consider what we inevitably miss when our focus is narrowed to fictional thought experiments of this type.

Recall that, on Held's account, a random collection of individuals can only be held responsible for failing to act collectively "when the action called for in a given situation is obvious to the reasonable person and when the expected outcome of the action is clearly favorable" (Held 1970: 476). Writing in 1970, Held anticipates much future conversation when she remarks, in passing, on the possible implications of her view for "political situations":

> If a reasonable person judges that the overthrow of an existing political system is an action that is obviously called for, he may perhaps consider himself morally responsible for the failure of the random collection of which he is a member to perform this action. If he thinks some action to change an existing political system is obviously called for, but is not clear about which action, he may consider himself morally responsible for the failure of the random collection of which he is a member to perform the quite different action of transforming itself into a group capable of arriving at decisions on such questions.
>
> *(480)*

A provocative example, to be sure. Revolutionary fervor aside, though, Held seems to be making a bid for theoretical simplicity and parsimony here. Having based her account on an analysis of a handful of relatively simple coordinated bystander cases, she seems to be suggesting that we can simply scale up to far more complex situations from there. Perhaps, then, we need rely on only a single set of tools when grappling with collective action problems of all sorts.

Held's gambit has more recently been taken up by Tracy Isaacs. Whereas Held starts with a case involving a strangler on the subway, Isaacs draws our attention to a group of children rafting down a river (Isaacs 2011: 243). Suddenly caught in rapids, hurtling helplessly toward a waterfall, the children will surely be killed if a random collection of onlookers does not join forces to intervene. Isaacs utilizes this thought experiment to argue that even a group of complete strangers can *presently* have a collective obligation to come to the aid of others, at least in situations where there is "a clear map between the situation, the required course of [collective] action and a collective agent" (ibid. 143). Scaling up to the question of what our current responsibilities are with respect to such complex problems as climate change, Isaacs argues that the members of a loosely structured group are collectively responsible for coming together and acting when—and only when—a collective action solution has, as she puts it, "come into focus" (ibid. 152). Harking back to Held's passing remarks, Isaacs suggests that the collective obligation to implement a given solution "exists in virtue of the clarity, by the standard of the reasonable person, of the collective action required" (ibid. 148). Hence, "Where there is a lack of clarity at the collective level, what is lacking is a clear picture of what collective course of action would effectively address the moral concern" (ibid.).

How often is this knowledge condition met?[7] I suspect it is met only rarely, in relation to a very specific set of problems. To see this, consider a revised version of Larry David's thought experiment. I call it "The Inverted Finale" because it features a case lacking all the distinguishing features of the *Seinfeld* paradigm.[8] My version invites us to imagine: *What would happen if Held's knowledge condition were incorporated into our practices of holding ourselves and others accountable? Whose collective inaction would be excused and, with time, taken for granted?*

Here is how the revised thought experiment unfolds: Jerry and friends are hanging out in front of a Manhattan diner. On a daily basis, and in full view and hearing of one another, they have each been participating in a variety of social practices that rely on energy-intensive, fossil-fuel dependent cycles of extraction, production, consumption, and waste (e.g., eating animal products, heating and cooling their spacious apartments, commuting in cars, and more). Although each of the four aims to cause as little suffering and death as possible, they know they are deeply implicated in situations they repudiate. Simply by living, eating, and throwing things away in a major U.S. city, they are caught up in broader systemic processes which they know are causing significant, ongoing harms to ecosystems and lives both near and far, and which are clearly unsustainable in the long run. They are aware of the many ways they benefit from the oppression of others and are also deeply damaged by the interlocking systems they play a role, however small, in reproducing. They understand that they, too, are being killed by those systems, however much more softly—that they, too, are neither the totally helpless "victims" of systemic outcomes, nor are they merely "standing by," unaffected and affecting none. Given their collective involvement in the ecological and social problems that keep them awake at night, they could hardly consider themselves "inactive." Simply by going with the flow, they are actively sustaining what they know to be unsustainable.

Noticing the weary expressions on his friends' faces, Kramer captures the moment on his camcorder. Meanwhile, Jerry, Elaine, and George crack self-deprecating jokes, debating who would be the first to be killed on *The Walking Dead*. Newman, Jerry's mail carrier, is every bit as aware as the others that his attempts at "ethical consumption" make little difference. He, too, has come to realize that there is no single, definitive collective action participation in which they could "solve" their shared predicament. Joining organized, long-term efforts to bring about systemic change would require significant commitment and could also involve a measure of risk and sacrifice. Even so, Newman feels frustrated that the New York Four are telling jokes while the world burns—frustrated enough to share his plight with a cop walking the beat. Confused, the cop looks Newman square in the eye: "What do you mean, '*they aren't doing anything*'? Aren't doing *what*, exactly? Talk to me when you've got a clear solution, wise ass." The upshot is clear: *pace* Held, Isaacs, and others, it is highly doubtful that we can simply scale up from the cases on which they focus, to the far more complex situations, such as climate change and global poverty, that they also claim to be offering resources for addressing.

Two lines of response are available here. First of all, those who remain sympathetic to the received way of thinking about responsibility for collective inaction might reject my description of the New York Four's predicament. In place of "The Inverted Finale," they might generate another thought experiment that makes Jerry's relationship to climate change seem a lot more like his relationship to a carjacking (the victims would be elsewhere, completely powerless; there would be no systemic dimensions to the problem; Jerry and friends would somehow be standing by, innocently, with no stake in the situation; and so forth). This would show that the types of problems I claim fall outside of the *Seinfeld* paradigm can be made to fit—or, at least, that specific aspects of those problems can be ignored for simplicity's sake. In that case, perhaps the New York Four are not off the hook for their collective inaction after all.

I find this response deeply unsatisfying. For one, I take it that an account of collective responsibility will only be useful to the extent that it helps us deal with the full range of problems that call for coordinated responses. Problems superficially, inaccurately, or otherwise falsely described, cannot be collectively dealt with, so our accounts need to approach the characterization of situations in an empirically rigorous way. Given that my description of the New York Four's predicament accurately captures some of its more salient features, and also seems applicable to several systemic problems other than those mentioned here, it stands to reason that situations of these types cannot be forced to fit the *Seinfeld* mold without considerable distortion. Unless it can be shown that situations with these features either do not or could not arise or are so rare as to be unworthy of mention, it will be difficult to find promise in the received approach.

Second, those still determined to take up Held's gambit might simply bite the bullet. They could accept that there is nothing strange about the cop's readiness to excuse the New York Four, insisting instead that it is Newman's frustration that cries out for justification. After all, there has to be a limit to the situations that a loosely structured group can be held morally responsible for failing to address, and it makes sense to draw the line at cases where there is no clear picture of what collective action would effectively address the concern. If the boundaries of collective responsibility ought to be drawn elsewhere, then a case to that effect needs to be made. Otherwise we are just trading intuitions and are unlikely to get very far.

This response fares no better. As I point out elsewhere (Doan 2016), the burden of proof lies with those who favor Held's knowledge condition, for that condition expresses a substantive view about the circumstances under which we should see ourselves and others as sharing responsibility for working together to address impending crises and catastrophes, not to mention many already present disasters. Yet it is hardly self-evident and has yet to be defended. So, an argument is owed in defense of the above-mentioned presumptions about the bounded nature of collective responsibility, and about the precise location of those boundaries.

It may make sense to draw a boundary in the place Held proposes. But I suspect that is only if we have already joined her in adopting a peculiarly *juridical* frame of mind. Although Held is concerned with questions of moral responsibility, she does invite us to consider such questions from the peculiar vantage of a judge or juror, reducing collective responsibility to collective *liability* and relying on a legal fiction for the sake of adjudication. But I doubt that we need to think like a state official to hold ourselves and others accountable for what we collectively fail to do (see Doan 2016; Young 2011). If adopting a juridical approach means we can no longer have meaningful conversations about our shared responsibility for addressing seemingly intractable systemic problems, then that is an approach to be avoided, not embraced.

Furthermore, I take it that part of the point of the practice of holding ourselves and others accountable for our collective inaction is to encourage each other to come together, get organized, and do what is required of us to reduce the amount of harm and injustice in the world. If we can only justifiably hold one another accountable when a clear solution has *already* "come into focus," then what are we to do about those problems that have no obvious, readymade solutions? How are we to handle those situations where it would be flatly unreasonable to expect the emergence of a single collective action that is perfectly "clear" to and "clearly favorable" for all involved? What about those situations where the people and institutions we have grown accustomed to looking to for answers either have none to share, or none at all? Here the received view is curiously silent.

Whereas it may seem inconsequential to draw a line around those situations we are already equipped to address with considerable confidence, the problems that make the New York Four weary are not so easily dismissed. Of course, the interrelated problems of climate change, ecological degradation, and global poverty do not suddenly resolve themselves when the cop refuses to make an arrest. Under these circumstances, what relief is there in saying to one another, "Well, at least we're off the hook"? Unless we find meaningful ways to hold ourselves and others accountable for coming together to address especially challenging problems *in spite of our shared not knowing how to go on*, we will be left without a valuable tool for protecting what matters.

In summary, the received approach to thinking about responsibility for collective inaction excludes from consideration a range of ecological and social problems that clearly call for coordinated responses, yet have no obvious, readymade solutions. Defenders of this approach must either distort such problems in ways that preclude the development of appropriate solutions, just to make assignments of responsibility intelligible, or else admit that unorganized groups bear no responsibility whatsoever for activating themselves. Neither option is acceptable.

One notable consequence of sidestepping systemic problems in general—and problems that existing institutions and practices are incapable of solving, in particular—is that the received approach ignores and renders irrelevant the epistemic agency and creativity of ordinary people. Suppose that the only problems loosely structured groups are collectively obligated to address are those for which clear collective action solutions have already, somehow, "come into focus." Oddly enough, we would never bear any responsibility for collectively analyzing especially complex, seemingly insoluble problems, even those we have a hand in creating and are harmed by; for cultivating each other's capacities to imagine new strategies; or for engaging in ongoing processes of collective learning, experimenting with, and revising those strategies over time. Some of us would probably find ourselves waiting around for others to dream up solutions, leaning on specialized institutions and authorities. Others would hope for sudden flashes of insight—flashes that are unlikely to ever come. Never calling upon one another to think for ourselves, our collective problem-solving capacities would likely atrophy from lack of use. Yet the problems would remain, growing worse all the while.

Instead of rendering the epistemic agency of ordinary people irrelevant, in the final section of this chapter I suggest that the production of new questions, ideas, and knowledge in and through collective struggle ought to be at the very center of future inquiry into collective responsibility. Rather than relying on thought experiments, I turn to a concrete case of people coming to each other's aid, exhibiting their collective brilliance under extraordinarily trying circumstances. I explore this case at some length, not to pump the reader's moral intuitions, or to defend an alternate set of criteria for collective liability, but in order to bring to the fore certain questions about collective responsibility that would otherwise go unasked.

14.3 Acting Together in the Midst of Disaster

> We must never forget these facts that made Hurricane Katrina a travesty: That climate change is creating unprecedented storms in size and intensity. Katrina was one of them. That ongoing ecological destruction in the name of profits has been perpetuated for more than a hundred years, including the destruction of wetlands and other natural barriers along the coastlines, allowing hurricanes to move further inland than ever before, in order to open up access to Gulf oil and commercial shipping routes. Next, it was that levees were built substandard by corruption and greed when contractors and some politicians knew they would never hold. And, finally, that the government response at all levels left thousands of people to die who had no means to evacuate due to health, age, and lack of funds, transportation, or connections. Individuals and families were trapped in their homes, on the streets, on their rooftops, and in their attics. Power reacted with brute force and criminalization of the people. It was criminal neglect. This was the latest in a long history of largely invisible disasters of neglect in these communities. To me, the levees became a symbol of the way that the corruption and arrogance of governments disregards the most vulnerable people.
>
> (crow 2014: 4)

When Hurricane Katrina devastated communities across the Gulf Coast in the summer of 2005, it became painfully clear to many people living in the U.S. that climate change was no longer some abstract or distant problem. As the above remarks from long-time community organizer scott crow suggest, the impacts of climate change[9] are shaped by a variety of factors—psychological, social, and systemic—including inadequate preparation, corruption, arrogance, greed, and deeply ingrained patterns of indifference and neglect. When the levees surrounding New Orleans gave way to surging coastal waters, all the amenities upon which residents had come to rely abruptly vanished. Many houses were swept away or consumed by floodwaters, while others were left smoldering in flames amidst sparking power lines and leaky gas mains. Water, electrical, and telecommunications infrastructures were downed or disconnected. Flooded cars, buses, and streets rendered the usual modes of transportation unusable. Jobs were swiftly relocated, rendered irrelevant, or disappeared. Meanwhile, opportunistic landlords raised rents amidst growing real estate speculation. Developers and investors scooped up bundles of properties for a song, often holding buildings left vacant and in disrepair, banking on rising values to come. Charter schools swooped in to replace an underfunded public school system left further in disarray, saddled with dozens of crumbling buildings: roofs leaking, mold spreading, immersed in a toxic soup of floodwaters laced with gas, debris, and animal carcasses.

While thousands of New Orleanians were voluntarily evacuated by government agencies in the days following the storm, many others were forcefully displaced to disparate locations hundreds of miles away, often without any means of returning home. The several thousand others whom the federal government simply left behind to fend for themselves, or who were unable or refused to be evacuated from their homes, were faced with the enormous challenge of surviving in post-Katrina New Orleans. The difficult situations of many remaining residents were exacerbated by the fact that official channels of support proved grossly incapable of addressing emerging needs, particularly in historically underserviced neighborhoods. In several overwhelmingly poor, largely black communities, state-sponsored and professional relief was either entirely absent, or unhelpfully, insultingly present, answering to needs that didn't exist and setting up bureaucratic hurdles that prevented people from accessing needed services.

In his 2014 book, *Black Flags and Windmills*, crow offers an extensive account of why so many people were compelled to rush *into* New Orleans with "emergency hearts" (65), precisely when the federal government was struggling to evacuate everyone they could manage. In his own case, it was a longstanding friendship with Robert H. King, a former member of the Black Panther Party, that first moved crow to journey from his home in Austin, Texas. King, who was living in New Orleans when Katrina made landfall, lost contact with crow when the levees broke. With the streets flooding and news of a citywide lockdown spreading, crow grew increasingly worried. When an acquaintance proposed that the two go in search of King, crow "had to know if he was all right" (ibid. 8). "As a community organizer who cares about people no matter where they might be," recalls crow, "I felt that it was my responsibility to aid those in New Orleans who, already marginalized, now had total devastation added to their burden" (8–9). After making an initial, particularly jarring trip into the city by boat, the search team turned up no signs of their friend, returning to Austin deeply shaken by all they had encountered along the way.

Several days later, upon receiving a call for aid from Malik Rahim, crow decided to make a second trip to New Orleans. Taking another opportunity to search for King, he also intended to contribute to relief efforts organized by those with deep roots in the city. Rahim, a veteran community organizer and former Panther, had helped run free breakfast for children programs in two of the most poverty-stricken housing projects in New Orleans. Calling from his house in the predominantly black neighborhood of Algiers, Rahim reported to crow: "we got racist white vigilantes driving around in pickup trucks terrorizing black people on the street. It's very serious. We need supplies and support" (ibid. 46).

By the time crow arrived, Rahim and his neighbors, including native New Orleanian Sharon Johnson, had already been struggling to find ways to provide basic aid to one another. "There was no Red Cross, no FEMA," writes crow. "There were no other options" (ibid. 50). On September 5, 2005, the trio decided to form a collective based at Rahim's home in Algiers, calling themselves the "Common Ground Collective" in honor of their lost friend King.[10] Within a week, the group grew to around fifty strong. Over the following months, its ranks swelled to several hundred, with mostly white, twenty-something, anarchist-oriented volunteers arriving from across the country. Common Ground was a community-initiated, all-volunteer organization with a mission "to provide short-term relief for victims of hurricane disasters in the Gulf Coast region, and long-term support in rebuilding the communities affected in the New Orleans area" (ibid. 229). Much of the group's work involved responding to seemingly intractable problems confronting those left behind, many of which were shaped, in part, by inept government and philanthropic responses. As crow recalls,

> We were seeing, in real time, what slowly filtered out to become painfully apparent worldwide. The state was off balance and unresponsive. The entities within it were failing to grasp the developing issues. The Red Cross wasn't doing any better. They were raising *billions* of dollars while people were still suffering. For me, it was the closest thing to seeing those in Power lose their stranglehold of control. We interpreted this as an opportunity to create an autonomous space where residents could establish self-determination over their future, be treated with dignity and respect, and have access to basic services that hadn't existed in years, if ever. We would begin relief work,

> without reliance on or interference from the state or professional aid agencies. We would prefigure the civil society we would like to see in the future.
>
> *(ibid. 65)*

I want to propose that an alternative approach to understanding collective responsibility can be assembled from the work of Common Ground—one that draws our attention to the collective accomplishments of ordinary people navigating impossibly difficult situations.[11] This approach can be summarized in three recommendations for future inquiry, to which I now turn.

14.3.1 Clear Paths or Paths Cleared?

Characterizing Common Ground as a "revolutionary aid organization," crow recounts their first three years in Algiers as "a story of ordinary people compelled to act for justice in an extraordinary situation" (ibid. 59, 4). Indeed, the collective's story is one of people joining forces to deal with problems that existing institutions and practices were not—and likely could not—address, thus exhibiting their collective brilliance in action. As a guide to understanding collective responsibility, crow's retelling of the story teaches us to focus not on what other people ought to have known at a given instant, but on *how those who came to each other's aid managed to generate new questions, ideas, and knowledge together, in and through collective struggle.*

For instance, next to Algiers in the much smaller, wealthier, whiter neighborhood of Algiers Point, a racist white militia had surfaced in the wake of the storm. Militia members hung hostile, stigmatizing signs (e.g., "You Loot, We Shoot") outside their homes and patrolled the streets of neighboring black communities in trucks, harassing and on several occasions, gunning down unarmed black men with impunity (Thompson 2008). "It was as if the dam of civil society that kept them from acting out their most racist tendencies had broken enough to allow their hatred to emerge," writes crow.

> Local authorities, with their racist attitudes toward the communities they were supposed to protect, stood by and let this militia function. There were bullet-riddled bodies of black men in the street, including the one that we tried to get picked up for days while it continued to decompose.
>
> *(crow 2014: 51)*

How would the collective and their neighbors protect themselves? Who would check these racist vigilantes, and how—with local law enforcement in complete disarray, at best, and passively or actively supporting racist terrorism, at worst? "In the stress of those days, I struggled to think through the unstable situation," writes crow (ibid. 59). Under circumstances unfamiliar to all involved, there was no dearth of clear solutions to the threat of racist violence left unpoliced. Nevertheless, drawing lessons from the community safety programs initiated by the Panthers in the late 1960s (see Newton 2009), and retailoring those experiments to suit a historically unique situation, members of Common Ground came up with the idea of setting up safety patrols, taking up a practice of community armed self-defense—a practice that crow notes was adopted reluctantly and as a last resort, following a series of violent confrontations (crow 2014: 55–58; cf. crow 2018). According to crow, "The presence of whites and blacks working together against the militia would later be cited by locals as one of the factors that helped ease tensions in that difficult time" (crow 2014: 54). "Self-defense opens up the possibility of changing the rules of engagement," he observes in retrospect. "It doesn't always make situations less violent, but it can help to balance the inequity of power" (ibid. 58).

Taking up arms to discourage racist violence also helped remaining residents direct their collective energies to addressing the scarcity of basic amenities. After establishing a measure of security for themselves and their neighbors, on September 13 the collective came up with the idea of setting up a distribution center at Rahim's home. The plan was to gather supplies on regular out-of-town excursions while coordinating larger deliveries from abroad. Within a matter of weeks, Common Ground was able to make a wide variety of goods and services available to Algiers residents, operating the distribution center "from 7 a.m. until curfew, seven days a week" (ibid. 115). With the help of a team of street medics, the group also established a more permanent first aid station in a nearby mosque, which quickly evolved into the Common Ground Health Clinic. This clinic—one of three the collective would eventually set up—still operates to this day, having morphed into a non-profit organization by the same name.

Common Ground went on to give birth to a wide range of programs organically, out of necessity, attending keenly to evolving local problems and needs with an optimistic, creative outlook on the future. As crow puts it, "Our intentions were to create permanent and sustainable solutions with and for those who were the most affected," grounded in the practice of solidarity and, eventually, "mutual aid" (ibid. 103, 165). For example, in addition to providing protection from white militias and distributing basic amenities, members also fought for displaced residents' rights to return; provided legal aid and safe shelter for women; pressured police for accountability and supported prisoners' rights; prevented housing demolitions, partly by gutting and repairing structures; used available legal means and direct action tactics to halt evictions; worked together with neighborhood councils; and helped create long-term food security through small-scale agricultural projects (ibid. 165, Appendix). The collective included a team of street medics and, eventually, nurses and doctors. In addition to establishing clinics, members engaged in Latinx health care outreach; cleaned up garbage and toxic floodwaters along streets and in houses; provided soil and water testing; offered bioremediation services for soils damaged by toxic substances; made counselling and social work services available, as well as massage, acupuncture, and herbal remedies; constructed compost toilets for families dealing with plumbing problems and water shutoffs; and planted community gardens that brought people together growing food.

Unlike state and professional aid organizations, Common Ground refused to see those whom they were serving as faceless or helpless victims, insisting instead on treating their neighbors as "active participants in the struggle to make their lives better"—that is, as *people* who were coming together "to struggle for survival, justice, and self-determination" (ibid. 103, 60). Rather than establishing relations of dependence between long-time residents, on the one hand, and relief organizations staffed by out-of-towners, on the other, the collective worked to support those most directly affected by the storm in taking charge of their own lives; in collectively analyzing deeply rooted problems in the course of developing solutions; and in rebuilding their own communities in sustainable, self-determining ways. While it would not be unreasonable to suppose that organizations such as FEMA and the Red Cross ought to be best positioned to deliver aid, the types of solutions that seemed clearest to these groups were actually among the problems Algiers residents would be forced to confront.

14.3.2 Inactive Groups or Groups in Action?

The array of ideas and experiments Common Ground managed to generate in the midst of severe instability, uncertainty, and hostility is truly astounding. So is the amount of collective learning that took place over those years, which later nourished a variety of developing projects, including the Occupy Sandy relief efforts that surfaced in 2012 (see Lustig 2012; Moore &

Russell 2011). Second, then, I want to suggest that the story of Common Ground teaches us to focus not on particular, supposedly singularly significant moments of collective inaction, but on *how such moments of astounding collective creativity emerge in the first place.*

As the philosopher John P. Clark points out in his foreword to the second edition of *Black Flags and Windmills*, collective responses to overwhelmingly complex problems do not just materialize out of thin air, even when they seem like genuine miracles. They certainly are not the result of sudden flashes of insight, nor of clear blueprints for collective action studiously absorbed by groups of strangers. Rather, "such miracles have deep roots" (crow 2014: xviii). The moment of Common Ground's emergence was "the product of many small but powerful transformative moments," adds Clark (2014: xix), not only in the personal lives of its founders, but in the lives and afterlives of the broader social movements from which the collective drew inspiration, volunteers, and material support, and to whom its members continually looked for hard-won lessons.

Some of those histories of collective struggle helped shape the place and people of New Orleans, including many who became involved in Common Ground. Other layers were national and global in scope—particularly in the cases of the Spanish anarchists during the 1930s, the Black Panthers during the 1960s and 1970s, and the Zapatista Army for National Liberation (EZLN) from the 1980s onward, whose work was especially influential in the formation of Common Ground. "In each of these political tendencies, people rose up to create initiatives that addressed complex and interrelated problems," observes crow.

> They didn't follow prescribed blueprints for revolution; they reimagined and reconfigured them. When they made mistakes, they learned more about themselves and the evolving situations around them, so as to be more effective. They were motivated by the love of humanity that drives us to create something better in the face of cynicism and repression.
>
> *(2014: 72)*

14.3.3 Conditions for Collective Blame or Brilliance?

Finally, the story of Common Ground teaches us to focus not on the conditions for collective liability and blame, but on *how to create the conditions for more such moments of collective brilliance in the lives of more people.*[12] These moments are clearly valuable, protecting people from impending harms while building towards more liveable futures. Moreover, we know that these moments have underlying conditions—not only in the initial hours and days when people find themselves thrown into states of emergency, but in the ongoing practices of mutual care and nurturance cultivated in their everyday lives, long before and after storms of various sorts.

I find crow's notion of the "emergency heart" useful in describing what motivates people to take up the responsibility we all share for making more such moments possible. Inspired by the words of Geronimo ji Jaga, the notion of the emergency heart encapsulates a deep feeling of love that "forms parts of the roots from which struggles grow" (ibid. 87). "Love drives what I call our *emergency hearts* to action and change in the face of repression and against all odds," writes crow. "The emergency heart is the feeling of empathy and compassion that motivates us to act now to end oppression and destruction. An emergency heart gets people into the streets to resist injustice and create something better" (ibid.).

Much as collective responses to overwhelmingly complex problems may seem to materialize out of thin air, the emergency heart may seem to beat for exceptional situations only, moving people to act in the now *of disaster*, in the midst of chaos and uncertainty. But there is another, more mundane sense in which the "state of emergency" is what arises between human beings whenever we find one another in assembly and set to work on assembling ourselves collectively. This everyday sense of emergency is, as Clark points out, "the normal condition of human beings in constant need of responsiveness to other human beings" (2014: xvii). Part of that shared need is a need to prepare each other to respond in situations where no clear and definitive responses are in the offing, and where no single portion of prior knowledge and skill will suffice. There are no sure-fire techniques for readying one another here, though there are plenty of past lessons from which to learn, and the story of Common Ground is but one worthwhile resource. Neither will there be any single, decisive moment where we collectively fail at the task of mutual preparation. As crow's retelling makes plain, it will take a good deal of patience and encouragement to sustain each other for the long haul—the creative patience of love in the midst of emergency.

14.4 Conclusion

In this chapter, I argued that the received way of thinking about responsibility for collective inaction is unhelpfully constraining. Not only does it exclude from consideration a range of systemic problems and crises that clearly call for coordinated responses, but in so doing, it ignores and renders irrelevant the epistemic agency and creativity of ordinary people. Perhaps these consequences would seem at least somewhat acceptable if the institutions and practices that have arisen over the past century were somehow capable of addressing each and every problem communities now face, and also equipped us to foresee and get out ahead of all possible complications down the line. As creatures in and of history, though, we should expect the emergence of new, more challenging situations in the wake of each solution proposed and implemented by fallible beings such as ourselves. Challenges such as these tend to encourage us to question those ways forward that have come to seem "clear" and "clearly favorable," to listen anew to and think differently with one another, and to rely on the collective resourcefulness and creativity of people in motion.

While exploring the work of Common Ground in post-Katrina New Orleans, I proposed an alternative approach to thinking about collective responsibility, expressed in summary form as three recommendations for future inquiry. When considering concrete cases of people acting together in response to seemingly intractable problems, I recommended that philosophers focus on how those who come to each other's aid manage to generate new questions, ideas, and knowledge together, in and through collective struggle; on how these moments of collective creativity emerge in the first place; and on how to create the conditions for more such moments in the lives of more people. The upshot of my proposal is that philosophical analyses of collective responsibility need to do justice to the existence of systemic problems, many of which cannot be solved by way of a single collective act, utilizing the epistemic resources and skills already at our disposal. Stories like that of Common Ground help us move beyond the limitations of the received view, which reduces collective responsibility to collective liability and, in so doing, narrows our focus to single, allegedly decisive moments of inaction, single-mindedly concerned with attributions of blame. Given that there are not always such singularly significant moments, particularly in the case of challenges both unforeseen and unforeseeable, it seems more important to start coming to grips with and acting upon our shared responsibility to develop each other's capacities for mutual responsiveness, preparation, and coordination in ongoing ways. As crow's words and work suggest, there is no special "now" when the emergency heart moves people into motion to create something better.

Whether and when we ought to hold ourselves and others accountable for our collective failure to take up this responsibility is no simple matter, particularly where stories of collective struggle are not well known or well studied. Perhaps by shifting our approach to thinking about collective responsibility, though, we might better enable one another to seize upon more opportunities for exhibiting collective brilliance in our everyday lives.

Notes

1 As Held explains, a "random collection" of individuals is a type of group distinguished by the fact that it has no decision-making procedure in place, and its members do not display much, if any, solidarity (Held 1970: 471).
2 The *reasonable person standard* is a legal fiction used to determine liability in criminal and tort cases. The term refers to a hypothetical person whose conduct exhibits average care, skill, and judgment. Thus, this person's conduct serves as a standard against which an actual person's conduct may appear negligent.
3 In an earlier paper (Doan 2016), I offer a critique of the epistemological assumptions undergirding this shared approach to thinking about collective inaction.
4 I understand *epistemic agency* in terms similar to Kristie Dotson, who focuses on "the ability to utilize persuasively shared epistemic resources within a given community of knowers in order to participate in knowledge production and, if required, the revision of those same resources" (Dotson 2014: 115).
5 I owe this formulation to Robin D. G. Kelley. As he points out, "Social movements generate new knowledge, new theories, new questions. The most radical ideas often grow out of concrete intellectual engagement with the problems of aggrieved populations confronting systems of oppression" (Kelley 2002: 8). With Kelley, I use the term *collective struggle* to refer to the collective efforts of aggrieved populations confronting systems of oppression and forcefully freeing themselves from systemic constraints.
6 I owe this formulation to Shea Howell.
7 I call it the *knowledge condition* because it implicitly references the cognitive states of the members of a random collection (Doan 2016: 6).
8 I draw inspiration here from Alexis Shotwell's thoughtful discussion of "constitutive impurity" (Shotwell 2016).
9 I understand *climate change impacts* in terms similar to Kyle Powys Whyte, who describes such effects as "arising based on the capacity of patterns of community relations to absorb local ecological alterations stemming from climate change," which may be more or less disruptive insofar as they can be absorbed by existing structures of organization without those structures needing to change (Whyte 2014: 601).
10 While giving a speech, King had once said: "If we as people are going to exploit anything it should be our *commonness*" (crow 2014: 96). King was eventually found, alongside his dog, Kenya. He told his friends: "I knew y'all would come" (ibid.).
11 I focus on the story of Common Ground not because the group's work is beyond criticism, but because it provides an illustrative example of people creating new cultural and economic practices together, through thousands upon thousands of collective acts.
12 While blame may sometimes be appropriate, its helpfulness in addressing the underlying problems is easily overstated. Partly for this reason, my work attends more to political than moral responsibility (Doan 2016).

References

"The Finale" (1998) *Seinfeld*. Season 9, episodes 23–4, NBC, May 14.
Clark, J.P. (2014) "Foreword to the Second Edition: In the Right Place, at the Right Time," in s. crow, *Black Flags and Windmills: Hope, Anarchy, and the Common Ground Collective*, 2nd ed., Oakland: AK Press: xvii–xxii.
Copp, D. (1991) "Responsibility for Collective Inaction," *Journal of Social Philosophy* 22(2): 71–80.
crow, s. (2014) *Black Flags and Windmills: Hope, Anarchy, and the Common Ground Collective*, 2nd ed., Oakland: AK Press.
crow, s. (2018) *Setting Sights: Histories and Reflections on Community Armed Self-Defense*, Oakland: PM Press.

Doan, M.D. (2016) "Responsibility for Collective Inaction and the Knowledge Condition," *Social Epistemology* 30(5–6): 532–554.
Dotson, K. (2014) "Conceptualizing Epistemic Oppression," *Social Epistemology* 28(2): 115–138.
Held, V. (1970) "Can a Random Collection of Individuals Be Morally Responsible?" *The Journal of Philosophy* 67(14): 471–481.
Isaacs, T. (2011) *Moral Responsibility in Collective Contexts*, Oxford: Oxford University Press.
Kelley, R.D.G. (2002) *Freedom Dreams: The Black Radical Imagination*, Boston: Beacon Press.
Lustig, J. (2012) "Occupy Sandy's Street Medics Go Door-to-Door in Coney Island," *New York Magazine*, November 6. http://nymag.com/daily/intelligencer/2012/11/occupy-sandy-goes-door-to-door-in-coney-island.html.
May, L. (1990) "Collective Inaction and Shared Responsibility," *Noûs* 24(2): 269–277.
Moore, H. and Russell, J.K. (2011) *Organizing Cools the Planet: Tools and Reflections to Navigate the Climate Crisis*, Oakland: PM Press.
Newton, H.P. (2009) *To Die for the People: The Writings of Huey P. Newton*, edited by Toni Morrison, San Francisco: City Lights Books.
Petersson, B. (2008) "Collective Omissions and Responsibility," *Philosophical Papers* 37(2): 243–261.
Shotwell, A. (2016) *Against Purity: Living Ethically in Compromised Times*, Minneapolis: University of Minnesota Press.
Tännsjö, T. (2007) "The Myth of Innocence: On Collective Responsibility and Collective Punishment," *Philosophical Papers* 36(2): 295–314.
Thompson, A.C. (2008) "Katrina's Hidden Race War," *The Nation*, December 17. Available at: www.thenation.com/article/katrinas-hidden-race-war/ (Accessed: 31 January 2019).
Whyte, K.P. (2014) "Indigenous Women, Climate Change Impacts, and Collective Action," *Hypatia* 29(3): 599–616.
Young, I.M. (2011) *Responsibility for Justice*, Oxford: Oxford University Press.

15
SHARED RESPONSIBILITY AND FAILURES TO PREVENT HARM

Shannon Fyfe

The notion of collective responsibility is often invoked in order to identify the persons and entities that can be blamed for an event that has occurred. Individual and collective blameworthiness for an event can be established through causal connections, intentions, relationships, or some combination of these features. Some argue that while we can identify group responsibility for actions, we cannot hold individuals or groups responsible for what they fail to do. Others are drawn to the notion of shared responsibility, which provides an opportunity to look at a harm that has occurred and identify the persons and entities that can be blamed for *failing* to act. Larry May offered an early account of shared responsibility that provided the resources to parse out shared individual responsibility for failures to act. What was novel about his account was its focus on this responsibility to intervene to prevent a harm, rather than a responsibility to refrain from interference.

In this chapter, I argue that a revised version of May's account of shared responsibility for wrongdoing can help us address important problems in the domain of collective inaction: namely, failures to prevent further harm. In section 15.1, I set up May's account of shared responsibility, focusing on the features that are most relevant for the issue of shared responsibility for collective inaction. In section 15.2, I explore what I consider to be the most compelling criticisms of May's view and suggest that his view should be more focused on achieving certain states of affairs than performing backward-looking accountability assessments. In section 15.3, I use this revised version of May's view to sketch a way to think about accountability for particular failures to prevent harm, where no specific individual or entity has the positive obligation to protect individuals or groups.

15.1 May On Shared Responsibility

Collective responsibility as a general term associates moral agency with group agents rather than individual agents. It refers to the causal responsibility and blameworthiness of groups, where moral responsibility is located in the group, as a collective, rather than in the individual members of the group. Some argue that the concept of collective responsibility is meaningless, claiming that responsibility can only be attributed to individuals who have their own intentions and engage in their own discrete acts. Those who defend the possibility of collective responsibility claim that some intentions and acts, and corresponding blameworthiness, can fairly be attributed to groups.

Shared responsibility is a particular form of collective responsibility. The term refers to the concept of individual group members each being held partially responsible for harm that is caused by the group's actions. We can think of the difference between group and shared responsibility in terms of distribution: group responsibility applies blame to the group as a whole, while shared responsibility applies blame to individual members of the group. Even if we accept the possibility of shared responsibility as collective responsibility, we might wonder if it is possible to fairly distribute blame among the individual members of a group. And if it is possible, when and how could shared responsibility exist?

Larry May provided an early account of shared responsibility in which he defends the possibility of such a distribution. In his 1992 book *Sharing Responsibility* he constructs an account of shared responsibility based on his view that the identity of individual moral agents is largely shaped by their communities. May acknowledges the connection between one's attitudes and one's behavior, but he does not see our attitudes as something over which we have sole control. He draws on the earlier existentialist work of Karl Jaspers and Jean-Paul Sartre to develop his own social existentialist understanding of a responsible individual, who cannot be seen in isolation. Rather, May claims that the emphasis of individual responsibility should be on "the kinds of things that one could do, or prevent from occurring, when one acts in combination with others" (May 1992: 24). May sees groups as "individuals-in-relationships," where individuals are the focus in terms of intention and action, but we must look to the group structure in order to explain the relationship between the individuals (May 1987). When it comes to assessing group responsibility, he argues that we should be focused on the capacity of a collection of persons to engage in joint action or articulate a common interest.

For May, the concept of shared responsibility allows us to expand the traditional concept of individual responsibility to acknowledge the social influence on our attitudes and the social nature of many acts. Accordingly, shared responsibility provides the tools for holding individuals responsible for things that were not directly caused by the individual. May's view of individual responsibility as something that is both unique to an individual and inextricably tied to the collective also grounds his concept of shared responsibility, which is meant to "divide responsibility among the members of a group, rather than to hold each member fully responsible or to hold the whole group collectively responsible" (May 1992: 37–8).

An attribution of collective responsibility relies on the identification of something over and above the individual contributions of each member of a group; but, since shared responsibility is about the aggregation of individual responsibility, May argues that it can be used to understand responsibility within groups that are less cohesive. Thus, he sees his account as particularly useful for situations in which a person made a "choice that contributed to a harm for which that person was then at least partially responsible" (May 1992: 36). May is focused on the *choices* that individuals make as what warrants their full or partial responsibility for harms, which involve both our actions and our attitudes. We are generally thought to be responsible for our voluntary behavior, whether intentional or negligent, if it results in a harmful event. May's view of shared responsibility allows for us to hold individuals responsible for voluntary actions and attitudes that were not intended to cause the harm, or may not have directly caused the harm.

There are several types of situations in which the need for the concept of shared responsibility arises, according to May. The first situation is when an individual makes a choice to conspire with another to engage in joint action. The fact that a choice was made by the individual is what warrants some amount of individual responsibility, but the fact that the individual's actions were not sufficient to cause the harm renders full responsibility inappropriate. Second, shared responsibility is appropriate when an individual takes a voluntary action, and this action is a necessary part of the harm, but the individual does not have any knowledge or intent of contributing to the harm that occurs. Again, it is the choice and its necessary contribution to the harm that warrants partial responsibility for the individual. Finally, and most controversially, May argues that there are situations in which an individual can be held partially responsible for choosing to maintain particular attitudes that increase the risk of harmful behavior on the part of others.

In each of these situations, there is more than one person who contributes to a harm. In the first scenario, there is a somewhat clearly constituted group, insofar as the two or more individuals have agreed to work together to facilitate the harm that occurs. In the second and third scenarios, however, the "group" is less cohesive. Some claim that a group cannot exist without a formal institutional structure, shared group intentions, and a commitment of the individual members of the group to the entity of the group as a whole (see, e.g., Gilbert 1996; 2014). But as previously noted, May understands groups in terms of the relationships between group members, arguing that "when a collection of persons displays either the capacity for joint action or common interest, then that collection of persons should be regarded as a group" (May 1987: 29–30). This capacity is located in the structure of the group rather than in the individuals, but this does not make the group exist independently of the individuals. Thus, May argues that a "group" can exist based on the *capacity* of the individuals for joint action, not the actual shared commitments and intentions.

May distinguishes between a corporation as an example of a group with significant organizational structure,[1] and a mob as an example of a group with little (if any) organizational structure, but which has come together for economic or political reasons. A mob, however, provides an opportunity for individuals to engage in actions that they would not be able to on their own, and May argues that social identification can play a role in creating shared attitudes and behaviors. He notes that:

> [g]roup members influence one another by a certain kind of socialization, often not fully recognized by the group members, in which the values of the group member tend to be reshaped so as to conform to the norms of the majority of the members of the group. Mob members influence each other in such a way that people are encouraged to act in pursuit of goals and in ways they would never have allowed themselves if they had been uninfluenced by fellow mob members.
>
> *(May 1992: 78)*

Take a group of individuals who have just witnessed an incident of unwarranted police brutality against a young man, a scenario I will refer to as *Mob*. In *Mob*, the individuals are outraged by the same event, and due to their shared outrage, begin yelling at the police officer and eventually flip over his police car. If a single individual had witnessed the act of police brutality, she would have been equally outraged, but she may not have been encouraged (or emboldened) by the presence of others to speak out against the police officer, and she certainly would not have been able to flip over his car. This scenario reveals that even in mobs, there can exist the capacity for sufficient shared intention and joint action, and relationships that allow for mutual influence. Thus, for May, a mob can constitute a group that could be held collectively responsible for harm.

But what about a putative group that is even less cohesive, one that is created out of circumstance and not shared interests? May uses a common example of a drowning child and a collection of bystanders on the shore (I'll call this coordinated bystander scenario *Beach*) to demonstrate what he means by "capacity for joint action." In the example, none of the individuals who hear the drowning child are capable of saving her on their own, but if they fail to coordinate a rescue attempt, "it may be implausible to say that their failure to act constitutes collective inaction" because they do not necessarily have the time to coordinate amongst themselves (May 1992: 111). May contrasts this example of a drowning emergency with a famine (which I will refer to as *Famine*), a situation in which there is more time for a putative group of individuals (or institutions) to develop the mechanisms necessary to coordinate group action. On May's view, the putative group in *Famine* could be held collectively responsible for failing to coordinate and failing to prevent harm, as well as individually responsible for failing to prevent harm. Shared responsibility, however, does not rely on the existence of a group, since it is based on the aggregation of individual responsibility.

Mob, *Beach*, and *Famine* bring up another important feature of shared responsibility, which is the manner of dividing responsibility. May explains how this happens as follows:

> Dividing responsibility for a harm is also different from assigning to each of several people full responsibility for a harm. Some or all members of a group may be assigned less than full responsibility for a harm in cases of divided or shared responsibility. When a person is assigned less than full responsibility for a harm, that person still is subject to blame, punishment, or shame for what has occurred, and should feel motivated to choose differently in the future, just as in a case of full individual responsibility. But, unlike full individual responsibility, shared responsibility calls attention to the way in which the actions or attitudes of a group of people resulted in a harm; that is, attention is focused on the way in which each of us interacts with others, rather than on the individual person as an isolated agent.
>
> *(May 1992: 38)*

Individual responsibility is to be shared among the various actors, and is to be divided fairly, but not necessarily equally. May notes that "some persons in [a] collective may be able, because of their various leadership skills, to be more effective in bringing these people to form a group able to act intentionally" (May 1992: 111). He defends a view of distributing responsibility that mirrors his ontological view of groups, which acknowledges an individual's choices, as well as the influence and potential that comes from the group. A purely individualist account of responsibility would focus solely on the individual's intentional decisions, and it wouldn't matter to the assessment of responsibility whether or not there were other actors or a putative group. May's view, on the other hand, takes into account that an individual may be influenced by others, and "thus it sometimes makes sense to view the individual's responsibility in a group as different from what it would be if there were no group" (May 1992: 112–13).

In *Mob*, it may be that one particular individual suggested that the group work together to flip over the police officer's car. Each individual member of the mob would be assigned some level of responsibility for the damage done to the police officer's car,[2] and the ringleader would receive a greater distribution of responsibility than the individual who stood back and cheered while the others flipped the car. On the shore in *Beach*, a CEO is likely more responsible than a teenager for failing to coordinate the pair of former Olympic swimmers to work together to save the drowning child. And in *Famine*, it may be that relief organizations with experience responding to large-scale crises receive more blame for the continued harm than a new nation-state with few resources.

It is important to note that in both *Beach* and *Famine*, it is collective inaction, rather than action, that results in harm. For the remainder of this chapter, I will focus on what seems to be the most crucial contribution of May's view of shared responsibility, which is his defense of individual responsibility for collective inaction. Some thinkers argue that while we can be held responsible for harm that we have intentionally caused, we may not be responsible for intervening where we are not the cause of harm (see, e.g., Kamm 1986; Sartorio 2005). As May argues, "[i]naction leads to serious harm in the world, just as certainly as intentional, active wrongdoing. Yet inaction, especially collective inaction, presents difficult problems for theories of responsibility" (May 1992: 105–6). But assuming we can make a normative claim that there are situations in which individuals or institutions are obligated to act to prevent harm, we must be able to identify which failures to act should be singled out as warranting blame, and how the responsibility for failures to act should be distributed among individual members of a group (or putative group).

As shown in *Beach* and *Famine* above, assessing shared responsibility for collective inaction requires an analysis of whether the collective had the capacity to act as a group. As May notes, assessment of this counterfactual, "Could the collection of people have avoided inaction?" proves much more challenging than an assessment of action, especially in the case of putative groups with no history of collective decision-making (May 1992: 109). If the putative group could not have reasonably been expected to act as a group, then a "collective" failure to act would only be a failure of each individual to act. But if the individuals could have acted otherwise, then they would have been individually responsible for harms resulting from the failure to constitute themselves as a group, and corresponding inaction. The kinds of omissions that a group might be responsible for include those harms that the group has done something to contribute to already, those harms about which they have created expectations that they would act to prevent, and those harms that they are uniquely situated to prevent. As for putative groups, May largely relies on a determination of what the rest of society sees as reasonable to expect, in light of existing norms.

Individual responsibility for action is more easily distributed, based on actual behavior, including acts of leadership or persuasion, as shown by the ringleader in *Mob*. Both individual and collective responsibility for inaction, according to May, is focused on capacity. Thus, an individual who could have used leadership skills to prevent harm should have a greater share of responsibility than those who were only capable of following orders. Yet May does not see assessment of moral responsibility for a harm as an endeavor to distribute a fixed number of "equal shares based on the number of people present in the group" (May 1992: 113). Rather, he claims that individuals should be required to do as much as they are capable of doing, which is based on an assessment of an individual's capacity, and which does not change in relation to the capacities of the other individuals in the putative group. This method of distribution also allows for a distinction between an individual who directly causes harm and individuals who fail to act, while still attributing some amount of blame to the indirect actors.

A final aspect of May's view of shared responsibility and collective inaction worth considering is how to hold individuals responsible for inaction. May claims that another difference between shared responsibility for collective action and shared responsibility for collective inaction is the corresponding moral weight. For May, the partial, shared responsibility is of a different kind than the guilt associated with full responsibility for directly causing harm. He suggests that shame is a more appropriate tool than guilt, since it is "directly related to a person's conception of herself or himself, rather than to explicit behavior (which is what guilt most commonly attaches to)" (May 1992: 120). His claim seems to be both descriptive and normative, as May sees an individual's failure to act as part of a collective as something that generates the moral feeling of shame, rather than guilt, because it relates to the association between one's own identity and the identity of the group. I will return to this aspect of May's argument in the next section, where I explore criticisms of May's account of shared responsibility for collective inaction.

15.2 Criticisms of May's View

As I argued in the previous section, May's view is important because it provides a mechanism for holding individuals responsible for inaction in situations where they could have prevented harm by coordinating with other, similarly situated individuals. He acknowledges that this creates a high standard for moral agents, but also argues that it should be inspirational, "calling attention to the need for people to look beyond their individual lives, to consider what they could accomplish in their communities through joint action" (May 1992: 118). I agree with May that any account of shared responsibility for collective inaction should be motivating, but I argue that his account needs to be modified if it is to meet this goal. In this section, I argue that May's view lacks the resources needed to be as motivating as he wants it to be, because it relies too heavily on a backward-looking assessment of responsibility and adopts the wrong reactive attitude. Accordingly, May's account should be revised if it is to address the sorts of pressing issues of harm and collective inaction I discuss in section 15.3.

Like May's accounts, most other accounts of collective responsibility and shared responsibility for collective inaction are retrospective, in that they take a particular harm and attempt to identify who (or what) can be held responsible for the harm (see, e.g., Copp 1991; Held 1970; Petersson 2008; Tännsjö 2007). It is easy to see why this is appealing: it allows us to create the kinds of counterfactuals that are necessary in order to generate responsibility for inaction. While we are not in an epistemic position to know exactly what was possible, we can know certain features of the individuals who failed to act, and we know the extent of the harm that occurred; and this can allow us to work backwards to create various counterfactuals. It is also a helpful way to think about responsibility if we want it to translate to the realm of legal responsibility. A criminal court can only assess the liability for a failure to prevent harm by looking backward at the mental state and actions of a defendant, establishing whether the defendant contributed causally to the harm, attributing an appropriate level of culpability, and delivering a correspondingly appropriate punishment. Even though it seems that in situations of collective inaction, a "repeat scenario" may be unlikely, a criminal verdict and punishment may have a deterrent effect on an individual in the future (insofar as one can be "deterred" from inaction). Regardless, judgments assessing criminal responsibility can allow communities that have suffered grievous harm to gain some closure and begin to move on.

Yet this retrospective look at collective inaction does not provide the same benefits as a forward-looking view of shared responsibility. Forward-looking responsibility establishes what individuals or other entities *should* be doing, not what they should have done in the past. Thomas Hill explains the difference between forward-looking responsibility and backward-looking responsibility as the difference between asking who is to blame and asking who is in a position, now, to do something (Hill 2010: 29). Robert Goodin has argued that a forward-looking view of responsibility requires us to see to it that a certain state of affairs obtains (Goodin 1985; 1995). The content of a state of affairs that is both desirable and possible also presents an epistemic challenge, and it cannot be outlined in detail. As Michael Doan argues, we don't necessarily know the collective action solution (and corresponding state of affairs) for many of the collective action problems we face, and thus our responsibilities should involve both collaborative inquiry and action (Doan 2016). Yet I contend that through this inquiry we can usually at least identify the relative desirability of certain states of affairs, and when we can do so, we can identify an obligation to act so as to avoid certain states of affairs with significant preventable harm.

Particularly when we think about ongoing crises like the one in *Famine*, there is good reason to think that there are many situations in which we have enough information to reasonably act to prevent future harm, and focusing on past collective inaction does not generate the same demand for action to mitigate the ongoing harm. Forward-looking responsibility can't get us to the same sort of analysis we do when we try to create a counterfactual to establish if a collective of individuals should have been expected to organize themselves into a group to prevent harm. However, it can give normative force to the moral responsibilities that are determined by the forward-looking analysis of future states of affairs, and demand that those states of affairs involve a world/nation/community with less suffering.

Tracy Isaacs offers such a forward-looking view of collective inaction, which she refers to as "collective obligation" to distinguish from backward-looking "collective responsibility" (Isaacs 2011; 2014). She gives her own example of a case in which several individual bystanders should work together to prevent harm to some children rafting nearby, and she goes on to argue that we should be focusing on our current and future "obligations" to perform particular acts. This part of her view, which frames responsibility as a prescriptive rather than an evaluative concept, is helpful for thinking about the right way to revise May's view of shared responsibility for collective inaction. Yet Isaacs is limited in her own ability to be prescriptive as well, because she is focused on collective obligations, rather than individual obligations as parts of a shared collective obligation. She claims that individual responsibility in collective contexts can only be understood in terms of collective responsibility, and she sees "no necessary connection between collective blameworthiness and individual blameworthiness" (Isaacs 2014: 43). Isaacs does see collective obligation as providing a useful framework for understanding individual failures to act, especially in terms of what role an individual might take in a potential response to harm. She agrees with May that with respect to collective action, "certain individuals are in a better position than others to direct the actions of the collective and to see that the collective's intention actions are consistent with its obligations as a collective" (Isaacs 2011: 134). This all seems right, since we can't understand collective inaction from a purely individualistic perspective, and individuals should be expected to engage in collective action based on their own abilities.

One concern we might have is that her focus on the collective is too attenuated to be properly motivating. While the moral *obligation* to act is distinct from the *motivation* to act, a case of collective inaction can sometimes be tied to the fact that no individual member felt the requisite motivation to act. On Isaacs' view, it looks like any given individual might be able to eschew her obligations, and the collective would have the same obligation to prevent future harm, only the roles would have to be redistributed among the group members. The individual could ostensibly avoid her individual obligation by removing herself from the putative group prior to an assessment of the collective obligation, and this may be more likely if she does not have properly motivating reasons to act. Again, the motivation is distinct from the obligation, but we should prefer a view that is motivating to one that is not. The benefit of May's view, revised to be forward-looking, is that the obligation is *shared* between the individuals, and each would be blameworthy for failing to fulfill her obligation.

My other main concern with May's view is that it relies on shame, rather than guilt, as the appropriate reactive attitude for individuals who share responsibility for harm. On a forward-looking view of shared responsibility, the aim is to motivate one to act so as to avoid both guilt and shame, and perhaps even to garner praise. We can distinguish between guilt, which is a feeling associated with an act or failure to act, from shame, which focuses on feelings about one's character. Bernard Williams distinguishes between guilt and shame as follows:

> What arouses guilt in an agent is an act or omission of a sort that typically elicits from other people anger, resentment, or indignation. What the agent may offer in order to turn this away is reparation; he may also fear punishment or may inflict it on himself.

> What arouses shame, on the other hand, is something that typically elicits from others contempt or derision or avoidance. This may equally be an act or omission, but it need not be: it may be some failing or defect. It will lower the agent's self-respect and diminish him in his own eyes.
>
> *(Williams 2008: 90)*

So while guilt is tied to something done (or not done), shame attaches to an assessment of one's identity. As Williams notes, guilt can be tied to reparation, or some other accounting for one's behavior. Shame, it seems, looks inwardly and is not tied to making changes outside of oneself.

With respect to the most controversial aspect of May's account, that individuals be held partially responsible for choosing to maintain particular attitudes that increase the risk of harmful behavior on the part of others, shame may be an appropriate reactive attitude. May argues that individuals who maintain racist attitudes, even though they do not engage in racist acts, might share responsibility with members of their racial identity group which do engage in racist acts, because their choice to maintain such attitudes increases the risk of these harms (May 1992: 46–54). When considering individual responsibility for this sort of collective inaction, which is tied to one's identity, it makes sense to look inwardly and see racist attitudes as character defects. This is accurate, regardless of whether or not such self-awareness is motivating enough to encourage change. But it is not sufficient, and to rely on this internal self-assessment is to deny the power of accountability, and deny the moral weight of making a choice not to intervene to prevent harm.

Guilt is a powerful backward-looking tool for acknowledging that one should have acted differently. But it can also be a powerful forward-looking tool for demanding that one meet a moral obligation to contribute to a certain future state of affairs. It encourages us to look at how the choices we make affect other people, and how we might be obligated to prevent harm at some point. Returning to Isaacs' term "collective obligation," it seems that we should look at our responsibilities to prevent harm as obligations in the first place, rather than failed responsibilities after-the-fact, and the prospect of guilt is better suited to encourage us to avoid collective inaction. Whether or not shame generates the motivation to become a less defective person, it does not obligate us to create certain states of affairs, namely states of affairs without suffering that could be prevented through collective action, and this should be a necessary feature of accountability. In the final section, we will look at two situations that illustrate why.

15.3 Shared Responsibility for Failing to Protect

I turn now to two case studies of potential failures to protect, one involving shared responsibility among individuals, and one involving a more complicated assessment of various sorts of entities that could be found to share responsibility. Both situations involve familiar harms that would invoke the need for collective action to prevent future harm. Given that I have argued for a forward-looking version of May's view that focuses on guilt rather than shame, each situation involves an ongoing harm which could potentially be stopped through collective action.

> *Flooded Community*: A natural disaster has endangered and stranded nearly all of the inhabitants of a particular waterfront community. Those who have survived thus far are trapped in areas of rising water and will not survive without a swift, coordinated rescue effort. A neighboring community survived relatively unscathed, and individual members of the neighboring community have the boats and other resources necessary

to rescue their trapped neighbors. However, many individual members of the community would have to work together in order to prevent the imminent loss of life in the flooded community.

Flooded Community is somewhat similar to the *Famine* example explained in section 15.1. There is an ongoing crisis, during which harm has already occurred. The bystanders have no pre-existing, special obligation toward the persons who are suffering, although they appear to be uniquely situated to help. There may or may not be time for the bystanders to organize themselves into a collective, make decisions, and prevent future harm, but it seems likely that at least some of the trapped neighbors could survive until the bystanders were able to collectively organize. Notable differences include the fact that the entities implicated by the potential responsibility for collective inaction are individual persons, not nation-states or large aid organizations, and the fact that the crisis is occurring in the community rather than on the other side of the world. The latter difference should not matter under May's account, since the relevant question of responsibility is about whether future harm could be prevented and does not rely on geographic proximity, other than that proximity might make one uniquely situated to assist. The former difference might matter, since on May's account a group can be responsible for omissions if it has indicated in the past a willingness to help in similar instances, and we can assume that international aid organizations would be expected to act in the face of famine, if not other nations. But May would likely argue that even if the community does not constitute a group already, if the individual members of the community could organize themselves in order to prevent harm to the trapped persons, they would share some responsibility if they failed to do so.

Thus, May would argue that the community's failure to organize to prevent harm to the flooded community should constitute collective inaction for which the individual members of the community would share responsibility, based on their personal abilities, and the appropriate reactive attitude for this failure would be shame. The result of this collective inaction would be that suffering was not prevented, and the individuals would be blamed for being the "kinds of people" who do not intervene to prevent suffering. The community and its individual members might take this opportunity to self-reflect, and change their attitudes so that they would be the kinds of people who would make different choices should a similar situation arise in the future.

On the revised version of May's account, the standard for what is morally required is not significantly changed, but the motivation for each individual to meet her obligation is reshaped. The individual community members would be focused on their actions, rather than their character, and on their obligation to ensure that a certain state of affairs materializes, if that is possible. In this case, it would be the state of affairs in which the greatest number of individuals are rescued from the rising water and survive. Individual community members would not be focused on what a backwards-looking assessment of their actions says about them; rather, they would see the flooded community as imposing a collective obligation on their own community, and derivative individual obligations on each member of the community. The prospect of guilt would be more likely to motivate each individual to act, rather than permitting certain individuals to eschew their responsibilities to the flooded community and leave the collective obligation to prevent harm on a smaller number of their fellow community members. The potential for shame might be an extra motivator for some individuals, but it would not be sufficient to obligate the individual community members to participate in the rescue effort. Thus, it seems more likely under the revised version that an outcome with fewer deaths is achieved for the flooded community.

Now, let's look at one final case with several alternative variables to see how they are impacted by the revised account of shared responsibility:

> *War-Plagued Nation*: A small nation is being unjustifiably attacked by a neighboring, much larger nation. The nation cannot stop the assault and it has already sustained numerous casualties. No one nation's army can stop the aggression, but presumably, the joint efforts of several nations and/or international organizations could cause the aggressive nation to cease its military operations in the small nation.

War-Plagued Nation is also similar to *Famine* in several respects. There is an ongoing crisis, during which significant harm has already occurred. Because the harm is ongoing, there is time for the putative group members to organize themselves into a collective, make decisions, and prevent future harm. The putative group members are themselves entities made up of individuals, thus each entity has its own organizational and decision-making structure. The putative group members may also be a part of an international organization that has some measures in place for decision-making with respect to similar crises, but these structures are notoriously ineffective. Some notable differences include the fact that the entities may have indicated a willingness (or even obligation) to assist with similar harms in the past, thus creating a special obligation to intervene. Depending on the other potential interveners, they may also be uniquely situated to assist. However, the entities implicated by the potential responsibility for collective inaction would likely risk the lives of individual persons in order to prevent future harm in the small nation. Given this risk, and absent a special obligation, May would likely argue that the entities should not be responsible for collective inaction. His account of shared responsibility is premised on the idea that intervention risks little or no harm to the individual actor. But if there is a special obligation, May's account of shared responsibility could be used to blame the entities that make up a putative group for failing to intervene in the small nation.[3]

If *War-Plagued Nation* constitutes an instance of collective inaction, May's account would blame the group for failing to intervene (especially if the group had a special obligation toward the small nation), or the putative group members for failing to organize to intervene in the small nation. Each entity would be partially blamed, based on its ability to contribute to the collective effort. The blame would manifest as a version of shame in which each entity was identified as a failure, or defective entity, for not intervening to prevent harm when the harm could have been prevented. The result of this collective inaction would be that suffering was not prevented, and the various entities might establish different values or policies to ensure that this sort of inaction did not happen in the future, or it might not be affected at all by the same character criticism that would impact an individual.

Instances of potential collective inaction that involve coordination between groups are an even clearer indicator of the need for a forward-looking view of shared responsibility. Again, to the extent that we are concerned with generating better states of affairs, we should be concerned with shared responsibility in the forward-looking sense, and assuming that the larger nation can be stopped from its aggression, a better state of affairs will be achieved by collective action (even if, to recognize the real life complexity of the situation, the group makes a decision to "act" but in a way other than through military intervention). Backward-looking responsibility for failures to intervene incentivizes waiting to see what happens, and provides an opportunity to rely on epistemic gaps to justify the reasons for inaction. Forward-looking responsibility encourages thoughtful weighing of information and options, as a collaborative inquiry among putative group members, but generates an obligation to avoid the worst outcomes, which in this case seem to be the continuation of the unwarranted violence.

Entities like international organizations and nation states are perhaps even less likely than individual persons to have their behavior changed by something akin to shame. These sorts of entities do not possess character traits, even if we find it possible to label organizations as "selfish" or "generous." International organizations are aimed at achieving certain goals and are likely only concerned with perception insofar as negative perception prevents them from achieving their goals. Nation states may be slightly more influenced by external (or even internal) criticism of the nature of national identity, but also only insofar as it prevents the nation state from achieving its domestic and international goals. Given the breadth and scope of international engagement, is unlikely that any one foreign policy decision would cause the rest of the global community to cease interactions with a particular nation state due to its "poor character." The potential for guilt, as a part of the forward-looking obligation to prevent worse states of affairs in a certain community and in the world overall, should encourage collective action at the outset.

We have seen how collective responsibility is limited to holding a collective responsible as a unit, when there are situations in which we want to hold individuals each partially responsible for harm caused, at least in part, by a collective action or failure to act. Larry May's influential account of shared responsibility provides many tools to do so, but as I have shown, it needs to be revised in order to properly obligate and motivate individuals and entities alike. There are plenty of cases in which collective action can prevent harm on a small scale, but it seems that a theory of shared responsibility should also be able to address some of the largest-scale problems we face today, such as inter-state violence, climate change, and famine. These are issues that have thus far proven intractable, in part because they require such large-scale coordination between states and between individuals, and in part because we don't necessarily know how to achieve the best solutions to these problems, but also because there are not positive, individualized obligations to intervene to prevent harm. I have argued that we need a forward-looking view of shared responsibility that directs each of us to act so as to avoid certain bad states of affairs, if not pursue certain good states of affairs.

Notes

1 Assuming collective responsibility is a possibility, corporations seem to be clear examples of the kinds of entities that could be held collectively responsible for harm.
2 In this example, I assume that there were voluntary, intentional actions taken on the part of the individuals in the mob. I do not give an overall assessment of the morality of protesting police brutality, even to the point of property destruction.
3 I only claim that May's account *could* be used to make this argument, although I do not think he himself would use it this way, given what he has written elsewhere about war and its potential to ever achieve a "certain state of affairs" i.e. a state of affairs that we know will contain less preventable harm than the alternatives.

References

Copp, D. (1991) "Responsibility for Collective Inaction," *Journal of Social Philosophy* 22: 71–80.
Doan, M. (2016) "Responsibility for Collective Inaction and the Knowledge Condition," *Social Epistemology* 30: 532–54.
Gilbert, M. (1996) *Living Together: Rationality, Sociality, and Obligation*, Lanham, MD: Rowman & Littlefield Publishers.
Gilbert, M. (2014) *Joint Commitment: How We Make the Social World*, New York: Oxford University Press.
Goodin, R.E. (1985) *Protecting the Vulnerable: A Reanalysis of Our Social Responsibilities*, Chicago: University of Chicago Press.
Goodin, R.E. (1995) *Utilitarianism as Public Philosophy*, New York: Cambridge University Press.

Held, V. (1970) "Can a Random Collection of Individuals be Morally Responsible?," *The Journal of Philosophy* 67: 471–81.
Hill, Jr., T.E. (2010) "Moral Responsibilities of Bystanders," *Journal of Social Philosophy* 41: 28–39.
Isaacs, T. (2011) *Moral Responsibility in Collective Contexts*, Oxford: Oxford University Press.
Isaacs, T. (2014) "Collective Responsibility and Collective Obligation," *Midwest Studies in Philosophy* 38: 40–57.
Kamm, F.M. (1986) "Harming, Not Aiding, and Positive Rights," *Philosophy & Public Affairs* 15: 3–32.
May, L. (1987) *The Morality of Groups: Collective Responsibility, Group-Based Harm, and Corporate Rights*, Notre Dame, IN: University of Notre Dame Press.
May, L. (1992) *Sharing Responsibility*, Chicago: University of Chicago Press.
Petersson, B. (2008) "Collective Omissions and Responsibility," *Philosophical Papers* 37: 243–61.
Sartorio, C. (2005) "A New Asymmetry Between Acts and Omissions," *Nous* 39: 460–82.
Tännsjö, T. (2007) "The Myth of Innocence: On Collective Responsibility and Collective Punishment," *Philosophical Papers* 36: 295–314.
Williams, B. (2008) *Shame and Necessity*, Berkeley: University of California Press.

16
COLLECTIVE GUILT FEELINGS

Björn Petersson

16.1 Introduction[1]

In *Complicity* (2001), Christopher Kutz admits that there are important differences between assigning responsibility to a group in a holistic manner and summing up judgments about individual responsibility. He nevertheless denies that a group in itself can literally be culpable. One of Kutz's reasons for refraining from saying that collectives can be guilty is that

> a collective cannot respond affectively to these expressions, only its constituent members can. The lack of affective counter-response is troubling, because the efficacy of responses of accountability partially depends upon affect. The responses of shame, guilt, and regret help to register the significance of the harm.
>
> *(Kutz 2001: 196)*

The view that evoking feelings of shame, guilt, and related social affective attitudes is essential to our practices of blaming and holding groups morally responsible is common, at least within a broadly Humean or Strawsonian tradition (Hume 1740; Strawson 1962). And the claim that groups can feel guilt, or indeed feel anything at all, appears to "stretch phenomenological credibility" (Smith 2008: 241). So, Kutz's worry seems legitimate.

There is a relatively rich literature on the social psychology of collective guilt and on how different kinds and degrees of experiences of collective guilt affect and are affected by the degree of group identification, and by other ingroup/outgroup attitudes and behavior.[2] Social psychologists regard the feeling of collective guilt as an existing phenomenon; one which is available for empirical studies. This may seem to undermine Kutz's objection. However, even in the context of empirical research it is still not clear exactly what assumptions research subjects commit themselves to when they express feelings of collective guilt. The studied phenomenon is social and hence collective in the broadest sense of the word – it is a feeling that requires an us/them categorization and it explains attitudes that are directed towards one's own group or other groups. However, it is unclear whether it is collective in the sense required to mitigate Kutz's worry. Empirical studies in this area typically focus on individual experiences and perceptions, and as Ferguson and Branscombe note in a research review, "it is not clear whether such measures actually assess collective guilt" (2014: 259). In other words, it is not clear whether empirical research supports the idea that groups as such can react with the kind of affective response that Kutz finds essential for assigning meaningful responsibility to them.

Section 16.2 is a brief elaboration of Kutz's assumption that a subject's capacity for guilt feelings is a reasonable condition for holding it morally responsible in a meaningful way. Section 16.3 maps current defenses of the possibility of collective guilt into two categories: positions that assign guilt feelings to groups as such but play down the phenomenological or experiential component in guilt feelings, and positions that do justice to our intuitions about the phenomenology of guilt feelings but understand collective guilt feelings in terms of individual experiences. Section 16.4 focuses on two examples of the first type of approach, by examining the analogy between collective and individual guilt from two different collectivistic viewpoints – Gilbert's plural subject theory of group guilt, and the suggestion from Gunnar Björnsson and Kendy M. Hess that standard functionalist arguments for basic corporate agency extend to reactive attitudes like guilt feelings. The fourth section presents an approach of the second kind: an individualistic but "perspectival" understanding of collective guilt, related to the "we-mode" approach to collective intentionality.

My tentative conclusion is that Kutz is right in assuming that groups as such cannot feel guilty in the relevant sense, but that guilt as felt by individuals can have a distinctively collective character, such that the feeling still may be an appropriate response to assignments of collective responsibility.

16.2 Blame and Guilt Feelings

Kutz's objection to collective responsibility rests on the assumption that evoking feelings of shame, guilt, and regret is an essential function of moral blame in general. It is beyond the scope of this chapter to defend this assumption, but like David Hume, John Stuart Mill, Richard Brandt, Alan Gibbard, and others, I will assume that it is basically correct.

Hume emphasizes that moral feelings, i.e. "pleasure and pain of that *peculiar* kind, which makes us praise or condemn" are social in character, and differ radically from feelings we have towards inanimate objects. They include love and hatred, pride, and humility (1739, book III, section 1:2). These are feelings of the sort that are bound up with "the very great importance that we attach to the attitudes and intentions towards us of other human beings, and the great extent to which our personal feelings and reactions depend upon, or involve, our beliefs about these attitudes and intentions" (Strawson 1962: section 3). Like Strawson, Hume understands moral praise and blame in terms of interpersonal feelings that typically involve a mutual affective concern – a desire or expectation that the other cares about my attitudes towards her, and that she has a similar desire for me to care about her attitudes towards me.

When John Stuart Mill characterizes morality as a system of social sanctions, the type of sanctions he treats as most important are self-reproach and feelings of guilt.

> For the truth is, that the idea of penal sanctions, which is the essence of law, enters not only into the conception of injustice, but in that of any kind of wrong. We do not call anything wrong, unless we mean to imply that a person ought to be punished in some way or other for doing it; if not by law, by the opinion of his fellow creatures; if not by opinion, by the reproaches of his own conscience.
>
> *(Mill 1863: 33)*

According to Richard Brandt, the essential element in the moral responsibility of a person X is that

> it is fitting or justified in itself for X to have some blaming attitudes, including... remorse towards himself, and for many other persons Y to have some blaming attitudes including retributive indignation towards X, and to express them in their behavior.
>
> *(Brandt 1958: 16–17)*

Alan Gibbard claims that "[t]o hold a person to blame for an action will then be to accept norms that tell him to feel guilty for having done it, and tell others to be angry with him for having done it" (Gibbard 1990: 150).[3]

In line with this, I will assume that to hold you responsible for some bad event is to have an attitude with a conative element towards you: The wish that you feel guilt for your involvement in the event. When you feel guilt for what you did, you feel bad about your actions and wish them undone, due to your demand for regard from others. (As Mill notes, this demand may be completely internalized and it does not necessarily require actual social interaction in each case.) Blame typically appeals to your demand for goodwill from others and your sense of having been part of the explanation of why something bad happened.

On the face of it, we blame the deceased, we blame psychopaths who allegedly lack the capacity to feel guilt,[4] and we even appear to blame inanimate objects like malfunctioning computers. On the view assumed here, it appears that we must dismiss such behaviors as nonsensical, since the blamer in such cases aims at a reaction she knows cannot be realized. A less dismissive strategy is to regard them as distinct forms of blaming-like practices, whose meaning in various ways are parasitic upon the basic sense of blame, sharing some but not all of its essential characteristics. The latter strategy is compatible with holding on to the idea that blame in that basic sense still occupies the most central "region in our moral thought" (Gibbard 1990: 52), and hence that the question of whether a certain type of being is capable of feeling guilt is of great moral relevance.

As Mill notes, guilt feelings may be regarded as negative moral sanctions, closely related to other forms of punishment. Although guilt feelings may have valuable functions, such as helping ameliorate damaged relations, prompting personal improvement etc., like other forms of punishment they are in themselves generally unwanted and unpleasant. This becomes obvious when we consider cases where guilt feelings occur but lack the usual positive effects, such as when people cannot help but feel strongly guilty about some innocent choice that by coincidence turned out to have disastrous consequences.[5] Such feelings are generally considered as bad for the person, and clearly constitute a form of suffering. The unpleasant quality of guilt feelings appears essential to their function as negative moral sanctions.

For the sake of argument, I will not commit myself to any conceptual claims about the phenomenological nature of unpleasantness but like Brandt in *A Theory of the Good and the Right* I will at least assume that one thing which unpleasant states have in common is a continuous motivational component. Other things equal, as long as you are in an unpleasant state you want to be relieved of it, and you want this because of the intrinsic nature of the state you are in (Brandt 1979: 35–42).[6]

16.3 Guilt Feelings and Phenomenology

The view that groups can have their own beliefs, desires, and intentions has been defended in different ways by Philip Pettit, Margaret Gilbert, and others (Gilbert 2000; Pettit 2003). This does not mean that they would be prepared to assign phenomenal consciousness to groups. Christian von Scheve's and Mikko Salmela's anthology on various perspectives on collective emotions (2014) illustrates the fairly broad philosophical and scientific consensus on phenomenology being absent in groups.[7]

Like Burleigh Wilkins, most would probably find the idea of guilt feelings with a "total absence of any phenomenological accompaniments... extremely puzzling" (Wilkins 2002: 152). While a more technical term like "emotion" has been given non-phenomenological interpretations, at least in the philosophical literature – as referring to an essentially conative state or a type of evaluative judgment, for instance – the word "feeling" typically refers to something *felt* by a subject, i.e. an occurrent subjective experience of a particular kind, or at least a disposition for such experiences. Non-phenomenological accounts of emotions are usually explicitly contrasted with feeling accounts, thereby implying that feelings, unlike emotions, by definition come with phenomenology. So, on the common use of the word "feeling," "feelings without phenomenology" is a contradiction in terms.

Nevertheless, in line with the widely accepted repudiation of groups as bearers of phenomenal experience, one natural move among philosophers defending collective guilt feelings is to question the essentiality of phenomenology in this context. Gilbert explicitly doubts that some phenomenological condition must be met for someone to have guilt feelings (Gilbert 2002: 141). Thomas Szanto argues that corporations can have negative reactive emotions, such as feelings of humiliation, which "are not individuated by their phenomenology" and Deborah Tollefsen makes a similar point (Szanto 2016: 271–2; Tollefsen 2003: 232). In their functionalist defense of corporate reactive attitudes, among them guilt feelings, Gunnar Björnsson and Kendy M. Hess "fail to see why purely qualitative aspects of a phenomenal point of view would matter" (2017: 282).

The natural alternative to stripping the notion of "feeling" (in "collective guilt feelings") of phenomenological connotations will be to reinterpret the notion of collectivity in a way that makes it possible to assign the feeling in question to individual group members rather than to the group as such. This appears to be in line with how the term is mostly used in empirical investigations or case studies of collective guilt feelings (see e.g. Pettigrove and Parsons 2012). Versions of this strategy have been defended, for example, by Stephanie Collins, who interprets normative ordinary language claims about organizational emotions in terms of the organization's duties to promote said emotions in their members (Collins 2018) and by Anita Konzelmann Ziv, who accounts for "collective guilt feelings in terms of individual members' we-feeling of guilt" (Konzelmann Ziv 2007).

In other words, given that no reasonable approach assigns phenomenal consciousness to collectives as such, we need to stretch the meaning of "collective guilt feelings" beyond the most natural reading, either by allowing for "feelings" without experiential components, or by assigning a "collective" attitude to individuals. If we allow for the first strategy, it seems reasonable to require at least that the functional analogy between individual and collective guilt is very strong, phenomenal differences aside. If we allow for the second, the challenge is to give an account of what it means for an individual attitude to be collective in a substantive and interesting sense.

16.4 Joint Commitment to Feel Guilt

According to Margaret Gilbert, there may be a radical disjunction between the intentions and beliefs of a group, and those of their members. This is the core of her account: "A population *P* has a collective intention to do *A* if and only if the members of *P* are *jointly committed* to intending *as a body* to do A" (2002: 125, also Gilbert 2000, 2006 and 2009). A population fulfilling this condition constitutes a *plural subject* of the intention to do A. A joint commitment is not a set of individual commitments, it is not created by individual decisions, and it "does not have parts" although it has implications for the parties.

On the plural subject account, groups can have intentions of their own, and Gilbert argues that they can have moral beliefs. Therefore, groups as such can be guilty of performing wrongful acts. Gilbert questions Kutz's claim that collectives cannot respond affectively to moral blame in the appropriate way. "In particular, I argue that there is an important sense in which a collective can feel guilt" (2002: 117).

On the plural subject account of collective action, it is clear that groups as such can be guilty of wrongdoing, and that the group's guilt may have no implications for the guilt of its members (Gilbert 2000, section 8.10). Gilbert argues plausibly that the individual member's feeling of guilt in such a case may be different from ordinary feelings of guilt over the member's own individual actions: the object of the member's guilt feeling is the collective action of the group in which she is a member, and such feelings may not be proportionate to the member's assessment of her personal contribution to the collective wrongdoing. As Gilbert notes, a "problem with rejecting such feelings is that people seem to have them" (2002: 134). We might ask whether they can be rationally justified – Gilbert quotes Karl Jaspers' description of the predicament of being unable to rid himself of guilt feelings for what other Germans did during the Second World War, while as a philosopher he found such emotions to be rationally refutable – but for the present purposes it is sufficient to accept that we can have such feelings, feelings that we have in virtue of our membership in a collective. Gilbert calls them "membership guilt feelings" and we might imagine other sorts of membership feelings, like membership sadness over a collective loss, or membership pride over a collective achievement (Gilbert 2002; Jaspers 1947).

Still, the occurrence of membership feelings of guilt does not imply any feelings of the group as such, or vice versa. For genuinely *collective* guilt feelings to occur, it is

> neither necessary nor sufficient for members of the group to feel membership guilt over an act of the collective... neither necessary nor sufficient for members to feel personal guilt over their participation or other act relating to the collective act... [W]hat is needed, to put it abstractly, is expressions of readiness on everyone's part to be jointly committed to feel guilt as a body.
>
> *(Gilbert 2002: 140)*

Gilbert's general plural subject account is formulated in terms of a joint commitment to intend as a body to *do something*. From such a commitment follows individual entitlements to actions from other members, and personal obligations to act so as to constitute with others an entity that acts "as a body." The language of commitments seems more appropriate for capturing collective agency than collective emotions, for the simple reason that while we commit ourselves to act in various ways, we do not normally seem to make commitments to feel anything. In later work, Gilbert articulates the core idea by saying that "roughly, the parties are jointly committed as far as possible to emulate, by virtue of the actions of each, a single body that intends to do the thing in question" (2009: 180). The reference to commitments to *act* so as to constitute a body that *does* something is still essential in this formulation.

We do not make decisions about what to feel, and more generally, we do not seem to have the capacity for voluntary shifts of attitudinal modes. I do not deliberately switch from fearing that *p* to hoping that *p*, grieving that *p*, or feeling guilty that *p*. Admittedly, there are pre-commitment devices, more or less efficient self-help methods, and other ways of attempting to affect one's emotions and motivation but those sorts of activities are not what the parties to the joint commitment to feel guilt as a body are committed to in Gilbert's examples of such cases. In her illustrations of collective guilt feelings, the act of *expressing* guilt feelings as a body is really what the parties to the joint commitment are committed to.

When Joe and Lisa have failed to look after Phyllis' daughter Mary properly and as promised during the weekend, thereby making Mary depressed, a joint commitment between Joe and Lisa is prompted by Lisa's expressing their guilt feelings to Phyllis, in the presence of John. This results in a commitment "to feel guilt as a body" but the function of that commitment is e.g. to make Joe "feel constrained to do and say things that echo or conform to Lisa's claim that she and Joe feel guilty about the way they treated Mary" (2002: 140). Certainly, this type of situation occurs, but note that these conditions may be completely fulfilled – Joe and Lisa may both be constrained by a joint commitment to do and say things that are consistent with feeling guilty as a body – without any of them actually feeling guilty about anything.

Gilbert explicitly stresses the latter possibility: "No one of these feelings [i.e. collective, membership, and personal guilt feelings] seems to carry another with it as a matter of logic" (2002: 142). On Gilbert's notion of collective guilt feelings, their collective behavior would suffice for assigning such feelings to this group, even if we know for certain that neither Joe nor Lisa cares about Mary or Phyllis, and that their initial expressions of readiness to enter the joint commitment to do the things that are significant of collective guilt is fully explained by, say, their desire to conform with socially accepted behavior.

Gilbert explicitly questions the idea that some phenomenological condition must be met for someone to have guilt feelings. Let us grant that the apparent absence of an independent phenomenology of the plural subject may, as Gilbert claims, be "no issue" for an account of collective guilt feelings (2002: 141).

My remaining worry is that nothing in the account gives us any reason to believe that the plural subject as such would care about being in this state. Joe and Lisa may each wish that they were not bound by a joint commitment to express guilt feelings as a body, but the account assigns no such wishes to the plural subject, which is distinct from Joe and Lisa. To assign such wishes to the plural subject would seem to require that yet another joint commitment comes into play – a commitment to express resentment over the first commitment, perhaps. This seems farfetched, and would clearly be an *ad hoc* move. So, I am inclined to think that the plural subject's Gilbertian guilt feelings lack the element of being unpleasant and unwanted that is essential to guilt feelings and their functions in relation to blame.

My contention is that while Gilbert sketches an interesting account of how members in a group may feel obliged to express certain emotions on behalf of the group, and of how in such situations collectively tainted emotions may occur in the minds of individual members, the properties that she assigns to the plural subject – the group as such – do not constitute guilt feelings in the sense that is tied to moral blame.

Nevertheless, I think that elements in her reflections on the phenomenology of collective guilt feelings point to an interesting sense in which individuals may have distinctively collective feelings of guilt. I will return to that issue in the last section.

16.5 Corporate Agency and Reactive Attitudes

In "Corporate Crocodile Tears? On the Reactive Attitudes of Corporate Agents" (2017), Gunnar Björnsson and Kendy M. Hess challenge anyone who finds it reasonable to regard corporations as agents in a basic sense but refuses to assign feelings of guilt, sadness, or indignation to them. The challenge is to "explain why the sort of arguments that support basic corporate agency do not extend to reactive attitudes" (2017: 293). Elsewhere in the text, they state their conditional argument more cautiously and merely claim that functionalist arguments for regarding corporations as agents will also show that corporations can have "the moral equivalent" of reactive attitudes or something "sufficiently similar" to reactive attitudes (2017: 274).

The strategy of Björnsson and Hess, as I understand it, is to establish, first, that if we accept functionalist arguments to the effect that corporations have basic agency, then we should also accept that they can be in states that are functionally equivalent to, for example, individual reactive attitudes like guilt feelings. Second, they assume that if the corporation's and the individual's states are functionally equivalent, then they are morally equivalent. The step from functional to moral equivalence could be problematized. Hess' and Björnsson's dismissal of the phenomenal point of view in this context indicates that they have a narrow sense of "functional equivalence" in mind, where references to subjective experiences are excluded. (Functionalism in a broader sense might admit that a specific attitude's functional role could include its relation to subjective experiences, or dispositions for subjective experiences.) On that kind of functionalism, we would have to say that e.g. a robot programmed to imitate a mammal's physical pain perfectly in terms of inputs and behavioral outputs is in a state that is functionally equivalent to the mammal's physical pain. It seems reasonable to think that a machine could be programmed in this way without being extremely complex or displaying AI in any substantial sense. Would this kind of functional equivalence entail moral equivalence? But I will disregard this issue in the following, and focus on the first step in the argument.

The standard argument for regarding corporations as independent agents is that corporations can make decisions, express beliefs and follow policies that do not reflect the views of their individual members. This is taken to prove that "corporate commitments are distinct from member commitments, and this remains true regardless of whether they conflict or cohere" (Björnsson and Hess 2017: 276). I agree. It is obvious that such discrepancies can occur when the corporation is undemocratic, but it is also a fact that no collective decision procedure that fulfils reasonable rationality constraints can guarantee an outcome that reflects the beliefs and desires of its members. This is Philip Pettit's main reason for thinking that groups have "minds of their own" with their own beliefs, desires, and intentions (Pettit 2003). It could also be the case in periods that no collective or individual decisions at all are made about the corporation's overarching goals and policies – corporate policies and commitments have simply been passed on from previous generations of members, and new members carry on executing those policies without contestation, "because that is how things are done" in this company, as Pettit says. As Björnsson and Hess note, members may continue acting on the corporation's commitments and make various decisions based on them in response to external events, and they may even adjust the relative weight of those commitments when they come into conflict, without necessarily embracing these commitments as individuals.

I accept that this kind of distinction between member commitments and corporate commitments is sufficient for admitting that there is a basic sense in which a corporation can be regarded as an autonomous agent. Assume also with Björnsson and Hess that desires, beliefs, and intentions need not have any essentially phenomenal qualities, and that a corporation's autonomy is no more undermined by the underlying control by its members than an individual's autonomy is undermined by her decisions being caused by underlying mechanisms.

My first worry concerns the next step in the argument: from ascribing basic agency to corporations on account of the distinction between corporate commitments and member commitments, to equating corporate beliefs and desires with individual beliefs and desires in the standard sense. What we have established is rather agency in a very basic sense. As Pettit admits,

> If we are to recognize the integrated collectivity as an intentional subject, then we must admit of course that it is a subject of an unusual kind. It does not have its own faculties of perception or memory... it is incapable of forming degrees of belief and desire in the ordinary fashion of animal subjects; its beliefs are recorded as on-off judgments, its desires as on-off intentions.
>
> *(2003: 182)*

What we may think of as a corporation's beliefs, desires, and intentions are "its commitments about how the world is, what goals to pursue, and how to act" (Björnsson and Hess 2017: 277). As far as I can see, there are essential functional differences between corporate commitments and the beliefs or desires of an individual. Take ACME's commitment to be environmentally responsible. Such a commitment typically consists in a directive expressed in a policy document or a declaration that may be internal or public. The directive, in turn, is the end product of an individual or collective decision process. The corporate directive is the consequence of a decision taken at a specific point in time. The function of the directive is to promote or restrict future behavior of the corporation in this or that direction. The proper functional analogy to this kind of organizational commitment in the individual case would be the adoption of a pre-commitment device (like making a public New Year's promise that I will be environmentally responsible in order to raise the cost for certain future choices, e.g. in terms of lost respect from those who heard my promise) rather than a continuous desire.

A full-fledged desire would be a continuous internal state of ACME, which explains why they took the specific decision to adopt this policy document, or would enable us to predict future commitments. But nothing in the description of what happens makes it necessary to postulate a state of ACME with that functional role. What explains how the directive came about is a specific individual or collective decision procedure (whose outcome admittedly need not reflect the views of ACME's members).

If I would like to be environmentally responsible and know that I fail to be so, I have a continuously frustrated desire, i.e. I am in a state, presumably unpleasant, making me disposed to act and think in various ways. If ACME has declared its commitment to environmental responsibility and fails to live up to it, there may be external sanctions of various kinds, and individual members may feel frustrated if they identify with ACME or sympathise with its stated policies. However, there is no reason to think that ACME as such thereby has a continuous frustrated desire. It has a policy document that was decided upon at a specific point in time. If ACME declares regret over its failure, this new declaration is the result of another individual or collective decision procedure.

My other worries are more empirical and concern corporate guilt feeling behavior in real life. My evidence is anecdotal, but to begin with I find it rather unusual for corporations or their official representatives to display behavior indicative of such feelings on the part of the corporation as such. On the contrary, it seems to me that when the representatives of a business company or a public authority want to express concern for the victims of some harmful act that the corporation has committed or contributed to, they typically do this in a personal manner, marking that they and possibly their colleagues *personally* feel for the victims and their families etc. rather than that the impersonal corporation does so.

It is true, as Björnsson and Hess state, that ACME as a corporation "might issue apologies and compensate victims because ACME's position is that this is what one does when one is responsible for some harm" (2017: 18). This could be a policy and a standard procedure in the company. Apologies and compensation are weak indicators of guilt feelings though. I might apologise and compensate you after having broken your vase even if both of us know that it was an accident and completely unintended. Compensation may be fully justified even in cases where it is clear that there is no moral guilt to begin with. In the context of tort law, the notion of strict liability often applies precisely to cases where people have been harmed by commercial products. In such cases there may be a common assumption that the company causing harm is also responsible for compensating the victims, regardless of any wrongdoing.

Moreover, we should not underestimate the role of pure business strategy as the explanation of why apologies and compensations are offered. Think of cases where the risk of costs for future lawsuits, fines, apologies, and compensations have been calculated and weighed against expected profit before the harmful decision is made.[8]

Even if my empirical speculations about corporate behavior are true, they would not by themselves show that it would be *impossible* for a corporation to display all the subtle behavioral signs that are significant of guilt feelings. If that happened occasionally, only an oversimplified form of behaviorism or role functionalism, identifying guilt feelings with its external displays, would force us to conclude that the corporation in such a single case feels guilt. Unless this happens regularly and typically, we have no reason to believe that the company is in a continuous state warranting predictions about future patterns of behavior in relation to guilt in new decision contexts and circumstances.

In line with what I said in the first section of this chapter, I think that guilt feelings like other reactive attitudes have an essentially social and involving character, reflecting our sensitivity to how we are regarded by others and our caring about how they believe that we regard them. Moreover, like Hume I do not find it improper to regard feelings of guilt as a specific form of pain – it is unpleasant to be haunted by guilt feelings. Both properties are, I think, central to the function of blame and guilt feelings in morality as a system of social sanctions.

Björnsson and Hess agree that the unpleasant nature of guilt feelings might be important for its role in practices of holding responsibility (even though they do not think that this is absolutely necessary for fully fledged moral agency, p. 288). They claim, though, that something like the motivational role of unpleasantness is an element in a corporation's moral equivalent of guilt feelings, "since an organization instantiating the moral equivalent of guilt… will be thrown into disruptive internal conflict, conflict of a sort that it is motivated to avoid" (2017: 288). That rests on their assumption that the organization as such desires to avoid changing its commitments and values, and that taking on the moral equivalent of guilt feelings requires such changes. It is not clear to me why an organization as such necessarily should be motivated to avoid changing its commitments (nor that companies displaying elements of guilt behavior typically make fundamental policy changes). That seems to presuppose that the organization is attached to its commitments in a stronger sense than the assignment of basic agency, consisting of on-off intentions, and on-off judgments, can justify.

16.6 Blaming Collectives as a Way of Evoking Collectively Tainted Guilt in Individuals

As Gilbert points out, we may distinguish between the feeling of guilt that a person may have over her personal contribution to a collectively produced effect, and guilt feelings that are directed at the collective behavior of one's group. It is evident that groups to which we belong in various ways can figure in the objects of our frustration or displeasure. I may not only feel guilty about what my group has done, but also be dissatisfied with its performance, worried about its future, or depressed over its declining reputation. Such attitudes can differ from my views or feelings about my own individual performance, future, or reputation. However, the mere fact that my personal preferences about my group can be frustrated, or that I can have unpleasant feelings over what my group has done or things that happened to it, does not invoke any need for a special category of desires or emotions. These may be ordinary first-person individual attitudes, albeit with a conception of the collective in their content.

Gilbert tentatively suggests that an individual may not only have membership feelings (or, as she says, "feeling-sensations") of this unproblematic kind – individual feelings directed at some aspect of one's group – but also that distinctively *collective* feelings may occur in the individual's mind.

When Gilbert discusses how the pangs of guilt feelings that a person may have due to some act that her group has performed should best be described – as pangs of personal guilt, membership guilt, or collective guilt – she says that although these phenomena are distinct, "from a phenomenological point of view, there may be no way of deciding this issue: a pang is a pang is a pang" (2002: 141). That caveat may be unnecessarily cautious. Among authors defending the possibility of genuine collective intentionality (without postulating group minds or plural subjects), it is not uncommon to associate certain intentional states with a collectively tainted phenomenal feature, a "sense of we-ness" (Pacherie 2012: 343) or "feeling of togetherness" (Zahavi 2015: 91). I think that there is some intuitive plausibility to this.

Consider again the case of Karl Jaspers. One way of understanding his predicament would be to say that although he was neither causally involved in the atrocities, nor felt any kind of sympathy for these deeds or the ideology they were driven by, he felt guilt for them from the perspective of the German people – a collective with which he identifies. The idea that individuals may identify with groups has been commonly expressed in social psychology at least since the 1970s (for an overview, see e.g. Tajfel and Turner 1986, who discuss group identification in relation to social identity theory) and I believe that it is quite common in various popular debates on collective phenomena – people are said to identify to various degrees with their sports team, ethnic group, political party, etc. In the present context, we need to give a more exact meaning to such expressions. My suggestion is that there is a sense in which you can experience the situation from the group's perspective.

To make that claim plausible it is not enough to appeal to phenomenological intuitions or introspective evidence. We should be able to give a functional characterization of this perspectival feature of our attitudes. Elsewhere I have suggested a way of developing such an account of the collective perspective, and I will not go into all details here but just give some hints about how I think one should proceed.[9] My approach relies on the common assumption that we can characterize intentional states functionally in terms of what would make them successful. Some types of attitudes, like perceptions and action intentions, are only veridical or successful if their object stands in a certain relation to the subject of intention – my intention to raise my arm is not successful unless *I* raise my arm by way of carrying out this very intention, to use a standard example from John Searle. Like François Recanati, I think that Searle is wrong in thinking that this implies that the subject of the intention (*I*) must figure in the *content* of the intentional state in question. When you perceive this text, a complete description of what makes your perception veridical must include a description of how the text is causally related to you and your experience, but the content of your perceptual experience is mainly the text. The content of the experience need not, and normally does not, include any conception of how the text is related to you. Moreover, we must distinguish between the subject of intention, which is a perspectival feature of some types of intentional states, and the ontological subject, i.e. the individual in whose head the intentional state resides. All intentional states have bearers, but some intentional states, like beliefs, need not have a subject of intention – it may not be necessary to refer to the believer when exposing the truth conditions for a belief.

As Recanati has argued, some types of intentional states admit of perspectival variation when it comes to time and place. This means that the context in which the content of the intentional state should be evaluated (according to its success conditions) need not be the context in which the ontological subject is situated when possessing the state. An episodic memory is not veridical if its object occurs in the present context, but is if it occurred in the context of an earlier perceptual experience, for instance. So, the point in time and space from which the content of an intentional state is conceived need not be "here" and "now." In a similar manner, I suggest that it is possible that some types of intentional states admit of perspectival variation when it comes to the subject of intention, i.e. that the subject of intention may be either "I" or "we."

So, my claim is that there is a coherent and analyzable sense in which "the subject is immanent in the attitude" (to borrow a phrase from Hans Bernhard Schmid[10]) without necessarily being part of its content, and that this allows for genuinely collective attitudes without requiring the existence of group minds or independent plural subjects.

This section proceeded from Gilbert's claim that individuals can experience collective feelings, and a phenomenological intuition about the plausibility of the claim that a sense of we-ness may accompany certain attitudes. The suggested functional characterization of how attitudes can be held from a group perspective does not *rely* on such phenomenological intuitions, but fits well with them. Perspectival features of a mental state may be part of the phenomenology of that state. As Recanati says, "there is absolutely no reason to consider that phenomenology supervenes on content in the narrow sense" (2009: 51).

According to Deborah Tollefsen, "one could understand collective emotions as those emotions that are expressed *through* the group members *qua* group members" (2003: 232). A collective guilt feeling is "the guilt one feels in response to the actions of one's own group" (Tollefsen 2006: 237). I agree that these kinds of feelings occur and that they are distinct from the guilt an individual may feel over her individual contributions to the collective act. Such feelings are what Gilbert (and I) call "membership guilt feelings," i.e. individual feelings directed at the collective action of the group in which the individual is a member. What makes my membership guilt feeling "collective" is its *object*.[11] But like Gilbert, I believe that individuals can have collective guilt feelings in a sense distinct from mere membership guilt feelings. I cannot only feel guilt *for* my group or what it has done. I can feel guilt from my group's perspective. What makes this kind of feeling collective is not its object, but its intentional subject.

This approach will not provide any grounds for taking literally the claim that groups as such can feel guilt, but it may capture some of the intuitions behind such claims. It gives an explication of how feelings and preferences in the individual mind can be based on the individual's identification with the group, and thereby have a genuinely collective character. Such feelings can be unpleasant even if there are no corresponding feelings of discomfort held from the individual perspective.

Let me return to Kutz's challenge against the idea of collective guilt. Kutz thinks that it would be pointless to hold collectives accountable, since they are unable to respond affectively. Blame must therefore be directed towards the individual accomplices (Kutz 2001: 196). I am sympathetic to Kutz's restrictive attitude to collective blame and sanctions, partly because of considerations in the previous sections of this chapter. If those considerations are correct then there may be no meaningful way of punishing the collective as such – collective blame, if effective, will merely make individual members feel guilty.

That said, I think that Kutz overlooks the possibility that by holding a collective responsible, we address its members in a way that is substantially different from what we do when we assign individual guilt. And although the collective as such is unable to respond affectively, its members may do so from the collective perspective. As Tollefsen says, the norms governing the relevant affective reactions might differ, and so might the motivational role of the distinct types of feelings evoked by assignments of individual and collective responsibility (2003: 232).

I would add that there is a motivational difference not only between the guilt I may feel over what I have done and the membership guilt I may feel over what we have done. There is also a difference in terms of motivation between feeling guilty as a member over what we have done and feeling guilty *from our perspective*. The latter but not the former kind of feeling fits in with the kind of "agency transformation" that makes a distinct motivational difference in certain problematic social choice situations, as Bacharach's work on "team reasoning" indicates (Bacharach 2006). In other words, the functions and consequences of affective responses that are collective in this sense may be substantially different from what we are after when we blame each member individually. This way of addressing them may be appropriate when the collective character of the action for which they are blamed needs to be stressed.

16.7 Conclusion

Reasonable conceptual analyses of "collective guilt feelings" face the choice between assigning such feelings to groups as such while playing down the phenomenal element in the notion of "feelings," or assigning them to individual group members while weakening the collectivistic element in the notion of "collective." By discussing two examples, I have tried to show that the first strategy is less viable than the second, due to functional dis-analogies between the group case and the individual case.

My concluding claim is that an essential function of holding a collective morally responsible is to make its members feel guilt, albeit from the group's perspective. Guilt feelings are reactive attitudes of an essentially social character, intimately connected with our view of others, and with our thoughts and wishes about their view of us. Such feelings are appropriate responses to moral blame. Guilt feelings are essential elements in a social sanction system that may not constitute the whole sphere of morality but at least, as Hume, Mill, Gibbard, and others noted, occupies the most central "region in our moral thought" (Gibbard 1990: 52). Like other negative sanctions, guilt feelings are in themselves unwanted and unpleasant even when they are justified and fulfil their function. Fairness therefore requires that blame for collective actions is directed towards properly delimited collectives, consisting of people whose membership features make them complicit in the act the group is blamed for. We need criteria of complicity that explain why Jaspers is unfair to himself when he feels guilty just in virtue of sharing nationality with the perpetrators of atrocities.

Very generally speaking, the two basic pillars of moral as well as legal accountability are *causal involvement* and *intent*. However, in accounts of co-responsibility for collective or corporate action, both of these conditions have been questioned. Due to causal or epistemic complications such as over-determination or undetectable causal links, philosophers like Christopher Kutz (2001) and Brian Lawson (2013) have argued that people sometimes should be held to account as accomplices to collective wrong-doing merely in virtue of participatory intentions, regardless of causal involvement. Because of possible discrepancies between a group's collective decisions and the beliefs and desires of its members, other philosophers, like Torbjörn Tännsjö (2007), have abandoned or at least played down the requirement of intent.

I am more optimistic about upholding these two basic requirements for co-responsibility. I also think that giving them up would either have unwanted implications for moral and legal security, or make assignments of co-responsibility toothless. But I have discussed both kinds of worries in some detail elsewhere (2008, 2013) and they do not affect the main points of the present chapter.

Notes

1 Versions of this chapter were presented at the "Responsibility in Complex Systems" conference in Umeå and at the Higher seminar in Practical Philosophy in Lund. I am grateful to participants in these events for valuable input. Special thanks to Olle Blomberg, Gunnar Björnsson, Mattias Gunnemyr, Ingvar Johansson, Gloria Mähringer, András Szigeti, and to the editors of this volume Deborah Tollefsen and Saba Bazargan-Forward. This work was funded by project grant 421–2014–1025 from the Swedish Research Council.

2 For an overview, see Ferguson and Branscombe 2014.

3 Mill's, Brandt's, and Gibbard's characterizations of moral blaming are all stated in terms of acceptance of norms directed at the blamed: the blamer thinks that the blamed "ought" to be reproached by his own conscience (Mill) or that it is "fitting and justified" for the blamed to have blaming attitudes towards himself (Brandt). The blamer "accepts norms" that tell the blamed to feel guilty (Gibbard). Insofar as the blamer believes that ought implies can, this means that the blamer implicitly assigns an ability to feel guilt to the blamed.

4 Moral blame towards psychopaths may seem difficult to explain away as non-genuine or insincere forms of blame. At the same time, "lack of remorse or guilt" is an important item on the standard psychopathy checklist (Hare 1980: 115). But to begin with, "psychopathy" is a contested concept, used as an umbrella term for various types and degrees of anti-social personality traits (Mullen 2007). Insofar as we hold real-life "psychopaths" responsible, this may be because we apply the term to people that have some anti-social dispositions but still display a sufficient sense of guilt and concern, or simply because we lack the medical and psychological insights necessary to understand their degree of moral impairment. It is not very controversial to assume that it *would be* improper to react with moral blame towards an individual fulfilling all the standard criteria for full-blown psychopathy. The debate about whether real-life "psychopaths" should be held morally responsible tends to focus precisely on the empirical question of whether they really lack the capacity to react morally in a proper way (Levy 2014; Malatesti and MacMillan 2014, 13–14).

5 I am thinking here of unjustified moral self-blame. As Richard Hare points out, in situations like these it may not be easy to sort out genuine moral remorse from mere regret, which can be equally strong and unpleasant but justified in spite of moral innocence (Hare 1981: 28). Bernard Williams famously argues that a certain kind of morally tainted regret which involves a need to compensate or restitute, "agent-regret," can be morally warranted when agents faultlessly cause harm to others (Williams 1981: 27–9). My point here, which is not affected by these claims, is just that guilt feelings in themselves are unpleasant, and that this feature can be brought out by considering cases of unjustified self-blame.

6 I assume here that the motivational component is a necessary element in unpleasantness, leaving it open whether e.g. a certain experiential quality or some other less operationalizable feature is necessary as well. Brandt assumes that the motivational analysis gives necessary and sufficient conditions though: "In short, an experience is pleasant if and only if it makes its continuation more wanted. The transposition for being unpleasant will be obvious" (1979: 40–1). As Brandt points out, the necessary motivational element does of course not rule out the possibility that your overall disposition is nevertheless to endure the unpleasant experience. There may be various factors extrinsic to the state of being unpleasant, counteracting your disposition to be relieved from it due to its intrinsic quality. You may believe that you deserve to suffer, or that the unpleasant experience is necessarily intertwined with something instrumentally valuable, for instance.

7 Among the 28 contributions, Hans Bernhard Schmid's stands out as the only one that appears to assign phenomenal experience to groups: "The claim is that there is a sense in which it is literally true that when a group of people has an emotion, there is one feeling episode, one phenomenal experience in which many agents participate" (Schmid 2014: 9). However, as Tom Cochran points out in a review, Schmid's analysis of the phenomenon, in terms of individuals having plural pre-reflective self-awareness, makes the position less radical than it may seem at a first glance (Cochran 2016: 471). And as Schmid himself makes clear further on, his "shared feelings" are actually "feelings had *by individuals*, not feelings had by *a group*" (2014: 13).

8 www.nytimes.com/interactive/2014/05/18/business/gms-ignition-problem-who-knew-what-when.html?_r=0

9 Also described in Petersson 2015, 2017.

10 Hans Bernhard Schmid "The Duty to Know What We are Doing Together," talk at ENSO IV, September 2015.

11 Tollefsen draws an illuminating analogy between feeling collective guilt and feeling genuine embarrassment for someone else's behavior, which I believe brings out a difference between our suggestions about collective guilt feelings (2003: footnote 26). On the perspectival account that I suggest here, collective guilt feelings are still essentially first person – they are about the collective and they are held from the same collective's perspective – a first person plural perspective. But if, instead, we think of collective guilt feelings as mere feelings *for* a collective, as I take Tollefsen to do, it seems possible, in principle, that I could have such feelings for a collective that I do not belong to, in analogy with my feeling embarrassment for another individual.

References

Bacharach, M. (2006) *Beyond Individual Choice: Teams and Frames in Game Theory*, Gold & Sugden (eds) Princeton: Princeton University Press.

Björnsson, G. and Hess, K. (2017) "Corporate Crocodile Tears? On the Reactive Attitudes of Corporate Agents," *Philosophy and Phenomenological Research*, XCIV:2, 273–98.

Brandt, R. (1958) "Blameworthiness and Obligation," in Melden (ed.) *Essays in Moral Philosophy*, Washington: University of Washington Press.

Brandt, R. (1979) *A Theory of the Good and the Right*, Oxford: Oxford University Press.

Cochran, T. (2016) "Review of Collective Emotions: Perspectives From Psychology, Philosophy, and Sociology," *Phenomenology and the Cognitive Sciences*, 15: 467–73.

Collins, S. (2018) "'The Government Should Be Ashamed': On the Possibility of Organisations' Emotional Duties," *Political Studies*, 66(4): 813–29.

Ferguson, M. A. and Branscombe, N. R. (2014) "The Social Psychology Of Collective Guilt," in von Scheve and Salmela 2014.

Gibbard, A. (1990) *Wise Choices, Apt Feelings*, Oxford: Oxford University Press.

Gilbert, M. (2000) Sociality and Responsibility, Lanham: Rowman & Littlefield.

Gilbert, M. (2002) "Collective Guilt and Collective Guilt Feelings," *The Journal of Ethics*, 6: 115–43.

Gilbert, M. (2006) *A Theory of Political Obligation: Membership, Commitment, and the Bonds of Society*, Oxford: Oxford University Press.

Gilbert, M. (2009) "Shared Intention and Personal Intentions," *Philosophical Studies*, 144: 147–67.

Hare, R. D. (1980) "A Research Scale for the Assessment of Psychopathy in Criminal Populations," *Personality and Individual Differences*, 1: 111–19.

Hare, R. M. (1981) *Moral Thinking*, Oxford: Clarendon Press.

Hume, D. (1740) "*A Treatise of Human Nature, Book III*," in Árdal (ed.) *A Treatise of Human Nature, Books Two and Three*, London: Fontana, 1972.

Jaspers, K. (1947) *The Question of German Guilt*, E. B. Ashton (transl.) New York: Capricorn Books.

Konzelmann Ziv, A. (2007) "Collective Guilt Feeling Revisited," *dialectica*, 61(3): 467–93.

Kutz, C. (2001) *Complicity*, Cambridge: Cambridge University Press.

Lawson, B. (2013) "Individual Complicity in Collective Wrongdoing," *Ethical Theory and Moral Practice*, 16(2): 227–43.

Levy, N. (2014) "Psychopaths and Blame: The Argument From Content," *Philosophical Psychology*, 27(3): 351–67.

Malatesti, L. and McMillan, J. (2014) "Defending Psychopathy: An Argument From Values and Moral Responsibility," *Theoretical Medicine and Bioethics*, 35: 7–16.

Mill, J. S. (1863) "Utilitarianism," in J. Bennett (ed. & rev.), *Early Modern Philosophy*, www.earlymoderntexts.com/

Mullen, P. E. (2007) "On Building Argument on Shifting Sand," *Philosophy, Psychiatry and Psychology*, 14(2): 143–7.

Pacherie, E. (2012) "The Phenomenology of Joint Action: Self-Agency vs. Joint Agency," in Seeman, A. (ed.) *Joint Attention: New Developments*, Cambridge: MIT Press, 343–89.

Petersson, B. (2008) "Collective Omissions and Responsibility," *Philosophical Papers*, 37(2): 243–61.

Petersson, B. (2013) "Co-responsibility and Causal Involvement," *Philosophia*, September 41(3), 847–66.

Petersson, B. (2015) "Bratman, Searle, and Simplicity," *Journal of Social Ontology*, 1(1).

Petersson, B. (2017) "Team Reasoning and Collective Intentionality," *Review of Philosophy and Psychology*, 8(2): 199–218.

Pettigrove, G. and Parsons, N. (2012) "Shame: A Case Study of Collective Emotion," *Social Theory and Practice*, 38(3): 504–29.

Pettit, P. (2003) "Groups with Minds of Their Own," in F. Schmitt (ed.) *Socializing Metaphysics: The Nature of Social Reality*, Lanham, MD: Rowman & Littlefield, 167–93.

Pettit, P. and Schweikard, D. (2006) "Joint Actions and Group Agents," *Philosophy of the Social Sciences*, 36: 18–39.

Recanati, F. (2009) *Perspectival Thought: A Plea for Moderate Relativism*, Oxford: Oxford University Press.

Recanati, F. (2007) "It is Raining (Somewhere)," *Linguistics and Philosophy* 30(1).

Schmid, H. B. (2014) "The Feeling of Being a Group: Corporate Emotions and Collective Consciousness," in C. von Scheve and M. Salmela (eds) *Collective Emotions: Perspectives from Psychology, Philosophy, and Sociology*, Oxford: Oxford University Press, 3–22.

Smith, N. (2008) *I Was Wrong: The Meanings of Apologies*, Cambridge: Cambridge University Press.

Strawson, P. F. (1962) "Freedom and Resentment," *Proceedings from the British Academy* (at The Determinism and Freedom Website, ed. Honderich).

Szanto, T. (2016) "Do Group Persons Have Emotions, or Should They?" in S. Rinofner-Kreidl and H. Wiltsche (eds), *Analytical and Continental Philosophy: Methods and Perspectives*, Berlin/Boston: de Gruyter: 261–76.

Tajfel, H. and Turner, J. C. (1986) "The Social Identity Theory of Inter-Group Behavior," in S. Worchel and L. W. Austin (eds) *Psychology of Intergroup Relations*, Chicago: Nelson-Hall.

Tännsjö, T. (2007) "The Myth of Innocence: On Collective Responsibility and Collective Punishment," *Philosophical Papers*, 36(22): 295–314.

Tollefsen, D. (2003) "Participant Reactive Attitudes and Collective Responsibility," *Philosophical Explorations*, 6(3): 218–34.

Tollefsen, D. (2006) "The Rationality of Collective Guilt," *Midwest Studies in Philosophy*, XXX: 222–39.

Von Scheve, C. and Salmela, M. (2014) *Collective Emotions: Perspectives from Psychology, Philosophy, and Sociology*, Oxford: Oxford University Press.

Wilkins, B. (2002) "Joint Commitments," *The Journal of Ethics*, 6: 145–55.

Williams, B. (1981) *Moral Luck*, Cambridge: Cambridge University Press.

Zahavi, D. (2015) "You, Me, and We: The Sharing of Emotional Experiences," *Journal of Consciousness Studies*, 22(1–2): 84–101.

17

COLLECTIVE RESPONSIBILITY AND ENTITLEMENT TO COLLECTIVE REASONS FOR ACTION[1]

Abraham Sesshu Roth

What are the implications for agency – and in particular, the idea of acting for reasons – if we are to take seriously the notion of *collective* responsibility? My thesis is that some cases of individuals subject to a collective form of responsibility and blame will force us to make sense of how it is that an individual can be *entitled* to collective reasons for action, i.e. entitled to a reason had in the first place by a plurality of individuals together rather than any one of them alone. This entitlement makes it possible for the collective reason to be a reason for which one acts, even if one's contribution on its own makes little or no difference in the collective effort. Although a full defense of this entitlement cannot be undertaken here, I will gesture at how this might work by suggesting that intentions function to preserve reasons for action.

17.1 Retrospective Responsibility and Prospective Reason for Action

When is it appropriate to blame someone? (We could of course consider occasions for praise – but I will tend to dwell on the negative.) Let S be a condition or state of affairs that is a candidate occasion for blame. For example, someone nearby just off shore is in distress and drowns. Am I to blame for not rescuing him? Without attempting an exhaustive account of responsibility, we might identify one important condition for responsibility by considering a particular sort of excuse to deflect blame. Specifically, I'm interested in the following schema:

(1) *Do something about it*: An agent is not responsible for S if he or she is never in a position reasonably to do something about it.

If one is to do something about S, and this requires one to Φ, then one thing we can say is:

(2) *Capacity:* An agent is not responsible for S if he or she is never able to Φ.[2]

A farmer, for example, is not responsible for the loss of her crops if in conditions of sudden and unforeseeable extreme drought she is unable to irrigate her fields. And I am not responsible for saving the drowning individual if I cannot swim, or am not trained, or there is no life-ring to toss, etc.

Even if this much is clear, our schema is likely to prompt a number of questions, and it will not be helpful for someone without some day-to-day familiarity with the notion of blame and responsibility. The schema for example won't inform us of what exactly counts as reasonable when it comes to doing something about S; how much sacrifice would it be reasonable to make in one's efforts? There is also the worry about the vagueness of the notion of *doing something about*. Presumably, to do something about some problematic S would be to act in such a way as to prevent S, or to ameliorate its effects. Or at least to act in such a way as to have some chance of doing these things. We are not given in (1) anything that says what sort of likelihood of success is needed, or the extent of amelioration, for one to count as doing something about S.

Though the schema leaves much unanswered, it does draw a connection between the largely retrospective notions of responsibility and blame on the one hand, and the more prospective notion of reason for action on the other.[3] At least, it does this so long as we maintain (I think quite plausibly) that to do something about S is to act *for* S-related reasons – such as avoiding or preventing S, or ameliorating the badness of S. Taking Φ-ing again to be such a doing, the schema would be

(3) *Look-back-look-ahead*: An agent is not responsible for S if she is never in a position reasonably to Φ for the S-related reasons.

Note that blamelessness with regard to S doesn't necessarily require that the agent Φ *for* those S-related considerations. One might Φ for other reasons; but so long as Φ is performed, the problematic consequences are averted and no blame is called for.[4,5] Still, I suggest that the possibility or capacity at some point of acting for S-related reasons seems to be relevant for responsibility: blame in the matter of S entails some capacity on the part of the agent to act for or in light of those considerations.[6]

Why think so? I take (3) as a plausible understanding of the uncontroversial thought in (1) that one cannot be blamed for S if one simply can't do anything about it. It is, of course, a part of the idea of being in a position to do something about S that one has the ability in (2) simply to perform the requisite Φ-ing. But beyond this, one must have some capacity to Φ *for the relevant reasons* – even if, as just noted, the Φ-ing one in fact does is not done for those reasons. What is it, after all, *to be in a position to do something about S* but to have the occasion to act in light of the S-related reasons? Without such a capacity one would not be able to perform the relevant Φ appropriately; one's Φ-ing would be haphazard with respect to the S-related considerations. If that's the case, then this is not really to be in a position to do something *about S*; one wouldn't be responsible in *this* matter. Similarly, if one is incapable of making sense of their Φ-ing in terms of the S-related considerations, to grasp the *significance* of their Φ-ing in light of S, then this too puts in question one's responsibility for S.[7] So it's not merely the ability to Φ that is a condition for responsibility for S; it's also the ability to Φ *for S-related considerations*.[8]

In light of this, let's work with the idea that the possibility reasonably to act for certain S-related reasons is a condition for responsibility and the appropriateness of blame (and praise) for S. If the agent has conducted herself faultlessly; if there simply was no obligation or reason with respect to S, then the agent cannot be blamed for it. Or if there was a reason to act with respect to S, but it simply would be unreasonable for the agent to undertake it given other demands she faces, then here too it is unclear how they can be blamed for it.[9]

Thus, with *Look-back-look-ahead*, the backward-looking notion of responsibility is connected with the forward-looking notion of acting for reasons. What implications might this have for collective responsibility?[10]

17.2 Collective Responsibility: Against Monolithic Agency

Sometimes one is responsible and blamed for something, alongside others. Consider the following case due to Björnsson.

> *Humiliation*: After the last class of the day, a group of high-school kids grabs the classmate lowest in the pecking order, successfully preventing him from catching the bus, leaving him with a long and humiliating walk home.[11]

Responsibility and blame here seem to be collective. The *bullies* are responsible for the student's humiliating walk. But how should this be understood?

One suggestion is to take seriously the idea of the group as itself an individual agent, albeit a *monolithic* one comprising a number of lesser individual agents. The group is something that acts for reasons, is responsible for what it does, and is subject to blame. Applied to the example, the bullies constitute an agent, and *it* is responsible for the kid's long and humiliating walk home. There is something *it* can do about this – viz., refrain from grabbing the kid, or stop individuals from doing so. The group could act on considerations related to (preventing) the humiliation of someone. But it doesn't do so, and thus is to blame.[12]

Seeing the group as an agent and a locus of responsibility in this way has the benefit of ensuring a straightforward version of *Look-back-look-ahead* – the connection between responsibility and reason for action noted above. The group's responsibility for the child's humiliating walk is linked to the possibility that it could have done something about it – namely, acted so as to prevent this from happening, i.e. for that reason.

Furthermore, there is the suggestion that it's *only* by thinking of the group as an agent that we can make sense of the sorts of considerations that matter in important cases of collective responsibility – such as our responsibility for large-scale environmental damage. Averting environmental disaster is not something about which any ordinary individual agent normally can make a difference. So it's not clear that this sort of consideration can count as a reason for an ordinary individual. Only something very big and quite extraordinary will be up for this challenge – something in the realm of the monolithic. At the same time, we might hold an agent constraint on reasons: a consideration is a reason for action only for something that is an agent.[13] If averting some large-scale disaster is a reason for action, it is only a reason for a monolithic agent. If that's right, and we also want to maintain *Look-back-look-ahead*, then collective responsibility must, in turn, be understood in terms of the reasons of this monolithic agent.

But invoking monolithic agency has its drawbacks. First, many find implausible the thought that the group itself really is an agent.[14] It might be thought an ontological extravagance to think of groups as agents, over and above the constituent individuals. There is the temptation to try to understand action ascribed to the group reductively, in terms of the agency of the constituent individuals. Whether or not such a reductive project can succeed, there is a further worry that many groups seem not – at least not stably – to satisfy the conditions that are often thought necessary for group agency, such as some sort of decision procedure, or an executive/authority structure. Even when a collective is not structured in this way, we might nevertheless want to assign collective responsibility. For example, a collection of passersby might be collectively blameworthy if they didn't get their act together to move heavy debris to aid an accident victim. But on the current proposal, since the passersby do not constitute an agent, there is no possibility of acting on a reason, and thus no collective responsibility (Held 1970).

Another concern with the monolithic agent view is that it is not clear how we are to connect the responsibility of the monolithic agent with that of the constituent individuals in such a way that each of the latter is implicated in what the collective does (Collins 2017: 578–9). For example, one might be employed as a low-level administrator in a gigantic corporation or educational institution, with little sense of the actual purpose of the institution. Such a *nine to fiver* might not share the aims of the collective, and is only involved so as to make a living and maybe pay for his children's education. And yet, he might be performing actions that are important for the functioning of the larger institution. His duties (maybe it involves security, or low-level administration, classroom instruction, or publicity) could be executed in ignorance of the real purposes of the institution. Indeed, it might be part of his selection and training that he not be in a position to understand the higher-level aspects of the organization and its function.

This case suggests that there is a sense in which one might be a part of a group in that one serves merely as a human resource for the group or organization's pursuit of its ends, without genuinely and wittingly *participating* in what the group does. I'm not suggesting that individuals who play a role in the functioning of some monolithic agency are generally exonerated when it comes to the blameworthy actions of the monolith.[15] However, the fact that such monolithic agency is compatible with constituent individual agents whose tasks are so narrow and regimented, and who are so ill equipped to understand what the larger entity is up to, suggests that locating an individual as a constituent in some larger agency is not yet to give an account for how he or she is subject to a form of collective responsibility and blame. This is to say that for cases of collective responsibility that can implicate a constituent individual, we need to secure some form of *Look-back-look-ahead* at the level of the constituent individual.

Indeed, the worry might be pressed further with the suggestion that the robustness of the agency attributed to the monolith or group points toward a dampening of the responsibility of the individuals; that is, it might be that robustness of agency at the group level might preclude a form of *Look-back-look-ahead* at the level of the individual. It is partly the lack of responsibility at the individual level that is a central component of Copp's case for taking seriously the idea that some group of individuals is an agent.[16]

In general, it seems possible that a group agent might have individuals who are human resource components – even components that are vital for its functioning as an agent – which (or who) do not figure as intentional or full-blown *participants* in the group's action. Thus, it's unclear what implication we are to draw about the responsibility of constituent individuals from the proposition that the group or collective is an agent in its own right. It could very well be that the individuals do not, or even cannot, exercise agency in a way that implicates them with respect to whatever it is that the group or monolithic agent might be responsible for. For all we know, when a monolithic individual is responsible for some S, the constituent individuals are exonerated with respect to it. That would be quite the opposite of what we were looking for.

It would seem advisable for our purposes, then, to set aside monolithic individual agency. I do not mean to suggest that monolithic agency has no role to play in any case of collective responsibility. Sometimes there will be a story about how constituent individuals are implicated in what the monolith does. But in many cases there is no monolith. And even if there is a monolith, an important part of the story of how individuals are implicated is left out. I think that to get a handle on collective responsibility, we need to ensure not merely the constituency of the relevant individuals, but the possibility of their *participation* as well. To that end, we need to look to collective action and shared agency.

17.3 Joint Action and Participation

A familiar distinction is that between joint action where the group is a structured collective and arguably counts as a novel agent (over and above the constituent individual agents), and joint action of an unstructured collective where the agents are the individuals and there is no novel group agent (Schwenkenbecher 2013: 3; Pettit & Schweikard 2006). It seems promising that by invoking the idea of collective action (joint action in the latter sense), we secure participation by constituent individuals in a way that appealing to the notion of a novel, monolithic individual agency need not.[17]

But recall that we were interested in understanding participation in order to make sense of the idea that the individual is in a position to act for the relevant reasons. That is, we need to secure *Look-back-look-ahead* at the level of the individual participant. It is not yet clear how the notion of collective or joint agency is supposed to do this. As it turns out, for some cases it seems straightforward how an individual might be in a position to act for the relevant reason, and so the case of being held responsible is clear. Other cases are more challenging and will require us to reconsider some assumptions about the nature of agency and acting for reasons.

First, the straightforward cases. Consider an amusing case described by Wringe.

> *Office*: Two people share an office. Due to bad weather the roof starts to collapse. The person who needs to be informed has to be informed by email. A has the technical expertise necessary to describe the damage to the roof in an informative manner, but doesn't know how to use email. B is a computer wizard who doesn't know the first thing about roofs. Between them, they can pass an informative message to the right person. Individually, neither of them can.
>
> *(Wringe 2014: 479)*

A and B are collectively responsible for informing someone of the roof damage, and they can do something about it by sending the email with the relevant information. But at the individual level it's also clear what each can do: A can compose the message, and B can send it. Neither satisfies something like *Capacity* (2) with respect to informing the relevant party. But together they do. And each is capable of performing the actions that would be required for the joint effort.

But recall that the capacity to perform the relevant action is not enough for responsibility. There is, in addition, the question whether one has reason to. Now, in this case, it seems that each participant *does* have the relevant reason. The need to inform the relevant party is a reason to compose a message in A's case and serves as a reason for what A does. Even if A can't accomplish the entirety of the task by himself (because the message must be sent by email and he doesn't know how to do that), he has a relevant reason for his part (composing the message) and thus can do something about the matter. Barring other considerations, it seems then that A satisfies *Look-back-look-ahead* and can be held responsible (alongside B) in the matter. Likewise for B with regard to sending the message that he himself cannot compose.[18]

But other cases, such as that of over-determination, pose a challenge for understanding how an individual can act *for the relevant reasons*.[19] We can get to a problematic case by stipulating in the *Humiliation* scenario that whether or not an individual participates in the bullying makes no difference for the humiliating outcome; the others will engage in bullying irrespective of what the individual does. Given that it makes no difference whether one joins in the bullying – that refraining or attempting to intervene won't change the humiliating outcome – it's not clear how one has a reason to do anything to stop the bullying. The principle is something like this:

> *Makes no difference*: Sometimes a morally significant outcome S results from the contribution of multiple individuals, and S would result irrespective of the actions of any one of the individuals. In that case, the individual has no reason in light of S to act one way or another.[20]

If something like this is true, then we lose our grip on a reason that figures as a condition for responsibility. In what sense, then, can one (along with others) be blamed for humiliating the child?

One reaction to the *makes no difference* worry is to reject *Look-back-look-ahead*, allowing for responsibility and blame, even in the absence of the relevant forward-looking reason to act on. Kutz (2002: 563) seems to defend a position like this. He describes these cases as involving a "mediated relation to harm, where injury is brought about through the actions of others ... many of them are cases where what any one individual does makes no difference; only together do individuals cause harm." He adds that

> It's a familiar fact of our moral and legal practices that we blame, punish and demand compensation from complicitous agents even though what they did made no difference ... . The puzzle arises because, if causal contribution is necessary to responsibility, then no one is responsible, for no one makes a difference ... . What complicitous responsibility centrally challenges is an appealing, intuitive principle of responsibility, that someone can only be responsible for events over which he had control.
>
> *(Kutz 2002: 563)*

Kutz says that "Once we have an analytical understanding of co-operation, a normative account of complicity follows suit" (2002: 563) On this view, an individual counts as "inclusive" author of actions performed by another agent when each has a participatory intention that joins them in a single collective endeavor; responsibility tracks this inclusive authorship.[21]

Seeing how responsibility tracks authorship is not controversial so long as we're talking about each author really contributing and making a difference. But what happens when we *don't* make a difference? Kutz (2002: 564) insists that the point still holds: "... in cases of full over-determination, when no individual really does make a causal difference, blame ... may still fairly lie."

How does this work? Take Kutz' case of the picnic (2000b: 154; see Nefsky 2015: 250–1 for insightful discussion.) We are setting up a picnic together. While I go to fetch a cooler from the car, you carelessly spread the blanket in such a way as to destroy a flowerbed. There is nothing that I could reasonably have done to make a difference to avoid the consequence; I did everything right – in particular, I can't keep a constant eye on you; you're not a child and have no record of reckless disregard for landscaping. And yet, Kutz suggests, I am partly accountable for the damage – though much less so than you, of course. Some support for this assessment might come from comparing my culpability as a participant in the joint action with that of some other picnicker on the other side of the park who had nothing to do with me and my careless picnic partner. That individual on the other side of the park seems not to be at all implicated in the damage to the flowerbed, whereas my culpability, though attenuated, is real. At least, that is the intuition. Thus Kutz concludes:

> Whatever the ultimate account of complicitous responsibility...will have to go at least partly by way of the participatory intentions of the agents – their will, independent of its effect, to join in a collective act that does injury. For in the absence of any salient individual causal contribution, surely it is the co-operation itself that explains responsibility. Implication follows participation.
>
> *(Kutz 2002: 564)*

Kutz is making the point that a lack of control need not preclude responsibility; but the point would seem to extend to our concern – the idea of acting for reasons that amount to doing something about S. As one of Björnsson's bullies, I am implicated as a participant in the activity. But because I can't make a difference, there is nothing really for me to do about the bullying and humiliation; there is no reason for me to act one way or the other.

If we accept Kutz' intuitions about the picnic case, then we do seem to have an instance of accountability and responsibility without having the relevant reason grounding it – without, that is, the reason that figures in doing something about the matter. Regarding Parfit's famous case of the harmless torturers, Kutz (2002: 564) says "Parfit himself struggles to accommodate consequentialist ethics to a form of responsibility that seems, on its face precisely independent of individual consequence." For our purposes the moral would seem to be that we don't need to secure *Look-back-look-ahead* at the individual participant level, so long as we have joint or collective agency.

Now, it may seem that Kutz has identified a way of thinking about responsibility without reason for action (assuming that his intuitions about the picnic case are compelling). But it is troubling to concede that for many of the cases where an individual makes no difference whereas a collective effort does address the matter, the individual participant in the collective effort is not acting for any relevant reason and so doesn't count as doing anything about the matter. On the contrary, it seems that the individual who is doing her part of some collective effort is very much doing something about the matter, and acting for the relevant reason.

This concern becomes clearer and more pressing when we recognize the possibility that one might not be a part of the collective effort. For all that Kutz has said so far, it seems that when one is not a participant in some collective effort to address some environmental problem, one is not accountable for not making an effort. Kutz might then suggest that in this case one should *join* in such an effort. But what would be the motivation or reason for doing so? It can't be the consideration that we would have thought would generate the reason to do something, such as averting environmental disaster or preventing the kid's humiliation as the case may be. After all, the worry was that the individual has no such reason in these *makes no difference* cases (Nefsky 2015: 261–3). But if we ask why one might have a reason to join a collective effort, it would be precisely the sort of consideration like addressing climate change. The central reason one would have thought one has for participating in a collective effort is undermined. I may have other reasons – like enjoying the company of people who share my concerns and values. But it might be more fun to play video games by myself; or maybe the company of other people who are more carefree and oblivious would offer greater prospect of enjoyment. Of course, I may *care* about the environment much more than video games. But the point is that that concern doesn't seem to translate into a reason for action when one's contribution doesn't make a difference.

Thus, even if we set aside the concerns about how to establish joint action, it seems that Kutz' proposal doesn't get right the reason that one takes oneself as having for doing one's part in the collective activity. It's not as if there is no reason that one might try to locate in Kutz' view. One might, after all, be concerned with accountability and blame. And if Kutz is right that one has accountability in this situation – and indeed there are views where mutual accountability is constitutive of joint action (Gilbert 1990; 2009) – then such a concern will generate reasons to act. But, though a possibility, this is not the sort of reason one naturally has for doing something in these sorts of cases. Accountability was not one's concern; doing something to avoid environmental disaster was (Nefsky 2015).

I suspect that the challenge raised for Kutz' approach points to the idea that accountability is not fundamental; the rightness of the action, or the reasons that make the action right are what really matter.[22] *Look-back-look-ahead* connects backward-looking responsibility and accountability with forward-looking reasons for action. But the important thought underlying

Look-back-look-ahead is that this isn't merely a connection or correlation; the forward-looking reasons that make the act the right thing to do (partially) explain or ground facts about blame and responsibility. The sort of pure accountability that Kutz has in mind for complicitous responsibility is problematically ungrounded.

That being said, I think that there is something right in Kutz' invocation of intention. This, after all, is what secures the individual participation needed for the individual agent to be implicated in collective responsibility. But we also need the access to reasons for action that make sense of what one is doing in participating.

17.4 Linking and Transmission

We are imagining in the *makes no difference* cases that it's the individual who doesn't make a difference, so it's unclear what reason he or she has for doing something about the matter. Whereas the collective might have the wherewithal to get something done, so the *makes no difference* consideration doesn't speak against the collective having a reason. It follows that if we can make sense of how an individual could act on the collective reason, then we might be able to see how an individual is subject to (collective) blame. That is, we could use a version of *Look-back-look-ahead* that connects an *individual* participant to a *collective* reason. We've seen that this is straightforward when the individual's contribution is necessary or significant for the collective outcome. But what about cases where it makes no (significant) difference what the individual does?

I hope enough now has been said to motivate making sense of the idea of an individual acting on collective reasons in *makes no difference* cases. It's quite another thing, however, to show *how* one can act for collective reasons in *makes no difference* cases. Although I won't be able to provide an adequate defense of that claim here, I will gesture towards the view that I think has some promise.

We should note, first, that there must *be* collective reasons if it's going to be possible for an individual to act on them. I took their existence for granted earlier, when discussing Wringe's case of the collective (A and B) reporting the damage to the roof. Wringe introduces the example as part of his effort to establish that there are collective reasons.[23] And some might want to resist that there really is a collective reason here, insisting that fundamentally each of A and B has an individual reason to contribute to a collective effort that has a good outcome. And, if that's the case, then all we have to say is that each is individually responsible for making a contribution. That might be an acceptable position to take in this case.[24] But then it's not clear what to say about other cases like over-determination where a participant doesn't make a difference and where it is harder to make sense of individual responsibility in a way that doesn't depend on collective responsibility.

For example, take an over-determination case due to Parfit – that of the firing squad (Parfit 1984), or take *Humiliation* described above. The contribution of each member of the squad makes no difference for the bad outcome, given what the others do. So no one has a reason not to shoot and, given *Look-back-look-ahead*, no one is responsible for execution. But, assuming that the execution should not take place, there seems to be reason *for the squad* not to shoot. It's not just that it would be nice for the squad not to. There is a reason for action, albeit not one that is to be understood individually, independent of what other individuals have reason to do.

Reflection on such cases and others suggests that we cannot make do simply with individual reasons/obligation. I will be taking for granted that there are collective obligations or reasons in what follows.[25]

I turn to the normative significance of collective reasons for the individual – specifically, the question of whether it's possible for an individual to act on collective reasons in *makes no difference* cases. It seems that we would need something like the following:

> *Linking Principle*: If I am (or could be) acting with others, and we have a collective reason to Φ, I am *entitled* to our reason for Φ-ing; and when I do my part in our Φ-ing, I am acting for that collective reason.

A couple of provisos would help to make this principle more compelling, one addressing cases where the collective effort is hopeless, and another where one's contribution would be superfluous. When the situation is hopeless, there is no collective reason to address the problematic S because there is simply nothing to be done. In the example of working against environmental disaster, perhaps too much damage has been done, and there aren't enough of us to remedy the situation so that it won't make a difference even if we all exerted ourselves to the utmost. As for the superfluous: knowing that enough people have already contributed would also preclude one from acting on the collective reason. Here there is a collective reason, but it wouldn't make sense of one's efforts since others have already acted on it.[26]

There may be other sticking points with the *Linking Principle*, even when supplemented with the provisos concerning the superfluous and the hopeless. One source of reluctance has to do with making sense of an individual's *part* or *contribution* in a collective act in the *makes no difference* cases. What counts as doing one's part, given how miniscule one's contribution is in some very large collective endeavors, or given that it makes no difference whether one performs the relevant act? In reply, I should say that I am not attempting to give an account of the metaphysics of aggregates; so I concede that I am taking for granted that we can make sense of what it would be to contribute to or be a part of some collective effort even in cases of over-determination or other forms of *makes no difference*. So, for example, we can make sense of the idea that one is doing one's part in the collective act of getting someone elected by, say, casting a vote (or canvassing, or making a campaign contribution, etc). Whereas, one is not (at least not in normal circumstances) doing one's part in that collective electoral effort if one is sitting on the couch twiddling one's thumbs or buying beer at the convenience store – even if in the *makes no difference* scenarios these latter acts arguably have as much of a chance of making a difference on the electoral outcome as the former. Still, supposing we take for granted the notion of contribution here, we can go on to ask about its normative or moral significance. The question that is our concern, then, is how it is that when one is casting a vote, one's reason for doing so is to get someone elected – even if from some individual perspective it makes no difference whether one casts a vote.

A fundamental issue with the *Linking Principle* concerns the nature of the practical cognition involved in the cases it describes, where one is entitled to collective reasons and can act on them, even in the *makes no difference* circumstances. That is, even where it seems that the justificatory force of the reasons would seem not to be immediately accessible to the individual. A promising approach to explaining how this might be possible invokes the reason preserving function of intention (Roth 2017).[27] Intentions play a role in preserving the reasons that figure in deliberation and decision-making, so that when the agent subsequently acts on the intention that issues from the decision, the agent acts for the reasons that went into that decision. For example, I might for various reasons decide and thereby intend to go to a party on the weekend. When it comes time to attend, I do not consider *whether* to attend. After all, I have already decided to go. I don't have to reconsider the reasons; nothing has come up to warrant revisiting the decision. I just straightaway act on the intention and head over (or perhaps think about how to get there, not whether to go). Nevertheless, when I go to the party, the reasons for which I go are the ones that went into my original decision and which I didn't reconsider (or need not have reconsidered) at the time of action.

The proposal is that something like this might apply to the collective case. Imagine, first, that one undertakes to decide whether to act on a collective intention to Φ. One would have to consider the reasons that support Φ-ing. But notice that in the *makes no difference* cases many of relevant reasons are not the individual's own; only the collective really has those reasons – precisely because what the individual would do doesn't make a difference. So if the individual qua individual must make a decision as to whether to act on a collective intention, she will be stymied; she can't act for the reasons that make best sense of the collective effort. The point, however, is that to think that an individual must decide on *whether* to act on a collective intention is not to appreciate how intentions function in one's practical thought. Thus, when it's time to act, one doesn't consider whether to act; rather, one acts *directly* on the intention (barring defeaters). And in doing so, one acts for the reasons that went into the decision and intention formation in the first place. So, in applying this idea to the case at hand: the individual acts *directly* on the collective intention without considering whether to do so, and thus without having to consider the reasons. But in executing the intention, the individual is entitled to and acts for the reasons that went into the collective decision. At least, that would be in keeping with the idea propounded in the previous paragraph that intention plays a reasons-preserving role. This would secure *Look-back-look-ahead* at a level that is appropriate for collective responsibility bearing on individual participants.

So, Kutz is right that intention matters, as was suggested earlier. But it matters not because it directly secures accountability/responsibility in a way that circumvents *Look-back-look-ahead*. Intention matters, rather, because it's a way of showing how *Look-back-look-ahead* applies in this case – by securing entitlement to forward-looking reasons that are otherwise not available for the individual to act upon.

The picture is one where what I am doing is just a part of what we're doing. In executing the collective intention, the relevant reasons for so acting are the collective reasons; one is entitled to and relies on the collective reasons. And what one is doing makes sense in those terms – the terms that we had thought were proprietary to the entire collective, and not the individual.

One's access to the collective reason is by way of acting directly on the intention. What happens when one considers oneself as an individual agent, acting on one's own? Then the force of the collective reason might be counteracted, and the *makes no difference* considerations could very well have a role to play in this undermining (but see below). But part of the idea of intention, be it collective or diachronic within an individual, is that of a rational stability that can resist revision. Sometimes, a proffered intention should be resisted – such as when the deliberation or values that led to it are confused or misguided, or the assumptions that were in place are no longer relevant, or conditions of communal trust sufficiently eroded. But these sorts of concerns hold for intentions generally, and are not peculiar to the intentions that serve to provide access to collective reasons.

Again, my remarks here are meant only as a gesture at how we might think about what it would be for an individual to act on collective reasons in the *makes no difference* cases. A fuller account would have to defend further the proposal about intentions playing a reason preserving function, not to mention the idea that this sort of reason preservation and entitlement can work not only diachronically within an individual, but between collective and individual levels.[28]

Also needed is a story about who or what *issues* the collective intentions for one to act on. We can imagine that in the case of structured collectives – institutions etc. – there might be conventional procedures by which decisions are made on the basis of collective reasons, and the corresponding intentions issued. But I think that even when there is no structured collective it is possible for an individual to form the relevant intention. The intention would not be (just) for the intender to act up, but for a collective. No doubt there will be externalist conditions on whether one succeeds in issuing such an intention. It might depend, for example, on whether sufficiently many others are like-minded so as to take up or issue the intention as well. Just when it might be possible to issue such an intention is something that demands further investigation.

I want to turn, finally, to an argument that suggests that the collective reason in the *makes no difference* cases, if there is one, cannot be a reason for the individual to act because it has no normative force for the individual in the first place. We need to identify where this argument goes wrong if we're to make sense of the idea of an individual acting for a collective reason. I think that the following captures how the argument is supposed to proceed:

(1) Suppose that there is a collective reason to Φ. E.g. someone's life will be saved if adequate funds are raised from numerous individuals for the purchase of some very expensive medication.
(2) The person is saved whether or not some one individual joins the collective effort. In particular, it makes no difference whether I am a part of the collective effort.
(3) So, there is no point for my being a part of the collective effort.
(4) Thus, I am not subject to the collective reason. The collective reason puts no normative pressure on me or any particular individual to make a contribution.[29]

I think that the proper response to the argument is to resist the step from 2 to 3. That is, from the fact that for any individual it makes no difference whether they participate, it does not follow that one person in particular – such as *I, myself* – can be excluded from the collective and not be subject to the normative force of the collective reason.

The diagnosis of what goes wrong with this step of the argument is that it mistakenly introduces a distinct, individual element in order to resist a collective line of practical thought. Thus, reasoning from one's own point of view, one might think: there is no point for me to make a contribution, since I don't make a difference; I may as well do something else, like go off and have a beer with a friend, or take a pleasant drive in my SUV, etc. I don't deny that one's interests (be they egoistic, altruistic or whatever) can come into conflict with some collective goal. But the argument was meant to show that there was no normative force to the collective reason in the first place, not that there was some distinct point of view from which one might resist the normative force of the collective reason. If we start with the collective reason, then the recognition that not everyone will need to make a contribution entails not that I will not have to but rather that *some individuals* or *some one* of us will not have to. It takes more than the thought that I don't make a difference to get to the conclusion that *I* am amongst those who have no reason to contribute.

The thought is that there is a collective reason, and for all that's been said, it is a reason for which I can act by acting directly on the relevant intention. My earlier objection to Kutz was that he wanted to secure responsibility while, in effect, conceding that the responsible agent has no reason. He was thereby ditching *Look-back-look-ahead*. I think that Kutz is too concessive to the *makes no difference* worry. Although the agent doesn't have the relevant individual reason for contributing, I am suggesting that there is a collective reason to which she's entitled, and for which she may act.

In this chapter I have investigated the *Look-back-look-ahead* principle that draws a connection between responsibility and reasons for action. If we are to apply this principle to cases of collective responsibility in which an individual might be implicated, it would help to make sense of the idea of an individual acting for a collective reason. My very preliminary suggestion as to how this might work draws on the thought that intentions might preserve and transmit reasons of a collective so that an individual acting on the intention is entitled to the collective reasons and acts for those reasons. The idea is modeled on how intentions function within an individual over time. In acting directly on a previously acquired intention, one acts for the reasons that went into so deciding. If this provides a suitable model for the collective case, then we might be able to preserve the connection between responsibility and reasons for action in those collective cases where *makes no difference* considerations make it hard to see what individual reason one has for doing one's part.

Notes

1 Some material in this chapter benefited from presentation to audiences in the philosophy departments at Davidson College, Ohio State University, Bowling Green University, and at the ENSO conference in Lund, Sweden. Thanks also to the editors for their comments.

2 We might wonder why someone is unable to Φ. Presumably we should add that the incapacity was non-culpable. This suggests that spelling out conditions for this sort of excuse will not yield a reductive account of responsibility, for the concept of non-culpability presupposes that of responsibility.

3 The importance in the collective context of forward-looking notions of reason, duty, or obligation, has been emphasized more recently for example in Isaacs (2014: 40); Wringe (2014: 474–5); Schwenkenbecher (2013: 2); Dietz (2016: 958). Important earlier discussion includes Parfit (1984); Jackson (1987).

4 Although Kant would say that the S-ing has no moral worth.

5 Sometimes Φ won't preclude S. But if Φ is really all one could have reasonably expected to do about S, then even if S comes about because of bad luck, it seems that one should not be blamed for S. And I would add that one is not to be blamed even if the Φ-ing one did do was not done to avert S, but for some other reason.

6 Culpable ignorance might pose a worry. Due to the ignorance, the agent was never in a position reasonably to do something about S. We might nevertheless want to blame him.

7 I am assuming that this is not due to some morally culpable ignorance or insensitivity on his part.

8 Does this make selfishness an excuse? The worry, I take it, is that the selfish individual might think they have no reason to act in light of S-related considerations if those considerations don't bear on his own interests. But this by itself doesn't mean that the individual is incapable of acting for such reasons – unless the selfishness is pathological.

9 These remarks should be qualified in light of important considerations stemming from phenomena of moral luck and agent regret (Nagel 1979; Williams 1981). See Kutz (2002) for a discussion that is sensitive to and accommodating of these considerations (perhaps overaccommodating to my taste). Nelkin (2019) also provides a very helpful overview.

10 *Look-back-look-ahead* is related to a reasons-responsive picture of moral responsibility. But it is more minimal as a thesis. First, the suggestion is only intended as a condition on responsibility; not as the makings of a complete compatibilist account of responsibility. Second, reasons-responsiveness is often thought of as involving a counterfactual condition (regarding what reasons the agent would be responsive to) that has a bearing on what actually prompts the action in question (e.g. McKenna (2013: 154) discussing Fischer and Ravizza (1998). But I'm not taking a position on what sort of counterfactual reasons-responsiveness has to be true for someone to count as acting for a reason. Indeed, Frankfurt style cases (Frankfurt 1969) suggest that one can act for a reason (arguably even do so responsibly) while lacking reasons-responsiveness, as McKenna notes. It is a substantive question whether one could act for a reason even if one lacked a counterfactual sensitivity.

11 Björnsson, "Shared Responsibility Refined," delivered at Society for Agency and Responsibility, Pacific APA, 2017. See also the firing squad example from Parfit (1984: §26).

12 Collins (2017: 578) describes such a view, though doesn't endorse it.

13 For discussion in favor of the agent condition, see Collins (2017: 584); Lawford-Smith (2015); Isaacs (2011: 23–70). Against: Schwenkenbecher (2013: 8; 2018: 111); Wringe (2014: 484ff; see his 2010).

14 But see Copp (2006); Pettit (2003); Rovane (1997); French (1979).

15 For a view that holds that such individuals are not exonerated, see Kutz (2000b: 156ff).
16 Copp (2006: §5). Copp imagines cases where individuals playing their roles act in morally unproblematic ways, and yet because of how their decisions are aggregated, the group behaves in a critcizable way. And this commits us to the group's responsibility – precisely because there is no responsibility to be assigned to the individuals.
17 See Schwenkenbecher's (2018: 117) discussion of Erskine (2014):

> if there is a duty to rescue the child and the passersby can come together to do so, then they each have an obligation to contribute to establishing the kind of group needed for rescuing it … this view requires a certain kind of group to be formed – not a group agent but a goal-oriented collective. Erskine thinks that all that is required of the individuals here is to act jointly. They need not form a – structured – group agent. This difference is reflected, for example, in the different way in which the coalition of the willing can be held responsible: responsibility ultimately distributes between the members of the group but does not sit at the level of the group as such.

18 Schwenkenbecher (2013: 9, 11) says something similar discussing Held's case of bystanders lending aid at the scene of a car accident, and attributes this view to Collins (2013). The bystanders have a duty to engage in joint action to prevent some assault, and this duty can hold for each individually (Held 1970: 479).
19 Schwenkenbecher (2013: 17) notes this, but doesn't address it.
20 See Nefsky (2015); also Parfit (1984); Glover (1975).
21 Collins (2017: 580) objects to Kutz, saying,

> If each of A, . . ., N intends to 'w together,' then there are N intentions, each held by a different individual. Nothing is implied about any of the individuals having any significant relation to any of the others or their intentions, such as a relation of control or influence or emulation between the intentions. So authorship for what the others do—if this is understood as implying individual remedial duties for what the others do— receives insufficient justification.

For Kutz, a *participatory intention* is an instance of the familiar notion of an intention had by an individual. But he *does* impose conditions on it: it has a distinctive content, and is had only when individuals in question are strategically responsive to each other, mutually open about their interaction, and committed to shared goals (Kutz 2000a: 7). So it's probably not fair for Collins to say that on Kutz' view there are no significant relations between the respective intentions of the individuals.
22 Again, I'm bracketing complications arising from moral luck. See note 9 above.
23 Wringe (2014: 79) suggests that collective obligations explain the corresponding individual obligations.
24 Although Schwenkenbecher has her doubts (2018: 114–15) and favors the idea that the individuals are jointly obligated.
25 Another case that has generated substantial discussion is that of Hi-Lo. See Bacharach (2006); Gold and Sugden (2007); Hurley (1989). For useful related discussion of sympathetic to collective reasons, see Parfit (1984: §26); Jackson (1987); Wringe (2014); Dietz (2016); Schwenkenbecher (2018).
26 See Nefsky (2015) on superfluity, and Björnsson forthcoming for discussion.
27 Compare Burge 1993 on how working memory might preserve the warranted status of beliefs throughout an episode of reasoning.
28 I see the project here as related in interesting ways to certain non-reductive treatments of epistemic warrant in cases of testimony. See also the discussion of identification in Anderson (2001: 31ff).
29 Related arguments are rehearsed by Nefsky (2015: 249); Dietz (2016: 979).

References

Anderson, Elizabeth. (2001) "Unstrapping the Straightjacket of 'Preference': A Comment on Amartya Sen's Contributions to Philosophy and Economics," *Economics and Philosophy* 17: 21–38.

Bacharach, Michael. (2006) *Beyond Individual Choice*, N. Gold & R. Sugden (eds.), Princeton: Princeton University Press.

Björnsson, Gunnar. (2017) "Shared Responsibility Refined," delivered at Society for Agency and Responsibility, Pacific APA, 2017.

Björnsson, Gunnar. (forthcoming) "On Individual and Shared Obligations," in M. Budolfsen, T. McPherson, & D. Plunkett (eds.) *Philosophy and Climate Change*. Oxford: Oxford University Press.
Burge, Tyler. (1993) "Content Preservation," *Philosophical Review* 102: 457–88.
Collins, Stephanie. (2013) "Collectives' Duties and Collectivization Duties," *Australasian Journal of Philosophy* 91: 231–48.
Collins, Stephanie. (2017) "Filling Collective Duty Gaps," *Journal of Philosophy* 114(11): 573–91.
Copp, David. (2006) "On the Agency of Certain Collective Entities: An Argument from 'Normative Autonomy'," *Midwest Studies in Philosophy* 30: 194–221.
Dietz, Alexander. (2016) "What We Together Ought to Do," *Ethics* 126: 955–82.
Erskine, Toni. (2014) "Coalitions of the Willing and the Responsibility to Protect: Informal Associations, Enhanced Capacities, and Shared Moral Burdens," *Ethics and International Affairs* 28: 115–45.
Fischer, John Martin, and Mark Ravizza. (1998) *Responsibility and Control: An Essay on Moral Responsibility*, Cambridge: Cambridge University Press.
Frankfurt, Harry. (1969) "Alternate Possibilities and Moral Responsibility," *Journal of Philosophy* 66: 829–39.
French, Peter. (1979) "The Corporation as a Moral Person," *American Philosophical Quarterly* 16(3): 207–15.
Gilbert, Margaret. (1990) "Walking Together: A Paradigmatic Social Phenomenon," *Midwest Studies in Philosophy* 15: 1–14.
Gilbert, Margaret. (2009) "Shared Intention and Personal Intention," *Philosophical Studies* 144: 167–87.
Glover, Jonathan. (1975) "It Makes No Difference Whether or Not I Do It," *Proceedings of the Aristotelian Society* 49.
Gold, Natalie and Robert Sugden. (2007) "Collective Intentions and Team Agency," *Journal of Philosophy* 104(3): 109–37.
Held, Virginia. (1970) "Can a Random Collection of Individuals be Morally Responsible?," *The Journal of Philosophy* 67(14): 471–81.
Hurley, Susan. (1989) *Natural Reasons*, New York: Oxford University Press.
Isaacs, Tracy. (2011) *Moral Responsibility in Collective Contexts*, Oxford: Oxford University Press.
Isaacs, Tracy. (2014) "Collective Responsibility and Collective Obligation," *Midwest Studies in Philosophy* 38: 40–57.
Jackson, Frank. (1987) "Group Morality," in Philip Pettit, Richard Sylvan, and Jean Norman (eds.) *Metaphysics and Morality*, Oxford: Blackwell, 91–110.
Kutz, Christopher. (2000a) "Acting Together," *Philosophy and Phenomenological Research* 61: 1–31.
Kutz, Christopher. (2000b) *Complicity: Ethics and Law for a Collective Age*, Cambridge: Cambridge University Press.
Kutz, Christopher. (2002) "Responsibility," in J. Coleman and S. Shapiro (eds.) *Oxford Handbook of Jurisprudence and Philosophy of Law*, Oxford: Oxford University Press: 548–87.
Lawford-Smith, Holly. (2015) "What We?," *Journal of Social Ontology* 1: 225–49.
McKenna, Michael. (2013) "Reasons-Responsiveness, Agents, and Mechanisms," in D. Shoemaker (ed.) *Oxford Studies in Agency and Responsibility Vol 1*. Oxford: Oxford University Press.
Nagel, Thomas. (1979) *Mortal Questions*, New York: Cambridge University Press.
Nefsky, Julia. (2015) "Fairness, Participation, and the Real Problem of Collective Harm," in Mark Timmons (ed.) *Oxford Studies in Normative Ethics*, 5: 245–71.
Nelkin, Dana K. (2019) "Moral Luck," *The Stanford Encyclopedia of Philosophy* (Summer 2019 Edition), Edward N. Zalta (ed.), https://plato.stanford.edu/archives/sum2019/entries/moral-luck/.
Parfit, Derek. (1984) *Reasons and Persons*, New York: Oxford University Press.
Parfit, Derek. (unpublished ms) "What We Together Do."
Pettit, P. (2003) "Groups with Minds of Their Own," in F. Schmitt (ed.) *Socializing Metaphysics: The Nature of Social Reality*. Lanham, MD: Rowman & Littlefield: 167–93.
Pettit, P. (2007) "Responsibility Incorporated," *Ethics* 117(2): 171–201.
Pettit, P. and Schweikard, D. (2006). "Joint Actions and Group Agents," *Philosophy of the Social Sciences* 36(1): 18–39.
Roth, Abraham Sesshu. (2017) "Entitlement to Reasons for Action," in D. Shoemaker (ed.) *Oxford Studies in Agency and Responsibility Vol 4*. Oxford: Oxford University Press: 75–92.
Rovane, Carol. (1997) *The Bounds of Agency: An Essay in Revisionary Metaphysics*, Princeton: Princeton University Press.

Schwenkenbecher, Anne. (2013) "Joint Duties and Global Moral Obligations," *Ratio* 26(3): 310–28.
Schwenkenbecher, Anne. (2018) "Making Sense of Collective Moral Obligations," in Hess, Igneski, and Isaacs, (eds.), *Collectivity – Ontology, Ethics, and Social Justice*, 109–32.
Williams, Bernard. (1981) *Moral Luck*, Cambridge: Cambridge University Press.
Wringe, Bill. (2010) "Global Obligations and the Agency Objection," *Ratio* 23(2): 217–31.
Wringe, Bill. (2014) "Collective Obligations: Their Existence, Their Explanatory Power, and Their Supervenience on the Obligations of Individuals," *European Journal of Philosophy* xxii: 472–97.

18

THE POSSIBILITY OF COLLECTIVE MORAL OBLIGATIONS

Anne Schwenkenbecher

The philosophical literature on collective agency, collective responsibility, social epistemology, and social ontology is burgeoning. Scholarly interest in 'collective' phenomena and theories reflects a persistent desire to tackle an old conundrum – the relationship between individual agents and the collectives they compose. The problem of reconciling these two perspectives is not one for philosophy alone.[1] There is a notable shift away from a strict individualism towards theories that reflect the fundamentally social, cooperative nature of human activities.

Philosophical enquiry and theorizing has in many ways traditionally been too focused on the individual: the ideal of the autonomous, well-informed, moral agent has dominated ethics, philosophy of action and epistemology for a long time (and arguably still does). In contrast, in political philosophy the question of an inwardly and outwardly just society is often raised without spending enough time exploring what kind of 'collective' a society is and how to understand the relationship between this collective and the individuals composing it.

This chapter attempts to shed light on the issue of collective moral obligations, that is, obligations that individuals in loose groups (as opposed to group agents) may have together.[2] I take moral obligations to be a basic feature of our moral repertoire. Put in the simplest possible terms, there are things we ought and things we ought not to do.[3] For instance, we ought not to harm others without good reason and we ought to assist those in need. Further, we might want to distinguish between *pro tanto* and *all-out* obligations. *Pro tanto* obligations are demands on us that give us some reason to act, but which can be overridden by other, more important reasons. All-out obligations are those we ought to meet *all-things-considered*, taking all the different moral considerations into account.

My contention in this chapter is that our moral obligations (*pro tanto* and *all-out*) can sometimes be collective in nature. By this I mean that moral obligations can *jointly* attach to two or more agents in that neither agent has that obligation on their own, but they – in some sense – *share* it or have it *in common*.[4] I will explain this in more detail below.

I believe that the notion of collective moral obligations fills a conceptual gap in philosophy. In a sense, one could say that moral philosophy has traditionally been concerned with the question 'what ought I to do?,'[5] while what we ought to do as communities has been the focus of political philosophy. But some of the things that we *together* can (and potentially ought to) do may be neither the political communities' responsibility nor straightforward individual obligations. Furthermore, even where some desirable goal or action is *primarily* the political community's responsibility, as a matter of fact, political agents (e.g. states and their institutions) often fall short of meeting their obligations. In either case, there may be groups of individual agents that can step up and produce the desired outcomes or perform the required actions. Examples include our joint ability to overcome collective action problems even in the absence of state action, such as closing (or reducing) the so-called global emissions gap (Blok, Hohne, van der Leun, & Harrison, 2012; Wynes & Nicholas, 2017). On a national scale, our ability to produce herd immunity against some infectious disease should be seen as collective. I will come back to these examples at the end of the chapter. My starting point will be a simpler, small-scale, real-world example of spontaneous collaboration between complete strangers:

> Ten passers-by witness a car accident in which a motorcyclist gets trapped underneath a car, which has caught fire on one side. Somebody has to act very quickly to pull him out the other side and in order to do so the car will need to be ever so slightly lifted. None of the passers-by can lift the car on their own and pull the man out, but together they can (without taking any undue risks to their own health and safety). As it happened, the people manage to lift the car and save the motorcyclist's life.[6]

For the sake of argument, let us assume that the following is the case: it is obvious to the witnesses of the accident that the man is in imminent danger and it is fairly clear what needs to be done to get him out of danger.

There are several scholars who argue that under circumstances such as these individual moral agents can be under a *collective obligation* (or have collective responsibility) to assist (Held, 1970; Isaacs, 2011; May, 1992; Miller, 2010; Pinkert, 2014; Schwenkenbecher, 2013, 2014, 2019; Wringe, 2005, 2010, 2016). Collective obligations, on their accounts, are distinct from and not reducible to individual obligations (to contribute to cooperative ventures, for instance).

In the following, I will distinguish different ways of spelling out such collective obligations. But before I do so, let me briefly talk about why anyone might think that we need the notion of collective obligations. One of the starting points of many debates on collective obligations is the observation that in cases like the one above, in order to produce the morally best outcome, or in order to perform the action most likely to secure that outcome, individual agents need to cooperate with one another and coordinate their individual actions. It takes more than one person's effort to make a difference to the person in need.

More generally, there is a class of actions (and outcomes) that cannot be performed (or produced) by one person on their own. They require at least two people in order to be realized and no one individual agent can guarantee the success of the collective endeavor. These cases are characterized by 'joint necessity.'[7] Playing a duet is a joint necessity type of activity. By definition, it cannot be done by one person. Another example is 'talking past one another.' Joint necessity can be *analytic* (as in the two examples just given), where it is part of what it means to do x that x is done by at least two people. Or joint necessity can be *circumstantial*, where as a matter of fact (rather than as a matter of principle), something cannot be done by one person, for instance, if it takes two or more people to lift a heavy table (or a car, for that matter).

We can further distinguish between *strict* and *wide* joint necessity.[8] For strict joint necessity to apply, the number of available contributors to a collective outcome equals the number of contributors minimally necessary to produce it. What it means to be an available contributor would depend on the outcome in question. For the motorbike accident described above, it would mean anyone close enough to see what is happening and able to make some kind of contribution. For strict joint necessity, the success of the joint venture is counterfactually dependent on each available contributor playing their part. It is entirely within my power to stymie any efforts of our duet playing and the same applies to you.

Wide joint necessity applies where there are more available contributors to a joint outcome than minimally necessary. There are many large-scale examples of wide joint necessity such as producing herd immunity (against a certain infectious disease), bridging the emissions gap (UNEP, 2017), or producing a referendum outcome in favor of marriage equality. In order for herd immunity against a particular communicable disease to be achieved it is not necessary that everyone who can safely be vaccinated be in fact vaccinated. Depending on the disease, the figure may be around 90 percent. What this means is that, in contrast to strict joint necessity cases, my unilateral defection in a wide joint necessity case does not *guarantee* collective failure and neither does yours. This might lead someone to the conclusion that therefore individual obligations to contribute to such goods are always less stringent. But I think this would be the wrong conclusion to draw, as I shall show below.

In many joint necessity scenarios, something morally important is at stake. Especially where lives are in imminent danger, people tend to share the intuition that those who could help ought to do so, e.g. those witnessing the motorbike accident ought to assist the trapped person. But this common intuition may create a dilemma, because, no individual can guarantee the success of the joint endeavor (or produce the desired collective good).[9] That is, individually, none of these passers-by can assist the trapped motorcyclist. Hence, it cannot be any individual agent's obligation to rescue him. They can only help jointly. So, whose obligation is it? We might want to say that it is the obligation of all of them together. But what does that mean? Is it the 'group' of passers-by that has the obligation to assist? Or is there 'merely' an obligation on each of us to do our best given others' actions? The answer is not straightforward. In my view, this impasse is regularly felt when we try to make moral decisions: it is the pull between the individualist option (to do something that is under one's individual control only) and the collectivist option (where the success of one's actions often depends on others' contributions).

Scholars have chosen different routes to answer the question about the locus of moral obligation in joint necessity cases. Roughly, they can be divided into two groups, which I will call 'conservatives' and 'revisionists.' Revisionist scholars will usually introduce new moral vocabulary and concepts to fill what they believe to be a gap in traditional moral theorizing where joint necessity is concerned. Many argue that there is some kind of group-level obligation (or responsibility) that applies to loose collections of individuals such as the passers-by in scenarios like our exemplary case (Held, 1970; Isaacs, 2011; May, 1992; Wringe, 2010). Other revisionists, including myself, speak of individuals holding joint obligations (Miller, 2010; Pinkert, 2014; Schwenkenbecher, 2013, 2014, 2019) or sharing obligations (Björnsson, 2014). Conservative scholars, in contrast, do not see the need for new conceptual tools, but attempt to resolve collective action puzzles in a way that is maximally continuous with existing theory. They tend to argue that joint necessity cases give rise to (perhaps slightly more complex than usual) contributory duties only. According to Parfit, for instance, each of the individual passers-by simply has an obligation to contribute if she thinks that enough others contribute to get the joint endeavor off the ground (Parfit, 1984). Collins and Lawford Smith would argue that each ought to take steps towards forming a group that can then act as an agent (Collins, 2013; Lawford-Smith, 2015).

I will not discuss the merits of these different types of approaches in any detail here, since I have done so elsewhere (Schwenkenbecher, 2018). The obvious downside of the conservative approach is that the obligation to produce the collective good (or to realize the joint endeavor) is not allocated. In our example, then, there is no obligation to free the trapped motorcyclist, even though individual agents have obligations to contribute.[10] Holly Lawford-Smith acknowledges this problem for the conservative approach, but bites the bullet because she thinks the advantages of this approach still outweigh its disadvantages (2015). In contrast, the obvious downside of the first type of revisionist approach is this: it seems to be built on the assumption that there is a (novel) entity, a group agent of sorts, that can not only act on the problem at hand, but has a sufficient level of unity such that it can hold a moral obligation (or be held morally responsible). Revisionist scholars have tried to avoid this kind of criticism by arguing that being an agent is not a necessary condition for being the bearer of a moral obligation as far as groups (or collections of agents) are concerned (Wringe, 2010).

However, my aim here is not to give an overview of the literature but to instead flesh out my own (revisionist) approach to collective obligations and show how it applies in a range of cases.[11] This approach, while revisionist, avoids the objection sketched above by refraining from postulating a group agent (even a putative or potential one) and instead conceiving of the obligations to assist in joint necessity cases as shared or 'joint.'

18.1 Jointly Held Obligations

What does it mean to say that a number of agents *jointly* hold a moral obligation? On my view, collective obligations are not a novel type of obligation, but are moral obligations held in a collective *mode*: I can individually hold an obligation to do *x* or we (for instance you and I) can jointly hold an obligation to do *x* (for instance where *x* is only collectively feasible). To jointly hold an obligation is a plural predicate – it can only meaningfully apply to two or more agents, very much like other (non-moral) plural predicates such as 'playing a duet' or 'walking past one another.' On this approach, the obligation that the passers-by in our example assist the trapped driver is a joint obligation; they hold it together.

Joint obligations give rise to further individual obligations. If you and I jointly have an obligation to lift a heavy table, then each of us has an individual obligation to do our part or make an effort towards the joint endeavor. But joint obligations do not reduce to individual obligations to play our part. In order to see why, let us return to wide joint necessity cases, where we have more potential contributors then minimally necessary for the success of the collective performance. Suppose that it takes two people to lift a heavy table, but three potential contributors are available. Suppose further, that two is also the maximum number of people who can successfully lift the table together, because of the way each needs to position themselves to lift it. So out of the three potential contributors only two should act. It cannot be the case that each of the three has an obligation to act (since a three-way effort will not succeed). Neither should we think that any combination of two people (out of the three) is obligated to contribute. Because if we did, we would either (i) arrive at an impasse where we could not say exactly which two people have these obligations (that is, we would arrive at the following disjunctive obligation: Either *a* and *b* are obligated to do their part in lifting the table together, or *b* and *c* are so obligated, or *a* and *c*). Or, (ii) we would have to make an arbitrary decision on which two people have these obligations.

Instead, I suggest that the joint obligation is on all three and the individual (contributory) obligations will be derived from it. For instance, we may all be under an obligation to see to it that two of us lift the table together and one of us makes sure not to interfere. In order to do this, we will usually have to communicate with each other. This may be non-verbal communication. In everyday life, we often coordinate our actions this way – just think of a scenario where some passers-by rush to help someone who has trouble lifting a pram into a bus while others stay behind ready to step up if necessary.

But we need not always be able to communicate with each other in order to acquire (and discharge) a collective obligation. Sometimes having the right information concerning the other agents' beliefs will suffice. Suppose that you and I live on opposite shores of a protected lake and in order to preserve the lake's sensitive ecosystem and keep its pristine water clean we are instructed (by the local council) to ensure that no sewage or gray water enters the lake. We also learn that every neighbor is being thus instructed. Now I can do my part of not allowing any polluted water to enter the lake and so can you. But neither of us can guarantee that the lake's water is not compromised. That outcome we can only produce together. Assuming that the pristine ecosystem is valuable and no overriding concerns exist, we are under an obligation to protect it. This obligation is held by both of us, jointly. It is not an obligation held by either of us, because neither can discharge it alone. Note that this does not require us to act together in the strict sense. Note also, that a joint plan is in place (via the local council's communication), which ascribes to each of us a clearly circumscribed role in the collective effort (and which, furthermore, communicates that very fact to each of us).

18.2 Collectively Available Options and We-Reasoning

So when exactly should we think of our obligations as collective? I shall explain the conditions in the following. To start with, I argue that two (or more) agents have a collective moral obligation to do x if x is an option for action that is only *collectively available* and if each of them has sufficient reason to rank x the highest out of the options available to them.

Let me explain what this means. In a scenario like that of the trapped motorcyclist each individual could reason in the following way: 'I can walk over and attempt to lift the car but on my own I will not be able to lift it. Trying to lift it will only make sense if several other bystanders also contribute.'

Naturally, most of us would probably make an attempt to get others to contribute (provided no countervailing circumstances obtain). But why is this so? To me it seems that the reason why one would try to establish collective action in this kind of scenario is because it seems like the (morally) best option.

Before I continue note two things here: I do not commit to a view on what actually *is* morally best in this scenario, that is, I make my argument independently of any *particular* substantive moral theory. Evidently, different substantive theories vary significantly in what they consider morally best. However, I am hoping that the example used here is one where the major moral theories and common moral intuitions converge. Further, note that calling an option 'morally best' does not imply that I am committed to some kind of consequentialism. The morally best option for a Kantian may be to respect someone's autonomy and for a virtue ethicist it may be to act in the way most constitutive of *eudaimonia*.

Returning to our individual decision-maker: Let us assume that she perceives the option as best where several passers-by lift the car together. It is important to note that this option is not actually available to *her* (alone), but it is only available to *them*. At the point of making her move to assist the trapped driver, our deliberator does not yet know exactly how many people will be needed and how many of the other passers-by are willing and able to contribute and who they are. Still, she acts on what she perceives to be the optimal option for acting in this case (jointly lifting the car) and she infers her own (and potentially others') individual contributory action(s) from that *collectively available* option.[12]

If that is what our individual deliberator does, then she *we-reasons*. This means that the starting point of her deliberation is not merely the options available to her (individually). Instead, she also includes in her deliberation those options that are only collectively available, such as lifting the car and freeing the trapped motorcyclist. She reasons from the top-down, so to speak. Starting from the best option (which is only collectively available) she derives individual contributory actions.

I am not alleging that someone who acts like our exemplary deliberator *necessarily* engages in we-reasoning, but empirical evidence suggests that people faced with similar scenarios regularly do (Butler, 2012; Butler, Burbank, & Chisholm, 2011). And my contention here is that they often should.

Let me now explain the idea of 'we-reasoning' in some more detail. The way I am using the term is slightly different from how similar ideas of reasoning from the collective perspective are employed, e.g. in philosophy of economics and (non-standard) game theory (Bacharach, 2006; Butler, 2012; Gold & Sugden, 2007; Hakli, Miller, & Tuomela, 2010; Sugden, 2015; Sugden & Gold, 2007; Tuomela, 2013).[13]

Importantly, I am adopting the term from its original context of decision-theoretic discussions of strategic interaction for the field of moral deliberation and decision-making. As moral agents, we regularly face problems wherein the outcome of our actions depends on how others choose. There are two ways of deliberating about our own choices in such cases. We can either think of our choices as best responses to others' choices (I-mode reasoning). Or we can think of our own choices as contributions to the collectively best option (even when we do not know how others are (likely) to choose) (we-mode reasoning).

Let me illustrate this by returning to the example of the trapped motorcyclist. The individual passerby might reason in the following way:

> If sufficiently many others contribute then the morally optimal thing for me to do is to also contribute (provided that this will make a difference to the outcome). If not enough others contribute then the morally optimal thing for me to do is not to try to lift the car on my own, but perhaps to call an ambulance or the police.

This would be an instance of I-mode reasoning (I am adopting this term from Hakli et al. 2010).

Or, the individual passer-by might reason differently:

> The morally best outcome is the one where several people join forces to lift the car and free the trapped driver. In order to secure the morally best outcome, each of us should make an effort towards lifting the car. I should get others to make an effort in lifting the car and signal to others my readiness to contribute to the joint endeavor.

Note that this involves two steps: (i) *we-framing* means to include collectively available options in one's option set when deliberating about which option is best and identifying an option that is only collectively available as optimal. In a second step, (ii) the deliberating agent determines her individual course of action as playing her part in the collectively optimal course of action. If this is how the individual passerby reasons about what she should do, then she is employing we-reasoning.[14]

There are many joint necessity scenarios where by default most of us would reason in this way. Not only would we include collectively available options in our deliberation (we-framing), but also we would take individual steps towards realizing those options as well as encourage others to take the necessary steps. This may (but need not) include communicating our intentions and goals to others, asking them to contribute, or distributing and coordinating tasks and roles. Often we will play our part without having information on what others are doing; we will take a gamble, so to speak (for instance when we are not diverting gray water into the pristine lake).

Sometimes, individual roles or contributory tasks will be clear from the very start. This may be because there exists a joint plan or a habitual pattern of actions for a particular joint endeavor. Take the example of jointly setting a table, for instance. Or a traditional dance or a tune that people know well enough to perform it together instantly.

At other times, it may be relatively straightforward for individual agents to jointly work out a plan and individual contributions if they can communicate with each other. The other day I asked a friend to help me lift my canoe onto the roof rack of my car. We had to adjust our individual contributory actions on the go, but it was fairly easy to do so. If we did this more often, we might form a habitual pattern and could possibly even do this without important communicative (for instance visual) cues.

There are other cases where such patterns, while not habitual or engrained, can be easily established by potential contributors without any need for communication between them. It may be obvious what the collectively best choice is and how each person can contribute to realizing it (as, for instance, in a Hi-Lo game kind of scenario[15]). One example would be voting in a referendum on a morally black and white matter, such as the right to have an abortion (as happened in Ireland recently) or the right of same-sex couples to marry (as happened in Australia recently).

But there are also cases where communication is difficult or even impossible and where individual agents cannot divine their contributions to the joint task without communicating to the other agents. Arguably, in those cases individual agents would be less inclined to we-reason. That is, they may be (and probably should be) less inclined to include options that are only collectively available in their moral deliberation and to take steps towards realizing those options.

18.3 Joint Ability and Ignorance

Further, we might say that in such cases the *joint ability* of potential contributors to perform an action or produce an outcome together is severely diminished. That is, there will be circumstances under which the success of joint action is so unlikely that a collection of agents cannot be said to have the level of joint capacity minimally required for ascribing an obligation to them.

Two agents, *a* and *b*, have joint ability[16] to do *x* if there is at least one combination of contributory actions such that

- these are genuine options *a* and *b* have, and, if both are performed in the right way, they produce *x*;
- both contributory actions are compossible;
- *a* and *b* are capable of performing these actions with a view to combining them.

Let me explain the last condition: Joint ability is not mere compossibility. Rather, agents must – in principle – be able to willingly combine their actions. That is, they must be in a position to *intentionally perform their contributory action as a contributory action*.[17, 18] There must be some reason for agents to form plural intentions in the most minimal sense as intentions the content of which is some collective endeavor (Ludwig, 2016).[19] This is important, because otherwise we could ascribe joint ability wherever an outcome could accidentally be jointly produced. But surely, the accidental production of any outcome by some agent (or group thereof) should not be mistaken for a *robust ability* to produce that outcome where this robust ability is the basis for ascribing moral obligations.

Joint ability, then, is highly context-dependent and particularly sensitive to shared (or even common) beliefs.[20] As such, joint ability can be deliberately generated in a given collection of agents by providing information related to collective goals and contributory actions.[21] In fact, public information campaigns concerning specific collective causes do precisely that: they communicate collectively desirable patterns of action and outline those individual contributory actions, which are most likely to produce the collective pattern. This does not only solve (or prevent) coordination problems, but it also generates joint ability in the sense that people may now reasonably form intentions concerning their contributory actions *as* contributory actions where perhaps such intentions would not normally have been formed. Where small-scale joint necessity problems are concerned, we commonly (and without thinking much about it) inform others of the problem at hand, the potential patterns of action that will resolve it and encourage others to make their contribution ('Do you mind giving me a hand with this? If you just [do *x*] then I will [do *y*]...').

In other words, knowing of possible joint initiatives to address collective action problems will reduce or remove *propositional ignorance* of the issue concerned. A person is propositionally ignorant of a proposition *p* if they do not know *of p* (Le Morvan, 2011). For instance, someone may have never heard of anti-microbial resistance and therefore will not form intentions to contribute to the reduction of such resistance by changing her dietary habits, for instance (Giubilini, Birkl, Douglas, Savulescu, & Maslen, 2017). Further, information campaigns may reduce or eliminate *factive ignorance*, that is, they may correct false beliefs on the matter at hand. For instance, people may believe that there is nothing we can do to stop run-away climate change, but we may learn that there are things we can each do that will have a significant impact on mitigating global warming (Blok et al., 2012; Dietz, Gardner, Gilligan, Stern, & Vandenbergh, 2009; Wynes & Nicholas, 2017). Factive ignorance, then, can also prevent agents from having reasons to form minimal plural intentions to perform their contributory action *as a contributory action*.

It is easy to see that in our main example, the case of the trapped motorcyclist, we will hardly need to worry about propositional ignorance. To each of the passers-by it is immediately obvious that the person is in need of help and that he must be pulled out from underneath the burning car. Where the respective (collective action) problem is less immediate (as is the case for problems concerning 'distant strangers,' for instance), propositional ignorance will become a major factor in collective apathy and inaction.

In our exemplary case, there may be some factive ignorance as to whether the random group of strangers is in fact capable of lifting the car and extracting the driver, but in the real-world case, the passers-by were confident enough to try. The more immediate a problem, the less likely it is that agents are propositionally ignorant concerning that issue. Factive ignorance, in contrast, can have all kinds of causes, including emotional and psychological factors, and as such is often difficult to combat.

If we think that forming intentions to act depends on having certain beliefs (as I have been alleging) then interesting questions arise where we think that an agent or a group of agents can be held responsible for their suboptimal epistemic position. Take the example where a group of agents is factively ignorant of some harm they are collectively causing and they therefore continue to perform the actions that in aggregation cause harm. For instance, this was the case before the climate greenhouse effect was widely known. On my account, people who lived during the industrial revolution were not in fact jointly able to prevent global warming because their epistemic position was not such that they could have formed the intention to reduce (or abstain from) their fossil-fuel burning activities as part of an effort to prevent global warming.[22] This is not because there were no (feasible or economical) alternatives to burning fossil fuels and neither is it because they were not (accidentally or incidentally) capable of preventing the release of massive amounts of greenhouse gases in the atmosphere, but rather because they could not have formed the relevant intentions to contribute to a joint effort to prevent aggregate harm, because they were ignorant of that harm. In other words, their ignorance undermined their joint ability. But were they responsible for that ignorance? And if so, can we say that they were culpable for their lack of joint ability?

I cannot discuss here which criteria should make us consider an agent blameworthy of her ignorance, but will simply point to some of the literature on this topic (Le Morvan, 2011; Peels, 2010, 2016; Rosen, 2003; Zimmerman, 2016). What we may be able to say, though, is that where a proposition is *public knowledge*, agents will be less justified in claiming ignorance. A proposition is public knowledge if (a) most people believe that the proposition is true and (b) most people believe that (a) is the case.

18.4 When Do We Have Collective Obligations?

To sum up what has been said so far: In order for two or more agents to jointly hold an obligation to address some joint necessity problem they must have joint ability to address that problem. We also discussed that in deliberating about the right (individual) course of action vis-à-vis collective action problems, agents regularly we-frame the case at hand, that is, they include options in their deliberation that are only collectively available, and they we-reason with regard to their individual contributory actions.

It is a necessary condition for collective obligations that potential collaborators facing a joint necessity case have grounds to privilege we-reasoning over reasoning in I-mode. But under which circumstances do agents have such grounds? It is easier to give negative conditions for when agents lack such grounds. For instance, they will have no grounds for engaging in we-reasoning if they do not recognize the problem as a joint necessity case. Further, they may not recognize a joint necessity case as a morally pressing problem in need of resolution. Or else they may not be aware of other agents' potential to contribute. Finally, they may have reason to believe that they are on their own with regard to the problem, because agents appear unwilling to contribute. However, if the problem is pressing enough, the conscientious agent must not give up at this point, but ought to attempt to secure the others' cooperation.

The picture of joint obligations drawn here aligns best with a non-objective view of moral obligations. On an objective view of moral obligations, we ought to do what is objectively best (or right) regardless of whether we *know* what that is. So even if we act conscientiously, on the basis of the best available information, and are rigorous in our decision-making, we may still fail to meet our actual moral obligations. Likewise, we may meet them accidentally. I do not have the space here to argue against the objective view of moral obligations and will instead refer the reader to Michael Zimmerman's work on this issue (1996, 2014).

The notion of collective obligations defended here, aligns best with what Zimmerman (1996) calls the prospective view of moral obligations.[23] To put it in a nutshell: on the prospective view, we ought to do what is prospectively best, that is, what our best bet is given the obtainable evidence and provided we have conscientiously availed ourselves of the evidence. This means that our moral obligations depend on our reasonable, justified (but not necessarily true) beliefs concerning the problem at hand.

The prospective view of moral obligations makes better sense of the intuition that agents have no collective obligation to address a joint necessity problem where they reasonably believe an individually available option to be superior to an only-collectively-available option. Or where they reasonably disagree on which collectively available option is best and they therefore cannot agree on a course of action. Or where they are unlikely to figure out the collectively optimal solution in the time available to them. These kinds of complications, where they cannot easily be resolved between willing agents, can cancel collective obligations.

To illustrate the prospective view of collective obligations, let us once more return to the case of the trapped motorcyclist: The passers-by are likely to include the option of (collectively) lifting the car and extracting the driver in their set of options for moral deliberation unless they have reason to believe, e.g., that there is no one available to help them. Of course, because the stakes are so high they may still try on their own to pull out the driver, essentially testing if the option of rescuing him is individually available. However, this action is simply a way of availing themselves of evidence in a conscientious manner. Passers-by will usually attempt to investigate others' willingness to contribute – this serves to determine which options are available to *them*[24] and, potentially, it can be the moment where individual roles or contributions are distributed. Further, it generates common knowledge amongst potential contributors, and therewith increases (or even establishes) joint ability. The same action can also deliver important information for each individual deliberator with regard to how others rank the available options and the extent to which they are willing to make their contribution. What they have an obligation to do will depend on what they have good reason to believe is the best option, given they have availed themselves of the evidence. That evidence will often include information about other agents' willingness and ability to contribute.

Such information will often be crucial for whether or not the *pro tanto* joint obligation becomes an all-out obligation. To reiterate, an all-out obligation is an obligation *all-things-considered*. Whether or not anyone (or any group) has an obligation all-things-considered depends on how highly a particular option for action ranks for the respective individual(s) amongst competing options. Or, in other words, it depends on whether the reasons that speak in favor of that option outweigh the reasons speaking in favor of any of the alternative options. Awareness of others' likelihood to contribute will strengthen those reasons in favor of the collectively available option, other things being equal.[25]

On my view of collective moral obligations, two or more moral agents jointly hold an all-out obligation to perform an action or produce an outcome corresponding to a collectively available option if each of these agents, provided that she is conscientious, …

(1) … has reason to believe that the collectively available option (joint rescue) is morally best;
(2) … has reason to include that option in her deliberation about her obligations (we-framing the problem);
(3) … has reason to deduce her individual course of action based on (i) and (ii) (we-reasoning about the problem) and the ability to do so;
And if the agent …
(4) … has no overriding obligations, is not unduly burdened by the task, and is jointly capable with the other(s) of discharging the task at hand.[26, 27]

The first three conditions may be met either consecutively or simultaneously. Further, we-framing (ii) and determining individual courses of action (iii) will usually (but not necessarily) mean that agents communicate amongst each other, even though this need not be verbal communication. If one of the passers-by in our example observes another placing their hands on the car in an attempt to lift it then they usually have a reason as per (ii) and (iii).

It is obvious now that our main examples came with a few implicit assumptions, which are responsible for the initial plausibility of the claim that the agents involved have some all-out duty to assist. This was necessary to get the argument off the ground. For instance, the scenarios were characterized by a certain moral simplicity. The features of the situations described were such that rescuing the person (or protecting the lake) would presumably be the morally best response. That is, most major moral theories would converge in their action recommendation. Further, in taking these scenarios out of context and discussing them at a certain level of abstraction we simply ignored other factors that would play a role for moral deliberation. For instance, we did not discuss any competing obligations that our passers-by (or the lakeside neighbors) may have, but simply assumed that there were none that would override the obligation to assist. Further, in the cases presented the objectively best option corresponded to the option that was perceived to be best by potential contributors (that is, the objective and the prospective view on obligations would align in these cases as to their action recommendation). Further, the joint rescue case is a one-off problem that requires no recurring sacrifice. Apart from moral simplicity, we also assumed epistemic simplicity: the problems were fairly obvious to an ordinary agent and so were the solutions. The number of potential contributors was manageable and they could communicate directly with one another. Naturally, more often than not these favorable conditions will not obtain. What impact do moral and epistemic uncertainty have on our collective obligations? The short answer is: the same impact as they have on our individual obligations. We frequently make decisions about what we ought to do under conditions of uncertainty and risk. As such, assumptions concerning which of our many *pro tanto* obligations become all-out obligations will always be somewhat approximate.

However, it may seem that *more* needs to be known or possibly investigated by individual agents if they are to jointly hold an obligation, compared to individually held obligations. This is true insofar as some knowledge concerning the others' willingness and ability to contribute to a joint endeavor are concerned. On the other hand, joint agency often calls for the sharing of (epistemic and other) expertise and burdens. Often, we do not *each* need to know how exactly to address some problem in order to jointly address it, as long as between us we have enough expertise to do so. In this regard, the threshold to acquiring collective obligations may in fact be lower than it is for individual obligations, or, put differently, the former may at times be more easily defeated than the latter.

18.5 Large-scale and Global Moral Obligations

Let me conclude by commenting on a controversial question, that has been receiving some attention in the literature: the problem of large-scale and even global collective obligations (Isaacs, 2011; Lawford-Smith, 2015; Schlothfeldt, 2009; Schwenkenbecher, 2013, 2017; Wringe, 2005, 2010). In the examples used above, I suggested that we may have collective obligations to mitigate climate change through aggregate emission reductions. But is this really so? Can we – meaning 'humanity,' or the 'global rich,' or 'citizens of industrialized nations' – really have collective obligations to resolve such problems? That is, can individuals forming part of large, dispersed, non-organized groups, have collective obligations to jointly bring about some outcome or perform some action?[28]

One of the challenges of making definitive claims about 'global moral obligations' is that the problems these obligations are supposedly meant to address are usually extremely complex, unlike the fairly simple cases discussed above. This increase in epistemic complexity brings with it a certain ambiguity and vagueness in the ascription of obligations and responsibilities, not just in the collective case, but for individual duties, too.

Having said that, we might say that *some* large-scale collective action problems really are *not* too complex to be addressed by large and dispersed groups with no significant level of organization if they are in a position to produce desirable outcomes by way of aggregating individual actions or their effects.

Here is one example: Herd immunity against some disease – that is, the absence of the pathogen causing it – is a public good that is only produced if in a given population the vaccination rate is above a certain minimum threshold. Where herd immunity is undermined by lower-than-necessary vaccination rates, those who cannot be vaccinated because they are too young, too old, or ill, are at risk of contracting the respective disease, which – in the worst case – may lead to death. Protecting these vulnerable groups from the respective disease is only collectively possible: a sufficiently high percentage of people in that population must be vaccinated. Here it seems easy to stipulate a collective obligation, at least for those groups to whom these causal links are known. Again, public information campaigns can further increase public knowledge of the interrelation of vaccination behavior and deaths from these often-archaic diseases. The collectively optimal pattern of action and individual contributory actions are obvious and they are generally not too costly.

Let me now return to the problem of climate change mitigation. Do we have collective obligations to address this problem through the combined effect of individual action choices? Clearly, climate change mitigation is much more complex a goal than herd immunity, for instance. Let me therefore make a conditional claim: If climate scientists are correct in assuming that aggregate individual behavioral changes can have a significant if not decisive impact on closing the global emissions gap[29] (Blok et al., 2012; Wynes & Nicholas, 2017) then I see no reason why we (capable citizens around the world[30]) should not in principle have an obligation to make those behavioral changes with a view to contributing to large-scale collective action on climate change. However, I believe that public knowledge concerning the gap and the measures to reduce it is currently insufficient for grounding an all-out collective obligation to reduce or eliminate the emissions gap.

The crucial role that direct interaction and communication play in coordinating spontaneous collective endeavors (such as the joint rescue of an injured motorist) and establishing the epistemic conditions for we-framing (and agency transformation) can potentially be fulfilled by other means, such as public information campaigns, blogs, social media, etc. when it comes to large-scale collective action. However, the latter will usually require greater levels of organization and leadership and where these are absent we may lack the prerequisites for holding collective moral obligations to address these issues.

Acknowledgments

The author gratefully acknowledges financial support from the School of Arts at Murdoch University (2017) and an Oxford Martin Visiting Fellowship by the Oxford Martin School (2017–2018) to conduct research for this chapter. Further thanks go to the editors, Deborah Tollefsen and Saba Bazargan-Forward, for their constructive feedback on earlier drafts of the chapter.

Notes

1 To give just three examples from outside philosophy: Behavioural economists like Michael Bacharach (2006) emphasize the importance of 'team reasoning' in strategic interaction, and evolutionary biologist

Michael Tomasello (Warneken, Chen & Tomasello, 2006) posits the adaptive advantage from 'collective intentionality' in our ancestors' thinking (Olson, 1971).

2 I am referring to group agents as described by List and Pettit (2011) or Tollefsen (2015).

3 I cannot say much more about this without abandoning the required level of generality. How moral obligations as such are grounded is a question that cannot be addressed here. In particular, I will refrain from committing to any 'substantive' moral theory.

4 To jointly have an obligation is a plural moral predicate, much like to play a duet is a plural non-moral predicate.

5 Exceptions include Donald Regan's and Derek Parfit's works (Parfit, 1984; Regan, 1980).

6 See www.telegraph.co.uk/news/worldnews/northamerica/usa/8761446/Trapped-motorcyclist-saved-by-bystanders-who-lifted-burning-car.html. There are countless other examples of strangers collaborating spontaneously to save the life of perfect strangers or to protect them from harm. See for instance www.abc.net.au/news/2014-08-06/man-freed-after-leg-trapped-in-gap-on-perth-train-station/5652486 (both accessed July 7, 2018). I have used structurally similar examples in Schwenkenbecher 2013, 2014, and 2019, and so have a number of other scholars, such as Collins 2013 and Wringe 2016.

7 I am adopting this term from Lawford-Smith (2012).

8 I first introduced this distinction in Schwenkenbecher (2017).

9 Another problem may arise if this turns out to be a wide joint necessity case, because it would then seem that in addition to being individually unable to guarantee the success of the collective endeavor, each passerby is also not strictly speaking necessary for its success. I leave this problem aside here and will return to it later.

10 Consequently, in a case of collective omission, no one would be blameworthy for the failure to free him. Further, if individual contributory obligations are understood as conditional, we run into the problem of mutual release. Simultaneous non-action by all potential contributors voids obligations of the kind 'I ought to help if the others do' (see Goodin 2012).

11 For a more detailed defence of this account, see Schwenkenbecher (2019).

12 An option for acting is 'collectively available' if it is an option for two or more agents acting (or producing an outcome) together, but not something an individual can do (or bring about). For instance, the option of getting married is not available to me as an individual. It is only available to me and another person together.

13 My notion of 'we-reasoning' is equivalent to what Hakli et al. (2010) called 'we-mode reasoning.' It differs from what Gold and Sugden (2007) and Sugden and Gold (2007) call 'team-reasoning' in that it is not a joint (or team) effort.

14 A more detailed account of the difference between I-mode reasoning and we-mode reasoning can be found in Schwenkenbecher (2019).

15 This is a payoff-matrix for a Hi-Lo game. We can easily imagine moral decision-making scenarios that have this structure. Even when each player is ignorant of the other player's choice, it seems obvious that they should pick option A.

		Player 2		
		A	B	
Player 1	A	Hi/Hi	0/0	Hi > Lo > 0
	B	0/0	Lo/Lo	

16 Joint ability is temporal and comes in degrees.

17 This requires at least that agents are able to conceive of a collective pattern of actions, which their own and other agents' individual actions could form part of. It does not require them to believe that others are likely to perform their contributory actions within the pattern, only to think that they could conceive of their individual actions as part of such a pattern. Stemplowska (2016: 286) argues that if we have good reason to believe that other agents are not in a position where they can conceive of their individual contributory actions as forming part of such a collective pattern, then a collective action should be considered unfeasible:

> [A]n action of each of three billion people touching his or her nose next Tuesday is correctly classified as unfeasible because there are not three billion people who could know next Tuesday

how to do it or that their individual contributions are needed. (Of course it remains open that this may become possible in future, in which case the action will become feasible then.)

(Stemplowska, 2016)

18 In a wide joint necessity case, the same clause applies. It must be possible for each to intentionally perform their contributory action, which may mean to refrain from contributing where their contribution is either superfluous or detrimental to the success of the joint endeavor.

19 I cannot go into the debate on collective intentions or 'we-intentions' here. Suffice to say that plural intentions in the minimal sense are not interlocking intentions (of the kind that Michael Bratman (2014) focuses on), but 'independent' individual intentions.

20 A belief that x obtains is *shared* between two agents if each agent believes that x obtains. It is a *common belief* if it is shared *and* if each agent knows that it is shared (first order common belief). See also (Roy & Schwenkenbecher, under review).

21 This is what Scott Shapiro refers to as a 'shared plan' (Shapiro, 2014).

22 One might extend this period of blameless ignorance to the second half of the twentieth century. I am assuming that Svante Arrhenius' discovery of the greenhouse effect towards the end of the nineteenth century was not public knowledge for a long time. However, at the very latest with the adoption of the UNFCCC in Rio de Janeiro in 1992, climate change and the greenhouse effects should have been widely known.

23 It should be noted, though, that Zimmerman is an individualist about moral obligations and would probably not subscribe to the idea of collective obligations defended here.

24 Bacharach (2006) and others (e.g. Butler et al., 2011) insist that we-reasoning involves what they call 'agency transformation.' This means that individuals consider the group the locus of agency, rather than themselves (see also Woodard, 2011).

25 Another way to put this is to say that it depends on which moral reason(s) for action outweigh all others (see e.g. Woodard, 2011).

26 It should be noted that these conditions are jointly sufficient for collective obligations, but are not all necessary. This is because such obligations can also arise in the absence of joint necessity where one person alone can produce a morally optimal outcome or perform the corresponding action, but it is a matter of fairness that another agent (or other agents) help her in doing so. Cases of joint obligations arising from distributive justice rather than joint necessity are not discussed here.

27 Finally, whether or not a *pro-tanto* collective obligation becomes an all-out collective obligation depends on whether or not for the contributing agents there are competing overriding (collective or individual) duties. Or, to put it differently, it depends on whether or not the group-based reasons for contributing to the collective endeavor weigh heavier than other reasons (on group-based reasons for action see Woodard, 2017).

28 This question is different from that of ascribing duties to group agents such as states or international organizations. The question of duties of the global citizenry (if you like) or humanity arises not least, because those (group) agents whom we would consider principally responsible are failing in resolving problems such as climate change or global poverty. However, I do not claim that states' and other political agents' failure to resolve these problems is the only or even the major source of joint obligations to address large-scale collective action problems.

29 The emissions gap is the gap between the level of emission reductions required for limiting global warming to maximally 2°C (with a high probability) and the emission reductions states have currently committed to (UNEP, 2017).

30 A fully-fledged argument for this conclusion would need to specify who counts as 'capable' in this regard. My first instinct would be to suggest anyone who has the economic, intellectual, and epistemic capacity to make such behavioral changes without incurring disproportionate costs. Obviously, this need not be tied to certain nationalities – it may well be that a rich person from Zambia is more 'capable' in this sense than a poor person from the United States.

References

Bacharach, M. (2006). *Beyond Individual Choice: Teams and Frames in Game Theory*. Princeton: Princeton University Press.

Björnsson, G. (2014). Essentially Shared Obligations. *Midwest Studies in Philosophy*, *38*(1), 103–120.

Blok, K., Hohne, N., van der Leun, K., & Harrison, N. (2012). Bridging the Greenhouse-gas Emissions Gap. *Nature Climatic Change*, *2*(7), 471–474.
Bratman, M. (2014). *Shared Agency: A Planning Theory of Acting Together.* Oxford: Oxford University Press.
Butler, D. (2012). A Choice for 'Me' or for 'Us'? Using We-Reasoning to Predict Cooperation and Coordination in Games. *Theory and Decision*, *73*(1), 53–76. doi:10.1007/s11238-011-9270-7
Butler, D. J., Burbank, V. K., & Chisholm, J. S. (2011). The Frames Behind the Games: Player's Perceptions of Prisoners Dilemma, Chicken, Dictator, and Ultimatum Games. *The Journal of Socio-Economics*, *40*(2), 103–114.
Collins, S. (2013). Collectives' Duties and Collectivisation Duties. *Australasian Journal of Philosophy*, *91*(2), 231–248.
Dietz, T., Gardner, G. T., Gilligan, J., Stern, P. C., & Vandenbergh, M. P. (2009). Household Actions Can Provide a Behavioral Wedge to Rapidly Reduce US Carbon Emissions. *Proceedings of the National Academy of Sciences*, *106*(44), 18452–18456.
Giubilini, A., Birkl, P., Douglas, T., Savulescu, J., & Maslen, H. (2017). Taxing Meat: Taking Responsibility for One's Contribution to Antibiotic Resistance. *Journal of Agricultural and Environmental Ethics*, *30*(2), 179–198.
Gold, N., & Sugden, R. (2007). Collective Intentions and Team Agency. *Journal of Philosophy*, *104*(3), 109–137.
Goodin, R. (2012). Excused by the Unwillingness of Others? *Analysis*, 72(1), pp. 18–24.
Hakli, R., Miller, K., & Tuomela, R. (2010). Two Kinds of We-Reasoning. *Economics and Philosophy*, *26*(3), 291–320.
Held, V. (1970). Can a Random Collection of Individuals be Morally Responsible? *Journal of Philosophy*, *67*(14), 471–481.
Isaacs, T. L. (2011). *Moral Responsibility in Collective Contexts*. Oxford University Press.
Lawford-Smith, H. (2012). The Feasibility of Collectives' Actions. *Australasian Journal of Philosophy*, 90(3): 453–67.
Lawford-Smith, H. (2015). What 'We'? *Journal of Social Ontology*, *1*(2), 225–249.
Le Morvan, P. (2011). On Ignorance: A Reply to Peels. *Philosophia*, *39*(2), 335–344.
List, C. & Pettit, P. (2011). *Group Agency: The Possibility, Design, and Status of Corporate Agents*. Oxford: Oxford University Press.
Ludwig, K. (2016). *From Individual to Plural Agency: Collective Action I.* Oxford: Oxford University Press.
May, L. (1992). Collective Inaction and Responsibility. In *Sharing Responsibility* (pp. 105–124). Chicago University Press.
Miller, S. (2010). *The Moral Foundations of Social Institutions. A Philosophical Study*. New York: Cambridge University Press.
Olson, M. (1971). *The Logic of Collective Action: Public Goods and the Theory of Groups*. Cambridge, MA: Harvard University Press.
Parfit, D. (1984). Five Mistakes in Moral Mathematics. In *Reasons and Persons* (Vol. 1, pp. 55–83). Oxford: Clarendon Press.
Peels, R. (2010). What is Ignorance? *Philosophia*, *38*(1), 57–67.
Peels, R. (2016). *Perspectives on Ignorance From Moral and Social Philosophy*. Routledge.
Pinkert, F. (2014). What We Together Can (Be Required to) Do. *Midwest Studies in Philosophy*, *38*(1), 187–202.
Regan, D. (1980). *Utilitarianism and Co-Operation* (Vol. 33). Oxford University Press.
Rosen, G. (2003). IV—Culpability and Ignorance. *Proceedings of the Aristotelian Society (Hardback)*, *103*(1), 61–84.
Roy, O., & Schwenkenbecher, A. (under review). Joint Agency, Loose Groups, and Pooled Knowledge.
Schlothfeldt, S. (2009). *Individuelle oder gemeinsame Verpflichtung?: das Problem der Zuständigkeit bei der Behebung gravierender Übel*. Paderborn: Mentis.
Schwenkenbecher, A. (2013). Joint Duties and Global Moral Obligations. *Ratio*, *26*(3), 310–328.
Schwenkenbecher, A. (2014). Joint Moral Duties. *Midwest Studies in Philosophy*, *38*(1), 58–74.
Schwenkenbecher, A. (2017). Gemeinsame Hilfspflichten, Weltarmut und kumulative Handlungen. *Zeitschrift für Praktische Philosophie*, *4*(1), 123–150.
Schwenkenbecher, A. (2018). Making Sense of Collective Moral Obligations: A Comparison of Current Approaches. In T. Isaacs, K. Hess, & V. Igneski (Eds.), *Collectivity: Ontology, Ethics and Social Justice* (pp. 109–132). Rowman & Littlefield.

Schwenkenbecher, A. (2019). Collective Moral Obligations: 'We-reasoning' and the Perspective of the Deliberating Agent. *The Monist, 102*(2), xx.

Shapiro, S. (2014). Massively Shared Agency. In M.Vargas & G.Yaffe (Eds.), *Rational and Social Agency. Essays on the Philosophy of Michael Bratman* (pp. 257–293). Oxford: Oxford University Press.

Stemplowska, Z. (2016). Feasibility: Individual and Collective. *Social Philosophy and Policy, 33*(1–2), 273–291.

Sugden, R. (2015). Team Reasoning and Intentional Cooperation for Mutual Benefit. *Journal of Social Ontology, 1*(1), 143–166.

Sugden, R., & Gold, N. (2007). Theories of Team Agency. In F. Peter & H. B. Schmid (Eds.), *Rationality and Commitment*. Oxford: Oxford University Press.

Tollefsen, D. (2015). *Groups as Agents*. Cambridge, UK: Polity Press.

Tomasello, M. (2014). *A Natural History of Human Thinking*. Cambridge, MA;London, England: Harvard University Press.

Tuomela, R. (2013). *Social Ontology: Collective Intentionality and Group Agents*. New York: Oxford University Press.

UNEP. (2017). *The Emissions Gap Report 2017.A UN Environment Synthesis Report*. Retrieved from https://wedocs.unep.org/bitstream/handle/20.500.11822/22070/EGR_2017.pdf?isAllo...

Warneken, F., Chen, F. and Tomasello, M. (2006). Cooperative Activities in Young Children and Chimpanzees. *Child Development, 77*, 640–663.

Woodard, C. (2003). Group-based Reasons for Action. *Ethical Theory and Moral Practice, 6*(2), 215–229.

Woodard, C. (2011). Rationality and the Unit of Action. *Review of Philosophy and Psychology, 2*(2), 261–277.

Woodard, C. (2017). Three Conceptions of Group-Based Reasons. *Journal of Social Ontology* (Vol. 3, pp. 107).

Wringe, B. (2005). Needs, Rights, and Collective Obligations. *Royal Institute of Philosophy Supplement, 80*(57), 187–207.

Wringe, B. (2010). Global Obligations and the Agency Objection. *Ratio, 23*(2), 217–231.

Wringe, B. (2016). Collective Obligations: Their Existence, Their Explanatory Power, and Their Supervenience on the Obligations of Individuals. *European Journal of Philosophy, 24*(2), 472–497.

Wynes, S., & Nicholas, K. A. (2017). The Climate Mitigation Gap: Education and Government Recommendations Miss the Most Effective Individual Actions. *Environmental Research Letters, 12*(7), 074024.

Zimmerman, M. J. (1996). *The Concept of Moral Obligation*. Cambridge: Cambridge University Press.

Zimmerman, M. J. (2014). *Ignorance and Moral Obligation*. Oxford: Oxford University Press.

Zimmerman, M. J. (2016). Ignorance as a Moral Excuse. In R. Peels (Ed.), *Perspectives on Ignorance From Moral and Social Philosophy* (pp. 77–94). Routledge.

19

INDIVIDUAL RESPONSIBILITY FOR COLLECTIVE ACTION

Michael Skerker

19.1 Introduction

This chapter will develop standards for assessing individual moral responsibility for collective action. In some cases, these standards expand a person's responsibility beyond what she or he would be responsible for if performing the same physical behavior outside of a group setting. I will argue that structural differences between two ideal types of groups—organizations and goal-oriented collectives—largely determine the baseline moral responsibility of group members for the group's collective action. (Group members can be more or less responsible for collective action beyond that baseline due to personal qualities like knowledge of the intended collective outcome.) The same individual physical behavior can make the member of a goal-oriented collective responsible for the entire collective action to an equal degree with her fellow group members, whereas the typical organization member is only responsible for his contributory action.

I will proceed with a culpability standard of responsibility in mind when I discuss individual responsibility. Many agree that culpability is the most morally satisfying standard of individual responsibility because actors are fully able to control the behavior for which they are deemed responsible. It follows that people can be instructed how they ought to behave; they can intentionally aim at that behavior; and they take conscious steps to reform if they miss the mark.

After the problem of assessing individual responsibility for collective action is exemplified with a thought experiment in section 19.2 and some key definitions are provided in section 19.3, the heart of the argument about individual responsibility in goal-oriented collectives and organizations will be presented in sections 19.4 and 19.5, respectively.

19.2 Problem Statement

Assigning individual responsibility for collective action can be a challenging proposition. I am going to use a thought experiment involving collective violent action, juxtaposing the actions of a service member and a militia member, to discuss the ideas of this chapter, but these ideas could be expressed by juxtaposing formal and informal groups in any arena, e.g. hospital employees vs. Good Samaritans rendering aid, fire-fighters vs. neighbors cooperating to put out a house fire, etc.

> Country A is fighting an unjust, aggressive war against country B while also conducting peace-keeping operations in nearby country C, which has been wracked by tribal violence.
>
> Archer is a mechanic in country C who fixes vehicles for one of the tribal militias. He eagerly volunteered to participate in its genocidal campaigns against rival tribes and was assigned to fix the militia's vehicles.
>
> Baker is a helicopter mechanic serving aboard country A's aircraft carrier, which is off the coast equidistant from B and C. He (with others) is responsible for daily maintenance on four of the squadron's attack helicopters, # 601–604. He is never informed about the missions of the various helicopter crews and performs daily maintenance on the copters regardless of their missions. A given copter may perform very different missions day to day.
>
> On a given day, copter 601 attacks enemy troops in country B; 602 bombs a hospital in country B; 603 supports troops protecting villagers from a militia in country C; and 604 is grounded, in need of spare parts.

It is at first difficult to assess Archer and Baker's responsibility for the collective actions they help to causally advance. It is not plausible to think that any level of causal contribution makes a contributor fully morally responsible for any ensuing unjust collective action. Through minute causal connections, nearly everyone in the world would be responsible for nearly every collective unjust act. It is similarly implausible to exonerate all except the direct perpetrators of unjust collective action, since all the violent actors in the above case depend on support personnel in order to be effective. Further, a slightly different argument exonerating all who act in complex collectives to perpetrate unjust acts would implausibly imply that all one needs to do to avoid blame for an unjust act is to bring an accomplice. Clearly, it is absurd to assert that an assault victim could blame her single assailant but could not blame anyone if beaten by a group of three people (Cooper 1972: 140; Erskine 2003: 21).

Having set aside the two most extreme arguments let us consider the two mechanics' contributions. Archer made possible some of the genocidaires' transportation. Is he then morally responsible for everything they did after they left his garage? He knew they planned to murder villagers, but Archer did not kill anyone; all he did was fix trucks. There were other mechanics working for the militia too, and the militia could have gotten to its destination eventually with different vehicles. If Archer is responsible or partly responsible for genocide, is he also responsible for things he (and maybe the other militia members) did not know they planned to do? If one of the genocidaires in Archer's truck also decides to desecrate a religious shrine while he is in the village, is Archer responsible for that "deviation" from the mission as well? Where does Archer's responsibility terminate? Is Archer responsible for child abuse if a genocidaire returns to his home village on Archer's truck after the massacre and beats his son?

Baker seems even farther removed from wrongdoing. Like Archer, all he did was fix some engines. Yet unlike Archer, he did not know any of the missions the helicopters were executing; as such he could not have intended his causal contribution to be in furtherance of a particular mission. Further, he did not have Archer's evil motive of contributing toward an unjust collective action. He was acting under orders, in an organization dependent on obedience for efficient functioning, which he plausibly believes is a good and vital institution. Yet helicopters cannot fly unless they are maintained by aviation mechanics. So is Baker responsible for a) his repairs alone, b) the lawful, but possible immoral, killing of enemy troops, c) the unlawful and immoral bombing of a hospital, d) the unjust war as a whole, d) saving villagers from a militia; or e) combinations of the above? Generally speaking, are members of groups responsible for their immediate individual actions, the proximate joint actions they advance with the help of their immediate sub-group, the ultimate large-scale action resulting from the coordinated action of the entire group, or all or two of the above? Further, how does the level of their personal knowledge or intentionality regarding the proximate and ultimate actions affect their responsibility for them?

19.3 Two Types of Groups

Distinguishing between two kinds of groups, organizations and goal-oriented collectives, will help assess Archer and Baker's moral responsibility for the collective actions they help to causally advance. As we will see, differences in these two ideal-type groups' internal structures will permit a theorist to ascribe the injustice of the collective action the group perpetrates in different ways to the group members.

Organizations are long-standing, formally-constituted groups with stable roles and rotating personnel, like companies, the military, religious orders, and government departments. The structure of organizations will typically determine what their members know, and therefore can intend, with respect to the collective actions the organization performs. *Atypical* organization members will know or intend things about the collective actions, in a sense, in spite of the organization's structure.

A key aspect of organizations important for us to address in order to understand the role played by organization members' individual intentions and motives is what some theorists call a corporate intention (French 1987; Isaacs 2011; Pettit 2003). Corporate intentions are not simply an aggregate of the group members' intentions, for two reasons. First, individuals cannot intend complex collective actions. If an intention is a kind of mental event that directs a specific, deliberate action, then an individual person cannot, strictly speaking, intend to win a baseball game; build a cruise ship; or win a war. These ends can only be accomplished through the collective action of groups. As we will see, a person can intend to do something to *contribute* to a collective end and can be motivated to see the fulfillment of the collective end.

Second, something functionally similar to an individual's intention is created through the organization's unique protocols, irreducible to any one organization member's intention. These protocols are what Seumas Miller calls "joint mechanisms" or Peter French calls "corporate internal decision structures" (Miller 2001: 174; French 1987: 143; Pettit 2003: 182; Isaacs 2011: 68), sets of interlocking behaviors such as a decision-making procedures or protocols for transmitting orders used to coordinate actions and bring about certain types of outcomes within organizations. Joint mechanisms allow for variations based on the participants' varying desires and inputs. For example, company bylaws might indicate that certain decisions are to be made by a board of directors through a vote, but each board member is free to vote as she wishes (Miller 2006: 174–6). It follows that the mechanism's output (a subordinates' carrying out orders, the outcome of a vote, etc.) can be contrary to some of the participants' preferences. Importantly, the resultant corporate intention may not reflect the personal intention of any of the participants (Isaacs 2011: 30).

Corporate intentions are functionally identical with human intentions in the sense that they have the same relation to corporate actions as individual intentions do to individual actions (Isaacs 2011: 30, 37; Pettit 2003: 179, 182–3). They lead the collective to act. A business's corporate intention, set by a planning team, such as "Model 4032 of item X will be produced in time for the third quarter" directs employees to engage in specific actions which will interact in such a way that the business produces model 4032 in the third quarter (described further below). The term "policy" might be profitably substituted for "corporate intention" but I will defer to received usage. To be clear, organizations are not super-persons with corporate urges, corporate emotions, and the like. Whatever we wish to call them: these intentions, "intentions," or policies are corporate in the sense that they are irreducible to the human intentions of any one group member.

Apart from organizations, much group action takes place in another kind of group relevant to our concern with group responsibility since it is a group voluntarily formed in order to accomplish some goal. A "goal-oriented collective" is an ad hoc group assembled by its members for the accomplishment of a particular shared goal—like a group of campers, picnickers, or bank robbers (Isaacs 2011: 24). Unlike organizations, characteristic members in goal-oriented collectives know the collective end the group exists to bring about and intend to make causal contributions in order to bring about that end because they are motivated to see its fruition. Whereas typical organization members have their knowledge of, and intentions toward, the organization's collective actions framed by the structure of the group, the influence between members' subjective states and the group structure flows the other way in goal-oriented collectives. Such groups get their characteristic features from their founding members' (and similarly disposed entrants') horizontally coordinated, meshing intentions to perform actions contributing toward the commonly identified collective end (Bratman 1999) and their identical motives to bring about the collective end that constitutes the group's raison d'etre. There may be ambiguous cases where ad hoc groups become more formalized over time and take on more of the qualities of organizations. I will refer to goal-oriented collectives in what follows as an ideal type. I do not claim that these are the only two types of groups, but these two clearly cover much of the collective contexts for action.

19.4 Responsibility for Ultimate Collective Actions in Goal-Oriented Collectives

Having discussed the difference between organizations and goal-oriented collectives, the next task is to ask if members of these groups can be individually responsible for their collective action and if the different structures of the group make a difference for member responsibility. For example, is Archer responsible for genocide, for the murders perpetrated by the genocidaires ferried on the particular trucks he fixed, or merely for fixing some truck engines? Is Baker responsible for fixing engines (his individual action), for airstrikes (a proximate collective action), or for the war (the ultimate collective action)?

We need to consider if the collective actions of organizations and goal-oriented collectives can be scaled down in such a way that the full moral weight of the collective action is present in the contributory action. I will discuss goal-oriented collectives first. The assassination of Julius Caesar is a familiar and easily imagined example of a goal-oriented collective action. I will use it as a reference for what follows. The collective action of a group of senators stabbing Caesar can be scaled down for the purpose of moral consideration to a single contributing action of one senator stabbing Caesar. We have no problem assessing each member's culpability for the collective action when we can scale down a collective action like this one that is the aggregate of largely identical actions. A culpability standard for individual action looks at the actor's power, knowledge, intention, and motive. Specifically, a culpability standard considers the actor's power to plan, commit, and complete an action; his knowledge (or awareness) of his action and its likely outcome; his personal intention to commit the action; and his motive to bring about the associated end. Such a standard finds sufficient material to analyze in the person of each senator to deem him culpable for the assassination. We come to the same conclusion of culpability for assassination whether we analyze a senator acting in concert with others or a senator assassinating Caesar on his own. Each Roman senator voluntarily performs a physical action in concert with others' identical performances—an individual action sufficient on its own to kill Caesar—fully aware that stabbing can lead to death; intending to stab him; and hoping he dies as a result.

It is important to note for what follows, that it is not the case that each senator would be culpable for assassination only in the event that each senator's contributory action was a lethal blow. Due to the nature of the collective action, each conspiring senator is culpable for murder even if his contributory was a non-lethal action, either for it being a non-lethal stabbing or it not being an act of violence at all. Had one of the conspirators acted alone in these cases, he would be culpable for assault, attempted assassination, or no crime at all. Yet operating as part of a cabal, he is culpable for assassination even if his sword thrust only grazed the dictator or if he only smuggled the swords into the Senate since he knowingly and intentionally joined a group that intended to kill Caesar and which did kill Caesar. While the case is intuitively clearer when the constituent physical behaviors are identical, culpability is equally shared even when members contribute diverse physical behaviors to the collective end.[1] When a person who wishes to achieve an outcome that is only possible through group cooperation knowingly joins a group expressly dedicated to the singular achievement of that end, he is using that group as a kind of instrument to achieve an end he values. Other group members act with him and in his name even when he is not directly contributing to a joint project since they would not be acting but for the existence of the group and the contributions of all its members. He should thereby be held responsible for everything the group does that is in line with the features that commended themselves to his membership—even if he did not know about the specific joint action in question (Kutz 2000: 122, 144, 155, 157; Bazargan 2013: 124; Narveson 2002: 191–2; Feinberg 1991: 62; Mellema 2006: 171; Runciman 2003: 47; Sadler 2006: 139; Fain 1972: 80).

Let us return to our thought experiment involving the mechanics. Archer wants to destroy the hated ethnic group; joins a militia he knows is bent on that end; and intends to fix engines as a contributory action furthering genocide. He does not necessarily know where the truck he fixes will go tomorrow, but knows it will serve the militia's purpose. To anticipate the argument to follow, Archer cannot claim to be ignorant of his group's actions in the way that someone in a large organization can reasonably claim ignorance of his group's action. Whereas an organization like a corporation or military may be engaged in activities broadly characterized as "generating profits" or "serving the state," the size, complexity, and compartmentalization of organizations blind most participants to the specific collective actions the organization performs. The breadth of the organization's general mission also prevents the theorist from assuming that participants' motives for contributing their work product is morally dubious since the broad corporate mission does not have the obvious negative moral status like that of a more narrowly-tailored group like a genocidal militia. It thus seems important to follow Isaacs in limiting a charge of complicity to entrants/recruits to goal-oriented collectives, excluding entrants/recruits to organizations (cf. Kutz 2000: 157; Bazargan 2013: 187).

Is Archer more or less responsible for genocide than the other members of the militia? It may be descriptively helpful to categorize different types of complicity within a group (e.g. recruiter, facilitator, encourager, etc.) (Mellema 2006). Yet I think it is appropriate to assign equal moral responsibility to all causal contributors rather than identify different levels of responsibility with different job descriptions in a goal-oriented collective. Responsibility for the collective action of a goal-oriented collective can be assigned in this way because all the traditional markers of culpability for individual immoral action are met on the part of each group member. While the behavioral aspect of their contributory action may be morally trivial unto itself, the participant's motive to bring about the unjust collective action and participatory intention to do anything to support the group's characteristic activity makes the participant "the inclusive author of the group's actions" (Bazargan, quoting Kutz 2013: 186). Thus, his motive and participatory intention change how we should identify Archer's action, from "fixing the engine" to "participating in genocide." Not only does the collective action depend on Archer's material contribution, but Archer is only fixing engines, rather than doing something more obviously problematic, because he volunteered to do whatever he was best suited to do in order to contribute to the end he shared with others. He joined the militia because he wanted to contribute to its characteristic work of genocide. Had there been enough mechanics, he might have been handed a machete and told to get after it. Archer is equally morally responsible for genocide and can be punished with an equal sentence alongside those who directly killed people.

An exception to this argument about equal responsibility would occur in a scenario where a goal-oriented collective lost some of the transparency that gives it the moral character highlighted here. Imagine a group is formed to support a political candidate: they hand out flyers, make phone calls in his support, etc. A faction within that group begins to engage in violent actions on behalf of the candidate. A member of the group who, reasonably, really had no idea what some of the members were doing would not be responsible for the political violence. It is conceivable that a goal-oriented collective might take on more of the aspects of an organization in this way.

19.5 Responsibility for Ultimate Actions in Organizations

By contrast, the characteristic collective action of organizations, what some call "irreducibly corporate actions," do not scale down to the individual contributory actions retaining the moral character of the macro action (Isaacs 2011; Erskine 2003; Runciman 2003; Fain 1972; Pettit 2003; French 1991; Copp 2006; Cooper 1972). In irreducibly corporate actions, very different contributory actions performed by actors with varying levels of knowledge about the wider enterprise are combined by means of a corporate intention to form a collective action. Bearing in mind a comparison with the scaling down of assassination-by-group to assassination-by-individual, the morally interesting aspects of an organization's actions and its component actions are often lost when we look at a member's contribution to that collective action. The moral character of the collective action is lost amongst its component actions because of the typical member's fractional causal responsibility for collective action, his blinkered epistemic position, and his compelled adoption (explained below) of the organization's corporate intention and motive.

For example, we can see Baker's control over, knowledge of, and intentions with respect to the helicopters' operations are negligible. While his helping to fix the engines is materially necessary for the airstrikes to happen, the repairs do not directly contribute to the airstrikes. He performs daily maintenance on the helicopters whether they are conducting airstrikes, performing patrols, rescuing shipwreck survivors, engaging in training missions, or sitting below deck. Baker does not know anything in particular about the airstrikes. He forms an intention to tighten certain bolts; lube certain valves; and perform computer diagnostics, merely because he was ordered to do so. Absent the actions of thousands of other people, his engine maintenance would have absolutely nothing to do with an airstrike.

One might suspect Baker's intention to fix the engines offers grounds for responsibility for the collective action, which the engine repairs make possible. Individual intentions offer grounds for responsibility for collective action in the case of goal-oriented collectives like the militia. In goal-oriented collectives, the actor forms the intention to perform a contributory act as a conscious contribution to a collective action he joined the collective to see occur. The group may have assigned him a specific task but he joined wanting to do *whatever* he could to contribute to the collective end. As argued in the previous section, this participatory intention is inculpating. In the case of military action and other irreducibly corporate actions though, the service member's intention to perform a contributory action is usually not a self-generated intention but a person-sized segment of the group's corporate intention impressed by others for actions contributing to still other agents' broader ends.

Why can we not claim that Baker is fixing the engine purely of his own volition like a typical member of a goal-oriented collective? Military actions are definitionally those actions consequent to orders passed down through the chain of command (e.g. a Marine playing a video game after returning from patrol is not performing a military action). Baker makes his commanding officer's interpretation and application of the corporate intention of winning the war his own insofar as he is acting as a professional (Isaacs 2011: 29). When people act qua professionals, they act according to their institutional procedures, which in the military context means following the lawful orders of superior officers in one's chain of command. A civilian who snuck aboard the ship and started repairing the helicopter engine simply because he enjoyed tinkering with engines would not be acting as a professional and would not be performing a military action. Thus, the corporate intention of fighting the war does not scale down to a participating service member's individual intention because Baker does not and cannot intend his contributing action as a military professional absent the larger chain of command compelling him to adopt its intention. He would not have the intention to fix the engine were he not in the military and would not have the intention to fix the engine as part of a collective military action were he in the military but not ordered to fix the engine.

This argument about transference of intentions requires further elaboration. How exactly does the corporate intention to win a war get translated into service members' individual intentions to perform specific actions? Given this broad corporate end of winning a particular war set by the president, subsidiary corporate intentions to accomplish subsidiary collective actions like neutralizing the country's air defenses are determined through joint mechanisms in planning cells, wherein a staff of flag officers and their advisers determine the war plans. These decisions are then imposed and communicated throughout the organization according to a particular procedure, at which point group members are institutionally obliged to act according to these directives, which is to say, to act as if the corporate intention was their own. Seumas Miller introduces some technical vocabulary regarding intentions that is helpful here (Miller 2001: 64). Type a) intentions are for the actor's own actions while type c) intentions are for someone other than the intending agent to do something, as when a teacher tells a student to complete an assignment. So the president has a type c) intention that the military defeat the enemy regime. In response, an admiral develops a type a) intention to give an order to move the carrier strike group into position; he also has a type c) intention that the rear admiral in charge of the relevant carrier strike group obeys his command. The rear admiral derives a type a) intention to give orders about particular headings and speeds of the strike group's ships to his subordinates based on his boss's type c) intention. Far down the chain of command, Petty Officer Baker derives a type a) intention to fix an engine consequent to his Senior Chief's type c) intention that he do so.

Not only are the agents' intentions the vicarious vestige of their superiors' intentions, rather than their own, the vector of transmission of these intentions and ends is "pushed" rather than "pulled." It is characterized by compulsion rather than voluntary choice. This vector means that the theorist has no grounds for assuming service members would have intentions for their contributory actions absent the institutional framework of the chain of command. The theorist cannot assume the service member natively has the intention to perform the action causally linking him to the collective action. Shortly, I will address atypical situations where the service member really does have the relevant intention.

A debate between individualist and collectivist philosophers on the subject of social ontology is relevant to this point regarding collective responsibility.[2] Collectivists look to some centralized, top-down structure like a corporate intention to give form and direction to a group whereas individualists see only individuals as having intentions and so whatever "thing" binds together and animates a group must be an abstraction, an aggregate of individual intentions, ideas, or actions. Individualists, in short, see *all* groups as animated in the manner of goal-oriented collectives, even if some collectives have more formal structures, hierarchies, and longevity. The morally interesting elements of a group's knowledge, intention, motive, and actions can always be reduced down, without remainder, to the contributing actions of the group's members.

The individualist picture is correct in the case of goal-oriented collectives like the genocidal militia in country C; the members create and drive the group. We have a sufficient picture of what is animating the collective action if we add up all the sentences describing the individual actions of those within the groups. There is no pre-existing executive command structure shaping and directing the members.[3] In the case of organizational action however, the individualist account does not account for the fact that the military, say, is oriented toward certain ends, and collective decision-making and communication structures like planning cells and chains of command are embedded in the organization before any recruits fill the barracks. Further, a popular political and social theory has inculcated recruits with values that lead them to privilege military role-based reasons over their personal intuitions. Therefore, that which drives service personnel to act on certain reasons is not accounted for when we add up all the sentences of the form "Petty Officer Baker did X after he chose to see his orders as action-guiding."[4] The structure producing the orders and the common reason personnel feel it is compulsory to make those orders action-guiding are not accounted for with this individualist account.

So now having clarified that the full moral weight of the collective action is not necessarily present in the organization member's contributory actions, we need to determine how far someone like Baker's responsibilities do extend. Differences between organizational and goal-oriented collective action set what I will call "the horizon of responsibility" at the *contributory action* for an irreducibly corporate action and at the *collective action* for a goal-oriented collective action for the same physical behavior. The horizon of responsibility is the demarcation of what action the actor might be culpable for. We have already discussed how Archer is equally morally responsible for genocide with the rest of the militia members because of his individual action. Yet Baker's contributory action *on its own* is insufficient to deem him culpable for an unjustified collective action if he is in an unjust war. His contributory action has to be referred to the collective action in order to discern if his material involvement with the unjust war makes him responsible for an unjustified action. For the purpose of assessing culpability, a service member is not committing an individual unjustified action but *contributing to an unjust collective action*. Baker is not performing an "unjust repair" (which would be possible if he deliberately neglected some crucial task out of animus towards the pilot), but "fixing a helicopter's engine in an unjust war." Such an individual contributory action may be morally trivial on its own since the full moral gravity of an irreducibly corporate action is not present in its contributory actions. The contributory action instead gets its moral weight in *reference to* the collective action, dependent on the agent's knowledge of and intentional state with respect to the collective action.

Again, this reference to the collective action contrasts with an individual or goal-oriented collective action in which the individual or contributory action is unjustified by itself. Archer and Baker are performing the same physical behavior but Archer's is richly morally capitalized from the start as "participation in genocide"—and his charge sheet in a court might state as much. Baker is only performing a discrete action of engine repair. The theorist is precluded from making a summary judgment about the culpability of an organizational actor like Baker but instead needs to consider his power, knowledge, and intentionality with respect to the unjust irreducibly corporate action in order to assign culpability for a contributory action. One must ask questions like the following. Does Baker have the freedom to avoid contributing to the unjust war? What does he know about the collective action? Does he intend his contribution to advance the collective action because he wants to see its fruition? How does he interpret the corporate intention of his organization?

With respect to that final question, an organization member's actions are typically more "the organization's" instead of their own, but organization members still have to interpret their orders and exercise discretion in the execution of their role obligations. Therefore, when we look to the individual responsibility of organization members for their contributory actions, we may have occasion to magnify the moral importance of their individual actions beyond the immediate impact of their physical behaviors. We need to take into account both the member's individual attributes and her role responsibilities in order to discern how she occupied the role and executed the task differently than other people in her position. In other words, we should not judge a general in the same way we would a civilian urging a group of people on to violence, but compare her to other generals in similar situations in order to see how she personally interpreted the corporate intention of the army and what creativity and wisdom she brought to her role. Typically, the individual actions of low-ranking organization members will not be morally rich because they are relatively banal unto themselves and because there is little room for the introduction of personal creativity. Higher ranking members' personal actions may be morally weightier because there is more room for the individual's personal moral qualities to play a role interpreting the corporate intention. Giving orders is especially significant as order-givers often have a lot of discretion to convert broad corporate intentions into specific action-guiding directives that in turn create the conditions for subordinates to engage in morally upright or morally defective actions (Skerker 2014: 220). Immoral or negligent orders make the order-giver responsible for what subordinates do pursuant to those orders.

Finally, an organization member *can* be individually responsible for the specific joint projects to which she contributes and/or the broader collective actions of her organization if she atypically knows about the specific unjust actions and contributes to them while motivated to see their fruition. All the requirements of culpability are here met, with participatory intention to be part of a group contributing to a specific collective outcome doing the inculpating work done by individual intention in fraught individual actions. So, for example, Baker can be equally jointly responsible with other knowing members of the crew of helicopter #602 for bombing a hospital if he knows about the effects of his contributory actions and is motivated to bring about the specific unjustified action. He is also equally jointly responsible with other similarly-motivated service members if he intends to contribute to bombing a hospital but does not know that his specific individual action is currently furthering that action. Baker is also equally responsible with other knowing or similarly-motivated personnel for the entire unjust war if he knows it is unjust and is motivated to bring about its unjust ends. In these cases, the organizational member effectively is using the organization like a goal-oriented collective, like an instrument for his personal unjust agenda, doing whatever he can to link his efforts with others to bring about unjust ends he favors.

In conclusion, our attention is drawn to the same potential components of culpability, like power, knowledge, intention, and motive in analysis of irreducibly corporate actions as in analysis of individual actions, but the different features of irreducibly corporate and individual actions or contributions to goal-oriented collective actions indicate different horizons for determining what the individual is responsible for. A close causal connection to the morally fraught action is less important for being deemed responsible for it in goal-oriented collective action than in individual action. We are also less likely to find the requisite levels of knowledge and intentionality to deem someone responsible for irreducibly corporate actions than for individual actions expressed in superficially similar physical behaviors. The contributor to an unjust irreducibly corporate action is potentially responsible for a much greater harm than if he committed an unjustified individual action but is also less likely than an individual actor engaging in identical physical behavior to be liable for *any* unjustified action.

19.6 Conclusion

Organizations are irreducibly responsible for their collective actions. Within an organization, each actor in the chain of command is individually responsible for his unique interpretation of the collective intention and unique contribution to collective action(s). Often, the actions of lower echelon organizational members will tend to be more fully defined by their roles, with higher echelon members freer to add more of their personal expertise and creativity. This account of responsibility is geared to the "ideal" circumstances of an organization in which the member is non-culpably ignorant of the collective action in question and not motivated to see its fruition. The member is morally responsible for the action in the way described in the last section if he actually does know about the specific collective action he materially advances (be it a proximate joint project or the organization's ultimate collective action) and intends his contribution to further that collective action because he is motivated to see its fruition.

A member of a goal-oriented collective is fully morally responsible along with all other members of his group for the collective action, regardless of the extent of his causal contribution or his knowledge of the specific action so long as it is consistent with the general purpose for which he joined the group. It follows that there is a heavier burden on entrants into goal-oriented collectives than into organizations to understand the scope of the group's actions.

Notes

1 Bratman (1999), Toumela (1984), and Gilbert (1989) discuss how group members' intentions mesh in an interdependent manner since one person forms an intention for a component of the collective action only because she knows her comrades are forming intentions to perform other components of the collective action.

2 Individualists describe collective action in terms of individual contributory actions, so that a tango, for example, is understood to consist of the lead dancer doing X and his partner doing Y. At its root, a tango can be fully described using sentences describing one dancer at a time. By contrast, collectivists argue that collective members' behavior can only be intelligibly understood in the context of their collective affiliation, so in this case, each dancer would be described as dancing a tango.

3 A goal-oriented collective might have a hierarchy though it is established by its like-minded members in order to accomplish a particular goal. In country C, tribe members who had come to see a neighboring tribe as an existential threat perhaps decided to "do what had to be done" and nominated some among them, military veterans, to lead the attacks.

4 Jeff McMahan argues that putatively collective actions can be reduced to individual actions with this reasoning, personal communication.

References

Bazargan, S. (2013) "Complicitous Liability in War," *Philosophical Studies* 165, 177–95.

Bratman, M. (1999) *Faces of Intention*, Cambridge: Cambridge University Press.

Cooper, D. (1972) "Responsibility and the System," in P. French (ed), *Individual and Collective Responsibility*, Rochester, VT: Shenkman Books, 133–50.
Cooper, D. (1991) "Collective Responsibility," in L. May and S. Hoffman (eds), *Collective Responsibility: Five Decades of Debate in Theoretical and Applied Ethics*, Lanham, MD: Rowman & Littlefield, 35–46.
Copp, D. (2006) "On the Agency of Certain Collective Entities: An Argument from Normative Autonomy," *Midwest Studies in Philosophy* XXX, 194–221.
Erskine, T. (2001) "Assigning Responsibilities to Institutional Moral Agents: The Case of States and 'Quasi-States.'" *Ethics and International Affairs* 15(2), 67–85.
Erskine, T. (2003) "Assigning Responsibilities to Institutional Moral Agents: The Case of States and 'Quasi-States,'" in T. Erskine (ed), *Can Institutions Have Responsibilities? Collective Moral Agency and International Relations*, New York, NY: Palgrave Macmillan, 19–40.
Fain, H. (1972) "Some Moral Infirmities of Justice," in P. French (ed), 77–92.
Feinberg, J. (1991) "Collective Responsibility," in L. May and S. Hoffman (eds), 53–76.
French, P. (1987) "The Corporation as a Moral Person," in L. May (ed), *The Morality of Groups*, Notre Dame University Press, 133–49.
Gilbert, M. (1989) *On Social Facts*, Princeton: Princeton University Press.
Isaacs, T. (2011) *Moral Responsibility in Collective Contexts*, Oxford: Oxford University Press.
Kutz, C. (2000) *Complicity: Ethics and Law for a Collective Age*, Cambridge: Cambridge University Press.
May, L. (2006) "State Aggression, Collective Liability, and Individual Mens Rea," *Midwest Studies in Philosophy* XXX, 309–24.
Mellema, G. (2006) "Collective Responsibility and Qualifying Actions," *Midwest Studies in Philosophy* XXX, 168–75.
Miller, S. (2001) *Social Action: A Teleological Account*, Cambridge: Cambridge University Press.
Miller, S. (2006) "Collective Moral Responsibility: An Individualist Account," *Midwest Studies in Philosophy* XXX, 176–93.
Narveson, J. (2002) "Collective Responsibility," *The Journal of Ethics* 6, 179–98.
Pettit, P. (2003) "Groups with Minds of Their Own," in F. Schmidtt (ed), *Socializing Metaphysics: The Nature of Social Reality*, Lanham, MD: Rowman & Littlefield, 167–93.
Runciman, D. (2003) "Moral Responsibility and the Problem of Representing the State," in T. Erskine (ed), *Can Institutions Have Responsibilities? Collective Moral Agency and International Relations*, New York: Palgrave Macmillan, 41–50.
Sadler, B. (2006) "Share Intentions and Shared Responsibility," *Midwest Studies in Philosophy* XXX, 115–44.
Skerker, M. (2014) "Seeking a Variable Standard of Individual Moral Responsibility in Organizations," *Ethical Theory and Moral Practice*, 17, 209–22.
Toumela, R. (1984) *A Theory of Social Action*, Dordrecht: D. Reidel Publishers.

20
COLLECTIVE RESPONSIBILITY AND THE ROLE OF NARRATIVE

Cassie Striblen

Imagine a situation where an African American family moves into an historically all white neighborhood. Their home is vandalized, racial slurs are painted in motor oil on their lawn, and they are sent threatening letters until they finally relent and move away. We would classify what happened as a hate crime. Who is morally responsible for this hate crime? Is it simply those who actively vandalized the home and threatened the family, or does responsibility extend further? Is it possible that "white people," as a group, bear some responsibility for the actions of those few active perpetrators? Is it even possible for a large social group, like "white people," to be morally responsible? Or, perhaps many members of a large social group can share responsibility, with each member bearing some portion of the burden? One place to begin looking for answers to such questions is within the philosophical debate over collective responsibility. In what follows, I delve into the debate to show that focusing on narrative might help us better understand responsibility for things like hate crime.[1] I further note how taking a narrative approach affects the issues of collective punishment, collective apology, and collective akrasia.

One common denominator in the debate is this: most participants assume that if groups are to be morally responsible they must mimic individuals in particular ways. Accordingly, how the individual is characterized is crucial as it can impact our understanding of the nature and moral significance of groups. Of course, there are various ways of defining individuals. One promising way, particularly when thinking about issues of moral responsibility, relies on narrative. The basic contours of narrative are very familiar. Narratives are stories that have a protagonist and a plot; these stories are typically divided into fiction (literature) and nonfiction (biography, autobiography, history, etc.). In the current context, our focus is on narrative as the autobiographical stories we create about our experiences that make our actions intelligible. They explain, to others and ourselves, why we do what we do. Such narratives are connected to questions of personal identity and ethics, which can in turn bear on questions of both individual and collective responsibility. In this chapter I provide a brief description of narrative in its connection to these questions, ultimately showing that a narrative understanding of individuals and groups might provide justification for ascriptions of certain kinds of collective responsibility, particularly for shared responsibility among members of large social groups.

20.1 History and Terminology

To situate the relatively new role of narrative in this debate, it is important to begin by clarifying some terms and assumptions. First, when philosophers apply ideas from the study of narrative to their own perennial questions, they employ what we might call a "narrative approach." The narrative approach is varied and includes figures such as Alasdair MacIntyre (1984), Martha Nussbaum (1990), Paul Ricoeur (1994), Richard Rorty (1989), Marya Schechtman (1996), Charles Taylor (1989), and Margaret Urban Walker (1998), among others. While there are legitimate criticisms of the narrative approach,[2] in this chapter I do not attempt to defend the approach itself; instead, I promote the methodological value of implementing such an approach when exploring questions of group-related moral responsibility.

Broadly speaking, there are three primary objections to the notion that groups are central to questions of moral responsibility. First, there is the idea that groups are nothing more than an aggregation of individuals and do not have minds of their own with which to form intentions; therefore, any responsibility simply disperses to the relevant individuals who actively perpetrated the harm in question. We can call this the reductive objection. Second, if group responsibility distributes equally to all members, regardless of their connection to the harm in question and simply in virtue of membership, then group responsibility is obviously unfair. We can call this the normative objection. Third, whether responsibility distributes to members or not, ascribing group responsibility is liable to exacerbate rather than repair intergroup harms. This is the practical objection. It will be my task here to propose how taking a narrative approach can help address all three objections.

To date, the debate over collective responsibility has largely concentrated on the first objection and the question of whether a group can form intentions, thereby qualifying as a moral agent in its own right. Following Peter French, groups have been divided into simple "aggregates" that do not survive varying membership (e.g., mobs, people on the beach right now) or more complex "conglomerates" that have a decision procedure for forming intentions (e.g., mission statements, operating manuals, etc.) and whose "identity is not exhausted by the conjunction of the identities of the persons in the organization" (1984: 13). Thus, the groups under consideration are typically highly organized (e.g., committees, corporations, nations) or are small "plural" groups (e.g., two people moving a piano).[3] Those who find that some groups can count as agents may be labeled "collectivists" and those who deny this may be labeled "individualists." Both individualists and collectivists seem to agree that groups must be more than simple aggregates if they are to factor into our determinations of moral responsibility.

Some collectivists assert that groups can qualify as full agents and potentially be morally responsible in a manner that is over and above their members (i.e., the non-distributive form).[4] Early in the debate, the phrase "collective responsibility" was typically applied only to the non-distributive form; however, the debate has evolved to include many other forms of group-related moral responsibility. For example, one can argue for a form of group-related responsibility that distributes to members (i.e., shared responsibility).[5] Shares might be distributed equally or they might be distributed in proportion to one's relationship to the harm. When speaking about both non-distributive and distributive forms, I use the more generic phrase "group responsibility." Non-distributive forms typically require that the group itself qualify as an agent, while importantly, distributive forms do not.[6] Nonetheless, the distributive and shared form, if it is to apply to large groups, must still explain how these groups are more than simple aggregates to address fully the reductive objection; otherwise, shared moral responsibility may be limited to small groups of active perpetrators who share an intention to do harm (e.g., co-conspirators in a bank robbery, only the active perpetrators of a hate crime). Moreover, the defender of shared responsibility must have a means of addressing the normative and practical objections. As I indicate below, shifting to a narrative approach can help counter all three objections to shared responsibility, especially for larger groups that do not neatly fit French's taxonomy. Indeed, many social groups that interest us—races, genders, ethnicities, religions—do not seem to fit. These intermediate sorts of groups do not have explicit decision procedures yet they do survive varying membership and achieve a kind of stability over time. How do we interpret such groups when it comes to questions of moral responsibility? Taking a narrative approach can provide one answer.

20.2 Narrative Construction of Individuals and Groups

Again, one assumption of the debate over group responsibility has been that the individual is the paradigmatic moral agent, which a group must mimic if it is to qualify as a moral agent. Although my view does leave room for such a possibility, and while Gallagher and Tollefsen (2017) and Tollefsen and Gallagher (2017) appear to push in this direction, I do not use narrative to pursue full moral agency for groups. Instead, I want to demonstrate that groups can be more than simple aggregations of individuals such that shared responsibility among members of larger social groups emerges. Put simply, I hope to show that the group structure can link members to harm in such a way that many come to share responsibility for it. In any case, given the way the nature of individuals frames the overall debate, it is important to investigate some of our assumptions about individuals.

Individuals are often referred to with the terms "persons," "subjects," "selves," or "agents," and I use these terms interchangeably here. According to Diana Tietjens Meyers, there are five "widely espoused and widely debated conceptions" of the individual moral subject (2004: 290). They are: the Kantian unitary self, the communitarian social self, the psychodynamic divided self, the feminist relational self, and the embodied self (293). We do not have space here to explore all the details of these five common views. What Meyers points out in her discussion is that each view highlights an important aspect of human experience; however, no single view can fully explain our experience. She asserts that we cannot properly acknowledge the essential complexity of moral subjects if we adopt one view and exclude all others. A narrative view of individuals, according to Meyers, has the potential to accommodate aspects of all five common views and in that way better represents our complexity (293).

In the group responsibility debate, the Kantian and communitarian views have been prominent. The Kantian view emphasizes universal reason in moral decision making and denies that group membership would impact such reasoning. In his discussion of group responsibility Jan Narveson (2002) adopts a Kantian view. In contrast, when adopting communitarian views, we may emphasize relationships, including group memberships, in the process of moral decision making. Larry May's (1992) view of individuals is broadly communitarian. It is no great surprise, then, that Narveson is opposed to group responsibility while May is in favor of it. It appears that embracing any one view of the individual can bias our perspective on group responsibility. If, as Meyers suggests, the narrative view can incorporate the sometimes conflicting concerns of all five moral subjects, then it has the potential to balance out the biases inherent in adopting any one view and may enable greater impartiality in our judgments of group responsibility. Therefore, it is to the narrative conception of subjects we now turn.

The notion that narrative is central to our experience as moral subjects arises in the context of the issue of personal identity, that is, how one remains the same self over time and despite change. It also arises more directly in ethics proper as a feature which contributes to one's counting as an intentional agent. The narrative conception of subjects I rely upon was initially developed by Marya Schechtman (1996) in relation to personal identity, and it has been extended in various directions by Diana Tietjens Meyers (2004), Hilde Lindemann Nelson (2001), and others. The basic idea behind a narrative conception of subjects is that subjects are fundamentally story-telling beings; our stories, even if they contain misperceptions and contradictions, enable us to explain and make sense of our actions across time. Schechtman's "narrative self-constitution view" proposes that

> individuals constitute themselves as persons by coming to think of themselves as persisting subjects who have had experience in the past and will continue to have experiences in the future, taking certain experiences as theirs. Some, but not all, individuals weave stories of their lives, and it is their doing so which makes them persons. On this view a person's identity…is constituted by the content of her self-narrative, and the traits, actions, and experiences included in it are, by virtue of that inclusion, hers.
>
> *(1996: 94)*

Schechtman holds that narratives, including past experiences and future hopes, are the means by which an individual generates a personal identity, a unique and enduring self. She recognizes that while narratives cannot supply the ontological basis of personhood (otherwise fictional characters would count as persons), they do enable us to interpret and to weave together the characteristics (beliefs, values, experiences) that make us who we are across time. The process of interpretation results in a standard image of the self against which we can measure the consistency of our beliefs and actions.

Importantly for our purposes, the narrative process does more than define and establish a self. It also provides the background for our moral deliberations. Schechtman clarifies that

> creating an autobiographical narrative is not simply composing a story of one's life—it is organizing and processing one's experience in a way that presupposes an implicit understanding of oneself as an evolving protagonist. A large part of what that entails is that the remembered past and the anticipated future exert an influence on the present—that they serve as its interpretive context, the lens through which it is experienced.
>
> *(142)*

Our practical and moral deliberations, and subsequent actions, are influenced by the narrative understanding of ourselves that we have created. It is in light of our past actions and future hopes that we consider our present options. We generate intentions and take actions that are sometimes inconsistent with our narrative understandings, of course, but the baseline narrative is there as a kind of standard measure. In addition, Meyers has argued that as we weave together a narrative with moral overtones, we can choose whether to emphasize Kantian, communitarian, psychodynamic, feminist, or embodied considerations; indeed, we can emphasize them all in our narrative, even when they contradict, making the narrative conception of selves more complex and in some sense more realistic than any one view alone (2004: 293).

Thus, if we accept the interpretations of Schechtman and Meyers, the benefits of adopting a narrative conception of individual moral subjects when considering group responsibility are twofold. First, we can embrace our essential complexity and temper the biases of the different standard conceptions of the moral subject. Second, we can readily see how narrative is a necessary feature of moral agency. Note that from a metaphysical perspective, one may have a narrative but no body (e.g., a fictional character), or one may have a body but no narrative (e.g., infants, those with advanced dementia). In either case, we would not assign moral agency or responsibility. It appears that, perhaps in addition to other things, both a body and a narrative are required for moral agency and responsibility. To demonstrate that something lacks a narrative may be a method for showing that it cannot be responsible.

At the moment, we have in hand a narrative conception of individual moral subjects. What I want to show next, by drawing on Nelson, is one process for how narrative individuals and narrative groups are constructed. In her work, Nelson connects narrative to identity politics and sees narrative construction and reconstruction of identities as central to the process of recognition for members of marginalized groups. She discusses individual moral subjects in terms of their personal identities. For Nelson, "identities are the understandings we have of ourselves and others" (2001: 6). Nelson argues that our identities, as conceived by ourselves and by others, can impact agency tremendously. To illustrate, she offers the example of having the identity of a doctor or surgeon. If one has such an identity, then one is trained for and allowed to cut into live human beings—otherwise, that action is prohibited. Thus, identity clearly affects moral agency and responsibility. Moreover, our identities require some confirmation from people and records outside ourselves; we cannot simply choose any identity.[7]

On Nelson's view, we use narrative to craft our personal identities; however, the process is not entirely under our control. We construct our personal identities by weaving together collections of various stories where the self is the protagonist but the self is not always the author. As she explains it

> personal identities consist of a connective tissue of narratives—some constant, others shifting over time—which we weave around the features of ourselves and our lives that matter most to us. The significant things I've done and experienced, my more important characteristics, the roles and relationships I care about most, the values that matter most to me—these form the relatively stable points around which I construct the narratives that constitute the sense I make of myself. The (backward-looking) stories of my connection to these things over time are explanatory: they explain to me who I am and it's this that is my own contribution to my personal identity. But my identity is also constituted by the stories other people construct around the things about me that seem most important to them. From neither the first nor the third-person perspective are the stories that constitute an identity entirely original; many contain stock plots and character types borrowed from narratives that circulate widely in the culture.
>
> *(72)*

Nelson elaborates on this description by offering three processes that are used to construct personal identities, what she calls first-person narrative activity, third-person narrative activity, and a drawing on master narratives. First-person narrative is the process over which the individual has the most control. It involves emphasizing what I take to be most important about me, especially the choices and actions that I feel reflect my deepest values. Third-person narrative activity happens when others tell stories (true or not) about us. In relation to groups, third-person narrative activity can come from others inside our groups, what I call "internal" narrative activity, or from others outside our groups, what I call "external" narrative activity. Internal narrative activity, especially for powerful groups, tends toward the positive (e.g., glowing family or national histories) while external narrative activity tends toward the negative (e.g., stereotypes). In either case, others are contributing to our narratives and our identities without our permission or control. Indeed, as Alasdair MacIntyre correctly remarked, "we are never more (and sometimes less) than co-authors of our own narratives ... .We enter upon a stage which we did not design and we find ourselves part of an action that was not of our own making" (1984: 218). Our lack of full executive control does not mean we lack all accountability for our identities, however.

The third process for constructing personal identities involves drawing on master narratives and is done at both the first and third-person levels. According to Nelson, master narratives are "the stories found lying about in our culture that serve as summaries of socially shared understanding" (6). Some obvious examples include classic literature and film, fairy tales, famous court cases and news stories, mythology, religious stories, and so on. These master narratives function as "repositories of common norms" and as such "exercise a certain authority over our moral imaginations and play a role in informing our moral intuitions" (6). They are publicly available and serve as a kind of shorthand for describing and judging ourselves and others. As Nelson points out, there are implicit and sometimes explicit norms in the master narratives that "tell us how we are supposed to understand the people (including ourselves) to whom we apply them" (85).

Master narratives characterize types, not tokens, so they apply to individuals *as members* of certain groups. The norms within a master narrative apply to me as an individual because I somehow fit a particular type or belong in a particular group (e.g., as a "woman" I cannot wear a tuxedo to a formal event without violating a norm). Certain behaviors are expected of individuals because they are members of certain groups. I can belong to a group according to my own estimation, or perhaps only in the estimation of others. I can act in ways that comply with established group norms (further endorsing and shaping them) or I can act in ways that disrupt those norms (questioning and altering them). In any event, the norms contained within narratives are group based, portraying whole groups and their members in specific ways. Given this, Nelson observes that social groups have identities which "are themselves narratively constructed" (71).[8] Although Nelson does not detail how the identity of a social group is constructed, we may use the individual case as a guideline. First-person, internal narrative activity would be contributed by group members themselves. When non-group members make contributions, that would constitute third-person or external narrative activity. All parties would rely on publicly available master narratives and the norms within.

Up to this point, I have attempted to show how racial groups, gender groups, ethnic groups, religious groups, and the like are composed of members (who have their own narratives), plus a group narrative, to which many people, both inside and outside the group, contribute. Within that group narrative are norms, which are shaped by and apply to group members, and which figure in the practical reasoning process of members as they consider their actions. As I describe shortly, the group narrative, and the norms within it, may provide a link between many members of large social groups and those members who actively perpetrate harm.

20.3 Narrative and Group Responsibility

Returning to French's distinction between conglomerates and aggregates, it appears that social groups are closer to the former. Social groups, like conglomerates, survive varying membership and have an identity "not exhausted by the conjunction of the identities of the persons in the organization" (1984: 13). Conglomerates possess rules of conduct for members and prescribe a hierarchy of roles for members. When one is a member of a particular social group there are prescribed norms as well, though perhaps there is not a set hierarchy as in conglomerates. In contrast, aggregates do not survive varying membership, do not have prescribed norms, rules, or roles, and do have reductive identities. Clearly, narratively constructed social groups are closer to conglomerates than aggregates; however, they differ in one very important way—they lack "decision procedures."

As a concrete example, we can think of decision procedures on the model of Robert's *Rules of Order* for deliberative assemblies. Narratively constructed social groups do not possess such decision procedures. For many in the debate, including myself, this means that social groups cannot form collective intentions and achieve collective agency. Feinberg (1991) and May (1992) have proposed that solidarity might enable collective agency, but one would be hard pressed to maintain that large social groups, such as races and genders, genuinely possess solidarity. While I am arguing that identity groups approximate conglomerates, I do not hold that narratives generate a unified or collective intention to perform particular actions the way a decision procedure or true solidarity might, so ultimately mine is not a collectivist claim. What I am arguing is that narratives provide irreducible structure to social groups in a way that is important to questions of group responsibility.

Taking a narrative approach to individuals and groups meets the spirit of the reductive objection by demonstrating that even if the group does not qualify as an agent, not everything morally significant about the group is reducible to individual members. The group is reducible in terms of the physical bodies that constitute it, but the group narrative is not. The irreducible group narrative and the norms it contains might function as a kind of causal artifact, linking many members (who contribute to the norms) to perpetrators (who then act on the norms). This is key because if the reductive objection cannot be met, if groups really are fully reducible, then the other objections do not even arise. All moral responsibility would simply be the result of individual, intentional, direct, and proximal action, case closed. However, once the reductive objection has been met, the narrative approach suggests additional possibilities for meeting the normative and practical objections. Moreover, as I outline below, it gives us new ways of interpreting collective punishment, collective apology, and collective akrasia.

While I do not have space to provide and defend all the particulars, I can offer a rough sketch of where an emphasis on narrative can lead.[9] Recall that according to the normative objection, ascribing "shared" or "distributed" responsibility necessarily implies that every group member is equally responsible for harm regardless of contribution.[10] This is an indefensible result, of course. On my view, shared responsibility is proportional to one's contribution. This idea is largely uncontroversial; corporate and criminal conspirators can share responsibility for harm, with those who intend and order the actions often having more responsibility than those who carry out the actions. In such cases, the link between conspirators and the harm is direct and proximal; however, when considering hate crime and shared responsibility among members of large social groups, the link is much less obvious. By focusing on narrative, I believe we can reveal the link. On a narrative account, individuals and groups are importantly constituted by their narratives. The content of those narratives, especially the norms embedded within, inform the moral deliberations of individuals. The norms reside or are archived in the narrative and are partly formulated through narrative. Members of social groups contribute to group norms as they live their everyday lives; they cannot avoid it.[11] When members of social groups contribute to a norm that promotes violence, and another member relies on that norm when formulating intentions and committing violence, then those contributing members share responsibility with direct perpetrators. Those with more influence on group norms, like public figures with public platforms, would bear a greater share of responsibility than "average" members.

For example, in the hate crime case I described at the start, perpetrators likely reasoned that they were operating according to a norm endorsed by most members, a norm which says roughly that "whites should resist residential integration with violence if necessary." The norm was a necessary aspect of the commission of violence but the perpetrator is not individually responsible for the norm. The faulty norm is the product of many member contributions over time and causally links many members to the harm. Additionally, the faulty norm has an historical force that must be actively dislodged; doing nothing functions as a contribution to maintaining the status quo norm and to maintaining ones' link to that norm. Thus, on a narrative account, if members do not want to share responsibility, they must live and speak in ways that displace faulty historical norms, that sever themselves from such norms, and that thereby complicate the group narrative.[12]

Note that on this account one can share responsibility without deliberately intending to support the faulty norm; instead, one's small share of responsibility can result from a kind of recklessness or negligence.[13] But, as Hannah Arendt reports in *The Life of the Mind*, "the sad truth of the matter is that most evil is done by people who never made up their minds to be or do either evil or good" (180). Although it goes against common perceptions, recklessness and negligence may account for more harm than does intentional action. In any event, this admittedly attenuated link to harm revealed by the narrative account may be insufficient to motivate individuals to behave differently. Nonetheless, the account does show that there can be a causal connection between many members of large social groups and harm caused by a few direct perpetrators, making it sometimes appropriate to say things like "many whites share responsibility for hate crime."

Even if one's share of responsibility is small and the direct perpetrator's share is large, making the distribution fair and acceptable, a narrative account of shared responsibility must still overcome practical objections. In general, the practical objections coalesce around the idea that ascribing shared responsibility to large social groups can only make intergroup relations worse, not better. Indeed, it is easy to observe that people are quick to assign group responsibility (although they are loath to accept it themselves)[14] and that they often seek retribution against any member of the "guilty" group. Moreover, we frequently direct anger at groups and occasionally admit to feeling group-related guilt.[15] There is clearly a need to address how individuals interpret group responsibility so that intergroup hostility is diminished rather than increased.

A narrative account of shared responsibility encourages us to recognize the different contributions made by different members, rather than equalizing contributions the way other notions of group responsibility might. We would have to acknowledge that some members are wholly innocent (e.g., those who act to dislodge the norm), that others are unintentional contributors, that some are quiet endorsers of faulty norms, and that a few are aggressors. Consciously noting these differences in contribution should curb the impulse to impose indiscriminate "punishment" on all members. It can also help us determine what sort of "shared punishment" would be appropriate. Direct perpetrators would face criminal charges, of course, but indirect contributors would also be punished by facing changes to their individual and group narratives. Their narratives would no longer characterize most individual members as innocent bystanders or the group itself as unblemished. In the aftermath of the Rwandan genocide, for example, truth commissions sought to give both survivors and perpetrators a platform for sharing thorough and accurate narratives.[16] In this way, survivors were able to tell their stories and demonstrate that they were worthy of respect and protection, while perpetrators honestly described and took responsibility for their actions. Here in the United States, at historical sites like colonial Williamsburg and Monticello, the full stories of slaves and their daily lives, along with the truth about slaveholding among the founding fathers, is now emphasized and demonstrates a desire for honest, and in that way healing, narratives. These kinds of "transitional justice" efforts merge nicely with a narrative account of shared responsibility because they prioritize getting the narratives right, in all their complexity. This is now recognized as a necessary step toward intergroup reconciliation.

An additional practice that can impact intergroup reconciliation is "collective apology." This occurs when a representative of a group publicly apologizes for a harmful act committed by the group or its members. Organized groups, like governments or corporations, might engage in collective apology. The city of Charleston, South Carolina, very recently issued an apology for its role in the slave trade (Gomez 2018). The apology rang hollow with some black residents; they felt the apology was not accompanied by a substantial change in government treatment of black residents. While my narrative account does not rule out collective apology on the part of organized groups, it does speak to why some black residents may be dissatisfied. Although the apology begins to alter the narrative for the city of Charleston, the norms involving how black residents are treated need to show substantial change. The lack of substantial change in treatment continues to be part of the city's narrative.

There are situations where collective apology might be welcome when done correctly; however, "shared apology" is not a practice that the narrative account can endorse. Because large social groups like races and genders do not have organized hierarchies and decision-making procedures, there is no appropriate representative who can make the broad public apology. An apology can be shared in the sense that members at the same level of contribution have the same content to their apologies, but each can only apologize for her own contribution. Ultimately, individual members, even very influential ones, do not have the power to unilaterally or instantaneously alter group norms. Like the narrative itself, change can only unfold in time. Our shared task is to direct that change.

Finally, a major reason individuals may not be motivated by this account to take on the task is not that their share of responsibility is so small, but rather that their efforts would not seem to make appreciable change. Group members might believe that all things considered it would be better to speak and act against faulty group norms, yet they fail to do so. This kind of akrasia might be labeled "shared akrasia" and it differs from standard examples of individual or collective akrasia. Philip Pettit has defended the possibility of "collective akrasia" for organized "self-unifying cooperatives" that are subject to Bayesian improvements in decision making (78); however, this form of akrasia would not cover large social groups. "Shared akrasia" emerges, I propose, when many members of a group achieve the same better judgment in relation to the same necessarily group-related issue, but each fails to act in accordance with that better judgment. Our registered voters who fail to vote, although they believe voting to be best all things considered, would display shared akrasia, for example. One explanation for such akrasia might involve what psychologists call "competence motivation," the desire to produce appreciable change in the world (White 1959: 329). Akrasia may result when we feel we cannot produce change and are demotivated to act. Voters often feel that their individual vote does not matter and members of large social groups may similarly feel that their protesting of faulty norms will not change the group norm. Taking a narrative perspective can help us curb shared akrasia by emphasizing that although the group norm is not going to change substantially in the short term, one's own narrative will. One's individual narrative will evidence that one acted against faulty norms and that one does not share responsibility in a particular instance, placing one on the "right side of history" and perhaps alleviating feelings of group related guilt. Thoreau and Gandhi talked about this in terms of preserving one's conscience, but we can also think of it as crafting one's narrative in a way that avoids shared akrasia. The more individual members who do this, the more quickly the group narrative and the group norms will change.

To summarize, taking a narrative approach opens up strategies for addressing many objections and issues surrounding group responsibility. In the end, narrative may link each of us to harms we would prefer to see as none of our business; however, if the account above is right, we do have the ability to avoid sharing responsibility when we recognize the influence we each have on our individual and shared narratives.

20.4 Conclusion

The questions that prompted this investigation involved trying to determine responsibility for a racially motivated hate crime. In part, given that races are ontologically contested and in many ways unwieldy, racial groups and other large social groups have not been the focus of the group responsibility debate. Instead, discussions of group agency for conglomerates or shared agency for plural groups have dominated. Entering the debate through this alternative path of narrative provides one way of targeting large social groups specifically. To review, as my account has it, racial groups possess narratives, contributed to by many, which contain norms. Some of those norms encourage harm and all members who have contributed to those norms share responsibility when those norms are acted upon. As a result, one's share of responsibility may be fractional, but it is not non-existent unless one has taken action to uproot the established faulty norm. The way to avoid responsibility, then, is to defy the faulty norms and contribute to changing the narrative.

Additional motivations for adopting a narrative approach were that the narrative conception of individuals appears to be more comprehensive than the other standard conceptions and that a narrative account offers promising ways of addressing the reductive, normative, and practical objections, plus issues of group-related punishment, apology, and akrasia. Of course, many aspects of this account have not been defended here and merit further scrutiny.[17] Larry May's (1992) account of shared responsibility among members of large groups is similar to mine in many respects, although he relies on "attitudes" and "climate" rather than "norms" or "narrative."[18] Nonetheless, many of the objections to his view, plus his replies and extensions, would be applicable to mine as well. Indeed, May and Strikwerda (1994) have extended his view to cover men's shared responsibility for rape. The narrative view I have sketched would likely corroborate May's conclusion. Overall, what I have attempted to demonstrate here is that the narrative approach is a novel and potentially useful tool for addressing one of our most vexing moral problems. For as Reinhold Niebuhr, Martin Luther King and others rightly remind us, "groups are more immoral than individuals" (292).

Notes

1 Acknowledgments: Some aspects of this chapter were published previously in: Striblen, C. (2013) "Collective Responsibility and the Narrative Self," *Social Theory and Practice* 39, 1, 147–165; Striblen, C. (2014) *Group Responsibility: A Narrative Account*, New York: Palgrave Macmillan.
2 See, for example, Arras (1997); Strawson (1994); Tomlinson (1997).
3 See, for example, Bratman (1999) or Gilbert (2000).
4 See, for example, Cooper (1968/1991); List and Pettit (2010); Tollefsen (2015).
5 See, for example, Feinberg (1991); May (1992); Striblen (2014).
6 Margaret Gilbert (2013) also offers the unique notion of "joint" responsibility, which she describes as non-distributive yet shared. Most proponents of shared responsibility hold that responsibility distributes in some fashion and most proponents of non-distributive responsibility hold that a group must qualify as an agent; she does neither.
7 Nelson (2001) provides a series of what we might call "reality" constraints on the narrative process (93–104).
8 Elsewhere (Striblen 2014) I describe how Nelson's view of groups can be expanded using both Anthony Appiah's (2005) view and a common view in sociology labeled "interactionism" (Turner 1987). This is to suggest, in part, that such a view of groups is neither idiosyncratic nor inconsistent with social science.

9 For a full account see Striblen (2014).
10 This objection appears in Lewis (1948).
11 This is an involuntarily acquired role responsibility, akin to becoming a "daughter." For a full explanation and defense see Striblen (2014). There I lean heavily on Appiah (2005); May (1992); and Mills (1997).
12 For a similar view on "taking" responsibility, see Held (2002).
13 Many who also lean toward a "collectivist" or "shared" stance still require intention and decision-making procedures. See, for example, Bratman (1999); Gilbert (2000); Tuomela (1991).
14 One motivation for this tendency identified by social science is called the Ultimate Attribution Error (UAE). For a fuller description, see Striblen (2014), ch. 2.
15 For a few examples of philosophical treatments of group-related moral emotions see Gilbert (2002); Jaspers (1961); Striblen (2007); Tollefsen (2003).
16 Such an "expressivist" justification for collective punishment is suggested by Golash (2010).
17 For a more fully articulated and defended account see Striblen (2014).
18 I eschew "climate" and "attitudes" in favor of "narrative" and "norms" in part because the former are ephemeral unless present in narrative; furthermore, I argue that May's view does not adequately distinguish perpetrator from victim group members in terms of their contribution to climate. For details see Striblen (2014), ch. 4.

References

Appiah, A. (2005) *The Ethics of Identity*, Princeton, NJ: Princeton University Press.

Arendt, H. (1971) *The Life of the Mind*, New York: Harcourt.

Arras, J. (1997) "Nice Story, But So What?" in H. L. Nelson (ed) *Stories and Their Limits: Narrative Approaches to Bioethics*, New York: Routledge.

Bratman, M. (1999) *Faces of Intention: Selected Essays on Intention and Agency*, New York: Cambridge University Press.

Cooper, D.E. (1968/1991) "Collective Responsibility," in L. May and S. Hoffman (eds) *Collective Responsibility: Five Decades of Debate in Theoretical and Applied Ethics*, Savage, MD: Rowman & Littlefield.

Feinberg, J. (1991) "Collective Responsibility," in L. May and S. Hoffman (eds) *Collective Responsibility: Five Decades of Debate in Theoretical and Applied Ethics*, Savage, MD: Rowman & Littlefield.

French, P. (1984) *Collective and Corporate Responsibility*, New York: Columbia University Press.

Gallagher, S. and Tollefsen, D. (2017) "Advancing the 'We' Through Narrative." *Topoi*. https://doi.org/10.1007/s11245-017-9452-1

Gilbert, M. (2000) *Sociality and Responsibility*, Lanham, MD: Rowman & Littlefield.

Gilbert, M. (2002) "Collective Guilt and Collective Guilt Feelings," *Journal of Ethics* 6, 115–143.

Gilbert, M. (2013). *Joint Commitment: How We Make the Social World*, Oxford: Oxford University Press.

Golash, D. (2010) "The Justification of Punishment in the International Context," in *International Criminal Law and Philosophy*, L. May and Z. Hoskins (eds) Cambridge: Cambridge University Press.

Gomez, M. (2018) "Charleston Apologizes for City's Role in Slave Trade," *New York Times*, June 19, 2018.

Held, V. (2002) "Group Responsibility for Ethnic Conflict," *The Journal of Ethics* 6, 157–178.

Jaspers, K. (1961) *The Question of German Guilt*, E.B. Ashton (tr) New York: Capricorn.

King, M.L. (1991) *A Testament of Hope: The Essential Writings and Speeches of Martin Luther King, Jr.*, James M. Washington (ed) New York: Harper Collins.

Lewis, H.D. (1948) "Collective Responsibility," *Philosophy* 24, 3–18.

List, C. and Pettit, P. (2010) *Group Agency: The Possibility, Design, and Status of Corporate Agents*, Oxford: Oxford University Press.

MacIntyre, A. (1984) *After Virtue: A Study in Moral Theory*, 2nd ed, New York: Oxford University Press.

May, L. (1992) *Sharing Responsibility*, Chicago: University of Chicago Press.

May, L. and Strikwerda, R. (1994) "Men in Groups: Collective Responsibility for Rape," *Hypatia* 9, 2, 134–151.

Meyers, D.T. (2004) "Narrative and Moral Life," in C. Calhoun (ed) *Setting the Moral Compass: Essays by Women Philosophers*, Oxford: Oxford University Press.

Mills, C. (1997) *The Racial Contract*, Ithaca, NY: Cornell University Press.

Narveson, J. (2002) "Collective Responsibility," *Journal of Ethics* 6, 179–198.

Nelson, H.L. (2001) *Damaged Identities, Narrative Repair*, Ithaca, NY: Cornell University Press.

Nussbaum, M. (1990) *Love's Knowledge*, New York: Oxford University Press.
Pettit, P. (2003) "Akrasia, Collective and Individual," in Stroud and Tappolet (eds) *Weakness of Will and Practical Irrationality*, Oxford: Clarendon Press.
Ricoeur, P. (1994) *Oneself as Another*, K. Blamey (tr) Chicago: University of Chicago Press.
Rorty, R. (1989) *Contingency, Irony and Solidarity*, Cambridge: Cambridge University Press.
Schechtman, M. (1996) *The Constitution of Selves*, Ithaca, NY: Cornell University Press.
Strawson, G. (2004) "Against Narrativity," *Ratio* 17, 4, 428–452.
Striblen, C. (2007) "Guilt, Shame, and Shared Responsibility," *Journal of Social Philosophy* 38, 3, 469–485.
Striblen, C. (2013) "Collective Responsibility and the Narrative Self," *Social Theory and Practice* 39, 1, 147–165.
Striblen, C. (2014) *Group Responsibility: A Narrative Account*, New York: Palgrave Macmillan.
Taylor, C. (1989) *Sources of the Self*, Cambridge, MA: Harvard University Press.
Tollefsen, D. (2003) "Participant Reactive Attitudes and Collective Responsibility," *Philosophical Explorations* 6, 218–234.
Tollefsen, D. (2015) *Groups as Agents*, Cambridge, UK: Polity Press.
Tollefsen, D., and Gallagher, S. (2017) "We-Narratives and the Stability and Depth of Shared Agency," *Philosophy of the Social Sciences* 47, 2, 95–110.
Tomlinson, T. (1997) "Perplexed about Narrative Ethics," in H.L. Nelson (ed) *Stories and Their Limits: Narrative Approaches to Bioethics*, New York: Routledge.
Tuomela, R. (1991) "We Will Do It Again: An Analysis of Group Intentions," *Philosophy and Phenomenological Research* 60, 249–277.
Turner, J. (1987) *Rediscovering the Social Group: A Self-Categorization Theory*, New York: Basil Blackwell.
Walker, M.U. (1998) *Moral Understandings: A Feminist Study in Ethics*, New York: Routledge.
White, R. (1959) "Motivation Reconsidered: The Concept of Competence," *Psychological Review* 66, 5, 297–323.

21
THE DISCURSIVE DILEMMA AND COLLECTIVE RESPONSIBILITY

András Szigeti

21.1 Introduction

This chapter offers a critical overview of arguments for non-distributive collective responsibility, which are based on a central problem of judgment aggregation, the so-called discursive dilemma. It also presents possible rejoinders to these arguments by individualists who deny the possibility of non-distributive collective responsibility.

Accordingly, the chapter has two main critical objectives. The first goal is to show that there is actually a whole family of responsibility-collectivist arguments which all take the discursive dilemma as their point of departure but reach the collectivist conclusion along different routes. It has not always been made sufficiently clear in prior contributions to this debate that the move from the discursive dilemma to responsibility-collectivism is by no means trivial and that there are different ways of forging the missing link. Cataloguing these "bridge arguments" is also important for the second goal of the chapter. This is to understand better what specific reasons responsibility-individualists may have for disagreeing with the collectivist.

Section 21.2 defines the notion of non-distributive collective responsibility at stake in the debate between individualists and collectivists. Section 21.3 introduces a general distinction between agency-based and responsibility-based arguments for collective responsibility. To provide some context, agency-based and responsibility-based collectivist arguments which do *not* use the discursive dilemma will be briefly summarized in this section as well. An example of the discursive dilemma is presented in section 21.4, while sections 21.5 and 21.6 discuss responsibility-based and agency-based arguments from the discursive dilemma and various individualist objections. Section 21.7 concludes.

21.2 Collective Responsibility

Collectives, as this term will be used here, are groups of human beings including formal organizations, various associations, and random assemblages of people. Responsibility-collectivism is the view that the moral[1] responsibility of at least some such collectives is something over and above the aggregate moral responsibility of individual group members. The phrase "over and above" can be made more precise in the following way. According to responsibility-collectivists it can be true that you have allocated all responsibility there is to be allocated for an action or an outcome to all individuals involved in that action or in bringing about that outcome, and still you have not allocated all the responsibility there is to be allocated for that action or outcome. Responsibility-individualism is the view that this is not possible.

The term "collective responsibility" will be used in this sense throughout this chapter. Such responsibility, if it exists, is moral responsibility ascribed to collectives in a non-distributive and non-summative sense. It is moral responsibility the group has *qua* group and it is not reducible to the moral responsibilities of its members.[2]

Furthermore, this concept of responsibility is robust, desert-based, backward-looking moral responsibility. In other words, collective responsibility discussed in this chapter is to be distinguished from collective responsibility understood as a (distributive or non-distributive) obligation incurred by the collective.[3] It is also to be distinguished from responsibility, which is ascribed to the collective just because there is some uncertainty about precisely which members of the group are responsible. A teacher may tell off the entire graffiti gang for defacing the façade of the school because she does not know which member(s) were the actual culprits.

In addition, the kind of responsibility in question is commonly thought to be necessary for the justifiability of a distinct range of reactive attitudes (e.g., guilt, resentment, blame, etc.) and normative consequences (e.g., sanctions, reparation, perhaps even punishment) (see Pettit 2007a: 174; Tollefsen 2003). If a group is collectively responsible in this sense, then as a group it can be blameworthy and praiseworthy and can be held responsible overtly. So collective responsibility of this kind is not merely causal responsibility, nor is it merely liability to answer for and redress harm (see Petersson 2007; Pettit 2007a; Petersson 2008). In short, responsibility-collectivists claim that at least some groups are morally responsible in the same sense as individual agents.[4]

21.3 Arguments for Collective Responsibility

21.3.1 Agency-Based and Responsibility-Based Collectivist Arguments

It is worth drawing a general distinction between two types of collectivist argument. *Responsibility-based arguments* are based on the idea that without attributing non-distributive responsibility to collectives we will have a "deficit in the accounting books" (Pettit 2007a: 194; see also French 1979: 214; Kutz 2000: 113; Copp 2006: 216; Braham & van Hees 2011; List & Pettit 2011: 214; Smith 2018, etc.). We can end up with such a deficit because in some cases no individual seems to be responsible for some morally objectionable event or state of affairs, or even when all individual responsibility is tallied up there still appears to be some normative residue.

Responsibility-based arguments aim to establish that it is not conceptually incoherent and makes much moral sense to ascribe non-distributive responsibility to collectives in some cases. Whether and in what sense such groups can be said to be agents may not be considered at all. If that question *is* considered, then the intuitive plausibility of the claim that responsibility entails agency may be used to show that groups can be agents (see especially Copp 2006: 216–17 for this strategy). In other words, one can argue from collective responsibility to collective agency.

However, some collectivists may not be inclined to make this last move. For one thing, one could deny the claim that responsibility implies agency altogether. Alternatively, one could argue that (*pace* Copp 2006) the claim does not apply to collectives in the same sense as to individuals. Thus, some may accept the general claim but try to show that whatever the collective is held responsible for can be traced back to the exercising of *individual* agency. In any case, the availability of these theoretical options shows that responsibility-based arguments can be made without a commitment to the possibility of (non-distributive) collective agency.[5]

By contrast, *agency-based arguments* seek to show that some collectives can be unproblematically described as agents possessing the same capacities that render individual human beings "fit to be held responsible" (to use Pettit's (2007a) apt formulation). Why should collectives be let off the hook for the bad things they do if they have a sufficiently similar set of abilities and functions as those in virtue of which individuals are morally responsible for their deeds? Just as responsibility attributions, such ascriptions of agency are intended non-distributively. This means that it is at least sometimes wrong to understand statements about group action such as "IBM successfully conquered the Japanese market" or "the Allied bombers set Dresden on fire" to be a mere shorthand for a conjunctive list of individual actions, e.g., "Bomber pilot$_1$'s bombing$_1$, Bomber$_2$'s bombing$_2$, Bomber$_3$'s bombing$_3$..., Bomber$_N$'s bombing$_n$ set Dresden on fire."[6] Rather, some such sentences refer to an "autonomous" (Pettit 2007b) or "irreducible" (McKenna 2006) collective group agent.[7] Note also that such a collective agent could be autonomous in the required sense even when its actions are realized by an individual acting on behalf of the collective, e.g., when a manager signs a contract for her company (French 1979). In any case, commitment to the possibility of such agents is usually expected to be consistent with ontological individualism (about which more in section 21.6 below), i.e., the view that all group-level properties, including agential properties, supervene on properties of individual group members (and possibly non-members).

As a further step then, such agency-based arguments may proceed to demonstrate that collectives are not only agents, but also *morally* responsible agents *qua* collectives (section 21.6 will discuss one way in which collectivists have tried to do this using the discursive dilemma). However, it is important to recognize that the second step in agency-based arguments is not trivial. It can be argued that while some collectives meet the conditions of agency, they do not meet the more exacting conditions of morally responsible agency either as a matter of empirical fact (see McKenna 2006) or because it is conceptually impossible for this to be the case.

21.3.2 Alternative Agency-Based and Responsibility-Based Arguments for Collective Responsibility

One type of responsibility-based collectivist argument which does not invoke the discursive dilemma has been applied to cases of collective omissions (Petersson 2008, etc.), cases of marginal individual contributions to collective harm (Kutz 2000, etc.), and cases of outcomes causally overdetermined by individual contributions (Kutz 2000, but cf. Parfit 1984). The thought is that such cases involve unjustifiable harms such that the sum total of all individual fault (if any) falls short of what would be commensurate with the harm in question. For example, each typical inhabitant of the metropolis upstream seems only to be marginally at fault for her contribution to polluting the river (after all, the individual contributions may be hardly perceptible). Yet pollution seriously wrongs inhabitants of the village downstream. If the same wrong had been caused by an individual, we would not hesitate to hold her responsible. So why not do the same in the case of the collective?

Another type of responsibility-based collectivist argument takes the Strawsonian approach to moral responsibility as its point of departure. If Strawsonian reactive attitudes such as resentment or indignation are fitting reactions to collectives, then collectives can be morally responsible (Tollefsen 2003).[8] This finding can be used to show "in a roundabout manner" that certain collectives can be agents since being the fitting addressee of reactive attitudes presupposes reasons-responsiveness or some kind of normative competence (Tollefsen 2003). Alternatively, it could be argued that for collectives to be the fitting targets of reactive attitudes they do not need to be agents in a non-distributive sense.[9]

An influential agency-based collectivist argument, which does not appeal to the discursive dilemma (but is a precursor to arguments from the discursive dilemma), was put forward by French (1979). The basic idea here is that we can ascribe intentions to collectives as wholes provided they instantiate certain structural features. The relevant structural features are most importantly, first, a clear and formalized division of labor, and second, a commitment to stable and long-term corporate policies (French 1979: 212). Moreover, it is argued that since we can ascribe collective intentions to corporations that exhibit such structural features, we also have good grounds to hold them collectively responsible.

Empirical support for the collectivist position has been forthcoming as well. It has been found that folk psychology is at least sometimes collectivist. People in certain situations seem willing to ascribe non-distributive blame and praise as well as agency to at least certain kinds of groups (Michael & Szigeti 2018). Folk, of course, may be wrong, but these empirical findings show individualism to be more revisionist than may have been assumed.

21.4 The Discursive Dilemma

The discursive dilemma arises because the aggregation of individual attitudes is subject to certain inescapable limitations.[10] Formal impossibility theorems demonstrate that there exists no aggregation procedure that could satisfy an intuitive set of criteria for deriving the collective view from those of the individual members. Here I will keep the formal discussion to a minimum in order to focus on the question how the discursive dilemma has been pressed into service by collectivists to argue for collective responsibility.

Tenure Committee is a by now classic example of the discursive dilemma.[11] Three members of a university's tenure committee have to decide whether to recommend awarding tenure to Dr. Borderline.[12] University by-laws for tenure state that excellence in areas of research, teaching, and service is required (and sufficient) for tenure. In the case of Dr. Borderline, in each of the three areas a majority of the committee vote that she has achieved the required standard of excellence. The committee therefore recommends awarding tenure to Dr. Borderline (Table 21.1).

The reason why the situation is dilemmatic is that all decision procedures available to the committee are problematic in terms of how they derive the collective decision from the judgments of individual members. In the previous paragraph the committee was described as using the so-called premise-based decision procedure. They took a majority vote on each criterion, letting the decision itself follow from these votes as the logical conclusion. The manifest problem with this decision procedure is that, as can be seen in Table 21.1, the committee recommends awarding tenure despite the fact that individually each member of the committee is against this.

The committee could use the conclusion-based procedure instead, where each member votes only on one question, namely whether or not to recommend awarding tenure to

Table 21.1 Tenure Committee

	Research?	*Teaching?*	*Service?*	*Tenure?*	
A	No (-p)	Yes (q)	Yes (r)	No -(p&q&r)	
B	Yes (p)	No (-q)	Yes (r)	No -(p&q&r)	
C	Yes (p)	Yes (q)	No (-r)	No -(p&q&r)	
A&B&C	Yes (p)	Yes (q)	Yes (r)	Yes (p&q&r)	No –(p&q&r)

Dr. Borderline. Since each member judges that Dr. Borderline fails to meet one of the three required criteria, the committee would not recommend awarding tenure. The problem with using this decision procedure is that the decision goes against the majority view regarding the suitability of Dr. Borderline in terms of each criterion. This will be particularly worrisome if the group's views on the premises have been made explicit and perhaps even communicated to Dr. Borderline earlier on.[13]

So, the committee faces a dilemma: if it embraces the premise-based procedure it will reach a decision not supported by any of its members; if it uses the conclusion-based procedure it violates consistency at the group level.[14] Impossibility theorems generalize this finding showing that the difficulty is not restricted to the premise-based and conclusion-based procedures. More precisely, what these theorems show is that there exists no collective judgment aggregation procedure which for any (rational) profile of individual judgments will both (i) guarantee responsiveness to the views of members on each of the issues involved, and (ii) yield collective judgments on these issues which are themselves consistent and complete (List & Pettit 2002).[15]

The negative result of impossibility theorems does not entail of course that decision procedures would meet various normative desiderata equally well. Among others, it has been argued that the premise-based procedure is under most circumstances a better "truth-tracker" than the conclusion-based procedure (Pettit & Rabinowicz 2001; Bovens & Rabinowicz 2006). Perhaps even more importantly, the use of the premise-based procedure may be required by moral, political, or legal norms (Pettit 2001; Chapman 2002; List 2006). Some also believe that only the use of the premise-based procedure enables the group to live up to fundamental demands of rationality (I will return to this last point in section 21.6 below).

At the same time, some other considerations actually favor the conclusion-based procedure. First, in some cases groups may want to put a premium on unanimity over simple majority. Second, the conclusion-based procedure may better safeguard against strategic voting (List 2006: 391). Third, the premise-based procedure is not *always* a better "truth-tracker" (Bovens & Rabinowicz 2006). Fourth, in some cases we may want to or have to take a stand on a logically complex proposition as a whole without having a firm view on one or more of the simple propositions constituting it. Fifth, decomposing a conclusion into premises is to some extent an arbitrary matter because those very premises can themselves be decomposed. Sixth, in many cases the same conclusion might follow from different and logically independent sets of premises. That is, different arguments may favour the same conclusion.[16]

21.5 Responsibility-Based Collectivist Arguments from the Discursive Dilemma

It is one thing to establish that in certain situations collectives face discursive dilemmas, it is another to use discursive dilemmas to show that collectives could in some cases be collectively responsible. In this section and the next, I will review arguments that seek to forge exactly such a link between the discursive dilemma and responsibility-collectivism.

21.5.1 The Simple Argument

Imagine that a premise-based decision procedure is in place. Imagine further that the decision taken is morally objectionable because it is unfair or harmful. Finally, imagine that the distribution of individual judgments or votes is exactly as in Table 21.1 above.[17] In such a case, who can be held responsible or blameworthy for the morally objectionable decision? If you have a complaint against the decision whom can you remonstrate with? Each member can point out that they were against the decision, and further, that none of them could foresee what decision their votes would lead to (see esp. List & Pettit 2011, 216). Therefore, the only appropriate addressee seems to be the collective as a whole.

Note that the underlying motivation for attributing responsibility to the group is similar to other responsibility-based arguments for collective responsibility surveyed above in section 21.3.2. The decision is objectionable because it is unfair or harmful. However, no individual seems to be at fault. So, unless we ascribe responsibility to the group as a whole, there will be a "deficit in the accounting books" (Pettit 2007a: 194).

On closer scrutiny, several objections arise, however. Granted, those finding themselves at the losing end of the decision may feel bad about the outcome. However, first, it is questionable whether the decision is morally wrong in the sense that it involves the violation of a moral norm or obligation. And second, it is hard to see why the collective would be responsible for the decision whether or not it is morally wrong.[18]

To take an example where the moral implications are more dramatic than in the case of a tenure decision, consider a panel of three deciding whether to grant parole. Let us stipulate that rules for granting parole determine three (and only three) conditions of eligibility for parole: the felon's criminal history and behavior while in prison must be satisfactory, the risk of granting parole must be low (e.g., no strong indicators of a tendency to reoffend), and suitable accommodation upon the prisoner's release must be assured. Let us further stipulate that the panel uses the premise-based procedure. The distribution of votes is as follows:

Table 21.2 The Parole Board

	Satisfactory record?	*Criminal reformed?*	*Accommodation suitable?*	*Parole?*	
A	No (-p)	Yes (q)	Yes (r)	No -(p&q&r)	
B	Yes (p)	No (-q)	Yes (r)	No -(p&q&r)	
C	Yes (p)	Yes (q)	No (-r)	No -(p&q&r)	
A&B&C	Yes (p)	Yes (q)	Yes (r)	Yes (p&q&r)	No –(p&q&r)

The prisoner is released because the premise-based procedure was used. And now suppose that he commits another crime while on parole. Victims of his most recent crime may well complain about the decision to release the felon. But who can the victims "remonstrate with"? It seems only the board as a whole since no member of the board was in favor of releasing the prisoner.

However, it is unclear that releasing the felon was morally wrong – despite the unfortunate outcome of the decision. Parole decisions always carry a significant risk of doing harm: either to the felon, in cases where she is kept locked up needlessly, or to the felon's victims, in cases of recidivism. So, the mere fact that the decision turned out to have regrettable consequences does not mean it was not justified as long as the risks were assessed with sufficient care. After all, many of our justified beliefs turn out to be false, sometimes with disastrous consequences.

Of course, it is possible that the risks involved have not been assessed by the individual members with sufficient care. In that case, these individual judgments should have been different and releasing the prisoner was indeed the wrong thing to do. So, in that case, the individual members could certainly be at fault. However, that conclusion is obviously not the one the collectivist is out to establish.[19]

By contrast, if individual judgments were as careful as they could be, then the only way the decision can be unjustified is if there is something wrong with the decision procedure used to aggregate them. And it is true that in this particular case the conclusion-based procedure would have been in some sense preferable, at least *ex post*. If the board had used the conclusion-based procedure, parole would have been denied and the criminal would not have committed another crime.

However, it does not follow from the fact that the premise-base procedure yielded a harmful outcome that its use was unjustified, let alone morally wrong.[20] As noted, the inevitable risk of recidivism upon releasing a felon must be balanced against risk of keeping someone locked up who deserves to be set free. Consequently, even if members of the board take a straw vote and are thus aware of the distribution of votes there is no reason for them *ex ante* to prefer the conclusion-based procedure that would have yielded the conclusion that parole should be denied.[21]

Collectivists may at this point grant that there was no wrongdoing in *Parole Board*. Nevertheless, collectivists could still insist that while the board is not collectively *blameworthy*, it is still collectively *responsible* for the decision. So, if the victims seek some recognition of the harm caused to them – say, by way of an apology or compensation – they should turn to the board as a whole.

Responsibility-individualists are likely to remain unconvinced. Even if they agree that victims may be entitled to some recognition for the harms suffered they will not accept that the normative basis for the victims' claims will be the collective's responsibility. The reason is that, arguably, if individual members of the collective are not responsible for the outcome, then whoever is responsible for instituting the premise-based procedure is not responsible for the outcome either. Consider *Parole Board* again. The premise-based procedure may have been instituted by an individual, by the board itself, or it may have been adopted spontaneously as a "natural" way of rendering the decision without any explicit reflection by anyone. It may seem that in the second and perhaps the third case the collective is responsible for the relevant outcome.

This conclusion, however, does not follow. According to the collectivist, the reason why no individual member of the board is responsible for the outcome is because each actually opposed that decision and none of them could foresee that their actual contributions would result in a decision which yielded the specific outcome. Lack of knowledge is of course a standard and familiar responsibility-undermining condition, so if this condition applies to the group members, then indeed most will grant that the individual group members are not responsible for the decision. What the advocate of the Simple Argument fails to notice, however, is that the same responsibility-undermining excuse applies to the act of instituting the premise-based procedure. It was not foreseeable that the premise-based decision procedure used by the board will cause harm because that harmful outcome depended on what the actual distribution of votes by the individual members would be. Now, by definition, at the time when the use of the decision procedure is instituted whoever institutes the decision procedure will not be able to foresee the actual distribution of votes by members of the collective which will use that decision procedure.[22] Therefore, whoever instituted the decision procedure can invoke the same responsibility-excuse, which, according to the collectivist, blocks the ascription of responsibility to individual members when the decision is taken. And so, it does not really matter what the etiology of the use of the premise-based procedure happened to be in *Parole Board*. Whoever instituted the procedure will not be responsible for the harmful outcome resulting from a decision which was reached using this decision procedure. *A fortiori* even if the board itself was responsible for instituting the premise-based procedure it will not be responsible for the outcome of the decision.

It is important to see that these findings have little to do with the specifics of the example analyzed above (e.g., the legal or institutional context in which parole boards or tenure committees operate). The general problem with the Simple Argument is that it fails to show that the collective decisions in question constitute the violation of a moral norm or obligation by the collective (or anyone). As long as the individual contributions to the collective decision are justified, the collective decision will be justified as well, and so the collective will not be at fault. Moreover, the Simple Argument even fails to show that the collective (or anyone) is responsible for the fact that the use of premise-based procedure has led to a potentially harmful outcome. It fails to show this because it was not foreseeable that the use of that procedure could lead to that outcome. The Simple Argument fails therefore to forge the required link between the discursive dilemma and responsibility-collectivism.

21.5.2 The Contingency Argument

A different kind of responsibility-based collectivist argument from the discursive dilemma avoids some of the problems just mentioned. The basis for this argument is that the collective's decision is contingent on the decision procedure (Copp 2007; Szigeti 2014a) in the sense that which decision will carry the day depends only on whether a conclusion-based or premise-based aggregation rule is used. One could argue that such contingency could be unfair or harmful in certain situations. This argument is made more plausible by the fact that in such situations the decision seems to be vulnerable to challenges by those who were negatively affected by it.

Imagine, for example, that in a variant of *Tenure Committee* if the candidate for tenure at a department is successful, then an adjunct, Dr. Secondbest, will have to be let go due to financial constraints.[23] If Dr. Borderline is refused tenure, Dr. Secondbest can stay. Now, if the premise-based procedure is used by the committee, then Dr. Secondbest can raise what seems to be a legitimate complaint – after all, no member was in favor of giving Dr. Borderline tenure. If, on the other hand, the conclusion-based procedure is used, then Dr. Borderline can protest – after all, the university's by-laws for tenure clearly state that excellence in the three areas of research, teaching, and service is sufficient for tenure.

So, the Contingency Argument differs from the Simple Argument in a crucial respect. The Simple Argument is based on the analysis of cases such as the *Parole Board* where it seemed that the use of a specific decision procedure, namely that of the premise-based procedure, led to a morally objectionable outcome. By contrast, the Contingency Argument seeks to locate the basis for the moral objection in the potentially worrisome contingency of the decision on the decision procedure used. Unlike in the case of the Simple Argument, this moral objection could apply whether a premise-based or a conclusion-based procedure is used.

Collectivists of course will also have to show that the collective as a whole should be the addressee of the relevant moral criticism. Their suggestion once again is that the members cannot be reproached for anything since they acted in accordance with the procedure in place and voted fairly and after careful consideration of the applicant's merits.[24] Consequently, if the complaint is justified, then the only plausible addressee of Dr. Borderline's or Dr. Secondbest's complaint will be the committee itself. Unless the committee is held collectively responsible for the unfairness of the decision, we will have a responsibility gap, i.e., a "deficit in the accounting books."

As in the case of Simple Argument, the individualist response will once again consist in, first, questioning whether the situation involves any wrongdoing, and second, whether the collective bears any responsibility with or without wrongdoing. As regards the first issue, there is a good case to be made that the Contingency Argument fails to identify any violation of a moral norm or obligation. Both the premise-based and the conclusion-based procedures are reasonable, impartial, and procedurally fair.[25] If so, then there is no room for challenges on the basis that some alternative decision procedure would have produced a different result.

Moreover, note that if it is true that the same kind and degree of unfairness results whichever decision procedure is used (just the victims will be different), then it follows that all options open to the committee were equally objectionable, and therefore, equally bad (or equally good). It is worth recalling here (see section 21.4) that the paradox of collective judgment aggregation, as demonstrated in the pertaining impossibility theorems, consists in the fact that it cannot be guaranteed that for any distribution of judgments held by rational individual members of a group the respective outcomes of the premise-based and the conclusion-based procedures will be the same. This is why there is no procedure that could guarantee outcomes against which nobody could raise a legitimate complaint. In that case, however, it is justified to opt for either decision procedure, and so it does not constitute a violation of a moral norm or obligation to choose one or the other.

Perhaps we do not have to take this to mean that there is no basis at all to, say, Dr. Borderline's (or Dr. Secondbest's) complaints. Arguably, there is something morally objectionable about the fact that someone's tenure (or dismissal) depended solely on whether the committee members' views are aggregated via the premises or via the conclusion. Thus, perhaps the decision could be unjust even if justified.[26] If so, then the demand for some recognition of the injustice or harm caused by the contingency may be appropriate, and the collectivist could argue that responsibility for the injustice caused by the contingency must be laid at the doorstep of the collective as a whole.[27]

It is, however, not clear why the committee should be singled out as responsible for the injustice (if any) suffered by the party at the losing end of the committee's decision. The contingency is nobody's fault. As we have seen, it is generated by the paradox of judgment aggregation exposed by the discursive dilemma. It may be true that nevertheless the losing party's bad luck should be compensated. In *Tenure Committee*, for example, one could consider repeating the procedure by adding a fourth criterion, or one could create a position for Dr. Secondbest, and so on. However, the crucial point is that the normative basis (if any) for undertaking some compensatory or remedial action of this kind is not the collective's responsibility.

21.5.3 The Collective Irrationality Argument

Collectives can be criticized for being irrational. Collectivists maintain that such a failure can itself constitute the ground for collective responsibility. Specifically, it is argued that certain groups can be collectively responsible for failing to meet fundamental demands of rationality such as coherence and conversability (List 2006: 365f).

First, in the case of many collectives we require that their current decisions *cohere* with past decisions (Tollefsen 2004; Pettit 2007a; Pettit 2007b; List & Pettit 2011). Imagine, for example, that in *Tenure Committee* (as in the version of the case discussed in Copp 2007) votes are taken on the three premises, the results are made public, but at a later stage a vote is taken on the conclusion as well (see also Pettit 2003). In such a case, the collective can be charged with incoherence because its position on the four propositions will be inconsistent.

Incoherence due to inconsistency is not just an epistemic failure, but can have morally problematic consequences. For example, in his analysis of *Tenure Committee,* Copp (2007: 380) argues that it would be unfair to deny tenure to Dr. Borderline who, having learnt about there being majority support for her within the committee for each criterion of tenure, had a legitimate expectation or even a right to receive tenure. In general, Pettit warns us that unless a collective takes steps to ensure group-level coherence, it will not be regarded as "an effective or credible promoter of its assumed purpose," and will not be taken seriously as an institution or organization (Pettit 2003: 177).[28] If the existence of the institution or organization serves an important moral purpose, then once again the collective's *epistemic* failure can also be *morally* wrong. But since the epistemic failure and the resulting moral wrong is the collective's fault, and not that of individual members (none of the members have voted inconsistently or could foresee the result of their individual contributions), the collective as a whole could be morally blameworthy and responsible for it.

Second, collectives can be criticized for failing to be *conversable.* In general, to be conversable means to be able and willing to provide reasons for one's views and attitudes (List 2006: 365). It is said that we expect many collectives to justify their decisions, policies, and operation by providing reasons for them, not least because this will also allow those affected by these decisions to challenge or contest them (Pettit 2001). Perhaps not all collectives must live up to such high standards, but those that are can be held responsible for failing to do so.[29]

Individualists are likely to complain that the Collective Irrationality Argument involves a *non sequitur.* Most of them will be quite happy to accept that groups can be irrational, and even that group-level irrationality can emerge even when members are fully rational.[30] Furthermore, they can also accept that some groups are expected to be coherent and conversable. In *Tenure Committee*, for example, the collective might be required to take a straw vote to avoid group-level inconsistency. Perhaps the straw vote is taken because members are familiar with the literature on the discursive dilemma. As a result, the committee may discover that it judges that *p*, and *q*, and *r* since there is a majority support for each of these propositions. However, it may also discover that it judges that -*(p&q&r)* because no individual member is in favor of awarding tenure. If this is the case, then the committee could change its "mind" and come around to embrace the judgment that *(p&q&r)* to resolve the inconsistency.

Individualists will reject the claim, however, that the *collective* is to be held responsible for the failure to meet the demands of rationality to which collectives are also subject to. They will argue that if inconsistency threatens the group's rationality because the group is confronted with a discursive dilemma (or for some other reason), then the threat of inconsistency will generate reasons for *individual members* to revise their attitudes regarding the propositions to be decided upon. Failure to consider these reasons will be an individual failure not a collective one. For example, strongly convinced that -*(p&q&r)* some individuals may refuse to allow the group to endorse *(p&q&r)*. Or they may not notice that there is a problem, or not care about it. In any case, as a result, the collective could fail to meet the relevant requirements of rationality, which in turn may or may not have morally problematic consequences. But the crucial point is that when this happens it will be the responsibility of the individuals who failed to provide for the rationality of the collective because they were not sufficiently attentive or were not in a position to do so. And conversely too, it is individuals, not the group as a whole, who ensure that the collective remains coherent and conversable by supplying reasons for voting for or against a decision.

21.6 The Agency-Based Collectivist Argument from the Discursive Dilemma

The agency-based argument from the discursive dilemma is typically combined with functionalism (or sometimes with the position known as interpretationism).[31] According to functionalists, any system can be classified as an agent provided (i) it generally forms consistent and evidence-based belief-like cognitive states about its environment, (ii) generally forms not incompatible or impossible desire-like conative states, and (iii) is generally capable of acting on these cognitive and conative states. However, demonstrating that some collectives are capable of meeting these requirements is not enough. It also has to be established that some collectives are *autonomous* agents. This is where the analysis of situations involving the discursive dilemma plays a crucial role. These situations seem to show that the collective can hold views autonomously from the members' views. In *Tenure Committee*, for example, the committee can be interpreted as judging that Dr. Borderline should receive tenure, even though no member holds that view.[32]

In general, if collectives can be autonomous agents, then it seems intuitively more plausible to eliminate potential "deficits in the accounting books" by ascribing responsibility to them. Agents can act wrongly and do bad things. If a collective as a whole is an agent in its own right, then it, sooner or later, will also end up doing wrong, and if so, then it will be responsible for doing so. The intuitive idea is clear enough, but of course the crux of the matter is who is responsible for how, morally speaking, the actions of collective agents turn out to be.[33]

We have already seen in section 21.5.3 that group rationality and individual rationality can come apart, perhaps because the premise-based procedure is in place. When this happens, individual members will embrace a view which as individuals they reject. Once reason is "collectivized" in this way the relevant individual actions will be guided by reasons that are reasons for the group, and so the actions undertaken by those individuals for those specific reasons may be seen as actions by the collective agent. The collectivist will describe such cases as follows:

> the group will count as a reasoning subject in the image of the reasoning subjects that we individuals constitute. It will exercise a sort of control over its own processes of judgment-formation that resembles the personal control associated with individual reasoning. The members will act together in implementing an intentional exercise of group control. And they will do this in respect of themselves as a unified center of attitude formation and enactment.
>
> *(Pettit 2007b: 513; see also List & Pettit 2011: 104; Rovane 2004)*

A considerable advantage of this approach is that it seems to be able to avoid the specter of metaphysical dualism, and at the same time preserve the autonomy of group rationality.[34] This is an advantage because all responsibility collectivists, and certainly those discussed in this chapter,[35] embrace ontological individualism (Zahle 2007; Epstein 2009). Ontological individualism is the view that group-level properties supervene on properties of individuals (List & Pettit 2011: 89). If so, then group rationality too, while autonomous, must supervene on individual reasoning and deliberation, and the actions of the collective agent must be carried out by individuals. But as we have said, this stricture of ontological individualism is fulfilled because even when individuals are guided by group reasons it is still individuals who act, i.e., on this collectivist account it remains true that, strictly speaking, it is always the manager(s) who sign(s) the contract or the soldier(s) who pull(s) the trigger, and so on. On the other hand, group rationality remains autonomous too – supervenient on but irreducible to individual rationality – because when these individuals undertake various actions, their actions are guided by the interests and purposes of the group. The enacting individuals' reasons will in effect be the collective's reasons.

The individualist will insist that this account still does not establish the responsibility of collective agents, which are said to emerge through the collectivization of reason. If we grant (as responsibility-collectivists who are ontological individualists also do) that it is indeed the job of individual agents to monitor the epistemic states of the collectives, then there seems to be no ground for attributing (non-distributive) responsibility to the collective – at least not in situations which involve the discursive dilemma. It may of course frequently happen that individual members indeed "hear the call of the group" (Pettit 2007b: 516), and enable the constitution of the collective agent, for example, by not insisting on their individual beliefs allowing the group to endorse (*p&q&r*) and act accordingly (e.g., release the felon or recommend awarding tenure to Dr. Borderline). If the relevant individuals are so disposed, then (let us grant for the sake of the argument) a collective agent may have indeed come into existence. However, once the story is spelled out in a piecemeal way as we have just done here, it becomes clear that any morally objectionable action by the collective will be unequivocally traceable to the individual members' actions. Notice that this objection remains forceful *even if* we set aside the individualist worries discussed in section 21.5 that collectives do not seem to be at fault in the relevant sense in situations involving the discursive dilemma. For example, the recommendation to award tenure to Dr. Borderline will be made because one or more individual members have chosen to allow the group to go with the premise-based procedure and endorse (*p&q&r*). Therefore, those individual members will be clearly identifiable as responsible for the decision who have allowed the group to take the decision that (*p&q&r*).

In sum, responsibility-collectivists are caught between a rock and a hard place because, on the one hand, ontological individualism and responsibility-collectivism do not seem to go together, but the metaphysics of ontological dualism is found so unappealing by most, on the other. On an ontologically plausible account of collective agency, failures by the collective will be clearly traceable to individual actions, and so even if the collective is an autonomous agent in some sense, individual members will be responsible for whatever is done by the collective. Conversely, if collectivists deny that failures of collectives are traceable to individual actions, then they will have no plausible, metaphysically unmysterious account to offer about how autonomous collective agency is supposed to emerge.

21.7 Conclusion

This chapter set out to show that the discursive dilemma did not obviously or trivially imply a responsibility-collectivist conclusion. It has catalogued the most influential "bridging" arguments from the discursive dilemma – some responsibility-based, some agency-based – which collectivists have used to reach such a conclusion. It has also offered a number of possible individualist replies to these arguments. It may not have swayed either individualists or collectivists. Nevertheless, it is hoped that at the very least it could help each side to get a better sense of what exactly it is they disagree about when discussing the moral implications of the discursive dilemma.

Notes

1 Unless otherwise specified, all references to responsibility in the following are to moral responsibility.

2 And thus, it is different, for example, from the individualist account of collective responsibility advocated by Miller & Mäkelä (2005). On the latter view of collective responsibility, distributive collective responsibility is ascribed to individuals who are jointly responsible with others for joint actions and their outcomes. Petersson (2008) also allows for distributive collective responsibility, which is for him a kind of individual responsibility that accrues to individuals on account of their participation in joint actions or omissions. Such shared responsibility is distributive, but the distribution need not be equal among different individuals depending on their respective contributions to the collectively brought about outcome.

3 On collective duties and their relationship to collective responsibility, see Collins (2017).

4 Why the debate between collectivists and individualists loses much of its interest without these presuppositions is well explained by Haji (2006).

5 The collectivist may choose either option discussed in this paragraph to reply to responsibility-individualists who reject responsibility-collectivism on the grounds that (i) responsibility presupposes agency, and (ii) collectives cannot be agents (see Haji 2006 and Miller & Mäkelä 2005 for arguments of this sort). The first option denies (i), the second option accepts (i) but argues that *X* can be responsible as long as *Y* is an agent and *Y* stands in the right kind of relationship to *X*.

6 A claim vehemently denied by Ludwig (2016) for action sentences with plural noun phrases in the subject (e.g., we), and by Ludwig (2017) for actions sentences with singular noun phrases (e.g., "the mob", "IBM").

7 It is frequently argued that only well-structured collectives with formalized decision procedures and a stable identity can be such agents.

8 Some may worry that Strawsonian reactive attitudes can only be fitting if their addressee is also capable of having such participatory attitudes. It is, however, not obvious that collectives are necessarily incapable of such reactive attitudes (Björnsson & Hess 2016).

9 For other responsibility-based arguments not based on the discursive dilemma, see for example Copp (2007). Gilbert's arguments (2000) for collective responsibility can also be characterized as responsibility-based because while she argues for the possibility of plural subjects these are not irreducibly collective agents. Shockley (2007) explicitly denies that collective agency is necessary for collective moral responsibility.

10 In our time, the problem was first introduced in jurisprudence as the "doctrinal paradox" (Kornhauser & Sager 1986; Kornhauser & Sager 1993). List & Pettit 2011 provide a useful overview of historical predecessors to the contemporary debate.

11 See also with minor variations, Chapman (2002); Tollefsen (2004); Bovens & Rabinowicz (2006); List (2006); Copp (2006); Copp (2007); Pettit (2007a); Pettit (2007b); List & Pettit (2011). Name of the candidate below is from Copp 2007.

12 *Tenure Committee* has been retained here as an example of the discursive dilemma in view of its prominent role in the literature. However, note that the case itself is not unproblematic because of course tenure is not awarded by a committee, but ultimately by the university through a complex decision-making process involving several levels in the institutional hierarchy. I have sought to sidestep that difficulty at least in part by using the formulation that the committee *recommends* awarding tenure. Miller (2007: 404–405) observes that Copp (2007) fails to distinguish clearly between the committee's and the university's responsibility.

13 As in Copp's version (2007) where the decision is taken in two stages: the committee first votes on the premises, and then in a separate procedure, also votes just on the conclusion.

14 Chapman (2002) argues that groups such as the committee face no real dilemma because there is a rational order of priority among the propositions to be decided upon. However, first, there is frequently no natural sequential priority of the propositions to be established ("One person's conclusion may be another person's premise," List & Pettit 2011: 78). Second, even if Chapman is right, this would only undermine some collectivist arguments from the discursive dilemma (such as the "contingency argument," see below), but not others.

15 In addition, the problem also generalizes for different logical relationships between the premises and the conclusion (disjunctive as well as conjunctive, see below), diachronic as well as synchronic relationships among the propositions, and for any deliberative agenda with more issues than two. For further generalizations and a formally rigorous treatment of these issues, see List 2006, List & Pettit 2011, and the extensive technical literature quoted there.

16 I owe the fifth and sixth points above to Wlodek Rabinowicz.

17 In the following, as is customary in the non-technical literature, I will only discuss the premise-based and conclusion-based decision procedures.

18 On some versions of the argument, the committee's decision is not just a function of the decision-making mechanism, but also that of the committee's joint commitment to accept the results of the decision-making process (which commitment may or may not be itself the result of a prior formal decision) (see esp. Pettit & Schweikard 2006). Another individualist response may be formulated against these versions of the argument: since each member accepted the result, each member is individually responsible for the group's decision. This objection, however, may be rejected by the collectivist on the grounds that the commitment to abide by the decision does not implicate members in the morally objectionable consequences of the decision if they voted against that decision. By analogy, by participating in the elections I may have to abide by the outcome of the elections whoever is elected, but

that does not mean that I incur any responsibility for the actions of the winning candidate if I voted against her.

19 See Miller & Mäkelä (2005), Mäkelä (2007), and Hindriks (2009) for different formulations of the objection that on a proper analysis of cases involving the discursive dilemma any responsibility either distributes to individual members or no one is responsible.

20 It is crucial to keep in mind here that the question concerns the link between a harmful outcome (i.e., in this case, the felon's relapse) and the use of a specific decision procedure. As noted in section 21.4, there may be various reasons – political, epistemic, or even moral – to favor one kind of decision-procedure over another. However, in examples such as *Parole Board* (and the isomorphic examples used by collectivists, see esp. Pettit 2007a: 197f. and Copp 2007) collectivists do not argue that there is something inherently wrong with the premised-based procedure. Rather, they try to show that given the use of the premise-based procedure the collective is to be blamed for the outcome of the decision.

21 It may be suggested that the risks associated with granting parole and those associated with denying it are not equal because it is a graver matter to release a felon who relapses than to keep one locked up who no longer poses a threat. This would be a morally questionable position, but even if we grant it for the sake of the argument, it will not help the collectivist because differential risks, if any, can be and should be taken into account by the individual board members when rendering their individual judgments.

22 A possible objection here could be this: The fact that *some possible* distribution of votes will cause harm is perfectly foreseeable even if we do not need to foresee the *actual* distribution of votes. The fact that we know some possible distribution of votes will cause harm seems to implicate all of those who use this decision procedure. In response, we can specify that what was not foreseeable was that the use of the premise-based procedure would lead to the harmful outcome rather than the use of some other decision procedure. That only becomes clear once the actual votes are in. Had the conclusion-based procedure been used, for example, other distribution of votes could have led to the same outcome (and given those distributions the premise-based procedure would not have led to the harmful outcome). Therefore, those deciding to use the decision procedure are not responsible for the harm because they could not foresee which decision procedure could have prevented the harmful outcome.

23 This is a modified version of the example used in Szigeti 2014a.

24 For arguments that in such situations the individual members may not be above moral criticism after all, see Chapman 2002; Mäkelä 2007; Miller 2007; Hindriks 2009.

25 To repeat, there may be some inherent epistemic, political, and moral reasons (briefly reviewed in section 21.4) to prefer one decision procedure over another. However, the moral objection here to the collective decision is not based on these reasons. See also note 20 above.

26 "[O]ne and the same act can be both unjust (to someone or other) and justified" (Feinberg 1970: 45).

27 See Copp (2007: 381): "the university was blameworthy for the decision or at least liable to apologize or to compensate Borderline even though no person was blameworthy in the matter or liable to apologize or to compensate Borderline."

28 In practice, many groups are committed to long-term objectives and a stable group identity. In such cases, coherence is usually best maintained by using the premise-based procedure. Pettit (2003: 177) and List & Pettit (2011: 83), however, show that the premise-based procedure is not always a preferable way of maintaining collective rationality because there may be no natural way of prioritizing certain propositions as premises (perhaps because there is no logical or diachronic order of priority to be made out among the propositions to be voted upon). In such cases, a "functionally inexplicit organizational structure" such as a "straw-vote procedure" may be required to eliminate potential group-level inconsistencies (see List & Pettit 2011: 83f.; Pettit 2007b). See note 14 above.

29 Once again, the premise-based decision procedure is often the best way to ensure that the desideratum of conversability is met. This is because the conclusion-based procedure does not make it possible to make explicit the collective's views on the reasons for the decision.

30 Similar lessons have been drawn from Arrow's theorem and the prisoner's dilemma (at least on some interpretations of it, see Parfit 1984: 89).

31 For the former see esp. List & Pettit 2011 as well as all of List's and Pettit's publications cited here. For the latter, see Tollefsen 2002b.

32 Although cases such as *Tenure Committee* are usually presented in terms of judgments regarding propositions (here: *p*, *q*, and *r*), the same propositions can be the objects of desires and preferences too. So essentially the same argument from the discursive dilemma can be run for the autonomy of collective desires and preferences.

33 It is not my brief here to discuss functionalism as a general account of agency. Nor do we need to take up the issue here how plausible it is to attribute autonomous cognitive or conative states to collectives. For insightful criticisms on both counts, see Ludwig 2016. Note also that some would reject the view that a group can be said to believe that *p* without any of its members believing that *p* (see Hakli 2007).

34 Note that even if it is successful, the collectivist solution outlined in this section here would only solve one of the difficulties regarding the compatibility of ontological individualism and collective agency. Szigeti (2014b) argues that the metaphysical implications of collectivism will still be quite onerous as non-distributive collective agency can be shown to undercut the agency of individual members of the collective.

35 Although Rovane (2004: 337) comes close to accepting dualism here: "human-size persons might initially decide to pool their efforts in a joint endeavor. If they implement their decision, they no longer maintain separate rational points of view."

References

Björnsson, G. and K. Hess. 2016 "Corporate Crocodile Tears? On the Reactive Attitudes of Corporate Agents," *Philosophy and Phenomenological Research* 94(2): 273–298.

Bovens, L. and W. Rabinowicz. 2006 "Democratic Answers to Complex Questions—An Epistemic Perspective," *Synthese* 150(1): 131–153.

Braham, M. and M. van Hees. 2011 "Responsibility Voids," *Philosophical Quarterly* 61(242): 6–15.

Chapman, B. 2002 "Rational Aggregation," *Politics, Philosophy and Economics* 1(3): 337–354.

Collins, S. 2017 "Filling Collective Duty Gaps," *Journal of Philosophy* 114(11): 573–591.

Copp, D. 2006 "On the Agency of Certain Collective Entities: An Argument from Normative Autonomy," *Midwest Studies in Philosophy* 30: 194–221.

Copp, D. 2007 "The Collective Moral Autonomy Thesis," *Journal of Social Philosophy* 38(3): 369–388.

Epstein, B. 2009 "Ontological Individualism Reconsidered," *Synthese* 166: 187–213.

Feinberg, J. 1970 *Doing and Deserving*. Princeton: Princeton University Press.

French, P. 1979 "The Corporation as a Moral Person," *American Philosophical Quarterly* 16(3): 207–215.

Gilbert, M. 2000 *Sociality and Responsibility: New Essays in Plural Subject Theory*. Lanham: Rowman & Littlefield.

Haji, I. 2006 "On the Ultimate Responsibility of Collectives," *Midwest Studies in Philosophy* 30: 292–308.

Hakli, R. 2007 "On the Possibility of Group Knowledge without Belief," *Social Epistemology* 21: 249–266.

Hindriks, F. 2009 "Corporate Responsibility and Judgment Aggregation," *Economics and Philosophy* 25: 161–177.

Kornhauser, L. A. and L. G. Sager. 1986 "Unpacking the Court," *Yale Law Journal* 96(1): 82–117.

Kornhauser, L. A. and L. G. Sager. 1993 "The One and the Many: Adjudication in Collegial Courts," *California Law Review* 81: 1–59.

Kutz, C. 2000 *Complicity*. Cambridge: Cambridge University Press.

List, C. 2006 "The Discursive Dilemma and Public Reason," *Ethics* 116(2): 362–402.

List, C. and P. Pettit. 2002 "The Aggregation of Sets of Judgments: An Impossibility Result," *Economics and Philosophy* 18(1): 89–110.

List, C. and P. Pettit. 2011 *Group Agency: The Possibility, Design, and Status of Corporate Agents*. Oxford: Oxford University Press.

Ludwig, K. 2016 *From Individual to Plural Agency (Collective Action I)*. Oxford: Oxford University Press.

Ludwig, K. 2017 *From Plural to Institutional Agency (Collective Action II)*. Oxford: Oxford University Press.

Mäkelä, P. 2007 "Collective Agents and Moral Responsibility," *Journal of Social Philosophy* XXXVIII(3): 456–468.

McKenna, M. 2006 "Collective Responsibility and an Agent Meaning Theory," *Midwest Studies in Philosophy* 30: 16–34.

Michael, J. and A. Szigeti. 2018 "The Group Knobe Effect: Evidence that People Intuitively Attribute Agency and Responsibility to Groups," *Philosophical Explorations* (in press).

Miller, S. 2007 "Against the Collective Moral Autonomy Thesis," *Journal of Social Philosophy* 38(3): 389–409.

Miller, S. and P. Mäkelä. 2005 "The Collectivist Approach to Collective Moral Responsibility," *Metaphilosophy* 36(5): 634–651.

Parfit, D. 1984 *Reasons and Persons*. Oxford: Oxford University Press.

Petersson, B. 2007 "Collectivity and Circularity," *Journal of Philosophy* 104(3): 138–156.
Petersson, B. 2008 "Collective Omissions and Responsibility," *Philosophical Papers* 37(2): 243–261.
Pettit, P. 2001 "Deliberative Democracy and the Discursive Dilemma," *Philosophical Issues* (supp to *Nous*) 11: 268–295.
Pettit, P. 2003 "Groups with Minds of Their Own" in F. Schmitt (ed) *Socializing Metaphysics*, New York: Rowman & Littlefield.
Pettit, P. 2007a "Responsibility Incorporated," *Ethics* 117(2): 171–201.
Pettit, P. 2007b "Rationality, Reasoning and Group Agency," *Dialectica* 61: 495–519.
Pettit, P. and W. Rabinowicz. 2001 "The Jury Theorem and the Discursive Dilemma," *Philosophical Issues* 11(1): 295–299.
Pettit, P. and D. Schweikard. 2006 "Joint Action and Group Agency," *Philosophy of the Social Sciences* 36(1): 18–39.
Rovane, C. 2004 "Rationality and Persons," in A. Mele and P. Rawling (eds) *Oxford Handbook of Rationality*, Oxford: Oxford University Press.
Shockley, K. 2007 "Programming Collective Control," *Journal of Social Philosophy* 38: 442–455.
Smith, L. 2018 "The Curious Case of Ronald McDonald's Claim to Rights: An Ontological Account of Differences in Group and Individual Person Rights," *Journal of Social Ontology* 4(1): 1–28.
Szigeti, A. 2014a "Are Individualist Accounts of Collective Responsibility Morally Deficient?" in Ziv A. Konzelmann and H. Schmid (eds) *Institutions, Emotions, and Group Agents*. Studies in the Philosophy of Sociality, vol 2. Dordrecht: Springer.
Szigeti, A. 2014b "Collective Responsibility and Group Control," in J. Zahle and F. Collin (eds) *Rethinking the Individualism-Holism Debate*. Synthese Library (Studies in Epistemology, Logic, Methodology, and Philosophy of Science), vol 372. Springer.
Tollefsen, D. 2002a "Collective Intentionality and the Social Sciences," *Philosophy of the Social Sciences* 32: 25–50.
Tollefsen, D. 2002b "Organizations as True Believers," *Journal of Social Philosophy* 33: 395–410.
Tollefsen, D. 2003 "Participant Reactive Attitudes and Collective Responsibility." *Philosophical Explorations* 6(3): 218–235.
Tollefsen, D. 2004 "Collective Epistemic Agency," *Southwest Philosophy Review* 20: 55–66.
Zahle, J. 2007 "Holism and Supervenience," in S. P. Turner and M. W. Risjord (eds) *Handbook of the Philosophy of Science*, New York: Elsevier.

22
BYSTANDERS AND SHARED RESPONSIBILITY

Linda Radzik

22.1 Introduction

This chapter explores the moral responsibilities of bystanders, and more specifically the ways in which witnesses to wrongs, harms, and other ills come to share responsibility with other parties. To hazard a rough definition, we might say that a bystander is a third party witness to an event or action. Describing the bystander as a third party implies the presence of other parties: one who proximately causes the event or performs the action in question, and perhaps also a second who is acted upon. In the case of a mugging, for example, the bystander is a third party to the mugger and the one being mugged. He is neither the wrongdoer, nor the victim; rather, he is a witness. Furthermore, a bystander is a witness who does not stand in any formal relation of authority with respect to the other two parties, as would a police officer who happens upon the mugging. The police officer is a witness, we might say, but the bystander is "merely" a witness.

I am interested in the figure of the bystander because, although "bystander" is a familiar category in both ordinary and scholarly discourse, it is both conceptually unstable and morally fraught (Brudholm 2005). Applications of the category often come under fire for denying relationships of causal influence and agency that are in fact present. He is not merely a witness; he is an actor. So, the bystander is not really a bystander at all, says the critic. At other times, the objections are more straightforwardly moral as, for example, with the slogans "no bystanders" and "don't be a bystander," which are becoming common on college campuses. Witnesses are capable of action, and often they *should* act in order to prevent bad outcomes. On this version of the criticism, although the witness may be properly described as a bystander, he is not "merely" a bystander. He is also a person who bears a kind of responsibility with respect to the ills unfolding before him.

This chapter surveys the variety of ways in which people who may appear at first to be bystanders, or mere bystanders, to wrongdoing, harm or danger might instead share responsibility with other actors. My discussion divides cases into three rough, non-exclusive categories: (a) shared responsibility for wrongs and harms; (b) shared responsibility to provide aid; and (c) shared responsibility to enforce moral norms. Categories (a) and (b) have received quite a bit of attention in the philosophical literature. In both cases, discussion generally decries the passivity of witnesses to suffering. The witnesses, in remaining passive, fail to recognize how they nevertheless contribute to wrongdoing or otherwise fail to satisfy their obligations to other people. In response, scholars and activists work to identify the sources of passivity and recommend measures to overcome them.

The internet and social media have, in many ways, made it easier to join in group actions both for good (e.g. crowd-sourcing medical research) and for ill (e.g. cyber-bullying). They have also led to an upswing in group actions related to category (c) listed above. In these cases, we see witnesses to wrongdoing take up the responsibility for enforcing moral norms, for example, by joining boycotts or naming-and-shaming campaigns against bad actors. Group actions like these can be appropriate and productive. But, they also raise a number of concerns, as suggested by the aggressive language sometimes used to describe these groups (e.g. "Twitter mobs") and what they do to their targets (e.g. "dragging" or "canceling" them). My modest goal for this portion of the chapter is to highlight some ways in which the responsibilities of witnesses to wrongdoing need to be more thoroughly theorized. But, furthermore, I want to suggest that these cases show that active bystanders are not always preferable to passive ones. Sometimes, it is better for witnesses to wrongdoing to remain mere bystanders.

22.2 Shared Responsibility for Wrongs and Harms

How might witnesses to the wrongful or harmful actions of other people share in the responsibility for those actions?[1] In our simple case of the mugging, the bystander bears responsibility for neither the wrong done (the assault on the victim, the theft) nor the harm caused (the victim's pain, fear and loss). As we will discuss in the next section, the bystander, in virtue of witnessing the assault, might have a responsibility to provide aid to the victim. But he does not appear to bear responsibility for the wrong or the harm themselves. The mugger is responsible, not him. In other cases, though, attempts to place responsibility for wrongs and harms solely on the party who proximately causes the ill in question will be illegitimate.

For example, in the aftermath of political atrocities, ordinary citizens often plead that the crimes were the responsibility of officials, and that they were merely bystanders. "I tortured no one, killed no one, 'disappeared' no one. The leaders, the police, and the soldiers did that." Yet surely citizens share in the responsibility for such atrocities if they actively encouraged others to act wrongly or helped put people in positions of power while knowing they were likely to perform such wrongs (Gilbert 2006; Mellema 2006). Parties who provided such forms of encouragement or empowerment to perpetrators in ignorance of their likelihood to act wrongfully may also share responsibility if their ignorance was itself culpable (May 1992). In cases like these, claims to be a bystander or third party are implausible; the party in question makes a causal contribution to the wrong.

A witness to another person's act of violence might also share responsibility for the wrong in virtue of omitting to act (May 1992; Mellema 2006). Suppose this witness could have prevented the wrong without facing any unreasonable forms of risk to herself, such as by warning the victim or calling for help. Here, the witness does not help cause the wrong, but she omits to prevent it. By judging her to share responsibility for either the occurrence of violence or its consequences, we are still judging her for something that is in her control.

Witnesses to other people's wrongdoing or harm-causing might also come to share in responsibility by making things worse or blocking efforts at improvement. For example, studies of bullying suggest that bullying typically takes place in front of an audience (Flaspohler et al. 2009). The presence of the audience both provides an incentive to the bully and exacerbates the humiliation and other ill effects for the victim. Audience members need not express approval of the bullying to have a negative influence; passivity is sufficient (Coloroso 2009; van Heugten 2011). Similarly, being a member of the group in whose name wrongs are done, without registering opposition, may render the bystander complicit in the wrong (Hill 1979; Harvey 1996; Crawford 2014). Passivity adds to the credibility of wrongdoers who claim to represent the group, as well as the sense of isolation or hopelessness suffered by the victims. In these ways as well, the witness's responsibility rests either in her making a causal contribution to the wrong or harm, or else in omitting to act.

An even subtler dynamic is at work in the case of opportunists who knowingly accept the benefits of wrongdoing perpetrated by others. For example, when the Nuremburg Laws pushed Jews out of various professions, those positions were snapped up by others, typically without any overt protest. Each of these opportunists might have claimed the status of a mere bystander by pointing out that the victim had already been ousted before she took the position. However, such opportunists helped perpetuate and normalize the system of oppression of which the particular wrongs from which they benefited were but a part.

Less intentional forms of benefitting from wrongdoing may also be grounds for sharing responsibility (Isaacs 2014). One of the pernicious features of institutionalized oppression, as a type of wrongdoing, is how difficult it can be for members of favored groups to avoid benefiting from injustice (Young 2011; Stahl 2017). Even those members of favored groups who are vocal opponents of the oppressive institutions in which they live may be unable to shed those advantages (Esquith 2013). For example, male allies who speak against the discrimination against women in the workplace are frequently treated as more credible than the women they defend. White allies against anti-black racism still enjoy advantages in education and employment. As such comparative advantages and disadvantages accrue, even those who try to be part of the solution remain part of the problem. In these cases, one might argue that, even if the unwilling beneficiaries are not culpable for the existence of the injustice, they share in the responsibility to rectify those injustices. An analogy here might be the moral responsibility of someone who unwillingly received stolen property to return it to the rightful owners.

Another very common way in which witnesses to the actions of others make things worse or block improvement is by providing markets for goods and services that are produced through wrongful or harmful practices (Zoller 2015). The business owners who actively engage in abusing workers or destroying the environment only do so because there are customers for their products. Perhaps these cases strain my definition of a witness to wrongdoing, since the consumer who helps provide a market may be quite distant, temporally and geographically, from the wrongs in question. Yet many of us have read or heard enough to be aware that such practices take place and that we are likely buying goods and services that are tainted by wrongdoing. It is extraordinarily difficult for consumers in contemporary Western markets to completely avoid complicity in such practices. Though information is often available on particular goods if one looks for it, taken all together, the time it would take to research all of one's consumer choices and locate better alternatives is significant. The effort and resources it would take to avoid these forms of complicity might well be better invested in traditional charitable work (Lichtenberg 2010).

In this section, I've identified various ways in which one who may claim to be a bystander instead shares in the responsibility for (what are still reasonably described as) others' misdeeds. Attributions of shared responsibility are often met with resistance, especially in cases of political atrocity and oppression like those I have used in my examples. In those cases, I have suggested that very large groups of people share responsibility for terrible wrongs. Widely distributed responsibility seems to entail widely deserved guilt, blame, and punishment; and to endorse guilt, blame, and punishment is to endorse suffering, humiliation, and loss. So, one might object, the arguments for shared responsibility I've defended here threaten to treat individuals in harsh ways that exceed what they deserve.

Yet this line of reasoning rests on at least two faulty assumptions. First, it assumes that attributions of shared responsibility for wrongdoing and harm-causing cannot differentiate among group members based on the significance of their individual contributions. Yet, our discussion already highlights such differentiations. Second, it assumes that to hold someone responsible for wrongs and harms is to punish, overtly blame and/or encourage feelings of guilt. The parties who make the largest and most direct contributions to wrongdoing might well deserve to be held responsible in these ways. But other modes of accountability will be more appropriate for those who play smaller, less direct, or less voluntary roles. Among those who share in negative responsibility, a sense of obligation may be more fitting than guilt, shame or remorse (May 1992; Thompson 2006; Young 2011). Rather than deserving censure and punishment, more marginal figures may only deserve to share the burdens of paying compensation, returning ill-gotten goods, repairing relationships with members of victimized groups, taking steps to prevent future wrongdoing, or preserving the memory of the past. These other modes of accountability need not carry the stigma we associate with guilt, blaming, and punishment; they are not as psychically threatening to those held responsible (Darby and Branscombe 2014). Indeed, some of these modes of accountability, such as repairing relationships, working to prevent future harms, and preserving memory, offer members of wrongdoing groups opportunities for building virtue and creating positive good in the world (Thompson 2006; Radzik 2014a).

One strand of the literature on the moral responsibilities of bystanders emphasizes the things individuals can do to recognize how they contribute to systematic oppression and other group-based ills (Hill 2010; Esquith 2010; Young 2011). Once individuals become more aware of themselves as actors in these dynamics, they can find ways to disrupt them, even if only through protest (Hill 1979; Harvey 1996). The overall message is that individuals can avoid or lessen their susceptibility to sharing in negative responsibility for the actions of others by becoming more active.

22.3 Shared Responsibility to Provide Aid

In this section, our attention shifts from a responsibility for wrongs or harms to a responsibility to provide aid. For example, while the bystander in the mugging case does not bear responsibility for the wrong (the assault), he is responsible for responding appropriately to the wrong by providing aid to the victim. Given that the theme of this volume is collective responsibility, I will choose for my examples the kinds of problems that can only be solved by groups of people working together. For a bystander to these sorts of problems, the question is whether he is responsible for joining in group actions to provide aid.

The least controversial way for a bystander to come to share such responsibility would be for her freely to volunteer to take it on. Assume that the bystander, though she might have an imperfect duty to act charitably, has no perfect duty to contribute to any particular charitable campaign. In making a promise to contribute to some group effort, she can come to have a perfect duty. Having thus committed herself, the individual may then face a number of difficult issues that accompany working in groups, including questions about when to defer to the group's decisions, oppose them, or leave the group (Thomas 1998; Kolers 2005).

Another way in which an individual may come to share in a responsibility to provide aid is by being responsible for some past wrong or harm, either by being solely, individually responsible or by sharing in the responsibility of a group (Radzik 2009; Isaacs 2014). Providing aid to improve a situation can be a means of making amends for wrongdoing. In cases like these, the term "bystander" no longer seems to apply. Wrongdoers are not bystanders, and once we determine that someone who appears to be a bystander shares in the responsibility for a wrong, then she is no longer best characterized as a bystander. Yet, people sometimes make amends for harming person S by providing aid to another person, T, whom they did not harm. For example, people who have injured or killed others while driving drunk sometimes dedicate themselves to organizations that educate other drivers against the perils of drinking and driving. The driver is a wrongdoer in relation to the person she harmed but merely a third party in relation to the drivers who receive the education and their potential victims. (Alternatively, one might argue that the driver wronged the community at large, as well as her particular victim, and is here making amends to the community at large. On this interpretation, the driver is not a bystander in relation to her audience.)

Making amends directly to victims is generally preferable. However, more indirect forms of amends that involve participation in joint efforts to solve social problems may yet be meaningful. Where victims are dead, unreachable, or resistant to further contact with the wrongdoers, aid to other people (especially those who relevantly resemble the direct victims) provides an opportunity for the wrongdoers to send appropriate messages of acknowledgment and regret, to reform their characters, and to help prevent similar cases of wrongdoing in the future (Radzik 2009).

In cases of group wrongdoing, and perhaps especially historical wrongdoing, forms of amends that consist in future-oriented efforts to do good remain appropriate for group members who share in the responsibility of the group while bearing little or no individual culpability for those wrongs. While guilt, blaming or punishment are morally problematic for such parties, shared responsibilities to preserve the memory of the past or to help guard against a repetition of those wrongs are not (Blustein 2008, Radzik 2014a).

In another interesting set of cases, individuals may be obligated to join in group efforts to provide aid in order to avoid sharing in responsibility for wrongdoing. Here I am thinking of cases in which the only way to avoid complicity in wrongdoing is by engaging in some sort of positive action. For example, since passively watching another person be bullied enhances the power of the bully to traumatize the victim, witnesses must act. In the case of bullying, collective actions that coordinate the efforts of the various types of members of school communities (including students, parents, teachers, and administrators) appear to be particularly effective in reducing harm (Olweus 1993; Pearce et al. 2011). So, an individual bystander to bullying might have a responsibility to learn about and participate in her school's anti-bullying campaign. However, providing aid to victims may not always enable bystanders to completely avoid sharing in the responsibility for wrongdoing. As mentioned in section 22.2, it can be quite difficult for members of favored groups to avoid perpetuating the wrongs and harms of institutionalized oppression.

This brings us to more straightforward cases of a responsibility to rescue, wherein a bystander sees someone facing a danger for which the bystander bears no individual or shared form of responsibility. For example, a bystander who witnesses a swimmer struggling in the water may have a duty to rescue him. In this sort of case, the label "bystander" seems to be descriptively appropriate, and our attention turns to the normative claim that one shouldn't remain a mere bystander.

Defenses of a moral duty to rescue often rest on a general duty of benevolence (Beauchamp 2008). Benevolence is typically regarded as an imperfect duty, in the sense that the one obliged is generally free to choose when and toward whom to exercise benevolence. However, the duty becomes required on a particular occasion in cases of serious peril. A number of caveats are typically attached, however. The bystander must be capable of performing the rescue. For example, she must be able to swim well enough to assist a drowning victim. There are also limits on the harms or dangers a bystander can be required to undergo in her attempt to perform the rescue.

Easy rescues are morally required of bystanders; dangerous rescues are generally considered supererogatory.

A well-known puzzle about the responsibility to rescue asks whether a random collection of individuals can be responsible for providing aid (Held 1970). We can pose the question in the form of a paradox. Imagine a number of people on a beach, who are unknown to one another, witness a stranger struggling in the water. Given the undertow, no individual can perform the rescue alone. However, if the bystanders would form a human chain, they could reach the troubled swimmer with little risk to themselves. One might argue that no individual has a duty to rescue the swimmer, since no individual can perform the rescue. Furthermore, no group of individuals has a duty to rescue the swimmer because no "group" exists. A group, in the sense of the word relevant here, is an *organized* set of persons, which is capable of making a decision and jointly executing it (Held 1970). The people on the beach are merely a random collection of persons, not a group of the kind required. So, paradoxically, no one on the beach has a responsibility to save the swimmer, though it seems abundantly clear that they could save him quite easily.

Common solutions to the paradox focus on the content of the individual bystanders' responsibilities (Held 1970; Collins 2013; Björnsson 2014). Rather than each individual having a duty to rescue the swimmer, each has the responsibility to form a group (at least until a sufficiently large group has already been formed) for the purpose of saving him. Since forming an effective group requires leadership, we might also add that each has a responsibility to take a leadership role (at least until an apparently competent leader steps up). Whereas Held suggests that random collectives and their members are only responsible when reasonable individuals can be expected to know how they should act, Michael D. Doan recommends rethinking that requirement, given that some of the pressing problems that require collective action (including complex environmental problems) are ones that no one yet knows how to answer (Doan 2016).

We might also consider the responsibilities of witnesses who are unable to perform or contribute to rescues. For example, John Gardner presents another variation on a drowning case (Gardner 2004). This time, the bystander stands on a cliff far above the beach, with no path that would lead him to the water in time and no means of calling for help. In Gardner's example, the bystander watches frantically from the top of the cliff, pulling his hair and running about in despair. Gardner asks whether the drowning provides the bystander with any reason to act. Michelle Madden Dempsey puts a spin on this question that fits our interests here, asking whether the bystander has any reason to contribute to a water safety campaign (Dempsey 2019).[2] Some might argue that, while the bystander has an imperfect duty to engage in acts of benevolence, as do we all, merely witnessing the drowning provides no reason for him to contribute his efforts to the water safety campaign as opposed to other worthy causes. While making a donation to water safety might help the bystander work through the trauma of his own experience, he has no duty to respond in this way.

However, others might argue that merely witnessing a wrongful or harmful event can provide one with a (defeasible) responsibility to act in some way that will ameliorate that kind of harm. If others are unaware of the dangers posed by this particular stretch of water, the argument for the bystander's responsibility to support water safety efforts is strengthened. Because he is in an unusual epistemic position with respect to this particular danger, his responsibility to contribute to this cause is stronger than other people's. Furthermore, even when nothing can be done to ameliorate the harm done to the drowning victim, there may be value in simply bearing witness to another person's suffering, especially where that person is unable to speak for herself (Blustein 2008; Givoni 2014; Gillespie 2016).

A third response to the clifftop witness case interprets it through a comparison with Bernard Williams' much debated category of agent-regret (Williams 1981). Williams presents us with an example of a faultless driver killing a child who has darted out into the road. While the driver is not blameworthy, there would be something objectionable about someone in this position who did not feel a form of regret or a sense of moral burden. Although the driver is not morally responsible for the death, he is responsible for responding to the death in ways that other people are not. Perhaps the clifftop observer is similarly responsible for responding with a kind of agent-regret for a faultless act of omission, namely for failing to act to help the drowning victim. But this would fall short of a responsibility to provide aid.

This section has identified a number of ways in which someone who is (apparently) a mere bystander to danger or suffering may share a responsibility to provide aid, and more specifically, to provide aid by joining in collective efforts. Unfortunately, decades of psychological studies suggest that bystanders are likely to remain passive even when the need for aid appears obvious and poses little personal cost or risk (Latané and Darley 1970; Latané and Nida 1981). Indeed, there is abundant evidence of a phenomenon called the "bystander effect": the more people who witness a person in dire need, the less likely it is that anyone will lend a hand (Latané and Darley 1970). Psychologists have offered a number of explanations for the bystander effect and other patterns of bystander passivity including: the diffusion of a sense of responsibility; pluralistic ignorance (wherein several bystanders each falsely believe that the others are untroubled by what is going on); routinization and desensitization; fear of embarrassment, retaliation, damaging relationships, or becoming too involved; and the belief that one will be unable to make a difference (Latané and Darley 1970; Scully and Rowe 2009).

As evidence for bystander passivity and the mechanisms underlying it has grown, researchers and activists have turned to the problem of counteracting these tendencies (Latané and Darley 1970; Staub et al. 1984; Staub 2011). One branch of such efforts, which has reached many college campuses and workplaces, provides "active bystander" training (Scully and Rowe 2009; Swan 2015).[3] The goal is to create campus and workplace cultures in which bystanders will be more likely to intervene to help people in need, especially in situations of sexual harassment, bullying, domestic and relationship violence, and rape. These training programs aim to increase awareness of the prevalence and harmfulness of these forms of abuse. They frequently share the psychological research mentioned above in hopes of disabusing people of the confidence that they would surely help if help were required. Active bystander programs are instead based on the belief that people must cultivate their abilities to spot problematic situations and, more importantly, to overcome the psychological and social factors that lead them to silence their internal alarm bells.

Active bystander training also typically shares a wide range of intervention techniques, emphasizing that intervention does not necessarily require confronting wrongdoers. Sometimes abusive dynamics can be diffused by introducing simple distractions. For example, bullying in the workplace can be interrupted by asking a long, boring question just as the boss seems to be building up to another outburst of abuse against a vulnerable colleague. Checking that an inebriated fellow party-goer has a safe ride home, or starting an innocuous but persistent conversation with the person who seems to be leading her away to another location, are easy ways to reduce the likelihood of potentially traumatic outcomes.[4]

One way of characterizing the message of such active bystander programs is that they aim to emphasize that bystanders do not stand fully outside of the events they witness. In this way, such programs echo some of the messages of the philosophical literature on responsibility summarized in this section. Bystanders have the power to act in ways that can influence outcomes for the better and they have the responsibility to help protect others. Moral responsibility requires bystanders to train themselves to notice dangers, to overcome the temptation to remain passive, and to influence the dynamics of the groups in which they participate so as to reduce risk suffering (Crawford 2009).

Another message of the active bystander movement is that we all share in the responsibility to change problematic cultural patterns of belief and behavior, including those that are known as "rape culture." Indeed, one might argue that failing to help change such cultural norms amounts to acquiescence in their continuation. In this way, debate about witnesses' shared responsibilities to provide aid intersects with discussion of witnesses' shared responsibility for wrongdoing.

22.4 Shared Responsibility to Enforce Moral Norms

One might argue that bystanders to wrongs and harms share a responsibility to provide aid specifically by contributing to the promulgation and enforcement of morally appropriate norms (Calhoun 1989, Springer 2013). The idea that ordinary community members have a duty to correct wrongdoers has a long history. We find versions of such a duty within Jewish, Christian, and Islamic traditions ("Rebuke and Reproof" 2007; Aquinas 2006: 2a2ae, Q. 33, Art. 1–8; Costello 1949; Cook 2000). The duty is variously conceived as a duty of justice owed to God or as a duty of charity aimed at helping the wrongdoer. On stricter versions, failure to fulfill the duty to correct wrongdoers "saddles one with responsibility for what one has failed to prevent" (Cook 2000: 571). For the most part, these discussions express a marked preference for rebuking wrongdoers in private.

These days, witnesses to other people's wrongdoing increasingly use public forums for enforcing moral norms. Most people in moderately affluent societies walk around with smartphones in their pockets that enable them to film problematic events in progress. Social media platforms such as Twitter and Facebook enable ordinary people to communicate with the public at large, that is, with anyone in the world who has an internet connection. Ordinary people can also join their voices with others who share their concerns relatively easily, such as through the use of hashtags and re-posting. In these ways, individual actions become, and are often intended to become, parts of collective actions. I suspect that the increasing preference for collective action is, at least in part, motivated by an interest to improve social norms, rather than simply to chastise specific wrongdoers.

Social media provides groups of bystanders with a broad variety of methods for holding wrongdoers accountable. These include identifying instances of moral wrongdoing, such as, the practice of publicly posting and sharing videos of wrongdoing. In the U.S., for example, many videos of police violence against minorities, taken by third-party witnesses, have been widely shared. Social media users also engage in "calling out" wrongdoing, for example, by pointing out morally objectionable aspects of other users' posts, such as discriminatory content (Teekah 2015; Cooper 2017). The gaze of the audience before whom the wrongdoer is called out is part of the shaming power of such interactions, even if the audience remains silent or passive. On social media, though, audiences often do not remain passive. Witnesses to accusations of wrongdoing publicly express condemnation of transgressors or support for victims. They call for political action, sometimes using online petitions. They organize or endorse consumer or cultural boycotts, or call on people who do business with wrongdoers to withdraw their support (for example, by asking companies to stop advertising on the websites or television shows of people accused of wrongdoing) (Borman 2015).

A number of arguments may be provided in defense of these public, group-based efforts to enforce moral norms. Arguably, a community does not really accept that a certain class of actions is wrong unless there are social practices in place that generally sanction such actions.

For this reason, one might argue, the responsibility to maintain moral standards for behavior is a responsibility that is primarily attributable to a group. This idea may shed light on the fact that many social media efforts to "name and shame" are aimed at forms of wrongdoing that have previously been widely tolerated, such as discrimination against transgender people and sexual harassment in the workplace. For example, the #MeToo movement appears to have started as bystanders to particular women's accusations of sexual assault or harassment reported that they too had been experienced similar mistreatment (Shugerman 2017). In so doing, they supported the credibility of the accusers and also created a greater awareness of both the prevalence and harmfulness of these forms of abuse. They aimed to change the culture—to establish norms against abuse and harassment as facts of social life and not mere ideals—which is something that can only be done through the combined efforts of large numbers of people.

By failing to enforce moral norms in some way, one might argue, witnesses to wrongdoing miss an opportunity to do good or provide aid to the wrongdoer (who needs to reform), the community as a whole, or the victim. Other arguments suggest that, in failing to enforce moral norms, bystanders commit wrongs themselves. At least in some circumstances, as we have already noted in sections 22.2 and 22.3, passivity in the face of wrongdoing makes one complicit. The particular wrong of contributing to a victim's sense of isolation by failing to respond is sometimes characterized as abandonment (Harvey 1996; Walker 2006; Gillespie 2016). More broadly, one might argue that in failing to correct patterns of injustice, one allows them to continue. In failing to enforce morality, one permits wrongdoing.

Yet, the social enforcement of moral norms, especially by the collective and public methods that I highlight in this section, raises a number of concerns. Let's begin by noting that being subjected to moral criticism is typically a humbling, emotionally painful experience. These emotions are magnified when criticism is public and combined with expressions of anger, indignation, or contempt. Public criticisms also predictably damage the target's reputation and reduce other people's willingness to interact with or trust her.

At least many of the practices discussed in this section can be characterized as a kind of informal, social punishment for wrongdoing (Radzik forthcoming). Even those actions that are not intended as punishment may well be experienced as punitive by their targets. Practices of punishment reasonably raise questions about proportionality. Because informal, social punishment is not controlled by a centralized authority (as are the punishments typically imposed by the state, schools or employers), it is notoriously difficult to match the degree of hard treatment to the wrongdoer's level of desert. Boycotts are easier to start than they are to stop. Even when the targets of the boycott have met the demands of the protestors, consumers may not hear this news or recall why it is that they have developed an aversion to the product. This problem is magnified when the only thing holding the boycotters together as a group is a hashtag.

Similarly, once "naming and shaming" campaigns get started, there is no controlling how many participants they will attract or what the ramifications of such attention will be. Journalist Jon Ronson details one example of an ordinary woman who posted a poorly formulated joke on Twitter that was interpreted as racist (Ronson 2015). Within hours, she had been condemned by tens of thousands of people, fired from her job, and turned away by her family. Longer-term, the effects resemble PTSD. While she may well have deserved the first condemnatory message and the second, at some point the punishment surely became excessive. These concerns are exacerbated by the fact that the internet never forgets. Records of one's transgressions remain easily discoverable indefinitely.[5]

Other criticisms of social punishment practiced by bystanders focus on issues of desert. Accusations of wrongdoing may be simply inaccurate, or overlook legitimate excuses or justifications. Targets may find it difficult to defend themselves online. Passionate condemnations make for flashier posts and re-posts than corrections of the record. Other problems involve the public shaming of things that are not morally wrong (such as weight problems), of people who should not be held accountable (such as young children), in language that is morally inappropriate in itself (including bullying and threatening language), and of moral wrongs and vices that are simply not the public's business. This last example raises questions about who has the authority to engage in the public moral criticism or social punishment of another person and on what grounds (Cohen 2006; Radzik 2011; Friedman 2013; Herstein 2017). John Stuart Mill, for one, argues that not every wrong should be subjected to the "moral coercion of public opinion," suggesting that some issues should be left to the wrongdoer's own conscience (Mill 1977: I.9). Figuring out where to draw that line is difficult, but some such line is appropriate. It is simply implausible that *everyone* has the authority to sanction *every* case of wrongdoing.

Other arguments against joining in social media campaigns that identify, condemn or punish moral wrongdoing might rest on the temptations to vice that such campaigns present. Intentions to hold wrongdoers accountable or support victims may mask deeper, less admirable motivations, such as a sense of self-righteousness, voyeurism, or cruelty (Simon 1989; Fullinwider 2005; Bicknell 2010). Indulging in the public shaming of others, while remaining anonymous oneself, contributes to these risks. While critics sometimes have legitimate reasons for remaining anonymous, including protection from unreasonable or excessive forms of retaliation, anonymity blocks accountability for their own choices.

Finally, public shaming and social punishment can be counterproductive. The pain and shame of such experiences may cause wrongdoers to reject correction without sincerely reflecting on whether it is apt. Public shaming is also commonly charged with having a chilling effect on speech. When expressing one's views comes with the risk of being publicly vilified, then one may reasonably decide that it is better not to express oneself at all. The result will be a loss of the benefits of discourse all around, including the retreat of individuals into "information bubbles" where they will only interact with like-minded people who will confirm their opinions. While there is certainly something to this concern, it is the sort of objection that tends to be raised opportunistically. Expressing moral criticism is "fighting the good fight" until it hits a bit too close to home. One might also worry that the objection is raised disproportionately often against people who have traditionally been silenced (Cooper 2017).

Reflecting on the disadvantages of these public, group-based forms of moral criticism may recommend the preference for rebuking wrongdoers in private (assuming, of course, that one has the proper authority to criticize at all). Privately correcting others may reduce the severity of the concerns about proportionality, desert and unintended consequences described above. However, we might also worry that practices of purely private correction are more likely to simply reproduce entrenched views about values, leaving less powerful victims isolated in smaller communities where their victimization may not be recognized or taken seriously.

22.5 Conclusion

In this chapter, I have surveyed a huge variety of scenarios in which people who may claim to be bystanders to cases of wrongdoing, harm, and danger nevertheless share in some form of responsibility with respect to the events they witness. Section 22.2 examined how witnesses may share in the responsibility for what are reasonably described as other people's misdeeds. Section 22.3 observed that some problems can only be solved when people act together and asked how people who witness such problems might have a responsibility to help solve them. In both discussions, I documented a tendency among writers on moral responsibility to encourage witnesses to see themselves as actors rather than bystanders. The passivity of witnesses is presented as morally problematic, and typically for good reason. Section 22.4 focused on the enforcement of moral norms as a collective action in which bystanders to wrongdoing may see themselves as sharing the responsibility to act. From one point of view, the responsibility to help enforce moral norms is just another responsibility to provide aid to others. From another point of view, one must take up the responsibility to enforce morality in order to avoid sharing in the responsibility for wrongdoing and injustice. But, the issues raised in section 22.4 suggest that active bystanders are not always preferable to passive ones in this context.

While there is a good case to be made for the view that ordinary people share some degree of responsibility for enforcing moral norms, the sheer destructive power of public naming-and-shaming campaigns indicates that sometimes it is better to correct wrongdoers in private or even to remain a mere bystander to another person's wrongdoing. A world in which anyone's misdeed is treated as everyone else's business is a frightening prospect. The era of social media in which we are living makes further discussion of the moral responsibilities of bystanders a pressing issue. Whose responsibility is it to enforce morality, and who ought to stay on the sidelines?[6]

Notes

1 In this chapter, I focus on witnesses who are individuals. For discussion of the responsibility of states that are witness to wrongdoing and suffering, see the literature on humanitarian intervention (Luban 2002; Evans 2002; Bellamy 2004).

2 Dempsey posed this question at a conference on Gardner's work at Wadham College, Oxford in 2018. A spirited exchange broke out in response. Thanks to Dempsey and to the audience members, who raised many of the points included here.

3 Specific training programs include Green Dot and Bringing in the Bystander. As Sarah L. Swan reports, active bystander training has been endorsed by a number of high profile entities, including the Obama White House, the Centers for Disease Control and Prevention, the American College Health Association and the World Health Organization (Swan 2015: 977).

4 For criticisms of active bystander programs see Swan 2015 and Radzik 2014b.

5 One response to these problems is European Union legislation defending a "right to be forgotten," which provides legal recourse to having certain information removed or blocked from internet searches (McNealy 2012).

6 Much of the research behind this work was supported by grants from the Alexander von Humboldt Foundation and the Glasscock Center for Humanities Research at Texas A&M. The author is grateful for that support, as well as for the helpful suggestions and support of Saba Bazargan-Forward and Deborah Tollefsen.

References

Aquinas (2006) *Summa Theologica*, trans. Fathers of the English Dominican Province, Project Gutenberg.

Beauchamp, T. (2008) "The Principle of Beneficence in Applied Ethics," *Stanford Encyclopedia of Philosophy*, Fall Edition. Available from plato.stanford.edu. [17 May 2018].

Bellamy, A. (2004) "Motives, Outcomes, Intent and the Legitimacy of Humanitarian Intervention," *Journal of Military Ethics* 3, no. 3: 216–232.

Bicknell, J. (2010) "Self-Righteousness as a Moral Problem," *Journal of Value Inquiry* 44, no. 4: 477–487.

Björnsson, G. (2014) "Essentially Shared Obligations," in P. A. French and H. K. Wettstein, eds., *Midwest Studies in Philosophy*, Vol 38 *Forward-Looking Collective Responsibility*, Boston, MA: Wiley Blackwell, pp. 103–120.

Blustein, J. (2008) *The Moral Demands of Memory*, New York: Cambridge University Press.

Borman, D. A. (2015) "Protest, Parasitism, and Community: Reflections on the Boycott," *Social Philosophy Today*, 31: 7–22.

Brudholm, T. (2005) "Surveying a Gap: A Philosophical Perspective on Historians' Responses to Discourses on the 'Bystanders,'" *Holocaust Studies: A Journal of Culture and History*, 11, no. 3: 1–23.

Calhoun, C. (1989) "Responsibility and Reproach," *Ethics*, 99, no. 2: 389–406.

Cohen, G. A. (2006) "Casting the First Stone: Who Can, and Who Can't, Condemn the Terrorists?" *Royal Institute of Philosophy Supplements*, 81: 113–136.

Collins, S. (2013) "Collectives' Duties and Collectivization Duties," *Australasian Journal of Philosophy*, 91, no. 2: 231–248.

Coloroso, B. (2009) *The Bully, the Bullied, and the Bystander: From Preschool to High School--How Parents and Teachers Can Help Break the Cycle*, updated ed., New York: William Morrow Paperbacks.

Cook, M. (2000) *Commanding Right and Forbidding Wrong in Islamic Thought*, New York: Cambridge University Press.

Cooper, B. (2017) "How Free Speech Works for White Academics," *Chronicle of Higher Education*, 64, no. 13: 8.

Costello, J. A. (1949) *Moral Obligation of Fraternal Correction*, Washington, DC: Catholic University of America Press.

Crawford, N. C. (2009) "No Borders, No Bystanders: Developing Individual and Institutional Capacities for Global Moral Responsibility," in C. R. Beitz and R. E. Goodin, eds., *Global Basic Rights*, New York: Oxford University Press, pp. 131–156.

Crawford, N. C. (2014) "War 'In Our Name' and the Responsibility to Protest: Ordinary Citizens, Civil Society and Prospective Moral Responsibility," in P. A. French and H. K. Wettstein, eds., *Midwest Studies in Philosophy*, Vol. 38 *Forward-Looking Collective Responsibility*, Boston, MA: Wiley Blackwell, pp. 138–170.

Darby, D. and N. R. Branscombe (2014) "Beyond the Sins of the Fathers: Responsibility for Inequality," in P. A. French and H. K. Wettstein, eds., *Midwest Studies in Philosophy*, Vol 38 *Forward-Looking Collective Responsibility*, Boston, MA: Wiley Blackwell, pp. 121–137.

Dempsey, M. M. (2019) "What We Have Reason To Do: Another View from the Cliff-Top," *Jerusalem Review of Legal Studies*, 19, no. 1: 141–154.

Doan, M. D. (2016) "Responsibility for Collective Inaction and the Knowledge Condition," *Social Epistemology*, 30, no. 5–6: 532–554.

Esquith, S. L. (2010) *The Political Responsibilities of Everyday Bystanders*, University Park: Pennsylvania State University Press.

Esquith, S. L. (2013) "The Political Responsibility of Bystanders: The Case of Mali," *Journal of Global Ethics*, 9, no. 3: 377–387.

Evans, M. (2002) "Selectivity, Imperfect Obligations and the Character of Humanitarian Morality," in A. Moseley and R. Norman, eds., *Human Rights and Military Intervention*, Brookfield: Ashgate, pp. 132–149.

Flaspohler, P. D., J. L. Elfstrom, K. L. Vanderzee, H. E. Sink, and Z. Birchmeier (2009) "Stand by Me: The Effects of Peer and Teacher Support in Mitigating the Impact of Bullying on Quality of Life," *Psychology in the Schools*, 46, no. 7: 636–649.

Friedman, M. (2013) "How to Blame People Responsibly," *Journal of Value Inquiry*, 47: 271–284.

Fullinwider, R. K. (2005) "On Moralism," *Journal of Applied Philosophy*, 22, no. 2: 105–120.

Gardner, J. (2004) "The Wrongdoing that Gets Results," *Philosophical* Perspectives, 18: 53–88.

Gilbert, M. (2006) "Who's to Blame? Collective Moral Responsibility and Its Implications for Group Members," in P. A. French and H. K. Wettstein, eds., *Midwest Studies in Philosophy*, Vol 30 *Shared Intentions and Collective Responsibility*, Malden, MA: Blackwell Publishing, pp. 94–114.

Gillespie, K. (2016) "Witnessing Animal Others: Bearing Witness, Grief, and the Political Function of Emotion," *Hypatia*, 31, no. 3: 572–588.

Givoni, M. (2014) "The Ethics of Witnessing and the Politics of the Governed," *Theory, Culture and Society*, 31, no. 1: 123–142.

Harvey, J. (1996) "Oppression, Moral Abandonment, and the Role of Protest," *Journal of Social Philosophy*, 27, no. 1: 156–171.

Held, V. (1970) "Can a Random Collection of Individuals be Morally Responsible?" *Journal of Philosophy*, 67, no. 14: 471–481.

Herstein, O. (2017) "Understanding Standing: Permission to Deflect Reasons," *Philosophical Studies*, 174, no. 12: 3109–3132.

Hill Jr., T. E. (1979) "Symbolic Protest and Calculated Silence," *Philosophy and Public Affairs*, 9, no. 1: 83–102.

Hill Jr., T. E. (2010). "Moral Responsibilities of Bystanders," *Journal of Social Philosophy*, 41, no. 1: 28–39.

Isaacs, T. (2014) "Collective Responsibility and Collective Obligation," in P. A. French and H. K. Wettstein, eds., *Midwest Studies in Philosophy*, Vol 38 *Forward-Looking Collective Responsibility*, Boston, MA: Wiley Blackwell, pp. 40–57.

Kolers, A. (2005) "Justice and the Politics of Deference," *Journal of Political Philosophy* 13, no. 2: 153–173.

Latané, B. and J. Darley (1970) *The Unresponsive Bystander: Why Doesn't He Help?* New York: Appleton-Century-Crofts.

Latané, B. and S. Nida (1981) "Ten Years of Research on Group Size and Helping," *Psychological Bulletin*, 89, no. 2: 308–324.

Lichtenberg, J. (2010) "Negative Duties, Positive Duties, and the 'New Harms,'" *Ethics*, 120: 557–578.

Luban, D. (2002) "Intervention and Civilization: Some Unhappy Lessons of the Kosovo War," in P. De Greiff and C. Cronin, eds., *Global Justice and Transnational Politics*, Cambridge, MA: MIT Press, pp. 79–115.

May, L. (1992) *Sharing Responsibility*, Chicago: University of Chicago Press.

McNealy, J. E. (2012). "The Emerging Conflict Between Newsworthiness and the Right to be Forgotten," *Northern Kentucky Law Review*, 39, no 2: 119–135.

Mellema, G. (2006) "Collective Responsibility and Qualifying Actions," in P. A. French and H. K. Wettstein, eds., *Midwest Studies in Philosophy*, Vol 30 *Shared Intentions and Collective Responsibility*, Malden, MA: Blackwell Publishing, pp. 168–176.

Mill, J. S. (1977) "On Liberty," in J.M. Robson, ed., *Collected Works of John Stuart Mill*, vol. 18, Toronto: University of Toronto Press.

Olweus, D. (1993) *Bullying at School: What We Know and What We Can Do*, Cambridge, MA Blackwell.

Pearce, N., D. Cross, H. Monks, S. Waters and S. Falconer (2011) "Current Evidence of Best Practice in Whole-School Bullying Intervention and Its Potential to Inform Cyberbullying Interventions," *Australian Journal of Guidance & Counselling*, 21, no. 1: 1–21.

Radzik, L. (2009) *Making Amends: Atonement in Morality, Law and Politics*, New York: Oxford University Press.

Radzik, L. (2011) "On Minding Your Own Business: Differentiating Accountability Relations within the Moral Community," *Social Theory and Practice*, 37, no. 4: 574–598.

Radzik, L. (2014a) "Historical Memory as Forward- and Backward-Looking Collective Responsibility," in P. A. French and H. K. Wettstein, eds., *Midwest Studies in Philosophy*, Vol 38 *Forward-Looking Collective Responsibility*, Boston, MA: Wiley Blackwell, pp. 26–39.

Radzik, L. (2014b) "Uncertainty in Everyday Life," *The Philosopher's Magazine*, Issue 66, 3rd Quarter: 77–83.

Radzik, L. (forthcoming) *The Ethics of Social Punishment: The Enforcement of Morality in Everyday Life*, New York: Cambridge University Press.

"Rebuke and Reproof" (2007) in M. Berenbaum and F. Skolnik, eds., *Encyclopedia Judaica*, Detroit: Macmillan Reference USA.

Ronson, J. (2015) *So You've Been Publicly Shamed*, New York: Riverhead Books.

Scully, M. and M. Rowe (2009) "Bystander Training Within Organisations," *Journal of the International Ombudsman Association* 2, no. 1: 1–9.

Shugerman, E. (2017) "Me Too: Why are Women Sharing Stories of Sexual Assault and How Did It Start?" *Independent*, online edition, 17 October, available from www.independent.co.uk. [17 May 2018].

Simon, C. J. (1989) "Judgmentalism," *Faith and Philosophy*, 6, no. 3: 275–287.

Springer, E. (2013) *Communicating Moral Concern: An Ethics of Critical Responsiveness*, Cambridge, MA: MIT Press.

Stahl, T. (2017) "Collective Responsibility for Oppression," *Social Theory and Practice*, 43, no. 3: 473–501.

Staub, E. (2011) *Overcoming Evil*, New York: Oxford University Press.

Staub, E., D. Bar-Tal, J. Karylowski, and J. Reykowski. (1984) *Development and Maintenance of Prosocial Behavior: International Perspectives on Positive Morality*, New York: Plenum Press.

Swan, S. L. (2015) "Bystander Interventions," *Wisconsin Law Review*, no. 6: 975–1048.

Teekah, A. (2015) "Lessons from SlutWalk: How Call-Out Culture Hurts Our Movement," *Herizons*, 29, no. 2: 16–21.

Thomas, L. M. (1998) "Moral Deference," in C. Willet, ed., *Theorizing Multiculturalism*, Malden, MA, Blackwell Publishing, pp. 359–381.

Thompson, J. (2006) "Collective Responsibility for Historic Injustices," in P. A. French and H. K. Wettstein, eds., *Midwest Studies in Philosophy*, Vol 30 *Shared Intentions and Collective Responsibility*, Malden, MA: Blackwell Publishing, pp. 154–167.

van Heugten, K. (2011) "Theorizing Active Bystanders as Change Agents in Workplace Bullying of Social Workers," *Families in Society*, 92, no. 2: 219–224.

Walker, M. U. (2006) *Moral Repair: Reconstructing Moral Relations After Wrongdoing*, New York: Cambridge University Press.

Williams, B. (1981) *Moral Luck*, New York: Cambridge University Press.
Young, I. M. (2011) *Responsibility for Justice*, New York: Oxford University Press.
Zoller, D. (2015). "Moral Responsibility for Distant Collective Harms," *Ethical Theory and Moral Practice* 18, no. 5: 995–1010.

PART III

Domains of Collective Responsibility

Part III of the Handbook focuses on the domains in which issues pertaining to collective responsibility arise, such as: collective responsibility in health care, in scientific communities, of the state, and of corporations. Stephanie Collins, though, begins this discussion in Chapter 23 with an investigation of collective responsibility as it pertains to international relations. She points out that the international arena is comprised of a network of overlapping collectives, including states, multinational corporations, non-government organizations – but also non-institutional and non-corporate ad hoc collectives, such as "the rich" or "the educated." Collins aims to determine which of these groups harbors moral responsibility. She begins by presenting an account of the conditions an entity must meet in order to qualify as a candidate for moral responsibility. On this account, it turns out that some states and intergovernmental organizations do indeed qualify in that they can be aptly described as morally responsible both retrospectively and prospectively. However, group entities such "the rich" and "the West" do not similarly qualify – they are not those sorts of entities to which moral responsibility can be attributed qua groups. That being said, Collins makes clear that members of such groups (whether they are individuals or collective agents) can indeed be morally responsible for the effects of their conduct; moreover, they might have a duty to transform themselves from an ad hoc group into the type of group for which moral responsibility is apt.

In discussing collective responsibility in the context of health care, Robert Downie, in Chapter 24, takes an even more metaphysically conservative approach. He maintains that only individual persons can be morally responsible. Nonetheless, the aims and values of the collectives in which such persons operate influence the decisions these individuals make. This phenomenon is especially pertinent in the context of health care in which doctors, patients, and bureaucrats operate or receive care under the aegis of a vast and highly regimented institution. In particular, Downie points out that hospitals typically operate as corporate bodies harboring the values and aims of commercial organizations. The same goes for pharmaceutical companies. The aims and values of these collectives ineluctably influence the moral decisions of professionals working in health care, especially when the individuals receiving health care have recently come to be conceptualized less as patients and more as consumers. Downie does not claim to provide a comprehensive account of who is responsible for the harms resulting from this paradigm shift. Rather, he aims to delineate where the problems of responsibility arise.

Turning from health care to the scientific community, Bryce Huebner and Liam Kofi Bright investigate, in Chapter 25, collective responsibility for instances of fraud among scientists. They begin with a review of an established explanation of this problem according to which scientific fraud is largely a consequence of the norms, rewards, and punishments, by which the "scientific credit economy" operates. Huebner and Bright seek to update this explanation by applying more recent and metaphysically sophisticated accounts of collective responsibility. Focusing on fraud within large-scale collaborative research and within ghost-written and ghost-managed research, Huebner and Bright argue that the scientific community as a whole is prospectively responsible for addressing scientific fraud by adopting norms and practices that diminish the incentives for perpetrating such fraud and which diminish the harmful effects of such fraud. In light of this, they suggest particular steps the scientific community might take.

The legal doctrines of *complicity* and *conspiracy* in the criminal law virtually cry out for accounts of collective responsibility. Christopher Kutz answers that call in Chapter 26 where he notes that the core of criminal law is individualistic in that the bearer of culpability is typically an individual, and the basis for that culpability is typically an individual action. The law, then, faces a doctrinal challenge: how do we extend individualistic legal principles in ways necessary to capture cases involving cooperative criminal wrongdoing? The task of the philosopher is to assess whether the resulting doctrinal principles assume philosophically defensible accounts of causation, intention, moral responsibility, and state punishment. Kutz's task in this chapter is to offer an "opinionated survey" of work on this philosophical problem; he focuses on the law of accomplice liability by considering, for example, the philosophical challenges that the indirect or superfluous contributions of criminal actors raise. In doing so, Kutz briefly considers attempts to resolve the conflict between the causation requirements implicit in the core of criminal law with the doctrine of accomplice liability. He ends by considering alternative kinds of liability for collective action.

Moving away from complicity and institutional responsibility, Avia Pasternak considers in Chapter 27 whether and to what extent citizens are responsible for what their state does. She notes that it is common practice to hold a state responsible for what it does. Does this mean that the state is blameworthy? If so, what about its citizens? We usually demand apology and compensation from blameworthy parties, and sometimes subject them to punishment. But the claim that the citizen of a state can be "on the hook" in this way for what her government does seems to violate an individualist doctrine according to which each individual is responsible solely for his or her own conduct and not for what the members of her group do. Pasternak reviews the existing literature on these issues, after which she carves out her own view by splitting the difference between blameworthiness and remedial responsibility. She argues that only those citizens who wrongly contributed or failed to prevent their state's wrongdoing are blameworthy for what their state does, and even then, only in proportion to the importance of those contributions. Nonetheless, she suggests that in a sufficiently just state, all or nearly all citizens are *remedially* responsible for the wrongdoing their state does in virtue of their status as members of the state.

No account of collective responsibility would be complete without a discussion of corporate responsibility, which is Amy J. Sepinwall's focus in Chapter 28 as well as Jeffery Smith's and Wim Dubbink's focus in Chapter 29. Corporations, on occasion, commit dreadfully harmful wrongs. Yet, as Sepinwall notes, it remains a point of contention whether it is apt to blame corporations qua corporations for such wrongs. Her goal is to help resolve this debate, in part by attending (as Pasternak does in the previous chapter) to the distinction between moral agency and blameworthiness. Specifically, Sepinwall argues that moral agency does not entail liability to blame. To be blameworthy, an agent must be capable of experiencing guilt. As a result, even if a corporation is a moral agent, it nonetheless lacks the capacities required for blameworthiness in that it lacks the ability to affectively feel guilt. Though corporations qua corporations are not blameworthy, Sepinwall argues that we might still be permitted to treat some of their constitutive members – such as the executives – as blameworthy for what the corporation does, even if they are not to blame for having done anything wrong qua individuals. In Chapter 29, Smith and Dubbink also investigate whether corporations qua corporations bear the sort of agency required for moral blame. But unlike Sepinwall, they focus not on the capacity to experience guilt, but on whether corporations possess the autonomy required for moral agency. In doing so, they distinguish between two kinds of autonomy: (1) functional autonomy by which we deliberately constrain actions in accordance with moral principles, and (2) a deeper autonomy by which we self-reflectively endorse those moral principles. Corporations, they argue, possess the first kind of autonomy but not the second. By making this distinction, Smith and Dubbink attempt to show that there is a sense in which both sides of the debate are right – and wrong – when it comes to whether corporations are moral agents.

23

COLLECTIVE RESPONSIBILITY AND INTERNATIONAL RELATIONS

Stephanie Collins

23.1 Introduction

Which entities bear responsibility in international relations? This chapter answers this question via four illustrative case studies: states, intergovernmental organizations, the affluent, and the West. Section 23.2 begins by distinguishing causal, retrospective, and prospective responsibility. The rest of the chapter focuses on the latter two, which, I assume, can be borne only by moral agents. Section 23.3 provides a permissive account of the conditions under which a collective is a moral agent and demonstrates that it applies straightforwardly to most states. Section 23.4 turns to a more contentious case: intergovernmental organizations. I argue that some IGOs are moral agents, and so are liable to retrospective and prospective responsibility. But this conception of collective moral agency is not as inclusive as one might hope. In section 23.5, I demonstrate that it straightforwardly does not apply to the affluent; in section 23.6, I demonstrate that it (somewhat less straightforwardly) does not apply to the West. The result is that neither "the affluent" (as a group) nor "the West" can bear retrospective or prospective responsibility—though they may well be candidates for causal responsibility, and their members are severally candidates for retrospective and prospective responsibility.

23.2 Responsibility

There are at least three senses of responsibility-for-an-outcome: causal, retrospective, and prospective. Causal responsibility occurs when one thing impacts or influences another. The causal responsibility of groups has been investigated extensively in the long-running social scientific debate between methodological individualists and holists. There, the primary question is whether groups are eliminable from our explanations about what causes what within the social world. I mention causal responsibility only because—as foreshadowed above—I will deny that certain collectives can bear retrospective or prospective responsibility. By denying that, I emphatically do not deny that they can bear irreducible causal responsibility. (In Collins, forthcoming B, I argue that ad hoc groups can bear group-level causal responsibility. See similarly List and Spiekermann 2013.) Causal responsibility does not entail any moral assessment, which contrasts with retrospective and prospective responsibility.

Retrospective responsibility is at issue in debates about blame, answerability, and accountability. It is sometimes called the "basic desert" sense of responsibility (Pereboom 2001) and is often used interchangeably with "blameworthiness or praiseworthiness" (Smiley 2010). If an entity has retrospective responsibility, then it is an appropriate target of reactive attitudes such as indignation, resentment, or gratitude. Several philosophers have developed theories of groups' retrospective responsibility (e.g., French 1984; Isaacs 2011: Pettit 2007).

Prospective responsibility is evoked when entities are attributed moral obligations or duties. I assume that obligations and duties are grounded in moral reasons that are presumptively decisive in decision-making: moral reasons that their bearer should, when deliberating about what to do, presume are not defeated, undermined, or outweighed by other reasons—even though this presumption will sometimes rightly be overridden. Again, there are several accounts of groups' prospective responsibility (see, e.g., *Midwest Studies in Philosophy*, 38(1)).

I will assume that all and only moral agents can bear retrospective and prospective responsibility. This assumption is based on three natural thoughts: responsibility attaches to actions; only agents can act (or refrain from acting); and all and only *moral* agents can consider moral reasons when choosing how to act. So, a collective can bear (retrospective and prospective) responsibility if and only if it is a moral agent. This assumption is disputed (Wringe 2016; cf., Collins, forthcoming A, chs. 2–3; Lawford-Smith 2015). I make the assumption so that I can focus on its implications for international relations.

My discussion will focus on whether a collective can *itself* bear responsibility—that is, whether a collective can bear responsibility that is distinct from the responsibility of its members. I assume that if this is possible, then it'll be possible for a collective to be responsible for some outcome without any of the members being responsible for it (as explained by, e.g., French 1984; List and Pettit 2001). This question differs from the question of whether individuals can together *share* responsibility for some outcome (on which, see, e.g., Björnsson 2014; Schwenkenbecher 2013). If the latter is possible, this doesn't entail that individuals can share responsibility for something for which none of them individually has responsibility. I take collective-level responsibility to be more contentious—and, therefore, more interesting. So, I put shared responsibility to one side.[1]

23.3 An Easy Case: States

I'll assume that, in the most general and abstract terms, a collective agent is composed of (at least two) human agents that are united under a rationally operated group-level decision-making procedure, while non-agential groups are composed of human agents that are not united in this way. The basic thought here is: a distinctly group-level decision-making procedure is necessary for distinctively group-level *deliberation*, which in turn is necessary for the group to be an agent distinct from (although supervenient upon and constituted by) its members. In this section, I'll say more about this conception of collective agency, primarily to demonstrate that it is held by the most powerful and prevalent actors in international relations: states. As we shall see, many (but not all) states are also *moral* agents. For reasons of length, my remarks here will be somewhat stipulative. (I develop this account of collective agency and collective moral agency in Collins, forthcoming A, ch. 6.)

I'll assume there are three jointly sufficient conditions for a decision-making procedure to be *group-level* and for individuals to be *united under* that procedure. When these three conditions are met, the individuals who are united are the collective's *members*. So I'll call them the "members" in what follows.

First, each member is committed (even if only tacitly) to abide by the procedure's results. This condition is important for enabling the collective to act in the world. After all, members are the physical constituents of collectives, so the collective can physically act only if it does so through the physical form of its members. But in order for the collective to reliably control these physical constituents, the constituents must be committed to enacting the collective's decisions. This commitment is *pro tanto*—it can be overridden—but the commitment is presumptively decisive in the individual's decision-making. Take the United Kingdom: its citizens' behavior largely reflects a *pro tanto* commitment to abide by the UK's decisions (that is, its laws). The commitment is *pro tanto* insofar as committed individuals might sometimes break laws for reasons of personal conviction, individual gain, or outright thoughtlessness. And perhaps the commitment is made under duress, thus not entailing any duties for members. But members' duties are not at issue here: all that's at issue is whether members are presumptively committed to the group's procedure; this commitment can exist even if it was coerced (Gilbert 2006). The general (even if not infallible) ability of the collective to determine its members' actions allows the collective to act through them. Importantly, there will be some citizens and some residents who don't meet this "commitment" condition—for example, staunch anarchists or children. These individuals are not members of the state *in the sense relevant to constituting the state as a morally responsible collective agent*. The state does not act through these individuals. (Which is not to say that they are not members for other purposes—for example, we might use the term "member" to indicate the people that have special claims to the state's resources.)

Second, the beliefs and desires that the collective's procedure takes as inputs—and the way the procedure processes those inputs to form decisions—systematically depend on the deference, votes, debate, contributions, etc., of its members, while being *operationally distinct* from the inputs and processes that any member uses when deciding for herself. This condition is important for locating the collective's agency as distinct from its members' agency. The collective's inputs and processes are operationally distinct insofar as: first, the beliefs and desires that are the outputs of the group-level procedure can have different content than the beliefs and desires that any of the members input into the procedure; second, its method for processing the beliefs and desires (that are produced by the procedure) is different from the method of any one member when deciding for herself; and third, the decisions it produces are not the straightforward conjunction of individuals' decisions. (On different kinds of group-level belief, and on the possibility of such distinctively group-level beliefs, see, e.g., Lackey 2016; List 2014; Mathieson 2006.)

Take the UK again. The beliefs, desires, and decisions of the UK systematically depend on the manifestos of political parties, the decisions of ministers, the judgments of judges and juries, and so on. The first two of these, at least, in turn systematically depend on the votes, letters, petitions, and so on, of citizens (and, sometimes, some non-citizen residents). So the UK's decisions systematically depend on those of its component members (though, again, citizens are not component members if they don't meet the commitment condition). Although this systematic dependence holds, the UK's beliefs, desires, and decisions are *operationally distinct* from those of its members, in the three ways outlined above: first, the UK can believe something (e.g. "a bespoke Brexit deal is possible") even while many, most, or even (in theory) none of the members personally believe this; second, the UK's methods for using its beliefs and desires to form decisions include parliamentary debates, Cabinet meetings, and so on—these are decidedly *not* the procedures that members use when using their own beliefs and desires to make their personal decisions; and, finally, the decisions of the UK are not just "Theresa May decides this and Boris Johnson decides that and… ." Instead, the UK resolves such disagreements to arrive at an unequivocal collective position (this is most clearly exemplified in the "collective responsibility" of Cabinet (Brady 1999)).

The third jointly-sufficient condition on a decision-making procedure's being group-level, and of individuals being united under the procedure, is that the enactment of the group's decisions requires actions on the part of the members, where those actions are properly understood as attributable to the collective. This third condition will hold if there is a particular interplay between the first two conditions: not only are individuals committed (so that the collective can, by and large, determine their actions-qua-members), and not only does the collective make decisions in a distinctive way, but the distinctively collective decisions and the actions of the committed individuals converge to make some actions of members attributable to the collective as such.

To illustrate, suppose the UK decides that it will teach its schoolchildren a particular curriculum. The enactment of this decision requires actions on the part of thousands of members: teachers, regulators, curriculum designers, and so on. The actions of a given teacher, when teaching this curriculum, are his or her own. But they are *also* properly attributable to the state, because they result from his or her commitment to abide by the state's distinctive decision-making procedure. To see this, we can imagine that the state takes the position that evolutionary theory will be taught in biology classes. To a teacher who doesn't believe evolutionary theory, his or her action of teaching evolutionary theory is his or her own—but it cannot be properly understood as due to his or her agency alone. He or she is acting as an organ, part, participant, or (I will usually say) member of the state. Without referring to the state, we cannot locate one of the decision-makers (alongside himself or herself) that is behind his or her action, since the group's decisions explain his or her action and he or she would not perform that action if acting in a non-member capacity.

As it is hopefully clear from the discussion of the UK, all states have collective agency. Of course, not all states have ordinary citizens as members (in the technical sense of membership at issue here): dictatorships and aristocracies, for example, will include a much narrower group of humans as members that meet the three conditions just outlined.

The idea that states are agents accords with the views of prominent international relations theorists (e.g., Erskine 2001; O'Neill 1986; Wendt 2004), and with the long tradition of realism in international relations theory. According to realism, states are rational and self-interested agents, who pursue their own power, preservation, and self-interest in perpetual tension with other states. Realism assumes that states are agents, but it does not impute *responsibility* to states, because responsibility requires *moral* agency. Yet in international political practice, states are treated as moral agents. For example, UN summit documents regularly attribute to states both prospective and retrospective responsibility (for discussion of how responsibility operates in the UN summit documents on the Sustainable Development Goals, see Bexell and Jönsson 2017).

Do states have moral agency? Moral agents are agents that can deliberate about, and act on, morally good reasons. Such deliberation and action plays a crucial role in prospective responsibility (an entity must be able to deliberate and act upon morally good reason if it is to fulfill its obligations) and in retrospective responsibility (we typically blame and praise only those entities that can deliberate and act upon morally good reasons). There is no conceptual roadblock to a collective being a moral agent. After all, human moral agents can recognize the morally good reasons that apply to agents other than themselves. If a collective's members are human moral agents, and so can recognize such reasons, then they will be able to (i) design a collective's decision-making procedure such that the procedure countenances the input of the morally good reasons that bear on the collective's decision-making, and then (ii) operate the procedure so it processes those reasons in the way morality demands of the collective, such that the collective forms its own intentions to act in response to those reasons. Of course, it's unlikely that any collective will respond to morally good reasons infallibly, but if infallibility were the standard for moral agency, then no human would be a moral agent. Our conception of moral agency should not require moral perfection, so this is not a conceptual roadblock to collectives' moral responsibility.

However, if a collective is *constitutionally incapable* (not in terms of composition, but rather in terms of governmental capacity) of taking morally good reasons as inputs and processing them, then the collective cannot be held morally responsible: it can neither bear obligations nor be blameworthy. This is the same for individuals: children, for example, cannot process moral reasons, and so lack obligations and blameworthiness. To be sure, in the case of a collective that's not morally responsible, the *founders* or perhaps *present-day members* might be responsible as individuals for the fact that the collective lacks moral responsibility. But the collective itself cannot be blameworthy for that fact, nor can it have an obligation to fix that fact. Thankfully, "being constitutionally capable of taking morally good reasons as inputs and processing them" is a low bar for a collective to meet. It requires only that (i) members be permitted (by the collective's decision-making procedure) to put morally good reasons as inputs into the procedure, and (ii) the collective has the minimal material and structural resources to deliberate upon those inputs. (For a similar, but more stringent, account of collectives' moral agency, see Hindriks, forthcoming.)

If members are not permitted (by the procedure) to present morally good reasons to the collective, then their attempts to do so will result in "stonewalling" by the collective. The collective is then the moral equivalent of a psychopath: rational, but amoral (Hindriks, forthcoming, also draws this analogy. The Nazi Party might be an example of such a collective). To picture this, imagine sitting on a committee and raising a consideration outside the committee's remit. While you have *tried* to present this consideration to the committee, the committee's constitution does not permit it to be considered—so the committee is constitutionally incapable of acting on that consideration. If the procedure does not permit *morally good* reasons to serve as inputs to the collective's deliberation, then the collective will not be able to act on such reasons. But if morally good reasons *can* be input into the collective's procedure, and if those inputs *are in fact* put into the procedure, then the collective will deliberate upon them—using such mechanisms as inter-member debate, member reflection, established collective practice, and so on. Such deliberation is not algorithmic or automatic: a collective's use of its procedures to deliberate upon morally good reasons is thus similar to the deliberation of human moral agents. It can be held prospectively and retrospectively responsible for the results of its deliberation.

How can a *state* have moral agency? By having fora in which members are permitted (by the group) to input morally good reasons into the group's decisions and within which deliberation on such reasons occurs. Examples of such fora include petitions and protests that are then discussed in the legislature; parliamentary debate in general; and election campaigns with subsequent voting (the slogans for which regularly appeal to citizens' moral sensibilities). By having such fora, a state is not just a collective agent, but also a *moral* collective agent. That said, states need not be democratic to be moral agents: conditions (i) and (ii) for moral agency are multiply realizable. Even a dictatorship or aristocracy can be a moral agent—just not one of which ordinary citizens are members.

However, it's possible that not all states are moral agents. This is because—arguably—not all states have decision-making procedures that permit their members to put morally good considerations as inputs into the procedure. Swaziland or the DPRK are perhaps examples of states that are agents. After all, even in an absolute monarchy—where the state has just one member, in the sense outlined above—that member's decision-making processes will differ when he is acting qua head-of-state than when he is acting qua individual. But such states are not *moral* agents, that is, capable of acting on morally good considerations or reasons. If a group's decision-making procedure has immoral goals as its absolute priority (the goal of maintaining the power of the leader, say), then feeding morally good inputs into the procedure may not be permitted by that procedure. Another way to say this is that morally good considerations are ruled out by the state's constitution: the state is a psychopath.[2]

Crucially, this is consistent with thinking that other entities—whether individual or collective—have obligations to *make* that state into a moral agent. For example, dictators may well have obligations to do so. After all, states' leaders are moral agents—constitutionally capable of having morally good considerations bear on their decisions. So, they are capable of bearing responsibility for the actions performed by the states they control. Even if the state's leader is a psychopath, *other* agents can bear obligations to act upon the state and its leader to render the state a moral agent. To be clear, I have not here *argued* that such obligations always exist. I just mean to emphasize that such individually-held obligations (and blameworthiness for not discharging them) are not ruled out by the fact that the relevant state is not itself a moral agent. If such individually-held obligations exist, then individuals can (and, often, should) be held blameworthy and culpable when the non-moral-agent state causes harm.

23.4 A Harder Case: Intergovernmental Organizations

The above notwithstanding, my conception of group agents is permissive—more permissive than other prominent conceptions (for example, the conceptions of French (1984), whose "corporations" have unchanging policies; List and Pettit (2011), whose "group agents" exclude dictatorial groups; and Rovane (1998), whose "group persons" must have a unifying project). To picture the permissiveness, imagine a group of five friends at the beach. Numerous decisions must be made: where to lay their towels, where to go for lunch, and so on. Such a group is likely composed of humans that are united under a group-level decision-making procedure. The procedure is likely *conversation-based consensus*. This procedure can become established simply by each member's taking a conversational and consensual stance to the various decisions—each asking the others where they would prefer to go for lunch, and why, until all agree. Such a procedure can be rationally operated, just so long as the group doesn't decide, for example, both to get burgers for lunch and not to get burgers for lunch. By taking part in the conversations (which can be done simply by staying silent to indicate indifference), each member tacitly commits to abide by the procedure's results. (This example illustrates another way in which my account is more permissive than List and Pettit's: they focus purely on groups that have formal "aggregation functions." The group of beachgoers has no such formal function.)

The group has different beliefs and desires, and processes them differently, than the members. This is what makes its beliefs and desires distinctively group-level. For example, Laura might prefer sushi for lunch, but upon learning the preferences of the others, partake in the consensus over burgers. We can even imagine that all members aim to please all others, but all are wrong about what the others want, so they end up using conversation-based consensus to go somewhere *none* of them wants to go. Here, the group desires something (having pizza, say) that none of its members desires. Thus, the collective forms desires in a way none of the individuals does when forming his or her desires. And because no member can unilaterally decide that the group will have pizza for lunch, its decisions are not the straightforward conjunction of individuals' decisions.

Finally, the enactment of the pizza-for-lunch decision requires that members act (by walking to the pizza place). These actions are attributable to the group in the following sense: the explanation of why any one of the individuals is walking to the pizza place requires referring to the fact that she's a committed member of a group that has decided to have pizza for lunch. She goes to the pizza place for lunch, but this action also partly constitutes the group's action of going there for lunch. The same considerations that led us to classify the UK as an agent also lead us to classify our beach-going group of friends as an agent.

I emphasize this application because it has implications for international politics. Specifically, collective moral agency extends to some groups in international politics whose decision-making processes involve informal diplomatic wrangling, power-play, self-interest on the part of members, and case-by-case bargaining amongst members. This includes some intergovernmental organizations (IGOs).[3]

An IGO is a group created by agreement between states, whose members are the states who made the agreement (or organs of those states), where that founding agreement determines the group's aims and operations (Union of International Associations 2015; ILC 2011: 2). Additionally, an IGO has a permanent secretariat, staff, and/or headquarters.[4] The IGO's continued identity depends upon temporal continuity in the *broad structure* of the secretariat, the staff relations, and the headquarter operations. This doesn't mean that a new IGO comes into existence every time there are changes in which individuals make up the IGO, but that sufficiently significant changes in the role structure would lead to a change in identity.

IGOs might aim to be maximally inclusive, such as the United Nations (UN) or International Criminal Police Organization. Or they might select members regionally (e.g., the African Union or the European Union), or historically or politically (e.g., the Commonwealth or the Francophonie). IGOs are hugely diverse—even more diverse than states. In what follows, I'll focus on those in the UN system, alongside the clearest cases of IGO agents, such as NATO, the European Union, or the World Bank. My aim is to show that at least *some* IGOs are moral agents, not that all are.[5]

In considering the possibility that IGOs are moral agents, one should not be concerned that the members of IGOs are collective agents. Any group with its own decision-making procedure is an agent that can make decisions, have goals, and perform tasks distinctly from its members. Some of these decisions, goals, and tasks might involve membership in a supra-group agent. This reveals the possibility of many levels of "nested" agency: the US State Department is a member of the United States, which is a member of the Security Council, which is a member[6] of the UN, and so on.

Are IGOs agents? They have members, which are agents (in this case, states). In joining the IGO, each member explicitly agrees to abide by the procedure's decisions (or at least, to abide by most of them: states can enter "reservations" when signing treaties, but when the reservations arise they can be treated in the way lawbreakers were in the above discussion of states). The members are given roles by the procedure, usually in the form of rights and duties listed in the IGO's founding and subsequent treaties. These membership-based rights include a right for the member to have influence over the collective's decisions, under the procedure. Yet the IGO's decision-making procedure is different from the procedure any one member uses when deciding for itself—often, an IGO's procedure is "negotiation and consensus amongst members." The IGO's decision-making procedure chooses actions the IGO will perform, member roles jointly sufficient for those actions, and an allocation of these roles amongst members. At the most general level, the actions might be the maintenance of international peace and security,[7] the facilitation of cooperation amongst states' law enforcers,[8] and so on; at a more specific level, the actions might be calling for restraint in civil wars, or training states' criminal investigators; even more specifically, it might be the issuing of a resolution regarding a particular conflict. Some IGOs are, therefore, agents.

What's more, the procedures of at least some (perhaps not all) IGOs permit members to bring morally good reasons to bear on the IGO's decisions. This permission—even encouragement—is implicit in the general actions described above: "maintaining peace and security" and "facilitating cooperation" require concern for the interests and perspectives of multiple agents. Indeed, many IGOs were set up specifically to bear retrospective or prospective responsibility. Consider, for example, the IGOs that are charged with enforcing various declarations, conventions, and covenants—such as the UN's Human Rights Committee, its Commission on Human Rights, its Human Rights Council, or the International Criminal Court. The moral outcomes at which these documents aim could not be produced if not for the relevant IGO, because each member state requires assurance that other member states will do their bit toward the moral outcome—otherwise, any state's performance of its own tasks would be inefficacious. What's more, no single state could have a prospective responsibility to, say, progressively realize the fulfillment of everyone's human rights—because no single state could do that (Collins 2016). Analogously, we can imagine a friendship group in which no member can, on his or her own, afford to buy enough pizza for the whole group. So if there is a prospective responsibility to produce the collective-level outcome (whether human rights or pizza), it had better be an intention held by the collective itself (whether IGO or friendship group)—on pain of violating the principle that "ought" implies "can." Once a relevant IGO is in place, there is an over-arching procedure that can organize states towards such collectively-attainable outcomes—and so, can bear prospective responsibility for doing so (and retrospective responsibility for not doing so). Indeed, many IGOs positively endorse this conception of themselves as responsibility-bearing collective agents—most prominently, the UN and the EU (on the EU's self-presentation as a moral actor, see Aggestam (ed.) 2008; Mayer 2017; on the UN's, see Bexell and Jönsson 2017).

This idea—that some IGOs are moral agents—accords with a growing consensus amongst international relations scholars. Kjell Engelbrekt (2015) points to the ease with which the Security Council's structure enables it to shirk its responsibilities. Anthony Lang, Jr., (2003) argues that the Security Council bore retrospective responsibility for the fall of Srebrenica, via its construction of "safe havens" that were not protected. Lang argues that (1) the structure of the Security Council—more so than the actions of any individual members—led to safe haven resolutions, and (2) the culture of the UN led commanders to make mistakes. Michael Barnett (2003) similarly argues that the UN's "cultural landscape" played a crucial role in the 1994 Rwandan genocide. The point to appreciate when considering these arguments is that the UN's *structure, constructions*, and *cultural landscape* are group-level features—they are not just the aggregation of the features of its members.

Similar arguments concern IGOs other than the UN. For example, Paul Cornish and Frances V. Harbour (2003: 121–3) argue that NATO undertook prospective responsibility to halt ethnic cleansing in Kosovo. More broadly, Desmond McNeill and Asunción Lera St. Clair (2009) analyzed the financial clout, economic expertise, delegated authority, and moral authority of various intergovernmental organizations: the UN Development Programme, the World Bank, UNESCO, and the Inter-American Development Bank. Their analysis took the *starting point* that "international organizations have a [prospective] responsibility to ameliorate poverty, [and] they also have a [prospective] responsibility to rise above the states that created them—should this be necessary in order to achieve their purpose" (McNeill and St. Clair 2009: 10–11). My analysis vindicates this starting point.

Yet this analysis will be contentious. Surely, one might think, IGOs are run by their members (states). So IGOs can make only the decisions that states permit. Yes, IGOs can and sometimes do provide "warrants," "approval" or "legitimacy" to states' actions (as Harbour 2004: 67 argues in defense of their status as moral agents). But they are not the ones executing the actions and their instructions are not always authoritative. Thus James Crawford asserts that, "[u]nlike states, international organizations do not possess general competence: they may only exercise those powers expressly or impliedly bestowed upon them" (2012: 184) and Chris Brown argues that Security Council authorizations are

> not the exercise of discriminating moral judgment by the council acting as a collective body, but ... the operation of political judgments based on calculations of interest. ... [m]uch of the time, because of the veto [powers of the five permanent members], they [the UN and Security Council] will simply be unable to act.
>
> *(2001: 92)*

We should therefore be skeptical of IGOs' agency—let alone their moral agency. Or so the thought goes.

Other IR scholars make more circumscribed, but still pessimistic, remarks about IGOs' agency. Kenneth Abbott and Duncan Snidal (2009) suggest that IGOs have independent capacities only insofar as the IGO can bring in third parties (such as NGOs or private actors) to act as intermediaries between IGOs and those actors (usually states) that IGOs wish to influence. Similarly, Frances Harbour (2004) looked at six cases of humanitarian intervention and found that in none did states base their decisions on IGOs' evaluations. And Gareth Evans points out, "[s]tates remain, for better or worse, and will be for the foreseeable future, the primary actors in international affairs. Intergovernmental organizations can only decide if their member states agree and can only act if their member states deliver..." (2008: 196).

Clearly, IGOs' moral agency is constrained: IGOs rely on members to *enact* the IGOs' decisions; members sometimes resist bringing morally good reasons as *inputs* to IGOs' decisions; IGOs are *set up* by members; and IGOs cannot act in *any and all* circumstances. How much of a problem is this for IGOs' capacity to bear responsibility? Not much of one. After all, individuals also face these constraints: individuals rely on their later temporal parts to enact present decisions; individuals have recalcitrant desires that sometimes prevent moral considerations from being considered by the individual (even if the individual would overall prefer to be moral); individuals are set up (raised) by other individuals; individuals cannot act in many circumstances. So if these constraints must be overcome in order for an entity to be a moral agent, then we jettison individual moral agency.

Perhaps one thinks that individuals don't face these constraints to the extent that, or in the way that, IGOs do. Even if that's right, it's still true that all collective agents face exactly these constraints. So if we jettison IGO moral agency, then we jettison all collective moral agency. One might accept this, and reason via *modus tollens*: given that IGOs are not collective agents, perhaps there are *no* collective agents—whether IGOs, states, beachgoers, or anything else. But this neglects three important facts about (some) IGOs' capacities. These capacities together demonstrate that IGOs are not problematically tethered to their parent-states, and therefore that they don't face the kinds of constraints that would warrant skepticism about their agency, and therefore that we needn't use their lack of agency as a premise in an argument against collective agency in general.

First, IGOs often *make possible* the multilateral coordination that is necessary for states to reliably bring about moral states of affairs. Often, IGOs do this by acting as fora within which states can coordinate their actions. For example, IGOs might intentionally provide states with the physical and administrative apparatuses states need to provide each other with the requisite assurance that they will φ if others φ. The fact that IGOs intentionally opt to offer such apparatuses points towards a special capacity *of IGOs*: the capacity to *encourage* and *facilitate* states' use of IGOs' apparatuses in this way. This is a matter of IGOs guiding and managing states, not vice versa.

Second, such inter-state coordination will sometimes require that IGOs don't just intentionally provide the *forum* for decision-making, but that IGOs are the decision-*maker* itself. Again, these are situations where the IGO guides states, rather than vice versa. Some outcomes require that multiple states agree on *how* they will decide, before the time for decision comes. This is more than just an agreement on a particular decision: it is the setting up of a group decision-making *procedure* to which they are all committed, which will come into effect under conditions on which they all agree, which will be used to make many future particular decisions. The use of such a procedure is *the IGO* making a decision. This is particularly clear in majoritarian IGOs, such as the Security Council and the World Health Organization.

Third, any given state cannot be guaranteed that the IGO will make the decision the state wants it to make. The quotations above suggest that *each* state is more powerful than the IGO. In fact, states *together* determine the scope of IGOs' powers. The power of any one state—even a powerful state like the United States—is weaker than that of the IGO, within the IGOs' scope of decision-making. Powerful states can of course "veto" certain IGO decisions (notoriously those of the Security Council), but they still are not guaranteed to have their preferred action permitted (Grigorescu 2007: 296–7; Steffek 2010; Woods 2003). IGOs' decision-making procedures are a result of complex and lengthy negotiations between members, with the result that members are often required to perform actions that they would not perform in the absence of the IGO (as demonstrated by Harbour's (2003) discussion of compromise in IGOs). The capacity to make decisions and distribute roles against the will of any one state gives an IGO a decision-making capacity that is distinct from the sum of members' capacities—and, once again, shows that (in some contexts) states are tethered to IGOs, not vice versa.

This is important, since holding an IGO responsible as a collective agent—in either the prospective or retrospective sense—is not the same as holding responsible the sum of the states that happen to constitute that IGO. This distinction is not always appreciated in international political practice. For example, the UN's 1999 report on the fall of Srebrenica asserted that

> The international community as a whole must accept its share of [retrospective] responsibility for allowing this tragic course of events by its prolonged refusal to use force in the early stages of the war. This responsibility is shared by the Security Council, and Contact Group and other Governments [...] as well as by the United Nations Secretariat and the mission in the field.
>
> *(United Nations 1999: par. 501)*

My analysis suggests that the Security Council, Contact Group, and United Nations Secretariat are all candidates for responsibility—prospective and retrospective. But the "international community as a whole"—understood as a collection of states and not identified specifically with the UN (or the UN General Assembly)—is not a moral agent.[9] To hold this informal group responsible is not the same as holding particular IGOs responsible. I take up such informal groups over the next two sections.

23.5 An Easy Non-Case: The Affluent

My conception of collective agency is permissive, but it's not as permissive as some might hope. In particular, it doesn't include groups such as "the international community," "the affluent" or "humanity." To settle ideas, I'll focus on "the affluent," but my remarks apply equally to the international community, humanity, carbon emitters, and so on. Each of these groups lacks a group-level decision-making procedure; however, we still might try to attribute responsibility to them, by pointing out that they are *potential moral agents*. The argument would be roughly: (1) the affluent have the potential to become a moral agent, and (2) if the affluent were a moral agent, then they would bear moral responsibility; therefore, (3) the affluent bear (perhaps putative) responsibility for making themselves into a moral agent.[10] One way to understand this is that the affluents' becoming an agent is the *means* towards the affluents' discharging their moral responsibility. Since the affluent have the ability to take this means (i.e., they have the ability to become an agent), the affluent have responsibility to take the means. The responsibility to take the means (become a moral agent) derives from their responsibility over the end (alleviating global poverty, for example).

The problem with this argument is that *becoming a moral agent* is either an action, or it is not. If it is an action—and if only agents can perform actions—then the affluent would need to be an agent before it could become an agent. However, this is impossible, because no entity is an agent before it has become an agent. But in that case, the affluent cannot have a responsibility to perform the action of becoming an agent as a means to discharging its responsibilities. Alternatively, perhaps becoming an agent is not an action. Then, becoming an agent is indeed something that can *happen to* the affluent. But it is not an action, so it doesn't look like something the affluent can have responsibility over.

A different way to argue that the affluent can have responsibility is to say that each affluent individual is retrospectively responsible for her individual actions that causally interacted with certain actions of other affluent people (leading to poverty, or climate change, or so on), and/or that each affluent individual has prospective responsibilities that require her to consider, and interact with, other affluent individuals (in order to alleviate poverty, or climate change, or so on). That is, we might point out that individuals' responsibilities have inter-related *content* or similar *explanatory origins*. This might be thought to suggest that the responsibilities are held by the collective *as such*.[11]

However, inter-related content of individual responsibilities does not suggest that the responsibility is held by the group per se. After all, almost all prospective responsibilities of all agents require their bearers to react to other agents, and almost all retrospective responsibility of all agents are responsibilities for actions that were linked with others' actions. For example, if I am retrospectively responsible for breaking my promise to you, then I have performed an action of promise-making, where that action is linked to your action of promise-accepting. Or if I am prospectively responsible for giving you \$10, then fulfilling that responsibility will require that I interact with you (or at least your bank account). If we said that all responsibilities-that-are-linked-with-other-agents'-responsibilities were responsibilities of a group that included those other agents, then the results would be bizarre: plainly, my retrospective responsibility for breaking my promise to you is not held by me-and-you; likewise, my prospective responsibility to give you \$10 is not held by me-and-you. By the same token, my responsibility to contribute to poverty relief might require that I interact with other affluent people, but this does not mean the responsibility is held by *the affluent* as such. Such a group cannot bear responsibility for international political problems.

23.6 A Harder Non-Case: The West

The final group that I'll consider is the West. Unlike the affluent, the West is united by a substantive common cause that's not held by all agents—roughly, the promotion of individual rights and free trade. "The West" is what Isaacs (2011) calls a "goal-oriented collective." To give my own gloss on this notion: each member of the group (1) holds the same goal, where it's out in the open between them that the goal is held by each (though it might be held only tacitly or implicitly); and (2) is disposed to act responsively to one another (insofar as they encounter one another) to realize the goal; however, the group (3) lacks group-level procedures for forming decisions, intentions, beliefs, and desires that are attributable to the group as such. Other examples of groups that meet (1), (2), and (3) include capitalists, environmentalists, human rights campaigners, and the oil lobby—all key players in international politics. To be clear, the members of these goal-oriented collectives each contribute to relevant collective agents—but there is no *one* collective agent to which they all contribute, so the group as a whole does not constitute a collective agent.

Other international relations theorists have similarly delineated this category of collective. "The West" is what Stephen Krasner seminally defined as a "regime," that is, a group united by "implicit or explicit principles, norms, rules, and decision-making procedures around which actors' expectations converge in a given area of international relations" (Krasner 1983: 2). Crucially, the "decision-making procedures" that Krasner references here are decision-making procedures held severally by each of the members—the procedures "converge" in that they have similar structures and goals, but there is one procedure for each member, rather than one overriding procedure that subsumes all members. Likewise, Mervyn Frost (2003: 94–8) analyzes groups whose members are engaged in a "dispersed practice." Within this category, Frost includes collectives bound together along religious, political, or linguistic lines—within which he includes "global civil society," "the West," and "capitalism" (2003: 99). I will take the West as a paradigm example of a goal-orientated collective (Isaacs), regime (Krasner), or dispersed practice group (Frost).

What are we to say about the moral responsibility of such entities? It is tempting to attribute moral agency (and, therefore, moral responsibility) to them, because of their common goal, shared dispositions, and shared ability to deliberate about morally good considerations. We might naturally say *the oil lobby frustrates climate legislation reform* or *the environmental movement should take more radical action*, meaning to attribute retrospective and prospective responsibility, respectively. International relations scholars do the same: Frost points out that his "dispersed practice" groups are in fact treated as responsible, and sometimes treat themselves as responsible (2003). Frost views such treatment as sufficient to *construct* or *establish* the moral agency of such entities. From a normative perspective, however, we should be wary of uncritically accepting the way entities happen to be treated. Our treatment of these entities as agents might be inappropriate. Instead, the question I want to address is: *should* we treat the West as a responsible entity?

From some theoretical perspectives, such treatment might make sense. For example, suppose "the West" includes all and only those states that favor individual rights and free trade (rather than also including the individual members of those states). One might then think the West meets the conditions Michael Bratman gives for a "shared intention": "[w]e each have intentions that we J, and we each intend that we J by way of each of our intentions that we J and by way of subplans that mesh" (Bratman 2014: 103). This will be the case where J is, for example, "slow China's economic rise." We might grant that the West can, in this way, have intentions. (Though it's worth noting that Bratman himself eschews such applications of his framework (Bratman 2014: 7).)

Still, I suggest, we should not grant agency—and, therefore, not responsibility—to the West per se. This is because the collective (or joint, or shared) intention was not formed *by the group*. That is, the West does not have a central core of agency—a *procedure* by which it can make official group-level decisions—at which it is possible for the group to produce that collective intention. Instead, the collective intention was formed simply via each agent (that is, each Western state) holding a certain intention, and intending to exercise it in ways that mesh with the others' like intentions. The West cannot intend anything that its state-members don't intend. That is to say: to be an agent (and, *a fortiori*, a moral agent), it's not enough that one has an intention, or acts intentionally. In addition, one's intentions must have a certain kind of causal history: one's deliberation, consideration, or reflection must be what produces the intention. But in a group like the West—considered distinctly from NATO or the European Union, both of which have the kind of agency discussed in section 23.4—there is no group-level capacity for such deliberation, consideration, or reflection. Such processes require that the entity act on *its own* reasons, not the conjunction of the reasons held by each of the members of the group. But a group can come to its own reasons only if it has its own distinctive goals and beliefs. This means that the West, per se, cannot bear prospective or retrospective responsibility—though its individual members can, as can collective moral agents that include those members as members (such as NATO or the EU).

23.7 Conclusion

Where are we to locate prospective and retrospective responsibility in international relations? I answered this question by starting with the (admittedly large) assumption that all and only moral agents can bear responsibility. I offered a characterization of moral agency, which I suggested was straightforwardly applicable to many states and (somewhat less straightforwardly) to some intergovernmental organizations. Things are less promising, however, when it comes to holding responsible a group whose members hold no goals in common (such as "the affluent"), or even groups that are united around a common cause (such as "the West").

Let me close with two important caveats. First, states' and IGOs' moral agency does not imply that states or IGOs are moral saints that should go unquestioned or unchallenged. Precisely because they have the *capacity* to deliberate upon morally good reasons, we should hold them accountable for their decisions—both good and (perhaps more often) bad. Second, members of non-agent groups can have responsibility (prospective or retrospective) for acting upon those non-moral collective agents—and upon non-agent collectives—in such a way as to transform them into collective moral agents. Likewise, non-members (including various moral collective agents) can have responsibility for such transformation of collectives. In this way, the fact that some entities in international politics do not themselves bear responsibility does not let anyone "off the hook" in the long run. Instead, by limiting our responsibility-ascriptions to those entities that are moral agents, we can be surer that we make demands only on those entities with the capacity to respond.

Notes

1 I thank Deborah Tollefsen and Saba Bazargan-Forward for pressing me to clarify this.
2 Erskine (2001: 82–3) considers but ultimately rejects a similar conclusion for "quasi-states". "Quasi-states" are moral agents on my criteria, which are more permissive than Erskine's.
3 The idea that IGOs are agents accords with public international law (Crawford 2012: 169–70). I've argued elsewhere that moral agency applies to even more informal groupings, such as some "coalitions of the willing" (Collins 2014; see also Erskine 2014).
4 I add this condition because it rules out the G7 and G20 as IGOs. While this deserves argumentation, it allows me to focus on the strongest examples, to demonstrate that at least *some* IGOs are moral agents.
5 I thank Richard Collins for pressing IGO diversity and encouraging the "some" claim.
6 In the sense defined in section 23.2—there is also a natural sense in which only states are "members" of the UN.
7 The most general aim of the United Nations is provided in Chapter I of its Charter (UN 1945).

8 The most general aim of the International Criminal Police Organization (INTERPOL) is "to enable police around the world to work together to make the world a safer place" by giving them "access to the tools and services necessary to do their jobs effectively" and "facilitating international police cooperation even where diplomatic relations do not exist between particular countries" (INTERPOL 2019).

9 I therefore agree with Brown: "there is no body that acts for the society of states *as a whole*" (2001: 98, emphasis original). However, in opposition to Brown, this is not because UN organs are not moral agents. It's rather because "the society of states" is not an agent, and no agent can act on behalf of something that is not itself an agent.

10 Arguments of this kind are made by May 1992: 109; Isaacs 2011: 145–51; and Wringe 2010: 222. These authors could be interpreted as arguing that each of the individuals in the group has a responsibility with the same content, rather than that the responsibility is group-level. Given this possible interpretation, I am considering this argument independently from its presentation by these authors. I thank Deborah Tollefsen and Saba Bazargan-Forward for pressing the alternative interpretation of these authors.

11 Young (2011: 180–1) implies something like this, though again one could make the "shared content of individual responsibilities" rather than the "group-level responsibility" interpretation ofYoung.

References

Abbott, K.W. and Snidal, D. (2009) "Strengthening International Regulation Through Transnational New Governance: Overcoming the Orchestration Deficit", *Vanderbilt Journal of Transnational Law* 42(2), pp. 501–78.

Acharya, A. (2017) "After Liberal Hegemony: The Advent of a Multiplex World Order", *Ethics and International Affairs* 31(3), pp. 271–85.

Aggestam, L. (ed.) (2008) *Ethical Power Europe*? Special Issue of *Ethics and International Affairs*, 84(1), pp. 1–143.

Barnett, M. (2003) *Eyewitness to a Genocide: The United Nations and Rwanda*. Ithaca: Cornell University Press.

Bexell, M. and Jönsson, K. (2017) "Responsibility and the United Nations' Sustainable Development Goals", *Forum for Development Studies* 44(1), pp. 13–29.

Biermann, R. and Koops, J.A. (2017) "Studying Relations Amongst International Organizations in World Politics: Core Concepts and Challenges" in Biermann, R. and Koops, J.A. (eds.) (2017) *The Palgrave Handbook of Inter-organizational Relations in World Politics*. London: Palgrave Macmillan, pp. 1–46.

Björnsson, G. (2014) "Essentially Shared Obligations", *Midwest Studies in Philosophy* 38(1), pp. 103–20.

Brady, C. (1999) "Collective Responsibility of the Cabinet: An Ethical, Constitutional or Managerial Tool?", *Parliamentary Affairs* 52(2), pp. 214–29.

Bratman, M. (2014) *Shared Agency: A Planning Theory of Acting Together*. Oxford: Oxford University Press.

Brown, C. (2001) "Moral Agency and International Society", *Ethics and International Affairs* 15(2), pp. 87–98.

Collins, S. (2014) "Are 'Coalitions of the Willing' Moral Agents?", *Ethics and International Affairs* 28(1) [online]. Available at: www.ethicsandinternationalaffairs.org/ 2014/are-coalitions-of-the-willing-moral-agents/ (Accessed: 25 January 2019).

Collins, S. (2016) "The Claims and Duties of Socioeconomic Human Rights", *The Philosophical Quarterly*, 66(265), pp. 701–22.

Collins, S. (Forthcoming A) *Group Duties: Their Existence and Their Implications for Individuals*. Oxford: Oxford University Press.

Collins, S. (Forthcoming B) "Collective Responsibility Gaps", *Journal of Business Ethics*.

Cornish, P. and Harbour, F.V. (2003) "NATO and the Individual Soldier as Moral Agents with Reciprocal Duties: Imbalance in the Kosovo Campaign" in Erskine, T. (ed.) (2003) *Can Institutions Have Responsibilities? Collective Moral Agency and International Relations*. Basingstoke: Palgrave Macmillan, pp. 119–37.

Crawford, J. (2012) *Brownlie's Principles of Public International Law*. 8th edn. Oxford: Oxford University Press.

Engelbrekt, K. (2015) "Responsibility Shirking at the United Nations Security Council: Constraints, Frustrations, Remedies", *Global Policy Volume* 6(4), pp. 369–78.

Erskine, T. (2001) "Assigning Responsibilities to Institutional Moral Agents: the Case of States and Quasi-states", *Ethics & International Affairs* 15(2), pp. 67–89.

Erskine, T. (ed.) (2003) *Can Institutions Have Responsibilities? Collective Moral Agency and International Relations*. New York: Palgrave Macmillan.

Erskine, T. (2014) "Coalitions of the Willing and Responsibilities to Protect: Informal Associations, Enhanced Capacities, and Shared Moral Burdens", *Ethics and International Affairs* 28, pp. 115–45.

Evans, G. (2008) *The Responsibility to Protect: Ending Mass Atrocity Crimes Once and For All.* Washington: The Brookings Institution.

French, P. (1984) *Collective and Corporate Responsibility*. New York: Columbia University Press.

Frost, M. (2003) "Constitutive Theory and Moral Accountability: Individuals, Institutions, and Dispersed Practices" in Erskine, T. (ed.) (2003) pp. 84–99.

Gilbert, M. (2006) *A Theory of Political Obligation: Membership, Commitment, and the Bonds of Social Society*. Oxford: Oxford University Press.

Grigorescu, A. (2007) "Transparency of Intergovernmental Organizations: The Roles of Member-States, International Bureaucracies and Non-Governmental Organizations", *International Studies Quarterly* 51(3), pp. 625–48.

Harbour, F.V. (2003) "Collective Moral Agency and the Political Process" in Erskine, T. (ed.) (2003), pp. 69–83.

Harbour, F.V. (2004) "Moral Agency and Moral Responsibility in Humanitarian Intervention", *Global Society* 18(1), pp. 61–75.

Hindriks, F. (Forthcoming) "Collective Agency: Moral and Amoral", *Dialectica*.

International Criminal Police Organization (INTERPOL) (2019), "About INTERPOL: Overview". [online] Available at: www.interpol.int/About-INTERPOL/Over view. (Accessed: 27 January 2019).

International Law Commission (ILC). (2011) *Draft Articles on the Responsibility of International Organizations*. [online] Available at: http://untreaty.un.org/ilc/texts /instruments/ english/draft%20articles/9_11_2011.pdf. (Accessed: 25 January 2019).

Isaacs, T. (2011) *Moral Responsibility in Collective Contexts*. Oxford: Oxford University Press.

Krasner, S.D. (1983) "Structural Causes and Regime Consequences: Regimes as Intervening Variables" in Krasner, S.D. (ed.) (1983), *International Regimes*. Ithaca: Cornell University Press, pp. 1–20.

Lackey, J. (2016) "What Is Justified Group Belief?", *Philosophical Review* 125(3), pp. 341–96.

Lang, Jr., A. (2003) "The United Nations and the Fall of Srebrenica: Meaningful Responsibility and International Society" in Erskine, T. (ed.) (2003) pp. 183–206.

Lawford-Smith, H. (2015) "What 'We'?" *Journal of Social Ontology* 1(2), pp. 225–9.

List, C. (2014) "Three Kinds of Collective Attitudes", *Erkenntnis* 79 (9 supp), pp. 1601–22.

List, C. and Pettit, P. (2011) *Group Agency: The Possibility, Design, and Status of Corporate Agents*. Oxford: Oxford University Press.

List, C. and Spiekermann, K. (2013) "Methodological Individualism and Holism in Political Science: A Reconciliation", *American Political Science Review* 107(4), pp. 629–43.

Mathiesen, K. (2006) "The Epistemic Features of Group Belief", *Episteme* 2(3), pp. 161–75.

May, L. (1992) *Sharing Responsibility*. Chicago: University of Chicago Press.

Mayer, H. (2017) "Is It Still Called 'Chinese Whispers'? The EU's Rhetoric and Action as a Responsible Global Institution", *International Affairs* 84(1), pp. 61–79.

McNeill, D. and St. Clair, A.L. (2009) *Global Poverty, Ethics and Human Rights: The Role of Multilateral Organizations*. New York: Routledge.

O'Neill, O. (1986) "Who Can Endeavour Peace?", *Canadian Journal of Philosophy* 16(1), pp. 41–73.

Pereboom, D. (2001) *Living Without Free Will*. Cambridge: Cambridge University Press.

Pettit, P. (2001) "Deliberative Democracy and the Discursive Dilemma"', *Philosophical Issues* (supp. to Nous) 11, 268–99.

Pettit, P. (2007) "Responsibility Incorporated", *Ethics* 117, pp. 141–201.

Rovane, C. (1998) *The Bounds of Agency: An Essay in Revisionary Metaphysics*. Princeton: Princeton University Press.

Schwenkenbecher, A. (2013) "Joint Duties and Global Moral Obligations", *Ratio* 26(3), pp. 310–28.

Smiley, M. (2010) "From Moral Agency to Collective Wrongs: Rethinking Collective Moral Responsibility", *Journal of Law and Policy* 19(1) pp. 171–202.

Steffek, J. (2010) "Public Accountability and the Public Sphere of International Governance", *Ethics & International Affairs* 24(1), pp. 45–68.

Union of International Associations (2015) "What Is an Intergovernmental Organization?" [online] Available at: www.uia.org/faq/yb3. (Accessed: 27 January 2019).

United Nations. (1945) *Charter of the United Nations*. [online] 26 June 1945. Available at: www.un.org/en/charter-united-nations/index.html (Accessed: 27 January 2019).

United Nations. (1999) *Report of the Secretary-General pursuant to General Assembly resolution 53/35: The Fall of Srebrenica*, Document A/54/549. New York: United Nations. [online] Available at: http://repository.un.org/handle/11176/227626 (Accessed: 25 January 2019).
United Nations Department of Public Information (UNDPI). (2012) "Secretary-General, Addressing Drake University Students on 'Global Citizenship', says no Issue can be Seen in Isolation as World Changes". UNDPI News and Media Division, New York. 19 October 2012. Available at: www.un.org/News/Press/docs/2012/sgsm14595.doc.htm (Accessed: 25 January 2019).
Wendt, A. (2004) "The State as Person in International Theory", *Review of International Studies* 30(2), pp. 289–316.
Woods, N. (2003) "Holding Intergovernmental Institutions to Account", *Ethics & International Affairs* 17(1), pp. 69–80.
Wringe, B. (2010) "Global Obligations and the Agency Objection", *Ratio* 23(2), pp. 217–31.
Wringe, B. (2016) "Collective Obligations: Their Existence, Their Explanatory Power, and their Supervenience on the Obligations of Individuals", *European Journal of Philosophy* 24(4), pp. 472–97.
Young, I. M. (2011) *Responsibility for Justice*. Oxford: Oxford University Press.

24
COMPETING COLLECTIVE VALUES
Moral and Causal Responsibilities in Health Care

Robin Downie

24.1 Problems and Approaches

Some philosophers maintain that only individual persons of mature age can be held morally responsible, but others argue that collective responsibility is also a legitimate concept. Those philosophers who wish to allow for collective responsibility usually distinguish between two different types of collective. Some collectives, they argue, have well-defined identities and decision-making procedures, such as large commercial businesses, or political entities such as the Cabinet in the United Kingdom's government. They are often called "corporations" (French 1984). A second candidate to be called a collective is one in which the group members identify themselves as group members and share attitudes, values, and aims (Feinberg 1968; French 1984: 13–14). An army might be an example of a collective of this sort. I have no objection to calling both types of organization "collectives" and indeed there may be some legal convenience attached to doing so. Collectives of both types exert considerable influence on the behavior of the individuals who work within them; they could therefore be said to have some causal responsibility for the behavior of their members. But my position is that moral responsibility remains with individuals. Nevertheless, it is of interest to consider how the aims and values of these collectives influence the decisions of the doctors, patients, and bureaucrats who work in or receive health care.

These two types of collective are involved in different ways in the delivery of health care. The shared attitudes and values of the medical profession are of course central but health care is affected in crucial ways by the fact that a great deal of it takes place in hospitals, which are corporate bodies with the attitudes and values of commercial organizations. Even in the UK, where health care is publicly funded, hospitals are obliged to meet various targets, including financial ones. These are set by non-medical external bodies such as government departments. Moreover, pharmaceutical companies, which are also corporate bodies, have a large impact on the delivery of health care. They too are under pressure to produce new drugs and to make profits for shareholders. Pressures from the aims and values of these different types of collective will affect the moral decisions and responsibilities of individual doctors working in health care. For example, there can be dilemmas for doctors caused by pressures from hospital management to meet targets, which may be at the expense of high quality care.

In addition to these complexities, it is important to note that the delivery of health care by doctors is currently, in the West at least, in a state of transition between different models of the doctor/patient relationship. Traditionally, the patient approached the doctor with a health problem, and the doctor made a diagnosis with a suggested treatment usually consented to by the patient. But at the moment, many patients approach the doctor with requests, or sometimes even demands, concerning the sort of treatment the doctor should provide. In other words, patients are becoming consumers of health care. And with this change, moral responsibility will become divided (Downie 2017). Doctors will remain morally responsible for supplying accurate information, but patients as consumers become morally responsible for making the choice of treatment.

In view of these several variations and complexities in the delivery of health care, it is unlikely that a clear picture of responsibility will emerge. But at least it can be shown where the problems of responsibility for the doctor and the patient/consumer arise. As a way into these problems, I shall begin by examining the morality of social roles and the type of responsibility involved, for doctors occupy social roles.

24.2 The Medical Role

We assume in everyday life that it is individuals who are to be held morally responsible for their actions, on the grounds that it is only individuals who can have the freedom of choice and prior knowledge that are considered to be the necessary conditions of moral responsibility. I shall not discuss the many challenges to this assumption. But my argument does require that I stress that the conception of the individual in the common assumption tends to be a thin one. The self which emerges from Cartesian, Kantian, or existentialist assumptions is one defined simply by an ability to choose, to have a rational will; it carries no social baggage. By contrast, I shall argue for a self which is social in nature (Macmurray 1970). Our identities are influenced or indeed constituted by values from many sources. From our arrival in this world, we assimilate values from family, high school education, professional education, newspapers, and influences of all kinds. In short, we take on the values of assorted groups and collectives. This means that the self which chooses is expressing collective values through individual choices. These collective values and attitudes are especially focused when we examine professional choices, especially those involved in the long tradition of health care. To enable me to conceptualize this point, I shall use the concept of a social role. I shall not argue for the thesis sometimes found in sociological literature that all actions and choices take place in a social role (Hindin 2007). My argument is less extreme: I shall assume only that the actions of doctors and other professionals in health care are carried out in a social role, a role which is constituted by a long history and contemporary expectations.

Over the years, the medical role has grown and developed. It is constituted by three main elements. The first is the Hippocratic element. Hippocrates was a Greek physician who was born around 460 BC. He and his School were dedicated to investigating the rational, scientific basis of medicine (Lloyd 1983: 29). This scientific approach ignores the individuality of patients and concentrates on what diseases have in common: it is assumed that diseases follow a pattern, the causal laws of which can be discovered. This belief is the foundation of Western, scientific medicine, expressed nowadays in the slogan or a pattern, the causal. It is the dominant value in the medical role at the moment and is the inspiration behind the algorithmic approach to patient care, which I shall discuss later. Many doctors in fact see medicine as an applied science, and they strongly value a scientific approach to disease.

The second element shaping the role is also Greek in origin: it is the tradition of Asclepius, a shadowy figure in Greek thought who was claimed to be the son of Apollo (the god of healing and the arts) by a mortal woman. Patients sought relief from their sufferings in the temples of Asclepius, where harmless serpents (*Coluber longissima*) lived. Their hypnotic gaze was thought to encourage healing to come from within the patient: as contrasted with the external interventions favored by the Hippocratic tradition, the Asclepian tradition stresses quiet waiting and listening (Hart 2000). Dr. Marie Therese Southgate, former Deputy Editor of the *Journal of the American Medical Association*, brings out the nature of the Asclepian tradition by means of a comparison with the approach of the artist. She argues that both have a common goal, to complete what nature cannot bring to a close: this is done, she suggests, by paying attention: "If we are attentive in looking, in listening, and in waiting, then sooner or later something in the depths of ourselves will respond" (Southgate 1997: xii). This approach draws attention to the mystique of a medical consultation and ascribes to the doctor an almost shamanic quality, corresponding to the hypnotic gaze of the healing serpents. In more contemporary, down-to-earth terms, doctors retain a high status in Western society and remain similarly respected and deferred to. Doctors are aware of this status and see it as part of the medical inheritance. The awareness of status contributes to the make-up of the role, although, as I shall suggest, the shamanic quality is under threat, or at least modification, from patient consumerism.

The third element consists of a combination of Greek and Christian influences. The Greek influence derives again from Hippocrates and his School. Hippocrates is usually given the credit for introducing the idea of ethics into medical practice. Even if medical students no longer take the Hippocratic Oath the idea of the values expressed in that Oath continues in forms modified by cultural changes. Medical ethics has of course greatly developed in the period since 1945 and doctors see ethics as central to their role. Medical law has also developed. But the regulations of medical law and ethics cannot cover what might be termed the adverbial side to ethics – the manner and extent of medical interventions. This is where the Christian influence has been powerful. The parable of the Good Samaritan (Luke 10: 30–37) tells of the good physician who has compassion and cares for a victim regardless of race, religion, or danger. There is a tradition that St Luke was a physician and certainly the New Testament Greek contains references to remedies from Greek medicine. This element is wider than the rights and duties of medical ethics – it stresses the centrality of dedication and vocation in professional practice.

These three elements – the Hippocratic/scientific, the Asclepian/shamanic, and the ethical/Samaritan – have created a sense of solidarity and shared values within the profession and have given rise to a mystique surrounding the medical consultation, not unlike the deference formally accorded to priests. Indeed, the views of doctors are sought on many matters wider than medical ones. It is convenient to encapsulate the three elements in the idea of a medical "ethos." The ethos pervades medical education and becomes part of the identity of the doctor qua doctor. When medical students graduate from medical school they accept a role constituted by this ethos. This is what it means to act as a doctor. The ethos has molded the role and therefore strongly influenced the actions and decisions emerging from it. Consider the following quotations, which are typical of contemporary attitudes:

> Medicine is one of the few spheres of human activity in which the purposes are unambiguously altruistic.
>
> *(New England Journal of Medicine 2000: 42)*

or:

> Altruism is the essence of professionalism. The best interest of patients, not self-interest, is the rule.
>
> *(American Board of Internal Medicine 1998: 5)*

These shared values and attitudes – the ethos – are cultivated through medical education. From the start of medical education, students are taught together and share a curriculum, which is largely similar for all students, and even extra-curricular activities reinforce the ethos through informal student societies, such as "year clubs." Such factors play a role in inculcating a sense of loyalty even in the earliest years of professionalization. This loyalty is directed partly towards the institution and its members, but also towards medicine itself. In later years, ways of relating to patients and other health workers, even in other institutions, become part of medical professionalism. The professional ethic of medicine is steeped in collective attitudes and values. Those values and attitudes constitute the role of the doctor and are expressed in the continuity of the ethos. The ethos, or the collective values of medicine, will causally affect medical policies and decisions, but moral responsibility enters the scene only if the individual is willing to go along with the ethos.

24.3 Role Acceptance

Social roles are accepted by the individuals who act in them. Insofar as individuals choose the role of doctor or other health professional, they are morally responsible for their choices. But again, there is need for some modification here; the collective values of society, or at least of certain social classes within society, are also determinants in these career decisions. For example, some young people entering medical school may have been highly influenced by their parents or high school. These authoritative bodies are expressing a collective view that being a doctor or health professional is a good thing. The young person's freedom of choice may thus be, to some extent and in some cases, totally compromised, and their moral responsibility is affected by a subtle kind of duress. Equally, the young person's knowledge of what they were letting themselves in for may have been skewed by another set of collective values – those expressed by the many fanciful medical soap operas. It could therefore be argued that these collective values will to some extent determine, or at least affect, the moral choices of some of those entering medical school. But of course, it is possible to leave medical school or resign the role, so these considerations perhaps amount to no more than the point that no action or decision is purely an individual one: all our decisions are to some extent influenced by the values of our society. But certainly, we can and do pass moral judgments on the morality of role acceptance. In view of the nature of the health care professions and their bearing on human good and harm, the responsibility for choosing the role of medical student is a moral one. Was the role chosen out of a sense of vocation or calling; in the hope of making money; or just because it seemed a respectable middle-class job? It is impossible to disentangle the factors that may affect such important decisions, but it is clear that to a greater or lesser extent, the assorted collective values of society as a whole will be important factors affecting individual responsibility.

Moreover, while collective values certainly affect the moral responsibility of trainees for their decisions to enter the health professions, collective values also play an important part in administrative decisions as to whether to accept applicants to medical schools. Applicants must pass certain tests of intellect and personality, and these tests will be the same for all applicants.

Many medical schools will also interview candidates and ask the same set of questions to each interviewee. The questions asked of the applicants and the assessment of their answers will again express the collective values of the health professions at a certain point in history. In this way, the continuation of the traditional ethos of the medical profession is ensured by the selection process.

24.4 Role Enactment

More important than the morality of role acceptance is that of role enactment. In view of the fact that the medical role exists as a set of rights, duties, and values independently of who is acting in the role, the free action of doctors is to a great extent limited by the role. We might put the point in other words by saying that the doctor is *authorized* by the collective values of the role to act only in certain ways. Or we might say that since doctors are *representatives* of their profession – they must act only in certain ways laid down by their collective. Their individual moral decisions will therefore be causally affected by the collective values of the medical tradition. More importantly, however, there is increasing insistence by professional bodies on treatment guidelines, protocols, and algorithms. These are thought to express the collective wisdom of the profession on the best management of patient care.

Consider the following extract from a book concerned, among other matters, with the way in which we are increasingly organized into networks so that each person is only a small step in a huge network of algorithms, and it is the algorithm as a whole that makes the important decisions. The author takes the specific example of hospitals and writes:

> Think about a modern hospital, for example. When you arrive the receptionist hands you a standard form, and asks you a predetermined set of questions. Your answers are forwarded to a nurse, who compares them with the hospital's regulations in order to decide what preliminary tests to give you. She then measures, say, your blood pressure and heart rate, and takes a blood test. The doctor on duty examines the results, and follows a strict protocol to decide in which ward to hospitalize you. [...] Specialists analyze the results according to well-known statistical databases, deciding what medicines to give you or what further tests to run. The algorithmic structure ensures that it doesn't really matter who is the receptionist, nurse, or doctor on duty. Their personality, political opinions and momentary moods are irrelevant. As long as they follow the regulations and protocols they have a good chance of curing you. According to the algorithmic ideal, your fate is in the hands of "the system", and not in the hands of the flesh and blood mortals who happen to man this or that post.
>
> *(Harari 2015: 160–161)*

There is clear justification for this, in that the most satisfactory result is likely to emerge from following the algorithm. For example, let us imagine that a general practitioner (GP) is interviewing a patient. She comes to the conclusion that the symptoms indicate a certain condition and treatment. Now, an experienced GP may have seen 50–100 similar cases. But the algorithm indicates that the symptoms should be fed into the computer, which contains information on 5 million cases. Hence, a more accurate diagnosis and treatment will emerge. But where is the responsibility here? The individual responsibility is that of the GP who followed the proper procedures, and presumably a computer programmer is responsible for correctly programming the data, but the data comes from innumerable sources (Susskind and Susskind 2015: 46–55). These sources amount to collective wisdom; they will express the best evidence base for the ailment in question. Even if a doctor thinks that this collective wisdom may not lead to the optimum treatment for a given patient, she may ignore her own judgment and go with the algorithm. There will always be a strong legal defense for the GP, to the effect that "I did what the protocol instructed." In other words, strong pressure comes from the "system," the collective. We might say that the treatment protocol acts as a kind of duress: even if the doctor thinks that in this case the protocol will not result in the optimum treatment for a patient, she puts her career at risk by ignoring it.

It might be said, of course, that there is certainly scope for discretion concerning ways of communicating and managing the patient. This is the "adverbial" side to treatment, mentioned earlier, concerning in what manner, when, and how much to communicate to a given patient. But even here, courses on "communication skills" have the effect, if not the aim, of stereotyping doctors' responses to patients, conveying the idea that there is a universal, teachable, and learnable skill in communicating. Hence, the scope for individual initiative and therefore individual responsibility is increasingly limited, even in matters such as communication.

My argument so far has attempted to highlight the manner in which even apparently individual decisions in health care are strongly influenced by the shared collective values and attitudes of doctors and nurses and the whole continuing ethos of medicine. These collective values influence or even determine the actions of individual health professionals, from their entry to the professions to their conduct within them. Doctors, perhaps more than any other group, identify with their values and recognize themselves and other doctors as belonging to a group that shares the same values. There is therefore at least some collective causal responsibility, deriving from the ethos, for individual moral medical decisions.

Many writers on collective responsibility are concerned with collective guilt. They are interested in whether groups or even whole nations can be blamed for bad actions (French 1972). But collective values can also have good consequences. As far as medicine goes, both good and bad consequences spring from its collective values. The good consequences are obvious, but health care can be an unpleasant and stressful job. Doctors often must work long hours and deal with blood, sweat, tears, and worse, so the collective values and attitudes here can be a support and an inspiration in dealing with difficult cases. This is widely recognized and doctors have a high status in Western societies. Moreover, the collective wisdom of the algorithm is likely to lead to optimum treatment. There is an important downside to this, however, which I shall discuss later.

24.5 Collective Values and Roles in Management

So far, I have discussed collective responsibility in health care in terms of the shared attitudes and values of doctors, which to a great extent and in various ways determine their actions and affect their moral responsibilities. But a very different kind of collective responsibility is also present in health care, because a great deal of health care takes place in hospitals or other large group practices. Hospitals are corporate persons, that have aims, values, and responsibilities that differ from medical ones. Two questions arise here: how does the existence of corporate persons, such as hospitals, affect my conceptual/philosophical claim that only human individuals are morally responsible; and how do the values of corporate persons such as hospitals causally affect the individual decisions, and therefore responsibility, of its employees such as doctors?

In answering the first question, I stress that the essential attribute of corporate personality is that, upon incorporation, the company becomes a legal person distinct from its members, such as its shareholders. The corporate person can then sue and be sued in its own name; does not cease to exist if its members die; and can have debts for which its members are not liable. Corporate personality is therefore a useful legal concept, but crucially, it is an *abstract* concept: it separates its responsibility from that of any group of individuals who happen to be members of the corporate person at any given time. Of course, the individual persons who are employed by the corporate person carry moral responsibility for their roles in the business of the corporate person, but (to answer my first question) the corporate person itself carries only *legal* responsibility and not *moral* responsibility.

A corporate person is a kind of collective familiar in politics and business: it has a clear structure, hierarchy, and decision procedure. An example of a structure of this kind is the Cabinet within the UK government. Its members are individually morally responsible for their own views and advice, but the Cabinet acts as a unitary body over important matters. It therefore carries the corporate responsibility of a legal person (French 1979: 297–317). Large businesses have a similar structure, and in the same way, are corporate persons that can be held responsible for their actions. But the responsibility in such cases is legal, rather than moral. Large hospitals or hospital trusts are in this category: they have boards of management and chief executives; maintain tight control of decision-making; and, if they run into financial difficulties, may be fined by governments. But note it is the corporate person, the trust, which is fined, but not the individual managers (although they may be sacked by the board of management). It is true as an empirical point that we do sometimes pass moral judgments on the corporate person as a whole, including hospitals, without especially thinking of the individuals who work in them. But this is a convenient fiction that allows the public to express their feelings through moral judgments.

My second question concerns the ways in which the attitudes and values of corporate persons, such as business or "the market," are liable to have a causal influence on the decisions of the medical staff that work within hospitals regarded as corporate persons. The values of business or "the market" were first stated by Adam Smith in 1776, and they have not been modified very much since that time. In a well-known passage in *The Wealth of Nations*, Smith tells us that it is not from the benevolence of the butcher, the baker, or the brewer that we expect our dinner, but from their regard to their self-interest (Smith 2008: 22). This passage is the classic statement of the view, taken as a given to the present day, that self-interest underlies all market transactions. Smith later expands this view by including competition and profits as essential to market transactions.

These are the values of market or business transactions; hospital trusts as corporate businesses will therefore be organized and administrated with those same values and aims. In terms of the concepts I have so far used, the role of manager or chief executive will be constituted by the values of institutional self-interest, the need to succeed in competition and to make profits. Just as the collective values of medicine permeate medical education, so business schools cultivate the values and attitudes of the free market. Moreover, the role enactment will also have been strongly influenced by management training: even if the chief executive was originally a doctor, the subsequent management training will have greatly modified the original medical values. It is therefore inevitable that the differences between the collective values of medicine and those of management are likely to lead to conflict. For example, in the UK, the need to meet government targets or satisfy shareholders may result in a decline in patient care; the emphasis will be on quantity of through-put rather than quality of care, which is likely to lead to poor morale among the medical staff. The collision between two sets of strongly held collective values does not make for coherent policies in health care, and it can create dilemmas of moral responsibility for the medical staff.

24.6 Patient Choice and Consumer Choice

The tensions between traditional medical values and those of business make for coherent policies in health care, and Western governments now encourage patients to see themselves as consumers of health care. Thus patient choice is stressed, but there is serious ambiguity in the conception of patient choice. The ordinary conception of choice enters medical practice via a term more commonly used in health care – consent, a foundation principle of medical ethics and treatment. Briefly, the doctor must provide adequate information on the treatment; suggest alternatives; and outline a possible action plan. Responsibility is therefore divided: the doctor takes responsibility for providing the information, the alternatives, and the action plan, while the patient takes responsibility for choosing or consenting to an offered action plan (Mason and McCall Smith 1994: 218–37).

But if patients adopt the role of consumer, they may wish to suggest their own alternatives. This can create three problems. The first is that of funding; however, I shall not develop this important issue, because although it raises serious problems for states and other providers of health care, funding is not one of the basic values of medicine. But the second problem is central to the medical ethos, that of the ownership of the knowledge base and the treatment options. Traditionally, medical knowledge was a preserve of the profession: influenced by the ethos, doctors would offer what they considered to be the best evidence-based treatments. But the internet has provided a challenge to this, and contemporary patients, as consumers of health care, may make suggestions or indeed demands concerning the treatments they want. Ownership of medical knowledge may therefore be disputed. The third problem concerns the locus of responsibility. In terms of the traditional ethos, the doctor was responsible for offering the treatments and the patient for consenting; but if the patient insists on having a certain treatment, the patient must take on the moral responsibility for that choice. If the patient's choice of treatment has been reached after discussion with his or her doctor, this change can be seen in a positive way, as creating a partnership between doctor and patient. But it certainly challenges the traditional medical ethos (Downie and Randall 2007: 182–185).

A consumerist-type problem can of course arise if there is disagreement between patient and doctor on optimum treatment. The UK and the United States seem to differ on this issue. In the UK, the Court of Appeal ruled that the courts could not require a medical practitioner to offer a treatment that the practitioner thought was contra-indicated. Lord Justice Balcombe went as far as to say: "[he] could conceive of no situation where it would be proper to order a doctor to treat a patient in a manner contrary to his/her clinical judgment" (*Re J* 1992: 625). On the other hand, in a survey of the literature in the US, it was claimed that doctors will almost always continue treatment if requested by patients or relatives, even if they regard it as futile (Paris et al. 1993). This view was supported by many US ethicists throughout the 1990s. Thus, Veatch and Spicer maintain that a physician is obliged to supply requested treatment, even if the request "deviates intolerably" from established standards or is in terms of the doctor's judgment "grossly inappropriate" (Veatch and Spicer 1992). I do not know what Veatch and Spicer mean by saying that a physician is "obliged" to supply "grossly inappropriate" treatment: such an obligation seems in direct conflict with the moral duty of a physician. But it is in accord with the consumerist maxim, "the customer is always right."

The point here may emerge more clearly if attention is drawn to the ambiguous term "best interests." It can be said that one merit of a consumer-based system is that it enables patients to achieve their own best interests. The assumption here is that patients know their own best interests, whereas traditionally, doctors decide what is in the patient's best interests and take responsibility for that decision. But there is a confusion here that arises from an ambiguity in the concept of "interest," an ambiguity between a psychological and a normative sense. "Best interests" in the psychological sense refers to choices arising from what people actually want to have: "autonomous choice" is usually interpreted in this way as expressing what the patient wants. But "best interests" in the normative sense refers to what a patient ought to have, whether he or she in fact wants the offered treatment or not. For example, it might be in a person's best interest to take some exercise or cut down on sugar, but he or she might not want to. As we say to the relative reluctant to accept the treatment, "It's for your own good." But in the framework or value-base of consumerism, the psychological and the normative senses will run together, for a person's best interest in such a framework or value-base is simply the satisfaction of his/her wants. On the other hand, in the framework or value-base of medicine, the psychological and normative senses of "best interests" are quite separate, and the doctor's professional duty is to offer treatments from the normative interpretation of "best interests." This normative view will have two components: a duty to promote the health of patients where possible, and a duty to take responsibility for the suggested treatment. Of course, the patient is entitled in law to refuse the doctor's offer of choices based on this normative view of best interests, even in cases where life-prolonging treatment is involved (British Medical Association 1999). But the central point is that the psychological sense of "best interests" expresses the value-base of consumerism, while the normative sense expresses that of medical professionalism. In other words, there is a conflict between two sets of collective values.

This conflict between the values and attitudes of medicine expressed through medical practitioners, and those of the free market expressed through management structures, can result in poor care for patients. For example, the management imperative to meet targets in the name of efficiency can conflict with the medical desire to spend time with patients, and thus care can be minimized to achieve through-put of patients. But the situation can become more confused when, as I shall go on to suggest, the solidarity of medical attitudes is in harmony with the solidarity of management attitudes with the aim of covering up serious mishaps.

24.7 Collective Cover-ups

When things go wrong, as they often do, the values and attitudes of both medicine and management can lead to the covering-up of serious failings in an attempt to preserve the reputations of both the medical professionals and management. For example, there has been increasing public concern about the covering-up or non-disclosure (as it is often called) of medical errors. In the US, for example, the Institute of Medicine reports that there are perhaps over a million preventable adverse events each year. It suggests that of these "adverse events", between 44,000 and 98,000 led to the deaths of patients. A note of caution should be recorded here, however, because the institute defines a medical error as "the failure of a planned action to be completed as intended or the use of a wrong plan to achieve an aim" (Institute of Medicine 2000). But that is a counterintuitive definition of an error: if I plan to meet you at 8pm for dinner and I am prevented from getting to the intended restaurant because of a transport breakdown, I have not made an error. And it is not uncommon for most of us – and especially within the complex world of clinical medicine – to have rational evidence-based plans, which for unforeseeable reasons do not work. Sometimes, for example, the standard, evidence-based antibiotic might not clear the infection because an unknown strain of bacteria has appeared. These failures are hardly "errors"; nevertheless, there are areas of health care in which there are justifiable concerns about non-disclosure. These usually concern poor care, sometimes amounting to negligence. According to an article in YouGov: "One in six British adults knows of someone whose poor treatment by the NHS has been covered-up – and majorities support sacking, prosecuting, and removing the pensions of staff found to be involved" (Dahlgreen 2013). Even allowing for some populist exaggeration from the people questioned in this survey, there is no doubt that cover-ups are of public concern.

There are several reasons why cases of poor treatment might be covered up. The first concerns the collective values of medicine, which encourage the closing of ranks. There is a smooth transition from the sharing of attitudes and a spirit of solidarity to a conspiracy of silence. The second is a legitimate desire not to upset the patient, especially when nothing can be done to put things right. The third, perhaps the most important, concerns fear of litigation. From the doctor's point of view, there may be a fear of disciplinary action, which could extend to a loss of license to practice. But even from the management point of view, there may be incentives to cover up. For example, the phenomenon of the ambulance-chasing lawyer is common enough, and patients and their relatives can easily be persuaded that they have been badly treated and are therefore entitled to financial compensation. Indeed, in the UK even if the courts find in favor of the hospital and not the patient, costs are likely to be awarded against the hospital. Hence, hospitals may settle out of court because this is cheaper. Again, however, hospital management may not want the bad publicity that comes from admitting to failures in care. At the very least, this would weaken their hospital's position in a competitive market. Hence, hospitals and their doctors – for different but understandable reasons – are inclined to play down significant adverse incidents. Collective attitudes here combine to work against good patient care. Once again, it may be a convenient fiction to speak of a collective cover-up and to attach moral blame to the hospital as corporate person, but the reality is that there has been a conspiracy of individual silences. Those who knew of the errors or poor treatment, and said or did nothing, are individually morally responsible.

Despite the understandable concerns of hospitals as corporate persons, however, the evidence seems to be that patients are less upset if there is disclosure of errors, provided that the disclosure is done in a compassionate way (Wu et al. 1997). Legal liability is another matter. Nevertheless, the American Medical Association's Council on Ethical and Judicial Affairs states that "concern regarding legal liability which might result following truthful disclosure should not affect the doctor's honesty with a patient" (American Medical Association 2007).

24.8 Conclusion

I have suggested that collective or widely shared values exist in health care. They derive from ancient traditions and are re-enforced by teamwork in professional situations and by the collectivization of treatment decisions by algorithms. But the situation in health care is complicated by the fact that hospitals also act as corporations or collectives with a different set of values – those of the market or of economics – which may be in tension with medical values. In addition, patients are increasingly taking on the role of consumers. This again will tend to clash with traditional medical values and will divide moral responsibility between doctor and patient-consumer. On the other hand, patient consumerism can be depicted as creating a new partnership between patient and doctor. But in the end, moral responsibility remains with individuals, although the collective aims and values of medicine, business corporations, and consumerism may all have causal responsibility for their impact on these moral decisions.

References

American Board of Internal Medicine (1998) *Project Professionalism*, Philadelphia: American Board of Internal Medicine.

British Medical Association (1999) *Withholding and Withdrawing Life-prolonging Treatment*, London: BMJ Books.
Dahlgreen, W. (2013) "One in Six Britons Know of NHS Cover-Ups Personally," *YouGov*, June 23 [online] Available at: https://yougov.co.uk/news/2013/06/23/one-six-britons-know-cover-ups-personally (Accessed: February 19, 2019).
Downie, R. (2017) "Patients and Consumers," *Journal Royal College of Physicians Edinburgh* 47: 261–265.
Downie, R. and Randall, F. (2007) "Choice and Responsibility in the NHS," *Clinical Medicine* 8(2): 182–185.
Edwin, A. (2009) "Non-Disclosure of Medical Errors an Egregious Violation of Ethical Principles," *Ghana Medical Journal*, 43(1): 34–39.
Feinberg, J. (1968) "Collective Responsibility," *Journal of Philosophy* 65: 674–688.
French, P. (1972) *Individual and Collective Responsibility: The Massacre at My Lai*, Cambridge: Schenkman Publishing Co.
French, P. (1979) "The Corporation as a Moral Person," *American Philosophical Quarterly*, 16(3): 297–317.
French, P. (1984) *Collective and Corporate Responsibility*, New York: Columbia University Press.
Harari, N. (2015) *Homo Deus*, London: Harvill Secker.
Hart, G. (2000) *Asclepius: The God of Medicine*, London: Royal Society of Medicine.
Hindin, M. (2007) "Role Theory," in G. Ritzer (ed.), *Blackwell Encyclopedia of Sociology*, London: Blackwell, 3959–3962.
Institute of Medicine (2000) *To Err is Human: Building a Safer Health System*, Washington, DC: The National Academic Press.
Lloyd, D. (1983) *Hippocratic Writings*, Harmondsworth: Penguin Books.
Luke 10: 30–37, *Holy Bible*. Oxford: Oxford University Press.
Macmurray, J. (1970) *Persons in Relation*, London: Faber.
Mason, J. and McCall Smith, R. (1994) *Law and Medical Ethics*, London: Butterworths.
New England Journal of Medicine [editorial] (2000) "Looking Back on the Millennium," *New England Journal of Medicine* 342(1): 42–49.
Paris, J., Schreiber, M. and Statter, M. (1993) "Sounding Board," *New England Journal of Medicine* 329(5): 354–357.
Re J (a minor)(wardship: medical treatment) [1992] 4 All ER 614. For discussion, see: Kessel, R. (1992) "British Judges Cannot Order Doctors to Treat," *Hastings Center Report*, 22(4): 3–4.
Smith, A. (2008 [1776]) *The Wealth of Nations*, K. Sutherland (ed.), Oxford: Oxford University Press.
Southgate, M. T. (ed.) (1997) *The Art of JAMA: One Hundred Covers and Essays from the Journal of the American Medical Association*, St. Louis: Mosby.
Susskind, R. and Susskind, D. (2015) *The Future of the Professions*, Oxford: Oxford University Press.
Veatch, R. and Spicer, C. (1992) "Medically Futile Care: The Role of the Physician in Setting Limits," *American Journal of Law and Medicine*, 18(1–2): 15–36.
Wu, A., Cavanaugh T., McPhee S., Lo, B. and Micco, G. (1997) "To Tell the Truth: Ethical and Practical Issues in Disclosing Mistakes to Patients," *Journal of General Internal Medicine* 12: 770–775.

Further Reading

May, L., and Hoffman, S. (1991) (eds.) *Collective Responsibility: Five Decades of Debate in Theoretical and Applied Ethics*, Maryland: Rowman & Littlefield.

25

COLLECTIVE RESPONSIBILITY AND FRAUD IN SCIENTIFIC COMMUNITIES

Bryce Huebner and Liam Kofi Bright[1]

Some people rely on scientific data to decide whether a particular physical condition calls for a medical intervention. Others rely on scientific data to decide what they should and shouldn't eat. Still others attend to data from social psychology, economics, or climate science to determine which social policies they should support, and which they should resist. In these cases, and many others besides, the reliance on scientific data can shape a person's practical engagements with the world. This is at least part of the reason why scientists who intentionally manipulate data to confirm their hypotheses, or who publish results that they know to be false, are thought to violate moral as well as epistemic norms.

Fortunately, many scientists are committed to getting things right, and to telling the truth as they see it. And this should make outright fraud and fabrication the exception rather than the rule. Yet, questionable research practices that fall short of fraud and fabrication persist across the sciences (Fanelli 2009; John et al. 2012). By dropping data points on the basis of gut feelings, refusing to publish data that contradicts their previous research, or citing papers that they take to be flawed or problematic, scientists can shape our understanding of the world in ethically problematic ways (Martinson et al. 2005). It is difficult to draw a precise boundary between these questionable research practices and cases of outright fraud. But at minimum, a scientist who commits fraud must knowingly enter what they take to be falsehoods into the scientific record (Bright 2017: 291). This can take the form of fabricating data; claiming to have carried out an analysis without actually doing so; or claiming to have support for a hypothesis after knowingly omitting data that defeat this support. In many cases, fraudulent practices are carried out by scientists who know that they are acting against scientific norms (cf. Fallis 2009). But individual intentionality becomes less salient when responsibility becomes more diffuse and distributed.

Research in social ontology and the philosophy of science has started to explore the questions about who should be held responsible for harms that emerge as a result of the structure of scientific communities. Such approaches shift attention away from questions about individual responsibility, and toward the role of scientific communities in shaping the collection, analysis, and dissemination of scientific data. In this chapter, we build on this trend by examining some of the effects that institutional factors and collaborative practices have on moral responsibility in scientific communities. We begin by summarizing an influential strand of thought in the sociological literature, according to which scientific fraud is likely to emerge as an effect of participating in the scientific credit economy under stress. We then turn to a recent account of the different kinds of collective responsibility that are at play in scientific communities. And with these preliminaries on the table, we turn to two contexts where the factors that are likely to foster fraud emerge within scientific communities: (1) large-scale collaborative research; and (2) ghostwritten and ghost-managed research. Finally, in light of these cases, we turn to questions about who should be held accountable for the bad outcomes of questionable or fraudulent research, and we argue that the scientific community as a whole should be held responsible for seeing to it that there is less scientific fraud, and that the harmful effects of fraud are mitigated.

25.1 A Theory of Fraud

Most scientists are concerned to pursue the truth, and many are concerned to produce elegant explanations of the phenomena they study. However, there is an enormous literature suggesting that scientists also operate within a *credit economy*, which rewards *priority* in accordance with scientific *norms* (e.g., Dasgupta and David 1994; Kitcher 1990; Latour and Woolgar 1979: ch. 5; Stephan 1996; Zollman 2018). In this section, we provide an account of each of these italicized terms, and show how fraud can emerge through the interactions between these variables. Put briefly, we claim that scientists do not just seek truth, they also seek credit for their work; that scientific credit is only awarded to those who are perceived as being first to establish matters of scientific interest (that is, those who are seen to have priority for a discovery); and that it is only awarded when research is thought to proceed in accordance with the norms that govern empirical research. However, we argue that there are some cases where the desire to seek credit can lead scientists to adopt questionable or fraudulent means of establishing priority for matters of scientific interest.

To begin with, most proponents of the theory of the scientific credit economy hold that scientists seek glory and esteem from their peers. Explicit markers of being held in high esteem include having numerous people cite one's work and discuss it favorably; receiving prestigious prizes or commendations; and having things like theorems, body parts, or disorders named in one's honor (cf. Cole and Cole 1970). They also include material and social advantages, such as the ease of finding a job, the location of the job that one receives, and the sorts of grants that one is likely to receive. Each of these factors, and many others besides, track and influence one's standing within the scientific community. A scientist with a high-status job is more likely to have their research cited widely and approvingly; further, having one's research cited widely and approvingly increases the likelihood that a scientist will receive grants to fund more research, and this in turn increases the likelihood of citation. Over time, the relationships between markers of status tend to stabilize, yielding mutually reinforcing and resilient evidence of one's standing within a scientific community.

Credit is typically attained through priority, that is, by being seen as the first scientist to have established some matter of scientific interest (cf. Merton 1957). And it is commonly acknowledged that ascriptions of priority are governed by scientific norms, which specify when something should be counted as a successful discovery. We use the term "norms" loosely, as a way of covering any form of behavior that a community expects you to engage in, and would think it improper for you to deviate from. We cannot survey the literature on the social epistemic consequences of scientific social norms here (e.g., Bright et al. 2018; Heesen 2017b; Longino 1990; Mayo-Wilson 2014; Rubin and O'Connor, forthcoming). However, for our purposes, the important point is that scientific norms govern which research topics are worth pursuing, where things should be published, and the conditions under which scientific claims should be evaluated. For example, it is a norm that scientific claims should be published in accredited venues, and not just distributed over email or social media; and it is a norm that accredited venues should have a process of peer review, which verifies that the epistemic and social norms of a particular research community are properly upheld (Zuckerman and Merton 1971). This peer review process should ensure that proper statistical procedures or experimental protocols are followed; it should ensure that past priority claims are acknowledged through citation; and it should ensure that fraudulent claims are not entered into the scientific record.

Where things go well, aspirant credit seekers will have their work verified as following the proper epistemic and social protocols. Their work will be published and publicized by the journal they have submitted to. And this will allow them to gain whatever credit the scientific community sees fit to dispense when priority is granted for the discovery. However, in some contexts the norms that govern the assignment of scientific credit through priority can also tempt people to commit fraud, even though there are scientific norms against doing so. For, while many scientists are committed to the pursuit of truth, "a more immediate objective often intrudes into vision, that of establishing credit" (Broad and Wade 1982: 52–3). And in some contexts, scientists may come to feel that fraudulent means are the only ones available for establishing priority on interesting discoveries. The pressure to pursue credit can therefore produce incentives to fabricate or manipulate data. This tends to happen where people's personal commitment to the restraining epistemic and social norms of science have been weakened; and this is especially likely where institutional pressures disincentivize the pursuit of truth, and where people begin to think that they will be able to get away with questionable research practices because pre-publication checking mechanisms turn out to be incapable of reliably detecting and preventing the publication of fraudulent research (cf. Ben-Yahuda 1986; Braxton 1993; Casadevall and Fang 2012; Sovacool 2008; Zuckerman 1984). What is important is that the desire for credit, and the ability to achieve it through establishing priority in accredited journals, can exist even where the commitment to the epistemic norms of science are either lacking or overpowered. In such cases, pre-publication checking mechanisms are rarely strong enough to prevent fraud from occurring.[2] Such effects are commonly acknowledged, even by those who are not entirely sympathetic to the standard theory of the cause of fraud. For example, a recent empirical study by Fanelli et al. (2015: 13), suggests that the motivation for committing fraud is "to gain an unfair advantage in the race for priority and success." And in a paper focused on the case of ghost-management in pharmaceutical research, Elliot and Landa (2010) argue that "the structural logic of pharmaceutical public relations [i.e., *the socially entrenched credit economy in pharmaceutical research*] prevents its practitioners from engaging in ethical scientific communication, even if, as individuals, they are well intentioned." We return to a more detailed account of these institutional pressures in section 25.3. But for now, we simply suggest that a plausible understanding of what generates scientific fraud must acknowledge the impact of the credit economy.

25.2 Kinds of Collective Responsibility

Contemporary science often includes groups as aspirant credit seekers. And in many domains, collaborative science is becoming the norm. This is partly because of the complexity of addressing scientific questions; and it is partly because of the increased likelihood of receiving funding for interdisciplinary projects. Haixan Dang (submitted) draws on recent work in metaethics to suggest that there are three ways of construing questions about collective responsibility in such scientific communities. First, there are questions about the parties to which a scientific outcome is attributable. Some scientific results are the result of individual efforts. Others are the result of the coordinated efforts of individuals working together. But in some cases, there will be a group who is attributable-responsible for an outcome, because of the claims that they make as a group, or the scientific procedures that they carry out as a group. Second, there are questions about who is answerable for a particular scientific claim. A group that is attributable-responsible for a scientific outcome will also be answerable-responsible for that outcome if they are in a position to produce the reasons that would justify it. As we argue below, answerability for scientific claims often becomes highly diffuse, in ways that make it impossible to find anyone below the level of a whole research team who is answerable-responsible for a scientific claim; and in some cases, it may be impossible to find any individual or group who is in a position to be answerable responsible for a scientific claim. Finally, there are questions about who should be held accountable for problematic scientific claims, and who should be praised for scientific insights; questions about accountable-responsibility turn on the proper target of praise or blame for a scientific product; and questions about the proper targets of reward or punishment for making scientific claims that are true, erroneous, or fraudulent. And in general, a group can only be held accountable for an outcome if they are attributable-responsible for it, and are in a position to adjust their behavior in light of the praise and blame that they receive.[3]

Our primary focus in this chapter is on collective responsibility for problematic scientific outcomes. However, numerous pressing questions about how to assign epistemic and moral responsibility to individuals and groups arise even in the context of good and neutral scientific outcomes (Heesen 2017a; Merton 1968; Strevens 2006). Specifically, there are questions about how credit should be divided among collaborators (Bruner and O'Connor 2017); and numerous scientific journals (e.g., *Nature*, *Science*, and *The New England Journal of Medicine*) have developed contributor policies that aim to make it clear who a scientific claim should be attributed to. In general, these policies are designed to clarify attributability, by recording the names of everyone who makes a relevant claim or carries out a relevant procedure. But by requiring all contributors to be listed as authors, they also help to make it clear who should be held accountable for problematic outcomes, and who should receive credit for the reported research. And they constitute attempts to guard against the intrusion of hidden influences and conflicts of interest, by making it clear who has made specific contributions to a scientific paper. Consequently, these policies embed collaborative research more firmly within the networks of norms that govern the scientific credit economy. Each researcher receives credit for their own contributions; and where all collaborators know who is responsible for which aspects of a scientific project, it is easier to track down the points where distortions have emerged.

Many contributor statements go beyond considerations of attributability, in an attempt to clarify these distributed structures of answerability and accountability. This shouldn't be a surprise, especially where scientific research impacts the way that people conceptualize core values such as health, wellbeing, and treatment options. Such ethical considerations may help to explain why the International Committee of Medical Journal Editors (ICMJE) recommends that someone should be counted as an author if and only if they have: (1) made a substantial contribution to the research design, or played a significant role in the acquisition, analysis, or interpretation of data; (2) drafted the manuscript or made substantial and intellectually significant revisions to it; (3) given their approval on the final version of the manuscript; and (4) agreed to vouch for the accuracy and integrity of all aspects of the research. These robust constraints on authorship are designed "to ensure that contributors who have made substantive intellectual contributions to a paper are given credit as authors, but also that contributors credited as authors understand their role in taking responsibility and being accountable for what is published" (ICMJE 2013). As a result, they draw considerations of attributability, answerability, and accountability together by specifying who carried out the research and writing, who can justify claims, and who should be held accountable if a problematic outcome arises.

This is all quite reasonable, as many forms of collaborative research preserve the unity of Dang's three proposed kinds of responsibility. Consider a small group of authors who toss a manuscript back-and-forth until they all agree that it is ready for submission (or who defer to statisticians and modelers when questions about their models arise). Such catch-and-toss collaborations preserve familiar forms of individual and shared responsibility, allowing each author to know who is able to address specific kinds of questions, and allowing collaborators to reconstruct justifications for their scientific claims where problems arise (Huebner et al. 2017). Perhaps more importantly, they preserve the ability of co-authors to trust one another to follow scientific norms, and to figure out where problems have emerged in the process of collecting, analyzing, or interpreting data (cf. Andersen 2013). So, each contributor can justify their own contributions and direct inquiries to collaborators where they lack relevant expertise: the scientists who are responsible for producing a scientific paper can be answerable for the claims that they make, and they can be treated as legitimate targets of praise or blame for the outcomes of their research.

In such contexts, scientific misconduct is typically performed by a single contributor—and while co-authors may be epistemically blameworthy for trusting a fraudster, they will rarely be morally culpable for the actions of that fraudster (Andersen 2014). There may also be cases where co-authors refuse to intervene on forms of misconduct that they are aware of; and in such cases, an agency-based approach to complicity may be relevant to the assignment of responsibility (Bazargan-Forward 2017). Such cases are likely to be relatively rare in small-scale collaborations; and even where they arise, we will typically be able to figure out who is answerable for scientific misconduct, and who should be held accountable if problems arise. However, these patterns of trust and deference can be compromised, and this can have an enormous impact on the relationship between attributability, answerability, and accountability for research outcomes (here too, we follow Dang; however, our conclusions diverge from hers). Specifically, we contend that accountability for mistakes can dissipate in massively distributed research groups, even where it is clear who a claim is attributable to, and who carried out various scientific tasks; and we argue that external values can compromise answerability, in part by obscuring lines of attributability. We consider these possibilities in sections 25.3 and 25.4 respectively.

25.3 Radically Collaborative Science

Some contemporary research is carried out by very large research groups consisting of multiple labs, from different scientific fields, working in different parts of the world. In such contexts, social and material pressures shape the collection, analysis, and interpretation of data; and local norms shape each researcher's decisions about when to treat something as data, and when to treat it as noise (Douglas 2004; 2009). The contributors to large collaborations also worry about tenure and promotion; they try to run successful labs; they try to place their graduate students in high-status positions; they strive to cultivate the respect of their colleagues; and they hope to receive grants that will fund their research. And in the large-scale collaborations that are becoming increasingly common in biomedical research and climate science, economic and political factors also come into play, shaping the way that data are collected, interpreted, and presented. In these respects, large-scale collaborations are not that different from any other scientific research; but in this context, such factors make it difficult to determine who is answerable for a scientific claim, and who is accountable when problems arise (for extended treatments of these issues, see Huebner et al. 2017; Kukla 2012; Winsberg et al. 2014).

The scientific questions addressed by large-scale collaborations require contributions from multiple researchers, who draw on tools and techniques from different disciplines, and who are working in different locations. And since these research communities are constituted by scientists who operate within partially distinct credit economies, and who make judgments on the basis of partially distinct networks of disciplinary skills and norms, their research outputs are typically shaped by "a chaotic web of micro-interests and local values that penetrate the study bottom-up" (Winsberg et al. 2014: 17). Numerous judgments are often made in parallel, and methodological adjustments are often made "on the fly in response to noncompliant research participants, unforeseen barriers to implementation and communication, surprising side effects, and so forth" (Huebner et al. 2017: 103). But the uncertainties that evoke such adjustments are rarely predictable in advance; and methodological adjustments are often made differently by different researchers, and at different stages of the research process.

In this context, subtle forms of epistemic distortion can emerge, even where everyone is committed to engaging in good epistemic practices. There is no obvious way to keep track of the impact of the adjustments that are made across the collaboration; and there is no way to know whether their effects will aggregate, cancel each other out, or amplify one another. At each stage of the research process, incoming data that has been shaped in accordance with local norms can be re-evaluated in accordance with locally salient considerations; and the impact of this fact is often obscured due to the individual or team who is responsible for writing papers and producing other research outputs. Since it is unlikely that they have participated in the collection or analysis of data, writers function as a distinct component of the collaboration, and they tend to write in accordance with their own normative assumptions about what is worth presenting and what can be ignored. Of course, the output of this process is typically interpretable. But it is often impossible to determine how the collaboration arrived at the reported results.[4]

To clarify the ethical implications of this situation, we return to Dang's (submitted) tripartite distinction regarding different kinds of responsibility. In radically collaborative research, papers and other research outputs are typically attributable to widely distributed networks of researchers, technicians, statisticians, and writers. And the author list on a publication typically constitutes at least a partial record of attributability (though technicians and lab managers may not be listed as contributors). But there is rarely any contributor who fully understands the roles that are played by all of the other researchers; and there is rarely any contributor who can vouch for the results of every other researcher (Winsberg et al. 2014; Wray 2017: 127). Consequently, such research cannot proceed in accordance with the constraints on authorship advanced by the ICMJE (2013). And as a result, the research can only be attributable to the collaborative group, who have collectively produced the relevant claims and carried out the relevant procedures. As information is propagated through a radical collaboration, this situation can be complicated by errors that are introduced as a result of explicit manipulation, or as an artifact of divergent norms operating in different parts of the collaboration; and where such errors are entered into the scientific record, it will be difficult to discover or correct them, as the precise locus of attributability for the error will be obscured by the size and complexity of the experimental or observational design. Where these errors yield problems with research outcomes, there may be no individual or collective agent who is in a position to produce the reasons that would justify a problematic claim; and if this occurs there will be no individual or group who can be answerable-responsible for the problematic claims that have been made (Huebner et al. 2017; Kukla 2012). Finally, when there is no one who controls all of the knowledge that is necessary to justify the procedures that have been used in the production of scientific claims in such a context, there will be no individual or group who can be a proper target of praise or blame for scientific outcomes; and this can yield a situation where individual, shared, and collective accountability all dissipate (Winsberg et al. 2014).

The scope of these kinds of research projects can thus compromise the otherwise stable link between the best features of the scientific credit economy and the process of scientific research. This can occur when highly distributed and massively interdisciplinary research leads to the breakdown of the norms that typically constrain individuals in the pursuit of scientific credit, because the communal oversight of adherence to those norms has been weakened. First, co-authors on such projects will often object to the retraction of a paper, attempting to hold on to any credit they have received for a massively multi-authored paper. Second, there is little motivation to take part in attempted replications of large-scale collaborative research projects with problematic implications. The credit one receives as the 164th author in a field of 400 authors is both minimal and diffuse; and the credit one would receive for pursuing a replication, which is not likely to establish priority, is even more minimal. Third, no one can reasonably be punished if problems arise within a large-scale collaboration, as both answerability and accountability become so diffuse in a network of hundreds of distributed researchers that it only makes sense to hold the collaboration as such accountable; unfortunately, attempts at censoring radical collaborations are likely to fail, since such collaborations are often kludged together for a specific purpose, and they often dissipate after the projects are completed. Fourth, and finally, this kind of research has a serious impact on the checking mechanisms that are typically at play in the peer review process. When "research projects engage a greater proportion of the scientists working in a specialty, there are fewer and fewer competent scientists available to referee the resulting research" (Wray 2017: 129ff). In the context of massively interdisciplinary research, which draws on many different research areas, it is unlikely that anyone is competent to evaluate the research project as a whole; consequently, the more limited pool of referees is likely to impose significant constraints on the ability of the scientific community to track cases of where questionable research practices are employed, or where fraud has been carried out.

Such collaborations thus compromise the checking mechanisms that serve to prevent fraudulent claims from being entered into the scientific record. And where problems emerge—whether unintentionally, or as a result of fabrication and manipulation—it becomes difficult, and perhaps impossible, to figure out who is answerable-responsible for the scientific claims that are made, and who should be held accountable when problems arise, even if it is possible to attribute a paper to the widely distributed research group. Intriguingly, similar problems arise where heavily managed and systematically biased research is produced in accordance with a single set of non-scientific values. Here too, questions arise about who is responsible for the production of a scientific claim, who is answerable for it, and who should be held accountable when problems arise.

25.4 Ghostwriting and Market Values

In recent years, for example, a troubling pattern has emerged in pharmaceutical research: despite strong evidence from clinical trials, as well as enthusiastic support from physicians, problematic outcomes emerge when people begin to use a drug (e.g., high rates of cardiovascular disease, diabetes, or hypertension, or suicidal ideation); we later learn that the drug company was aware of the potential for problems before the drug went to market, that they actively worked to downplay the risks of using the drug, and used ghostwritten publications to get the drug quickly and efficiently to market (Elliot and Landa 2010). This pattern began to emerge in the late-1990s, as drugs such as Paxil, Neurontin, Fen-Phen, and Zoloft triggered a range of aversive effects; and there are many detailed accounts of these cases (see Sismondo and Doucet 2010 for a review). In pharmaceutical research, it is often necessary to increase the efficiency and speed of publication; and professional writers are often used to ease the pressures on researchers and clinicians, who may have little time to write a paper. And in these cases, and many others besides, research was either carried out or written up "on behalf of pharmaceutical companies, and then published under the name of academics who had played little role earlier in the research and writing process" (Sismondo 2007: 1429).

By definition, these forms of ghostwriting must remain hidden from view, so we don't know how commonplace they are. Moreover, there is little consensus about how to understand the ethical implications of ghostwriting. It is widely assumed that moral problems are likely to arise when professional writers are employed to rush a paper to publication, and when research is guided by the interests of pharmaceutical companies. Philosophers and journal editors have worried that using industry-sponsored ghostwriters can compromise the pursuit of truth by centering market values; and it is sometimes suggested that plagiarism, or a nearby violation of academic integrity, occurs when a scientist puts their name on a paper that they have played little role in writing or revising (Anekwe 2010; McHenry 2010). We contend that ghostwriting also yields a countervailing force that can compete with, and perhaps overcome, the allegiance to the epistemic norms of science. And given the theory of fraud outlined in section 25.1, this is precisely the kind of situation that one ought to be concerned about.

When professional writing services are used in pharmaceutical research, the roles of various named authors often remain obscure. In several cases, there is evidence that industry interests have played a role at every possible point during the research process: from the specification of experimental design, to the analysis and interpretation of data, ghost-managed research aims to make it "easier for pharmaceutical companies to use scientific research to market their products" (Sismondo and Doucet 2010: 275). But achieving these ends requires both increasing the prevalence of research supporting a product in the academic literature, and doing so in ways that make use of high-impact journals, with the assistance of prominent scholars, universities, or research institutions. Put differently, within the existing scientific credit economy, ghost-written articles can only be useful as marketing tools if "they appear to come from a disinterested source" (Moffatt and Elliott 2007: 27). And where there is evidence of a robust conflict of interest, scientific norms preclude the publication and dissemination of data. To work around these norms, pharmaceutical companies have taken advantage of the fact that many academics are willing to participate in ghost-managed research; as credit seekers, academics "have a strong interest in publications, particularly in prominent journals" (Sismondo and Doucet 2010: 275). And this is what leads to cases where pursuing scientific truth is disincentivized, while the desire to pursue credit by co-authoring problematic research is enhanced.

It is worth pausing to make it clear why someone would willingly accept credit for a paper, when they played no role in its production. As we see it, two related factors are at play in shaping this kind of situation:

(1) Industry-sponsored and ghost-managed research tends to be placed in higher-impact journals, and it tends to be cited more frequently than non-industry-supported research (Healy and Cattell 2003; Sismondo and Doucet 2010: 278). In part, this may be because strategic "publication plans" are used to shepherd industry-supported research through the publication process, from the presentation of research at high prestige conferences, to the placement of publications in prominent journals; and professional writers are paid to write compelling and readable articles on the basis of this research. Consequently, medical journals may be more likely to publish ghost-managed research. But in part, this may also be because pharmaceutical companies often purchase large numbers of reprints to distribute to physicians (Sismondo and Doucet 2010: 275).

(2) Existing norms governing scientific authorship allow some people to put their names on nearly completed papers. Cultures of honorary authorship allow the leader of a large lab to be listed as an author, even where they have contributed little to a manuscript. And authorship is sometimes conferred on the basis of theoretical contributions that were made in conversation. There may be good reasons to worry about the prevalence of these practices. But on their own, they need not compromise the pursuit of scientific truth.

Through the interaction of these factors, a situation emerges where a scientist might come to believe that they can get away with putting their name on a ghostwritten paper. And in this context, they have some incentive to use this low-cost strategy of pursuing academic credit. Of course, many scientists will refuse to take part in this kind of research, as scientific norms play a more significant role in their decision-making than do industry norms. However, the social organization of this kind of research does open up the possibility of engaging in questionable research practices, and potentially fraudulent behavior.

Industry-financed writers can take advantage of this situation to produce articles that promote a company's interests, while a "key opinion leader" accepts credit for a paper that they have played no substantial role in writing (McHenry 2010). Such practices obscure the role that industry interests have played in determining which data are presented and which data are ignored; and this makes ghost-authored papers look like they are ordinary contributions to scientific knowledge. But perhaps more significantly, ghostwriting and ghost-management can bring about the diffusion of collective moral responsibility in a way that is similar to the diffusion of responsibility that emerges in the context of large-scale collaborative research (see Kukla 2012). To see what this amounts to, we return to Dang's (submitted) tripartite distinction between different kinds of responsibility.

To begin with, where papers are ghostwritten, it becomes much more difficult—if not completely impossible—to figure out who a scientific product should be attributed to. In the most extreme cases, the named authors have not made any substantial contribution to the research design, and they have not played any significant role in the acquisition, analysis, or interpretation of data; further, they have not drafted the manuscript, or made substantial and intellectually significant revisions to it. They have simply signed off on the final version of the manuscript. Put somewhat differently, it is not just that the causal story is complicated (as it was in the cases we discussed in section 25.3), attributable-responsibility is compromised in these cases because the people who are given credit for the relevant research have played no causal role in its production. Consequently, papers are attributed to people who are in no real position to vouch for the research, or to offer justifications where they are called upon to do so; and this means that there may be no one who is answerable-responsible for the research product. That said, the presence of a ghostwriter doesn't itself compromise answerability and accountability. These further problems arise precisely because ghost-managed manuscripts are produced with the intent of obfuscating the role of monetary interests; and where such interests can be hidden, this will increase the potential for manipulations of data that accord with the interests of pharmaceutical companies. Put somewhat differently, where research is ghost-managed and where manuscripts are ghostwritten, considerations of attributability are intentionally distorted; and this is done in a way that makes it difficult for anyone to figure out who precisely is answerable-responsible and who is accountable-responsible for the research.

The research guiding decisions that are made in this context are "rarely, if ever, made by isolated individuals" (Biddle and Kukla 2017: 229). They are typically made by loosely connected networks of pharmaceutical representatives, researchers, scientists, and professional writing companies. This distribution and obfuscation of attributability causes a situation where answerability becomes diffused, as no identifiable individual or group has the capacity to produce the reasons that would justify a scientific outcome; and the diffusion of accountability follows, as there is no identifiable individual or group who is a proper target of praise or blame for the scientific outcome, and no identifiable individual or group who is justly accorded reward or punishment for making claims that are true, erroneous, or fraudulent. While there may be some cases where it is possible to figure out who collected, analyzed, and interpreted the data for a ghostwritten paper, the lack of transparency at every level of the research process can make it impossible to figure out who is answerable, and who should be held accountable for problematic research. And pushing on the named author or "key opinion leader" will at most lead to the acknowledgment that they appended their name to a research product they did not really contribute to. The result is that, where corporate influences intrude, and where conflicts of interest distort the pursuit of truth, both answerability and accountability can be compromised. Where pressures from industry shape research decisions from the top-down, they will tend to privilege market interests over the pursuit of scientific truth (Moffatt and Elliott 2007; Sismondo 2009). This pressure opens up the possibility of fraud, as well as other questionable research practices. And since ghostwritten papers are designed to bring a product rapidly to market, or to increase its market share, the norms governing the author's behavior are likely to be those of the market, not those of the scientific community. In this context, supporting data will often be highlighted, while contradictory findings will tend to remain unpublished. And this can yield distortions of the scientific process, which can have massively problematic effects.

As with the cases we discussed in the previous section, these kinds of ghost-managed and ghost-authored research make it difficult to assign responsibility for fraudulent research to any particular individual. Epistemically, it is often unclear who the pertinent claims should be attributed to, even where there is a fact of the matter. In the case of widely distributed research, it is not clear that anyone is actually answerable or appropriately accountable—no one stands in the right kind of relationship to provide a justification or to be held accountable if the results of a study are inappropriate. In the case of ghostwritten research, by contrast, the intentional obfuscation of authorship makes it at least impractical to design institutional mechanisms that can be used to hold people accountable for the research that they have actually done. Where fraudulent claims emerge, there will be someone who is causally responsible for entering the problematic claim into the scientific record. But it is not the named author; and the process that leads to the production of the claim is likely to be such a complex and intractable mixture of legitimate science and industry-based interests that it will be impossible to track down where the distortion was introduced in the research process. What is more, since the group membership and structure is opaque for the same reasons the individual contributions are, it is just as difficult to hold the group answerable or accountable for any wrongdoing. If there are many cases where no individual nor research group may be held accountable for fraud, this leads naturally to the next question: what ought to be done to ameliorate fraud?

25.5 Communal Responsibility for Ameliorating Fraud

The standard theory of fraud affects the dominant theories of how to respond to scientific fraud. It is commonly suggested that attempts to address the prevalence of scientific fraud should aim to reduce alienation from the norms of science and to increase respect for more distinctively scientific norms (e.g., Bright, forthcoming; Nosek et al. 2012, though see Bright 2017 for a note of skepticism). An alternative suggestion is that we can do more to encourage the effective use of checking mechanisms (e.g., Bruner 2013; also discussed in Lee 2013; Romero 2016). Whichever response is preferred—they are not inconsistent—such solutions proceed in a technocratic vein, by assessing the extent to which the causes of fraud can be addressed so as to ensure that there is less of it. We, however, are interested in a more distinctively moral question: who ought to be morally responsible for reducing the prevalence of fraud?

In an ideal world, each individual would work to avoid making fraudulent claims, and each individual would hold others accountable where fraud was detected. Over time, this would become the norm, yielding a fraud-free science. But fraud has not been eliminated, incentives to commit fraud remain in place, and we cannot plausibly assume full compliance with scientific norms. So we must look for non-ideal strategies for ameliorating the problematic effects of fraud, including the spread of falsehoods, the failure of policies based upon false beliefs, the erosion of trust in the scientific literature, and the breakdown of respect for the norms that allow for epistemically successful publications.

Here too, we build on Dang's three senses of "collective responsibility." As we noted above, someone is attributable-responsible if they made the pertinent claim or carried out the relevant procedure. We can typically attribute fraudulent claims or procedures to particular scientists. Doing so can become difficult or impossible in the two cases we have just discussed; but even here, there must be some individual or group who is causally responsible for producing a claim, even if we can't figure out precisely who is attributable-responsible for it. And this can yield situations where standards of answerability and accountability become difficult to establish. Recall that someone is answerable-responsible for a claim if they are in a position to produce the reasons that would justify it. Answerability for scientific claims (fraudulent or not) is often diffuse, and whole research teams may sometimes be collectively answerable-responsible for scientific claims. Moreover, in the kinds of cases we have discussed above, answerability tends to break down, generating a situation where no one can answer for problematic claims. Perhaps the scientific community as a whole might somehow be answerable for fraudulent claims that arise in such cases, though difficult questions remain as to what this would amount to. Finally, someone is accountable-responsible if they are the proper target of praise or blame for a scientific product, or if they are justly accorded reward or punishment for making claims that are true, erroneous, or fraudulent. Given the highly social nature of science, we contend that the most plausible thing to say is that the community as a whole is accountable for fraud; and to the extent that we are justified in treating individuals as accountable for fraud, this is because this is a plausible way for the community to fulfill its responsibility for preventing and ameliorating the mal-effects of fraud. This is a complex and contentious claim, so it will help to work through it in more detail.

What does it mean to say that the scientific community as a whole is accountable for the amelioration of fraud? On the one hand, the scientific community is unlikely to satisfy any plausible theory of the constraints on agency. As a "community," it is far too dis-unified, and far too widely distributed, to carry out any sort of coordinated and intentional actions; moreover, even where trends do emerge within this community, they are rarely under the rational control of any individual or collective agent. So the community, understood as an agent in its own right, is probably not the right place to look in attempts to change the norms and expectations that give rise to fraudulent action. That said, there is another sense in which the scientific community can be held accountable for the emergence and prevalence of fraud. The members of the scientific community are causally responsible, *qua* members of the scientific community, for the norms that govern attributions of priority within the scientific credit economy. No individual can determine which norms are accepted by the community. And no individual can change problematic norms where they become stable. But when scientists act together as members of the scientific community, they can begin to shift the salience of expectations to act in particular ways. And over time, this can lead to a shift in the way that the scientific community as a whole operates.

Social norms do not float free from the expectations of the individuals in a community. But at the same time, the expectations that the individuals within a community have depend on the patterns of behavior that are observed within interconnected networks of social actors. As members of a norm-governed community, scientists tend to share numerous values, at least in the minimal sense that they each see themselves, and they each see one another, as possessing the standing to demand compliance with scientific norms. And this tends to be true even where expectations regarding norm compliance are not grounded in joint commitments or shared intentions (cf. Hedahl and Huebner 2018). As a result, the stability and prevalence of the norms that allow fraud to emerge can be properly attributed to the networks of social actors who constitute the scientific community. Moreover, since the presence of fraud depends on the presence of norms and incentives that are inherent in the network structure of the scientific credit economy, ameliorative strategies will require a shared commitment among the members of that community to transform the content and the salience of the norms governing scientific practice. So when we claim that the community as a whole is accountable for fraud, what we mean to suggest is that the proper target of praise and blame in the case of fraud is the interconnected network of scientists, who act in accordance with their roles as community members, and who shape the salience of scientific and credit-seeking norms.

Only the community as a whole has the power to bring about the reforms that could increase or decrease the prevalence of fraud in the non-ideal world. There may not be an agent which constitutes the scientific community, but effective anti-fraud action can only happen through change that works upon this diffuse network of interlinked scientists, enforcing norms and constituting credit through their praise and esteem, and thus generating different expectations about risks and reward. But this must occur through the actions of individual scientists, who are working to reshape the credit-seeking economy. According to the theory outlined in section 25.1, scientific fraud tends to arise as a result of the incentive structure that scientists operate within, as well as the efficacy of the social norms that scientists are supposedly subject to. When fraudulent claims are entered into the scientific literature, there is always some individual or identifiable group to whom the claim is properly attributable. But no individual or group that is smaller than the whole community has the power to modify the credit system, or to shape the norms that will increase or decrease the prevalence of fraud in the non-ideal world that we inhabit. As such, we contend that only the community as a whole can see to it that there is less fraud; that the scientific community as a whole must actively work to minimize scientific fraud, and that it collectively should be praised or blamed for arranging itself in ways that yield greater or lesser amounts of fraud.

As to how this responsibility should be discharged, we think the scientific community is broadly on the right track already. We should bring credit incentives into line with obeying epistemic norms of science, foster respect for those norms, and avoid anomie. As such, educational institutions should do their best to inculcate and encourage a sense of honesty and allegiance to the epistemic norms of science (Du Bois 1898). Initiatives such as encouraging pre-registration to ensure fraudulent research practices do not yield accredited publications ought to be supported (van 't Veer and Giner-Sorolla 2016). Moreover, robust uses of checking mechanisms via replication (OSC 2015), and attempts at multi-method triangulation (Munafò and Davey Smith 2018), should be used to ferret out false claims that have already been entered into the literature, making it less likely that scientists will gain lasting priority credit for claims that are false. Together, these practices will help disincentivize fraud. Additionally, mechanisms should be put in place to ensure that taking part in such practices is rewarded in the credit economy. This might involve favored access to funding, rewards, or publication venues for studies of the required form. Finally, where there is evidence of malpractice, ensuring that there are procedures in place for retraction and punishment will further disincentivize fraudulent behavior. This may involve making individuals or groups answer for the instances of fraud they commit. But individual instances of fraud are always embedded in larger social patterns; and the agent that is answerable for regulating these patterns is the scientific community that is constituted by networks of interacting individuals and institutions.

Notes

1 Both BH and LKB made substantial contributions to the writing and revision of this chapter; and both authors approved its submission.

2 While it is not exactly the same phenomenon, the problem of the garden of forking paths (Gelman and Loken 2013) also contributed to the replication crisis by creating situations in psychology where checking mechanisms could not track norm compliance, while the temptation to establish priority and gain credit remained strong.

3 Dang (submitted) is primarily concerned with questions of epistemic responsibility. But she does note in passing that similar issues are likely to arise in the context of collective moral responsibility. We agree, and we argue in the remainder of this chapter that questions about moral and epistemic responsibility are deeply connected, at least in the context of questions about scientific responsibility. Following Dang, we also suggest that an account of collective moral responsibility in science must begin by acknowledging that these three kinds of responsibility can converge or diverge as a result of the organization of a scientific research group.

4 Drawing on an argument advanced by Lenhard and Winsberg (2010: 256–7), we might see such collaborations as kludged architectures, which display a sort of fuzzy modularity: each research group is organized in accordance with the norms of their local credit economy, so their data and inferences are shaped by a mixture of principled science and locally salient practices of credit-seeking; and the interactions between these groups shape the content of the information that is propagated through such collaboration, as data are continuously exchanged between research groups, and as queries are made for more data or further interpretations.

References

Andersen, H. (2013) "Epistemic Dependence in Contemporary Science: Practices And Malpractices," in L. Soler, S. Zwart, M. Lynch, and V. Israel-Jost (eds), *Science After the Practice Turn in the Philosophy, History and Social Studies of Science*, London: Routledge, 161–73.

Andersen, H. (2014) "Co-author Responsibility: Distinguishing Between the Moral and Epistemic Aspects of Trust," *EMBO reports* 15(9): 914–18.

Anekwe, T.D. (2010) "Profits and Plagiarism: The Case of Medical Ghostwriting," *Bioethics* 24: 267–72.

Bazargan-Forward, S. (2017) "Complicity," in M. Jankovic and K. Ludwig (eds), *The Routledge Handbook of Collective Intentionality*, London: Routledge, 327–37.

Ben-Yehuda, N. (1986) "Deviance in Science—Towards a Criminology of Science," *British Journal of Criminology* 26(1): 1–27.

Biddle, J., and Kukla, R. (2017) "The Geography of Epistemic Risk," in K. C. Elliott and T. Richards (eds), *Exploring Inductive Risk. Exploring Inductive Risk: Case Studies of Values in Science*, New York: Oxford University Press, 215–37.

Braxton, J.M. (1993) "Deviancy From the Norms of Science: The Effects of Anomie and Alienation in the Academic Profession," *Research in Higher Education*, 34(2): 213–28.

Bright, L.K. (2017) "On Fraud," *Philosophical Studies* 174(2): 291–310.

Bright, L.K. (forthcoming) "Du Bois' Democratic Defence of the Value Free Ideal," *Synthese*: 1–19.

Bright, L.K., Dang, H., and Heesen, R. (2018) "A Role for Judgment Aggregation in Coauthoring Scientific Papers," *Erkenntnis* 83(2): 231–52.

Broad, W., and Wade, N. (1982) *Betrayers of the Truth*, New York: Simon and Schuster.

Bruner, J.P. (2013) "Policing Epistemic Communities," *Episteme* 10(4): 403–16.

Bruner, J.P., and O'Connor, C. (2017) "Power, Bargaining, and Collaboration," in T. Boyer-Kassem, C. Mayo-Wilson, and M. Weisberg (eds), *Scientific Collaboration and Collective Knowledge: New Essays*, Oxford: Oxford University Press, 135–57.

Casadevall, A., and Fang, F.C. (2012) "Reforming Science: Methodological and Cultural Reforms," *Infection and Immunity* 80(3): 891–6.
Cole, J.R., and Cole. S. (1970) *Social Stratification in Science*, Chicago: University of Chicago Press.
Dang, H. (submitted) "Epistemic Responsibility in Science."
Dasgupta, P., and David, P.A. (1994) "Toward a New Economics of Science," *Research Policy* 23(5): 487–521.
Douglas, H. (2004) "Prediction, Explanation, and Dioxin Biochemistry: Science in Public Policy," *Foundations of Chemistry* 6(1): 49–63.
Douglas, H. (2009) *Science, Policy, and the Value-Free Ideal*, Pittsburgh: University of Pittsburgh Press.
Du Bois, W.E.B. (1898) "The Study of the Negro Problems," *The Annals of the American Academy of Political and Social Science* 11(1): 1–23.
Elliott, C., and Landa, A.S. (2010) "Commentary: What's Wrong With Ghostwriting?," *Bioethics* 24(6): 284–6.
Fallis, D. (2009) "What is Lying?," *The Journal of Philosophy* 106(1): 29–56.
Fanelli, D. (2009) "How Many Scientists Fabricate and Falsify Research? A Systematic Review and Meta-Analysis of Survey Data," *PLoS One*, 4(5): e5738.
Fanelli, D., Costas, R., and Lariviere, V. (2015) "Misconduct Policies, Academic Culture And Career Stage, Not Gender or Pressures to Publish, Affect Scientific Integrity," *PLoS One* 10(6): 1–18.
Gelman, A., and Loken, E. (2013) "The garden of forking paths: Why multiple comparisons can be a problem, even when there is no 'fishing expedition' or 'p-hacking' and the research hypothesis was posited ahead of time," Department of Statistics, Columbia University. [online] Available at: www.stat.columbi a.edu/~gelman/research/unpublished/p_hacking.pdf [Accessed: 15 March 2019].
Healy, D., and Cattell, D. (2003) "Interface Between Authorship, Industry and Science in the Domain of Therapeutics," *The British Journal of Psychiatry* 183(1): 22–7.
Heesen, R. (2017a) "Academic Superstars: Competent or Lucky?," *Synthese* 194(11): 4499–518.
Heesen, R. (2017b) "Communism and the Incentive to Share in Science," *Philosophy of Science* 84(4): 698–716.
Hedahl, M., and Huebner, B. (2018). "Sharing Values," *Southern Journal of Philosophy* 56(2): 240–72.
Huebner, B., Kukla, R., and Winsberg, E. (2017) "Making an Author in Radically Collaborative Research," in T. Boyer-Kassem, C. Mayo-Wilson, and M. Weisberg (eds), *Scientific Collaboration and Collective Knowledge*, Oxford: Oxford University Press, 95–116.
ICMJE (2013) www.icmje.org/recommendations/browse/roles-and-responsibilities/defining-the-role-of-authors-and-contributors.html.
John, L.K., Loewenstein, G., and Prelec, D. (2012) "Measuring the Prevalence of Questionable Research Practices with Incentives for Truth Telling," *Psychological Science* 23(5): 524–32.
Kitcher, P. (1990) "The Division of Cognitive Labor," *The Journal of Philosophy* 87(1): 5–22.
Kukla, R. (2012) "'Author TBD': Radical Collaboration in Contemporary Biomedical Research," *Philosophy of Science* 79(5): 845–58.
Latour, B., and Woolgar, S. (1979) *Laboratory Life: The Social Construction of Scientific Facts*, Princeton: Princeton University Press.
Lee, C.J. (2013) "The Limited Effectiveness of Prestige as an Intervention on the Health of Medical Journal Publications," *Episteme* 10(4): 387–402.
Lenhard, J., and Winsberg, E. (2010) "Holism, Entrenchment and the Future of Climate Model Pluralism," *Studies in History and Philosophy of Modern Physics* 41(3): 253–62.
Longino, H.E. (1990) *Science as Social Knowledge: Values and Objectivity in Scientific Inquiry*, Princeton: Princeton University Press.
Martinson, B.C., Anderson, M.S., and De Vries, R. (2005) "Scientists Behaving Badly," *Nature* 435(7043): 737–8.
Mayo-Wilson, C. (2014) "Reliability of Testimonial Norms in Scientific Communities," *Synthese* 191(1): 55–78.
McHenry, L.B. (2010) "Of Sophists and Spin-Doctors: Industry-Sponsored Ghostwriting and the Crisis of Academic Medicine," *Mens Sana Monographs* 8: 129–45.
Merton, R.K. (1957) "Priorities in Scientific Discovery: A Chapter in the Sociology of Science," *American Sociological Review* 22(6): 635–59.
Merton, R.K. (1968) "The Matthew Effect in Science: The Reward and Communication Systems of Science are Considered," *Science* 159(3810): 56–63.
Moffatt, B., and Elliott, C. (2007) "Ghost Marketing: Pharmaceutical Companies and Ghostwritten Journal Articles," *Perspectives in Biology and Medicine* 50(1): 18–31.

Munafò, M.R., and Davey Smith, G. (2018) "Robust Research Needs Many Lines of Evidence," *Nature* 533(1): 399–401.
Nosek, B.A., Spies, J.R., and Motyl, M. (2012) "Scientific Utopia II: Restructuring Incentives and Practices to Promote Truth Over Publishability," *Perspectives on Psychological Science* 7(6): 615–31.
Open Science Collaboration (OSC) (2015) "Estimating the Reproducibility of Psychological Science," *Science* 349(6251): aac4716.
Romero, F. (2016) "Can the Behavioural Sciences Self-Correct? A Social Epistemic Study," *Studies in the History and Philosophy of Science: Part A* 60(1): 55–69.
Rubin, H., and O'Connor, C. (forthcoming) "Discrimination and Collaboration in Science," *Philosophy of Science.*
Sismondo, S. (2007) "Ghost Management: How Much of the Medical Literature is Shaped Behind the Scenes by the Pharmaceutical Industry?," *PLoS Medicine* 4(9):e286.
Sismondo, S. (2009) "Ghosts in the Machine: Publication Planning in the Medical Sciences," *Social Studies of Science* 39(2): 171–98.
Sismondo, S., and Doucet, M. (2010) "Publication Ethics and the Ghost Management of Medical Publication," *Bioethics* 24(6): 273–83.
Sovacool, B.K. (2008) "Exploring Scientific Misconduct: Isolated Individuals, Impure Institutions, or the Inevitable Idiom of Modern Science?," *Journal of Bioethical Inquiry* 5(4): 271–82.
Stephan, P.E. (1996) "The Economics of Science," *Journal of Economic Literature* 34(3): 1199–235.
Strevens, M. (2006) "The Role of the Matthew Effect in Science," *Studies in History and Philosophy of Science Part A* 37(2): 159–70.
van 't Veer, A. E., and Giner-Sorolla, R. (2016) "Pre-registration in Social Psychology—A Discussion and Suggested Template," *Journal of Experimental Social Psychology* 67: 2–12.
Winsberg, E., Huebner, B., and Kukla, R. (2014) "Accountability and Values in Radically Collaborative Research," *Studies in History and Philosophy of Science: Part A* 46: 16–23.
Wray, B.K. (2017) "The Impact of Collaboration on the Epistemic Culture of Science," in T. Boyer-Kassem, C. Mayo-Wilson, and M. Weisberg (eds), *Scientific Collaboration and Collective Knowledge: New Essays*, New York: Oxford University Press.
Zollman, K.J.S. (2018) "The Credit Economy and the Economic Rationality of Science," *Journal of Philosophy* 115(1): 5–33.
Zuckerman, H. (1984) "Norms and Deviant Behavior in Science," *Science, Technology, & Human Values* 9(1): 7–13.
Zuckerman, H., and Merton, R.K. (1971) "Patterns of Evaluation in Science: Institutionalisation, Structure and Functions of the Referee System," *Minerva* 9(1): 66–100.

26
COLLECTIVE ACTION AND THE CRIMINAL LAW

Christopher Kutz

26.1 Introduction

Let us begin with the story dominating world news at the time of this writing (and which is sure to be a matter of historical memory): the legal investigations into the actions of United States President Donald Trump—before and after his election—related to his dealings with his lawyers, business partners, lovers, and foreign powers. Among the questions posed by these investigations are: what rules control the relation of the business organizations owned by the President to his duties as President? Did the President and other members of his campaign and staff act collectively, with members of the Russian government, to trade changes in U.S. law for help in the U.S. election or other private benefits? Are nominally legal acts of a President (firing the then-director of the Federal Bureau of Investigation, pardoning convicted criminals, etc.) made illegal when done in coordination with outside parties? Did the President and his attorneys work to modify the testimony of actual and potential government witnesses?

These questions largely concern the legal regulation of government officials and political candidates. Others are squarely matters of criminal law, including cooperating with a hostile foreign power to interfere in an election and obstructing a lawful investigation. While some of the acts thus far alleged may be matters of strictly individual criminality, most of them involve groups of individuals working together in ways that are prohibited by law. This is the domain of collective action within the criminal law. Within the Anglo-American legal system, which anchors my discussion, the key concepts are those of *complicity* and *conspiracy*. Together, these doctrines provide ways of assigning retrospective criminal liability to actors—and hence, prospectively, of deterring potential ones—in cases where the individuals do not themselves attempt or perform all the acts of a given crime, or in which the full scale of the harm resulting from the crime cannot be assigned to any individual.

The need for complicity and conspiracy doctrines arises from the personal and act-centered core of criminal responsibility. In the core model, someone is guilty of a crime when he personally performs a criminal act or produces a socially harmful result (e.g., threatening someone with a weapon), with the intention of performing that act or producing that result. But in many cases of interpersonal action, some of the people don't perform those acts or produce those results. Instead they suggest or endorse those actions, or help with planning or provide other kinds of logistical support. Morality and a realistic sense of social policy tell us that many of these ancillary acts are wrong and socially dangerous. So the doctrinal problem within criminal law is how to extend legal principles in order to capture at least some of these cases outside the core. The philosophical problem is whether the resulting doctrinal principles cohere with more general conceptions of moral responsibility, legitimate state punishment, and the underlying conceptions of causation and intention that provide the skeletal architecture of criminal law.

In what follows, I offer an opinionated survey of work on that philosophical problem, focusing particularly on the law of accomplice liability. There are, of course, many other ways that theories of collective action impinge upon law, not least in the way that collective action generates law—for instance, through legislation, collegial adjudication, and hierarchical systems of precedent and coordination. And there are interesting philosophical questions about how models of collective action can and should inform other departments of law, including the law of armed conflict, the law of labor and social organization, and family law. I will touch on some of these questions, but the central example will be criminal law. I proceed by first laying out the moral terrain on which criminal doctrine is built, then looking at the difficult questions presented by indirect or superfluous contributions by criminal actors. I briefly discuss some attempts to reconcile the broad sweep of accomplice liability with the causation requirements at the core of much criminal law. And I conclude with a look at other forms of liability for collective action.

26.2 Moral and Metaphysical Foundations for the Criminal Law of Collective Action

Criminal law is grounded in, and limited by, conceptions of moral responsibility. While there are substantial disputes whether one should understand criminal responsibility as simply that area of moral responsibility enforced by the state, virtually all criminal law theorists agree that the legitimacy of state-imposed liability is threatened if people are routinely punished for acts for which they bear no proportionate moral responsibility.[1] The starting point for a philosophical inquiry into complicity law should be a sketch of its moral foundations. As individuals, we are routinely capable of thoughtlessness, avarice, and nastiness. The things we do under such conditions can gravely harm friends and strangers alike—harming their feelings or their lives. The drunk driver, the sociopathic con artist, the rapist: acting on their own, they wreck lives and dreams. We are also capable of individual virtue, thoughtfulness, and compassion. Seeking no glory, we give comfort to the sick, mentor the young, and give time and money to good causes. And in many of these cases, we touch and better lives and ideals.

But the really significant harms and wrongs of life—the looming incineration of our planet, the genocides, the systems of social hierarchy, etc.—are not the products of us acting alone. They reflect collective choices, intersecting plans, organized groups, and deliberately composed systems of incentives and reward. Likewise, the great achievements of freedom and equality: though led sometimes by individuals, they are products of social movements, alliances of parties, shared deliberation by voters, and implemented by agencies, armies, and bureaucracies.

In causal terms, history's greatest heroes and villains are collectives not individuals. To be sure, Hitler, Stalin, and Tamerlane attract biographies, and their individual decisions and acts were crucial to history's unrolling. But on their own, they could not cause the tens of millions of deaths laid at their feet. They achieved their monstrous results with the cooperation of hundreds of thousands of collaborators. Collective action in much less dramatic form is also at the root of many of our most pressing contemporary problems. Some of these forms of collective action are deliberate, as when a corporate board decides to lobby for reduced carbon emissions controls, or when a non-governmental organization (NGO) comes to a disaster to provide medical aid and relief. Some of these forms of collective action are best described as aggregative—as when individuals behave in response to a common set of incentives and signals—and knowingly together cause harm—as when individual social media users participate in an informational network that becomes a vector for deliberate political sabotage—or good—as when individuals each donate small amounts to the NGO above, and together make possible the aid intervention. And sometimes the chief issue is the *inaction* of the collective, as when potential voters fail to turn out, allowing the election of scoundrels and fools; or groups of critical workers refuse to act as their bureaucracy directs, thus undermining a policy of deliberate cruelty.

The morality of collective action—or, better put, the moral valence of collective acts—is of course a central topic of moral, social, and political life. And it has attracted a significant body of important philosophical inquiry. Such inquiry has typically taken three forms (although sometimes combined): first, an analytical account of collective agency, which is meant to generate support for claims about praise and blame, or responsibility more generally, for the individuals involved in these acts; second, an account of the ways moral responsibility—including future-directed, action-guiding claims of duty—attach to groups (collectives) as such; and third, an account grounded in politics and normative sociology, about how the collectives construct a social ontology that legitimates persisting forms of inequality and subordination. Much of this work, this author's included, has a frankly normative aim of its own: to stir individuals towards reflecting on the collective context of apparently individual choices, moving them thus to desist from causing harm, or towards banding together to alleviate it.

Put aside metaphysical speculations as to whether collections of agents can be said, non-reductively, to act. Indulge in the legal fictions of corporate acts and acts of state. It is indisputable that whenever a collective acts (or fails to act), individuals have acted (or failed to act). A crowd surges against a barrier—only because each person has stepped forward and pushed against those ahead. A country elects a president—only because millions have cast ballots, others have tallied those ballots, others have certified their results, and many more have accepted as legitimate those results. How do we assess individual responsibility in such cases? Each individual has acted—but no individual's act seems to have made a difference to the outcome. However, if many had not acted as they did, the harm would have been averted. This is the moral problem of parallel, marginal individual action, involving accumulations of similar individual acts with tiny or invisible effects. A proper analysis of the moral significance of these acts must look to, and beyond, questions of individual causal significance to broader concepts of "making a difference," threshold-crossing, and what Derek Parfit famously called "moral mathematics."[2]

Another difficult category of individual responsibility lies in the domain of non-parallel but individually significant acts, when the moral value of one act is affected by another's distinct act. One such case might be the furnishing of a means to another's bad end, when one person sells a crowbar to another planning to use it in a burglary; or a doctor provides medical aid to someone being tortured by an intelligence service, knowing that the victim will be tortured again if he survives. These acts are non-parallel because they involve individuals contributing in different forms to a result. In these cases the individual act, taken on its own, is morally innocent, even beneficent. But added to the latter's act, it may make the difference between the success or not of the intended wrong.

The term "complicity" finds its technical, legal sense in such cases, and also its core moral sense, when the moral liability of one person depends on the acts of another. But the term may be more broadly used for the broader category of parallelism. As a first-order matter of morality, time presents two different types of questions that individuals might pose for themselves in such cases, or others might pose to them or about them: *ex ante*, what should individuals do—act or refrain, given the significance of their acts when summed or otherwise aggregated with those of others? Second, *ex post*, if harm has been done (or good, for that matter), what responses are appropriate, whether of blame and sanction, or praise and reward? Both questions hinge on the question of how the moral valence of one's own act is affected by its inclusion in a broader class of similar acts.

Some cases present primarily causal/metaphysical puzzles rather than moral ones. When the intent of the peripheral parallel actor, or aider or abettor, is clear and maleficent, a character judgment is easily assessed; and practices of shunning or reprobation have secure consequentialist anchors. Intent, as a matter of moral theory and social practice, drives a judgment of retrospective blame or prospective avoidance. Cases in which the individual act is surplus, or otherwise irrelevant to the scale of the harm, can matter for questions of the *scale* of moral responsibility or legal liability, whether to punishment or compensation. Think of one vote to elect a demagogue, when the margin of victory is far greater than one vote (and can be predicted to be so). Or a plant manager letting out a small amount of toxic discharge, aware that it is a common practice, and that the amount from one discharge has no determinable effect. As a metaphysical matter, whether these actors have causally contributed to a wrong requires some wrestling with ordinary and even refined conceptions of causation. Moral philosophers divide on the best metaphysical account of causation: whether it is a matter of logical, counterfactual dependence ("c caused e" is true if and only if, if c hadn't occurred, e would not have occurred); conditional dependence ("c caused e" is true if and only if c is a non-redundant element of a set of other non-redundant conditions sufficient for the occurrence of e); probabilistic relations ("c caused e" is true if and only if the occurrence of c raised the probability of e's occurrence); or a brute, singular physical relation involving the transferal of forces.[3] And there is room for further debate regarding criminal law's (or tort's) distinctive use of the term "causation" and whether it means anything more than, roughly, "the sort of relation for which liability is appropriately imposed, and for which a normatively constrained *sine qua non* relation is the best approximation."[4]

But descriptive metaphysics is less the issue than normative significance. We might agree that the cause of the house's burning down was both the faulty circuit and the failure of the fire department to turn up in time to dowse the flames—even though the metaphysically parsimonious would not recognize the omission as a genuine cause. While fire investigators and tort lawyers might further disagree about which is to count as the cause, that disagreement lies in policy, not philosophy. The issues of overdetermination and inter-agent causation presented by complicity are similar. The central issue of causation lies in the attribution of relative degrees of significance, more than in the resolution of the puzzles of overdetermination. Philosophers can solve the metaphysical problem by articulating conceptions of causation—for instance, the "NESS" test,[5] according to which each contributor to an overdetermined event can count nonetheless as a part cause of the event. Imagine, for example, one hundred people each tossing a match onto a wooden porch. No one match can generate enough heat to set the porch afire, but some number jointly can. Stipulate that the minimal number of matches for ignition is 50. In this case, each match thrower can be deemed a non-redundant element of a set of 50 match throws that were jointly sufficient for the event. Presto, the metaphysical puzzle of overdetermination is solved! Not so the normative problem: each match thrower can still say, "Sure, hold me responsible for the reckless throwing of a single match. But I cannot be responsible for the fire on the porch, because it would have happened regardless of whether I threw mine." To justify a non-trivial sanction for participating in the total arson, we need a moral, normative account that goes beyond the metaphysical.

One way to address normative significance is to make use of the idea of being responsible for an attempt—that is, to treat an agent as liable so long as the agent's act is of a *type* that generally causally contributes to the realization of a wrong (even if here it did not). If no typical excusing conditions are in place, we can treat the act as sufficiently anti-social in motivation, and risky in other iterations, that some form of sanction is warranted (or praise in the beneficent cases). It can also be the basis for a warranted judgment of character, and reveals the nature of the relations between the peripheral agent and those towards whom his ill-will or indifference is expressed.

The hardest puzzles are generated on a strictly Kantian account, because a peripheral agent could pass the relevant Kantian moral filters. Kantians require us to act in ways that accord with rules that all can defensibly follow. In principle, each match thrower can say, "I only throw matches when I know it won't make a difference, because there are a sufficient number of other match-throwers so that my act is superfluous." But even here, a proper understanding of the agent's intentions—which necessarily include coordinating around others' acts, if not identifying with them to accomplish a joint goal—makes it appropriate to assess the act in relation to that collective outcome. And so moral responsibility is warranted even in these metaphysically troublesome cases. We may summarize the case as follows: philosophical argument can support ordinary moral practices; the harms brought about collectively by several persons can be a basis for the warranted recrimination of a single agent, independent of any individually significant causal contribution. As a general matter, such recrimination is grounded in the intentional orientation of the agent—how she understands her actions in relation to what others do.

There are a number of different philosophical approaches, largely grounded in the philosophy of action, which provide further structure to this claim: that intentional or knowing contribution to an event produced through multiple individual acts is a sufficient basis for warranted response. Accounts by myself, Margaret Gilbert, Holly Lawford-Smith, Seumas Miller, and Julia Nefsky are among the contributions to this literature; many others are discussed, criticized, and defended elsewhere in this Handbook.[6] Some of these philosophers, following the lead of Michael Bratman,[7] build cooperation out of dense networks of individual intentions, coupled with reciprocal conditions ("I'll do this, if you'll do that"). Others, among them notably Margaret Gilbert, understand cooperation as built up not out of ordinary, first personal intentions ("I'll do this, if you'll do that"), but as reflecting a more radically social form of agency ("I'll do this as part of *our* doing that"). My view falls in the latter camp: I understand collective agency as composed of individuals orienting their agency around a goal or activity they understand as irreducibly joint. In the focal case, this is a matter of individuals having "participatory intentions" to do their part in a collective act.

Much of this scholarship raises questions that go beyond the issues within accomplice liability, such as the difference between bare coordination and full cooperation; the ethical obligations that arise from (and may be constitutive of) cooperation; the ontology of social groups; and the reducibility of participatory intentions to ordinary individual intentions. But there is important carry-over, and potential cross-fertilization, between law and philosophy in this area. The first site of convergence concerns the basic structure of the accomplice's intent, whose distinctive character is illuminated by the philosophical concepts of joint action and intentionality. But the real value may lie in the contributions of philosophy of action to two other standard questions within complicity law: the alienated accomplice and the knowing facilitator.

26.3 Collective Action, Complicity, and Criminal Law[8]

The above sketch of the moral foundations of responsibility for collective wrongs puts us in a position to translate these abstractions into the most concrete legal context in which they arise: criminal law. The standard model of criminal liability is beautiful in its simplicity. Imagine a crowd outside a nightclub. The proverbial shot rings out, a person falls, and a suspect is identified and charged with the killing. The law of homicide prohibits the taking of life without excuse or justification. A jury must answer two questions as a result: first, a question about conduct and causation, or *actus reus*: did the suspect cause the victim's death, by firing a shot that hit the victim and ended his life? Second, a question about the defendant's mental state, or *mens rea*: did the suspect cause this death intentionally, or was he aware of the risk he was imposing, or—at the least—would a reasonable person have been aware of that risk? If the answer to both questions is yes, then the defendant will be convicted of some form of homicide, depending on his degree of deliberateness or awareness.

Saying that these are easy questions does not imply that their answers are easily forthcoming: the basic facts will be in dispute, and coincidences may complicate the answer. Perhaps the suspect genuinely believed it was a toy gun, or cigarette lighter, that he was demonstrating; if no, no *mens rea*, and no liability. Or perhaps the victim had simultaneously collapsed from a drug overdose moments before he was shot; if so, then no causation. Nonetheless, the basic liability package is clear: a responsible defendant (i.e., capable of rational self-regulation) who acts intentionally or otherwise culpably to cause social harm, and in fact does so.

No moral theory of punishment hesitates here. A Kantian could not reasonably universalize a maxim of doing deliberate or indifferent lethal harm in a world in which we must expect reciprocal concern from others; a state agent would be charged with respecting the equal dignity of the victim, in relation to the killer, and thus be obliged to punish. Hence, we may call for retribution, in the form of a social principle of deliberately harming those who deliberately harm others. No utilitarian could think such behavior socially worthwhile, in the absence of any special justification. We must inflict suffering, lest this defendant or others be emboldened by the success of his anti-social behavior. And with the deliberateness or other form of culpability established, no liberal could object to the infliction of punishment on someone who so chose to flout the norms of criminal law. While skepticism is possible, for example, about the role of moral luck or freedom of the will, the basic conceptual questions of moral culpability and liability to punishment are basically overdetermined in the single actor case.

Now add another actor: two patrons are squared off and angry, when a third person in the crowd hands a gun to one of them, saying "give him what he deserves." The fighter handed the gun shoots and kills. Clearly, he is guilty of some form of homicide, and morally responsible for that act. But both morality and law insist that the fact that only he pulled the trigger does not exhaust the question of responsibility. The onlooker with the gun also contributed to the death—notwithstanding that it was the shooter's decision whether to pull the trigger, and independent of whether the shooter might have killed with a knife instead. The act of handing a gun to another itself causes no harm and violates no legal norm, assuming it is not being handed to someone prohibited from holding arms. But this basic principle, that indirect contribution to someone else's bad act can render one responsible for that act, is subject to a vast range of philosophical challenges.

Consider some more elaborated legal and literary examples:

(1) Stewart bears a grudge against Roger. When Frank says that he is thinking of breaking into Roger's house, Stewart offers to keep a lookout on the street, and to whistle if police approach. No police approach; Frank successfully burgles Roger.
(2) Iago, seeking to frame an innocent, persuades his jealous commander Othello that his wife has been unfaithful. Iago plants evidence, insinuates Desdemona's betrayal, and then, as Othello's jealousy rises to fever pitch, suggests that Othello strangle her. Othello does and is charged with murder, but is convicted only of manslaughter, on the ground that most

people, in the circumstances, might have behaved in similar fashion, and so is not fully responsible for his acts. Is Iago guilty of a more serious crime?

(3) Maxwell, a member of a Protestant Irish militant organization, was asked to drive his car to the home of some Catholics, thus leading a car containing four strangers to the home. Maxwell did not know what specific crime was intended, although he knew it was a "military operation" of some sort. Is Maxwell guilty of the attempted bombing of a bar conducted by the four strangers?[9]

Many moral-philosophical puzzles arise from the collective aspect of these cases. First, what justifies the liability of the aider, whom law calls a "secondary party" ("S"), given that he has done nothing intrinsically harmful, or that otherwise directly violates a legal rule, in contrast to the "Principal Actor" ("P"), who does the breaking, strangling, bombing? The lookout for a burglary does not enter the house. The getaway driver harms no one. Why is intent, plus some (legally) innocuous action, enough to justify loss of liberty or other severe penalties? Second, relatedly, why should (as in most jurisdictions) S be liable to the same punishment as P? In general, accomplices are punished as though they were principals—even though they have not themselves directly caused harm. Shouldn't there be a default reduction in liability? (Of course, some accomplices, namely those like Iago who instigate crimes, may arguably be more responsible than the direct perpetrators.) Third, and conversely, why is a "specific intent" to cause the harm generally required for an accomplice's liability, but not for a direct actor's? In general, for crimes grounded in a result (e.g., homicide), knowing that you will, or likely will, produce the result is enough to be treated as if you intended the result—for instance, throwing a rock at a window to see if it might bounce off (because you wonder idly if the window is plexiglass) counts as intentionally breaking the window. But in criminal law, doing something that you knowingly or strongly suspect will aid someone else in committing a crime does not make you liable for the crime. Selling ammunition from a gun shop to someone with a balaclava mask in his rear pocket doesn't make you an accomplice to his robbery (though you may be morally reprehensible). So why is accomplice liability limited in such cases, where moral responsibility would extend across the bridge of collective action? After all, many cases of collective (though not cooperative) action involve precisely such hand-offs, where there is immediate cooperation around a single task, but longer-term divergence of goals.[10]

These questions arise within criminal law, in relation to the formal concepts of intent and cause. They also reflect a specific dialectic within criminal law, between its backward-looking, retributive structure, and the forward-looking, risk-reducing aims that have become an increasing part of its modern justification. A retributive view of criminal law puts pressure precisely on the difficult points of interpersonal causation and joint activity, while an instrumentalist conception, like that embodied in the U.S. Model Penal Code, rests on vaguer grounds, such as whether a given defendant has manifested some form of social dangerousness, independent of the causal efficacy of the particular role he played.

We can sketch the basic elements of accomplice liability crudely as follows: someone is liable for the conduct of another as an accomplice if, prior to the other's attempt at or commission of a criminal act, the first person does or says something that could assist or encourage the second in the commission of the act, where the act of the first is done with the intention that the second in fact engage in the criminal act. The conduct, or *actus reus*, element of complicity is evidently broad, and defined only in relation to acts of assistance or encouragement (including inducement); the mental, or *mens rea*, element is accordingly narrower, and requires that the accomplice have an intent closely analogous to that of the principal. Thus, one does not become an accomplice to another's burglary merely by pointing out to someone loitering on the street that a house has a window open. Rather, one needs to point out the window with the specific intent that the addressee enter with the aim of permanently depriving the owners of property. Stewart's attitude towards the crime is more than mere glee at its happening. He has "made it his own," in the famous phrase of American judge Learned Hand, and linked his will to it, such that he has oriented his agency around it. He thinks of himself—and has made this a matter of common knowledge with Frank—as one of "us" engaging in the crime. Just as we distribute credit and blame alike to members of collectives who act together, recognizing in our moral response the character of their shared agency, so we distribute criminal liability in similar measure.

Within criminal law theory, there have been refined debates about whether the interpersonal connection can necessarily be deemed causal, as doctrine (especially in the United Kingdom) sometimes suggests. The problem is not so much one of peripheral parallel actors in relation to an overdetermined harm. Rather, the question is whether the Secondary agent can be said to (partly) cause the Principal agent to act by aiding or encouraging, so as to cement her own independent connection to the resulting harm. John Gardner and I divide on the question, for example.[11] Gardner insists that *any* contribution by an accomplice intended to encourage or aid the crime—whether or not it makes a difference, satisfies the doctrine's causal requirement. I, by contrast, argue that the best way to understand the criminal significance of an accomplice's contributions is by seeing them as attempts to influence the crime, whether or not they are causally relevant. This is to treat the causal requirement in complicity law as a kind of legal semi-fiction: the accomplice's acts have to have been of the right type, and to have occurred in the neighborhood of the principal's crime, with the requisite intent, but any further causal investigation is irrelevant.[12] Michael Moore has also recently argued, in turn, that complicity doctrine as a whole can be dissolved, and replaced piecemeal with the ordinary elements of individual criminal liability: secondary parties who contribute to harms by (partly) causing them—for instance, Mafia bosses whose orders initiate killings—are just killers causing death using people (with guns) as weapons; and non-causal accomplices can instead be thought of as principal actors who through their acts raise chances of harm, though they do not themselves cause it.[13] Moore's argument is clever, but perhaps not ultimately persuasive, in large part because both our general conception of moral responsibility—and associated doctrines of criminal law—rebel against treating forms of encouragement or persuasion short of duress as sufficiently direct to merit being put on the same footing as pulling triggers, pouring gasoline, hauling off stolen goods, and the other acts constitutive of the criminal law. Moore's proposal threatens to obscure the way accomplice liability involves a distinctive, but still responsibility-generating, form of association with criminal harms, while placing a great deal of evidentiary pressure on proof of causation or risk.[14]

For these purposes, however, the relevant point is that whether through a legal fiction of a token-level causal relation, or whether through a broader notion of causation, Aiders and Abettors are deemed to be closely enough connected to resulting harms that liability can be justified in retributive terms. There are, to be sure, instrumental reasons for doing so as well: collective criminality may pose greater social risks, through the division of labor and the scaling of effort, and hence deterrence of the ancillary members is important. But the foundational moral logic is one of recognizing complicity as a species of joint activity within our broader social ontology.

Now, to say this is not yet to justify the equivalence of accomplice and direct liability—i.e., the co-equal liability of Stewart (who stands and does nothing) and Frank, who breaks in.

Indeed, in most legal systems, if Stewart had reason to think Frank might be armed, and Frank while burgling shoots the homeowner, both are liable for murder. The notable jurisdictional exception is Germany, where aiding accomplices are given a significant discount from their principals' sentencing, although inducing accomplices are given no such discount.[15] This seems anomalous, given that Frank's act of shooting can only be described as a killing, while Stewart's act of standing alert cannot be described as a killing at all. Simply on linguistic grounds, it seems wrong to label Stewart equally a killer.

Of course, the moral valences can be reversed, as in the example of Iago. Othello is guilty at the least of voluntary manslaughter, and perhaps even second-degree murder, depending on a jury's sympathies for the torments of misplaced sexual jealousy or the reasonableness of his suspicions. But Iago's case is more complicated. Othello is too strong to be considered a victim, and Shakespeare is clear that honor alone does not compel him to kill—the murder arises more from his own insecurities, and proceeds with fair deliberation. But Othello is still essentially moved by a world of false clues Iago constructed around him. Iago, meanwhile, is not subject to the specific irrationality of sexual jealousy; Desdemona's killing is the object of his plot, not an outbreak of passion. He is a deliberate murderer, without question. While Othello is more than a mere instrument of Iago's will, Iago's greater culpability is supported by the distinctive nature of his plan—the way it incorporates Othello's agency within.

The interchangeability of accomplice and principal liability is peculiar because, in the case of attempt liability—arguably the closest analogue to accomplice liability—the dominant pattern in legal systems is a systematic reduction in punishment for incomplete harms. More generally, empirical moral psychology tends to assign weight to an agent's proximity to harm; and legal systems tend to reflect such conventional morality, except in the case of Mafia kingpins. Nothing decisive follows from this fact of our moral psychology, but it does suggest that the justificatory burden should be significant for the principle of equal punishment. Or, to put it another way, it seems anomalous for accomplice liability to be so Kantian when much of the rest of criminal law reflects more luck-sensitive intuitions. It may be that the best explanation for not discounting accomplice liability is simply that there are too many cases of the Iago sort, where intuitions and even reflective moral judgments conflict, and it would be a waste of public resources to make fine distinctions between criminal actors, each of whom has manifested an anti-social animus. But such pragmatism does not satisfy the general liberal presumption against punishment beyond what is socially useful and fair. This is an area where more philosophical work can be done.

The last point that complicity law helps us to make involves the fundamental concept of *alienated participation*, exemplified in the example of Maxwell. An alienated participant is someone indifferent to the success of the venture as a whole (perhaps because he does not profit from it), but who nonetheless deliberately contributes to the venture. Individuals participate in collective ventures for a variety of reasons, including desire to profit, or fear of repercussions if they refuse. In any of these cases, an accomplice put to trial might say, "I didn't intend to help the principal succeed—I was just doing my job." In general, the defense fails, unless the pressure brought to bear on the accomplice is so great that it constitutes the legal excuse of duress.

Maxwell was tapped by the Ulster Volunteer Force to lead a car of men he knew were up to no good to the location they requested, where they subsequently planted a bomb. In his defense, he said he neither shared their mission nor knew the plan they meant to carry about; hence he lacked the specific participatory intent to further their pipe-bombing of the inn. Under a certain understanding of participation, that would be correct. Indeed, the language of American complicity law suggests that one needs "a stake in the venture," something more than a mere association, to be an accomplice.[16] But the language is misleading if it suggests that the accomplice must be subjectively attached to the mission of the principal. The actual standard in law is functional, not subjective: one is deemed to satisfy the standard if one's acts are guided counterfactually by the principal's aim—however one feels about that aim. Now, it may simply be that the court did not believe Maxwell's claim to be alienated from the goal. But under general principles of complicity law, whatever Maxwell's feelings about the bombing, he could be found liable as an accomplice. This is because his acts are fully described, functionally and dynamically, as helping the Irish Republican Army find their target: his agency, over the course of his driving, is fully oriented around that goal. Criminal sanctions aimed at deterring or punishing assistance of unlawful acts will look to this functional characterization.

There are, to be sure, marginal cases. Contrast Maxwell's situation with that of a gas station attendant filling the IRA car.[17] The attendant may knowingly provide aid, but assuming his motivation was not one of helping in the bombing, his intentional act is plausibly described in terms of the one-off goal of filling the tank with gas, which had a known effect. Filling a gas tank involves cooperation around the micro-tasks of engaging in conversation and completing the payment transaction. It may, if the getaway car is running low on gas, be the difference between criminal success and failure. But the gas attendant is not generally regarded as one of the members of the criminal gang. Criminal legal systems divide on how to treat such cases. Generally speaking, English and civil (including international criminal) law make knowing or foreseen provision of aid or encouragement a basis for criminal liability, while most U.S. jurisdictions do not. Notably, in France, Vichy collaborator Maurice Papon was held liable for crimes against humanity when he transported French Jews to the Nazis, knowing of their eventual fate though without any interest in bringing it about. A major task for philosophical analysis is determining whether joint action mediated through mere knowledge of effects should be treated as equivalent to jointly goal-oriented activity, or less culpable than the latter, or not at all culpable.[18]

Lessons from more basic philosophy of action serve well here: the distinction between intentional (purposive) action and action done with the awareness of side effects is real, and thus crucial to understanding how we integrate specific aims into our more general plans. As both Bratman and Duff have argued, while our decisions to act incorporate our awareness of the consequences of those acts, there remains a difference between, say, acting with the intent to cross a lawn, knowing it will track the snow, and acting with the intent to track the snow.[19] In the second case, but not the first, failure to produce the tracks will result in a shift in plans, perhaps a redoubling of the path. The difference, in other words, goes to the core of intentional agency.

Having the analytical distinction in hand does not resolve the moral or legal treatment of someone who acts knowing that effects will be produced. While the distinction may not be relevant to the permissibility of the action, it will bear on the character of the agent, contributing to both a retributive assessment and a calculation of the risk posed by him. As T.M. Scanlon notes, it would be peculiar to think, for example, that the permissibility of an act might vary, simply in virtue of the attitude taken by the actor—for example, a bombing raid might be deemed permissible if done by a pilot who seeks a military target, knowing of civilian collateral casualties, but be impermissible if done by a pilot seeking civilian casualties, aware that a military target will be taken out.[20] Nonetheless, we might decide that a distinction between the two cases is relevant to our treatment of the pilots, for one might pose a greater risk of escalating violations of the law of war. The interplay of strongly pragmatic motives and moral considerations makes the law of war an especially promising context for investigating these questions, as in the work of Saba Bazargan-Forward and Seth Lazar.[21]

26.4 Other Dimensions of Collective Action and Liability

I began this chapter with the example of the criminal investigations surrounding President Donald Trump, and the suspicions that he and his campaign "colluded" with Russian state actors to gain an advantage in the election. As Trump's defenders have frequently commented, there is no crime of "collusion" to be found in the criminal statutes. Treating him as an accomplice would also seem a poor fit for criminal liability. Take, for example, what has been cited by the U.S. Department of Justice as a successful effort by Russian intelligence to hack into U.S. Democratic Party email servers, and then to release the hacked emails for general distribution through Wikileaks.[22] That act itself involved principal, direct actors (the hackers who typed the relevant commands), as well as many secondary parties—the Russian intelligence and political actors who ordered them to do so. Julian Assange and other staff at Wikileaks could be arguably treated as accessories-after-the-fact, like those who fence stolen goods for thieves, and so also derivatively responsible.[23]

It is of course possible that Trump or his campaign associates aided or encouraged this hacking and release of the emails in advance, in which case their liability as accomplices would be straightforward. But what is likelier—even as a matter of fiction, if we wish to treat the example this way—is a more complicated relation to the Russian efforts, whereby there was an understanding between members of the campaign and members of the Russian state that the Russians would work to support Trump (primarily by undermining his opponent), in exchange for efforts to create more favorable policies towards Russia. Such an understanding would be morally and politically corrupt, inasmuch as it trades covert foreign interference in a democratic process for policy outcomes—this is the basis of opprobrium attached to the idea of "collusion." But it would still be hard to link the U.S. actors as accomplices, if they did not know what specific acts the Russians planned to do.

"Conspiracy" is criminal law's solution to the problem of how to extend liability to individuals who act in concert with others to achieve criminal ends, but without necessarily making distinctive causal contributions to those crimes, or knowing much at all about the other actors and their plans. Typically, all that is required for conspiracy liability, in Anglo-American and civil law, is for two or more people to agree to participate in the commission of crime.[24] The punishment for a conspirator can be greater than that for the crime that is planned, and will apply even if the conspiracy never gets past the planning stages. Individuals are routinely found liable for conspiracies when they are part of a loose network of individual nodes, with little or no sense of the full set of other conspirators. Moreover, under U.S. federal law, many state laws, and in international criminal law, members of a conspiracy whose crimes are realized will be treated as though they were in fact accomplices in each of the crimes that was committed—even if they lack the specific intention and knowledge that is otherwise required for accomplice liability.

The great breadth and flexibility of conspiracy law makes it an extremely useful tool for state authorities, who can bring cases against individuals for participating in the planning of crime (on the basis of evidence of discussions, say), despite the lack of any more specific evidence of their role in the crimes. Such breadth is said to be essential for prosecuting, and so deterring, organized crime.[25] There are many questions philosophers might ask about the moral and political principles supporting or limiting legitimacy of such broad liability (even if in particular cases, liability seems wholly appropriate). Among other issues, conspiracy liability can seem to interfere with the proper liberty of political or labor discussion, and indeed there is a long history of state use of conspiracy law to repress labor and political activity. But there are also questions that are best answered from within the theory of collective action. Among these questions are: what constitutes an "agreement" when details remain to be filled in, most plans are yet to be laid, and individual participants may have highly conflictual understandings of their joint aim?

Because conspiracy liability is, essentially, liability for a collective mental object—an agreement—it therefore requires a theory of collective intentionality. And so philosophy has an invitation to step into the breach. The issues around conspiracy are quite similar to those surrounding topics in contract law, as well as statutory interpretation, albeit the latter topics require and receive much more fine-grained treatment. Take the example of the individual who served on occasion as the driver for Osama bin Laden: could he be regarded as a co-conspirator in bin Laden's larger plans? This is a threshold existence question that asks whether the individual's conception of his role meshes with other participants' understandings: did he think of this as a single drive, a drive to enable a specific terrorist operation, or a standing role in a terroristic organization? Answering that question is not necessarily easy, but once it is answered, liability follows.[26] By contrast, in a case of contract or statutory interpretation, courts need to determine not usually whether there was an agreement, but the specific content of the agreement as all sides understood it. This is a much more difficult matter, and frequently requires assessment not just of a collective intention among the parties, but how inherently ambiguous or unforeseen circumstances should be handled.

There has been some philosophical work on this question, specifically in relation to conspiracy. I have argued that the idea of a "participatory intention" can play a help role: participatory intentions are individual intentions to orient one's own activity around a shared goal.[27] Individuals will have, perforce, very different subjective conceptions of shared goals, given different levels of knowledge and motivation. What criminal law requires, making sense of a conspiratorial agreement, is an objective conception of the least extensive state of affairs that jointly would satisfy individual participant attitudes. If you believe I am driving you to the bank to commit a robbery, while I only believe I am driving you into midtown, the overlap in our participatory intentions (to ride together) includes only the ride, not the bank robbery. By contrast, if you believe I am driving you in order to help you rob the bank as part of our plan to dismantle capitalism, while I understand myself only as enabling the bank robbery, then our joint intention is now to rob the bank, but not dismantling capitalism. If this is a jurisdiction that treats conspirators as consequently also accomplices to further crimes, then having the right philosophical conception of collective intentions can have dramatic consequences.

While I have focused thus far on criminal liability and collective action, I will note the closely related topic of civil liability. In the private law in both Anglo-American and European countries, liability for harms brought about by collective action is shared among partners, industrial colluders, and assigned to employers—but largely excluded from shareholders, unless their ownership of the harm-doing company is itself fraudulent. The default proposition, that partners in a joint business enterprise bear individual liability for the harms realized by the whole, largely expresses rock-bottom moral common sense. But some of the specific rules of liability are more questionable, such as the general rule that each partner may be personally liable for the whole of the harm, do not track this moral sense (this is called "joint and several" liability). Such rules of collective liability are justified on the grounds that it is unfair, within an adversarial legal system, to make the victim sue each partner to recover fully; partners can, after paying off the victim, recover from each other. But this represents at best a way of working within a liability system that itself lacks much normative justification, given the extraordinary ratio of litigation costs to recovery by victims. A wholesale philosophical rethinking of liability in these cases is due.

More problematic yet is the strong default rule that shareholders, even in privately held corporations, bear no liability beyond the value of their shares for harms done by their company.

Take, as examples, shareholders in an oil company that fails to adhere to safety and environmental standards, and so causes an environmental catastrophe; or private equity majority owners of an arms manufacturer, whose weapons are easily modified for maximum lethality and are used in a gun massacre. The companies in these cases would be liable, to be sure (barring special protective legislation, that is). If they are cleverly structured, they will not have enough assets to cover the full potential costs of their harms, and their shareholders can walk away. The justification for such a policy is the instrumental need for companies to be able to raise significant amounts of capital investment; minimizing the financial risk to shareholders induces them to invest more. But this seems patently inadequate as a normative defense of limited shareholder liability, because it permits an extraordinary asymmetry: there is no upside limit on the profits shareholders can reap from a firm, but there is a firm limit on their downside liability—a limit purchased at the expense of potential accident victims.

I have argued in prior work for the importance of bringing a philosophical challenge to this aspect of law's treatment of collective action, but philosophy has not rushed in to fill the gap.[28] There is significant philosophical work on the morally and legally unproblematic, if ontologically mysterious, question whether corporate entities as a whole can be held liable for accidental or deliberate harms.[29] Whether or not one treats corporate personality as a legal fiction or moral truth, the coordinated activities of the managers and employees make corporations an apt and responsive target for civil liability and even criminal penalties. But the limitation of liability on their capital investors greatly restricts the constraining force of legal norms. Given the dramatic potential and actual harms facing the earth that arise from joint economic and social activity, much of it through deliberate state and corporate decisions, the field of civil liability and state responsibility present much the most urgent matters. I hope that philosophy will follow.[30] This is a matter of understanding the promises and limits of law as a way of engaging us in the most urgent collective action problem of all: restraining our joint carbon emissions so as to prevent our planet from burning to a crisp.

Notes

1 While criminal law has pockets of so-called "strict liability"—criminal responsibility for harmful or risky outcomes even if the criminal actor was not even careless in producing the outcome, such as the liability of a business owner for selling mislabeled pharmaceuticals—these are seen as morally dubious, and best limited to certain kinds of regulatory concerns.

2 Parfit (1986), ch. 3.

3 These positions are associated with, among others, David Lewis, J.L. Mackie, and Richard Wright. For a very useful summary, see Michael Moore (2011).

4 The quoted phrase is mine, approximating Hart and Honoré (1959); see also Honoré and Gardner (2010).

5 "NESS" stands for "Necessary Element of a Set of jointly Sufficient" conditions. The idea was first articulated by Hart and Honoré, then named, refined and elaborated by Wright (1985), especially pp. 1788–98.

6 See, e.g., Gilbert (1996); Lawford-Smith (2016); Kutz (2000); Miller (2006); Nefsky (2011).

7 Bratman (2014).

8 Material from this section is drawn and revised from my contribution to Deigh and Dolinko, *Oxford Handbook of Philosophy of Criminal Law* (Kutz 2011).

9 Director of Public Prosecutions for Northern Ireland v. Maxwell [1978], 1 W.L.R. 1350.

10 See Bratman, "Shared Cooperative Activity," in *Shared Agency*, for the distinction between coordinated and fully cooperative activity, where the latter involves complex sharing of goals.

11 See Kutz (2007); Gardner (2009), ch. 3.

12 Take, for example, the case of a spectator at an illegal fight who, among thousands, shouts encouragement at the fighters (who would be fighting whether or not there was any shouting). Criminal law

could properly treat him as an accomplice to the fight, but I think there is no plausible account of causality, including the NESS test, which would treat the shouts as actual causal contributors. See *Wilcox v. Jeffery*, 1 All E.R. 464 (1951).

13 See Moore (2007). There are a few other doctrines that can sweep up some remaining difficult cases, for example forms of vicarious liability imposed because of a relationship between parties (such as an employer for an employee), where liability is thought important for deterrence and other incentive effects.

14 For these and other doubts, see Duff (2007).

15 Strafsgesetzbuch Secs. 27, 49(1).

16 This is the language of Judge Learned Hand in *United States v. Peoni*, 100 F.2d. 401 (2nd Cir. 1938).

17 Imagine a world (as in Oregon) where gas station attendants exist.

18 See, for a general discussion, Lepora and Goodin (2013), ch. 4.

19 Bratman (1987) ch. 10; Duff (1990).

20 Scanlon (2010), ch. 1.

21 Bazargan-Forward (2013); Seth Lazar (2016).

22 Grand Jury for the District of Columbia, "US Indictment of 12 Russian Intelligence Officers" (July 13, 2018), located at https://assets.documentcloud.org/documents/4598947/DOJ-indictment-of-12-Russian-intelligence.pdf

23 Although accessories after the fact did not necessarily aid or encourage the crime (they may have arrived on the scene later), their liability is justified on the two-fold crime that expectations of their later assistance make the crime likelier to happen; and their knowing profit from an unambiguously criminal prior act makes them morally culpable. It is a form of what I call "causeless complicity."

24 Typical of conspiracy statutes is the catch-all U.S. statute, 18 US Code §371: "If two or more persons conspire either to commit any offense against the United States, or to defraud the United States, or any agency thereof in any manner or for any purpose, and one or more of such persons do any act to effect the object of the conspiracy, each shall be fined under this title or imprisoned not more than five years, or both."

25 For a discussion of the policy issues, and a defense of its importance to combat the special nature of collective criminality, see Katyal (2003).

26 In the case I allude to, concerning Salim Hamdan, Hamdan was actually acquitted of conspiracy charges, on the argument that he did not understand himself to be playing a role in the larger criminal enterprise, and so lacked the requisite criminal intent.

27 See my ch. 3, in Kutz (2000), as well as Ohlin (2008). The topic of collective intentionality, writ more broadly, has of course attracted much more attention. Most relevant to these questions is the theory of law developed by Scott Shapiro. Shapiro (2011) argues that law is best understood, in Bratmanian terms, as a form of joint planning, and that this conception entails specific consequences for a theory of legal interpretation. Work by Gilbert (2000); Pettit (2001); and Tollefson (2015) is also very valuable for these topics.

28 See my *Complicity*, ch. 7.

29 See, among others, the works of French et al. (1992) and Pettit (2007).

30 Some of these inquiries are initiated by the authors, including me, in Aust (2011).

References

Aust, H.P. (ed) (2011) *Complicity and the Law of State Responsibility*, New York: Cambridge University Press.

Bazargan-Forward, S. (2013) "Complicitous Liability in War," *Philosophical Studies* 165: 177–95.

Bratman, M. (1987) *Intentions, Plans and Practical Reason*, Cambridge: Harvard University Press.

Bratman, M. (2014) *Shared Agency: A Planning Theory of Acting Together*, New York: Oxford University Press.

Director of Public Prosecutions for Northern Ireland v. Maxwell [1978], 1 W.L.R. 1350.

Duff, R.A. (1990) *Intention, Agency and the Criminal Law*, Oxford: Blackwells.

Duff, R.A. (2007) "Is Accomplice Liability Superfluous," *University of Pennsylvania Law Review* 156: 444–52.

French, P.A., Nesteruk, J., and Risser, D.T. (eds) (1992) *Corporations and the Moral Community*, New York: Holt Rinehart & Winston.

Gardner, J. (2009) "Complicity and Causality," in *Offences and Defences: Selected Essays in the Philosophy of Criminal Law*, New York: Oxford University Press, 57–76.

Gilbert, M. (1996) *Living Together: Rationality, Sociality and Obligation*, Lanham, MD: Rowman & Littlefield.

Gilbert, M. (2000) *Sociality and Responsibility*, Lanham, MD: Rowman & Littlefield.
Grand Jury for the District of Columbia, "Indictment of 12 Russian Intelligence Officers," *United States of America v. Netyksho*, 1:18-CR-00215 (ABJ), July 13, 2018. [online] Available at www.justice.gov/file/1080281/download (Accessed: 11 April 2019).
Hart, H.L.A., and Honoré, A. (1959) *Causation in the Law*, New York: Oxford University Press.
Honoré, A. and Gardner, J. (2010) "Causation in the Law," E.N. Zalta (ed), *The Stanford Encyclopedia of Philosophy* (Winter 2010 ed.) [online] Available at https://plato. stanford.edu/archives/win2010/entries/causation-law/ (Accessed: 11 April 2019).
Katyal, N. (2003) "Conspiracy Theory," *Yale Law Journal* 112: 1307–98.
Kutz, C. (2000) *Complicity: Ethics and Law for a Collective Age*, New York: Cambridge University Press.
Kutz, C. (2007) "Causeless Complicity," *Criminal Law and Philosophy* 1: 289–305.
Kutz, C. (2011) "The Philosophical Foundations of Complicity Law," in J. Deigh and D. Dolinko (eds), *The Oxford Handbook of Philosophy of Criminal Law*, New York: Oxford University Press, 147–67.
Lawford-Smith, H. (2016) "Difference-Making and Individuals' Climate-Related Obligations," in C. Hayward and D. Roser, (eds), *Climate Justice in a Non-Ideal World*, Oxford: Oxford University Press, 64–82.
Lazar, S. (2016) "Complicity, Collectives, and Killing in War," *Law and Philosophy* 35: 365–89.
Lepora, C., and Goodin, R. (2013) *On Complicity and Compromise*, New York: Oxford University Press.
Miller, S. (2006) "Collective Moral Responsibility: An Individualist Account," *Midwest Studies in Philosophy* 30(1): 176–93.
Moore, M. (2007) "Causing, Aiding, and the Superfluity of Accomplice Liability," *University of Pennsylvania Law Review* 156: 395–444.
Moore, M. (2011) "Causation in the Criminal Law," in J. Deigh and D. Dolinko (eds), *The Oxford Handbook of Philosophy of Criminal Law*, New York: Oxford University Press, 168–93.
Nefsky, J. (2011) "Consequentialism and the Problem of Collective Harm: A Reply to Kagan," *Philosophy & Public Affairs* 39: 364–95.
Ohlin, J.D. (2008) "Group Think: The Law of Conspiracy and Collective Reason," *Journal of Criminal Law and Criminology* 98: 147–206.
Parfit, D. (1986) "Five Mistakes in Moral Mathematics," in *Reasons and Persons*, New York: Oxford University Press. Ch. 3.
Pettit, P. (2001) "Collective Intentions," in N. Naffine, R. Owens, and J. Williams (eds), *Intention in Law and Philosophy*, Ashgate: Aldershot.
Pettit, P. (2007) "Responsibility Incorporated," *Ethics* 117: 171–201.
Scanlon, T.M. (2010) "The Illusory Appeal of Double Effect," in *Moral Dimensions*, Cambridge, MA: Harvard University.
Shapiro, S. (2011) *Legality*, Cambridge: Harvard University Press
Tollefson, D. (2015) *Groups as Agents*, New York: Polity Press.
United States v. Peoni, 100 F.2d. 401 (2nd Cir. 1938).
Wilcox v. Jeffery, 1 All E.R. 464 (1951).
Wright, R. (1985) "Causation in Tort Law," *California Law Review* 73: 1735–828.

27

COLLECTIVE RESPONSIBILITY IN THE STATE

Avia Pasternak

It is common practice to hold states responsible for their wrongdoings. Consider the following examples: in the aftermath of World War II, West Germany accepted responsibility for the crimes of the Holocaust, and transferred compensatory payments to the State of Israel and to diaspora Jewish survivors (Colonomos and Armstrong 2006). In 1991 the United Nations Compensation Commission held Iraq responsible for its invasion of Kuwait, and imposed on it compensation payments to the individuals, businesses and states that were harmed by its actions. In 2015 CARICOM – the umbrella organization of Caribbean states – issued demands of apology, compensation and investment in rehabilitation against European States, in light of their historical involvement in the transatlantic slave trade (CARICOM 2015).

It is also a common view that citizens are responsible for their state's wrongdoings. Consider the following examples: In 1947 the German philosopher Karl Jaspers wrote an influential text – *The Question of German Guilt* – where he identified four different senses in which German citizens share guilt for the Nazi administration's crimes (Jaspers 2000). In 2014 dozens of Israeli military intelligence officers signed a letter in which they announced their refusal to continue to serve in the Israeli military, in light of its record of human rights violations, and their responsibility as citizens to oppose them (8200 Refusniks letter 2014). And (by far more controversially) in 2005 a terrorist blew himself up on a crowded London Underground train. He justified his actions by referring to the responsibility of British citizens for the British government's policies in the Middle East (*Guardian* 2005).

However, recent philosophical literature suggests that assertions about state and citizens' responsibility are not as straightforward as they might appear. Even the few examples I mentioned raise various challenges. The first is conceptual: In what sense are states and citizens responsible for wrongdoing? Does the claim translate into the idea that a state and its citizens are *blameworthy* for wrongful policies? Does it follow that they ought to apologize, or offer compensation, or be punished when they commit such wrongs? These are all very different meanings of what being responsible means, with various practical implications. A second challenge is normative: the idea of collective responsibility that underpins claims about state and citizens' responsibility might appear to be in tension with common individualist sensitivities, according to which people should be held responsible for what *they* do and not for what other members of their groups do. In their discussion of state responsibility in international law, Crawford and Watkins (2010: 290) phrase this worry well:

> In virtually every case of state responsibility, the population that is eventually called upon to carry the costs of responsibility includes members who are, by any standard, morally blameless. [... This] may seem as unfair and ethically backwards as the treatment meted out under primitive systems of collective responsibility in which whole tribes or nations are subject to reprisals.

Finally, even if we are able to resist these conclusions, and to offer a solid argument for why citizens are responsible for their states' actions in a way that does not violate our individualist sensitivities, there is the question of the scope of that responsibility: Are citizens always responsible for their state's wrongdoings, or might some citizens be off the hook? And does the argument apply equally to all regime types, from radical totalitarian states to advanced democracies?

Each of these questions has received attention in the burgeoning literature on collective responsibility in the state. My goal here is to provide an overview of these debates and to highlight what I think are some of the most promising solutions they offer to these challenges. The chapter develops as follows. I first overview the various conceptual ways in which states and citizens might be responsible for state wrongdoing.[1] I then turn to whether, and how, states are responsible in their own right for their wrongful policies. Finally, I explore whether individual citizens are responsible (in the various senses I identify) for the wrongs committed by the state.

27.1 Collective Responsibility: Conceptual Clarifications

As discussed elsewhere in this volume, the term responsibility has multiple meanings. Authors on collective responsibility in general, and on collective responsibility in the state in particular, offer various typologies and definitions (e.g. Goodin 1987; Miller 2007). For the purposes of this chapter I shall use a broad distinction between two meanings of the term. The first denotes culpability or blame (I will use these terms interchangeably). A blameworthy agent is liable to, or deserves to be met with, appropriate reactive attitudes for her transgression: resentment, anger and (in the case of a legal violation) legal punishment. Blame in this sense attaches only to agents who acted (or failed to act) in ways that brought about (or failed to prevent) a wrong; who acted (or failed to act) in a culpable state of mind (i.e. purposely, knowingly, recklessly or negligently), and who had sufficient level of control over their choices and actions (Fischer 1999).

The second conception of responsibility is what David Miller (2007) refers to as 'remedial responsibility'. It concerns the tasks or duties agents need to perform in order to fix a wrong. In the context of state wrongdoing these remedial liabilities are likely to involve the following tasks: (1) to put an end to the ongoing unjust policy (as argued by the Israeli Refusniks), (2) to compensate those who were harmed by a wrongful policy (as did Germany and Iraq), (3) to offer remedies that go beyond direct compensation to the victims (as demanded by the CARICOM committee) and perhaps even (4) to take steps to ensure that similar wrongs will not occur again (e.g. by introducing new regulations or new institutions).

This distinction between culpability and remedial responsibility bears some similarity to Iris Marion Young's influential distinction between 'backward-looking' and 'forward-looking' responsibility (Young 2004: chapter 4). Young introduces these terms in her discussion of responsibility for 'structural injustices'. Such collective injustices (e.g. the appalling working conditions in the global apparel industry) are caused by the uncoordinated interactions of vast numbers of individuals operating under shared practices and norms. Young argues that we should avoid attributing 'backward-looking responsibility', which blames specific individuals for their past contributions to these wrongs, and instead focus on the forward-looking 'political responsibility', which requires agents to engage in a political process of change. I shall return to Young's cautions against backward-looking responsibility later in the chapter, but for now it's important to note that culpability and remedial responsibility are both 'backward' and 'forward' looking: if an agent is culpable for wrongdoing, then most likely she will have some forward-looking remedial obligations to compensate the victim, to offer an apology and perhaps even to incur punishment (Tadros 2011). Furthermore, as David Miller (2001) points out, like culpability, remedial responsibility can be grounded in backward-looking factors (i.e. factors that relate to facts that happened in the past): for example, people can be responsible for putting a wrong to the right because they have caused that wrong, because they have benefited from it or indeed because they are morally responsible for it.

I now turn to examine what *collective* responsibility means. A useful distinction here is between 'corporate' and 'shared' (or collective) responsibility. Corporate responsibility describes the responsibility of a group, over and above that of the members. For example, public international law holds states (rather than their individual citizens or members of cabinet) liable to pay compensation for their wrongdoings (Crawford 2007). Shared (or collective) responsibility refers to the responsibility of individuals for what they do together in groups, in light of their contributions for the collective wrong. The extent and scope of each member's share of responsibility depends on her position in the group and her relation to the collective harm. Sometimes, each member of the group plays such a pivotal role that each shares responsibility for the collective wrong itself. Consider for example a gang of three criminals, who co-plan a bank robbery and divide the task between them: A is the lookout, B is the getaway-car driver and C opens the safe. In this case, given their respective roles as co-planners and executors of the crime, we would commonly think that A, B and C all share responsibility for the bank robbery itself (cf. May 1992: 38). But in other cases, such as wrongdoings committed by very large or highly hierarchical groups (like the typical state), some members play a much less pivotal role in the planning and execution of the wrongdoing. As we shall later see, in such cases it is far less clear that each member is fully responsible for the wrongdoing itself. Precisely these cases raise concerns about holding people unjustly responsible for things that are beyond their control.

27.2 Holding States Responsible

Article 1 of the ILCC Articles on State Responsibility clearly states that 'every international wrongful act of the State entails the international responsibility of that State' (Crawford 2007: 77). Public international law is also clear that this responsibility is corporate – it attaches to the state itself – a complex system of legal and political institutions that are coordinated under a single decision-making process – rather than to specific individuals within it (see discussion in Crawford 2007: 28–36).

But although the idea of state responsibility is common in legal practice, several philosophers remain uncomfortable with that idea (Hindriks 2014). Normative individualism, the view that what fundamentally matters, morally speaking, are individual humans (and perhaps other sentient beings) might seem in tension with the claim that states are in themselves actors that are morally responsible for their actions. After all, the objection goes, states lack the relevant attributes to be moral agents: as corporate agents they are not real persons, they have no minds of their own and do not engage in moral reasoning.

Therefore, it would be nonsensical to blame them for their wrongdoings. Furthermore, at least on some views of punishment, which see it as a form of moral dialogue with a perpetrator, it would also make little sense to punish states, given their lack of dialogical capacities.[2] Perhaps there are pragmatic reasons to treat states as fictional, legal persons, and to assign them some forward-looking compensatory duties, but ultimately, moral responsibility for state policies lies with the individuals who play their role within the state apparatus (Fabre 2016).

However, recent voices in the burgeoning literature on corporate agency challenge these assertions. These views hold that groups can be moral agents in their own right, and morally responsible for what they have done, over and above their members. One highly influential account of corporate moral responsibility has been offered by Christian List and Phillip Pettit (2011). They focus on structured groups with central decision-making procedures and enforcement mechanisms. As List and Pettit show, such groups cannot rely on a simple majoritarian decision-making process, as it is likely to lead to conflicting beliefs and goals at the group level. In order to maintain rationality over time, such groups must adopt a decision-making procedure that 'collectivizes reason': i.e. it collects members' beliefs and desires on various separate premises, and then aggregates them on the basis of a logical combination. When groups adopt this type of decision-making process (and they often do), their beliefs and goals become 'functionally independent' from those of their members, and the group can end up 'having beliefs' or desires that are distinct from what some or even all group members believe and desire. As List and Pettit conclude, such groups have a 'mind of their own', which supervenes upon, but is functionally independent of, the minds of their individual members (65–72). Given that such groups have a mind of their own, they can qualify as moral agents, who understand and respond to moral reasoning. As List and Pettit conclude, a corporate entity of this type is the appropriate subject of moral evaluation, and 'has to answer as a whole for what it does at the corporate level, drawing on the resources provided by its members' (163).

List and Pettit's influential account of corporate moral agency has been used to show that states too are moral agents (Tanguay-Renaud 2013; cf. Erskine 2001): they are unified organizational actors, which set and follow laws and principles, and which have stable decision-making processes and binding authority structures that ensure organizational autonomy and rational consistency over time (e.g. constitutions, defined role responsibilities and internal accountability mechanisms). Their decision-making processes 'collectivize reason' in the way List and Pettit suggest and therefore they can meet the requirements of moral agency. As such they can be morally responsible when they act wrongly (e.g. declare an unjust war) or negligently (e.g. fail to prevent a culture of implicit racism). If we accept this view, it follows that states are not just responsible in a thin, legal sense. Rather, they are the appropriate subjects of reactive attitudes like anger and resentment, directed at the state itself, as the agent that plans and orchestrates the actions of its members. This idea gives further grounding to current legal practices, and also suggests they can be taken a step further. Currently, international law does not recognize states as criminal wrongdoers, and does not subject them to criminal punishment. But if states are moral agents, then there may be good reasons to expand criminal international law so that it applies to them as well (whether this is a change that is feasible, given the structure of international relations, is a separate question) (see Tanguay-Renaud 2013; Wringe 2016: 154–177).

List and Pettit developed an influential framework for thinking about corporate moral agency in general and that of states in particular. However, as some commentators have noted, their novel conception of corporate moral agency also opens up a host of questions about the moral status of corporate agents and their place in our moral universe. For example, should corporate moral agents follow the same normative standards we deploy for individual agents, or might they have their own special morality? And if states are indeed moral agents, over and above their members, does it also follow that they have moral rights which deserve protections in and of themselves? These important questions require further exploration in existing literature.

27.3 Citizens' Moral Responsibility

I have explored so far the idea that states are corporately morally responsible for their wrongful policies. But what about their citizens? Much attention has been paid in recent years to the question of the responsibility of individual group members for collective harm in general, and for state harm in particular. I'll examine these debates first with relation to moral responsibility and then with relation to remedial responsibility. As I noted in the introduction, the idea that citizens are to *blame* for their government's actions raises concern for normative individualism, given that one of its key tenants is that guilt, or blame, may attach only to offending actors, in light of their own state of mind and actions. As Joel Feinberg famously put it, 'there can be no such thing as vicarious guilt' (Feinberg 1968: 676). Blaming a citizen for the wrongdoings committed by her government, just because she is a citizen of that state, violates this widely accepted principle. However, on the other hand, even supporters of the idea of corporate moral responsibility warn against it becoming a form of blanket exoneration for all citizens, who might use it to argue that they are 'only acting on behalf of the truly responsible party, the State itself', and are therefore immune from either moral or criminal liability (May 2005: 139).

Clearly, even when it is the state that commits a serious wrongdoing, there will be at least some individual members within the state who will share the blame.[3] This applies most clearly to high-level officials and policymakers, who have prominent influence on the state's decision-making process. One interesting puzzle in this context concerns the gap between policy-makers' actions and the actual wrongdoings: often policymakers are not the direct perpetrators of the wrongs committed on behalf of the state. They contribute to the shaping of the state's decision to, for example, engage in an unjust war, but they do not fight or commit human rights violations on the ground. Are they morally responsible for acts that they themselves have not taken part in? Scholars of international criminal law suggest that the answer to this question is positive: leaders of states are responsible for crimes committed by their soldiers when they have ordered these crimes, and even when they are merely aware of them and failed to prevent them (May 2005: 139–143).

In his discussion of the normative foundations of prosecutions of crimes against humanity, Larry May goes even further. He argues that central policymakers such as heads of state are morally (and criminally) responsible for the very collective wrong the state commits – e.g. engagement in an unjust war – because they are the ones who set the intentions of the state, so its criminal state of mind can be attributed to them (140). However, this claim is in tension with the corporate moral agency I have described earlier. As we saw, on that account, the state's mind is not reducible to the state of mind of any of its individual members, including its policymakers. Precisely for that reason, as Tracy Isaacs suggests, all members of an organization, including policymakers, share responsibility for their *contributions* to the state's collective wrongdoing (Isaacs 2011: 106–111). These contributions might be central and even essential for the wrong to have taken place, and such factors will increase the seriousness of the relevant individual wrongdoing. Only in some very rare cases, an individual might be in such a pivotal position within the state as to be morally responsible for the state's wrong itself (as were the three criminals in my earlier example). And even then we should not assume that holding such individuals responsible for their contributions to the state wrongdoing substitutes holding the state responsible as well.

Holding policymakers morally responsible for state wrongdoing may seem fairly straightforward. But what about ordinary citizens?[4] Do they share the blame for what their government does? In answering this question it is worth noting that the line between 'policymakers' and 'ordinary citizens' is not that easy to draw. At least in democratic states (and to an extent in some non-democratic states as well), citizens can be 'policymakers' too in the sense that they contribute to the decision-making process and to the execution of state policies: they vote for the political parties in charge and have various other formal and informal channels of influence on their political representatives. They also pay the taxes that are used to execute state policies, and they contribute to the state apparatus by obeying the state laws. If, as we saw, policymakers can be morally responsible for their contributions to state wrongdoing, should not ordinary citizens be blamed as well? A negative answer to this question might follow from Young's analysis of backward-looking responsibility. As I mentioned earlier, Young warns against holding ordinary individuals to blame for their participation in collective structural injustices which, she explains, are 'produced and reproduced by large numbers of people acting according to normally accepted rules and practices'. In such scenarios each participant's contribution to the outcome is untraceable, and therefore it is not at all clear that it makes any difference for which one can be blamed (Young 2011: 100). For example, it is impossible to draw a direct causal link between a single citizen's income tax payments and her state's engagement in, say, violations of the codes of just war in the course of a military operation. The state mechanism is such that specific contributions are not linked to specific outcomes.

Furthermore, Young points out that most participants in structural injustices do not act with the relevant guilty state of mind. Their contributions to the ongoing injustice are the outcomes of habitual conventions and practices. Those who perform them do not intend to contribute to the wrong, and they don't engage with 'explicit reflection on the wider implications' of what they do (107). Not only that, but third, refusing to contribute to the state apparatus can be extremely difficult. Ordinary citizens participate in their state in a wide variety of ways, and it is hard to see how one can entirely abstain from making such contributions. Even if that were possible, it is likely to entail high personal costs. Given all these difficulties, one might draw the conclusion that pointing the finger of blame at citizens for the wrongdoings of their governments is misguided. And it might also be counterproductive: rather than motivating citizens to act against the wrong they are part of, a 'rhetoric of blame in public discussion of social problems [...] usually produces defensiveness and unproductive blame-switching' (Young 2004: 378–379). As I noted earlier, Young suggests that we should instead engage in a different 'forward-looking' strategy, which assigns all citizens the role of bringing an end to their state's wrongdoing, regardless of their share of the blame for it.

Young offers a powerful critique against backward-looking responsibility in the context of collective structural harms. However, might she be letting ordinary citizens off the hook too quickly? In answering this question we should separate her strategic and substantive critiques against the 'rhetoric of blame'. Whether or not blaming ordinary citizens is politically counterproductive is by and large an empirical question, which cannot be settled here. But it's worth noting that some commentators argue that blame (and praise) can actually play a constructive role and incentivize actors to 'seek good actions in the future and avoid bad ones' (Nussbaum 2013: ii).[5] Setting this strategic question to the side then, Young's substantive critiques of the backward-looking model of responsibility have been critically examined in recent debates. Some authors suggest, *pace* Young, that attributing blame for participation in structural injustices is possible: first, because a contribution need not make a traceable difference to the outcome in order to satisfy the causality condition of moral responsibility (for extended discussion see for example Kagan 2011; Nefski forthcoming); second, because individuals who contribute to a collective wrong need not necessarily intend to commit that wrong: it suffices that they are aware that their actions contribute to some wrongdoing (Lepora and Goodin 2013: 80–81); and third, all agree that if citizens have no choice but to contribute to their state wrongdoing, they are excused. But it is far from clear that all citizens are equally coerced to contribute to their state's wrongdoing. More affluent citizens, for example, often have the resources to cope with the legal and financial costs of civic resistance to state injustice, including the refusal to contribute to the state apparatus (Thoreau 1991). In fact, as Eric Beerbohm (2012) has argued, especially in democratic states, where public officials are acting in the name of the citizens, citizens, and especially those with the resources to do so, have a democratic duty to engage in political activity to ensure that their representatives act justly. Beerbohm's notion of democratic duty is closely related to Young's claim that citizens have a forward-looking political responsibility to resist structural injustices. But, as Beerbohm points out, what follows from it is that, when citizens negligently fail to comply with their forward-looking political duties (i.e. assuming that the costs of such engagement are not too high for them), they become blameworthy for their failure, and for its consequences. Young's plausible assertions about forward-looking duties then have important backward-looking implications which might be overlooked, given the sharp conceptual distinction she draws between forward- and backward-looking responsibility: if one has a duty to resist injustice, and one fails to do so without a reasonable excuse, then one becomes morally responsible for her contribution, via omission, to the ongoing occurrence of the injustice (Nussbaum 2013: xxi).

To conclude the point, on the one hand, sweeping attributions of blame to whole populations (as from the terrorist in the example that opened this chapter) are wrong and misguided. Holding citizens and policymakers responsible for state wrongdoing must take into account their own actions, omissions, intentions and choices. But, on the other hand, ordinary citizens cannot use the collective nature of state wrongdoing as a shield against attributions of personal blame. Given their citizenship status and their inevitable contributions to the state apparatus, each citizen has a special responsibility to ensure that unjust policies are counteracted. What, and how much, each citizen is expected to do is a complex and difficult question. But clearly citizens who have the capacity to act and yet do nothing to resist unjust policies, even when the costs of resistance are fairly low, share some blame for the consequences. Given the limited scope of their actual and potential contributions, the scope of their blame will be fairly low. But it may justify some moral responses: self-reproach and shame (Abdel-Nour 2003), and some moral censure from fellow or other citizens.

27.4 Citizens' Remedial Responsibility

I now turn to examine the question of citizens' remedial responsibilities. As we saw in previous sections, it is commonly assumed that when a state commits a wrongdoing, it incurs forward-looking remedial duties to address that wrong, including investing resources to end the wrong, compensation to its victims and investing resources in correcting the factors that led to the wrong (e.g. faulty decision-making procedures and culture). On the corporate account, these duties fall on the state in the first instance. But in order to execute them, clearly the state must draw on its citizens' resources, e.g. in the form of increased taxes or reduced services. This has been referred to as the 'distributive effect' of state responsibility (Pasternak 2011). Is there a normative justification for it?

One affirmative answer to this question is provided by Stephanie Collins (2016). As we saw earlier, there are various factors that determine which agents are responsible for putting a bad situation right, including moral responsibility for the wrong, benefit from the wrong, association with the victims and even mere capacity to act. Collins argues that once we identify the source of the state's remedial duties to put the bad situation right, we can justify the distribution of the burden amongst the citizens, as long as it is done in accordance with the same factor that grounds the state's remedial duties. For example, if the source of the state's remedial duties is its moral responsibility for the wrongdoing, then citizens who also share moral responsibility for the wrong should be expected to share the burden, in proportion to their level of blame. Here, as we saw in the previous section, various factors will determine citizens' level of blame and corresponding share of the burden: the centrality and proximity of their contributions to or omissions from the state wrongdoing; the extent to which they knew, or should have known that they were contributing to a wrongdoing; how enthusiastically they were acting; and the extent that they could have avoided contributing in this way (Lepora and Goodin 2013: chapter 4).

Collins' 'source-tracking' model gives a sound rationale for why, and when, citizens are remedially responsible for the state's wrongful policies, and – importantly – her rationale is compatible with normative individualism, as each citizen's burden is determined in light of their own actions and omissions. But one difficulty this model faces is that it is hard to implement in practice, given the size of the state, its complex structure and the varying levels of blame of the different actors within it. Collins (352) points to some ways of addressing these difficulties. For example, she argues that taxation can target activities that we consider wrongful contributions to state wrongdoing (e.g. in the context of climate change injustice, the state can raise resources by taxing polluting activities). However, even if these proposals are implemented, it is hard to avoid the conclusion that given the highly complex structure of the state, and the type of information the source-tracking model requires, it is going to be impossible to fully implement it. Indeed, if we look at political practice (e.g. the cases of German and Iraqi reparations I mentioned earlier), we find that usually states deviate from this model and instead use resources from the general tax pool to pay for their wrongdoings. Does doing so constitute a wrong against the citizens who are not to blame for their government policies (e.g. those who protested against the wrong), or who bear less blame than, say, high-ranking policymakers? Or can a distribution that does not track blame be normatively justified? In the rest of this section I will explore two models that offer a positive response to this question.

The first model is developed by Anna Stilz (2011), and revolves around the idea of democratic authorization. Stilz's starting point is Kant's theory of legitimate state authority. Kant famously argues that all persons have a basic, natural right against unjust interference from other agents, and also a basic, natural duty to respect the freedom of others. These rights and duties justify the existence of the state, because they can only be respected under a joint political authority which will coordinate individuals' actions and subject them to shared laws. A state that performs these functions has the right to be obeyed by its subjects, and it is also authorized by them, in the sense that they grant it the right to act in their name. But not any state that subjects citizens to its laws is authorized by its citizens. Rather, the state must pass a threshold of moral acceptability: it must respect its citizens' basic liberal freedoms, guarantee their equality before the law, comply with basic requirements of distributive justice and give all citizens equal democratic rights. Stilz argues that when a state complies with these conditions, its policies are authorized by each of its citizens, even those who disagree with a specific policy. For even when a citizen disagrees with a specific policy, given that the state crosses the threshold of moral acceptability the policy remains a 'plausible interpretation' of what the state may do in her name. In that specific sense, each citizen's will is 'implicated' in the state's policies, and each citizen 'has a reason to "own up" to what an authorized state does' (Stilz 2011: 198; cf. Parrish 2009). Owning up means accepting a share of the task of discharging the state's remedial responsibilities when it acts wrongly. Importantly, each citizen's share of the burden need not necessarily be determined by her level of moral responsibility.[6] What grounds citizens' remedial duties is the fact that as free and equal members of the state, their will is implicated in their government's actions. Stilz's model seems well placed to justify a distribution of the burden that is spread amongst all citizens. Even citizens who protest against the unjust policy of a reasonably just state are implicated in it, and ought to share the burden.

However, one lingering worry concerns this account's core claim that citizens authorize the reasonably just state to act in their name, and that therefore they are implicated in its actions. As we just saw, according to Stilz, the authorization is objective – it is grounded in the characteristics of the state itself and not in the citizens' subjective perceptions of their citizenship status. But, as David Miller (2004: 245) points out, a core guiding principle in matters of distributing collective responsibility is that 'as far as possible, we want people to be able to control what benefits and burdens they receive'. Arguably, the claim that citizens authorize their state and share responsibility for its policies regardless of their own subjective attitudes to these policies is an overly restrictive requirement, which gives citizens too little control over the extent of their remedial responsibilities.

A different attempt to explain citizens' remedial responsibilities, which does pay attention to their internal attitudes, revolves around the concept of collective action. There is by now a very rich literature on the meaning and normative implications of this concept (see Roth 2017). One influential model within that literature is offered by Christopher Kutz (2000). He suggests that '[c]ollective action is the product of individuals who orient themselves around a joint project' (67). Kutz argues that all participants of collective action share a participatory intention to act as part of the group or to contribute to a collective outcome. Furthermore, he argues that when agents intentionally participate in a collective action, they become the 'inclusive authors' of that act – part of the 'we' who performed the act. As such, they are complicit in it and remedially responsible for its outcomes (122). These obligations, he explains, 'mirror the nature of their participation' as members of a joint venture (201).

Like much of the literature on collective action, Kutz's analysis focuses primarily (but not exclusively) on relatively small-scale groups like military units and business corporations. However, some authors (e.g. Jubb 2014; Pasternak 2013; cf. Kutz 2002) have argued that the model of participatory intentions could be scaled up to the state itself, and can explain why citizens are remedially responsible for their state's policies.[7] The idea here is that the state is a site of collective action, and that citizens are acting together in their state, as they perform their various roles in it (paying taxes, obeying the law, voting, etc.). Performing such actions amounts to orienting oneself around a collective project, that of maintaining the authority of the state and its ability to execute its plans. As participants in the state itself, citizens are inclusive authors of its policies – they are part of the 'we' who decides upon and executes these policies. They therefore ought to share in the task of undoing the wrongful impacts of their state policies.

Like Stilz's democratic-authorization model, this model can justify a distribution of the burden that does not track each citizen's personal moral blame. The explanation is related to the subjective, intentional feature of participation in collective action. When people decide to orient themselves around a joint project, they take certain risks upon themselves: when we act together with others, we lose some control over the action and its consequences. Sometimes the result is beneficial to us, but sometimes it incurs unexpected burdens on us. This will be the case, for example, when a source-tracking distribution of the burden of the type Collins envisions is too difficult or too costly to implement. In such scenarios, it is not unreasonable to expect of all citizens who intentionally participate in their state to also participate in the task of assisting their state in discharging its remedial responsibilities. This would simply be a burden that they risk having when they engage in collective action of this type. But given that the justification for this burden revolves around citizens' intentional stance, it gives citizens more control over the scope of their liabilities than Stilz's objective account. Indeed, this account is able to explain the remedial responsibilities of citizens even in states that fail to pass the standard of moral acceptability. Consider again the case of Nazi Germany. This regime surely did not pass Stilz's test of moral acceptability. Yet many people might think that it was not unjustified to impose duties of compensation on its population in the aftermath of the war. As Robert Jubb (2014: 60–61) explains, one way to support this common intuition is by reference to the popular support on which the Nazi regime relied, and the general consensus on its right to rule. Many citizens in Nazi Germany were intentional participants of the regime, and hence shared remedial responsibility for its wrongdoing (regardless of whether their support was morally excused).

Given this approach's emphasis on the import of citizens' subjective, internal stances towards their state, at least some of its advocates (e.g. Pasternak 2013; for a critique see Jubb 2014) suggest that intentional participation generates remedial duties only when it is genuine. Genuine intentional participation does not mean consent. Clearly, citizens do not consent to become members of their state – most of us are born into our citizenship status, and few of us have the option of giving it up without considerable cost. What I mean by genuine participation is that citizens do not view their citizenship status as something that is forced on them against their will, and that they would give up if they could. When individuals do view themselves as coerced to take part in a collective venture that they deeply resent, it seems wrong to argue that they ought to take responsibility for the outcome; if anything they are the victims of that collective project rather than its inclusive authors. But when citizens endorse their citizenship status, in the weak sense that they do not resent it, and would not have given it up if the opportunity was there, they are genuine participants in this collective venture.[8] In reasonably open states, which respect their members' basic rights, people are free to develop their attitudes towards their citizenship status (Pasternak 2013; for a related account see Miller 2007). And many, indeed most, citizens in such reasonably decent states do not see their citizenship status as something that is forced on them against their will, even when they disagree with their current government's policies. Consider again the Israeli refusniks' letter which I mentioned earlier: it seems that these soldiers' membership in their state is in fact a constitutive part of their identity, and the reason they see themselves under the duty to act when they disagree with its policies.

Unlike Stilz's democratic-authorization model then, the intentional-participation model seeks to hold citizens responsible and at the same time to give them some control over the extent of that responsibility by leaving open the option that they reject their citizenship status. But here too challenges remain. First, not all agree that the models that explain collective action in the context of relatively small groups can be scaled up to the state: the highly complex and hierarchical nature of the state, which places citizens at a great distance from actual policymaking, casts doubt on the extent to which citizens are indeed intending to take part in each of its actions, and the extent to which its actions are attributable to them (see discussions in Shapiro 2014; Lawford Smith 2019). Second, the model seeks to leave open the door for citizens to negate their responsibility for their state's actions, but the fact that it relies on the internal attitudes of citizens for doing so raises important challenges: How can policy track these attitudes? And what do citizens need to do in practice in order to show that their participation is not genuine, especially given that, as a matter of fact, most cannot leave their state?

To conclude, I have explored in this section various models for justifying citizens' remedial responsibilities for their states' wrongdoing. These various models attempt to balance between, on the one hand offering a justification for the distributive effect that gives citizens adequate control over their responsibilities, and on the other hand offering a model of distribution that states can adopt in practice. As we saw, the various models I discussed offer different answers to the correct balance between these two considerations. But they also share some important insights. First, they confirm that many, indeed most citizens in reasonably just states will share some remedial responsibility for their state's wrongdoing. Second, they all suggest that we should be much more cautious about assigning remedial responsibilities in states that do not pass some threshold of moral acceptability. Consider the oppressed citizens of a dictatorship like North Korea. While they contribute to their state policies, and at least some of them do so enthusiastically, none of the models I discussed here would support the claim that they are either morally or remedially responsible for their government's policies. Given the dire conditions in North Korea, it is clear that most ordinary citizens will have valid excuses, from coercion to extreme manipulation, that will exonerate them from moral responsibility for their limited contributions to their state's policies. And the fact that the North Korean State fails to meet basic standards of moral acceptability implies that its citizens are not genuinely participating in it, and that its actions are not reasonable interpretations of their rights (Jubb 2014). It follows then that often in those regimes that commit the most egregious human rights violations, collective attributions of responsibility to the citizenry are the least plausible.

27.5 Conclusions

This chapter has provided a review of recent debates on states' and citizens' collective responsibility. As we saw, recent philosophical literature on the nature of corporate agency has given a boost to the idea that states are morally responsible agents, and that when they do wrong they are the appropriate subjects of moral reactions, from resentment to anger and even criminal punishment. On the other hand, as I emphasized throughout, we should be careful not to conflate our moral reactions to the state with our moral reactions to its citizenry as a whole. Moral blame attaches only to citizens who wrongly contributed to, or failed to prevent, their state's wrongdoing, in proportion to the centrality of these contributions to the wrongdoing. But according to at least some models, remedial responsibility can be distributed amongst all, or nearly all, citizens in light of their membership status in the state (assuming the state complies with the conditions I outlined).

These assertions have important pragmatic implications. For example, they can help to assess the various demands for compensation for state wrongdoing with which I opened this chapter. As we saw, most of these demands were targeted at wrongdoer states, in light of their atrocious actions. However, at the same time, given the corporate nature of the state and the distributive effect, it was the populations of these countries who felt the impact of burden. The analysis here cast doubt on the normative justification of this burden in some of the cases: Iraq, for example, was ruled at the time of its invasion of Kuwait by a highly oppressive and brutal regime. Given its treatment of its own population it is highly questionable whether the population should have been held remedially responsible for the regime's crimes.[9] This is not to deny that the victims of this state's atrocities ought to have been compensated. But the discussion here suggests that when the state fails to meet certain conditions, the international community ought to look for alternative compensation schemes that would not excessively burden the population of the wrongdoer states (see some suggestions in Fabre 2016: 166–168). On the other hand, the analysis suggests that were the democratic states that participated in the 2003 invasion of Iraq demanded to pay compensation for the serious harm they inflicted on the Iraqi population, then the distributive effect of that burden could be justified to American and British citizens, in light of the democratic nature of their state and/or their participation in it. Furthermore, many of these citizens, who regularly contribute to the democratic state and who had sufficient information about its policies, share at least some level of blame for the wrongdoings committed on their behalf.

Notes

1 My focus here is on responsibility for wrongdoing. States and citizens can be responsible for policies which are not wrongful and even praiseworthy, and that responsibility may carry with it various entitlements (e.g. to the fruits of a beneficial policy).
2 For a review of these critiques see Wendt 2004.
3 List and Pettit note that, conceptually, there can be cases where a group agent is to blame but none of its citizens will share the blame (166). But in reality it is hard to see how such cases can come about.
4 Another important question, which I lack the space to discuss here, concerns the moral responsibility of non-citizens for state policies: for example, the responsibility of migrant communities for the policies of their hosting states, or the responsibility of diaspora communities for the policies of the state with which they have strong cultural ties.
5 The impact of blame would change from context to context. For example, post-conflict societies often avoid using a blame-based model when apportioning reparations for the crimes committed during a recent conflict, precisely because of concerns about the disastrous political effects this model might bring, including instigation of further conflict.
6 Stilz is careful to separate moral blame and forward-looking task responsibility. She thinks that, given that many citizens have done nothing wrong, and object to their state's policies, they do not share blame for what it does. Nevertheless, the state is authorized to act in their name, and in that sense their will is implicated in its actions and grounds their task responsibility (Stilz 2011: 194–195)
7 Another influential work that understands citizenship as collective action is offered by Margaret Gilbert (2006).
8 On this weak-endorsement view, a citizen need not harbor especially positive views of her state. The citizen may be indifferent to her state, or have merely instrumental reasons to take part in it. Such weak attachments are sufficient to ground genuine participation.
9 For analysis of the German case see Jubb 2014. The CARICOM committee claims raise additional challenges about state responsibility for past wrongdoing. See Butt 2008 for a good starting discussion on this issue.

Bibliography

Abdel-Nour, F. (2003) "National Responsibility", *Political Theory*, 31: 693–716.
Beerbohm, E. (2012) *In Our Name: The Ethics of Democracy*, Princeton: Princeton University Press.
Butt, D. (2008) *Rectifying International Injustice*, Oxford: Oxford University Press.
CARICOM (2015) "Reparations for Native Genocide and Slavery" available online at: www.caricom.org/reparations-for-native-genocide-and-slavery [accessed 20 September 2018].
Collins, S. (2016) "Distributing State Duties", *The Journal of Political Philosophy*, 24: 344–366.
Colonomos, A., and Armstrong A. (2006) "German Reparations to the Jews after World War II: A Turning Point in the History of Reparation". In P. De-Greiff (ed.), *The Oxford Handbook of Reparations*, Oxford: Oxford University Press.
Crawford, J. (2007) *The International Law Commission's Articles on State Responsibility: Introduction, Text and Commentaries*, Cambridge: Cambridge University Press.
Crawford, J., and Watkins, J. (2010) "International Responsibility". In S. Besson and J. Tasioulas (eds), *The Philosophy of International Law*, Oxford: Oxford University Press.
Dodd, V., and Norton-Taylor, R. (2005) "Video of 7/7 Ringleader Blames Foreign Policy", available online at www.theguardian.com/uk/2005/sep/02/alqaida.politics [accessed 20 September 2018]
Erskine, T. (2001) "Assigning Responsibilities to Institutional Moral Agents: The Case of States and Quasi States", *Ethics and International Affairs* 15: 67–86.

Fabre, C. (2016) *Cosmopolitan Peace*, Oxford: Oxford University Press.
Feinberg, J. (1968) "Collective Responsibility", *The Journal of Philosophy*, 65: 674–688.
Fischer, J. M. (1999) "Recent Work on Moral Responsibility", *Ethics*, 110: 93–139.
Gilbert, M. (2006) *A Theory of Political Obligation: Membership, Commitment, and the Bonds of Society*, Oxford: Clarendon Press.
Goodin, R. (1987) "Apportioning Responsibilities", *Law and Philosophy*, 6: 167–185.
Hindriks, F. (2014) "How Autonomous Are Collective Agents? Corporate Rights and Normative Individualism", *Erkenntnis* 79: 1565–1585.
Isaacs, T. (2011) *Moral Responsibility in Collective Contexts*, Oxford: Oxford University Press.
Jaspers, K. (2000) *The Question of German Guilt*, New York: Fordham University Press.
Jubb, R. (2014) "Participation in and Responsibility for the State", *Social Theory and Practice*, 40: 51–72.
Kagan, S. (2011) "Do I Make a Difference?" *Philosophy & Public Affairs*, 39: 105–141.
Kutz, C. (2000) *Complicity: Ethics and Law for a Collective Age*, Cambridge: Cambridge University Press.
Kutz, C. (2002) "The Collective Work of Citizenship", *Legal Theory*, 8: 471–494.
Lawford Smith, H. (2019) *Not In Their Name: Are Citizens Culpable for Their State's Actions?* Cambridge: Cambridge University Press.
Lepora, C., and Goodin, R. (2013) *On Complicity and Compromise*, Oxford: Oxford University Press.
List, C., and Pettit, P. (2011) *Group Agency*, Oxford: Oxford University Press.
May, L. (1992) *Sharing Responsibility*, Chicago: Chicago University Press.
May, L. (2005) *Crimes against Humanity: A Normative Account*, Cambridge: Cambridge University Press.
Miller, D. (2001) "Distributing Responsibilities", *Journal of Political Philosophy*, 9: 453–471.
Miller, D. (2004) "Holding Nations Responsible", *Ethics*, 114: 240–268.
Miller, D. (2007) *National Responsibility and Global Justice*, Oxford: Oxford University Press.
Nefsky, J. (forthcoming) "How You Can Help, without Making a Difference", *Philosophical Studies*.
Nussbaum, M. (2013) "Introduction" in I. M. Young (ed.), *Responsibility for Justice*, Oxford: Oxford University Press.
Parrish, J. (2009) "Collective Responsibility and the State", *International Theory*, 1: 119–154.
Pasternak, A. (2011) "Sharing the Costs of Political Injustice", *Politics, Philosophy, Economics*, 10: 188–210.
Pasternak, A. (2013) "Limiting States' Corporate Responsibility", *Journal of Political Philosophy*, 21: 361–381.
Roth, A. S. (2017) "Shared Agency". In E. N. Zalta (ed) *The Stanford Encyclopaedia of Philosophy*, available online at https://plato.stanford.edu/archives/sum2017/entries/shared-agency/ [accessed 20 September 2018).
Shapiro, S. (2014) "Massively Shared Agency". In M. Vargas and G. Yaffe (eds.), *Rational and Social Agency: The Philosophy of Michael Bratman*, Oxford: Oxford University Press.
Stilz, A. (2009) *Liberal Loyalty: Freedom Obligation and the State*, Princeton: Princeton University Press.
Stilz, A. (2011) "Collective Responsibility and the State", *Journal of Political Philosophy*, 19: 190–208.
Tadros, V. (2011) *The Ends of Harm: The Moral Foundations of Criminal Law*, Oxford: Oxford University Press.
Tanguay-Renaud, F. (2013) "Criminalizing the State", *Criminal Law and Philosophy*, 7: 255–284.
Thoreau, H. D. (1991) "Civil Disobedience". In H. A. Bedau (ed.), *Civil Disobedience in Focus*, London: Routledge.
Wendt, A. (2004) "The State as Person in International Theory", *Review of International Studies*, 30: 289–316.
Wringe, W. (2016) *An Expressive Theory of Punishment*, London: Palgrave Macmillan.
Young, I. M. (2004) "Responsibility and Global Labor Justice", *The Journal of Political Philosophy*, 12: 365–388.
Young, I. M. (2011) *Responsibility for Justice*, Oxford: Oxford University Press.
8200 Refusniks Letter (2014). Available online at: https://modiinletter.wordpress.com [in Hebrew] [accessed: 20 September 2018].

28
SHARED RESPONSIBILITY FOR CORPORATE WRONGDOING

Amy J. Sepinwall

Corporations, for all their good, sometimes cause legendary harms without justification or excuse. The transgressions include peddling products carrying undisclosed serious health risks, defrauding shareholders, unconscionably exploiting workers, pocketing customers' money, furthering or even participating in gross violations of human rights, and recklessly poisoning our environment. This should not surprise us. Individual wrongdoing is hardly anomalous and, when individuals get together, especially in institutionalized groups, the potential for wrongdoing is ever present, and perhaps even enhanced (Katyal, 2002). We should expect that tendency to be even more prevalent in a culture dominated by the thought – mistaken though it is (Stout, 2002) – that the law requires managers to maximize profits for corporate shareholders, which can incentivize perverse, or even criminal, behavior.

What is perhaps surprising is the difficulty we face in responding to these corporate acts. To be sure, it is highly common to find excoriations of the transgressing corporation in newspapers, on social media, and in public discourse. But among philosophers and legal scholars, there has been longstanding, heated, and seemingly intractable debate about whether it is *appropriate* to blame the transgressing corporation (see, e.g., Donaldson, 1980; French, 1984; Velasquez, 1983; Hasnas, 2012; Hess, 2014; Ronnegard, 2015; Silver, 2006). Conflict arises too over which, if any, of the corporation's members we may rightfully blame for its wrongs (Sepinwall, 2015).

In this chapter, I aim to draw out the reasons for the persistence of this debate, and to make progress toward its resolution. Some of the confusion arises because of the corporation's murky moral status. There is much disagreement about whether corporations qualify for moral agency. But there is also, I shall argue, confusion about the relationship between moral agency and blameworthiness. On a widespread understanding of moral responsibility, if one satisfies the criteria for moral agency then one is appropriately liable to blame for one's wrongdoing. I seek to pull apart the concepts of moral agency and blameworthiness. I shall argue that even if the corporation is a moral agent it lacks an additional capacity necessary to make a moral agent an appropriate target of blame. The additional capacity I have in mind is the capacity to experience guilt. I aruge that only a being with affect can experience guilt and, because corporations have no affect, it follows that corporations cannot be blameworthy in their own right for their wrongs. But I do not conclude that we must then resign ourselves to treating corporate wrongs like natural disasters or cosmic injustices. Instead, I end by arguing that the norms governing corporate officeholders license our taking some of the corporation's members to be blameworthy for its wrongs, even if they are not at fault. Executives in particular, I shall argue, share responsibility for corporate wrongdoing irrespective of whether they culpably contributed to or failed to prevent those wrongs. In short, this chapter aims to draw out the problems with treating corporations as morally responsible in their own right, and urges instead that we assign blame directly to the corporation's members in a manner befitting the shared nature of responsibility in hierarchical institutional settings.

28.1 Corporate Moral Responsibility

At the time of its collapse, Arthur Andersen was one of the Big Five accounting firms. But as a result of its role in the Enron scandal, Andersen was forced to shutter its business. Employees at the firm had shred documents that were known to be material to an SEC investigation into Andersen's oversight of Enron's accounting – an offense that led to the firm's conviction for obstruction of justice. Andersen had to surrender its license to audit public companies and, barred from its main line of business, the firm was forced to fold.

Andersen's conviction raises numerous questions of philosophical interest relating to the possibility of joint action and the proper assignment of responsibility. For example, at the midpoint in its deliberations, the Andersen jury was at an impasse. Each juror believed that at least one Andersen employee culpably ordered the document shredding but the jurors could not agree about *which* employee that was. Assuming that the jury had deadlocked over the identity of the culpable employee even while each member believed that some employee was culpable, could the jury *as a body* have concluded that *an* employee impermissibly ordered the document shredding? For example, could the jury have found that Andersen had ordered the shredding of documents if six jury members believed that only employee Jones had ordered the shredding and the other six members believed that only employee Smith had done so? This is a question about determining when individual group members' acts amount to an act of the group and, if so, what the nature of the group act is. Questions of this kind will arise for any account that aims to conceptualize a "joint agent" (Bratman, 2014) or a "plural subject" (Gilbert, 2000), as some take the corporation to be (List and Pettit, 2011). But the Andersen case raises a second question: Suppose that the jury members succeeded ultimately in agreeing upon the identity of the perpetrator. (In point of fact, they did each converge in identifying a single employee who committed the predicate offense of corruptly persuading others to obstruct justice by shredding documents (Eichenwald, 2002).) Was it then appropriate to hold the firm as a whole morally responsible for that employee's crime?

That question has two different meanings, and I begin our inquiry by drawing out the distinction between them.

28.1.1 Ascribing Acts and Assigning Responsibility

It is clear that corporations can act only through individuals. Still, as I and others have argued at greater length (French, 1984; Hess, 2014; Sepinwall, 2016a), this constraint is consistent with corporate agency. Corporations can and do function as agents even though they require individuals to carry out their acts. In this respect, they are like armies, which carry out their own operations even though they require individual agents to perform the maneuvers of which the operations consist. One way to see that corporations act is to consider that some acts can be attributed only to the corporation qua group agent. For example, corporations can merge, dissolve, enter into contracts, and so on. To be sure, all of these acts require that individuals *do* some things – in particular, the underlying acts that together effect the merger, dissolution, conclusion of a contract, etc. But the corporation's, e.g., entry into a contract is its own act – none of the individual members of the corporation have entered into the contract (none of them, for example, is bound by the contract's terms in his or her individual capacity), nor has the aggregate of them entered into the contract, which again would entail that every one of them is individually bound by the contract's terms.[1] Moreover, the corporation has in a sense directed the individual actions that together constitute its act – it gives the individuals in question a *reason* to act as they did, and it outlines the chain of command that integrates their individual contributions (French, 1984). The corporation's intentions reside in its directions. While there is much more that could be said in defense of corporate agency, I assume it in what follows, for I aim to argue that it makes no sense to blame the corporation where it commits wrongs. One who denies that the corporation can act at all has independent reason to deny that the corporation is an appropriate object of blame.

When we ask whether a corporation is morally responsible for some act, we might have two very different things in mind. First, we might be asking: *when* may we ascribe an act of some corporate employee to the corporation itself? That is, when should we take an employee's act to be her own – off the clock, or outside the scope of her employment? And when should we take her act to be an act of the corporation? After all, it will be appropriate to blame the corporation for a wrongful act of an employee only if that act is properly ascribable to the corporation. So, in any case where there is a question of the corporation's blameworthiness, we must first ask a prior question about whether the wrong in question is properly ascribed to the corporation. Call this a question of *act ascription*. This is an ontological question about how we link up acts and agents, deciding which agents own which acts. But there is a second question: Once we determine that an employee's act is an act of the corporation, and that the act is morally wrong, *whom* may we blame? In particular, is the corporation an appropriate target of censure? Call this a question about the proper *assignment of blame*. Having determined that the employee's wrongful act is properly ascribed to the corporation does not automatically entail that the corporation should be held morally responsible for that act because it is not clear that corporations are the kinds of entities that can bear moral responsibility in their own right. Or, more formally, it is not clear that corporations are *moral agents*.

Before elaborating on the debate about corporate moral agency, it will be useful to note that the literature on corporate moral responsibility is rife with accounts that conflate the ascription and assignment questions. Scholars have come up with creative and oftentimes compelling theories for ascribing employee wrongdoing to the corporation in whose service the crime is committed. For example, on a "reactive fault" account, an employee's wrong is ascribable to the corporation because the wrong is ongoing or recurring; the corporation has had ample opportunity to end or deter the wrong; and the corporation has failed to do so (Fisse and Braithwaite, 1993; Laufer, 1994). On a "corporate ethos" account, the wrong is ascribed to the corporation when the corporate culture promoted it (Bucy, 1990). Most straightforwardly, where the corporation is organized around a criminal purpose, virtually any employee wrong carried out in the service of the corporation's aims will involve the corporation in a crime. Each of these accounts can justify our concluding that the wrong of some employee is a wrong of the corporation. But none of them establishes that the corporation is therefore morally responsible. In other words, these accounts answer an ontological question about *when* a corporation acts. But the accounts are advanced as offering more than this. They promise to answer a *normative* question about whether corporations are morally responsible for the acts they commit where those acts are wrong.[2] Answering the ontological question, though, does not in fact settle the normative question.

To see this, consider that there is no inconsistency in recognizing that an individual has committed a wrong and yet there is some feature of her that forecloses our finding her morally responsible. Most relevantly here, a person who is below the age of moral maturity, or who operates under cognitive or emotional deficits that undermine her moral agency, is not blameworthy for her wrongs. She lacks one or more capacities necessary to ground our taking her to be morally responsible. This may be because of a permanent deficit afflicting her (e.g., she is cognitively challenged and so cannot reliably distinguish between right and wrong) or instead because she is temporarily compromised (e.g., she has been hypnotized or drugged or otherwise made incapable of exercising her moral agency). So it is possible for an individual agent to commit wrongs for which she is not morally responsible.

There is no reason to think that the situation for corporate agents is any different. Corporations can act. They can, in particular, commit wrongs, understood here as the infliction of harm without justification or excuse (Gardner, 2005). That they can do so does not yet entail that they are blameworthy for those wrongs.[3] They would turn out to be blameworthy only if they satisfied some further conditions, and I will go on to deny that they do. But we should pause first to consider why some other theorists have been at such great pains to establish that corporations are indeed moral agents and thus appropriately liable to blame when they transgress.

There is much at stake in the question of corporate moral agency. In the most acute cases, a corporation unjustifiably imposes massive harm and yet there is no one individual who culpably contributed to that harm. If it turned out that the corporation was not a moral agent we would appear to have wrongdoing for which no one was answerable. One might think that pragmatic necessity therefore *entails* corporate moral agency. Otherwise, corporations would be able to perpetrate wrongs with impunity. I turn to accounts that seek to leverage pragmatic considerations in support of corporate moral agency before examining accounts that defend corporate moral agency more directly.

28.1.1.1 A Residue from Corporate Wrongs

Recently, a handful of theorists have explored discursive dilemmas as part of an effort to argue that a corporation (or other institutional group) can be morally responsible for an act even if no member of the group would be morally responsible for that act (Pettit, 2007; Copp, 2006; List and Pettit, 2011).[4] Discursive dilemmas arise where a group decision procedure yields a decision for the group to which none of its members would assent. To see how this works, consider a committee decision procedure that asks each member of the committee to vote on a Y/N question by voting on a series of sub-questions, and the votes on the sub-questions are then aggregated to determine the outcome for the committee itself. It is logically possible for the aggregated vote – i.e., the *group* decision – to come out one way even though an aggregation of each individual member's votes on the sub-questions would have had the decision come out the other way.[5] In such cases, these theorists argue, it is only the collective, and not its members, who may be held morally responsible for the consequences of the decision (see, e.g., Copp, 2006).

Philip Pettit argues that the "permanent possibility" that the group decision will diverge from that of each of the group's members "indicates that … the members will have to create a group agent that comes apart in a manner from the way that they are individually disposed" (p. 183). The positing of a group agent is then a rational response to the possibility of discursive dilemmas.[6] But this group agent must do more than render coherent individuals' acts or decisions on behalf of the group. Where the group arrives at a decision that none of its members endorses, the group must bear responsibility for that decision. As Pettit explains it, there stands to be "a deficit in the accounting books, and the only possible way to guard against this may be to allow for corporate responsibility of the group in the name of which they act" (p. 194). The idea of a "deficit" or "residue" motivates much of the literature defending corporate moral responsibility (List and Pettit, 2011; Dempsey, 2013). The worry is that corporate harms for which we cannot distribute full responsibility to the corporation's individual members will leave us with a remainder – an apparently intolerable state of affairs demanding that the corporation incur the responsibility that remains along with the blame it warrants (cf. Garrett, 2015).

In response to these accounts, one might well wonder what the remainder consists in and why it must be assigned anywhere. If no individual member is to blame, it is not clear why we should think there has been a collective wrong. To be sure, in cases where one experiences a setback to one's interests, it might well be more satisfying to assign moral fault somewhere. But the mere satisfaction that the assignment would produce does not entail that the fault *must* be assigned somewhere, less still that it must rest with the group (Miller, 2006, p. 187). Corporate harm that results from the aggregation of individual contributions, all of which are innocent in their own right, might involve nothing other than sheer bad luck. If (contrary to fact) the explosion of British Petroleum's (BP's) Deepwater Horizon leading to the massive oil spill in the Gulf of Mexico had resulted only from a system malfunction that could not have been prevented, along with one or more blameless human errors, then we would have to accept that the spill, as devastating as it was, was just a massively unfortunate accident (National Commission, 2011). We could, of course, still hold BP accountable in other ways – notably, we could require that it pay to clean up the Gulf. But we would have to consign ourselves to the fact that there was no one and nothing to blame (cf. Wolf, 1985).

In some cases where no individual acted in a blameworthy fashion, then, we might conclude that the corporation is blameless too. In other cases – including cases of discursive dilemmas – we might instead allow that members of the corporation *are* blameworthy, qua members, even though each of them is individually blameless all-things-considered. This, I take it, would be the appropriate way to respond to individuals who participate in a group decision, each deciding in favor of the morally wrong option but for reasons that are innocent in themselves (cf. Copp, 2006, 214–220). Consider, for example, the board of a private prison corporation as it faces a multi-factor decision about whether it should lobby the government to increase mandatory minimum sentences for non-violent crimes. The board ends up voting in favor of lobbying – a decision that, I assume, would be morally wrong (see Hughes, 2018; Isaacs, 2018) – but each individual member has a justification or excuse for his or her contributions to the wrong. For example, one of them, who would have voted against lobbying, had to miss the meeting at which the decision was made to stay home with a sick child. Another always follows the lead of the missing member and, given that he was not present and she had not done the work to know which way to decide, she simply voted with the majority, knowing that her vote would not make a difference to the result. Yet a third member genuinely but mistakenly believes that current prison sentences provide insufficient deterrence, etc. In cases like this, David Copp has argued that "no member is all-in blameworthy" (Copp, 2007, 373). So, on Copp's account, we may not assign moral responsibility to any of the individual members.

I do not believe that we are compelled to Copp's conclusion that there is no individual moral responsibility in cases where each group member has a justification or excuse for his contribution to the group act. Copp can view each of the individuals in his hypotheticals as blameless only because he presupposes that conflicting reasons and duties can fully cancel one another out. Yet those who subscribe to the notion of a moral residue (e.g., Williams; Marcus) will have no trouble making sense of the idea that the members who were subject to these conflicting obligations bear guilt for the obligation the conflict forced them to forsake. Further, even if one rejects the idea of a moral residue one would still not need to conclude that there is a responsibility deficit that only corporate moral responsibility can fill. One could allow the group's responsibility to redound equally to its members, as an account of shared responsibility would mandate, or one could "apportion[] responsibility among the members of a group ... *as and to the degree to which each contributed* to the group act" (Ludwig, 2007, 411). We should prefer corporate moral responsibility to these alternatives only if the corporation genuinely can bear responsibility in its own right.

28.1.1.2 Corporate Moral Agency and Blame

What we need in addition to a theory that answers the question of ascription is an account that establishes that the corporation is the kind of actor that is an appropriate target of our judgments of moral responsibility and the blaming responses those judgments prompt. One can seek to argue for or against this conception of the corporation in two different ways. First, one can identify the necessary and sufficient conditions for moral agency and then argue that the corporation does or does not possess them. Alternatively, one can identify the rationale for our blaming practices and then argue that blaming the corporation does or does not satisfy that rationale (Tollefsen, 2015). The first strategy is unpromising given the deep disagreement over just what the necessary capacities for moral agency are, let alone whether the corporation possesses them (see Sepinwall, 2016a). The second strategy, by contrast, is, I believe, decisive. To refute the idea that the corporation is an appropriate object of blame, it will suffice to show that blaming the corporation cannot achieve the end that blaming in general seeks. To be sure, the second strategy cannot avoid pursuing some of the considerations explored in the first – once we determine the end of blame, we will need to assess whether the corporation has the capacities that that end presupposes. But the inquiry will be more focused for it is possible that the conditions for full moral agency are not entirely co-extensive with those for being an appropriate object of blame. Of relevance here, it might be the case that some capacity in addition to those necessary for moral agency is required in order for one to be an appropriate object of blame. Indeed, that is just the line I will pursue, arguing that the capacity to experience guilt is necessary for being an apt target of blame even if it is not necessary for moral agency.

To begin: how can it be that someone is a moral agent and yet not liable to blame for their wrongdoing? The disconnect between the concepts of "moral agent" and "blameworthy" arises because, in asking what it takes to be a moral agent, we are often asking a prospective question – namely, is this individual or entity capable of judging right and wrong and acting in line with that judgment? But in asking whether someone is blameworthy, we are always asking a retrospective question – namely, would it be appropriate to blame this entity or individual for what he has done?[7] And it is possible for someone to reliably render moral judgments and act on those judgments and yet to not be blameworthy even when she decides to do something she correctly assesses to be wrong all-things-considered.

To see what I have in mind, consider Mr. Spock: he is cool-headed and entirely capable of abiding by his will (cf. Charland, 1998; Warren, 1973). If he intentionally harms someone else without justification or excuse, we can imagine that he has done so after a suitable process of deliberation, assigning all of the relevant moral considerations their due weight, nonetheless deciding to pursue the morally wrong course of action, while in complete control of his will. Why then might we find this Mr. Spock, who has dispassionately chosen to commit a wrong, an inappropriate object of blame?

To be clear, the question is not whether it would be appropriate all-things-considered to *blame* Mr. Spock. Sometimes, we rightly withhold expressions of blame, or we refrain from blaming at all (i.e., forming whatever attitudes or experiencing whatever emotions blame involves – more on this below), because of circumstances surrounding the wrongdoing. If, for example, the wrong was minor (Spock dismissed a reasonable proposal with undue harshness) and Spock was having a particularly bad go of it (leading a crew that threatens insubordination, and facing the prospect that his shuttlecraft won't have enough fuel to return to the *Enterprise*), then the victim of the crime might decide not to blame Spock. What would that involve?

On one possibility, the victim would choose not to *express* blame – she would hold her tongue, rather than reproaching Spock. But I want to consider a more dramatic possibility: she might forswear blame altogether. To do so, the victim would not need to disavow the judgment that Spock had acted wrongly in injuring her. For blame does not consist merely in a judgment of wrongdoing. If it did, two co-felons' gleeful celebrations of their successful crime – which rest on a judgment that they have done something wrong – would be an instance in which each blames the other. So the belief that they have done wrong cannot be all that blame consists in (e.g., Wallace, 2011, p. 348; Coates and Tognazzini, 2012). Instead, blame has an essential emotional component. It is this component that the victim would forswear were she to decide not to blame Spock.[8]

In forswearing the emotional component of blame, the victim would decide not to resent Spock. As such, she would forego the phenomenological correlates of anger (the state of excited negative emotion), along with whatever else resentment entailed (e.g., perhaps a desire for retribution). Further, in forswearing resentment, the victim would, I submit, desist from blaming altogether. But why should that be? One answer to that question can be found in accounts of blame that conceive of it as essentially constituted by the reactive attitudes. Peter Strawson offers the seminal account (1962 and 1993). For Strawson, our assignments of moral responsibility are constituted by the emotional responses we have to the attitudes and intentions of others as these are displayed in their actions (1993, pp. 49, 56–57). When it comes to wrongdoing, these reactive attitudes consist of a perspective-based triad of emotions – guilt, for our own wrongdoing; resentment, for wrongdoing against us; and indignation, for wrongdoing aimed at others (Strawson, 1993). Importantly, for Strawson, these reactive attitudes are not the *products* of a finding of blameworthiness. Instead, they constitute that finding. As Gary Watson puts it, on a Strawsonian account, "to regard oneself or another as responsible just is the proneness to react to them in these kinds of ways under certain conditions" (1987, 256–257). As such, for Strawson, there can be no blame without the moral emotions.[9]

I want to suggest a different way of foregrounding the essential role of the reactive attitudes in blame. While reactive attitude theorists typically focus on the emotional experiences of the *blamer*, I shall now argue that a capacity for emotion on the part of the *blamee* is necessary for blame to have uptake. It is because Spock lacks a capacity for emotion that he cannot be blameworthy.

To see this, consider the practical ends that blame seeks. Theorists offer different accounts of the function of blame. For example, we blame to register an impairment in our relationship with the offender (Scanlon, 2008), to record a demerit in the offender's moral ledger (Zimmerman, 1988), to communicate that the offender's act was wrong (Duff, 2003); to "protest" (Hieronymi, 2004) the offender's act, and perhaps also to punish (exposure to blame being painful in its own right) (Sepinwall, 2016b). At least the last two of these, I contend, require emotion if the end they seek is to be achieved (cf. Wolf, 2011).

Start with protest. As Pamela Hieronymi describes it, when we warrantedly judge that someone has wronged us, "our first response is, and ought to be, anger and resentment. … In resentment the victim protests the trespass, affirming both its wrongfulness and the moral significance of both herself and the offender." Hieronymi argues that that resentment is critical to blame by focusing on the change wrought by forgiveness. When we forgive, she describes, we do not renounce the judgment that the offender has wronged us. Instead, forgiveness involves giving up a different judgment – namely, the judgment that the moral significance of the wrong and one's worth stand in need of affirmation. That is the judgment that grounds one's resentment. When the offender atones, he makes it the case that the blamer no longer has reason to hold that judgment; as a result, "resentment loses its footing" (24) (cf. Rosen, 2015). So one change forgiveness brings about is to move the blamer from a state of anger to a state where anger makes no sense.

But anger is crucial not just for the blamer's stance but for the blamee's as well. For blame to function as protest, the blamee's emotions must be engaged too. Hieronymi describes the protest as a "claim" or a call to attention. Importantly, it is not just the content of the victim's claim – namely, that she has been wronged – that does the calling; the anger itself plays an essential role here. "Anger … seeks to set things right by demanding the recognition of a wrong." Angry blame does so by making manifest the pain the offender has caused. It allows the offender to see the effect of his transgression in all its force. The empathic offender – the one who can appreciate the blamer's pain – cannot help but feel pain himself, knowing that he is the source of the anger that he is, through blame, intended to absorb (see Sepinwall, 2016b).[10] In short, anger brings the wronging to light.

One who is inured to anger, like Spock, will not experience the protest *as* protest. In this respect, Spock is like a young child who knows she has broken a rule in, say, deliberately knocking over her brother's block structure but who does not and cannot react to her brother's rebuke with any kind of moral emotion at all. She can see that her brother is upset, and she can see that she is the cause of that upset – more specifically, that her rule-breaking act is the cause of his upset. She may fear sanction or retaliation. But she, like Spock, cannot experience the distinctive pain of guilt.[11] For Hieronymi, blame is meant to induce that pain; the anger in blame is meant to convey the full force of the wrongdoing. Blame will not then have its intended uptake if its target is insensitive to the protest blame conveys.

Anger is necessary for blame to function as punishment too. Butler's Sermons are frequently quoted as one wellspring for the view that resentment (which again I take to be constitutive of blaming) aims at punishment: He describes resentment as a "weapon put into our hands by nature, against injury, injustice, and cruelty" (116; see, e.g., Hieronymi), which aims for "the misery" of the offender (127). I have articulated blame's punitive dimensions at greater length elsewhere (Sepinwall, 2016b). For now I want to focus on this "misery" and why it is that we should understand inflicting it to be among blame's key functions.

Hieronymi understands anger as indispensable to calling the offender to repair his wrong. But on a punitive account, blame already goes some way toward rectifying the status imbalance that the wronging wrought between the offender and his victim. It does so at least in part by inflicting pain. To borrow from Jean Hampton's general understanding of punishment, the punitive dimension of blame functions to debase the offender, by subjecting him to the pain of being an object of reproach (1992). Blame, that is, already effects the end of restoring the status of the victim that protest seeks by treating the offender as one who *deserves* pain and then inflicting that pain to right the moral balance.[12]

Now, if all of this is right, then blame crucially relies on the blamee's having the emotional bandwidth to receive the blame as protest and punishment. But that is just what those like Spock lack. More specifically, there are two ways in which one might understand Spock's infirmity. On one understanding, what Spock lacks is the ability to *feel* guilt, or to appreciate first-hand the blamer's experience of anger. As such, the missing piece is a capacity for affect. On a second understanding, what Spock lacks is the capacity for guilt *tout court*. The thought here would be that dispassionate guilt – guilt with no phenomenological correlates – is not guilt at all. I am inclined to this second view, according to which emotions necessarily involve their felt aspects (see Hurley). But I will not aim to defend that view here, nor need I rely on it. It suffices for my purposes to establish that blame's essential ends require affect. For it is on this basis, we shall now see, that blaming corporations falters.

28.1.2 Corporations as Irrational Targets of Blame

If blame aims to inflict pain on the offender – as a matter both of having him appreciate the full force of his wrongdoing and having him incur punishment – then the target of blame must have the capacity to experience pain. If the offender does not have this capacity then blame will fail to achieve its end. It is clear that the corporation has no capacity for pain. This is just the reality underpinning the by-now clichéd lament that the "corporation has ... no body to kick" (Coffee, citing Baron von Thurlow, 1981). If I am right that a capacity to experience pain is necessary for blame to achieve its ends, and if the corporation lacks a capacity for pain, then it follows that it makes no sense to blame corporations.[13] To be sure, we might still have reason to offer statements condemning morally impermissible corporate conduct and even to experience and express outrage when we do so. We would offer these statements, perhaps in an enraged state, to let others know that we take it to be the case that no one should act as the corporation has, and to affirm the victims' sense that they have been treated in a way that no moral agent should treat another. But we could not rationally be protesting the corporation in the sense that we were calling *it* to appreciate its wrongdoing; nor could we be seeking to punish it through our expression of blame. For again the corporation would be insensible to our call or our punishment.

But perhaps corporate blame need not rely on the corporation's own capacities. For what if we could preserve the protest and punitive dimensions of blame by directing the pain underpinning these functions to the corporation's individual members? Deborah Tollefsen has something like this strategy in mind when she argues that we can secure a capacity for corporate remorse by relying on the capacities for guilt of the corporation's members (Tollefsen, 2003).

Contra Tollefsen, I am not convinced that members' "vicarious" feelings (Tollefsen, 2008, 12) can secure the ends of blame.[14] If blame aims at making its target feel bad, then those who blame the corporation aim (however misguidedly) to make *it* feel bad. The fact that someone else will feel bad won't suffice to make corporate blame sensible. The corporation will not itself have absorbed the blamer's anger, and so his blame will not have had its intended uptake. So recruiting members to feel on the corporation's behalf will not overcome the corporation's inability to feel in its own right.[15]

I take the foregoing arguments to ground at least a deep skepticism about the appropriateness of blaming corporations, though perhaps not a decisive argument against doing so. Yet even if it turns out that the corporation can bear blame, it behooves us to consider whether targeting the corporation is the only, let alone the best, way of blaming when the corporation commits a wrong.

28.2 Shared Responsibility for Corporate Wrongdoing

In the previous section, I examined the possibility that the corporation could shore up its ability to function as a rational target of blame by recruiting its members to do the feeling-work that the corporation itself cannot do. For the reasons adduced there, I doubt that that possibility would render intelligible our blaming corporations. But there is a more straightforward way in which the corporation's individual members should figure into an account of moral responsibility for corporate wrongdoing: At least some of these members are appropriate targets of blame in their own right. I have in mind here not just the individual malefactors, who obviously deserve blame for their own wrongful acts, but others within the corporation who engaged in no wrongdoing themselves: not only did they not contribute to the wrong, but they did not even know about it in advance; nor ought they to have known about it. Put more perspicuously, these corporate members are not individually at fault and yet, I shall argue, they nonetheless deserve blame.

In so arguing, I set myself against what might be called the fault principle – namely, the principle that one is blameworthy for some wrong only if one is at fault as regards that wrong, where being at fault involves having negligently, knowingly or intentionally contributed to a wrong without justification or excuse. The fault principle is the paradigmatic ground of inculpation for individuals in contexts involving arms-length interactions. But fault is not a prerequisite for blameworthiness when it comes to intimates, as I have argued elsewhere (Sepinwall, 2017). Nor is fault a prerequisite for blameworthiness when it comes to institutional actors, as I shall now argue (see also Sepinwall, 2015).

To begin, it will be useful to identify who among the corporation's members is liable to be blamed without fault. I focus here on high-level managers (i.e., those individuals occupying executive positions) for two reasons. First, the ground of blameworthiness I go on to adduce rests upon the corporate member's loyalty or solidarity and I take it that, of all the corporation's members, executives are most subject to norms of loyalty and solidarity. Second, executives have the greatest capacity to control the corporation's activities. To be clear, the idea is not that executives, in virtue of their control, could have prevented the wrong and so bear blame for failing to do so (cf. *United States v. Park*, 1975). If control were relevant in that way, then we would be squarely in the realm of the fault principle. Instead the thought is that the ability to exert control functions as a necessary precondition for eligibility for blame. Efficiency-based divisions of labor make it the case that low-level workers have too little control over the conditions of their work, with harmful consequences for their sense of self and their health too (Wilkinson, 2000). I take it that this is unfair (see Elizabeth Anderson, 2017). It would, as a result, be wrong to demand sincere loyalty or solidarity from these workers, so they are not eligible for faultless blame on the account I advance.[16]

Executives, I have suggested, bear an obligation to experience loyalty to their firm and solidarity with their fellows (cf. May, 1987). These obligations reflect a particular ethos appropriate to work in corporations, which consist of "teams" (Blair and Stout, 1999; Ian B. Lee, 2011). But they also follow from the nature of corporate production: it is frequently difficult, and perhaps even impossible, to individuate contributions to a corporation's work product. Even where a subset of employees works on a discrete project, the output of that project results not just from the contributions of those employees but also from the managers who assembled them and came up with the project idea, other employees who might have laid necessary groundwork or offered feedback along the way, higher-level managers who structured departments and working groups such that the project members could in fact come together, and so on.[17] Given these various contributions, there may be a large set of members of the corporation who bear responsibility for all of the corporation's acts even though their connection to some of these acts might be tenuous.

In this way, loyalty and solidarity are not norms separate and apart from the nature of corporate organization. Instead, they flow from that organizational structure – they are the feelings and attitudes workers enmeshed in that structure ought to have. For those workers who enjoy high power and status in the corporation, we can treat loyalty and solidarity as genuine obligations, such that failure to experience them properly subjects the workers in question to reproach.

The obligations of loyalty and solidarity entail in turn several commitments and dispositions. For one thing, the executive should see her interests as aligned with those of the corporation, such that she experiences the corporation's successes as a boon to her, and the corporation's misfortunes as reasons she has to lament (see Fiss, 1976). For another, when it comes to praise or blame, the executive's self-understanding should reflect the norms of loyalty and solidarity. This has interestingly divergent implications for the self-assessments the executive ought to make. Where the corporation has had a success, the executive should not single herself out for praise, even if that success was due in significant measure to her own contributions. Taking credit, even if it is her due, would betray the solidarity with her co-workers that she ought to experience, seeing them all as working toward a shared goal, in a team-like spirit. She should, in other words, demur in the face of praise directed at her personally, at least in the first instance. (If the praising party insists on having her accept individual credit, she might eventually accede, graciously. But it is important that she go through several rounds of this dance of praise and deflection, for it is an important embodiment of the team spirit that should pervade her orientation to her position. Were she to claim or accept individual credit too readily, we would rightly think that she had unduly minimized the contributions of others and also troublingly deviated from the norm of solidarity that binds her.)

While the executive should resist taking credit even where she is significantly responsible for the corporation's success, she should also readily take on blame even where she is not significantly responsible for the corporation's misstep. The solidarity that makes credit-taking improper entails as well that blame-taking is appropriate, and indeed required, again at least in the first instance. As such, when outsiders blame the corporation, the executive should not step outside of her team to point an accusing finger at the co-workers who in fact participated in the corporation's wrong. Instead, she should stand alongside them to absorb the blame that is all of their due.

Now, with all that said, two qualifications are in order. First, the thought is not that the executive can never disclaim personal responsibility. Just as she could properly accept individual praise or credit after she had made clear that she recognized others' contributions to the corporation's success, so too she can gently seek to distinguish herself from the malefactors after she has made clear that she accepts moral responsibility for the corporation's wrong irrespective of her own contributions to it. The important point is that she may not lead with a disclaimer; nor may she deny that the corporation's agency is bound up with her own, such that she comes to bear moral responsibility for its wrong, irrespective of her responsibility for it.

Second, the norms governing the executive's role do not require, or even permit, the executive to ignore individual contributions to wrongdoing in every context. Instead, it may be important that the executive seek to identify the individual malefactors in order to root them out, and to diagnose what institutional failures allowed them to proceed as they did. Nor do the executive's obligations of loyalty preclude her blowing the whistle in order to bring wrongdoing to light. Loyalty to the corporation entails as well that the executive aim to safeguard it from committing, or continuing to commit, wrongs. It is only at the moment when the corporation is targeted for blame that the norms pertaining to the executive's role function to foreclose individualized assessments. In particular, solidarity with her fellows demands that, when outsiders aim their blaming protests and punishment at the corporation's members, she stand alongside them to absorb the blame that is her and their due.

The foregoing has sought to leverage the normative underpinnings of executive office-holding to establish that the executive ought to take herself to be blameworthy for a corporate wrong whether or not she is at fault for it. But even if she ought to do so, what makes it the case that outsiders to the corporation may take her to be blameworthy too? Elsewhere I have argued that outsiders should do so to reinforce the norms of holding this kind of office (2015). But that way of putting the point suggests a "proleptic" (Fricker) or prudential rationale. More accurately, I now think, the reasons we may take the executive to be blameworthy are the very conceptual and normative reasons she has to view herself as blameworthy. What it is to hold an executive position within a corporation is to be a legitimate target of blame for corporate wrongdoing. And it is right that this should be so. Executives' liability to blame is part and parcel of norms that are beneficial, and perhaps even necessary, for corporations to function well. Solidarity and loyalty forge and cement the team aspects that foster the corporation's joint activity. So there is much good to be had from having executives adopt this stance.

But why must we insist that they retain the stance in the face of corporate wrongdoing? For example, an amoralist might suggest that we need not take the bad with the good: executives should enact and insist on solidarity and loyalty during normal corporate operations, for the sake of promoting productivity and good morale, but discard them when the corporation is called to account. But matters cannot be arranged so shrewdly. For, if solidarity and loyalty are ever genuinely to be operative, they cannot be turned off when convenient. Indeed, if anything, their presence becomes credible only if and when exhibiting them comes at a cost. The moment when others direct their blame at the corporation for its wrongdoing represents one such instance. For the reasons I have offered, executives are the appropriate targets of that blame.

28.3 Conclusion

When corporations commit wrongs, we rightly feel that it is imperative to cast blame somewhere. But the corporation itself cannot bear this blame if we understand that the ends of blame – crucially, protest and punishment – presuppose a capacity for pain and guilt and we see that the corporation has neither. The proper targets for the anger that corporate wrongdoing elicits are instead those members of the corporation who are expected to exhibit loyalty to it and solidarity with their colleagues. Executives are the paradigmatic members of the corporation in this regard. Corporate executives thus share responsibility for corporate wrongdoing. And unlike the corporation, they are susceptible to feeling blame's bite.

Notes

1 Aggregates are groupings of individuals fully reducible to the individual members. One defining feature of an aggregate is that there is no organizational structure that allows the grouping to act in a unified way, such that acts of some of them can be attributed to them all. For example, "the set of individuals on the 92 bus this morning" is an aggregate. For more on aggregate groups and their opposites (i.e., associations), see French, 1984; Held, 1970.

2 While I focus here on moral responsibility for wrongful acts my comments apply *mutatis mutandis* for moral responsibility for commendable acts.

3 How could an entity that does not qualify for moral agency commit a wrong? When I refer to instances when a corporation commits a wrong, I am using shorthand. The full formulation would be something like, "when a corporation commits an act that would constitute a wrong were it to have been committed by a moral agent."

4 It is important to note that the pragmatic arguments theorists offer in support of corporate moral agency are not meant to stand alone. These theorists supplement their pragmatic arguments with capacity-based accounts of corporations, in an effort to show that the corporation contains the capacities necessary for moral agency. I address their capacity-based arguments in section 28.1.1.2.

5 To borrow an example from David Copp (2006, 211): Suppose that a three-person committee, consisting of A, B, and C, is charged with making faculty tenure decisions on the basis of three dimensions of performance: research (R), teaching (T), and service (S). Each committee member votes up or down on whether the candidate has a satisfactory record of each of R, T, and S. So long as a candidate gets at least two-thirds "up" votes on each of the three dimensions, the committee will decide in favor of that candidate's tenure. Were any of the individuals to vote directly on the candidate's tenure, however, it would need to be the case that the candidate received an "up" vote on all three dimensions. After all, no one would want to approve a tenure candidate who had a sub-par research, teaching, or service record. Now suppose that A alone finds the candidate deficient on R, B alone finds the candidate deficient on T, and C alone finds the candidate deficient on S. The candidate will receive a majority of "up" votes on each of the three dimensions; the committee as a whole, then, will approve the candidate's tenure. But none of the committee members would have voted in the candidate's favor because each found the candidate to be deficient on one dimension. It is in this way then that the voting procedure can produce results that no individual would endorse.

6 David Sosa takes issue with Pettit on this point. He notes that, for Pettit, "groups are under pressure to collectivize reason," and he argues that "this represents a striking contrast with the case of the individual person. The important thing about individual persons is not what practical pressure they are under to be rational: the demand on a person to be rational is *constitutive*" (2008, 222–223).

7 More precisely, the question should include not just what the entity or individual has done but what he has associated himself with in a way that renders him liable to blame.

8 Other theorists contend that what is essential to blame is its conative component (Sher, 2006; Scanlon, 2008). I am skeptical (see Sepinwall, 2016b) that blame necessarily involves a desire that the wrongdoer not have been the sort of person who would offend (Sher), or an inclination to distance oneself from the wrongdoer (Scanlon). But the more important claim on the account advanced here is that, whatever else blame involves, it necessarily involves felt emotions. If blame also necessarily has a conative component then it would be the case that forswearing blame entailed forswearing that component too.

9 This isn't to say that anger must be felt on each and every occasion when it is expressed. It is only to say that blame paradigmatically involves angry feelings, and that the cool blamer could nonetheless be worked up into a state of anger under the right conditions.

10 Putting the point this way implies that the psychopath, or anyone incapable of empathy for that matter, is not an appropriate object of blame. I endorse that implication although I do not seek to defend it here.

11 Of course, one might resist the analogy, claiming that, unlike Spock, the child does not grasp the intrinsic force of the rule. By contrast, Spock knows not only that, e.g., destroying another's work is against the rules but also that it *ought* to be against the rules, that it is the way of the universe that there should be a rule against wanton destruction because wanton destruction is wrong. In response to the claimed disanalogy, one might concede that Spock can grasp some of the features that make wanton destruction wrong but contend that neither the child nor Spock can fully appreciate its wrongful character – in Spock's case because he cannot know what it is like to experience the malice and suffer the disappointment that the destruction entails.

The more general thought is this: it might be the case that a lack of emotion rules out not just certain moral reactions but also deep moral knowledge (see Sepinwall, 2016b). To the extent that feeling the force of a moral rule requires empathy – e.g., knowing what it would feel like to be on the receiving end of the conduct the rule prohibits – it may be that those who lack a capacity for moral emotion (or any emotion) would have only a shallow knowledge of right and wrong.

That knowledge would be shallow in two respects. First, as just described, the force of the moral rules even someone like Spock could recognize would be weak. Moral rules would function for him like the rules of etiquette of some alien species would function for us – we could commit them to memory and aim to practice them but could not find any of them intrinsically motivating in its own right (although we would presumably harbor a background motivation not to offend that secured our adherence to all of them).

Spock's knowledge of right and wrong would be shallow in a second respect, for in fact moral knowledge cannot comprehensively be committed to memory in advance. Instead, moral discernment requires the capacity to extend moral principles to novel situations. To the extent that this extension requires in turn a capacity for empathy, someone like Spock will again be compromised. If he cannot know what it will feel like to be on the receiving end of the contemplated conduct, Spock will again be without the resources to know how the rule applies or extends.

All of this suggests an impairment that may reach beyond Spock's capacity to be blameworthy; it may implicate his ability to function as a moral agent altogether. I do not explore that possibility further for it suffices for my purposes to establish it makes no sense to blame Spock even if he is adequately capable of fulfilling the conditions for moral agency, including the capacity to judge conduct as morally right or wrong.

12 Some have objected to the claim that blame necessarily has an emotional component by pointing to instances when a person blames without emotion (Sher, 2006. Cf. Wallace, 1994; Hurley, 2007). I address these objections elsewhere (Sepinwall, 2016b). I am at any rate concerned here with the necessity of emotions on the part of the blamee (i.e., the target of blame), not the blamer, and so I will not consider these objections further.

13 Mitchell Haney has argued that, because corporations lack a capacity for guilt, they also lack for moral motivation: the corporation does not care about the moral quality of its acts for their own sake and so it cannot be self-motivated to rectify the wrongs it commits (2004). All of that is congenial to the arguments I offer here but it is worth noting two points of divergence between Haney and me: First, Haney is primarily concerned with the corporation's capacities for *taking* responsibility – in particular, by reforming itself. By contrast, I am concerned not so much with the corporation's responses to its own wrongdoing as with the responses of the moral community. And my emphasis is not on how the community can get the corporation to avoid wrongdoing in the future but instead with whether it can get the corporation to experience guilt over its past acts. Second, Haney maintains that corporations are members of the moral community even though they cannot self-regulate through guilt. Like Haney, I believe that we can and should continue to hold corporations to moral rules and sanction corporations when they deviate from those rules. We should, in other words, treat corporations as morally responsible for their acts. But if, as I have argued, corporations are not susceptible to blame then I am doubtful that they belong in our moral community. Blaming is a central practice within that community. While I do not develop the thought here, I would venture that our moral community should consist only of those who can not only discern right from wrong and act accordingly but also relate emotionally to their own wrongs, whether revealed through self-evaluation or the blame of others.

14 Tollefsen raises the notion of feeling for the corporation vicariously (2008, 12), but that notion would seem to make sense only if the corporation can feel in its own right, which Tollefsen denies. Our capacity to feel for others almost certainly depends on their being able to feel for themselves. Thus we can mirror the emotions of other humans; we cannot do so for entities that have no feelings of their own. So if corporations have no feelings of their own and I am right that members' feelings should not count as the corporation's, then members cannot vicariously experience the corporation's feelings.

15 In later work, Tollefsen allows that the ways in which the corporation differs from individual moral agents might entail that we subject the corporation to something less robust than moral responsibility – a form of treatment she terms "accountability," following Mitch Haney (2004) (Tollefsen, 2015). This is an intriguing suggestion and it certainly tracks some of our moral practices – in particular, it justifies our expectations that corporations will compensate the victims of their wrongs and perhaps also undertake the rituals around apology and expressions of remorse. But the possibility that corporations are proper targets for this thinner form of moral address does nothing to undercut the position I stake according to which corporations are inapt targets of blame qua protest and punishment. To reiterate, protest and punishment (in the form of angry blame, not material sanctions) presuppose that their target can feel guilt. Insofar as accountability comes into the picture precisely because corporations cannot feel guilt, the fact that corporations can be morally accountable offers no support whatsoever for the prospect of their being appropriately subject to blame given the ends of blame that I adduce here.

16 But suppose some low-level employees *do* experience loyalty to the firm and solidarity with the other employees of their corporation, even though loyalty and solidarity ought not to be expected of them. Are they then blameworthy? Not on the account I go on to advance. Executives ought to conceive of the corporation's acts as their own, and take responsibility accordingly. Outsiders to the corporation may blame executives for corporate wrongs both as a way of honoring and reinforcing the norms mandating that executives see their agency as entwined with the corporation's and also because that entwinement is real, as I go on to explain. (See also Sepinwall, 2015.) But blaming low-level employees, whose agency is not entwined with the corporation's, for the corporation's wrongs is like blaming a Francophile who has no political connection to France for France's transgressions. The mere fact that the Francophile takes herself to be bound up with France's acts give us no reason to see her that way; nor does it give us a reason to treat her as if she deserves credit or blame for France's acts. Of course, if France becomes hell-bent on evil then there is something for which we ought to blame the

Francophile – namely, her loyalty to an evil regime. By the same token, if a low-level employee remains steadfastly committed to her corporation even as, she knows, it transgresses we may blame her too for her loyalty. But we may not blame her for the corporation's acts for they are not hers. With that said, I leave open the possibility that some other account of shared responsibility could ground responsibility on considerations that do apply to low-level workers.

17 I note also that clerical and janitorial staff contribute to the product by supporting the workers and work environment in various ways. I do not list them in the text because I believe they are foreclosed from contributing in other ways that subject one to praise and blame for corporate acts, as I explained in the preceding note.

References

Anderson, Elizabeth. 2017. *Private Government: How Employers Rule Our Lives (and Why We Don't Talk about It)*. Princeton, NJ: Princeton University Press.

Blair, Margaret M. and Lynn A. Stout. 1999. 'A Team Production Model Theory of Corporate Law'. *Virginia Law Review* 85(2): pp. 248–328.

Bratman, Michael. 2014. *Shared Agency: A Planning Theory of Acting Together*. New York: Oxford University Press.

Bucy, Pamela. 1990. 'Corporate Ethos: A Standard for Imposing Corporate Criminal Liability'. *Minnesota Law Review* 75: p. 1095.

Butler, J. 1729. *Fifteen Sermons Preached at Rolls Chapel*. London: J. and J. Knapton, 2nd edition.

Charland, Louis C. 1998. 'Is Mr. Spock Mentally Competent?' *Competence to Consent and Emotion, Philosophy, Psychiatry, & Psychology* 5 (1): pp. 67–81.

Coates, D. Justin and Neal A. Tognazzini. 2012. 'The Nature and Ethics of Blame'. *Philosophy Compass* 7 (3): pp. 197–207.

Coffee, John C., Jr. 1981. '"No Soul to Damn: No Body to Kick": An Unscandalized Inquiry into the Problem of Corporate Punishment'. *Michigan Law Review* 79 (1981), p. 386.

Copp, David. 2006. 'On the Agency of Certain Collective Entities: An Argument from "Normative Autonomy"'. *Midwest Studies in Philosophy* 30 (1): pp. 194–221.

Copp, David. 2007. 'The Collective Moral Autonomy Thesis'. *Journal of Social Philosophy* 38 (3): pp. 369–388.

Dempsey, James. 2013. 'Corporations and Non-Agential Moral Responsibility'. *Journal of Applied Philosophy* 30 (4): pp. 334–350.

Donaldson, Thomas. 1980. 'Moral Agency and Corporations'. *Philosophy in Context* 10: pp. 54–70.

Duff, R. A. 2003. 'Punishment, Communication and Community'. *Debates in Contemporary Political Philosophy*, edited by Derek Matravers and Jonathan E. Pike, pp. 387–407. Routledge, in association with the Open University, Print.

Eichenwald, Kurt. 'Andersen Guilty in Effort to Block Inquiry on Enron'. *New York Times*, June 16, 2002, p. YNE-1.

Feinberg, Joel. 1965. 'The Expressive Function of Punishment'. *Monist* 49 (3): pp. 397–423.

Fiss, Owen M. 1976. 'Groups and the Equal Protection Clause'. *Philosophy and Public Affairs* 5 (2): pp. 107–177.

Fisse, Brent and John Braithwaite. 1993. *Corporations, Crime and Accountability*. Cambridge: Cambridge University Press.

French, Peter A. 1984. *Collective and Corporate Responsibility*. New York: Columbia University Press.

Fricker, Miranda. 2016. 'What's the Point of Blame? A Paradigm Based Explanation'. *Noûs* 50 (1): pp. 165–183.

Gardner, John. 2005. 'Wrongs and Faults'. *Appraising Strict Liability*, edited by Andrew P. Simester, p. 51. Oxford: Oxford University Press.

Garrett, Brandon L. 2015. 'The Corporate Criminal As Scapegoat'. *Virginia Law Review* 101 (7): pp. 1789–1853.

Gilbert, Margaret. 2000. *Sociality and Responsibility*. Lanham, MD: Rowman & Littlefield Publishers, Print.

Gilbert, Margaret. 2002 'Collective Guilt and Collective Guilt Feelings'. *Journal of Ethics* 6 (2): pp. 115–143.

Haji, Ishtayaque. 2010. 'Psychopathy, Ethical Perception, and Moral Culpability'. *Neuroethics* 3 (2): pp. 135–150.

Hampton, Jean. 1984. 'The Moral Education Theory of Punishment'. *Philosophy and Public Affairs* 13 (3): pp. 208–238.

Hampton, Jean. 1992. 'An Expressive Theory of Retribution'. *Retributivism and Its Critics*, edited by Wesley Cragg, pp. 1–25. Stuttgart: F. Steiner, Verlag.
Haney, Mitchell R. 2004. 'Corporate Loss of Innocence for the Sake of Accountability'. *Journal of Social Philosophy* 35 (3): pp. 391–412.
Hasnas, John. 2012. 'Reflections on Corporate Moral Responsibility and the Problem Solving Technique of Alexander the Great'. *Journal of Business Ethics* 107 (2): pp. 183–195.
Held, Virginia. 1970. 'Can a Random Collection of Individuals be Responsible?'. *Journal of Philosophy* 67: pp. 471–481.
Hess, Kendy. 2014. 'The Free Will of Corporations (and Other Collectives)'. *Philosophical Studies: An International Journal for Philosophy in the Analytic Tradition* 168 (1): pp. 241–260.
Hieronymi, Pamela. 2004. 'The Force and Fairness of Blame'. *Philosophical Perspectives* 18 (1): pp. 115–148.
Hughes, Robert. 2018. 'Imprisonment and the Right to Freedom of Movement'. *Rethinking Punishment in the Era of Mass Incarceration*, edited by Chris W. Surprenant, pp. 89–104. New York, NY: Routledge.
Hurley, Elisa A. 2007. 'Working Passions: Emotions and Creative Engagement with Value'. *The Southern Journal of Philosophy* 45: pp. 79–104.
Isaacs, Dan. 2018. 'When Government Contractors May or May Not Spend Money On Political Speech'. *Journal of Business Ethics* (forthcoming).
Katyal, Neal K. 2002. 'Conspiracy Theory'. *Yale Law Journal* 112: pp. 1307–1398.
Laufer, William. 1994. 'Corporate Bodies and Guilty Minds'. *Emory Law Journal*. 43: pp. 647–730.
Lee, Ian B. 2011. 'Corporate Criminal Responsibility as Team Member Responsibility'. *Oxford Journal of Legal Studies* 31 (4): pp. 755–781.
List, Christian and Philip Pettit. 2011. *Group Agency: The Possibility, Design and Status of Group Agents*. Oxford: Oxford University Press.
Little, Margaret. 1995. 'Seeing and Caring: The Role of Affect in Feminist Moral Epistemology'. *Analytic Feminism* 10 (3): pp. 117–137.
Ludwig, Kirk. 2007. 'The Argument from Normative Autonomy for Collective Agents'. *Journal of Social Philosophy* 38: 410–411.
Marcus, Ruth Barcan. 1980. 'Moral Dilemmas and Consistency'. *The Journal of Philosophy* 77: 121–136.
May, Larry. 1987. *The Morality of Groups*. Notre Dame: University of Notre Dame Press.
May, Larry. 1993. *Sharing Responsibility*. Chicago, IL: University of Chicago Press.
Miller, Seumas. 2006. 'Collective Moral Responsibility: An Individualist Account'. *Midwest Studies in Philosophy* 30 (1): pp. 176–187.
National Commission. 2011. *Deep Water: The Gulf Oil Disaster and the Future of Offshore Drilling*. Washington, DC: U.S. Government Printing Office.
Pettit, Philip. 2007. 'Responsibility Incorporated'. *Ethics* 117 (2): pp. 171–201.
Ronnegard, David. 2015. 'How Autonomy Alone Debunks Corporate Moral Agency'. *Business and Professional Ethics Journal* 32 (1): pp. 77–106.
Rosen, Gideon. 2015. 'The Alethic Conception of Moral Responsibility'. *The Nature of Moral Responsibility*, edited by Randolph Clarke, Michael McKenna and Angela M. Smith, pp. 65–88. Oxford: Oxford University Press.
Scanlon, T. M. 2008. *Moral Dimensions: Permissibility, Meaning, Blame*, Cambridge, MA: Harvard University Press.
Sepinwall, Amy. 2012. 'Guilty by Proxy: Expanding the Boundaries of Responsibility in the Face of Corporate Crime'. *Hastings Law Journal* 63: pp. 101–145.
Sepinwall, Amy. 2015. 'Crossing the Fault Line in Corporate Criminal Law'. *Journal of Corporation Law* 40 (2): pp. 101–145.
Sepinwall, Amy. 2016a. 'Corporate Moral Responsibility'. *Philosophy Compass* 11(1): pp. 3–13.
Sepinwall, Amy. 2016b. 'Blame, Emotion and the Corporation'. *The Moral Responsibility of Firms*, edited by Eric. W. Orts and N. Craig Smith. Oxford: Oxford University Press.
Sepinwall, Amy. 2017. 'Faultless Guilt: Toward a Relationship-Based Account of Criminal Liability'. *American Criminal Law Review* 75: pp. 521–570.
Sher, George. 2006. *In Praise of Blame*, Oxford: Oxford University Press.
Sherman, Nancy. 1997. *Making Necessity of Virtue*. Cambridge: Cambridge University Press, Print.
Silver, David. 2005. 'A Strawsonian Defense of Corporate Moral Responsibility'. *American Philosophical Quarterly* 42 (4): pp. 279–293.
Silver, David. 2006. 'Collective Responsibility, Corporate Responsibility and Moral Taint'. *Midwest Studies in Philosophy* 30 (1): pp. 269–278.

Smith, Robert J. 1984. 'The Psychopath as Moral Agent'. *Philosophy & Phenomenological Research* 45 (2): pp. 177–193.
Sosa, David. 2008. 'What Is it Like To Be a Group?'. *Social Philosophy and Policy* 212: pp. 222–223.
Starkey, Charles. 2008. 'Emotion and Full Understanding'. *Ethical Theory and Moral Practice* 11 (4): pp. 425–454.
Stout, Lynn. 2002. 'Bad and Not So Bad Arguments for Shareholder Primacy'. *Southern California Law Review* 75: pp. 1189–1212.
Strawson, Peter F. 1993. 'Freedom and Resentment'. *Perspectives on Moral Responsibility*, edited by John Martin Fischer and Mark Ravizza, pp. 45–66. Ithaca, NY: Cornell University Press.
Tollefsen, Deborah P. 2003. 'Participant Reactive Attitudes and Collective Responsibility'. *Philosophical Explorations* 6 (3): pp. 218–234.
Tollefsen, Deborah P. 2008. 'Affectivity, Moral Agency, and Corporate-Human Relations'. *APA Newsletter on Philosophy and Law* 7 (2): pp. 10–13.
Tollefsen, Deborah P. 2015. *Groups As Agents*. Cambridge, UK: Polity.
United States v. Park, 421 U.S. 658 (1975).
Velasquez, Manuel. 1983. 'Why Corporations Are Not Morally Responsible for Anything They Do'. *Business & Professional Ethics Journal* 2 (3): pp. 1–18.
Wallace, R. Jay. 1994. *Responsibility and the Moral Sentiments*. Cambridge, MA: Harvard University Press.
Wallace, R. Jay. 2011. 'Dispassionate Opprobrium: On Blame and the Reactive Sentiments'. *Reasons and Recognition. Essays on the Philosophy of T. M. Scanlon*, edited by R. Jay Wallace, Rahul Kumar and Samuel Freeman, pp. 348-372. New York: Oxford University Press.
Warren, Mary A. 1973. 'On the Moral and Legal Status of Abortion'. *Monist* 57 (1): 43–61.
Watson, Gary. 1987. 'Responsibility and the Limits of Evil: Variations on a Strawsonian Theme'. *Responsibility, Character and the Emotions*, edited by Ferdinand Schoeman, pp. 256–286. Cambridge: Cambridge University Press.
Wilkinson, Richard G. 2000. *Mind the Gap: An Evolutionary View of Health and Ineqality*. London, UK: Weidenfeld & Nicolson.
Williams, Bernard. 1981. *Moral Luck*. Cambridge: Cambridge University Press. doi: 10.1017/CBO9781139165860
Wolf, Susan. 1985. 'The Legal and Moral Responsibility of Organizations'. *Nomos XVII: Criminal Justice*, edited by R. Pennock and J. Chapman, pp. 267–286. New York: New York University Press.
Wolf, Susan. 2011. 'Blame, Italian Style'. *Reasons and Recognition: Essay on the Philosophy of T. M. Scanlon*, edited by R. Jay Wallace, Rahul Kumar, and Samuel Freeman, pp. 332–347. New York: Oxford University Press.
Zimmerman, Michael. 1988. *An Essay on Moral Responsibility*, Totowa, NJ: Rowman & Littlefield.

29

CORPORATE MORAL RESPONSIBILITY AND THE EXPECTATION OF AUTONOMY

Jeffery Smith and Wim Dubbink

Recent discussions about whether corporations are capable of being held morally responsible have, in large part, turned on whether corporations possess the capacities required to be a moral agent. Advocates of corporate responsibility hold that corporations indeed possess these capacities, even if in a manner distinct from individuals (cf. Hess 2014; Hess 2013; List and Pettit 2011; Pettit 2007; Copp 2006; Arnold 2006). Critics of corporate responsibility invoke arguments to maintain that corporations are incapable of possessing these capacities. The exact conditions for moral agency come in and out of view within these two camps and are the subject of continued debate (Phillips 1995; Velasquez 2003; Rönnegard 2013; Rönnegard and Velasquez 2017; Copp 2006; Donaldson 1982; Sepinwall 2012; Sepinwall 2017).

We intend to focus this discussion on two issues that bear on whether, and to what extent, corporations are capable of being held morally responsible. First, we provide an explanation as to why corporate responsibility is important and a feature of prevailing social institutions; specifically, we maintain that there is a political expectation in modern societies to attribute a level of moral responsibility to corporations. A corollary of this presumption is that corporations are taken to possess certain characteristics that warrant thinking of them as moral agents. This political need gives rise to a second, larger question about how a corporation's moral agency can be established rather than simply presumed.[1] To address this matter we critically examine recent attempts to put forth a metaphysically-grounded defense of corporate moral agency. We will focus on one key component of moral agency, specifically the autonomy of corporations, and whether recent attempts to ground corporate autonomy are plausible. We ask whether those that defend the possibility of corporate autonomy have provided a sufficient philosophical defense of corporate moral agency.

While we are sympathetic to these recent attempts, our exploration will ultimately help in drawing an important contrast between two types of autonomy that moral agents can possess. This contrast will allow attributions of responsibility to corporations while also demarcating at least one important way that corporations, unlike individuals, are not autonomous. In brief, we argue, first, that there is a functional form of autonomy that presumes a capacity on the part of an agent to deliberately restrain its actions in accordance with moral principles and, second, a deeper form of autonomy that implies a kind of self-reflective endorsement of those moral principles. The former type of autonomy is consistent with a correlative sense of moral agency that takes corporations to be the sorts of entities that can restrain their activities consistent with the demands of morality; the second sense of autonomy is linked to a type of moral agency that ultimately cannot be attributed to corporations but is characteristic of moral personhood.

In section 29.1 we provide a brief excursus that describes why modern market economies are implicitly designed to presume a level of moral agency on the part of corporations. We then turn in section 29.2 to examine some recent attempts to ground corporate moral agency in the possibility of corporate autonomy. Thereafter we turn to a more systematic exploration of the two above-mentioned senses of autonomy in section 29.3 before concluding. In the end, by distinguishing two senses of autonomy, we hope to bring some clarity to the two competing intuitions that, on the one hand, take corporations to be morally responsible for their conduct as an institutional matter, and, on the other, corporations lack some of the basic features that are associated with ascriptions of moral responsibility.

29.1 The Pragmatics of Corporate Moral Responsibility

There are numerous pragmatic reasons to think of corporations as moral agents that are capable of being held morally responsible for their conduct. Consider that we speak as if corporations are the authors of their own action (or inaction) and that such action (inaction) is evaluated against certain moral expectations. Newspaper articles routinely discuss, for example, "Volkswagen's act of fraud" or how "BP should properly compensate communities on the Gulf Coast." In these instances, we seem to understand that corporate action reflects freely undertaken, deliberate acts by the corporation itself, orchestrated by norms, decision making processes and moral commitments that extend beyond the specific intentions, actions or attitudes of its members. Those who dismiss these sorts of linguistic practices bear the burden of developing a detailed explanation as to why we describe corporate conduct in these morally-laden ways.

Corporations are also taken to be morally responsible agents through various institutional arrangements. Industry associations representing corporate interests and socially-minded stakeholder initiatives have established compliance expectations that set forth moral standards for corporate conduct. The Pharmaceutical Research and Manufacturers of America (PhRMA), for instance, has developed the *Code on Interactions with Health Care Professionals* designed to reduce conflicts of interest among medical doctors and improve the delivery of medicines to patients by limiting the type of marketing and promotion undertaken by pharmaceutical firms (PhRMA 2017). These sorts of efforts presume that corporations not only can elect to comply (or not) with those norms but that it is within the purview of firms to develop sophisticated, corporate-level decision making systems to satisfy those norms. There is also wide recognition among non-governmental organizations and other advocacy groups that corporations must "do good" and contribute to the public's interest above and beyond what is required by law. The entire notion that corporations can be held criminally liable—a unique feature of law in the United States—presumes that corporations are blameworthy for their decision making and conduct (Diskant 2008; Sepinwall 2012).

One way of explaining these pragmatic ascriptions of corporate moral responsibility is to conceive of capitalist political economies as presuming the very possibility of corporate responsibility. Corporate discretion over the investment of capital and the production of goods and services within the market, as well as the attendant social authority that flows from this discretion, conveys an expectation that the realization of certain "morally important social values" like liberty, respect, honesty, fairness, and distributive justice, as well as other dimensions of human well-being, such as public health and knowledge, are impacted by firms through their policies and business practices (McMahon 2012). This political expectation implicitly relies on the premise that corporations can exercise their discretion and authority in morally principled ways and that they can be held responsible when they do not.

This presumption of responsibility reflects a liberal view of how responsibilities are to be shared and institutionally divided within a well-ordered society (cf. Lindblom 2001: 60–83). In a market economy decisions regarding investment and production are decentralized and delegated to private actors, most notably corporations. The state could retain authority over these matters; however, by seeking to harness the social welfare gains that accompany a privatization of certain investment and production decisions, it is reasonable to expect that any latitude exercised by corporations in the market is done so in a way that is consistent with other moral objectives. So understood, the political expectation that corporations be taken to be responsible agents and respect the demands of a morality arises out of a specific aim of modern societies to enhance social welfare through decentralized economic decision making while enabling the realization of other moral values. Modern polities "need corporations to be morally responsible because the social welfare benefits of corporate discretion are best realized when corporations become moral as well as market actors" (Dubbink and Smith 2011).

But a mere pragmatic presumption that corporations can be saddled with moral responsibilities—even if grounded in a larger political theory—is not enough. It may be tempting to think that the "justification for treating a [corporation] as a responsible agent [should be] tied to the aims and purposes of the wider social activity" in which corporate activity "plays a part" (Hussain and Sandberg 2017: 84).[2] However, in order for this presumption to make sense, there need to be grounds for ascribing to corporations the capability of exercising their economic discretion in a morally responsible fashion. Why does it make sense within our institutional settings to take corporations to be capable of being morally responsible agents? A crucial component of the pragmatic expectation of moral responsibility, thus, is that it is actually supported by certain capacities associated with agency. The central question is whether it makes sense to think of corporations as capable of morally-directed, voluntary action and whether corporations themselves are the authors of their own conduct.

This is where the metaphysical debates taking place around corporate responsibility become relevant. Those discussions have centered on the discovery of characteristics that allow us to ground our manners of speaking and ideals behind our political aspirations. The question, then, is whether this literature has made progress in providing a philosophical foundation for ascriptions of moral responsibility to corporations.

29.2 Corporate Judgment and Restraint

Peter French (1979) famously argued that corporations are the authors of their own conduct—and therefore agents—because their actions are the result of corporate internal decision making structures (CIDs), which "accomplish a subordination, and synthesis of the intentions and acts of various … persons into a corporate decision" (212). Corporations that undertake action according to a process prescribed by a CID, thus, have done so on the basis of a corporate intention to realize an objective (or objectives).

One way to interpret French's insight is to note how CIDs preserve corporate-level intentions. A corporation is thought to have an intention in virtue of the processes prescribed by a CID (cf. Arnold 2006; Bratman 2014). And, in virtue of this intention, a corporation is thought to possess a sufficiently independent level of agency to warrant our ascriptions of responsibility. The problem, however, with this focus on corporate intentions is that intentions are a necessary but not sufficient quality of a morally responsible agent. Indeed, this was the initial concern expressed by Thomas Donaldson in his original response to French:

> [French's] view assumes that anything which can behave intentionally is an agent, and that anything which is an agent is a moral agent. But some entities appear to behave intentionally which do not qualify as moral agents. A cat may behave intentionally when it crouches for a mouse. We know that it intends to catch the mouse, but we do not credit it with moral agency ... . A computer behaves intentionally when it sorts through a list of names and rearranges them in alphabetical order, but we do not consider the computer to be a moral agent ... . One seemingly needs more than the presence of intentions to deduce moral agency.
>
> *(Donaldson 1982: 30)*

For Donaldson moral agents not only are intentional entities but also demonstrate a decision-making process that is of a moral nature. This extends beyond the identification of a decision-making process, simpliciter, to include a process whereby moral reasons are sought out and utilized as part of formulation of what action is intended. "To be a moral agent, something must have reasons for what it does, not simply causes for what it does, for something to be a moral agent, some of those reasons must be moral ones" (Donaldson 1982: 30).

This call for moral reasoning that frames corporate intentions is straightforward enough. The presence of moral considerations, as well as deliberate consideration of—and responsiveness to—those considerations for proposed courses of action is part of what we count as an agent capable of morally responsible conduct. French's later work acknowledges this basic point (1996, 2017).

A deeper examination of this expectation is borne out in Phillip Pettit's recent defense of "incorporating" moral responsibility (2007). He maintains—evoking Donaldson's call for responsiveness to moral considerations—that moral agency demands that the would-be agent can: (a) make an autonomous choice in situations where moral values are relevant; (b) exercise reflective judgment to compare and evaluate different moral values in those situations; and (c) is prepared to exercise restraint over what course of action to take in order to facilitate that judgment. Moral agency, in brief, expects that the agent is autonomous, capable of holistic judgment, and able to exercise restraint, all with respect to moral principles (List and Pettit 2011: 153–156).[3]

The capacity for judgment and restraint are straightforwardly found within CIDs, such as corporate constitutions, shared behavioral norms, by-laws, board decisions and other day-to-day managerial processes. Kendy M. Hess (2014) has recently made the case that these elements make up a corporate "structure" that unifies corporate agents and allows a single point of view from which various commitments about fact and value guide a corporation's action. This point of view provides a corporation a "unique orientation to the world" and forms the basis of the planning that constitutes the corporation's intention; moreover, it forms the basis of the ability to respond to situations by adjusting plans or established patterns of conduct by integrating new information and other values-based considerations. The capacity for judgment is functionally built in to the collective structures that overlay the conduct of individuals.

A similar story can be told for the capacity of restraint. Corporate structures provide the mechanisms through which corporate conduct is limited or prescribed. This may even be the case despite the fact that some individual members may not agree with those limitations or believe that the limitations are not forthcoming from the point of view prescribed by the structure. Again, as in the case of corporate judgment, restraint of the corporation arises out of shared structures that produce practical results above and beyond the beliefs, intentions and attitudes of individual members. Corporations restrain their own conduct on the basis of practical results generated within corporate decision making structures.

Pettit and Hess understand the capacity for judgment and restraint to be guided by moral considerations. So the explanation as to how corporations can exercise judgment and self-restraint include the use, integration and application of moral principles within corporate decision making structures. Corporate decision making structures stand above the decisions made by individual members of the corporation. They provide both direction and authorization for members to act on behalf of the corporation, reflecting the procedural outcomes of the "corporate charter and by-laws as interpreted and amended by the board of directors, corporate management, and market forces" (Hasnas 2017: 601).

The level of moral agency suggested by the capacities of judgment and self-control conveys the idea that corporations are entities that are capable of examining actions with respect to certain moral commitments and then implementing policies that meet those commitments. The demands of morality have a disciplining function within corporate structures and corporations, and, in virtue of those structures and the guidance they provide individual members, are themselves capable of engaging, with intention and deliberateness, activities consistent with the demands of morality.

The disciplining function of moral principles within corporate decision making structures is what allows for the political account of corporate moral responsibility sketched above. Corporations are social institutions that are capable of acting independent of mere external constraint. They can act with restraint and such restraint can be shaped against the background of moral concerns that are integrated into corporate decision making structures.

29.3 Corporate Autonomy

The capacities for judgment and restraint imply that corporations possess reasons for their decisions and actions. As Pettit notes, implicitly acknowledging Donaldson's original objection to French, corporate judgment and self-restraint are "reason-sensitive" in that judgments and acts of self-restraint arise within the justifications found within corporate decision making structures (Pettit 2007: 188). These structure-derived reasons exist independently of whatever (related) reasons individual members may have to endorse the actions undertaken by the corporation.

This exposes an assumption about the nature of reasons; in particular, if we presume that corporations lack minds, it suggests that reasons may not be mental states but, rather, states of affairs. This is a noteworthy result, but one that will not occupy our attention at this moment. But the idea that corporations possess and act upon reasons (whatever the metaphysics involved turn out to be) moves us closer to an examination of Pettit's first criterion for corporate responsibility, namely that corporations are autonomous.

To say that corporations have autonomy, for Pettit, means that their reasons for action are theirs independently. Their reasons are theirs to be identified, had and acted upon.

> Autonomy is intuitively guaranteed by the fact that on one or more issues the judgment of the group will have to be functionally independent of the corresponding member judgments, so that its intentional attitudes as a whole are most saliently unified by being, precisely, the attitudes of the group.
>
> *(184)*

So, using the examples from above, if Volkswagen's corporate decision making structures produced a decision to initiate a compensation program for its defrauded customers, or if BP's board and management decided to work with local communities to formulate plans to restore inland wetlands harmed by its operations in the Gulf of Mexico, there are reasons that those corporations have to respond in the manner that they do. Pettit argues that if we can understand a corporation's reasons as its own reasons, then it is reasonable to infer that the corporation is acting autonomously.

The most natural way to argue against the possibility of there being corporate reasons for action is to give an account of how what seem to be the independent reasons held by a corporation are actually reducible to a function of reasons held by its individual members. This is exactly the move that Pettit and others, including Hess, try to anticipate. Hess argues that there can be "discontinuity between the commitments that exist at the collective, corporate level and the commitments that exist at the individual, member level" (Hess 2014: 241–242). This divergence can be illustrated in a variety of cases. Explicit decisions that result from corporate structures (say those decisions made by an executive leadership team) may not reflect the judgments of individual members. Corporate decisions also result from "distributed" decision making where otherwise "piecemeal" decisions of individual members set in motion collective action which, while becoming accepted within the overall decision making structures of the corporation, do not reflect the reasoned commitments of individual members.

> [Distributed decision-making] is a bit like assembling a car, with each member contributing one fact or decision and then passing the project on to the next without any member being in a position to see the on-going collective actions that the corporate agent will reliably enact as a result of their individual choices.
>
> *(Hess 2013: 325)*

Hess goes on to explain that corporate policy can be built up from these distributed decisions over time. This creates circumstances where the commitments expressed through corporate action diverge from the commitments of its individual members.

The independence of corporate decisions, thus, is conceivable because there are situations where the executive and distributed nature of corporate action escapes scrutiny or endorsement from individual members. These sorts of discontinuous cases illustrate what Pettit refers to as "discursive dilemmas" that show how a corporate decision cannot be understood as a "majoritarian" function of its members' attitudes or intentions (Pettit 2007: 181; Pettit 2003). David Copp agrees, noting that corporate decision making structures provide enough resources to establish a perspective from which the corporation itself can be described as a "rational unity":

> [Corporations] can face situations to which its members can respond by "collectivizing reason"--by adopting a decision procedure that forces the [corporation] to achieve a kind of rational coherence among the resulting decisions and judgments. Having done this, a [corporation] is an "integrated collectivity" and an "intentional subject" in its own right, capable of making decisions that its members would not support, capable of achieving a rational unity in its beliefs, intentions, and actions, and open to a kind of rational criticism if it fails in a relevant way.
>
> *(Copp 2006: 194)*

Hess takes this to mean that a corporation is not just a "very complicated puppet" but is an independent agent in its own right with its own beliefs, desires, commitments and, seemingly, any other "agential moral property" that we would normally attribute to individual agents (cf. Copp 2007: 369). And "having their own [reasoned] commitments and their own actions, corporate entities are agents with their own obligations and their own responsibility" (Hess 2014: 244–245).

Corporate autonomy on this line is thought to be established through the irreducibility of practical reasons, which can only be attributed to the corporation. But is this sufficient? Is the autonomy of an intentional actor established simply by the presence of reasons that only it possesses? Are there other dimensions to autonomy beyond the "rational unity" that corporate decision making structures provide?

29.4 Two Senses of Autonomy

Autonomy, at bottom, expresses the idea that an agent is capable of reflecting upon certain grounds of action and deciding whether those grounds are good—or sufficient—to act in a certain manner. This is what leads David Rönnegard to think that autonomy "involves an agent's ability to hold a vantage point that is distinct from the agent's desires and allows the agent to choose which desire to act upon" (2015: 134). Autonomy is not about the capacity to choose, per se, but a unique ability to form "second-order" intentions based on a scrutiny of "first-order" desires, presumably through the exercise of reason.

But this only gets us so far. The ability of an agent to examine and form intentions about whether to act on her desires is only part of the story. To get clearer on whether corporations are capable of autonomy, we have to ask whether having independent reasons, i.e., reasons that are the agent's own, sufficiently encapsulates what we mean by having the autonomy necessary for *moral* agency. One way to press this point is to think about autonomy within the Kantian tradition. Human agents, for Kant, are autonomous because they not only possess reasons to act in this or that way, but those reasons are reasons guided by principles that do not merely make reference to subjective goals, interests or ends that the agent possesses. So the fact that one has a life plan with certain ends, perhaps which she has herself endorsed, is not what fully characterizes her autonomy; rather, another necessary dimension to her autonomy is that that very process of how she sets ends within her life—and how she carries out action plans in accordance with those ends—are bounded by other practical requirements which make no reference to the particular ends that she possesses. The presence and recognition of these practical requirements, which guide the process of practical reasoning in general, are characteristic of the capacity to be autonomous.

Put in slightly different Kantian terminology, certain practical requirements are derived from the fact that one's action should conform to a universal law and, in turn, this formal expectation structures the deliberative activities of morally responsible agents. An agent has autonomy not simply because they recognize and institute reasons for action, which are their reasons, but that some of their action plans are governed by requirements that make no reference to the specific ends an agent possesses. The unique moral status of such requirements follows from this formal requirement; they bind the agent to act in certain ways regardless of who they are, what life they have created for themselves or what subjective interests they possess. To be autonomous, thus, is to take the requirements embedded within the very idea of a universal law as having normative authority for oneself.

Can the type of corporate autonomy described by Pettit and Hess be captured along similar Kantian lines? Consider initially that the corporate capacities of judgment and self-restraint could be premised on a respect for certain principles that are universal in form; that is, a corporation's deliberation about how to conduct business and the regulation of its own behavior by its own decision making structures could very well take account of principles that have significance apart from the corporation's economic interests (e.g., sales growth, market share or profitability). Perhaps this is exactly what corporations like Volkswagen are doing when, over time, they adapt their conduct on the basis of coordinated, internal decision making that places priority on principles that proscribe fraud or prescribe compensation to those who have been negligently harmed. Responsible corporations can take account of, and consistently prioritize, principles in their operational decisions.

The question, however, is not whether corporations can consistently integrate into their decision making structures certain moral requirements. We could imagine a range of situations where an agent begins with some principled commitment and then competently applies that principle to determine in some of those situations that her action should be constrained or altered in order to uphold the principle in question. Perhaps this is what agents who respect positive law are doing when they decide to tailor their conduct according to what legal restrictions are enforced by the state. They look at what kinds of cases are subsumed by the law's requirements and then adjust their conduct accordingly.

But the question at hand is whether corporations themselves are capable of taking principled requirements as normative independent of the economic goals they happen to have. Autonomy on the Kantian line is not simply the ability to institute a moral principle but the recognition that the moral principle is an authoritative consideration independent of one's subjective interests. But, here again, some may counter that corporate decision making structures permit even this type of recognition. Corporate decision making structures could allow for a consideration of moral principles alongside economic aims and the structures could indeed embody a shared commitment to those principles. Morality could remain normative for the corporation in that moral principles are taken to be overriding considerations that limit or constrain how business is conducted.

This answer is problematic along one key dimension. The normative authority of moral principles for agents is found in a very special moment of practical recognition. The ability to act on reasons that are not tied to one's subjective interests is an important component of the freedom exhibited by Kantian agents; but there is an additional component, namely the moment in which agents recognize that their conduct is governed by principles which they give themselves. This "positive" dimension of our freedom is unique. Being autonomous is not simply being free from external causes. It is being subject to practical constraints for which the agent is herself the author. "To conceive of a person as having [autonomy] is to think of the person as having … in some sense necessarily imposed [principles] on oneself by oneself as a rational agent" (Hill 1992: 87).

Another way of putting this point is to recognize that "the source of the normativity of moral claims [is] … found in the agent's own will, in particular … that its claims are ones she is prepared to make on herself" (Korsgaard 1996: 19). The practical grip of moral principle is born out of the very capacity to reflectively endorse courses of action and that very capacity presupposes an appeal to general laws that are authored by the agent. This recognition of authorship is, at bottom, a capacity for "self-consciousness" about "our own actions [that] confers on us a kind of authority over ourselves" (Korsgaard, 1996: 20).

Cast in this light it may be clearer now why critics of corporate moral responsibility may be reluctant to assign the capacity of autonomy to corporations (Rönnegard 2013). The moment of "self-consciousness" that is presupposed by autonomy is not necessary for Pettit's three criteria to be met. Judgment, deliberation and the existence of independent, corporate grounds for action do not rely upon the corporation's structural assessment that the grounds for its action are governed by laws that it gives itself. This defining feature of autonomy—not just self-authorship of morality but the self-recognition of this fact—is absent in the case of corporate actors. Pettit's criteria may be helpful in explaining why we attribute a level of moral responsibility to corporations; but the criteria do not provide sufficient grounds to think that corporate decision making structures give rise to a sense of corporate self-awareness that would be a marker of the corporation's autonomy. The introspective moment where an agent phenomenologically has direct contact with the awareness that her reasons are her reasons, derived from principles that she has authored, is not present for corporations.

It might be noted, then, that the discussion about whether corporations are morally responsible involves two senses of autonomy in the context of corporate action. There is, first, an *administrative autonomy* that accompanies the corporate capacity to judge and deliberate about how to act and how to enact policies that are consistent with principled moral commitments. The political conception of corporate responsibility that we put forth in section 29.1 can allow for—and even require—this functional sense of autonomy. Corporate decision making structures and the leadership roles that board members and managers have within these structures presume that the reasons possessed by corporations are the corporation's reasons. Corporate action prescribed by its internal decision making structures is autonomous in that there is no other subject of action, but for the corporation itself. Corporations are capable of being held morally responsible in virtue of the capacity to independently incorporate moral considerations into their deliberation and judgment about how to conduct business.

The *moral autonomy* expressed within Kantian thought demands more, however. It presupposes that the corporation's principled moral commitments are not simply accepted constraints on deliberation and judgment; rather, if corporations are autonomous in this second sense, those commitments have normative validity independent of the corporation's operational objectives and their validity is anchored in an act of self-reflective endorsement completely divorced from those objectives. Autonomy is, at bottom, a capacity of agents that is born out of their experience of their own independence and freedom in deciding how to act (Guyer 1996).

29.5 Moral Autonomy and Moral Personhood

This last point is important. Advocates of a more robust account of corporate autonomy may simply object that the Kantian emphasis on the phenomenal experience of the self-authorship of morality is an analytic move that immediately—by fiat—excludes corporations from possessing moral autonomy. This objection is understandable; but, apart from appealing to the intuitive sense of unified selfhood that individual agents possess, the move is supported by the fact that moral autonomy underwrites our attributions of moral personhood. Insofar as there are strong intuitions against thinking of corporations as moral persons, the lack of moral autonomy described above could prove useful in explaining this intuition.

Some readers may recall that French (1995) jettisoned his early belief that corporate decision making structures provide the ground to attribute personhood to corporations in favor of the more modest position that corporations are moral agents without being fully moral persons. This shift by French was the result of criticism that the mere presence of internal decision making structures and corporate intentions does not sufficiently establish personhood. Corporate decisions need to be accompanied by the presence of reasons, held and recognized by the actor to whom we ascribe agency.

Again, through a Kantian lens, this connection between practical reasoning and personhood has a straightforward explanation. The formal constraint that one's actions conform to a universal law also expresses a necessary, "priceless" value placed on the very capacity to reason, i.e., the "humanity" in oneself and others. The special status of being a moral person simply amounts to possessing humanity; to be a moral person is to possess the very capacity to which a rational agent necessarily ascribes "incomparable" value. The inescapable recognition of this "necessary end" arises at the moment of self-experience where an agent asks herself "what should I do"? (Hill 1992). A moral person is one whose identity, including the ability to determine for oneself how to act and develop a life plan, is inseparable from the capacities needed to engage in self-directed, rational examination of one's subjective circumstances.

The central point here is that in making the case that corporations do not possess moral autonomy, we have a clear way to explain why corporations are also not moral persons (cf. Hess 2013: 333–334). Corporations are not moral persons because personhood flows from the presence of moral autonomy.

This line against corporate moral personhood opens up immediate avenues to explain why individual agents have entitlements to basic liberties and citizenship protections but corporations do not. Emergent debates in American jurisprudence about corporate rights, such as the right to political expression and religious freedom, are interesting when placed alongside claims that corporations are autonomous agents. One might ask: if corporations are indeed independent, autonomous actors, then why would we not take seriously the idea that they possess the moral entitlements associated with being autonomous? (Hasnas 2018). On what grounds could we be philosophically comfortable that corporations have autonomy but also assert that they do not possess the rights that flow to autonomous actors? The problem seems to be that the more advocates of corporate moral responsibility attempt to provide richer and richer accounts of the properties of agency—such as autonomy—the more difficult it is to resist the assignment of moral entitlements to corporations if they possess those attributes.

The legal rationale in recent decisions by the United States Supreme Court do not rely on any ascription of autonomy to corporations, at least in any sense being discussed thus far. In *Citizens United v. Federal Election Commission* (2010), for example, the Court found that corporate spending on political campaigns or issues is a social conduit through which political speech occurs; as such, there can be no legal limits placed on the amount of corporate spending in these areas because such limits would violate the First Amendment of the Constitution which prohibits laws that abridge the freedom of political speech. Some commentators loosely speak of this decision as granting corporations a "right to free speech," which, at best, may be misleading (cf. Hasnas 2017). Nonetheless, as an institutional matter, the "right" of individual citizens to engage in political speech finds its legal expression in the First Amendment; as such, it is natural to think that allowing unregulated corporate spending on political matters is tantamount to granting corporations a "right" to free speech, which begs the question of whether there are suitable philosophical reasons to support this extension of the First Amendment.

The distinction between administrative and moral autonomy provides a solution to the problem of what, if any, grounds exist to grant corporations rights that would normally be granted only to individuals. Moral principles can limit the conduct of corporations within their decision making structures and corporations can be held responsible when they fail to adequately take account of moral principles when conducting business. What corporations do not have, however, is a recognition that those moral commitments are normative independent of the decision making structures through which their actions are undertaken. As long as corporations lack moral autonomy, and thereby lack moral personhood, the inherent dignity possessed by moral persons does not extend to corporations. The basis for certain kinds of entitlements, such as expression, political participation and religious freedom, is therefore lacking for corporations. While there is undoubtedly more to be said about this line of analysis, it seems like this is fertile ground to defend a form of corporate autonomy without being concerned that corporations have the same rights as individual actors with moral autonomy.

Second, the denial of moral personhood to corporations that is sketched above also helps provide an explanation as to why we hold corporations morally responsible in the limited, administrative sense, without also extending other important moral attributes to corporations that we associate with being a full moral agent. Amy J. Sepinwall, for example, notes how moral responsibility requires the presence of "reactive attitudes" among moral agents (Sepinwall 2012; Sepinwall 2017: 144–145). Guilt, shame and remorse are attitudinal responses that we would expect of actors to whom we ascribe agency, and thereby hold responsible for immoral conduct. To the extent that such attitudes are affective states, and that corporations "have no capacity for affect," it may be appropriate to describe the type of agency possessed by corporations as functional but not fully moral because corporate agency is not accompanied by the entire range of experiences we expect of those we hold morally responsible. Sepinwall adds that without these reactive attitudes, it makes little sense to blame corporations for immoral conduct. This echoes a long-standing reservation held by Susan Wolfe that the presence of blameworthiness is a necessary attribute of an actor that acts irresponsibly, especially if we seek to punish the actor (Wolfe 1985).

There is, of course, a complex Kantian explanation as to why reactive attitudes are important. Reactive attitudes and other affective states provide direction and insight for an agent to help her "see" what is deliberatively salient in deciding how to act. Kant himself makes it "clear that moral perfection requires the development of feelings compatible with and conducive to those intentions that are dictated by pure reason alone" (Guyer 1996: 30). Indeed, given that humans are affective creatures, a "free practical will" cannot lead agents to moral action without what Kant calls a "disposition of the feeling for practical ideas" (Guyer 1996: 30). "The contingent nature of the self (in particular its [affective] embodiment) is not conceived of as an inevitable enemy of rational nature, but as a potential ally that we have a duty to cultivate" (Sherman 1995: 369). One might reasonably understand that the interface between reason and affect—and the awareness of their duality—is what actually forms the basis of moral personhood.

29.6 Conclusion

We argued in the opening sections of this discussion that modern, market economies presume a degree of moral responsibility on the part of corporations. The discretion and decision making latitude given to corporations implies an expectation that corporations make business decisions in a way that respects an array of moral considerations. This political conception of corporate moral responsibility helps explain a number of institutional arrangements that rely on corporations acting in a morally responsible fashion.

In order for this presumption to withstand philosophical scrutiny, however, it should make sense to think of corporations as being morally responsible agents. This requires careful engagement with a deeper, metaphysical question about agency; at the same time, this is an opportunity to draw some important distinctions between types of agency, in particular the type of autonomy that is exhibited by different actors. At the heart of corporate autonomy is a question of whether there are independent, corporate acts for which grounds for action can be attributed to the corporation—as a whole—as opposed to its individual members.

In one sense of autonomy—what we called administrative autonomy—an explanation can be given for our willingness to think of corporations as morally responsible agents. Corporate decision making structures provide a framework of norms, governing rules and managerial processes that generate corporate reasons to act. Insofar as those structures can integrate a consideration of moral principles, corporations are morally responsible for adhering to business practices that do not run afoul of the demands of morality. In another sense of autonomy—moral autonomy—the independence of an agent's reasons for action is, by itself, insufficient. Autonomy in this sense requires an additional moment in which the moral principles guiding one's actions are normative because they are principles authored by the agent. This captures the deepest sense of self-governance expressed by the term "autonomy." We argued that corporations do not have the capacity for this type of reflective endorsement but, instead, can only integrate moral principles as given constraints on how to pursue their other economic interests.

The distinction between administrative and moral autonomy therefore helps explain the multiple intuitions we have about corporate moral responsibility. It explains standing behind our institutionally-backed intuitions that corporations are the proper objects of our moral scrutiny. We can intelligibly hold them responsible in virtue of the fact that they are agents who can independently judge and restrain their actions in accordance with moral principles. It also helps explain why those institutional intuitions do not license us to make inferences about corporate agents that mirror our inferences about individual agents. Put differently: corporations are moral agents but they do not retain the status of moral persons.

Notes

1 Another example of a position that presumes corporate moral responsibility is David Silver's (2005) argument that ascriptions of corporate responsibility have credence because our practices (including legal practices) hold corporations blameworthy for wrongdoing. Here, as in our own political conception of corporate moral responsibility, there remains a need to justify those practices (cf. Sepinwall 2017: 159–160).

2 We disagree, in part, with Hussain's (2017) treatment of this issue; whereas he makes the case that a "functionalist" account of responsibility can be given for why we hold corporations responsible for their conduct, his focus remains on how corporations can be held liable or financially responsible when they pursue business practices that are harmful, fraudulent or otherwise negligent. But his account is focused on how corporations should be treated through law, not whether there are any underlying attributions of moral responsibility to corporations. To address this matter, we cannot simply focus on how corporations are treated legally but how we understand their capabilities for agency, which relies on the "metaphysical" issues that Hussain prefers to avoid.

3 We have adapted our descriptions of Pettit's criteria based on the interpretation offered by Hasnas (2018).

References

Arnold, D.G. (2006) "Corporate Moral Agency," *Midwest Studies in Philosophy* 30(1): 279–291.

Bratman, M.E. (2014) *Shared Agency: A Planning Theory of Acting Together*, New York: Oxford University Press.

Citizens United v. Federal Election Commission, 588 U.S. 310 (2010).

Copp, D. (2006) "On the Agency of Certain Collective Entities: An Argument From 'Normative Autonomy'," *Midwest Studies in Philosophy* 30(1): 194–221.

Copp, D. (2007) "The Collective Autonomy Thesis," *Journal of Social Philosophy* 38(3): 369–388.

Diskant, E.B. (2008) "Comparative Corporate Criminal Liability: Exploring the Uniquely American Doctrine Though Comparative Criminal Procedure," *Yale Law Journal* 118: 126–176.

Donaldson, T.E. (1982) *Corporations and Morality*, Englewood Cliffs: Prentice Hall.

Dubbink, G.W. and Smith, J.D. (2011) "A Political Account of Corporate Moral Responsibility," *Ethical Theory and Moral Practice* 14(2): 223–246.

French, P. (1979) "The Corporation as a Moral Person," *American Philosophical Quarterly* 16(3): 207–215.

French, P. (1995) *Corporate Ethics*, Wadsworth: Wadsworth Publishing Company.

French, P. (1996) "Integrity, Intentions and Corporations," *American Business Law Journal* 34(2): 141–156.

French, P. (2017) "The Diachronic Moral Responsibility of Firms," in C. Smith and E. Orts (eds.) *The Moral Responsibility of Firms*, Oxford: Oxford University Press.

Guyer, P. (1996) *Kant and the Experience of Freedom*, Cambridge: Cambridge University Press.

Hasnas, J. (2017) "Does Corporate Moral Agency Entail Corporate Freedom of Speech?" *Social Theory and Practice* 43(3): 589–612.

Hasnas, J. (2017) "The Phantom Menace of the Responsibility Deficit," in E.W. Orts and N.C. Smith (eds.) *The Moral Responsibility of Firms*. Oxford: Oxford University Press.

Hasnas, J. (2018) "Should Corporations Have the Right to Vote? A Paradox in the Theory of Corporate Moral Agency," *Journal of Business Ethics* 150: 657–670.

Hess, K.M. (2013) ""If You Tickle Us…": How Corporations Can Be Moral Agents Without Being Persons," *Journal of Value Inquiry* 47(3): 319–335.

Hess, K.M. (2014) "The Free Will of Corporations (and Other Collectives)," *Philosophical Studies* 168(1): 241–260.

Hill, T.E. (1992) *Dignity and Practical Reason In Kant's Moral Theory*, Ithaca: Cornell University Press.

Hussain, W. and Sandberg, J. (2017) "Pluralistic Functionalism About Corporate Agency," in E.W. Orts and N.C. Smith (eds.) *The Moral Responsibility of Firms*, Oxford: Oxford University Press.

Korsgaard, C.M. (1996) *The Sources of Normativity*, Cambridge: Cambridge University Press.

Lindblom, C.E. (2001) *The Market System: What It Is, How It Works, and What to Make of It*, New Haven: Yale University Press.

List, C. and Pettit, P. (2011) *Group Agency: The Possibility, Design, and Status of Corporate Agents*, Oxford: Oxford University Press.

McMahon, C. (2012) *Public Capitalism: The Political Authority of Corporate Executives*, Philadelphia: University of Pennsylvania Press.

Pettit, P. (2003) "Groups with Minds of their Own," in F. Schmitt (ed) *Socializing Metaphysics*, Lanham, MD: Rowman & Littlefield, pp. 167–193.

Pettit, P. (2007) "Responsibility Incorporated," *Ethics* 117(2): 171–201.

PhRMA (2017) *Code on Interactions with Health Care Professionals*, retrieved from www.phrma.org/codes-and-guidelines/code-on-interactions-with-health-care-professionals

Philips, M.J. (1995) "Corporate Moral Responsibility: When It Might Matter," *Business Ethics Quarterly* 5(3): 555–576.

Rönnegard, D. (2013) "How Autonomy Alone Debunks Corporate Moral Agency," *Business and Professional Ethics Journal* 32(1–2): 77–107.

Rönnegard, D. (2015). *The Fallacy of Corporate Moral Agency*. Dordrecht: Springer.

Rönnegard, D. and Velasquez, M. (2017) "On (Not) Attributing Moral Responsibility to Organizations," in E.W. Orts and N.C. Smith (eds.) *The Moral Responsibility of Firms*, Oxford: Oxford University Press.

Sepinwall, A.J. (2012) "Guilty By Proxy: Expanding the Boundaries of Responsibility in the Face of Corporate Crime," *Hastings Law Journal* 63(2): 411–454.

Sepinwall, A.J. (2017) "Blame, Emotion and the Corporation," in C. Smith and E. Orts (eds.) *The Moral Responsibility of Firms*, Oxford: Oxford University Press.

Sherman, N. (1995) "Reasons and Feelings in Kantian Morality," *Philosophy and Phenomenological Research* 55(2): 369–377.

Silver, D. (2005) "A Strawsonian Defense of Corporate Moral Responsibility," *American Philosophical Quarterly* 42(4): 279–293.

Velasquez, M. (2003) "Debunking Corporate Moral Responsibility," *Business Ethics Quarterly* 13(4): 531–562.

Wolfe, S. (1985) "The Legal and Moral Responsibility of Organizations," *Nomos* 27: 267–286.

Wolfe, S. (2015) "Responsibility, Moral and Otherwise," *Inquiry* 58(2): 127–142.

PART IV

Applied Issues in Collective Responsibility

Part IV of this handbook applies theories and accounts of collective responsibility to real-world problems, including collective responsibility for: war, global poverty, climate change, conspiracy theories, environmental injustice, and institutional racism. Part IV begins with a discussion in Chapter 30 of collective responsibility – or rather, complicity – in the context of warfare. Saba Bazargan-Forward points out that most combatants play highly subsidiary roles in the war they fight. The result is that most contribute very little to the harms their side causes. On what grounds, then, can they be morally liable to be targeted by the enemy? Bazargan-Forward's aim is to provide an account explaining how and why cooperation dramatically expands the scope of responsibility. He argues that, typically, when we undertake shared action, we establish a division of agential labor in virtue of which each of us has the putative authority over the other that they do their part, where this authority is cached out in terms of Razian protected reasons. He argues that acting in accordance with this putative authority serves as a basis for mutual inculpation; the result is that each of us can be responsible for what we together do irrespective of our causal contributions to that cooperatively committed wrong. The result is that individual soldiers can be on the hook for what their comrades do.

The harms of war, as egregious as they are, pale in comparison to the harms of poverty and famine. In Chapter 31, Violetta Igneski investigates the claim that we have collective duties of beneficence to the worst off. She begins by arguing that collective duties of beneficence should be taken seriously in moral and political theory. After summarizing current debates on whether unstructured collectives can have such duties, she turns to her own view. She defends the claim that even when the collectivities we are concerned with are not group *agents*, they can nonetheless have a duty *qua* group to prevent a harm or wrong when there is evidence available that the group possesses the capacity to do so. On this view, the duty of the group *qua* group grounds the duties of its individual members. Igneski ends by exploring the implications for individual agents given their role in the various collectives of which they are a part.

No investigation of collective responsibility as it applies to the real world would be complete without a discussion of the most destructive collective action dilemma of our time: climate change. In Chapter 32, Holly Lawford-Smith and Anton Eriksson note that to mitigate the harms of climate change, we need to cut greenhouse gas emissions. Yet, given the magnitude of the changes required, it seems that the duties to cut emissions do not fall on any given individual. It seems, then, that the duty to address climate change must fall irreducibly on collectives. Lawford-Smith and Eriksson accordingly argue as much. In particular, they maintain that the duty to mitigate climate change falls centrally on states. Lawford-Smith and Eriksson go further, however, by arguing that states possess collective moral agency and count as culpable emitters in their own right. That is, states do not merely have a duty to address the emissions that their citizens or privately owned corporations cause. In addition, states are themselves, *qua* states, morally responsible for the copious emissions they cause.

The proliferation of unfounded conspiracy theories is also an eminently salient topic these days – and one that often involves collective action. In Chapter 33, Juha Räikkä investigates whether and how conspiracy theorists are collectively responsible for what they together do. In doing so, he distinguishes between (1) developers and publishers and (2) ordinary believers and disseminators of conspiracy theories. Räikkä argues that the responsibility of developers and publishers is different from that of the ordinary believers and disseminators. Nonetheless, these groups are severally and jointly collectively responsible for what they together do, in three ways. First, the ordinary believers and disseminators share responsibility for diminished trust in major social institutions. Second, developers and publishers typically support one another by acting jointly, which results in joint responsibility for what they together do. Third, developers and publishers are collectively responsible for failing to establish organizations and institutions devoted to propounding only those theories that satisfy virtuous epistemic norms and principles.

Returning to collective responsibility as it pertains to the environment, Kenneth Shockley notes in Chapter 34 that we often approach this issue by asking *who* is blameworthy, collectively or otherwise, for environmental injustice. This is, he points out, a backward-directed approach to responsibility. Shockley argues, however, that a focus on blame might not be the best way to address environmental injustice. He urges us to consider our forward-directed duties to alter the social practices and institutions that enable the institutional wrongdoing in the first place. Accordingly, Shockley argues that those capable of doing so harbor a 'forward-directed shared responsibility' to change the institutional environment in which environmental injustice occurs. Those individuals who fail to act appropriately can be held responsible, in the backward-directed sense, for that failure. We are, then, collectively responsible for environmental injustice in this sense: we share a duty to change our institutional environment.

Michael Hardiman closes Part IV with a much-needed discussion of collective and individual responsibly for institutional racism – i.e., racial oppression of the sort perpetrated by social institutions for which no individual is necessarily to blame. He raises the following question: does institutional racism let individuals off the hook? Hardiman argues that it does not. Racist individuals in racist, 'colorblind' racist institutions – i.e., institutions that promote racial inequality even in the absence of racist attitudes – can be held to account for the institution's racism. Likewise, nonracist individuals in racist institutions who simply 'do their jobs' are still on the hook for enabling such institutions to promote its problematic goals. (Such individuals are likely to be guilty of 'indifference racism' in any case). So, according to Hardiman, the structure of institutional racism does not exonerate the individuals who work in such institutions, even if said individual are not themselves racist.

30
RESPONSIBILITY FOR SHARED ACTION IN WAR

Saba Bazargan-Forward

30.1 Background

In international law, the legal permission to target combatants derives from their status rather than their conduct. That is, what makes an individual a legal target is not whether she poses a threat, but whether she qualifies as a combatant (though a civilian directly participating in hostilities thereby qualifies as a combatant). According to international law, a combatant 'may be attacked at any time until they surrender or are otherwise *hors de combat*, and not only when actually threatening the enemy' (Solis, 2010, p. 202).

On the *orthodox view*, the morality of war parallels international law with respect to the laws pertaining to the legal permission to target combatants. The most influential defender of the orthodox view is Michael Walzer. He argues that all active-duty combatants – even those whose actual contribution to the war is small or nonexistent – are morally permissible targets since they are all 'currently engaged in the business of war' (Walzer, 2000, p. 43). By having made themselves into combatants they have made themselves dangerous.

The orthodox view, though, has been heavily criticised, most prolifically by Jeff McMahan (McMahan, 2009). He argues that whether you pose a threat is neither a necessary nor a sufficient condition for losing your right not to be killed. A combatant does not lose her right to be killed when she poses a morally justified threat, no more than the victim of an attempted mugging loses her right not to be attacked when she engages in necessary and proportionate self-defence. Hence, combatants who are fighting in accordance with the rules of war and in furtherance of morally just aims have done nothing to lose their right against being killed. Put differently, such combatants are not morally liable to be killed.

On this *revisionist view*, combatants who are acting in furtherance of a war's unjust aims have indeed forfeited their right against being subjected to necessary and proportionate defensive violence. They are potentially liable to be killed, in that killing them does not wrong them provided that doing so is necessary to achieve a sufficiently important good. Such a combatant is morally liable because (and only if) she is responsible for her contribution to an end which violates the rights of others. So, a combatant who scrupulously targets solely military installations and personnel still thereby makes herself liable to be killed defensively if she does so in furtherance of an unjust aim, whereas her targets, by attacking her, are *not* morally liable to be killed if their attack is a necessary and proportionate act in furtherance of a just aim.

So, on McMahan's revisionist view, only combatants responsible for contributing to an unjust cause (or against a just cause pursed by unjust means) are morally liable to be targeted. It is what you do – not your status – that determines your liability in war. If this is correct, the orthodox view is mistaken in its claim that all combatants are morally entitled to kill enemy combatants.

The revisionist view faces a challenge, though. On the revisionist view, a combatant is morally liable to be killed only if she contributes to an unjust cause (or to a just cause unjustly). Moreover, that contribution must be substantial – so substantial that she loses the right against being subjected to necessary and proportionate lethal violence. However, a significant portion of combatants, such as those who occupy subsidiary support roles, contribute very little to the war being fought. Indeed, most combatants never see combat. If, on the one hand, these combatants are *not* morally liable to be killed, then how do we distinguish the liable combatants from the non-liable ones? Waging a morally just war would seem to be pragmatically impossible.

Anticipating this problem, McMahan argues that the threshold for liability is quite low; as a result, virtually all combatants acting in furtherance of an unjust aim will likely be morally liable to be killed (McMahan, 2009).[1] Other responses are possible, though. Bradley Strawser, in defense of the revisionist view, argues that we should drop the bivalent distinction between combatant and noncombatant in favor of a more complex scheme in which we track levels of liability based on reasonable perceived liability (Strawser, 2011). Still others maintain that appealing to the liability of combatants cannot justify intentional killing in war. For example, Janina Dill and Henry Shue argue that most combatants participating in furtherance of an unjust aim do not contribute enough to make lethal attack necessary and proportionate (Dill & Shue, 2012).

Recently, a different strategy for defending the revisionist view has emerged. Some have argued that most combatants – including those whose contributions to an unjust aim are insignificant – are typically morally liable to be attacked because they are engaged in shared action. For example, Adil Ahmad Haque argues that each participant is morally responsible not just for her own contribution to that shared action, but for the shared action itself. He says, "[i]n general, persons are morally liable to defensive killing only if they pose unjust threats directly, *jointly with others*, or indirectly through others they control" (my emphasis) (Haque, 2017, p. 57). So when combatants cooperate in furtherance of a mission, each is typically responsible for what they together do, since "members of a military unit performing coordinated roles in a combat operation are paradigmatic joint perpetrators" (Haque, 2017, p. 59). Haque elaborates further:

> several people *jointly* kill another by together performing a joint action that causes the other's death, without subsequent intervening agency by others and, typically, without which the victim would not have died. [...] For example, if A restrains V while B stabs V to death, each performing coordinated roles in a common plan, then A and B together kill V. Importantly, joint actions are the actions of each participant, not solely the actions of the last participant to perform her role or only the actions of those participants without whose participation the plan would not have succeeded. For example, in the previous case, A and B together kill V even if B's participation was counterfactually unnecessary because V would not have resisted. What we do, I do. When we kill, I kill.
>
> *(Haque, 2017, p. 65)*

This view has an intuitive appeal; indeed, Haque isn't the only one to have proffered it.[2] Yet we need to provide grounds for this view. We cannot just stipulate that when individuals cooperate in furtherance of a shared goal, each cooperator can end up responsible for more than what she causes. To treat this as a bedrock claim is problematic since the intuition seems to conflict with the equally plausible pronouncement that each of us is morally responsible only for what is within her own causal reach. What we need is an account explaining how and why cooperation dramatically expands the scope of responsibility.[3] It's my aim here to provide such an account and to apply it to war.

My argument, in brief, is this. We share an action in the relevant sense when we coordinate and combine our actions in furtherance of doing something together, as when we walk together or paint a house together (to take canonical examples from Gilbert [1990] and Bratman [1992]). In typical cases, when you and I are engaged in shared action, I will take myself to have authority over you that you do your part (whatever that might be) and you will likely take yourself to have authority over me that I do my part (whatever that might be), where in both cases this authority is cached out in terms of protected reasons. A protected reason to do ϕ is comprised of a first-order reason to do ϕ and a second-order reason to exclude certain competing considerations from deliberation pertaining to ϕ. (See Raz, 1977; Raz, 1990, pp. 35–84)). This authority you and I take ourselves to have over the other is grounded in the agreement we made to participate in the shared action. In arguing for this view, I will focus in section 30.2 on the two most influential accounts of shared action: Margaret Gilbert's and Michael Bratman's. I then argue in section 30.3 that where I take myself to have authority over you that you do ϕ, and where you subsequently do ϕ, thereby conforming to the protected reasons you take there to be, I thereby end up morally responsible for what you do. Of course, if you choose to do ϕ in part because of me, then I might be morally responsible for what you do in virtue of my causal influence on your voluntary conduct (intervening agency notwithstanding). But I argue that there is another, separate basis for thinking that I am morally responsible for what you do. Irrespective of my causal contributions to your conduct, the very fact that I have putative authority over you that you do ϕ can ground my moral responsibility for what you do should you abide by that claim I have against you.

Why is this so? Normally, my intentional conduct has the function of enacting the practical reasons I take there to be; concomitantly, the practical reasons I take there to be have the function of normatively guiding my conduct. However, it is possible for me to attribute to you the role of enacting those practical reasons; should you accept that role, I thereby change the object at which my practical reasoning is directed. Its object is no longer my conduct, but rather yours. That is to say, the practical reasons I take there to be have the function of guiding your conduct, and your conduct has the function of enacting the practical reasons I take there to be. In this way, we establish a division of *agential* labor, in that I count as the 'decider,' and you count as the 'doer.'

We assess conduct partly by assessing the practical reasons for which it was done. So, to morally assess *your* conduct, we need to repair to the practical reasons *I* take there to be insofar as I count as the decider in the division of agential labor we've established. So, if my practical reasons are morally problematic, then I am responsible for a wrong-making feature of your conduct. The result, then, is that I am at least partly morally responsible for what you do (though my responsibility in no way diminishes yours).

To be clear, the claim here is not that I am morally responsible for what you do in virtue of having influenced your motivations (though that too might be a basis for moral responsibility). Rather, the basis of my responsibility for your conduct is constitutive rather than causal. *Your conduct has the function of enacting the practical reasons I take there to be; so, by adopting morally problematic practical reasons, I constitutively determine, from afar, the purpose of your conduct.* Insofar as that affects the moral assessment of your conduct, I am on the hook for that difference I make. I call this 'authority-based moral responsibility.'

The upshot is this. The decider is morally responsible for what the doer does *qua* doer. Such cases might be better described as proxy agency or extended agency rather than shared agency, insofar as the doer acts not to achieve some mutually desired or shared end but rather out of a perceived obligation to the decider. But the basis for inculpation in these cases applies also to shared action as well. Any given participant in typical instances of shared action has authority over the other participants that they do their part, in that she has a claim against them yielding a protected reason for them to do their part. The practical reasons she takes there to be has the function of normatively guiding their conduct in that regard, and their conduct has the function of enacting the practical reasons she takes there to be. So, given the authority-based argument for responsibility, she is morally responsible for what they do should they conform to those reasons. Because this is true of every participant, the result is that each participant is morally responsible for what they together do – irrespective of the degree to which they causally contribute to what they together do. Finally, in section 30.4, I argue that the account provides a basis for thinking that an individual soldier in a war is responsible for more than what she causes or the difference she makes.

30.2 Putative Authority and Shared Action

Normally, you decide whether to do some action ϕ by considering the reasons for and against ϕ. Things are different, though, when you decide what to do in response to someone you believe to be authorized to tell you what to do with respect to ϕ. The reason to do ϕ in such a case derives not from the merits of ϕ itself, but from the very fact that the authority has a claim against you that you do ϕ. H.L.A. Hart points out that regardless of how widely authorities differ in what they require of us, they all provide us with the same reason for compliance: the very fact that the authority has a claim against us that we so act (Hart, 1990, p. 101).[4] In addition, the putative authority's claim against you that you do ϕ provides a reason to exclude certain competing first-order reasons from further deliberation pertaining to ϕ. (The authoritative claim does not exclude *all* competing reasons, however; the zone of exclusion varies with the command and the context in which it is given.)[5] The combination of the first-order reason to act in accordance with the authoritative claim against you, and the second-order reason to exclude from deliberation certain competing first-order reasons, yields what Joseph Raz calls a *protected* reason (Raz, 1977; Raz, 1990, pp. 35–84).

Deference to authority, then, requires doing what the authority commands precisely because the authority commands it. In this respect, the commands of an authority serve to 'settle the matter' for you within a particular domain of conduct. To be clear, though, someone you believe to have authority over you needn't actually issue a command that you do ϕ in order for you to have what you take to be a protected reason to do ϕ. It is enough if you believe that, in virtue of the person's authority over you – that she has a claim against you that you do ϕ.

There is, of course, a vast literature on what constitutes legitimate authority, and even whether such authority is possible, especially in the context of whether governments are justified in compelling its citizens to obey laws. But here I limit myself to authority between individuals. Suppose you accept a promise I made. The reasons to fulfill a promise are in general protected (see Raz, 1986, pp. 35–37). So, if I promise to you that I will do ϕ, then we both take it that you have authority over me with respect to ϕ, by deciding whether or not to hold me to that promise. If you decide to hold me to that promise, then we both take it that you have a claim against me that I do ϕ, where, by our lights, that claim provides me with a protected reason to do ϕ.[6]

I will argue that participants in shared action have authority over one another – even in cases of shared action *among equals*. In what follows, I focus on the two most influential accounts of shared action – the accounts developed by Margaret Gilbert and by Michael Bratman.

30.2.1 Margaret Gilbert's Account

On Gilbert's account, shared activity requires that each participant individually express their willingness to be committed with others to act as a body, thereby resulting in a 'joint commitment.' The participants thereby form a 'plural subject' (Gilbert, 2006, p. 134). I will use an example to explain what each of these terms means.

Suppose you and I agree to bake a cake for our colleague's potluck. Each of us does not *individually* agree to bake our colleague a cake; that would result in *two* cakes. Instead, we each individually express willingness to be committed to baking a cake together. It is in this respect that we 'act as a body' – we coordinate our efforts in furtherance of baking the cake as would a single individual. By doing so we together form a 'plural subject' – an entity to which intentional action and propositional attitudes can be attributed (Gilbert, 2006, p. 145).

On this account, a joint commitment is not the aggregate of a commitment I make to you and of a commitment you make to me. Instead, a joint commitment is a commitment we both become party to, when I express my willingness to bake the cake with you and you express your willingness to do the same. Though the commitment is held by a plural subject, this does not mean that the commitment is held by a "single centre of consciousness" or a "distinctive form of 'subjectivity'" (Gilbert, 2006, p. 134). Instead, the commitment is held, simply, by those bound to it – me and you.

On Gilbert's view, joint commitments entail a normative relationship between the individuals who are party to the commitment. By forming a joint commitment, each of us is obligated to do his or her part in furtherance of baking the cake together. And each of us has a claim against the other that he or she do the same. If I neglect to live up to those obligations, you would be justified in rebuking me (Gilbert, 1990). Rescinding the joint commitment or otherwise releasing any individual from the requirements of participation requires unanimous concurrence from all the persons party to the commitment (Gilbert, 1999; see also Gilbert, 1990).[7]

Gilbert makes clear that relevant obligations are 'directed' in that if I fail to do my part in baking the cake, you have an agent-relative complaint against me; but it isn't a moral complaint (Gilbert, 2009, 2008, p. 497).[8] The relevant obligations are not moral obligations (Gilbert, 2009, p. 178). The result is that individuals party to a morally wrongful shared activity have claims against each other that they do their part even though these claims generate no moral reasons in favor of doing their part.

It seems, then, that on Gilbert's view the *merits* of the joint commitments do not affect my obligation to you that I act in accordance with the joint commitment; neither does it affect your claim against me that I act in that way. Put differently, once I'm party to a joint commitment, the obligation that I have to act accordingly does not derive solely from whether it is a good idea to do so, but from the claim that you have against me that I so act. By agreeing to be part of a joint commitment, I thereby *grant* you authority over me, which grounds a claim that you have against me: the claim that I do my part in the shared activity. Once I have agreed to be party to the commitment, I have a reason to act accordingly. Moreover, your claim against me that I do my part gives me a reason to exclude from the zone of deliberations certain contrary reasons that might otherwise be relevant. For example, the fact that I do not feel like doing my part ought not to serve in my deliberations as a reason against doing my part. The result is that once I agree to do my part, no further deliberation is practically required from me in the absence of new information.[9] I have a reason to act in accordance with the claim you have against me, and a reason to ignore competing reasons. The result is that my reason to do my part is protected.

It might seem strange to think that equals – i.e., individuals in a non-hierarchical relationship – can have authority over one another.[10] But in shared activity, the authority I have over you and you have over me is only the authority that you fulfill the terms of the commitment you made. The claim that each of us has over the other is that the other do his or her part, *sans phrase*.[11] Absent some further agreement, you lack a claim that I do my part *in the way that you specify*. If, in baking the cake together, you tell me to melt the butter before mixing, but my mother always told me to use it cold, you needn't cease to deliberate and do as you're told, since the authority I have over you does not extend to specifying how you are to mix the batter.

The upshot is that on Gilbert's view, joint commitments by default establish relationships in which individuals party to that arrangement enjoy authority over one another which grounds mutual claims against each other that they do their part in the shared action. Such claims yield protected reasons to conform with the joint commitment they have made.

30.2.2 Michael Bratman's Account

Bratman has developed a competing, reductive account of shared activity (Bratman, 1993, p. 11); Bratman, 1999, pp. 108, 129). It is reductive in the sense that he analyzes shared activity in terms of shared intentions, which in turn are analyzed wholly in terms of first-personal intentions held by individuals.

On this view, shared intentions are instantiated in an arrangement of individually held intentions across multiple persons. These shared intentions reflect the commitment each individual has to what they are doing together, rather than merely a commitment to her own role in those plans. Inasmuch, each participant intends the *entirety* of the shared activity. So, if you and I intend to bake a cake together, our respective intentions do not refer to our own respective acts but to the joint act of baking a cake. Put more generally, each participant has an intention of the form *I intend that we J*, where J refers to the joint activity in which the intending agents participate (Bratman, 1992). Though such an intention refers in its content to an action performed by a collective, the intention is still *personal*, in that the intention is held by an individual rather than a group (Bratman, 1999, pp. 122–123).

As participants in shared activity, the ordinary norms of individual planning agency – such as consistency and coherence – apply to our interpersonal intentions. So, for example, suppose again that you and I share an intention to bake a cake. We share this intention only if each of us intends that we bake a cake. But the norms of consistency and coherence require more than this. We need to formulate a complex of interrelated personal intentions that interdepend in the right way. In particular, our plans must *mesh*. That is, our respective intentions instrumental to or constitutive of our shared intentions – our 'subplans' – need not be identical, but they do need to be mutually compossible as a result of intending as much.[12] The resulting set of interdepending individual attitudes composes a shared intention. Each participating agent must intend that they achieve the activity together, in part because of the other participant's corresponding intention; and it must be common knowledge between them that their subplans in furtherance of that activity are consistent.

In discussing Gilbert's view, Bratman rejects her claim that obligations are constitutive of shared action (Bratman, 1999). He admits that individuals engaged in shared activities will often create mutual expectations, which in turn might create moral obligations to fulfill those obligations, in accordance with something like Timothy Scanlon's principle of fidelity.[13] But on

Bratman's view, these obligations are incidental consequences of, rather than essentially intrinsic to, shared action.[14] As such, he maintains that it is perfectly possible to embark on shared activities absent any such obligations.

If something like Bratman's account of shared actions is correct, then they will not necessarily establish relationships in which each participant has an authoritative claim against the other yielding protected reasons for them to do their part in the shared action. This is because shared activity only contingently results in mutual promissory obligations among the participants. If the participants explicitly or implicitly promise to do their part in furtherance of their shared activity, then it is the promise, rather than the shared activity per se, that yields mutual authority among the participants. The fact remains, though, that typical instances of shared action will include implicit agreements among the cooperators. And since these agreements themselves yield protected reasons, the result is that on Bratman's account, shared action typically yields protected reasons for participants to do their part.[15]

30.3 Authority-Based Moral Responsibility

So far, I have argued that on two influential accounts of shared action the participants involved in shared action will either necessarily or typically take themselves to have authority over one another, where this, in turn, yields what the participants take to be protected reasons in favor of compliance. In what follows I will argue that when we both believe that I have an authoritative claim against you that you do ϕ, and you subsequently conform to that claim, I am morally responsible for what you do irrespective of my causal influence on your conduct (which isn't to say that you are any less responsible for what you do). Such a view is in keeping with the moral upshot of the claim we began with, that in war "[w]hen we act jointly, your act is my act; when you act on my orders, your act is my act" (Haque, 2017, p. 60). The first is a shared action, the second is proxy action; both involve authority claims and so in both cases I am responsible for what you do.

30.3.1 Establishing an Agential Division of Labor

Suppose Person A asks Person B to assault a particular innocent. In response, Person B promises to do so. In this case, A and B have established an *agential* division of labor, in that Person A counts as the 'decider' and Person B counts as the 'doer.' Person A counts as the decider in the sense that she has the function of normatively determining whether Person B is to commit the assault, by either holding him to his promise or releasing him from it. And to say that Person B counts as the doer is to say that she has the function of acting accordingly. But what does it mean for someone to have a 'function'? And how does someone attain a function?

All functions have an end – an aim at which the function is normatively directed. We can characterize a function in terms of a protected reason to act in accordance with the function's end. This elegantly captures the nature of a function: it imposes upon us a particular end and (possibly) a particular means by which to achieve that end, while simultaneously delimiting deliberative freedom by excluding some (and possibly all) competing considerations from the balance of reasons. So, to say that Person A has the function of deciding whether Person B is to commit the assault, and to say that Person B has the function of acting accordingly, is to say that they both treat A's directives to B pertaining to whether he should commit the assault as *settling that matter* for Person B, in that A's directives yield protected reasons for B.

Recall, though, that protected reasons also characterize *authority*. Person A and Person B believe that A has authority over B that B do ϕ if they both believe that A's claim that B do ϕ provides a protected reason for B to do ϕ. So, one way to characterize the functional relationship between Person A and Person B is in terms of the authority Person A has over Person B. This is because both authority and functional roles are cached out in terms of protected reasons. The upshot, then, is this: the protected reasons resulting from the promise which Person B makes and Person A accepts grounds both the putative authority Person A has over Person B, and the function each of them has with respect to each other.

The idea that Person A's claim against Person B settles the matter for B – in that B takes himself to have limited deliberative say in the matter – might seem to overstate the role that the promise plays in B's motivational economy. Suppose that if fulfilling the promise were not beneficial to B, he would renege on it. Or suppose B decides to go through with the promise he made only after deliberating about the merits of committing the assault, in that he re-considers the advantages of doing so, of getting caught, whether he feels like doing it, and so on. In these cases, Person B seems to be violating the deliberative injunctions imposed by his protected reasons, even if he ultimately decides to go through with the assault.

Nonetheless, so long as B believes that the promise provides a protected reason to commit the assault, then by B's own lights, Person A has the authority to settle the matter for him, and to exclude further deliberation about the matter. If he denies *that*, then he has not made a sincere promise. So long as they both believe that A has a claim against B where that claim yields a protected reason for B to commit the assault, then the functional relationships characterizing the division of agential labor between them remain in place, even if B's commitment to the protected status of that reason is less than perfect.

In summary: Person A and Person B establish an agential division of labor in which A functions as the decider and Person B functions as the doer. Each has this function in virtue of their belief that A's claim against B yields protected reasons for B to act accordingly. That is, each has the function that they do in virtue of the putative authority that A has over B. And that authority is grounded in the promise that B makes and A accepts.

Clearly, both A and B are severally and fully morally responsible for the ensuing assault. Person A is responsible partly in virtue of the causal role she plays in convincing or motivating Person B to commit the assault. But in what follows, I will argue that A is also morally responsible on different grounds: in virtue of the role she plays as the 'decider' and the role Person B plays as the 'doer.' This will have consequences for responsibility in the context of shared action in general, and in war specifically.

30.3.2 Responsibility in an Agential Division of Labor

When Person B commits the assault, his victim is entitled to an explanation of what happened. She has an interest in ascertaining the wrongdoer's *practical reasons* for acting in the way that he did. Whether and why the wrongdoer believed the harm to be warranted is morally relevant to assessing the wrongful conduct.

But what type of practical reason is morally relevant to assessing the conduct? A *fact-relative* practical reason is a practical reason that there actually is – a consideration that counts in favor of acting in a particular way. A *belief-relative* practical reason is a practical reason that a deliberator *takes there to be* in favor of acting in a particular way. To morally evaluate Person B's conduct, his victim would need to know B's belief-relative practical reasons for harming her. That is, she is entitled to demand that he explain what he thought spoke in favor of harming her.

The relevant belief-relative practical reasons are those that the wrongful conduct in question had the function of enacting. The purpose of practical reasoning, is, after all, to normatively guide conduct by determining what ends to pursue and how to pursue them. Concomitantly, the purpose of conduct (or at least intentional conduct) is to enact the practical reasons the actor takes there to be.

Clearly, B's conduct had the function of enacting some of his own practical reasons of which there might be a variety. Person B might have committed the assault partly because he promised to do so, and partly because he enjoyed it, and partly because he was paid to do so, and partly because he wanted to earn Person A's respect, and so on. Suppose, though, that like most people Person B thinks that when we make a promise, we make a commitment to the person to whom we make the promise, and that this gives us a protected reason to fulfill the promise irrespective of whether we benefit from doing so. This isn't to say that B is motivated solely or even mostly by that sense of commitment. Neither does it suggest that B is so committed that he would follow through with the promise even if he thought doing so wouldn't benefit him. Rather, Person B registers the commitment he made as *a* reason – albeit a defeasible one – to fulfill the promise.

But if the relevant belief-relative practical reasons are those that the wrongful conduct in question had the function of enacting, then they will include not only B's reasons, but A's as well, since A has the function of specifying whether B is to commit the assault, and B has the function of acting accordingly, given the division of agential labor the two of them established. Recall that these dovetailing functions arise from the promise which B made and which A accepted; by accepting the promise, A thereby issues a protected reason for B to commit the assault unless A demands otherwise. Recall also that the purpose of intentional conduct in general is to enact the practical reasons we take there to be. So, if A gives B the go-ahead (or otherwise refrains from instructing Person B to stand down), and B subsequently commits the assault, B's conduct will have had the function of enacting the practical reasons A takes there to be in favor of committing the assault.

This means that, if we evaluate conduct by addressing the belief-relative practical reasons that the conduct has the function of enacting, then we ought to evaluate B's conduct *by adverting to A's practical reasons*. So, if the victim wants to know all the belief-relative practical reasons behind the decision to commit the assault, she needs to address not just Person B, but Person A as well. In this way, the practical reasons A takes there to be serve as a basis by which we evaluate what B does. To the extent that the practical reasons A takes there to be are morally problematic, *Person A is responsible for a wrong-making feature of Person B's conduct*. After all, if we evaluate conduct by addressing the belief-relative practical reasons that the conduct has the function of enacting, and if Person A's belief-relative practical reasons are problematic, then Person A has made it so that Person B's conduct is morally problematic as well.

To be clear, the claim here is not that Person A is morally responsible in virtue of having influenced Person B's motivations (though that too might be a basis for moral responsibility). Rather, the basis of Person A's responsibility for Person B's conduct is *constitutive* rather than causal. Person B's conduct has the function of enacting the practical reasons Person A takes there to be; so, by adopting morally problematic practical reasons, Person A, from afar, constitutively determines the purpose of Person B's conduct. Insofar as that morally affects an assessment of Person B's conduct, Person A is on the hook for that difference he makes.

If A is responsible for a wrong-making property of the conduct in this way, then A (in addition to B) is a proper object of the victim's reactive attitudes in response to the wrong she has suffered. The result is that when B fulfills a claim that they both believe A has against B, Person A can be morally responsible for the harm Person B inflicts quite apart from the causal role A plays in that harm. I will call this the 'authority-based argument for moral responsibility.'

Of course, in the example under consideration, A is also *a cause* of B's conduct; so it goes without saying that B's victim can blame not just B but A for the harm she has suffered. In this case, the authority-based grounds for moral responsibility is largely otiose. But in cases of shared action where each participant's causal contribution is morally insignificant, the authority-based grounds for moral responsibility will play an important role in inculpating the participants, especially in war. I turn to this next.

30.4 Shared Action in War

Let us return now to shared action. I argued in section 30.2 that when we undertake a shared action, each participant takes herself to have a claim against every other participant that she does her part in the shared action, where these claims yield what the participants take to be protected reasons to so act. In effect, we each believe that we have authority over the other that they do their part in the shared action. Given the authority-based argument for responsibility in section 30.3, it turns out that each of us is morally responsible for what the other does in the context of shared action, irrespective of our individual causal contributions.

If this account is correct, then causal over-determination (whether concurrent or pre-emptive) in the context of shared activity is no impediment to responsibility. Suppose many individuals together agree to assist one another in furtherance of some shared action ϕ which each of them hopes to promote. Though each participant's contribution to ϕ is negligible, together they achieve ϕ, which, we can suppose, constitutes a substantial harm. On a standard, causal account of moral responsibility, any given participant is responsible at most for her contribution to what she causes, which by hypothesis is negligible. But given the authority-based argument for moral responsibility, any given participant will be potentially responsible for up to the sum total of what all the participants together do, provided that they are participants in shared action.

We have an argument, then, for the view that an individual acting cooperatively with others can be responsible for more than her contribution to what she causes. For example, Haque writes:

> when individuals indirectly or jointly threaten to kill they are *directly* liable [...] In these cases, we do not kill one person to prevent another from killing; instead, we kill one person to prevent her from killing through or with others. It follows that most direct participation in hostilities on behalf of an unjust cause falls within the paradigm case of moral liability to defensive killing.
>
> *(Haque, 2017, p. 66)*

The authority-based argument for moral responsibility can ground this view. Each soldier engaged in shared activity will end up responsible for what the other soldiers do, in virtue of the claim that each has against every other soldier that they act in ways conducive to the shared actions of which they are a part (as discussed in sections 30.2 and 30.3). This means any given soldier is morally responsible for what *other* soldiers do in conformity with the claims she has against *them*; likewise, every other soldier is morally responsible for what *she* does in conformity with the putative claims that they have against *her*.[16]

This authority-based argument for moral responsibility, though, might seem to prove too much when applied to the context of war. It seems to have as a consequence that each soldier is responsible not only for what she does but for what every other soldier on her side does as well. This is because each soldier might be described as participating in the shared activity in which the war itself consists. This would suggest, for example, that a private manning a traffic-control checkpoint, who personally kills no one, is responsible for *all* the deaths that her side causes in that war. Surely this is implausible. Indeed, Haque briefly pauses to consider the possibility that "combatants involved in a collective war effort, irrespective of their function, engage in 'massively shared agency,' coordinated not through mutual responsiveness to each other's intentions and actions but instead through a mutually accepted authority structure that assigns roles and integrates tasks." Accordingly, "[t]hese combatants may be said to collectively pursue unjust war aims." But Haque ultimately rejects this view; "only those combatants who pursue unjust war aims by directly, indirectly, or jointly posing unjust threats are morally liable to defensive killing" (Haque, 2017, p. 90) (footnote omitted).

The authority-based argument for moral responsibility, however, does not have the absurd consequence that each soldier is responsible for the entirety of what her side does. This is because protected reasons can vary in their strength. For example, soldiers in a squad on a reconnaissance mission have authoritative claims against one another in virtue of the shared activity in which they are participating. They also have authoritative claims against other soldiers in other squads, which together compose the platoon of which they are a part, where that platoon in combination with other platoons composes a company, which together with other companies form a battalion, then a brigade, a division, and finally an army. And a soldier in an army has authoritative claims against other combatants in other branches of the military.

But as we telescope outward in this way, the claims the combatants have against others will typically weaken, in that the protected reasons they yield will weaken.[17] Recall that a protected reason to do ϕ is comprised of both a first-order reason to do ϕ, and a second order reason to exclude from deliberation certain reasons against doing ϕ. The constitutive first-order reasons obviously admit of degrees; but the exclusionary reasons do so as well. They admit of degrees by way of the size of the exclusionary zone the second-order reasons set. Depending on how we specify the scalarity of the reasons the authoritative claims yield, there is room for the view that a typical soldier bears little responsibility for what the vast majority of the other combatants fighting in the war do – and yet is responsible, e.g., for what her platoon does on a mission in which she is participating.

There is another way in which the authority-based responsibility avoids the consequence that each combatant is responsible for what every other combatant does. In a hierarchically organized collective command structure, subordinates have the function of following the orders issued by their superiors, but not vice versa. That is to say, the orders superior officers issue to their subordinates are protected, whereas subordinates lack the standing to issue such orders to their superiors.

Given the account I have developed, superiors will be morally responsible for what their subordinates do in conformity with the orders they issue. This isn't to say, though, that subordinates cannot be responsible for what their superiors do. Though subordinates lack the standing to issue specific commands to their superiors, the subordinates still have a general claim against them that they fulfill their most basic roles as superiors. That is, superiors *owe it to their subordinates* that they function as superiors. For example, suppose a captain, *apropos* of nothing, ceases acting as such; his subordinates have the standing to complain. There is, then, a kind of authority that subordinates have over their superiors, albeit quite attenuated in comparison to the authority that the superiors have over them. The upshot is that responsibility will (as we might expect) accrue at the higher echelons of command.

It might seem that when soldiers obey orders, they are not engaging in shared action, properly speaking, with their superiors. After all, the soldier might be wholly unaware of the purpose of the orders she has been given, and as such cannot be described as 'sharing an end' with her superior. These cases seem more akin to proxy agency than shared agency, insofar as the subordinate is implementing the will of the superior rather than implementing what they together will. But a subordinate obeying the orders of a superior might still be described as participating in a shared action in the following sense: the soldier knows that the only way to achieve certain ends – such as accomplishing a mission, or winning a war, or protecting the country – is to defer to her superiors. Under this description, she does indeed share an end with her superiors; it so happens that the best way to help achieve that end is by deferring to them.

What about soldiers, though, who are largely alienated from those aims? They might not care whether the mission is achieved, the war is won, or the country protected. In this case, the soldier's superior is still inculpated in what the soldier does *qua* soldier, given the authority-based argument for responsibility. Likewise, the soldier will still be inculpated in what her comrades do when they act their part by virtue of the claim she has – whether she exercises it or not – that they do their part accordingly.

This is, of course, just the beginning of developing an account of cooperative responsibility in war. The armed forces of technologically advanced countries are immensely complicated institutions; that complexity is imported into how warfare is organized, administrated, and executed. I have here only scratched the surface of how authority-based moral responsibility might apply to responsibility in the context of warfare. But I hope to have shown that this principle can provide war ethicists operating within a revisionist account of the morality of war with the resources for showing that an individual soldier in a war can be responsible for more than what she causes or the difference she makes. The result is that even those soldiers who contribute little or nothing to an unjust aim of which she is a part can be morally liable to be targeted. This helps dissolve the pragmatic difficulty with which we began: that of determining who is and isn't morally liable given the revisionist account of war.

Notes

1 But see Lazar (2010).

2 See Lepora and Goodin (2013, p. 8), and Miller (2006, pp. 177–178, 181), who adopt versions of this view.

3 One might try to causally ground the claim that each soldier is responsible for what they together do in the following way. Any given soldier participates because other soldiers participate. In this respect, each soldier exerts a small, aggregable causal influence on every other soldier. (This is assuming we can make sense of degrees of causation. For a recent overview of this issue, see Kaiserman [2018]). But even then, each soldier will end up responsible for only a small fraction of what they together do, which will likely fall short of what's necessary for liability to be killed.

4 For helpful discussion, see Shapiro (2002), Owens (2008), and Westlund (2011).

5 For helpful discussion, see Shapiro (2002, pp. 406–407) and Owens (2008).

6 See (Owens 2008, 2012) for an extended discussion of promise-making as conferring authority.

7 Gilbert uses the mutual obligation condition to criticize accounts that analyze shared activity in terms of "personal intentions" (Gilbert, 2008), such as that defended by Bratman (see below).

8 For more on the 'bipolar normativity' characteristic of directed obligations, see Darwall (2004). See also Roth (2004) who characterizes the obligations characteristic of shared activity in terms of "contralateral commitments."

9 Of course, as a matter of *morality*, more deliberation would be required if the shared activity or my role in it is morally wrongful. But there would be nothing *practically* problematic in treating the matter as settled given that I have already made myself party to the joint commitment.

10 On Gilbert's view, hierarchically organized shared activity would itself be established by further shared activity (Gilbert, 2008, p. 180).

11 Of course, we need a way to determine what exactly counts as 'your part' in the shared activity. For more on this, see the discussion of Bratman in the next section.

12 For example, if my subplan is to bake the cake with frosting, and your subplan is to bake a chocolate-flavored cake, and I have no preference about the cake's flavor and you have no preference about frosting, then our subplans mesh. The result is the following account of shared intention. We intend to J if and only if:

1. (a) I intend that we J and (b) you intend that we J.

2. I intend that we J in accordance with and because of 1a, 1b, and the meshing subplans of 1a and 1b; you intend the same.
3. 1 and 2 are common knowledge.

13 See Scanlon (1998, p. 304). For discussion of Scanlon's principle as it relates to shared activity, see Shiffrin (2008). For discussion of mutual obligation in the context of shared action, see Roth (2004).

14 Some, in addition to Gilbert, have criticized Bratman's account on this point. See for example Roth (2004).

15 There is space for views between Gilbert's account (in which shared mutual obligations are constitutive of shared activity) and Bratman's view (in which shared activity only contingently results in mutual obligations). For example, Facundo Alonso (2009) argues that we can accommodate the normative significance of shared intention without having to claim that interpersonal obligations are constitutive of shared intention; instead, on his view, shared intentions necessarily present a *basis* for interpersonal obligations.

16 The authority implicit in shared action has an important feature in common with a Razian service-conception of authority: both yield protected reasons. See Raz (1979). But there are important differences. According to the service conception, soldiers are morally required to defer to their superiors only if by doing so they are *more* likely to do what's right than they would be if they acted on their own judgment. The deference characteristic of normative agentive functions, on the other hand, is established by the decision to participate in shared action.

17 This depends on much more than how the military is organized; for example, a particular battalion in the army might happen to work more closely with a particular Air Force wing than they do with other battalions – the strength of the authoritative claims that the involved combatants have against one another will reflect that fact. For more analysis see Bazargan (2012).

References

Alonso, F., 2009. Shared Intention, Reliance, and Interpersonal Obligations. *Ethics*, 119, pp. 444–475.

Bazargan, S., 2012. Complicitous Liability in War. *Philosophical Studies* 165(1):177–195.

Bratman, M., 1992. Shared Cooperative Activity. *The Philosophical Review*, 101(2), pp. 327–341.

Bratman, M., 1993. Shared Intention. *Ethics*, 104, pp. 97–113.

Bratman, M., 1999. Shared Intentions and Mutual Obligation. In: *Faces of Intention*. Cambridge: Cambridge University Press, pp. 130–141.

Darwall, S., 2004. *Respect and the Second Person Standpoint*. Proceedings and Addresses of the American Philosophical Association, pp. 43–59.

Dill, J. & Shue, H., 2012. Limiting the Killing in War: Military Necessity and the St. Petersburg Assumption. *Ethics & International Affairs*, 26(3), pp. 311–333.

Gilbert, M., 1989. *On Social Facts*. Princeton, NJ: Princeton University Press.

Gilbert, M., 1990. Walking Together: A Paradigmatic Social Phenomenon. *Midwest Studies in Philosophy*, 15(1), pp. 1–14.

Gilbert, M., 1999. Obligation and Joint Commitment. *Utilitas*, 11, pp. 143–163.

Gilbert, M., 2006. *A Theory of Political Obligation*. Oxford: Oxford University Press.

Gilbert, M., 2008. Two Approaches to Shared Intention: An Essay in the Philosophy of Social Phenomena. *Analyze & Kritik*, 30, pp. 483–514.

Gilbert, M., 2009. Shared Intention and Personal Intention. *Philosophical Studies*, 144, pp. 167–187.

Haque, A., 2017. *Law and Morality at War*. Oxford: Oxford University Press.

Hart, H., 1990. Commands and Authoritative Legal Reasons. In: *Authority*. New York City: New York University Press, pp. 92–114.

Kaiserman, A., 2018. 'More of a Cause': Recent Work on Degrees of Causation and Responsibility. *Philosophy Compass*, 13(7), pp. 1–10.

Lazar, S., 2010. The Responsibility Dilemma For Killing in War - A Review Essay. *Philosophy & Public Affairs*, 38(2), pp. 180–213.

Lepora, C. & Goodin, R. E., 2013. *On Complicity and Compromise*. Oxford: Oxford University Press.

McMahan, J., 2009. *Killing in War*. New York: Oxford University Press.

Miller, S., 2006. Collective Moral Responsibility: An Individualist Account. In: P. A. French, ed. *Midwest Studies in Philosophy*. Minneapolis, MN: Wiley Blackwell, pp. 176–193.

Owens, D., 2008. Rationalism About Obligation. *European Journal of Philosophy*, 16(3), pp. 403–431.

Owens, D., 2012. *Shaping the Normative Landscape.* Oxford: Oxford University Press.
Raz, J., 1977. Promises and Obligations. In: *Law, Morality and Society: Essays in Honour of H.L.A. Hart.* Oxford: Clarendon Press.
Raz, J., 1979. *The Authority of Law.* Oxford: Clarendon Press.
Raz, J., 1986. *The Morality of Freedom.* Oxford: Oxford University Press.
Raz, J., 1990. *Practical Reasons and Norms.* Princeton, NJ: Princeton University Press.
Roth, A., 2004. Shared Agency and Contralateral Commitments. *The Philosophical Review*, 113(3), pp. 359–410.
Scanlon, T., 1998. *What We Owe to Each Other.* Cambridge, MA: Harvard University Press.
Shapiro, S., 2002. Authority. In: *The Oxford Handbook of Jurisprudence.* Oxford: Oxford University Press, pp. 382–339.
Shiffrin, S., 2008. Promising, Intimate Relationships, and Conventionalism. *Philosophical Review*, 117(4), pp. 481–524.
Solis, G. D., 2010. *The Law of Armed Conflict: International Humanitarian Law in War.* New York: Cambridge University Press.
Strawser, B. J., 2011. Walking the Tightrope of Just War. *Analysis*, 71(3), pp. 533–544.
Walzer, M., 2000. *Just and Unjust Wars: A Moral Argument With Historical Illustrations.* 3rd ed. New York City: Basic Books.
Westlund, A., 2011. Autonomy, Authority, and Answerability. *Jurisprudence*, 2(1), pp. 161–179.

31
COLLECTIVE DUTIES OF BENEFICENCE

Violetta Igneski

Bystanders who have witnessed a car accident have a duty to call for help and to coordinate their efforts to pull the injured to safety. The member states of the United Nations have an obligation to collaborate and find sustainable ways to reduce extreme poverty and fulfill the UN Sustainable Development Goals. The European Union must enact and implement a plan to humanely protect refugees fleeing war zones and landing at their borders and shores.[1] When we make these intuitively plausible claims, we are saying that as long as the groups or collectivities in each of these scenarios (i.e., bystanders, member states, the EU) can, within reasonable limits, rescue the injured, fulfill the SDGs or protect the endangered refugees, they have a duty to do so.[2] More specifically, we are saying that these groups have collective duties of beneficence.

It has long been argued that keeping the analysis of moral responsibility and obligation solely at the level of individuals fails to capture significant normative elements of situations where groups have acted together to bring about collective harms and wrongs for which no individual can be held responsible. The literature in collective responsibility considers what kinds of groups can be held responsible; the conditions under which groups can be said to be responsible agents; and also, how (and when) responsibility distributes to its individual members (Cripps 2013; French 1984; Isaacs 2011; Kutz 2000; May 1992). More recently, a parallel debate has emerged that explores not what groups can be held responsible for (in a backward-looking sense), but rather, whether and under what conditions groups or collectives have responsibilities (in a forward-looking sense)—or what I will be calling "duties" or "obligations." Though we commonly say that groups like bystanders or the UN member states have moral duties, either to refrain from violating rights or causing harms, or even to act together to prevent harms or protect rights, how should we understand these obligations? Notice that it is one thing to say that a corporation such as British Petroleum (BP) violated duties (certainly legal, plausibly also moral) when its negligent and reckless actions led to a deadly explosion and a devastating oil spill in the Gulf of Mexico, and quite another to say that the affluent or perhaps all of humanity, as a group, have a duty to end extreme poverty.

The focus of this chapter will be on making sense of these latter, more controversial claims, that unstructured groups or collectivities that are not agents (or at least not yet agents) can have obligations—that is, collective obligations of beneficence—and that these collective obligations have moral implications for the members of these groups. This is a challenge because it is commonly accepted that only moral agents have obligations, and none of the groups of bystanders, the UN member states or the European Union states are (collective) moral agents. So we must either be prepared to surrender these intuitively plausible judgments, or else explain why it is that these collectivities and their individual members are obligated to do anything at all.

I have three main aims in this chapter. My first aim is to motivate the idea that there is something normatively significant about collective duties of beneficence such that our moral and political theorizing must broaden its focus beyond individual duties. My second aim is to give an overview of the current debates on collective duties of beneficence with a particular focus on unstructured collectives or groups as duty-bearers. In doing so, I set out three different ways of conceiving of the collective duties of unstructured collectives: as the duties of a group entity, as the duties of individuals taken jointly, or as an aggregate of individual duties. After surveying these various views, I defend the idea that even when the collectivities we are concerned with are not group *agents*, when there is evidence that the group of individuals has the necessary capacity to prevent a harm or wrong and the individuals are aware (or should be aware) of this, they have a duty, as a group, to prevent that harm or wrong. And it is this duty of the group *qua* group that explains and grounds the duties of its individual members. My third and final aim is to consider a few important questions that arise for individual agents concerned about what their individual obligations are given their part in various collectivities.

To start, I will unpack the concept of collective duties of beneficence: they are *duties of beneficence*; and they are held by *collectives*.

31.1 Duties of Beneficence

Moral agents, individual and collective, are bearers of many different types of duties: there are legal duties, contractually specified duties, duties not to harm, remedial duties, and many others. My focus in this chapter will be on duties of *beneficence*. In a general sense, duties of beneficence are moral duties to benefit someone or make them better off. They are typically considered to be *positive duties* in the sense that they require duty-bearers to take certain actions, and are contrasted with *negative duties* to refrain from certain actions. So, if one agent punches another in the face or dumps oil in the ocean, she has violated a negative duty she has not to harm. But if an agent passes by a drowning child or hears of a famine in her region, assuming she has the necessary capacity to help, she has a positive duty to do what she can to help. Though negative duties may have more widespread acceptance (even among libertarians and egoists), positive duties of beneficence hold a prominent position in the dominant normative theories (among them are utilitarianism, sophisticated consequentialism, Kantianism, virtue ethics, pluralistic deontological theories, etc.). That is, on almost any ethical theory, agents have a duty to rescue the drowning child or contribute to famine relief within a certain limit of risk and cost. While the existence of duties of beneficence is virtually uncontested, their thresholds and limits are still the subject of vigorous and healthy philosophical debate.

In this chapter, I understand duties of beneficence in a narrower sense: not as duties to make people better off in general, but as duties to provide for each other's most basic needs or the preconditions of our agency. Another way of putting this is that there is a distinction to be made between duties to make someone better off and duties to aid. Barbara Herman (1984) puts the distinction in a helpful way when she distinguishes between helping someone pursue their ends and enabling them to be pursuers of their ends: she calls the latter "a duty of mutual aid." The duty to aid takes priority over the duty (if there is such a duty) to help a friend pay for a well-deserved vacation or help a stranger build a monument to their god (Scanlon 1975). This narrower duty to aid generally aligns with the commonsense usage of duties of beneficence.

How one justifies and grounds moral duties will vary depending on one's normative commitments. I will take it as granted that there are moral duties, but I will specify briefly two preconditions of the existence of moral obligations that will be especially relevant in the debate about collective duties of beneficence. The first is the *agency condition*, according to which only (moral) agents can bear moral obligations. Agents can deliberate, respond, and act on the basis of reasons, so it is appropriate to hold them accountable for the actions they undertake and also to demand that they act in certain ways and follow certain norms. As will become evident, not all of the groups that we might think are subject to moral obligations are actually moral agents. So, we need to consider whether we should reject or modify the agency condition, or modify our intuitive judgments. The second is the *capacity condition* according to which only agents with the capacity to perform an act or meet a goal can have an obligation with respect to that act or goal. This condition is in line with the commonly accepted "ought implies can" precept. As we will see, we might agree with former UN Secretary General Ban Ki Moon's famous assertion that "we are the first generation in human history that can end extreme poverty" but wonder if it necessarily means that this is something we can immediately accomplish. And if this highly dispersed and unstructured group must engage in significant coordination and take many steps before it is able to meet such a lofty goal, we may wonder if we ought to judge it to have the requisite capacity now. And if not, we may wonder if it is possible for humanity to have a collective duty at all.

31.2 Collective Duties or Duties of Collectives

Before we go into the details of how to best conceive of collective duties of beneficence, we might ask what necessitates discussing *collective* duties at all that could not be fully expressed by discussing individual duties. A great number of global problems such as extreme poverty, climate change, and the refugee crisis require collective solutions if they are ever to be solved. If we think that there is a moral imperative to solve these problems, the question arises, who is morally obligated to do something about it? When the harms or wrongs at issue are discrete instances that can be addressed by an individual, we may look to specific individuals to address them. In such instances, the attribution of an obligation to an individual agent is straightforward. But when the harms and wrongs are widespread and on a large scale, or when there simply are no individuals with the capacity to respond, addressing them requires a collective solution.

The general idea that aiding the needy requires the coordination and collaboration of a great number of people, and so should be conceived of as a collective duty, is not a new idea, but it has not been subject to the same level of scrutiny in the past as it has in recent years. Liam Murphy, for one, has written about beneficence as a cooperative project rather than an individual aim (2003). On Murphy's view, beneficence is a shared duty and its demands are distributed across all persons in fair shares, such that the compliance effects are distributed equally. Notice that even though Murphy is talking about a collective duty, he does not impute the existence of a group or collective agent that has a duty. The duty-bearers are individuals. The focus of Murphy's analysis is to show that by conceiving of beneficence as a collective enterprise, the demands on individuals would (likely) turn out to be less onerous than on more traditional consequentialist accounts. Though the collective duty of beneficence is at the center of his account, the duty-bearers are individuals and their duties of beneficence are duties to take on a share of the collective project.

Garrett Cullity (2004) has also argued that in response to global poverty and great need we have collective duties of beneficence. The duties are collective on his view mainly because the problem is vast, and addressing it requires a collective solution such as building effective and efficient development agencies and supporting them financially. For Cullity, the moral requirement of beneficence starts as an individual aim (that we have in common with others) and becomes a collective aim when we see we can achieve it more effectively together. Overall, Cullity's view that individuals have shares of a collective duty (that increase in conditions of partial compliance) seems to be individualistic in the sense that he does not impute the existence of a group that has a collective duty that is then distributed to individual members. But, unlike Murphy, he makes certain comments that gesture toward the possibility of a more collectivist interpretation: consider when he says there is a collective requirement for which "we together are the subject" (Cullity 2004: 60). That said, neither Cullity nor Murphy have much to say about the nature of collective duties or how to understand the subject of the envisioned collective duty.

A deeper analysis is important because not just any type or form of collective is a candidate for bearing duties. Do all the women in the world count as a relevant collective that can bear a moral duty? Perhaps not; but the corporation Microsoft does. What about the fans at a Blue Jays game? It is important to work out what features are necessary for groups to be considered appropriate candidates for duty-bearing. And even those collectivities that turn out to be appropriate candidates will likely differ in terms of whether and how their collective duties distribute to their members based on their structure.

31.3 Structured and Unstructured Collectives and Collective Duties

Corporations and other highly structured organizations are moral agents due to their collective intentional structures that are expressed through their policies, decision-making procedures, and actions (Erskine 2003; French 1979; 1984; Isaacs 2011; Pettit 2007; Tollefsen 2015). Peter French (1979) has argued that it is the corporate structure that grounds the corporate agency of the collective rather than the intentions of the individual members. Expanding on this view, Christian List and Philip Pettit (2006; List 2011) developed an account of group agency, according to which group agents have the ability to form representational or goal-seeking states; are rational; and have the capacity to act and intervene in the world. Moreover, group agents are novel agents, in the sense that they have their own intentional structures that are not simply reducible to the intentions of their individual members, such that the group may hold judgments and take actions that are not directly continuous with the individual judgments and actions of its constituent members. They can have their own beliefs, desires, and intentions; respond to reasons, deliberate, and act; and, as such, can be the proper subject of normative demands. Kendy M. Hess and Gunnar Björnsson (2014) further argue that collective agents have the capacities required for reactive attitudes (such as guilt or indignation) that some claim are necessary for moral agency.

Philosophers such as Margaret Gilbert (1990), Michael Bratman (1999), Christopher Kutz (2000), Seumas Miller (2001), and Raimo Tuomela (2007), among many significant others, have further expanded the class of collective agents beyond highly structured corporate agents, each in their own way, to include collectivities considered to be agents in virtue of their members' commitments to a joint goal, or their shared, collective or participatory intentions toward a joint or shared goal aimed at a collective act. We can call the collective agents in this broad category that pursue joint goals through collective actions, such as a group of friends painting a house or the group that perpetrated the Rwandan genocide, "goal-oriented collectives" (Isaacs 2011). Though less structured than corporations, it is their collective intentional structures that give rise to collective intentions and collective actions.[3] Tracy Isaacs (2011) adopts a strongly collectivist and non-reductive version of this view to advance her argument that there are two distinct levels of responsibility (collective and individual) in the case of both corporations and goal-oriented collectives, and that responsibility is not simply reducible to the individual responsibility of the members.

Collective or group agents are subject to moral duties just as individuals are. But not all collectivities will meet the criteria necessary for the group to be deemed sufficiently organized or to hold the necessary attitudes and capacities to be considered an agent. Consider again a group of bystanders witnessing a car accident where a victim remains trapped; a group of states that have unwillingly received an influx of refugees at their borders; and all of humanity who has the capacity to bring an end to extreme global poverty. None of these collectivities is a collective *agent*, and claiming that these unstructured groups have moral obligations seems to run afoul of the agency condition. Nonetheless, it is common to think that these collectivities—what some consider to only be random groups—have certain obligations towards the accident victim, the refugees, and the impoverished, respectively; and that accordingly, they ought to get together, develop a plan to respond, and act on it.

The question is how we should understand the claim that these unstructured (non-agent) groups and their individual members have a collective duty. Is the collective duty not really a duty of a collective, but merely an aggregate of the duties of the individuals, and thus fully reducible to individual obligation? Is it a duty of the individuals jointly, such that the duty is not entirely reducible to the individual obligations of the individual members? Or is it the duty of a collective entity or group, distinct in a significant way from the duties of the individual members? I will consider each of these ways of understanding collective duties (and their duty-bearers) in unstructured group contexts, highlighting some of the more prominent challenges and criticisms that have been raised against each (Schwenkenbecher 2018).

The first view is a reductive individualistic view (hereafter, simply the individualistic view) of collective duty, because it views the duty of a collectivity simply as the duties of the individual members to do something (individually) themselves (Collins 2013; Lawford-Smith 2012). So, in the case of the car accident, if we say the bystanders have a duty to rescue the trapped victim, what we are saying is that each of the bystanders has a duty to do their part in the action required for the rescue. This may entail helping to organize the group so they can act effectively together and participate in the rescue effort by each doing one's part. In the case of global poverty, it may entail working with others to form effective group agents and make individual contributions toward the collective goal of ending poverty.

One strength of the individualistic view is that it isn't vulnerable to the agency objection. Even though the collectivity is unstructured and isn't a collective agent, there is no denying that each of the individual bystanders is an agent. Given that the individualist does not posit the existence of any group entity, the demands are placed solely on the individuals and the analysis is kept at the level of individual duties. However, the individualist is left to explain what is demanded of each individual bystander and how these individual obligations come about.

Assuming that no individual bystander has the capacity to rescue the person trapped in the car, while also respecting the capacity condition, it would follow that no individual has a duty to rescue the victim. But this leads to an apparent weakness of the individualistic view: namely, contrary to what we might expect, there is no entity that has *a duty to rescue the victim*, even if the group of bystanders can easily do so by working together. The only candidate for the duty to rescue is an agent that has the capacity to carry it out, but here, there is no such agent. The individualist will only say that there are a number of individual agents that have individual duties to contribute their parts. But we might ask, what is their contributory obligation a part of? And how do the individuals come to have their individual duties? Such a duty could only exist in a collective context where there are others who also have parts to play. But put in individualistic terms, if none of the individuals do their parts (or not enough of them do) and the victim isn't rescued, no one can be held to account for failing to rescue because no one had a duty with that content. At most, each individual can be blamed for failing to do her part. The disadvantage of this conception is that it doesn't fully capture the nature and scale of the moral demands that impinge on the group—that is, to rescue the trapped person. The individualist can bite the bullet here and say this is the best we can do in cases where there is no collective agent. But others may see the fact that no agent holds a duty to rescue (nor can be held accountable for the failure to rescue) as reason to reject the individualistic view.

Another problem for the individualistic view arises out of the conditional nature of the individual obligations. That is, if we assume that coordinated or collective action is required to effect the rescue and that an individual's action in isolation won't have any effect, individuals would only have duties to do their parts in the rescue if the other bystanders do their parts. I can hold up one end of a heavy crowbar to try to pry open the doors of the car, but unless someone else picks up the other end, there is no compelling reason for me to do so. The individualist could not say that the two of us are still obligated to act together to rescue. Thus, when the collective duty is fully reducible to a series of conditional individual duties, we are unable to capture the idea that the bystanders have a duty to aid, and that their resulting duty remains even when some do not participate. It may very well turn out that there is nothing effective that the remaining individuals can do, and so, after communicating their readiness and trying to pursue other potentially effective avenues, there is nothing they can do that will help. In response, the individualist would not merely say that these (well-intentioned) individuals aren't blameworthy for failing to act because there was nothing they could do, but would say that they aren't blameworthy because they never had a duty to act.

The next two views I consider are both non-reductive, and so each, in its own way, aims to capture the idea that there is more to a collective obligation than an aggregation of individual duties. I'll first consider the view that understands the collective duty as a joint duty that the individuals have to perform together. Then, I'll turn to the view that understands the collective duty as a collective duty of a group *qua* group. On these views, the individual duty to contribute to the collective goal arises from and is explained by the joint or collective obligation (Cripps 2013; Erskine 2003; Igneski 2018; Schwenkenbecher 2014; Wringe 2005).

A plausible way of understanding the obligation of the bystanders or the UN member states is as a joint duty that they (i.e., the bystanders and the member states) have to perform an action (or actions) together. The idea is that when a group of individuals, jointly, has the capacity to perform a morally mandatory action (such as save an accident victim), they have a joint duty to do so. On this view, the collective duty isn't fully reducible to a series of individual duties to do one's part, but rather, the individuals jointly have a collective obligation; that is, the collective obligation is a joint obligation or, as it is sometimes put, a shared obligation (Björnsson 2014; List and Pettit 2006; Pinkert 2014; Schwenkenbecher 2014). We can also refer to this view as a "non-reductive individualistic" view. "Non-reductive" because individuals don't just act individually toward the shared goal, but "act with the belief that others contribute to that same goal and with the intention to jointly perform an action" (Schwenkenbecher 2014: 62); and "individualistic" because even though the duty is shared, it falls only onto individuals.

When a group of individuals acts jointly, there is something that they do together, apart from their individual actions, an action that they together perform (Pettit and Schweikard 2006: 21). And when a group of individuals has an obligation to act jointly, there is something that they have an obligation to do together, apart from their individual obligations—an action that they together are obligated to perform. This view is able to capture the common intuition that when there is a collective duty, it will typically target a collective action, an action beyond the reach of any individual agent.

In recent work, Anne Schwenkenbecher develops the joint duty view, giving the following proposal: a plurality of agents *a*, *b*, and *c* have a collective moral obligation if

> (1) There exists a specific morally significant joint-necessity problem *P*, such that agents *a*, *b*, and *c* can collectively, but not individually, address *P*.
> (2) Conscientious moral deliberation leads all of them (or a sufficiently large sub-set of them) to believe that some collectively available option *O* is morally optimal with regard to *P*.
> (3) *A*, *b*, and *c* (or a sufficiently large sub-set of them) are in a position to determine individual (or joint) strategies to realize *O* and to achieve *P*.
>
> *(2018: 19)*

One advantage of the joint duty account is that it gives us a more intuitively appealing way of conceiving of the content of the collective duty than did the individualistic account. Where the individualist was unable to say that, in the case of a failure to act, a duty to rescue was violated (instead only being able to say that individual persons failed to do their individual parts), on the joint duty account, the individuals jointly have a duty to rescue and if they fail to act jointly to rescue, they violate their collective duty. The "they" here are the individuals jointly.

Another advantage of the joint duty account is that it is not vulnerable to the agency objection because the individual participants are all agents. However, it is important to note that unlike the individualist who reduces the collective duty into a series of individual duties, on the joint duty view, the collective duty is not simply reducible to an aggregation of individual obligations, insofar as there is a collective duty in which the group of individuals shares. That said, there is no talk of the duty of groups as such, over and above the duty of the individual participants. As Schwenkenbecher puts it: "talking of 'groups' seems quite superfluous" (2018: 118).

The individualist will think that the joint duty account goes too far in the collectivist direction when it resists reducing collective obligations to a collection of individual obligations. But the collectivist will question whether conceiving of responsibility or obligation as a joint duty of the individual participants is able to sufficiently explain how it is that the individuals have obligations without recognizing a distinct and prior collective obligation from which they are derived.

More robustly collectivist accounts take the duty-bearer of the collective obligation to be a collective entity. Virginia Held has argued that an unstructured group, or what she calls a "random collection," can be held morally responsible for "its failure to act as a group" (1970: 477). Her central example is of a group of passengers on a train that fails to prevent a murder when they can easily have done so. For Held, a random collection of individuals is responsible for failing to act "when the action called for in a given situation is obvious to the reasonable person and when the expected outcome of the action is clearly favorable" (1970: 478). Though reasoning about backward-looking responsibility, if we extend her claims to forward-looking responsibility or obligation, we would say that an unstructured group can have an obligation to perform an act.

Bill Wringe, with his more expansive understanding of what unstructured collectivities can hold duties, has argued that humanity, as a whole, is a global collective with a collective obligation (2014). On his account, the obligations of individual human beings are derived by and explained by the prior obligations of the collective of which they are a part (Wringe 2010). Applying this interpretation to the scenario we have been considering: it is the group "bystanders witnessing the accident" that holds an obligation to rescue the trapped victim, and each bystander has a derivative individual obligation to do her part in the collective response.

Even if a collectivist were to consider humanity to be a global collective, this does not imply that she is taking the view that humanity is an agent (say, in light of its internal intentional structure or collective decision-procedure) as surely it is not (at least not before they commit to a collective goal and pursue it together). It is open to the collectivist to view the unstructured collective as a putative or potential collective agent, either along the lines of a potential goal-oriented collective or, in some instances, a potential highly structured organization. Either way, the main claim is that we have good normative and explanatory reasons to recognize two distinct levels of obligation—the collective and the individual—such that there is a collective obligation that falls on the collectivity, and also a derivative individual obligation that falls on the individual members.

The collectivist view is intuitively appealing because it captures the idea that there is a collective or group that has a duty to rescue, and that if the individual members fail to act, they—together, as a group—violate the duty to rescue. Of course, if the group under consideration was already a group agent there would be no worry. But when the collective is a group of bystanders or all of humanity, we must consider how it fares against the agency objection.

There are a few different ways one might respond to the agency worry. Wringe has one response: we should distinguish between the entity to which the obligation is addressed and the entity that is the duty-bearer. Doing so allows us to say that we address all of humanity (as a group) with the duty to end global poverty and that individual persons—who have the requisite agency to bear duties—are the duty-bearers. Thus, on his view, potential agents that are currently unstructured collectivities can be the subjects of actual duties (Wringe 2010; 2014).

Another approach is to attribute the collective obligation to a *putative* collective agent instead. Putative groups are groups "in which people are sometimes capable of acting in concert but in which no formal organization exists" (May 1992: 109). Larry May claims that if a putative group participates in harm through inaction, the members share responsibility, but he follows Held by endorsing an exception for cases of putative groups that could have developed a sufficient structure in time to avoid inaction (*Id.*). In this latter case, collective responsibility can attach to the putative group.[4]

In order to avoid the difficulties of a view that attributes actual obligations to putative agents, Isaacs (2011) modifies May's view and attributes putative collective obligations to putative collective agents. For example, the member states of the UN may not currently constitute a group agent, but we can consider them as a putative agent; and, once the members take the necessary steps, they will become an actual agent. This route avoids the agency objection rather than responding to it, since it doesn't dispute that it is only collective agents that have actual obligations. The challenge with this interpretation is then to show how it is that individual members get actual obligations. Deriving actual individual obligations from actual collective obligations is one thing, but deriving actual individual obligations from putative collective obligations is tricky. And it seems that this is exactly what is required in order to explain why individuals have obligations to form actual collectives that can be the bearers of actual duties.

I want to suggest that in the cases of the bystanders, the EU, and the UN member states, all instances where it is reasonable to hold that the collectivity has the capacity to meet a morally mandatory goal, the collectivity has an actual collective duty to do so. We would only say that an unstructured group has the capacity to act in some way if it has the capacity, through the actions of its members, to become sufficiently organized to so act. On this view, we would say that the collectivity currently has mediated capacity and once its members take the necessary steps (such as coordinating and collectivizing), they will have immediate capacity (Igneski 2018; Pinkert 2014). The collective's mediated capacity gives individual members (who are agents) reason to act to take the necessary steps required for the group to become an effective collective agent.

Take humanity as an example. We do not think that humanity is an agent, nor that it has the immediate capacity to end poverty. However (and I will assume that this is true), there is good evidence to think that if human beings were to take steps to coordinate and organize (something I'm also assuming here that they have the capacity to do), they could together, as a group, effectively act to end poverty. Moreover, human beings can reasonably be expected to know that there are steps that they can take to achieve this goal. This gives humanity an actual duty to end poverty and gives human beings individual duties to take the necessary steps to becoming an effective collective agent.

Recall my earlier reference to the UN General Secretary's assertion that we are the first generation in human history with the capacity to end poverty. Unless we have reason to dispute this assertion or to think that we are unable to organize ourselves to act effectively, we can say it follows that humanity has an obligation to end poverty. Notice that we could not have said this 200 years ago, as 200 years ago, humanity did not even have the mediated capacity to end poverty, given how widespread poverty was and given the lack of capacity for global communication and coordination.

This response challenges the agency condition because it holds that to have a moral obligation it is sufficient that one is a potential agent. But it is important to reiterate that not just any potential agent can bear an obligation. An unstructured group, which is composed of a plurality of individual agents, can only be the subject of moral obligations if it has the capacity to act to meet a morally mandatory goal, even if intervening steps must first be taken by the individuals that compose the group to enhance the group's capacity to take immediate action. It is the very fact that the group as such is capable (even in a mediated sense) that obligates the individuals to take the intervening steps in the first place.

Wringe makes a similar point when he says "it seems plausible that if a collective is (merely) a potential agent, it is capable of doing any of the things which it would have the capacity to do if it were appropriately organized" (Wringe 2014: 176). As long as we consider the unstructured group to have the capacity to act intentionally, even if it is a mediated capacity, we should consider it to have sufficient capacity and agency (initially in a potential state) to be the bearer of moral duties.

31.4 Individual Duties to Collectivize and to Contribute to the Collective Goal

All the views I have surveyed, even those that reject the idea that non-agent groups can have duties, will agree that individuals can have duties with respect to collective goals like rescuing accident victims. Where they differ is in their explanation of why the individuals have those duties. The individualist will say that they are individual duties all the way down, whereas the joint duty and collective duty accounts will derive the individual duties from joint duties and collective duties respectively.

Given that the collectives are unstructured and that, practically, the members must act to sufficiently organize themselves to achieve their collective goal and discharge their duties, there is both a practical and moral imperative to do so. Held was willing to hold a random collection of individuals responsible for failing to act when the called-for action was obvious and the outcome was clearly favorable; however, she also argued that when

> the action called for is not obvious to the reasonable person, a random collection may not be held responsible for not performing the act in question, but, in some cases, may be held responsible for not forming itself into an organized group capable of deciding which action to take.
>
> (1970: 476)

Stephanie Collins (2013) calls these "collectivization duties": they are duties individuals have, to take steps toward forming a collective that can achieve the collective goal. This is a duty the individuals have to transform the group so they are immediately capable of achieving their moral goal. This might entail forming a goal-oriented collective agent or, in some cases, a more highly structured organization. And, in addition to the individual duty to collectivize, and while the collectivity is in the process of collectivizing, we can further add that, when individual members are capable of making a contribution, they also have duties to contribute to the collective goal "in the meantime" (Igneski 2018). For example, a UN member state such as Canada, who has the necessary resources, will have an obligation to do its part to contribute to the UN Sustainable Development Goal of providing clean drinking water to all persons, while it is waiting for the international community to sufficiently organize and develop the necessary infrastructure and institutions to meet it together in its entirety.

The discussion thus far has engaged with some of the main theoretical debates surrounding collective duties of beneficence. Beyond these more foundational questions, there are many unresolved issues and questions that remain. In the final section of this chapter, I will address two sets of pressing questions pertaining to collective duties of beneficence that arise from the perspective of individual members. The first set asks how responsibility for the failure to fulfill a collective duty of beneficence distributes to individual members: is the collective responsible; the individual members; or both? What are they responsible for? And to what extent can they be blamed for their failures? The second set asks if the failure of some members to fulfill their share of the collective duty increases the shares of complying members who have already done their fair shares, such that they are morally required to do more. And relatedly, are individual obligations conditional upon the participation of others?

31.5 Individual Responsibility for Failing to Fulfill the Collective Duty of Beneficence

As can be expected, one's answer to who is responsible for failing to fulfill a collective duty of beneficence will depend on one's conception of collectives and the particular type of collective involved. Corporations and other such highly structured group agents are the most straightforward. The group itself, like any other agent, is held responsible for failures to fulfill their duties. I mentioned earlier that one feature of corporate agents is that responsibility does not always distribute to its members. But this does not mean that individuals do not hold any responsibility at the individual level. The group's formal decision-making procedures and various other structures distribute responsibility to members relative to their role in the organization. Consider again BP's reckless and negligent actions leading to a deadly explosion and a massive marine oil spill that killed 11 workers and countless marine wildlife, and caused significant and ongoing environmental damage. The corporation, a collective agent, was held morally and legally (including criminally) responsible for the harms it caused. This moral and legal liability did not translate to the individual liability of its individual members.[5] That's not to say that certain corporate leaders and decision-makers and others in relevant roles were not morally responsible, but certainly, the responsibility of the collective did not distribute automatically or equally to all members and perhaps not at all to some (take, for instance, an intern whose job it was to answer the phones).

A parallel point can be made for positive duties of beneficence. When the collective agent is a corporation, the corporation is responsible, as a group, for failing to fulfill the duty of beneficence, and some of its members will be held individually responsible, while others will not, depending on their role. Consider an employee who developed a community outreach proposal in which her corporation would engage in numerous activities to address poverty in her community and also make an impact on environmental issues, but the management team refused to fund the initiative. If the corporation has a duty to aid in this situation and they haven't taken any other steps to fulfill it, there is a case to be made for holding the corporation collectively responsible and (some) members of the management team individually responsible for some share, while not attributing responsibility or blame to the conscientious employee.

But when the collective is less structured and not (or at least not yet) a collective agent, questions about individual responsibility and blame for failures to fulfill duties are even more difficult, because there aren't tightly prescribed roles and procedures for allocating shares to members. So work needs to be done to determine individual fair shares based on the individual's capacity, responsibility, and role within the group, and for the group to communicate this to its members. The responsibility of individual members is a function of what a particular person's share was and to what extent they fulfilled or attempted to fulfill it. Notice also that a more determinate answer to this question will depend on one's views on the next question I will discuss; namely, under conditions of partial compliance, do individual shares increase, so that those who have already complied with their share of the collective burden are required to do more? This is relevant because, if they are required to do more, we might ask if they are blameworthy if they don't pick up the slack.

31.6 Collective Duties of Beneficence and Partial Compliance

Individual members of collectivities are required to do their shares in fulfilling a collective duty. Typically shares are distributed to individuals according to some appropriate principle. Sometimes a fair and just distribution is going to be an equal division; sometimes it will be distributed according to capacity, need, responsibility, etc. No matter what the principle is, the share is typically determined under ideal circumstances on the assumption that each complies with her obligation. But our circumstances are not ideal, and individuals regularly fail to comply with their shares of collective obligations. We see the consequences around us: extreme poverty, refugees with no secure path to residency, an environmental crisis that continues to worsen. In the face of these consequences, those who have complied with their shares might ask if they are obligated to pick up the slack of non-compliers. That is, is more required of some individuals in order to fulfill the duty of beneficence?

Unsurprisingly, there is no consensus. Some argue that individuals are only required to do their fair share and should not be compelled to pick up the slack (Miller 2013; Murphy 2003). Others argue that individual shares increase under partial compliance. On this view, the collective requirement and the individual shares are recalculated in light of the remaining need (Cullity 2004). The fact that someone has already done her fair share does not undermine the fact that she still has good reason to aid if she can do so at reasonable cost. In a similar vein, others, agreeing that the remaining need still grounds a duty to aid, argue that compliers have a duty to pick up the slack of non-compliers (Karnein 2014; Kuosmanen 2013; Stemplowska 2016).

Both sides of this debate have merit, and I will briefly sketch a view that captures the appealing aspects of both. We can both reject the idea of redistributing greater shares of collective duties of beneficence to complying agents, and also hold that the basic needs of others always provide us with a reason to aid, thus making our individual duties to aid more demanding under conditions of partial compliance. On this view, it is important to keep our various duties distinct; we have individual duties to aid and we have individual shares of collective duties to aid. Our individual duties to aid are onerous in conditions where there is a great deal of need and undemanding in conditions where there is no need (if that is even possible). Under conditions of partial compliance, many persons fail to fulfill their share of the duty and thus greater need remains. Under these conditions, to redistribute the share of a noncomplying agent to a complying agent is to fail to treat them as equals (assuming the shares were distributed according to a fair procedure); it is to place greater demands on some because they are conscientious. That said, even if these conscientious agents do not inherit a greater share of the collective duty, as I am suggesting they should not, more will be required of them as individual moral agents in light of the more demanding individual duty of beneficence that bears on them in light of the widespread non-compliance of their fellow duty-bearers.

31.7 Conclusion

We may think that bystanders have a collective duty to rescue the victim of an accident, that the EU ought to work together to protect the basic rights of fleeing refugees, and that UN member states have a collective duty to meet the SDGs. Some of us may even think that humanity has a collective duty to eradicate global poverty. The preceding discussion aimed to unpack some of the theoretical complexities, highlight some of the exciting debates, and indicate some of the recent progress made in conceptualizing collective duties of beneficence. We seek these advances not merely to provide conceptual clarity or for purely theoretical purposes; as moral agents, we seek to understand our place in the world and the types of moral demands that impinge on us. When thinking about what we owe to those who do not have secure access to their most basic needs, we must consider that by acting together with others, we can accomplish much more than if we act alone; and so, that we have collective duties to do so.

Notes

1 Though I single out the EU in this example (mainly because, as I write this, the member states of the EU are in negotiations on how to collectively deal with a new influx of predominantly Syrian migrants/refugees escaping violence and persecution), one can make the case that even though the states who are confronted with migrants at their borders may have a special obligation with respect to these migrants, the crisis impacts the wider international community and moreover obligates them to participate in a collective solution.

2 A word about the terminology I will be employing: I will be referring to a plurality of individuals or a plurality of agents as "groups" or "collectives" or "collectivities." Not all groups or collectives are agents in their own right; when they are, I will refer to them as group agents or collective agents.

3 Cripps goes even further to argue for a non-intentionalist model of collectivity. On her account, a set of individuals constitutes a collectivity if and only if they are mutually dependent on each other for the satisfaction of their fundamental interests. She then is able to appeal to our collective self-interest in climate change mitigation to ground a collective duty of "the Young" to organize themselves to mitigate climate change (Cripps 2013, especially ch. 2).

4 Cripps adopts a similar strategy but puts it in terms of a "potential collectivity" and, in some contexts, a "should-be collectivity," where the latter describes "a set of individuals who would constitute a collectivity were they to espouse some goal and who ought (morally) to do it" (2013: 59).
5 Though several onsite managers were charged for acting negligently in their supervision of safety tests, and some others were charged with obstructing justice for covering up information relevant to the investigation, the corporation's executives were not charged.

References

Björnsson, G. (2014) "Essentially Shared Obligations," *Midwest Studies in Philosophy* XXXVIII: 103–20.

Bratman, M. (1999) *Faces of Intention: Selected Essays on Intention and Agency*, Cambridge: Cambridge University Press.

Collins, S. (2013). "Collectives' Duties and Collectivization Duties," *Australasian Journal of Philosophy* 91: 231–48.

Copp, D. (2006) "On the Agency of Certain Collective Entities: An Argument from 'Normative Autonomy'," *Midwest Studies in Philosophy* 30(1): 194–221.

Copp, D. (2007) "The Collective Moral Autonomy Thesis," *Journal of Social Philosophy* 38(3): 369–88.

Cripps, E. (2013) *Climate Change and the Moral Agent: Individual Duties in an Interdependent World*, Oxford: Oxford University Press.

Cullity, G. (2004) *The Moral Demands of Affluence*, Oxford: Oxford University Press.

Erskine, T. (2003) "Making Sense of Responsibility in International Relations: Key Questions and Concepts," in T. Erskine (ed), *Can Institutions Have Responsibilities? Institutional Moral Agency and International Relations*, New York: Palgrave MacMillan, 1–16.

Feinberg, J. (1968) "Collective Responsibility," *The Journal of Philosophy* 65(21): 674–88.

French, P. (1979) "The Corporation as a Moral Person," *American Philosophical Quarterly* 16/3: 207–15.

French, P. (1984) *Collective and Corporate Responsibility*, New York: Columbia University Press.

Gilbert, M. (1990) "Walking Together: A Paradigmatic Social Phenomenon," *Midwest Studies in Philosophy* 15: 1–14.

Gilbert, M. (2006) "Who's to Blame? Collective Moral Responsibility and its Implications for Group Members," *Midwest Studies in Philosophy* 30(1): 94–114.

Goodin, R. (2012) "Excused by the Unwillingness of Others?," *Analysis* 72(1): 18–24.

Held, V. (1970) "Can a Random Collection of Individuals be Morally Responsible?," *The Journal of Philosophy* 67(14): 471–81.

Herman, B. (1984) "Mutual Aid and Respect for Persons," *Ethics* 94(4): 577–602.

Igneski, V. (2018) "Individual Duties in Unstructured Collective Contexts," in K.M. Hess, V. Igneski, and T. Isaacs (eds), *Collectivity: Ontology, Ethics and Social Justice*, Lanham: Rowman & Littlefield, 133–52.

Isaacs, T. (2011) *Moral Responsibility in Collective Contexts*, Oxford: Oxford University Press.

Karnein, A. (2014) "Putting Fairness in Its Place: Why There is a Duty to Take Up the Slack," *The Journal of Philosophy* CXI(11): 593–607.

Kuosmanen, J. (2013) "Perfecting Imperfect Duties: The Institutionalisation of a Universal Right to Asylum," *Journal of Political Philosophy* 21: 24–43.

Kutz, C. (2000) *Complicity: Ethics and Law for a Collective Age*, Cambridge: Cambridge University Press.

Lawford-Smith, H. (2012) "The Feasibility of Collectives' Actions," *Australasian Journal of Philosophy* 90(3): 453–67.

List, C. (2011) *Group Agency: The Possibility, Design, and Status of Corporate Agents*, Oxford: Oxford University Press.

List, C. and Pettit, P. (2006) "Group Agency and Supervenience," *The Southern Journal of Philosophy* 44: 85–105.

May, L. (1992) *Sharing Responsibility*, Chicago: University of Chicago Press.

Miller, D. (2013) "Taking Up the Slack? Responsibility and Justice in Situations of Partial Compliance," in *Justice for Earthlings: Essays in Political Philosophy*, Cambridge: Cambridge University Press.

Miller, S. (2001) *Social Action*, Cambridge: Cambridge University Press.

Murphy, L.B. (2003) *Moral Demands in Nonideal Theory*, New York: Oxford University Press.

Pettit, P. (2007) "Responsibility Incorporated," *Ethics* 117, 2: 171–201.

Pettit, P. and Schweikard, D. (2006) "Joint Actions and Group Agents," *Philosophy of the Social Sciences* 36(1): 18–39.

Pinkert, F. (2014) "What We Together Can (Be Required to) Do," *Midwest Studies in Philosophy* XXXVIII: 187–202.
Scanlon, T. (1975) "Preference and Urgency," *Journal of Philosophy* 72(19): 655–69.
Schwenkenbecher, A. (2014) "Joint Moral Duties," *Midwest Studies in Philosophy* XXXVIII: 58–74.
Schwenkenbecher, A. (2018) "Making Sense of Collective Moral Obligations: A Comparison of Existing Approaches," in K. Hess, V. Igneski, and T. Isaacs (eds), *Collectivity: Ontology, Ethics, and Social Justice*, London: Rowman & Littlefield, 109–32.
Stemplowska, Z. (2016) "Doing More Than One's Fair Share," *Critical Review of International Social and Political Philosophy*, 19(5): 591–608.
Tollefsen, D. (2015) *Groups as Agents*, Cambridge: Polity Press.
Tuomela, R. (2007) *The Philosophy of Sociality*, Oxford: Oxford University Press.
Wringe, B. (2005) "Needs, Rights, and Collective Obligations," *Royal Institute of Philosophy Supplement* 80(57): 187–208.
Wringe, B. (2010) "Global Obligations and the Agency Objection," *Ratio* 23(2): 217–31.
Wringe, B. (2014) "From Global to Institutional Obligations," *Midwest Studies In Philosophy* 38: 171–186.

Further Reading

French, P., and Wettstein, H. (2014) "Forward-Looking Collective Responsibility," *Midwest Studies in Philosophy* XXXVIII.
Isaacs, T., Hess, K., and Igneski, V. (2018) *Collectivity: Ontology, Ethics and Social Justice*. Lanham, MD: Rowman & Littlefield.
May, L., and Hoffman, S. (eds) (1991) *Collective Responsibility. Five Decades of Debate in Theoretical and Applied Ethics*, Lanham, MD: Rowman & Littlefield.

32

ARE STATES RESPONSIBLE FOR CLIMATE CHANGE IN THEIR OWN RIGHT?

Holly Lawford-Smith and Anton Eriksson

32.1 Introduction

One of the most pressing moral challenges of our time is climate change. Over the past 150 years, the global temperature has risen 0.85°C and is threatening to reach a global average of up to 4.8°C before the end of the century (IPCC 2014: 40, 77). The problem with a warmer climate is an increased risk of adverse climatic effects. Some of these include heatwaves, droughts, floods, and rising sea-levels, all of which will have harmful impacts on both current and future generations. For instance, the Intergovernmental Panel on Climate Change (IPCC) predicts that a warmer climate will give rise to deaths from excessive heat, increased food shortage, and displacement of people, among other things.

Warming is caused by an increase in the global concentration of greenhouse gases (GHGs), such as carbon dioxide (CO_2), methane (CH_4), and nitrous oxide (N_2O). GHGs are mainly emitted through the burning of fossil fuels, such as coal or petroleum, with additional emissions resulting from activities such as deforestation and agriculture. Despite a growing awareness of the dangerous effects of emissions, atmospheric concentrations of GHGs have been rapidly growing in the past 50 years. Since 1750, humans have increased the concentration of CO_2 in the atmosphere by around 40 percent, and half of that amount has been emitted since the 1970s (IPCC 2014: 44–5).

In order to halt the dangerous effects of climate change, we need to start making deep cuts in emissions. Many people are skeptical that this could be a responsibility *individuals* have, given the magnitude of the problem, and the negligible effects of an individual's action on it (see, e.g., Sinnott-Armstrong 2005). But if it isn't, then it must be a responsibility *collectives* have.[1] We take collective responsibility to be the group-level responsibility of a singular, and not a plural, subject. That is, collective responsibility is a property of the group itself and cannot be reduced to responsibility of the members of the group.

In this chapter, we will argue that there is collective responsibility to mitigate climate change and to reduce global GHG emissions. There are many collectives potentially responsible for climate change: companies, environmental organizations, consumers, and lobby groups all either contribute in a serious way to climate change or have a significant capacity to affect emissions, compared to individuals. In spite of this, it's commonly held that climate change can only be solved by government action (Broome 2012: 36; Gardiner 2011: 75–6; Vanderheiden

2004: 144). States are the main political units in the international community, and the negotiating parties to international climate agreements. For that reason, we are going to focus in this chapter on the responsibility of *states* as collective moral agents.

We're in good company in thinking about states as the principal agents when it comes to climate change. Others focus on some variant of this: "countries" (Neumayer 2000: 186–7; Pickering and Barry 2012: 670; Shue 1999: 534);"states" (Shue 1999: 534; Zellentin 2014: 260, 265–8); and "nations" (Miller 2009: 128) (see also discussion in Berkey 2017, esp. fn. 5). And it makes sense to think this way, because states, after all, have the power to coordinate the emitters within their territory, whether through incentives or through sanctions.

Still, while much focus has been placed on states as central actors in *taking* responsibility for climate change, they have not necessarily been identified as culpable emitters of GHGs in their own right. In order to say that they are, it needs to be shown that states are not merely proxies or intermediaries for other things within the state territory, such as the citizens or privately-owned corporations. It could be that states do not themselves emit, but that companies and citizens within their borders do. In order to show that states are collectively responsible—in the strongest sense that comes from being culpable—for mitigating climate change, we need to show that they are genuinely causally responsible for significant quantities of emissions.

We shall assume that only *agents* are the kinds of entities that can act and bear responsibility (Lawford-Smith 2015).[2] In order to make the case that states are responsible collectives, then, we shall have to see whether they satisfy the conditions for collective moral agency. We'll address that question in section 32.2, then turn to the question of whether states are emitters in their own right in section 32.3. Section 32.4 considers the moral implications of this, section 32.5 answers several objections, and section 32.6 concludes the chapter.

32.2 Collective Moral Responsibility

We take *collective* responsibility to be the responsibility of a collective agent. In contrast, *individual* responsibility is the responsibility of an individual agent. Insofar as a collective entity bears responsibility for an outcome, it does so in its own right, meaning that the responsibility befalls the collective, and not necessarily any of its constitutive parts.[3] In order for something to be collectively responsible, it needs to be an agent. Not all collective entities, however, qualify for collective agency, not to mention collective *moral* agency. In order to separate those groups that qualify as agents from those that don't, we therefore need an account of agency.

The last couple of decades have seen increased development in the debate over philosophy of the social world, including groups. Consequently, there are a number of different accounts of collective agency. We shall look at what we take to be the most prominent of these—that of Christian List and Philip Pettit—and apply it to the case of the state. (For space reasons, we will only run through one account. But for discussion of a range of accounts, and whether states count as collective agents relative to them, see Lawford-Smith forthcoming, ch. 3.)

List and Pettit take there to be three necessary conditions for agency (List and Pettit 2011: 20).[4] First, in order for something to be an agent, it must possess the capacity for having representational states. These are representations or beliefs that depict the world. Second, it needs the capacity for having motivational states. These are desires, which motivate the agent to act. What's important here is that the relevant type of mental states in humans—beliefs, desires—have a functional role equivalent in non-human agents (List and Pettit 2011: 21). Third, it needs the capacity to process these intentional states and then act on them. Like List and Pettit, we shall only focus on those collectives that survive changes in membership—i.e., those that retain their identity even though some of their constituent parts change (List and Pettit 2011: 31–2; see also Ritchie 2013).

In addition, List and Pettit require that in order to qualify as an agent, a collective must fulfill some minimal level of rationality and autonomy. For our purposes, it suffices that a collective is rational in the sense that it cannot hold inconsistent beliefs and desires (List and Pettit 2011: 37). To count as autonomous in List and Pettit's sense, the collective's mental states must be independent from the members' mental states (List and Pettit 2011: ch. 3). We interpret this requirement in a weak way: the collective decision *can* depart from any individual's decisions (rather than *must* depart). It could be that one or several members have the same belief content as the collective, but that the beliefs are independent because the members and the collective arrived at their beliefs through different processes.

So far, we haven't said anything about *moral* responsibility. On List and Pettit's account, when a collective agent faces a normatively significant choice, it is fit to be held responsible if and only if it has the capacity to make normative judgments and has the control necessary to choose between the morally relevant choices (List and Pettit 2011: 155–6). In total, this gives us seven distinct conditions, namely: capacity for the functional equivalents of beliefs and desires; the ability to process and act on them; capacity to survive membership changes; (capacity for) rationality; autonomy; and (capacity for) normative judgment.

The question, of course, is whether states can be said to meet the above conditions. If they can, then they are *candidates* for being culpable for climate change, and having a serious responsibility to mitigate emissions as a result. Before we try to establish whether the state is an agent, though, we first need to say something about what the state *is*. For simplicity, we are going to assume that states are governments (see discussion in Lawford-Smith forthcoming, ch. 4), as opposed to citizenries (see Lawford-Smith forthcoming, ch. 3; cf. Lawford-Smith and Collins 2017; Collins and Lawford-Smith manuscript). We use the term "government" in a broad sense that doesn't just include the executive branch consisting of the head of state and ministers. Rather, it includes *all* of the elected officials and employees within the legislature, the executive, and the judiciary, and other key branches of government, such as the police and the military. In short, it includes the organized political unit that exercises authority over the state's territory and population. (It need not necessarily include local political entities, such as city councils, given their relative independence from the rest of the state.)

To take an example, the Swedish state is the organized political unit that exercises authority over the geographical territory known as "Sweden" as well as over the Swedish people. This entity consists of the executive government, including the Prime Minister and the cabinet ministers who head the different ministries. But it also encompasses the parliament (the *Riksdag*, which has legislative power) and the courts that together comprise the judiciary. In addition, it also includes a number of different government agencies administered by the executive government and the parliament. These include, but are not limited to, the Swedish Armed Forces, law enforcement, the central bank, and the Swedish Tax Agency. Can this political unit be a collective agent? We think so.

For starters, this entity survives changes in membership. To take an example, the exchange of one of the ministers of the executive government for someone else does not change the identity of the government. Next, the government routinely forms beliefs about the world and holds desires about how to engage with it. The formation of these intentional states can be made based on voting—as when the parliament passes legislation—or be consensus-based—as when the executive government makes a decision. Based on these beliefs about how the world is, and desires about how the world should be, the government then proceeds to act, e.g., by the executive government implementing the decisions of the parliament or the relevant branch of the state, such as the Swedish Tax Agency, law enforcement, state-owned enterprises, or the military. The state thus intentionally *acts* on its beliefs and desires.

Rationality is ensured since the government has the capacity to revise inconsistent beliefs and desires, for instance by consulting with advisors and committees. Regarding autonomy, we only required that it is possible for the decisions of the collective to depart from the members' decisions. In this way, the government achieves autonomy because it's possible, for example, that the decision each minister of the executive government agrees to is not what they actually want, but what they each think that the others want. Finally, since it has the capacity for beliefs, and nothing stops these from being moral in nature, the government has the capacity for forming normative judgments. Insofar as the state is in control of its normatively significant choices, it is therefore fit to be held morally responsible.

So far, then, we have shown that, if we accept List and Pettit's account of agency, the state can be a collective agent, capable of bearing moral responsibility. The next question is whether states are responsible, in the strongest sense that comes from being culpable, for mitigating climate change.

32.3 States' Emissions

As we have said already, states are often assumed to be the main parties responsible for climate change. Commentators have cast states as players in a global "tragedy of the commons," where their self-interest predicts increasing emissions, in tension with the reduced emissions that would be in the interest of all states taken together. States are appropriate bearers of responsibility for climate change, because it is within their control to introduce policies that will restrict the emissions of the individuals and companies within their territories, like a carbon price or an emissions cap. On this understanding, we talk about "Australia's" emissions, but we don't really mean that these emissions come from the actions of the Australian government. The state is a proxy for the agents within its borders, in particular the companies and corporations that operate there, and to a lesser extent, the individual citizens who live emissions-intensive lifestyles there. This means that the actions performed by agents within the state territory are attributed to the state itself. But this way of conceiving of the state for the purpose of addressing the climate change problem sidesteps the question of whether states are culpable emitters in their own right. For them to be so the emissions need to be the result of the actions of the government, not merely of those agents who are active within the territory it governs.

What's at stake in this question? If states are culpable emitters, then their responsibility strengthens; no longer will they have a responsibility to mitigate as mere proxies for the emitters that lie within their territory and jurisdiction. Rather, they will have a responsibility to mitigate based on culpable involvement in creating climate change. What we want to do in this section is establish that states are culpable emitters, and argue that this further strengthens their obligation to take strong action on climate change, particularly in terms of mitigation. We'll run this discussion using the example of Australia, a representative high-emissions state. Let's start with direct emissions.

An important branch of any government is its military.[5] The Australian Defence Force consists of the Army, the Navy, and the Air Force, and employs over 80,000 people. It is the largest government emitter, producing more emissions than Fiji, the Solomon Islands, Timor-Leste, Vanuatu, and Samoa combined; and about as many emissions as one of Australia's large privately-owned corporations, Telstra, at 1.5 megatons (1 megaton = 1 million tons) of CO_2-e (carbon dioxide equivalents) per year (Thomas 2017). To put this in perspective, it is still dwarfed by the emissions of Australia's largest emitter in 2016–17, which was AGL Energy Ltd at 43.4

megatons. But it, in turn, dwarfs the emissions of Australian individuals, which vary between 3–30 tons of GHGs per year per person (Australian Greenhouse Calculator 2018). So even if we were only concerned with the GHGs of the military in thinking about the Australian state as a culpable emitter, the military would give us a solid foundation for thinking that it is.

Another important source of direct emissions for the state is those companies that are owned by Australia, either at the level of national government, or at the level of federated states (which have their own partially autonomous governments in Australia). These are so-called "government business enterprises," or "state-owned enterprises." Because we know (antecedently) that the energy, transport, and agricultural industries are large contributors to climate change, we'll focus on mentioning companies involved in those sectors rather than giving an exhaustive list.

The Australian government's enterprises include Airservices Australia (servicing the aviation industry), ASC Pty Ltd (building ships for the Navy), Australia Post (the main mail service), Australian Rail Track Corporation (managing Australia's rail network), NBN Co (operating the national broadband network), and Snowy Hydro Ltd (an electricity provider).

Australia has eight semi-autonomous states, the Australian Capital Territory (ACT), New South Wales (NSW), Northern Territory (NT), Queensland (QLD), South Australia (SA), Tasmania (TAS), Victoria (VIC), and Western Australia (WA). We'll just mention the four states with the highest populations, as representative: VIC (5.9 million), NSW (7.6 million), QLD (4.8 million), and WA (2.6 million) (World Atlas 2017). VIC's government business enterprises include Port of Melbourne (the largest port in Australasia for containers and cargo) and Port of Hastings (another container port), as well as Snowy Hydro (an electricity company), and VicTrack (a rail track corporation). NSW's government business enterprises include three energy companies (Ausgrid, Endeavour Energy, and Integral Energy); four transit companies (New South Wales Trains, RailCorp, Sydney Trains, and State Transit Authority); and three ports (Newcastle Port Corporation, Port Kembla Port Corporation, and Sydney Ports Corporation). QLD's government business enterprises include six energy companies (CS Energy, Energex, Ergon Energy, Powerlink Queensland, Stanwell Corporation, and Tarong Energy) as well as three ports (Port of Brisbane, Port of Townsville, and Port of Mackay). Finally, WA's government business enterprises include three energy companies (Horizon Power, Western Power, and Synergy) and two public transport companies (Transwa and Transperth).

It would be time-consuming indeed to work out all the government business enterprises for Australia, and track each of their annual emissions (including yearly historical emissions) to get an estimate of a total. But to give the flavor of an answer, in 2014–15 the total Scope 1 and 2[6] combined emissions of QLD's CS Energy were 13,284,260 tons of CO_2-e. NSW's Ausgrid were 968,547 tons and Endeavour Energy were 613,072 tons; QLD's Energex and Stanwell Corporation were 951,544 tons and 14,786,967 tons, respectively. This is already a total of 30,604,390 tons of CO_2-e, and it's not even close to a full accounting of all the government business enterprises of all eight states of Australia (Clean Energy Regulator 2017). Two of the top ten corporate emitters in Australia in 2016–17 were government business enterprises: Stanwell Corporation at third place with 18.6 million tons (and that's only Scope 1 emissions, so a significant increase from the 2014–15 reporting just mentioned), and CS Energy at fifth place with 14.1 million tons (also only Scope 1 emissions) (Clean Energy Regulator 2018). In other words, even this limited accounting puts government business enterprises between the highest and second-highest corporate emitters in Australia. Once we'd done the full accounting, it would not be surprising to see the Australian government overtake the top emitter (which is AGL Energy Ltd, with 43.5 million tons in 2016–17).

An influential recent paper tracked 63 percent of cumulative global carbon and methane emissions across a 260-year period to just 90 entities referred to as "carbon majors" (Heede

2014). This might look like evidence that we should shift away from talking about states as culpable emitters and start talking about carbon majors instead. But as we've just shown, government business enterprises are among the big emitters. In fact, a breakdown of the 90 carbon majors that were the focus of Richard Heede's analysis revealed 50 to be investor-owned, 31 to be state-owned, and 9 to be nation-states. That's 44 percent of the carbon majors turning out to be not corporations but, ultimately, states.

Of course we could go on, but at this point it is more interesting to shift to indirect emissions. So far, we've been interested in the emissions of particular branches or organizations of the state, using Australia as a running example. But what is interesting about the state is the control that it exercises over the agents within its jurisdiction. We're not going to make the familiar point that the state could introduce better climate change policy, and thereby reduce emissions. That is true, but we don't think this omission—as egregious as it is—is sufficient to make the Australian state culpable for the emissions of all agents within its jurisdiction. The high emissions lifestyles of individuals, and the huge emissions produced by companies and corporations, implicate the agents who produce them, and we're happy enough for now to maintain that the buck stops there. But what about in industries where there is a minister, with a portfolio attaching to a government department, directly responsible for advising on policy related to that industry?

For example, as of March 2018, the ministers for the Department of Infrastructure, Regional Development, and Cities were Michael McCormack, John McVeigh, Paul Fletcher, and Keith Pitt (the more specific Departments for Transport exist at the state level). Just as we might hold the Department of Immigration and Border Protection responsible for Australia's shocking policy on asylum-seekers, we might also hold the Department of Infrastructure, Regional Development, and Cities responsible for Australia's public transport infrastructure policy, particularly where this fails to be extensive enough to reduce the emissions from private car use. It seems to us that there are a number of government departments that have responsibility for policy that would affect the mitigation of GHGs one way or another, so that we can say that Australia's emissions totals depend on what these departments (and perhaps ministers) do. That too implicates the Australian state as an emitter in its own right.

This should not be confused with the proxy view described above, according to which emissions in a particular territory are attributed to the state that governs it. Those emissions belong to other agents. In contrast, certain policies will allow or prohibit these emissions, as a direct result of decisions by government. While these emissions are indirect, they are thus nonetheless a product of the state's own actions.

32.4 Moral Implications for States

The question we started with was whether there is any collective responsibility for climate change. We've focused on the specific collective that is the state, and we've answered in the positive. States are culpable emitters in their own right, and not merely proxies for other agents that reside (or have legal personhood) within the geographical territory over which the state has jurisdiction. But what are the implications of this? After all, commentators both academic and political have assumed that states are responsible for a portfolio of responses to climate change, from mitigation through adaptation to compensation (Caney 2012). Haven't we just gotten to the same conclusion by an alternative route?

We think not, for one important reason. The obligations that agents end up with are stronger or weaker, and have different content, depending on the reasons why agents have them. You have a stronger obligation to not do harm than to not allow harm (Foot 1967). Being the beneficiary of an injustice gives you stronger reasons to help its victim than to help other needy people (Lindauer and Barry 2017: 675). Duties grounded in considerations of justice are stronger than duties grounded in considerations of humanity (Lawford-Smith 2012).

If states are only *proxies* for emitters, then their obligations are comparatively weak. The "Polluter Pays" argument for the distribution of mitigation obligations among historically high-emitting states is a version of the idea that the agent who caused or contributed to an injustice is the ideal agent to repair it. Its success in the case of climate change depends on the targeted agent in fact being the polluter. But on the mere proxy view, the state is not the polluter. In fact, on a view like ours, which excludes citizens from membership in the state and focuses on the government, it would not be appropriate to account for the state's emissions as the total of all emissions produced within the geographical territory. Accounting for the state's emissions in that way could generate at best an "Ability to Pay" view, where the state has the greatest ability to mitigate climate change, because it is uniquely positioned to exercise control over those who emit within its territory (on the different distributive principles, see, e.g., Caney 2010; Garcia 2014; Huseby 2015).

But our intuitions from ordinary moral philosophy tell us that obligations that come from an ability to act are substantially weaker than obligations that come from having caused the situation requiring action. The thief is the primary bearer of an obligation to either return the stolen goods or provide compensation to the victim of her theft. Compare this obligation against that of a wealthy bystander who merely happened to see the theft happen. We generally think the bystander has no obligation at all, at least in circumstances where the thief herself can be made to fulfill her obligations. Where she can't, the bystander will be the last in a long line of candidate obligation-bearers (e.g., if a third person benefited from the theft, the obligation will fall to her first).

To put this in more general terms: the stronger the moral connection between the victims of a harm and a candidate obligation-bearer, the more cost the candidate obligation-bearer is required to take on (the more demanding her obligations, and the less she can appeal to costliness to get herself off the hook) (Collins ms). The moral connection we're interested in here is *having contributed to causing the victims' situation*. High-emitters are large proportional contributors to the harms that are being and will be brought about by climate change. The state—or at least, rich industrialized states like Australia—is a high-emitter.

32.5 Objections

We've argued above that there's a strong moral connection between the state and those who will be harmed by climate change. States have a responsibility to take action on climate change *because* they are high emitting collective agents (they are high emitters in their own right), and not just because they have control over high emitters (other agents, both individual and collective) within their territory. We're not taking a stand here on the specific content of the responsibilities this leaves states with, although we think that because states' emissions make a causal contribution to total global emissions, which in turn harm people all over the world, there's a good case to be made that serious mitigation action is necessary, whatever else states must do.

In making this argument, we disagree with John Broome (2012: ch. 4–6). Broome discusses both duties of justice and duties of goodness, and argues that individuals' duties not to emit—either by eliminating their personal emissions or by offsetting them—are duties of justice. But he thinks states' duties to mitigate emissions are duties of goodness. That is to say, states' duties to mitigate climate change are one instantiation of their general duties to make the world better. One justification Broome gives for this is based on the "non-identity problem," namely that the identity of future persons depends on the timing of when they were conceived (for the original discussion of the non-identity problem, see Parfit 1984: ch. 16; see also Broome 2012: 61–2). Individuals' emissions do not make enough of a difference to affect the identities of future persons, so we must limit our claims about the harm they do to people who are already alive. This is not much, but it is still something, and because they have a general duty to do *no* harm rather than *not much* harm, they'll have a duty of justice to eliminate or offset their emissions.

States' emissions are much more significant, but this means they plausibly do make enough of a difference to affect the identities of future persons. They'll do harm to current persons in the same way as individuals' emissions do, but we won't be able to capture the much greater amount of harm they seem to do to future persons—at least so long as we use a conception of harming as making someone worse off than they otherwise would have been. If this is the conception of harm that informs what counts as an injustice, then we'll be unable to capture the extent of the harm states' emissions seem to do in the language of injustice.

For Broome, this is a good reason to instead characterize states' duties to mitigate emissions largely in terms of goodness. Luckily, this is more plausible for states than it is for individuals: because states have a powerful reach, they can make a difference to GHG emissions in a way that individual citizens cannot. Furthermore, states have a strong mandate to promote the good of their citizens, and a weaker but nonetheless important mandate to promote the good of others outside the state. One way they can do this is by taking action on climate change, which will likely have consequences for their own citizens among many others. States can thus promote the good by taking action on climate change.

We can resolve this disagreement by resolving the non-identity challenge, so that it's open to us to maintain that states' emissions do harm at the magnitude that our intuitions tell us that they do. (That is to say, it's no use establishing that they emit a lot more as agents in their own right than we might have thought, if we're then forced to discount most of the effects of those emissions because they're effects on future rather than current persons.) Two solutions are promising here. The first appeals to an impersonal rather than person-affecting account of harm (Hare 2007: 516–19; Hartzell-Nichols 2012: 103–4). States' GHG emissions harm future persons *de dicto*, that is, whoever those future persons may turn out to be. Those people are worse off than other people in their situation could have been. But states' emissions do not harm future persons *de re*; that is, they do not harm specific future people, because those people very likely owe their existence to the high emissions actions of the state (see also discussion in Eriksson ms). The reason why Broome holds that states' emissions don't harm future persons is because he is only concerned with harm *de re*. Appealing to doing harm *de dicto* thus grants that future people can be harmed by states nonetheless.

The second appeals to a non-difference-making understanding of harm. Instead of thinking of injustice in terms of actions that make a person worse off than she otherwise would have been, we think of it in terms of actions that are bad for a person. The key insight here is that actions can be bad for a person even when they don't make her worse off, for example, because they violate her rights, or because they put her below some threshold level of wellbeing, or because they deprive her of certain important resources or capabilities (see, e.g., Rivera-Lopez 2009; Steinbock 2009; Velleman 2008). We might think people have a right to live in a world without severe resource scarcity, or a huge refugee problem, or the threat of statelessness, or compromised health through pollution, for example. The shortcoming of this solution is that it cannot account for emissions as harmful when they are not bad for people in one of these ways, even when they leave people worse off *de dicto* than they could have been for what look like bad reasons (e.g., the emissions relate to luxury goods that the emitters could easily have foregone).

On both the *de dicto* (impersonal) understanding of harm, and on a non-difference-making understanding of harm, states' emissions do harm, and they do it at the magnitude we argued for in section 32.3, rather than only in the restricted form allowed in Broome's discussion (2012).

32.6 Conclusion

We're endorsing a version of the Polluter Pays Principle that is premised on a more defensible understanding of the state. Instead of considering the state as a proxy for all the agents in its territory, we've considered a plausible understanding of the state itself and asked whether on that understanding the state is a collective agent. We've argued that it is. This might have threatened to undermine the responsibility of the state for climate change, given that it no longer includes all emissions activities in the territory, e.g., those of ordinary citizens, small-business, and investor-owned corporations. However, we've argued that it doesn't, because the government itself includes numerous branches, departments, and organizations that are themselves high-emitters, and these emissions accumulate to make rich, industrialized states like Australia culpable emitters. Our argument here should not be taken to imply that none of the other distributive principles create responsibilities for the state. We think it's probably true that a state like Australia's climate change obligations are compounded by the fact that it has benefited from its historical emissions, and that in virtue of being rich and industrialized it has an enhanced capacity to take action. We've been focused on what we take to be the *strongest* source of obligations, not what we take to be the *only* source of obligations. In sum: there is collective responsibility for climate change, and it's right where we thought it was, but for reasons other than we might have originally believed.

Notes

1 This does not exhaust the logical space of options, because there could also be no responsibility, but we'll dismiss that possibility here. Additionally, some philosophers argue that responsibility can be *shared* among individual agents (see e.g. Björnsson 2014; Pinkert 2014; Schwenkenbecher 2013). Since this responsibility resides at the individual level, though, we take this to be a species of individual, and not collective, responsibility.

2 There is thus no collective responsibility befalling, say, the set of affluent consumers in western countries, who together cause high GHG emissions, because this is not the kind of entity that can act (Lawford-Smith 2018).

3 There is a further question about the responsibility of the individual members of a responsible collective.

4 List and Pettit's terminology differs slightly from ours, in that they call theirs an account of *group*, rather than *collective*, agency.

5 Interestingly, the emissions from military activities were exempted from national GHG inventories in international negotiations up until the Paris Agreement in 2015.

6 As defined by Greenhouse Gas Protocol; see their "FAQ", online at www.ghgprotocol.org/sites/default/files/ghgp/standards_supporting/FAQ_0.pdf (accessed: 27 March 2018).

References

Berkey, B. (2017) "Benefiting from Unjust Acts and Benefiting from Injustice: Historical Emissions and the Beneficiary Pays Principle," in L. Meyer and P. Sanklecha (eds) *Climate Justice and Historical Emissions*, Cambridge: Cambridge University Press.

Björnsson, G. (2014) "Essentially Shared Obligations," *Midwest Studies in Philosophy* 38(1): 103–20.

Broome, J. (2012) *Climate Matters: Ethics in a Warming World*, New York: Norton.

Caney, S. (2010) "Climate Change and the Duties of the Advantaged," *Critical Review of International Social and Political Philosophy* 13: 203–28.

Caney, S. (2012) "Just Emissions," *Philosophy & Public Affairs* 40(4): 255–300.

Collins, S. (manuscript). "Relational Duties and Overdemandingness," as at 31 August 2018.

Collins, S. and Lawford-Smith, H. (manuscript) "Are the Citizens of a Democratic State a Collective Agent?," as at 31 August 2018.

Eriksson, A. (manuscript) *Omitting to Emit*, PhD Thesis, University of Sheffield, as at 19 May 2018, Chapter 3.

Foot, P. (1967) "The Problem of Abortion and the Doctrine of Double Effect," *Oxford Review* 5: 1–5.

Garcia, R. (2014) "Towards a Just Solar Radiation Management Compensation System: A Defence of the Polluter Pays Principle," *Ethics, Policy and Environment* 17(2): 178–82.

Gardiner, S. (2011) *A Perfect Moral Storm: The Ethical Tragedy of Climate Change*, Oxford: Oxford University Press.

Hare, C. (2007) "Voices from Another World: Must We Respect the Interests of People Who Do Not, And Will Never, Exist?," *Ethics* 117(3): 498–523.

Hartzell-Nichols, L. (2012) "How is Climate Change Harmful?," *Ethics and the Environment* 17(2): 97–110.

Heede, R. (2014) "Tracing Anthropogenic Carbon Dioxide and Methane Emissions to Fossil Fuel and Cement Producers, 1854–2010," *Climatic Change* 122: 229–41.

Huseby, R. (2015) "Should the Beneficiaries Pay?," *Politics, Philosophy, and Economics* 14(2): 1–17.

Intergovernmental Panel on Climate Change (IPCC) (2014) "Climate Change 2014: Synthesis Report. Contribution of Working Groups I, II and III to the Fifth Assessment Report of the Intergovernmental Panel on Climate Change" [Core Writing Team: R.K. Pachauri and L.A. Meyer (eds)] Geneva, Switzerland: IPCC.

Lawford-Smith, H. (2012) "The Motivation Question: Arguments from Justice and from Humanity," *British Journal of Political Science* 42: 661–78.

Lawford-Smith, H. (2015) "What "We"?" *Journal of Social Ontology* 1(2): 225–49.

Lawford-Smith, H. (2017) "The Comparative Culpability of Stratospheric Aerosol Injections and Ordinary Carbon Emissions," *Ethics & International Affairs* 31/4.

Lawford-Smith, H. (2018) "Does Purchasing Make Consumers Complicit in Global Labour Injustice?" *Res Publica* [early view].

Lawford-Smith, H. (forthcoming) *Not in Their Name*, Oxford: Oxford University Press.

Lawford-Smith, H. and Collins, S. (2017) "Responsibility for States' Actions: Normative Issues at the Intersection of Collective Agency and State Responsibility," *Philosophy Compass* 12/11.

Lindauer, M., and Barry, C. (2017) "Moral Judgement and the Duties of Innocent Beneficiaries of Injustice," *Review of Philosophical Psychology* 8: 671–86.

List, C., and Pettit, P. (2011) *Group Agency: The Possibility, Design, and Status of Corporate Agents*, Oxford: Oxford University Press.

Miller, D. (2009) "Global Justice and Climate Change: How Should Responsibilities Be Distributed?" *Tanner Lectures on Human Values* 28: 117–56.

Neumayer, E. (2000) "In Defence of Historical Accountability for Greenhouse Gas Emissions," *Ecological Economics* 3: 185–92.

Parfit, D. (1984) *Reasons and Persons*, Oxford: Oxford University Press.

Pickering, J., and Barry, C. (2012) "On the Concept of Climate Debt: Its Moral and Political Value," *Critical Review of International Social and Political Philosophy* 15: 667–85.

Pinkert, F. (2014) "What We Together Can (Be Required to) Do," *Midwest Studies in Philosophy* 38(1): 187–202.

Ritchie, K. (2013) "What are Groups?" *Philosophical Studies* 166: 272.

Rivera-Lopez, E. (2009) "Individual Procreative Responsibility and the Non-Identity Problem," *Pacific Philosophical Quarterly* 90: 99–118.

Schwenkenbecher, A. (2013) "Joint Duties and Global Moral Obligations," *Ratio* 26(3): 310–28.

Shue, H. (1999) "Global Environment and International Inequality," *International Affairs* 75: 531–45.

Sinnott-Armstrong, W. (2005) "It's Not My Fault: Global Warming and Individual Moral Obligations," in W. Sinnott-Armstrong and R. Howarth (eds), *Perspectives on Climate Change*, Elsevier.

Steinbock, B. (2009) "Wrongful Life and Procreative Decisions," in M. Roberts and D. Wasserman (eds) *Harming Future Persons*, New York: Springer.

Thomas, M. (2017) "What the ADF Can Learn from the US Military Response to Climate Change," *The Strategist*, 12 January 2017. [online] Available at www. aspistrategist.org.au/adf-can-learn-us-military-response-climate-change/ (Accessed: 26 March 2018).

Vanderheiden, S. (2004) "Knowledge, Uncertainty, and Responsibility: Responding to Climate Change," *Public Affairs Quarterly* 18(2): 141–58.
Velleman, D. (2008) "Persons in Prospect," *Philosophy & Public Affairs* 36: 221–88.
Zellentin, A. (2014) "Compensation for Historical Emissions and Excusable Ignorance," *Journal of Applied Philosophy* 32: 258–74.

Websites

Australian Greenhouse Calculator, "3. Households and GHG emissions," [online] Available at www.epa.vic.gov.au/agc/r_emissions.html#page-1/! (Accessed: 26 March 2018).
Clean Energy Regulator, "Corporate Emissions and Energy Data 2014–5," 27 October 2017. [online] Available at www.cleanenergyregulator.gov.au/NGER/National%20greenhouse%20and%20energy%20reporting%20data/Corporate%20emissions%20and%20energy%20data/corporate-emissions-and-energy-data-2014-15#Greenhouse-and-energy-information-by-controlling-corporation-201415 (Accessed: 27 March 2018).
Clean Energy Regulator, "National Greenhouse and Energy Reporting, 2016–7 published data highlights," 5 March 2018. [online] Available at www.cleanenergyregulator. gov.au/NGER/National%20greenhouse%20and%20energy%20reporting%20data/Data-highlights/2016-17-published-data-highlights (Accessed: 26 March 2018).
World Atlas, "Which Australian States/Territories Have the Highest Density of Population?," [online] Available at www.worldatlas.com/articles/which-australian-states-territories-have-the-highest-density-of-population.html (Accessed: 27 March 2018).

33
CONSPIRACY THEORIES AND COLLECTIVE RESPONSIBILITY

Juha Räikkä

33.1 Introduction

Political conspiracies are good examples of collective action. The plan to assassinate Roman Emperor Nero (The Pisonian Conspiracy), the 20 July plot against Adolf Hitler (Operation Valkyrie), and the plan to unleash terror attacks on the American people in order to justify a full-scale invasion of Cuba (Operation Northwoods) all included organized cooperation among the members of the plots. These conspiracies were unsuccessful, but many conspiracies have met their goals. For example, as a result of Russian conspiracy, Grigori Yefimovich Rasputin was murdered in 1916 in Saint Petersburg. Successful conspiracies also include the plot that led to the 1953 Iranian coup d'état, the conspiracy that helped Bolivians to execute Ernesto Che Guevara in 1967, and hundreds of other political conspiracies. Professional historians commonly refer both to unsuccessful and successful conspiracies when they explain political incidents of the past.

As opposed to conspiracies, *conspiracy theories* need not be based on collective action. It would be misleading to claim that conspiracy theorizing is always a collective activity. In principle, an individual person can create and disseminate a conspiracy theory – for instance, a theory that concerns Pearl Harbor, John F. Kennedy's murder, Princess Diana's death, or 9/11. However, almost always conspiracy theories are closely tied to cooperation and joint action. Individual conspiracy theorists can get new ideas by listening to other conspiracy theorists. Sometimes conspiracy theorists work in groups (Olmsted 2011). When they do, conspiracy theorizing is a collective action that resembles, to some extent, actions of other groups whose members are epistemically dependent on each other and select their own members – groups as diverse as religious communities and scientific research groups. Believing in conspiracy theories should be distinguished from conspiracy theorizing. But even believing in an alleged conspiracy suggested by conspiracy theorists is social in the sense that we accept certain beliefs much more readily when we know that others have those beliefs (Fricker 2006, 225; Lackey 2011, 71). Skillful conspiracy theorists know this and make use of social networks that disseminate their theories quickly and effectively.

In this chapter, I will ask why conspiracy theorists are collectively responsible for their activities. I will distinguish between (1) *developers and publishers* and (2) *ordinary believers and disseminators* of conspiracy theories. Developers and publishers are *active conspiracy theorists*, and their responsibility is different to that of the ordinary believers and disseminators. However, they both are "collectively" responsible, or so I argue. I will point to three different ways in which conspiracy theorists are "collectively" responsible. First, the ordinary believers and disseminators decrease the level of trust in major social institutions or, at least, increase the risk that the trust will lessen, and they share responsibility for that. Second, the active conspiracy theorists get support from each other and act in that sense jointly, sometimes even in groups. Third, the active conspiracy theorists fail to establish an organization that would guide its members along the lines of investigative journalists, or some other group that has its own principles – although they could establish such organization as a group.

However, let us start by considering briefly what conspiracy theories are and why conspiracy theorizing, taken as a whole, is morally problematic. I will concentrate mainly on political conspiracy theories rather than theories that concern Elvis, the antichrist, or UFOs.

33.2 Conspiracies and Conspiracy Theories

Conspiracies are usually revealed by leakers who are either members of the plots or people who are otherwise close to conspirators and know enough. The news is checked and published in newspapers and elsewhere – sooner or later. Sometimes conspiracies are revealed by the investigative journalists independently of the leakers, but typically the investigations start only when there is already a clue, namely, a leak. Big organizations often have their own monitoring systems against corruption and plotting, and the state authorities should watch and double check that everything goes well. But everything does not always go well. Anti-corruption authorities, national health authorities, food safety authorities, medical agencies, patient safety agencies, environmental protection agencies, traffic control authorities, and radiation and nuclear safety authorities all reveal conspiracies – for instance, related to the origin of the (fake) food, or to the (wrong) construction materials used in nuclear plants, or the (misleading) information about emissions of cars. The state authorities are not infallible, and the scientific community and the public media should monitor their actions and statements, as well as possible. Still, conspiracies may go unnoticed, and some conspiracies are revealed only after a long period of time, if ever. Such revelations are usually made by historians or by people who confess their secret role in some operation that belongs to history. A striking feature related to the revelation of conspiracies is that they are seldom revealed by "conspiracy theorists," although they are the only people who are explicitly interested in revealing conspiracies. If conspiracy theorists have any role in revealing conspiracies, it is that they provide others with a motivation to study further some political or economic issue.[1]

What are conspiracy theories? One way to characterize them is to say that they are explanations of political events that have two key features:

A. *Conspiracy Criterion.* They refer to (actual or alleged) conspiracies or plots.
B. *Conflict Criterion.* They conflict with a received explanation of the same political event so that the relevant epistemic authorities, more or less unanimously, find the conspiracy claim strikingly implausible, after considering the claim.

A. Conspiracy Criterion. Conspiracy theories refer to conspiracies and plots. If an explanation of a political event does not refer to a conspiracy or a plot, it cannot be a conspiracy theory. Conspiracies can be done for good or bad reasons. To say that a group of people "conspired" is not to say that their secret cooperation was, all things considered, wrong. Operation Valkyrie was a conspiracy, but there are many who would say that the members of the plot that aimed to murder Hitler had an excellent moral justification for their plan. It seems clear that conspirators need not have "nefarious intentions" (Keeley 1999, 117; cf.Van Prooijen and Acker 2015, 753), although conspiracy theories tend to refer to vicious conspiracies. However, we can say that secret cooperative activities whose aims and nature conflict with the so-called positive morality (that reflects our *de facto* moral commitments) or with specific *prima facie* duties (e.g. a duty not to kill anyone) are usually called "conspiracies," especially if the members of the cooperation have a certain position, and if the goal of their activities differs from the goal they are authorized to pursue. Conspiracies involve secret cooperation, but that does not mean that the conspirators must *meet secretly*. When a gang of criminals or terrorists commits a crime and some sort of deception is involved, people may talk about a conspiracy or a "terrorist plot."

B. Conflict Criterion. An explanation that refers to a conspiracy as a prime cause of some political event is not a conspiracy theory if it is and has always been completely consistent with the shared opinion of the relevant *epistemic authorities*. It is important to distinguish between conspiracy theories and ordinary *conspiracy explanations*. They both explain political events by referring to a conspiracy. History books are full of conspiracy explanations, but the books are not supposed to represent conspiracy theories. The difference between conspiracy explanations and conspiracy theories is that a conspiracy explanation is supported by the relevant epistemic authorities, while a typical conspiracy theory is not supported by them and would probably get much media attention were it shown to be true (cf. Keeley 1999, 116; Levy 2007, 187; Räikkä 2018, 211). By epistemic authorities I refer to the knowledge-producing institutions that, among other things, reveal conspiracies (although it is certainly not their main task). Epistemic authorities thus include institutions as diverse as mainstream media, investigative journalists, various state authorities and agencies, the scientific community, professional historians and so on. Our reliance upon the expertise of others is very extensive and almost automatic. Although the epistemic authorities work imperfectly and make mistakes, they are still the main social institutions that we use in the acquisition of our beliefs. Their trustworthiness is a default stance in the formation of our beliefs (cf. Coady 1992, 7; Adler 2002, 136; Fricker 2006, 225; Lehrer 2006, 145; Lackey 2011, 71). Of course, critical and rational people often doubt the information provided by the epistemic authorities, but the doubting is usually based on beliefs that are supported by the other views of the same authorities – and not, say, by the views of gurus or witches. In general, we *know* about the failures of epistemic authorities because they have produced information that helps us to notice the failures. Conspiracy theories do not get the status of being a "rival scientific theory," or anything like that; instead, epistemic authorities consider them strikingly implausible.[2]

Experts' opinions often conflict with one another, and then lay persons may have a hard time in choosing between disagreeing experts (Goldman 2011, 116; Guerrero 2017, 181). In these cases it may be advisable to leave the issue open, or use some external criteria to evaluate experts and their opinions – criteria such as how well an expert has done before and what the other experts in the same field think about her. Evidence of the expert's interests and possible biases vis-á-vis the question at issue may also be important (Goldberg 2011, 105; Goldman 2011, 116; Ritola 2012, 675; Guerrero 2017, 169). In usual cases, a novice cannot make her judgment by evaluating relevant evidence directly, however good her "epistemic environment" happens to be. Conspiracy theorists sometimes argue that people should evaluate evidence themselves instead of passively accepting mainstream news and information provided by epistemic authorities. Unfortunately, in most cases, that requirement is too demanding, as we are ordinarily dependent on others' opinions (although public participation in scientific research and citizen science provide examples that show that we are not *completely* dependent on experts, and that experts can be dependent on citizens).[3]

These two defining features (A and B) of conspiracy theories allow us to ask whether conspiracy theories are plausible or implausible. There are many who think that conspiracy theories (that is, alternative explanations that refer to alleged conspiracies) can be rather plausible, given the amount of conspiracies in history (Basham 2003; Pigden 2007; Dentith 2018). However, it seems more natural to think that conspiracy theories are *prima facie* implausible. As far as we trust that, generally speaking, epistemic institutions work tolerably well, and that we are justified in acquiring our beliefs in the way we do, the suggestions inspired by conspiracy theories are not plausible. A belief in the existence of conspiracy is quite likely to be unjustified when many epistemic authorities, more or less independently of each other, assert that the plausible explanation for an event does not require postulation of a conspiracy. It is unlikely that someone else is able to identify and interpret the evidence more reliably than most of the experts, or that all the defenders of the non-conspiratorial explanation are simply liars. Badly corrupted and totalitarian societies aside, the claims characteristic to conspiracy theories rarely have good grounds. When epistemic authorities reject conspiracy theories they do so because the theories lack sufficient evidence and do not meet rational scrutiny. In this respect, conspiracy theories resemble forms of pseudoscience, such as climate science denialism and so-called alternative medicine ("Silver water is healthy"). The claims of pseudoscientists can be true, perhaps, but it is unlikely that they are.[4]

33.3 Ethics and Conspiracy Theories

Why is conspiracy theorizing morally problematic? It is commonly known that conspiracy theories can produce and have produced socially undesirable consequences. As argued by Karen Douglas and others, when a conspiracy theory gets publicity, some people usually start to believe in it and that in turn can influence their behavior (Douglas and Sutton 2015). The list of potentially or actually harmful conspiracy theories includes theories that deal with vaccination, the extent of anthropogenic climate change, and various ethnic and religious groups. Of course, conspiracy theories may have desirable results as well, perhaps (Clarke 2002, 134). For instance, they can teach us to be critical and conscious citizens, and they can force authorities to further investigations. However, some of the negative consequences have been rather serious. Actions against the Jews have often been fueled by murky conspiracy theories (Swami 2012). Campaigns against vaccination have caused deaths in some countries, and these campaigns typically involve conspiracy theories and not merely information about the parental rights and risks of some vaccines (Craciun and Baban 2012). It can be argued that science denialism and conspiracy theories pose "a serious threat to human health and the long-term sustainability of human civilization" (Hansson 2017, 39; cf. Hansson 2018).

However, it is important to notice that not all conspiracy theories "fuel violence" (Sunstein 2014, 32) or are otherwise immediately dangerous. Claims such as "Shakespeare was somebody else" and "the moon landing was faked" are formally speaking conspiracy theories, as they go against official narratives and refer to conspiracies, but they hardly make people kill each other. If there is something wrong in disseminating these claims as facts although the relevant epistemic authorities deny them, it is not their immediate fatal effects.[5] It seems that the question is of sowing doubt.

It has often been said that conspiracy theories "undermine democratic debate" (Sunstein and Vermeule 2009, 226), impair confidence in the information system and fact-gathering agencies, and lessen general trust in "the behavior and motivations of other people and the social institutions they constitute" (Keeley 1999, 126). There is probably some truth in this claim, although the issue seems more complicated than is usually thought. Conspiracy theories belong to democratic debate. They may make the relevant epistemic authorities improve and clarify the "official" explanations of political events or, in any case, remind us of the grounds of the received explanations. Obviously, a single conspiracy theory does not undermine democracy or cause epistemic or social distrust. Brian L. Keeley (1999, 126; 2003, 105) has argued that accepting a conspiracy theory leads to the situation in which a conspiracy theorist must make "claims of larger and larger conspiracies" and is thus driven to "pervasive skepticism of people and public institutions" – at least when the evidence for a theory fails to obtain and the believer wants to hold onto the view. Keeley seems to exaggerate, however. Most conspiracy theories do not begin with global social skepticism nor do they end with it. Typical conspiracy theories concern a relatively small group of people, and the alleged conspirators are often even named. The "Everyone is involved!" move is very rare.

It is important to notice that hundreds of conspiracy theories have been around for decades, including theories that "the Pearl Harbor attack wasn't a surprise" and "Kennedy's murderer didn't act alone." Millions of people have believed and do believe in these and similar theories (Aaronovitch 2010). Still, until recently, the epistemic and social trust in major institutions (such as mainstream media, official bodies, and academia) has been at a reasonably high level for instance in the U.S. and Western Europe – in comparison to many badly corrupted countries where people find it completely irrelevant what major newspapers and national or local authorities say about this and that (cf. Uslaner 1999). We should not think that conspiracy theorizing *has caused* the collapse of trust in democratic debate, public institutions, and media. It has not.[6]

However, conspiracy theories can be problematic just because they move us closer to the society where people have cynical distrust in public institutions and authorities. In such societies people are unable to make rational long-term plans and reasonable investments, for example. The information problem in totalitarian and badly corrupted countries is not that the authorities and fact-gathering institutions always provide false information. The problem is that it is almost impossible to know whether the information provided is false or not, and people cannot take a default stance that information is trustworthy, that is, reliable and sincerely presented. Thus they cannot make the decisions concerning the proper course of action by presuming that the information provided is probably correct (cf. Govier 1997; Ullmann-Margalit 2004; Welch 2013). Conspiracy theories are steps that actively further our way to a society where people do not trust. By manifesting distrust, conspiracy theories undermine the grounds of the default stance that institutions and information provided by them are trustworthy. A dissemination of a single conspiracy theory is of course only a small step, but it *is* a step. Taken together, conspiracy theories form a threat to the presumption of trustworthiness, although, in fact, there are no grounds for a general suspicion (as there are in totalitarian societies).[7] Conspiracy theories are therefore morally problematic, whether or not some of them may turn out to be true – which is unlikely.[8]

In fact, conspiracy theories seem to be *more problematic* than other forms of sowing confusion and doubt. As opposed to science denialism or creationism, for instance, conspiracy theories tend to involve libels and false accusations that surely raise moral questions (Räikkä 2014, 80). We could say that by conspiracy theorizing a bad thing is realized in a particularly bad way, that is, through libels and accusations against innocent people.[9] Some conspiracy theories, such as the one that claims that "Nobody Died at Sandy Hook" school shooting tragedy, show no concern for the feelings of the victims' family members (Fetzer and Palecek 2015).

33.4 Collective Responsibility for Conspiracy Theories

I have argued that, in democratic and fairly uncorrupted countries, conspiracy theorizing is *prima facie* wrong, as it undermines the reasonable and socially important presumption that the major fact-gathering institutions are, generally speaking, trustworthy and truth-conducive. The question arises whether conspiracy theorists are collectively responsible for their theories and, if they are, what is the sense of "collective responsibility." In this context it is helpful to distinguish between (1) *developers and publishers* and (2) *ordinary believers and disseminators* of conspiracy theories. The distinction between these two groups is not altogether clear – surely the developers and publishers tend to disseminate their theories – but I think the separation is still useful. Developers and publishers are *active conspiracy theorists*. It seems that there are at least three different ways in which conspiracy theorists are collectively responsible for the threat they create on the presumption of trustworthiness. Let us consider all of them one by one. The first concerns actions of ordinary disseminators, the second concerns actions of developers and publishers, and the third concerns *omissions* of developers and publishers. A more thoroughgoing discussion of the notions of collective responsibility and shared action can be found from the first part of the book.

33.4.1 Actions of Ordinary Believers and Disseminators

The dissemination of unverified information is not morally unproblematic, especially when one should be aware that it conflicts with what is told by the relevant epistemic authorities, and when it is likely that the information will be taken more or less seriously – that it may decrease the level of trust in social institutions and make someone believe in a conspiracy that does not exist. A parent who distributes an anti-vaccine conspiracy theory in her Facebook or Twitter accounts by sharing a link surely knows that the information provided is "unofficial," to say the least (Kata 2010). Of course, she may have good intentions in sharing the information, and her worry about vaccines or a particular vaccine can be real. She may have "subjective justification" for her position. But this does not relieve her from all moral responsibility. When millions of peoples disseminate thousands of conspiracy theories (and rumors and denialist fake news) the consequences for the general presumption of trustworthiness of the main social institutions can be serious. An individual person is partly responsible for increasing the risk that we fall into a society that suffers from the lack of trust – however small the risk may be at the moment.

The ordinary dissemination of conspiracy theories can be compared to littering. Litterbugs may appreciate a clean environment but refuse to do their own share. They do not care about the bad example they provide. Although a single litterbug's contribution can be small and harmless in her own eyes – maybe she is cleaning out her car or a bag – the overall effect may be quite unpleasant, especially if others do not have enough resources to prevent the harm. Both the ordinary disseminators of conspiracy theories and litterbugs are responsible for their conduct – they should realize what they are doing. Although the question is of the possible overall impact of the actions committed by individual persons, the talk about "collective responsibility" is appropriate. The undesirable effects are produced *together*, and it seems that conspiracy theories provide an example of "unintentional collective action" here (Chant 2007, 255). Participants *share* the responsibility for the undesirable outcome (cf. May 1992). *Shared responsibility* does not require shared intentions or shared goals.

33.4.2 Actions of Developers and Publishers

Some conceptions of collective responsibility require that there must be we-intentions, or joint commitments, or decision-making procedures, or mutual obligations (Gilbert 2013; Tuomela 2013). However, to say that several people are collectively responsible for a harm does not entail the view that they compose a group which is itself the bearer of responsibility. In other words, collective responsibility does not entail group responsibility, and active conspiracy theorists can be collectively responsible without being responsible as a group. Notice also that "joint action" – a cooperative action that does not involve a commitment to special roles on the part of the individual participants – might suffice for collective responsibility. It seems clear that *active conspiracies act jointly*.

People who develop and publish conspiracy theories are usually interested in revealing conspiracies, and the dissemination of conspiracy theories cannot succeed without some platform (such as internet chat rooms). The question about the origin of conspiracy theories varies case by case, but often individual conspiracy theorists get ideas for their theories by following other conspiracy theorists and that, in some cases, conspiracy theorists work together in groups (Sunstein 2014, 22; cf. Cassam 2016, 163). The groups, in turn, may be connected to one another – an example would be the 9/11 Truth Movement that consists of various groups. Although the links between the active conspiracy theorists are sometimes pretty loose, there *are* some links. In particular, the members of the active wing are capable of communicating with one another, if not directly, then indirectly via other people who also study the possibility of hidden, unrevealed conspiracies. Although the dissemination of conspiracy theories happens largely in ordinary people's personal networks on the internet, or in the "alternative media" (Fine and Ellis 2010, 111; Del Vicario et al. 2016, 554; Stein 2017, 168), the active conspiracy theorists get support from each other and share the attitude of distrust. They are willing to transmit the attitude to others. Since conspiracy theorists act jointly, they can be held *collectively responsible in that sense*.

The active conspiracy theorists should realize what they are doing. Quassim Cassam (2016, 169) argues that conspiracy theorists are not necessarily responsible and blameworthy, as their "intellectual vices" are not within their control. In Cassam's view, "we should be willing to admit the possibility" that the conspiracy theorists just cannot help themselves, and "we should refrain from being excessively moralistic" (Cassam 2016, 169). This view, however, confuses intellectual vices and actions that they may cause. Surely a person who has developed a conspiracy theory could decide not to publish it. If she does not know that the theory is unverified and clearly controversial, she certainly *should know* it, and thus she should decide not to publish it.

33.4.3 Omissions of Developers and Publishers

It is important to notice that the number of active conspiracy theorists is considerably smaller than the number of ordinary believers and disseminators. This raises the question whether the active conspiracy theorists could transform "a collection of people into an organized group or collectivity," as is sometimes the case (Held 1970, 479). Conspiracy theories are developed all around the world, but that should not prevent the founding of an association or a union. Many worldwide groups have their own organizations. Arguably, the active conspiracy theorists could relatively easily turn "into an organized group capable of taking action requiring a decision" (Held 1970, 479). If so, then the failure of not transforming seems to be a fault *that should be attributed to the active conspiracy theorists as a group*. Furthermore, it is a moral fault, since there is certainly a moral reason to associate, namely, the reason that without an organization they cannot regulate the publishing of theories that are far too implausible to deserve public attention. Seen in this way, the active conspiracy theorists are collectively responsible for failing to establish an organization that would guide its members along the lines of investigative journalists, or some other group that has its own principles, however freely formulated. Conspiracy theories are harmful, but they could be less harmful, if some of them were censored.

In principle, an international "union of independent social critics" (or whatever) could prevent some of the risks that the development and publishing of conspiracy theories create. I say "some of the risks," as it is clear that not all of the active conspiracy theorists would join in such an association: they would suspect a conspiracy behind the scenes of "the Fifth Estate" (Burnett 2005, 11). Furthermore, not all conspiracy theories are published in detailed articles or books, although many of them are (Turner 1993; Meyssan 2002; Smith 2004; Fetzer and Palecek 2015). Conspiracy theories are often immediate reactions to some dramatic events, and the "theories" are expressed in a few sentences and published in the internet chat forums or by tweets. No association could prevent such reactions that are all too natural for many people: big events must have big causes (van Prooijen 2012). Notice also that conspiracy theorists are often rivals, and that the *content* of the possible regulations of the independent critics would hardly be too demanding. In all likelihood, the rules would allow the publication of doubts that are quite poorly supported by appropriate documents, just in order to create critical public discussion. Still, we could say that failing to take steps toward an organization or an association is a moral fault. An international association would not be meaningless – whatever we think about the value and acceptability of the activity that is regulated. Collective self-regulation is in many cases very effective. For the active conspiracy theorists, an association should be a welcome addition, not only from a moral point of view, but also from a strategic point of view. The fewer ridiculous conspiracy theories around, the more seriously are the rest considered by the agencies that should investigate them further. Of course, it is quite unlikely that the active conspiracy theorists would in fact organize their action. But that does not bear on the question of whether they should.

No doubt, it can be objected that collective self-regulation would not work in the context of conspiracy theories. Given that conspiracy theories are *prima facie* implausible, conspiracy theorizing cannot be "done well," in the same way that pseudoscience cannot be done well. This objection, however, misses the target of (possible) self-regulative actions. The point of regulative rules would not be to develop "epistemically good conspiracy theories." Rather, the rules would only limit the number of terribly bad and the most offensive theories by censoring them. If we cannot reach the ideal world, we should improve the non-ideal world.

It can also be objected that an organization could *increase* the credibility and influence of conspiracy theories. Suppose that the active conspiracy theorists would organize their action and put some limits on public conspiracy theorizing. That would have the desirable effect that the amount of completely implausible and insulting conspiracy theories would decline. Arguably, however, the conspiracy theories that would be around might get *more* support from people, as they had now passed a sort of critical evaluation, a referee process. That could *increase* the popularity of conspiracy theories. If so, one could argue that, after all, the active conspiracy theorists should not organize their action. However, the evaluation of the consequences of "organized conspiracy theorizing" is a complicated matter. It is hard to establish that the undesirable consequences of having a "union of conspiracy theorists" would be larger than its desirable effects.

32.5 Concluding Remarks

It is not clear that we possess any knowledge at all which is not in some way dependent on testimony. In social life, it is important to be able to make rational long-term plans and reasonable investments, and a precondition of these is that people can take a default stance that the social institutions we use in the acquisition of our beliefs are trustworthy. Considered as a whole, conspiracy theories seem ethically problematic, as they form a threat to the presumption of trustworthiness, although there are no grounds for a general suspicion (totalitarian societies aside). Conspiracy theorists can be held collectively responsible for conspiracy theorizing. First, ordinary believers and disseminators share responsibility as they increase the risk that we fall into a society that suffers from the lack of trust – however inadvertently they act in their own networks. They *share responsibility* for outcome. Second, active conspiracy theorists that develop and publish conspiracy theories *act jointly* and get support from each other and share the attitude of distrust. Their joint action constitutes their collective responsibility. Third, active conspiracy theorists are collectively responsible for *not taking action* that could prevent harms that unmonitored conspiracy theorizing causes. They could prevent some harms *together as a group*, but they have chosen not to prevent them. In this sense they are clearly responsible collectively.

I have assumed that conspiracy theories conflict with the views of the relevant epistemic authorities that we use in the formation of our beliefs. I have also assumed that we are justified in presuming trustworthiness, despite the fact that researchers can make serious mistakes and mainstream media is far from perfect, say, in terms of news coverage and reliability. We know about the failures of epistemic authorities mainly because they have produced information about the failures. Given that the fact-gathering institutions work, generally speaking, tolerably well, conspiracy theories are implausible – although they need not be false.[10] Of course, a person who would like to defend conspiracy theories can deny the distinction between conspiracy theories and conspiracy explanations, claiming that all the explanations that refer to conspiracies are "conspiracy theories," including those supported by the epistemic authorities (Dentith 2016, 587). Such a move may have some grounds, but it would not do justice to the fact that most people do not call all the explanations that refer to conspiracies or plots "conspiracies theories." If we want to describe conspiracy theories accurately, so that the concept reflects ordinary usage, we must distinguish between conspiracy theories and conspiracy explanations – the explanations that we know from history books and mainstream newspapers.

As opposed to conspiracy explanations, conspiracy theories have a bad reputation (Husting and Orr 2007; Coady 2012, 122; Koerth-Baker 2013; Dentith 2016, 587) and deserve it, at least to some extent. Because of that, there are people who would like to deny the dissemination of the theories by law (Lavik 2016, 75). Others think that the state should secretly intervene in groups that develop and publish those theories. Cass R. Sunstein and Adrian Vermeule (2009, 219), for instance, have defended "a cognitive infiltration of extremist groups." I do not think that anything as radical as these suggestions follow from the ethical problems of conspiracy theorizing. Conspiracy theories are a part of democratic civic discussion and, in principle, they can force epistemic authorities to improve and clarify the received explanations. In some cases, further investigations have started in part due to flourishing conspiracy theories and rumors. Of course, those who defend aggressive state action against conspiracy theorizing tend to claim that they are interested only in *false* conspiracy theories, but the problem is that it is hard to know for sure whether a particular conspiracy theory is false or not. Although conspiracy theories are *prima facie* implausible, given the conflict with the relevant experts, single conspiracy theories should be evaluated on a case by case basis, by concentrating on evidence. For instance, the claim that authorities have illegally concealed some worrying information concerning vaccine research may be unlikely, but surely it deserves appropriate attention.

It seems that conspiracy theories are bound to result almost any time there is a political event that shocks masses of people (cf. Olmsted 2009). But it also seems that in most cases multi-agency research commissions are bound to result from such events. Their aim is to provide the official explanation and a credible alternative to conspiracy theories, although this task is seldom explicitly mentioned. An interesting question is who should be invited to participate as members of such commissions. The present practice is to leave out at least conspiracy theorists – an understandable decision indeed – but if the aim is to stop conspiracy theories and rumors, such a practice may not be the best possible.

Acknowledgments

I have benefited from the possibility of discussing the themes of this chapter with the audiences of the Philosophy Research Seminar at the University of Turku and the Philosophy Research Seminar at the University of Helsinki. I would like to thank Lee Basham, Julien Giry and Brian L. Keeley for their helpful comments. Special thanks to the editors of this volume.

Notes

1 Sometimes conspiracies get publicity surprisingly slowly even if they are revealed. Sue Curry Jansen and Brian Martin write that the NSA spying scandal (the Echelon spying system) was originally revealed many years ago, but got more publicity only in 2013: "People who study government surveillance have long been aware of Echelon and related programs, but most of the wider public was unaware until Edward Snowden's 2013 revelations" (Jansen and Martin 2015, 665).

2 The news about the Watergate conspiracy conflicted with the information provided by the Nixon administration, and the theory did not get support from any relevant epistemic authorities in the beginning. However, as a "conspiracy theory" the Watergate theory was quite extraordinary, and there are many who would not call it with that name (at least, not any more). The developers of the theory were professionally responsible and they seem to have worked *within* the relevant epistemic authority (i.e. media) rather than outside and against it. In this sense, the Watergate theory brings to mind claims such as "Marco Polo never actually went to China, and he and the publisher of his book deceived people." This claim is *not* commonly considered a "conspiracy theory," although it refers to a conspiracy and conflicts or conflicted with the received anthropological view (that Polo went to China). The relevant epistemic authorities never find the conspiracy claim *strikingly implausible*. An example of a theory that most epistemic authorities have found strikingly implausible is a claim (supported by some biologists) that genetically modified food will soon kill millions of people, but the truth is kept secret. The question is of a conspiracy theory.

3 Most of us trust in the testimony of the official investigators, but testimony leads to the acquisition of knowledge only under some circumstances – not all circumstances (cf. Lehrer 2006, 145; Foley 2001, 24). Conspiracy theorists encourage us to ask *when* testimony suffices for the acquisition of knowledge, and surely that is an important question. Presenting the question is not to deny that almost everything we know depends in some way or other on the testimony of others (Code 1987, 168; Coady 1992, 7; Adler 2002, 136; Fricker 2006, 225; Lackey 2011, 71).

4 Conspiracy theories may resemble pseudoscience in another respect too. Some pseudoscientists (e.g. those who work for the tobacco industry) produce cultural ignorance deliberately – not merely because they are gullible and naïve (cf. Hansson 2017). The same seems to be true of some conspiracy theorists. Although most conspiracy theorists are serious about their theories, it is likely that some conspiracy theories are on the market partly because of political reasons or because the responsible artists make good money by writing best-sellers about topics that are hot enough – topics such as the alleged fatal effects of genetically modified food (see e.g. Smith 2004). At the same time the authors are able to induce doubt among people, as do some of the pseudoscientists who create fake controversies here and there.

5 Of course, there are many reasons why people shun conspiracy theories and find the pejorative usage of "conspiracy theory" appropriate. One of the reasons is that conspiracy theories tend to question beliefs that are very important for people – beliefs that they *want* to be true. (If somebody tells you that the food you have eaten for years will probably kill you someday, you certainly hope that she is wrong, and this desire will undoubtedly help you to sustain your belief, and eventually conclude that the person who dares to question your belief must be on the wrong track.) In that sense, conspiracy theories are annoying and disturbing. (Cf. Räikkä and Basham 2018.)

6 I argue that conspiracy theories undermine the reasonable and socially important presumption that the major institutions are trustworthy. But surely one of the reasons why conspiracy theories are popular in the first place is that people do not have sufficient trust in governments, the media, and academia. American culture has often been characterized as a "conspiracy culture" (Hofstadter 1966; Vankin 1991; Fenster 1991; Pipes 1997; Melley 2000; Knight 2002; Barkun 2003; Uscinski and Parent 2014), but that does not mean that trust in public institutions has totally collapsed. Of course, there are many who are worried about the present level of trust, and who also think that there may not be sufficient grounds for trust, especially when it comes to politics (see e.g. Ferguson 2017; Basham 2018). In politics, epistemic authorities have proven disastrously unreliable, and many have taken notice of recent history and understandably distrust the practice in which very few determine the beliefs of almost everyone else. Sheila Jasanoff (2017) writes about the "moral panics about the reliability of public knowledge." An interesting thing is that the supporters of conspiracy theories who claim that epistemic authorities are untrustworthy seem to trust in the authorities when the authorities reveal conspiracies. In *these cases* the authorities are considered perfectly trustworthy. (To say that epistemic authorities are not trustworthy corresponds to saying that institutions that are usually considered as epistemic authorities are *not* epistemic authorities.)

7 My argument concerns the development, publishing, and dissemination of conspiracy theories rather than *believing* in them. Arguably, however, distrust (as an instance of not believing someone) can be morally problematic *as such* – if there is not a specific reason for it (cf. Baier 1986). As pointed out by J. L. Austin (1946), if A tells B that p and B does not believe her, A can justifiably feel insulted. Following Linda Zagzebski (2012, 124), we may want to add that A can justifiably feel insulted even "if B does believe what A tells him, but only because B possesses evidence that A is reliable" and speaks sincerely in this circumstance, and "would not have believed what A says otherwise." (Cf. Adler 1997, 451; Hinchman 2005, 563; Moran 2006, 297; Owens 2006, 119.) Possibly, this observation gives us a further explanation why we find the distrust manifested in conspiracy theories morally problematic. We feel that usually there is no specific reason not to believe what the relevant epistemic authorities tell us, but people who believe in conspiracy theories still refuse to believe the authorities. Such distrust may look insulting, although mistrust a person differs from mistrust an institution.

8 Conspiracies are relatively common, judging from the amount of revealed conspiracies and the frequency of the revelations, but this does not imply that conspiracy theories are plausible. They are not. Conspiracy theorists rarely manage to show the existence of conspiracies that were initially denied by the epistemic authorities. Conspiracies are revealed despite conspiracy theories, not because of them. Since the relevant epistemic authorities have done their job well, and we have relied on their testimony and expertise, we know about conspiracies. Normal adult persons are generally aware that conspiracies happen and that conspiracies are as common as corruption, bribery, and nepotism.

9 A conspiracy theorist is not a person who encourages us to epistemic abstinence or agnosticism. She does not teach us not to choose our sides when the issue is unclear. On the contrary, a conspiracy theorist says that we should choose our side, namely, the side that goes against conventional wisdom and mainstream. Conspiracy theorists are not "just asking questions" and warn us, say, about the mainstream newspapers' biased expressions and negligence of certain news items. They present positive theories. Conspiracy theorists are usually sincere – they report what they think – but often a conspiracy theorist gets motivation for conspiracy theorizing from her prejudices, say, about ethnic minorities, public health authorities, or intelligence agencies (Räikkä 2009, 463).

10 Perhaps the representatives of the information-gathering institutions *are* sometimes insincere. According to Brian Martin (2010, 215), supporters of "dominant scientific theories sometimes attack competing, less favoured theories in ways that conflict with expectations of proper scientific behaviour." Lee Basham (2018, 73) argues that "some conspiratorial scenarios, even if well evidenced, are too 'toxic' for our usual institutions of public information to disseminate to the public, or even investigate." M. R. X. Dentith (2018, 17) thinks that "our society might look open in a way that it is not."

References

Aaronovitch, David, *Voodoo Histories: The Role of Conspiracy Theory in Shaping Modern History* (Riverhead Books, New York 2010).

Adler, Jonathan E., "Lying, Deceiving, or Falsely Implying", *The Journal of Philosophy* 94 (1997), 435–452.

Adler, Jonathan E., *Belief's Own Ethics* (The MIT Press, London 2002).

Austin, J. L., "Other Minds" (1946) in his *Philosophical Papers* (Oxford University Press, Oxford 1979).

Baier, Annette, "Trust and Antitrust", *Ethics* 96 (1986), 231–260.
Barkun, Michael, *A Culture of Conspiracy: Apocalyptic Visions in Contemporary America* (University of California Press, Berkeley 2003).
Basham, Lee, "Joining the Conspiracy", *Argumenta* 3 (2018), 73–92.
Basham, Lee, "Malevolent Global Conspiracy", *Journal of Social Philosophy* 34 (2003), 91–103.
Burnett, Thom et al., *Conspiracy Encyclopedia* (Collins & Brown, London 2005).
Cassam, Quassim, "Vice Epistemology", *The Monist* 99 (2016), 169–180.
Chant, Sara Rachel, "Unintentional Collective Action", *Philosophical Explorations* 10 (2007), 245–256.
Clarke, Steve, "Conspiracy Theories and Conspiracy Theorizing", *Philosophy of the Social Sciences* 32 (2002), 131–150.
Coady, C. A. J., *Testimony: A Philosophical Study* (Clarendon Press, Oxford 1992).
Coady, David, *What to Believe Now* (Wiley-Blackwell, London 2012).
Code, Lorraine, *Epistemic Responsibility* (Brown University Press, London 1987).
Craciun, Catrinel and Adriana Baban, "Who Will Take the Blame? Understanding the Reasons Why Romanian Mothers decline Hpv Vaccination for Their Daughters", *Vaccine* 30 (2012), 6789–6793.
Del Vicario, Michela, et al. "The Spreading of Misinformation Online", *Proceedings of the National Academy of Sciences of the United States of America* 113 (2016), 554–559.
Dentith, Matthew, "When Inferring to a Conspiracy Might Be the Best Explanation", *Social Epistemology* 31 (2016), 572–591.
Dentith, Matthew, "Expertise and Conspiracy Theories", *Social Epistemology* 33 (2018).
Douglas, Karen and Robbie Sutton, "Climate Change: Why the Conspiracy Theories Are Dangerous." *Bulletin of the Atomic Scientists* 71 (2015), 98–106.
Fenster, Mark, *Conspiracy Theories: Secrecy and Power in American Culture* (University of Minnesota Press, Minneapolis 1991).
Ferguson, Niall, *The Square and the Tower: Networks, Hierarchies and the Struggle for Global Power* (Allen Lane, London 2017).
Fetzer, Jim and Mike Palecek, *Nobody Died at Sandy Hook: It Was a FEMA Drill to Promote Gun Control* (Moon Rock Books, USA 2015).
Fine, Gary A. and Bill Ellis, *The Global Grapevine: Why Rumors of Terrorism, Immigration, and Trade Matter* (Oxford University Press, New York 2010).
Foley, Richard, *Intellectual Trust in Oneself and Others* (Cambridge University Press, Cambridge 2001).
Fricker, Elisabeth, "Testimony and Epistemic Autonomy" in J. Lackey and E. Sosa (Eds.), *The Epistemology of Testimony* (Clarendon Press, Oxford 2006), 225–250.
Gilbert, Margaret, *Joint Commitment* (Oxford University Press, Oxford 2013).
Goldberg, Sanford C., "'If That Were True I Would Have Heard about It by Now'", in A.I. Goldman and D. Whitcomb (Eds.), *Social Epistemology: Essential Readings* (Oxford University Press, Oxford 2011), 92–108.
Goldman, Alvin I., "Experts: Which Ones Should You Trust?" in A.I. Goldman and D. Whitcomb (Eds.), *Social Epistemology: Essential Readings* (Oxford University Press, Oxford 2011), 109–134.
Govier, Trudy, *Social Trust and Human Communities* (McGill-Queen's University Press, Montreal 1997).
Guerrero, Alexander A., "Living with Ignorance in a World of Experts" in R. Peels (Ed.), *Perspectives on Ignorance from Moral and Social Philosophy* (Routledge, New York 2017), 156–185.
Hansson, Sven Ove, "Science Denialism as a Form of Pseudoscience", *Studies in History and Philosophy of Science* 63 (2017), 39–47.
Hansson, Sven Ove, "Dealing with Climate Science Denialism", *Climate Policy* 2018. https://doi.org/10.1080/14693062.2017.1415197
Harding, Luke, *Collusion: Secret Meeting, Dirty Money, and How Russia Helped Donald Trump to Win* (Penguin Random House, New York 2017).
Held, Virginia, "Can Random Collection of Individuals Be Morally Responsible?", *The Journal of Philosophy* 67 (1970), 471–481.
Hinchman, Edward S., "Telling as Inviting to Trust", *Philosophy and Phenomenological Research* 70 (2005), 562–587.
Hofstadter, Richard. *The Paranoid Style in American Politics and Other Essays* (Jonathan Cape, London 1966).
Husting, Ginna and Martin Orr. "Dangerous Machinery: 'Conspiracy Theorist' as a Transpersonal Strategy of Exclusion." *Symbolic Interaction* 30 (2007), 127–150.
Jansen, Sue Curry and Brian Martin, "The Streisand Effect and Censorship Backfire", *International Journal of Communication* 9 (2015), 656–671.

Jasanoff, Sheila, "Back from the Brink: Truth and Trust in the Public Sphere", *Issues in Science and Technology* 33 (2017).

Kata, Anna, "A Post-Modern Pandora's Box: Anti-Vaccination Misinformation on the Internet", *Vaccine* 28 (2010), 1709–1716.

Keeley, Brian L., "Of Conspiracy Theories", *The Journal of Philosophy* 96 (1999), 109–126.

Keeley, Brian L., "Nobody Expects the Spanish Inquisition! More Thoughts on Conspiracy Theory", *Journal of Social Philosophy* 34 (2003), 104–110.

Knight, Peter, (ed.) *Conspiracy Nation: The Politics of Paranoia in Postwar America* (New York University Press, New York 2002).

Koerth-Baker, Maggie. "Why Rational People Buy Into Conspiracy Theories." *The New York Times Magazine*, 21 May 2013.

Lackey, Jennifer, "Acquiring Knowledge from Others" in A.I. Goldman and D. Whitcomb (Eds.), *Social Epistemology: Essential Readings* (Oxford University Press, Oxford 2011), 71–91.

Lavik, Trugve, "Climate Change Denial, Freedom of Speech and Global Justice", *Etikk i praksis. Nordic Journal of Applied Ethics* (2016), 10 (2), 75–90.

Lehrer, Keith, "Testimony and Trustworthiness" in J. Lackey and E. Sosa (Eds.), *The Epistemology of Testimony* (Clarendon Press, Oxford 2006), 145–159.

Levy, Neil, "Radically Socialized Knowledge and Conspiracy Theories", *Episteme: A Journal of Social Epistemology* 4 (2007), 181–192.

Martin, Brian, "How to Attack a Scientific Theory and get Away with It (Usually): The Attempt to Destroy an Origin-of-AIDS Hypothesis", *Science and Culture* 19 (2010), 215–239.

May, Larry, *Sharing Responsibility* (University of Chicago Press, Chicago 1992).

Melley, Timothy, *Empire of Conspiracy: The Culture of Paranoia in Postwar America* (Cornell University Press, Ithaca 2000).

Meyssan, Thierry, *9/11: The Big Lie* (Carnot Publishing, London 2002).

Moran, Richard, "Getting Told and Being Believed" in J. Lackey and E. Sosa (Eds.), *The Epistemology of Testimony* (Clarendon Press, Oxford 2006), 272–304.

Olmsted, Kathryn, *Real Enemies: Conspiracy Theories and American Democracy, World War I to 9/11* (Oxford University Press, New York 2009).

Olmsted, Kathryn, "The Truth Is Out There: Citizen Sleuths from the Kennedy Assassination to the 9/11 Truth Movement", *Diplomatic History* 35 (2011), 671–693.

Owens, David, "Testimony and Assertion", *Philosophical Studies* 130 (2006), 105–129.

Pigden, Charles R., "Conspiracy Theories and the Conventional Wisdom", *Episteme* 4 (2007), 219–232.

Pipes, Daniel, *How the Paranoid Style Flourishes and Where It Comes From* (The Free Press, New York 1997).

Räikkä, Juha, "The Ethics of Conspiracy Theorizing", *The Journal of Value Inquiry* 43 (2009), 457–468.

Räikkä, Juha, *Social Justice in Practice* (Springer, Heidelberg 2014).

Räikkä, Juha, "Conspiracies and Conspiracy Theories", *Argumenta* 3 (2018), 205–216.

Räikkä, Juha and Lee Basham, "Conspiracy Theory Phobia" in J. Uscinski (Ed.), *Conspiracy Theories and People Who Believe Them* (Oxford University Press, Oxford 2018) 178-186.

Ritola, Juho, "Critical Thinking Is Epistemically Responsible", *Metaphilosophy* 43 (2012), 659–678.

Smith, Jeffrey, *Seeds of Deception* (Green Books, London 2004).

Stein, Richard A., "The Golden Age of Anti-Vaccine Conspiracies", *Germs* 7 (2017), 168–170.

Sunstein, Cass R., *Conspiracy Theories and Other Dangerous Ideas* (Simon & Schuster, New York 2014).

Sunstein, Cass R. and Adrian Vermeule, Conspiracy Theories (January 15, 2008). Harvard Public Law Working Paper No. 08-03; U of Chicago, Public Law Working Paper No. 199; U of Chicago Law & Economics, Olin Working Paper No. 387.

Swami, Viren, "Social Psychological Origins of Conspiracy Theories: The Case of the Jewish Conspiracy Theory in Malaysia", *Frontiers in Psychology* 3 (2012), 280.

Tuomela, Raimo, *Social Ontology* (Oxford University Press, New York 2013).

Turner, Patricia, *I Heard it Through the Grapevine* (University of California Press, Berkeley 1993).

Ullmann-Margalit, Edna, "Trust, Distrust, and in Between" in R. Hardin (Ed.), *Russell Sage Foundation Series on Trust* (New York, Russell Sage Foundation, New York 2004), 60–82.

Uscinski, Joseph E. and Joseph M. Parent, *American Conspiracy Theories* (Oxford University Press, Oxford 2014).

Uslaner, E. M., "Democracy and Social Capital" in E. Warren (Ed.), *Democracy and Trust* (Cambridge University Press, Cambridge 1999), 121–150.

Van Prooijen, Jan-Willem, "Suspicions of Injustice: The Sense-Making Function of Belief in Conspiracy Theories", in E. Kals and J. Maes (Eds.), *Justice and Conflicts* (Springer, Heidelberg 2012), 121–132.

Van Prooijen, Jan-Willem and Michele Acker, "The Influence of Control on Belief in Conspiracy Theories: Conceptual and Applied Extensions", *Applied Cognitive Psychology* 29 (2015), 753–761.

Vankin, Jonathan, *Conspiracies, Cover-Ups, and Crimes: Political Manipulation and Mind Control in America* (Paragon, New York 1991).

Welch, Shay, "Transparent Trust and Oppression", *Critical Review of International Social and Political Philosophy* 16 (2013), 45–64.

Zagzebski, Linda Trinkaus, *Epistemic Authority: A Theory of Trust, Authority, and Autonomy in Belief* (Oxford University Press, 2012).

34
ENABLING COLLECTIVE RESPONSIBILITY FOR ENVIRONMENTAL JUSTICE

Kenneth Shockley

34.1 The Responsibility to Take Responsibility

> It all came back to the concept of justice, for Love Canal families felt that they had been sacrificed on the altar of profit and power. ... Activists wondered: Would the government be so apathetic about hazardous waste in an affluent area? ... As more toxic waste sites were discovered after 1978, and more hazardous waste facilities were planned for the future, they fell into a familiar geographical pattern: certain places – particularly blue-collar locales and communities of color – faced greater toxic threats.
>
> *(Newman, 2016, p. 172)*

The harms that generate environmental injustice are commonly understood to be matters of collective responsibility. As Robyn Eckersley reminds us, "environmental protection is generally accepted as a public good, and the task of preventing environmental degradation is widely understood as a collective responsibility" (2016, p. 346). But the nature of this collective responsibility is far from clear. The aim of this chapter is to provide some clarification.

One challenge to assigning collective responsibility for environmental injustice is that despite the long string of corporate malfeasance, governmental misconduct, and individual misdeed there is seldom a single agent, collective or otherwise, on whom to pin moral responsibility. This challenges our intuitive response to a harm or injustice: identify a culpable agent who caused that harm or injustice and assign blame accordingly. We can think of this typical approach as a backward directed approach to responsibility. But this focus on blameworthy actions that have already occurred may not always be the best way of addressing the harms of environmental injustice. In cases of environmental injustice we are responsible for more than just what we have done, directly. The scope of responsibility is broader. When our concerns are more with the background conditions that enable environmental injustice, we should also consider our forward directed responsibilities to change the social practices and institutions that constitute those background conditions, what we will here call our institutional environment (Wringe, 2014). We will see in what follows that by distinguishing forward and backward directed responsibility we can clarify the connection between collective responsibility and environmental justice. As environmental justice is dependent on what Iris Marion Young (2006, 2013) has referred to as *structural* injustice, and our focus is on the social conditions that disadvantage one group over another, responsibility for injustice is often better framed in terms of our forward directed responsibility for generating or reforming social practices and institutions. This chapter will argue that those who can effect change bear a forward directed shared responsibility to address the institutional environment in which environmental injustice occurs. While we cannot hold individuals responsible for what is out of their control, we can hold individuals responsible for failing to respond to the structural concerns animating Eckerlsey's intuition that environmental justice is a matter of collective responsibility. And, in some cases, we can hold them responsible, in a backward directed sense, for having in the past failed to satisfy this forward directed responsibility.

The chapter will proceed as follows. Section 34.2 will introduce environmental injustice and its relation to structural injustice. In section 34.3 the chapter will address what has elsewhere been called the programming account of collective responsibility (Shockley, 2007), according to which responsibility is warranted in cases where the (causal) role of a collective is ineliminable in characterizing the harm, wrong, or injustice. This provides a means of framing the connection between moral responsibility and collective responsibility more productively: we are responsible in a forward directed sense in those cases where addressing the moral wrong requires changing the institutional environment rather than (merely) assigning blame. In section 34.4 the chapter will outline the particularly significant role institutions and organizations play in providing the causal connection between individual actors and changes in the institutional environment. In section 34.5 the chapter will focus on the prospective shared responsibilities individuals have for addressing environmental justice. A brief conclusion will return us to the central theme of the chapter, that as individuals we have shared responsibilities for not only what we have done, but also what we have allowed and what we might have prevented. In cases where, together, we reasonably could have changed our institutional environment, we have a shared responsibility for not having done so. These shared responsibilities to make changes to our institutional environment provide the sense in which we are collectively responsible for environmental injustice.

34.2 Structural Environmental Injustice as a Matter of Collective Responsibility

While the precise definition of environmental justice is contested (Schlosberg, 2007), Kristin Shrader-Frechette provides this helpful characterization:

> Environmental Justice requires both a more equitable distribution of environmental goods and bads and greater public participation in evaluating and apportioning these goods and bads... . evidence indicates that minorities ... who are disadvantaged in terms of education, income, and occupation not only bear a disproportionate share of environmental risk and death, but also have less power to protect themselves.
>
> *(2002, p. 6)*

Particularly in light of Shrader-Frechette's definition we might think of environmental justice as no more than a distributional problem. Indeed, the effects of environmental injustice – from air pollution to water contamination to climate change – are indeed typically expressed through distributional concerns. However, the patterns taken by these distributional concerns indicate the underlying social, political, and institutional structures of society are key contributors to environmental injustice (Shrader-Frechette, 2002; Walker, 2012; Carmin and Agyeman, 2011). Eckersley's appeal to collective responsibility is intended in part to remind us that environmental justice is a matter of public concern, a responsibility we all have to alleviate conditions that systematically disadvantage one group at the expense of another.

> Unlike individual injustices, where undeserved harms can be traced to the willful or negligent acts of identifiable 'culprits,' structural injustices are undeserved harms that are collectively produced through recurrent social practices that are considered 'normal' and therefore non-blameworthy.
>
> *(Eckersley, 2016, pp. 346–347)*

Similarly, the problems of environmental justice are not primarily individual or distributional, but, as we will see, structural.

Along these lines it is common to frame environmental injustice as a form of structural injustice, yet despite the common appeal to structural injustice a formal account is elusive. On Iris Marion Young's influential account,

> Structural injustice exists when social processes put large categories of persons under a systematic threat of domination or deprivation of the means to develop and exercise their capacities, at the same time as these processes enable others to dominate or have a wide range of opportunities for developing and exercising their capacities.
>
> *(Young, 2006, p. 114)*

We can think of the structure that frames Young's account in terms of the systems of practices, laws, and expectations, the institutional environment, that makes the circumstances in which an individual acts so remarkably different, and, on occasion, so unfair. When a person is unable to vote because voting is only allowed during hours when that person is required to work, when a person is unable to relocate as required by their employer because there is no reliable childcare at their new location, when a person is unable to find housing that will provide a healthy and safe environment for her children, in all of these cases the institutional environment generates structural injustice (See Young, 2013, pp. 43–74). In such cases, the institutional environment in which individuals make their decisions is structured in a way that certain individuals face challenges that others do not. Fairness is systemically compromised, and environmental injustice threatens.

While the dependence of environmental injustice on our institutional environment is well established in the environmental justice literature (Bullard, 2000; Agyeman, 2013; Schlosberg, 2007), we can see this most clearly through a brief examination of three instances of environmental injustice.

Love Canal. In the late 1970s residents of the Love Canal development, just to the east of Niagara Falls, New York, discovered that their homes had been built on or in extremely close proximity to a stew of toxic chemicals. While the precise composition of the chemicals was not publicly known, the chemical stew was widely understood to be highly toxic, and "no fewer than four major reports on Love Canal confirmed the presence of chemicals in homes" (Newman, 2016, p. 105). The health and well-being of locals was severely compromised. In the face of these threats to health and well-being, residents wanted out. However, they did not have the financial resources to leave without selling their homes (Newman, 2016, p. 102), and for obvious reasons they were unable to do so. Local residents "felt trapped in their own home[s]" (Newman, 2016, p. 109). They looked to an institutional or governmental response to facilitate their exit. But through a failure to recognize their predicament and need for relocation, it took years for any substantial support to be provided. Indeed, lack of political recognition and the corresponding lack of voice constituted a problem perhaps more severe than the economic challenges posed by relocation. The lack of voice of those in Love Canal, and the vulnerability exacerbated by that lack of voice, was not the result of the decisions made by those in Love Canal. Nor was it the fault of any one individual or collective agent. The problem came from institutional failures and social processes involving disposal of waste and the lack of oversight of waste disposal, the lack of corporate accountability, the failure of institutional oversight, economic pressures, and political inaction. The people of Love Canal faced a threat to their well-being and to a flourishing life, and their predicament was, initially, barely recognized.

Of course, environmental toxins were not limited to Love Canal, and their wider distribution points to a more general problem, anticipated in this chapter's epigraph. In the very different responses to the largely white community at risk in the Love Canal case, and the largely black community at risk in the Carver Terrace case (Shrader Frechette, 2002, p.7), we can see that the structural features of environmental justice are complex, many layered, and pervasive. They are interwoven with structural racism, classism, regionalism, and the wide range of group differentiated vulnerabilities that permeate society more generally. Many of the problems that generate the unequal burdens of environmental pollution are tied to the failure to recognize the power differentials that allow for those who find themselves in a certain social or geographical situation to be subject to grave environmental harms.

Transnational E-Waste. While the residents of Love Canal suffered from their unchosen proximity to toxic pollution from decades past, problems of environmental injustice arise with equal clarity and severity in the international arena. Through its comparative economic and political power, the developed world is able to draw the benefits of development while offloading the burdens and costs of that development. As described in a wide range of environmental justice literature (Walker, 2012; Shrader-Frechette, 2002; Carmin and Agyeman, 2011; Lepawsky, 2018), the cross-border movement of discarded and recycled electronics – cell phones, televisions, computers, printers, and the wide range of electronics so central to our contemporary world – provides a distressingly clear example of environmental injustice. Despite the 1989 adoption of the Basel Convention on the Control of Transboundary Movements of Hazardous Wastes and their Disposal (Basel Convention, 2018), many parties have used loopholes surrounding recycling (along with outright violation of the convention) to transfer unwanted waste from the developed world to the developing world (Walker, 2012; Pellow, 2006, 2007; Basel Action Network, 2002, 2005, 2018). Those who bear the costs of this "e-waste," through efforts at salvaging metals and other valuable materials, are dependent on the illicit practices that provide them with this "resource." Under awful conditions the electronic goods generated for the use of the powerful and wealthy are "recycled" by those who could never afford those items, who need the meager economic benefit that comes from the scrap material salvaged from those items, who suffer the health consequences of working in highly toxic environments with no protective equipment, and who are compelled by the pressures of politics and economics to compromise their economic opportunities, physical health, and environmental well-being (*Guardian*, 2009; *Pacific Standard*, 2018). Apart from the costs of this injustice in terms of the physical health of those working to salvage economically valuable materials from the waste, the case of e-waste points to the ability of power differentials to enable the exploitation of economic vulnerabilities half the world away (Lepawsky, 2018, pp. 71–91). With few economic, social, or personally viable options, and little or no political voice to contest these conditions, background economic and political pressures compromise one group for the sake of another, something akin to what Bullard (1992) calls "environmental blackmail." Those who bear the costs are seldom recognized by those who use the products that are later salvaged, even as those who use the products benefit from the ability to have their products recycled. As Lepawsky (2018) points out, the need for reuse and repair lends itself to further vulnerabilities and demonstrates that the problem is not merely the dumping of e-waste, but a failure to recognize the voice, interests, and needs of those who serve as part of the chain of recovery, reuse, and disposal. The problems associated with dumping e-waste go well beyond questions of distribution; they result from a failure of recognition as well (Walker, 2012; Bullard, 1990).

Climate Change. A further dimension of environmental justice can be seen in the case of the differential effects of climate change. Whereas Love Canal and the problem of e-waste focus on environmental pollution in geographically discrete locations, the burdens of climate change are global in distribution. However, that global distribution is far from equal (Caney, 2014; Shue, 2014; Schlosberg, 2012; Hayward, 2007). We expect populations that are economically less powerful, politically stifled, and geographically less mobile to bear the brunt of climate change. And these same populations – from the poor in urban regions of coastal nations to citizens of island nations to farmers working in climate compromised agricultural zones – have minimal voice in generating policy to mitigate emissions causing climate change or to adapt to its consequences. The lack of distributional fairness of the burdens associated with our response to and the consequences of climate change is not entirely the result of the decisions of some collective agent, even if some of the harms and injustices associated with climate change could have been avoided or mitigated by the actions of various state actors. The cause of the injustice, the lack of fairness and imbalance of burdens and benefits on vulnerable populations, is largely a matter of economics, politics, and broad social conditions, that is, our institutional environment. These conditions allow the globe's wealthy to live lives that generate carbon footprints that will affect them less than the vulnerable, and to do so in a way that renders inaudible the voice of those who suffer. The problem is as much a matter of recognition as it is of distribution. As Robyn Eckersley (2016) has argued, the unjust distribution of the harms associated with climate change, and the responsibilities we have to address those harms, are largely matters of structural injustice.

Unifying these examples, the underlying environmental injustice has a recognitional component binding distributional problems to the institutional environment in which those distributional problems occur (Young, 1990, 2013; Frasier, 1998, 2000; Bullard, 1990; Alternet, 2016). In the cases referenced above, environmental injustice arises out of failures of recognition: "they stand in a position of being vulnerable" (Young, 2013, p. 45) to a set of threatening conditions out of their control and unacknowledged by the powerful. The voice of those subject to environmental injustice is unheard. That is to say, "part of the problem of injustice, and part of the reason for unjust distribution, is a lack of the recognition of group difference" (Schlosberg, 2007, p. 15). On this view, the distributional injustice that is often the clear expression of environmental injustice "comes directly out of social structures, cultural beliefs, and institutional contexts" (Schlosberg, 2007, p. 15). The need to recognize the social and institutional underpinnings of injustice, particularly in light of the power differentials between affected populations, makes clear that the relevant problems of justice are structural. It remains to be seen how the suppression of voice and the structural concerns that animate environmental injustice, matters of the institutional environment which seem largely to be out of the control of individual agents, can be a matter of collective responsibility.

34.3 Collective Responsibility as Explanatory Ineliminability

As a conceptual matter, there are certain events that can only be plausibly characterized by invoking groups or collectives. One person cannot storm the Bastille, but through the interdependent actions of many it was stormed. One person cannot (typically) change a community's attitude of acceptance toward an immigrant community. Yet even without judicial or legislative action that change may take place. One person may make changes to their own emissions behavior, but the effects relevant for global emission levels are found at the level of communities, nations, or humanity writ large. Even if they contribute to it individual actions and attitudes differ *in kind* from collective actions and attitudes (Gilbert, 2013; Tuomela, 2006, 2013; Pettit, 1993, 2003; but see Chant et al., 2014). Some phenomena require appeal to collectives and groups to explain their occurrence, even as we recognize the ontological dependence of those phenomena on individual agents. Whether we think of the masses storming the Bastille, a culture's changing attitude toward certain forms of social behavior, or the pollution of nearby streams and rivers, there are some phenomena, and some harms, that can only be described by appealing to groups. The cases of environmental injustice described above are such phenomena. One cannot explain the injustice of Love Canal, the nightmare of e-waste, or the systemic pattern of climate-based vulnerability without reference to group-based vulnerabilities, group-based harms, and the structural features that enable those harms. But what is the connection between individual actors and those structural features that constitute the institutional environment? It seems implausible that, at least generally, individual actors alone can directly effect change on the structures that generate injustice (Eckersley, 2016, p. 353). When there is no group-level *agent* involved, the connection between moral responsibility and group-level phenomena is not always obvious.

Traditionally, accounts of moral responsibility are based on what agents voluntarily choose to bring about. In the language introduced above, these are typically backward directed accounts.[1] Building off this more traditional treatment of moral responsibility, accounts of collective moral responsibility typically start by developing analogous requirements on either agency or the capacity of a collective to choose.[2] These accounts often make collective responsibility parasitic on notions of collective agency, whether by appeal to collective intentionality (Bratman, 1999, 2013; Tuomela, 1989, 2013), a unified plural subject (Gilbert, 2000, Velleman, 1997), or the deliberative and representational capacities of groups (Pettit, 2004; List and Pettit, 2011). Generally, these accounts focus on a causal connection between the occurrence of a harm and the actions of an agent. While this approach is helpful in those cases where the focus of inquiry is on assigning blame, it requires collective responsibility to be dependent on collective agency. It has little to say about cases of collective phenomena without collective agency. Such accounts may not help us address cases where the individual actions of large numbers of seemingly nonculpable agents aggregate to form great, even catastrophic harm. After all, as Jamieson (2012, p. 196) puts it, we are now in an era where through the aggregate effects of climate change we might destroy the world without any individual agent bearing morally responsibility for that destruction. Responsibility might well be shared across more than one individual in ways that do not require a robust collective intention, capacity, or agent.

Whereas collective responsibility is responsibility *of* a collective, *shared* responsibility is responsibility of individual members of a group for something done in concert with other members of that group. As Larry May puts it,

> When a group of people shares responsibility for a harm, responsibility distributes to each member of the group. When a group is collectively responsible for a harm, the group as such is responsible...Shared responsibility does not depend on the existence of a cohesive group since it concerns only aggregated personal responsibility.
>
> *(May, 1992, p. 38)*

We will see below that while shared responsibility is responsibility *of* individuals, the ability of individuals in concert to make changes in their institutional environment provides an avenue for connecting individual responsibility, in this shared sense, with structural and environmental injustice. However, the form of shared responsibility that May advocates is focused on the attribution of blame, a backward directed approach to responsibility (see Young, 2013, p. 111). As those who point to the connection between collective responsibility and environmental justice more generally are interested in what collectives are responsible for in a less distributed, and less backward directed sense, we will need to look further.

A different way of thinking about collective responsibility, one that shifts the emphasis to the contribution of individuals and the avoidance of future harms, would be to focus on explaining the causal role groups have in bringing about states of affairs through the actions of constituent members. One such account, the programming account of collective responsibility, relies on the explanatory ineliminability of collective entities for making sense of harms (or goods) that result from the actions or behaviors of those entities (Shockley, 2007).[3] In such cases we say the collective *programs* for the production of the state of affairs even when the collective is not an agent. For example, we might understand a mob to be collectively responsible for burning down a city without thinking that the mob constituted an *agent*. The harm, burning down the city, could not have taken place without the mob. More importantly, individual acts of arson in isolation wouldn't *explain* the burning down of the city. Only by framing individual actions in aggregate, conceptualizing these complementary actions as collective phenomena, can we speak of the kind of event that is the burning down of the city. While individuals might be responsible for acts of arson, they are not, qua individuals, responsible for burning down the city. That responsibility falls, collectively, on the mob. Explanatory ineliminability – the sense in which we cannot reasonably talk about the harm without appealing to the mob – provides a means of attributing collective responsibility when the actions of constituents together lead to a consequence that cannot be attributed to them other than as a whole. In the same way the best explanation for a square peg not fitting into a round hole is not by appeal to the molecules that collide but by the incompatibility of squareness and roundness, the best explanation for burning down the city is by appeal to the mob, not to individual persons (Pettit, 1993; Pettit and Jackson, 1992). The aggregate actions of individual actors (arson, etc.) constituted a collective phenomenon that "programmed" for the distinctively collective harm (the burning down of the city). This account still leaves open the possibility that individuals may be morally responsible for actions that contribute to that collective harm. While without collective agency there may be no backward directed moral responsibility on the part of the mob itself, there may well be for individual members of the mob in virtue of their shared participation in the act (May, 1987).

The programming account provides a helpful way of characterizing the connections between seemingly innocuous individual actions and environmental justice, and does so in a way that, as we will see below, connects individual moral responsibilities to collective responsibility. Collective responsibility is framed in terms of the way collectives control for the production of collective or group phenomena. This is expressed through the explanatory ineliminability of those collectives in characterizing the harm or injustice. Crucially, this control does not require collective agency, and so is particularly well suited for cases where the harms and injustices to be addressed are structural rather than agentive. Given the importance of structural considerations to matters of environmental justice this is a vital question to be addressed. For the citizens of Love Canal, the exploited populations suffering from e-waste, and the vulnerable populations facing climate change, all suffering from structural vulnerabilities and recognitional injustice, the question is more than merely theoretical. But precisely how do we connect individual moral responsibilities to environmental injustice? The answer, we shall see, lies in the role played by institutions in addressing structural injustice, and thereby environmental injustice.

34.4 Focusing on Institutions

But what are institutions? On one account, institutions are sets of rules, formal or informal, and some shared understanding of those rules that governs actors' interactions (Young, 2013; Oran Young, 2016; see also Gardiner, 2017). Frank Hindriks and Francesco Guala provide a helpful characterization of the three most common accounts of institutions:

> According to the rule-based conception, institutions are behavioral rules that guide and constrain behavior during social interaction, while according to the equilibrium-based conception institutions are equilibria of strategic games. The third account of institutions... . conceives of institutions as systems of constitutive rules that assign statuses and functions to physical entities – for example pieces of paper that are to be used as money.
>
> *(2015, p. 461)*

The first view has the advantage of providing a descriptively rich characterization of our commonsense notion of institutions such as property or marriage, and the second has the advantage of providing the right sort of incentive structure to capture the way institutions motivate the coordination of individual behavior. The third view, that institutions provide rules for assigning meaning to physical objects, captures the sense that institutions provide a means of (in Searle's (1995) terms) constructing social reality. Through institutions we can create meaning in objects (e.g., turn a simple piece of paper into money). And through this constructive process we can develop more formal institutions, which here we will call organizations, robust enough to be candidates for collective agency.

As Hindriks and Guala (2015) point out, these positions are not inconsistent (see also Guala, 2016). Following Hindriks and Guala's analysis, we can take institutions to be systems of rules in equilibria that regulate behavior, provide incentives for those subject to the institution to abide by those systems of rules, and serve as the foundation for more formal organizations (but see Rabinowicz, 2018). On this conception, institutions provide coordinating control over the behavior of individuals subject to those institutions; this makes them invaluable for explaining group-level behavior. Most importantly for our purposes, to the extent that institutions are ineliminable in our responses to group-level phenomena, particularly in addressing the structural vulnerabilities and group-based exploitation so central to environmental justice, they are a necessary means of satisfying our shared responsibilities. Whether systems of law, convention, and practice that allow us to coordinate our action – like the institution of property or the institution of money – or more formal institutions – organizations like the Environmental Protection Agency or nongovernmental organizations – institutions serve as instruments through which we can make changes in the conditions that allow the exploitation of vulnerabilities. Institutions provide a means of causally connecting individual agents to the structural background so central to instances of environmental injustice, and on which Young was so focused.

Of course, a causal link between the generation of harms and a collective phenomenon that programs for that harm is not sufficient to attribute collective moral responsibility (List and Pettit, 2011, p. 158). Collective agency is required for that, either in the backward directed sense of being responsible for what it, as a collective, did, or in the forward directed sense of being required, as a collective, to perform some action or effect some change. Following List and Pettit (2011, p. 158) groups are morally responsible agents if they, collectively

(1) face "a normatively significant choice, involving the possibility of doing something good or bad, right or wrong"
(2) have "the understanding and access to evidence required for making normative judgments about the options" and
(3) have "the control required for choosing between the options"

The central idea for our purposes is that for a group (a collective, in the language being used in this chapter) to be morally responsible it must both have the autonomous capacity to make choices and be responsive to those choices in a way that reflects the moral character of the choice. How and to what extent groups are able to make autonomous choices and respond appropriately to good or bad, right or wrong, is beyond the scope of this chapter (but see Searle, 1995; List and Pettit, 2011; Gilbert, 2013; Tuomela, 2013). However, our more formal institutions and organizations may well be capable of functioning as collective agents. And, as we will see below, developing or generating organizations from our institutions, following the pattern of the citizen response to Love Canal, provides a means of developing responsible agents, and so the possibility of discharging our shared responsibilities through those developed collective agents. To the extent that we are able to be collectively responsible for environmental injustice, it is through these more formal institutions. If shared responsibilities for environmental injustice are ever to be matters of collective moral responsibility – matters of responsibility *of* a collective – the required collective agents will have to be entities capable of making changes to the institutional environment that makes structural injustice possible.

But any responsibility to generate collective agents appears to present a conundrum for the intuition that we have a collective responsibility for environmental justice. Without collective agency we cannot be collectively responsible in a backward directed sense. But then while we might have a shared responsibility to develop organizations or formal institutions capable of being collectively responsible, we cannot have a collective responsibility to do so, at least not without appealing to some other collective agent. Individuals are simply not the right sort of agents. On the other hand Jamieson's (2012) thought points to our causal impotence with respect to our institutional environment (see also Sinnott-Armstrong, 2005) and so to our seeming inability to be responsive to environmental injustices as individuals. In the face of such impotence we cannot be morally responsible for changes to that environment. In the next section we will explore an alternative that makes this conundrum less troubling.

34.5 Individual Responsibility for Enabling Collective Responsibilities

If collective moral agency is rarely found in cases of environmental injustice, where should we look for the distinctively moral dimension of our responsibility for environmental injustice? One way to begin to broach this question, following Young, is to ask how individuals contribute to the commission of environmental injustice. The programming account of collective responsibility points to an answer that connects individuals to collective responsibility. If we can effect change in the circumstances that engender environmental injustice by engaging with institutions, we have a prima facie responsibility to do so. We have these direct responsibilities. However, as is often the case, these direct responsibilities do not capture the breadth of our responsibilities. While our individual efforts may not have a significant effect on the reduction of wetlands, on strip mining, on overfishing, or on the institutional environment of Love Canal, the e-waste trade, and climate change, together we might well be able to act to support or generate policies that can have such an effect. In short, in addition to any direct responsibilities we have for our actions as individuals, we have a responsibility to contribute. As institutions constitute shared enterprises, shared means of coordination and cooperation that are affected by our efforts, they provide a means of influencing the conditions supportive of environmental injustice. But can the effort of a single individual to affect our institutional environment be sufficient to respond to the structural challenges of environmental injustice? Some might find this doubtful.

On one common line of thinking, if an individual action does not directly affect a harmful outcome, or is not otherwise independently prohibited or permitted, then that individual cannot have a responsibility not to perform that action (Sinott-Armstrong, 2005). However, I suggest this account of responsibility is much too limited (Shockley, 2016). In addition to such direct responsibilities we should think of our ability to bring about change in terms of the indirect effects we might have if we act through intermediaries, in this case, institutions. We can see this anticipated in Young's (2013, pp. 106–113; see also 2006) shift from thinking about responsibility as culpability to thinking in terms of our ability to influence our social environment. While individuals may have difficulty effecting change alone, they can leverage their shared responsibilities and coordinate efforts to influence their institutional environment through shared practices and expectations of one another. The contributory approach advocated here allows us to think of responsibility in terms of how we might positively alter the background conditions that support structural injustice, generally through our ability to influence institutions that mediate between our individual actions and those background conditions that program for structural change. The focus on the moral responsibility of individuals to make their contribution brings in an explicitly moral dimension, one that bears heavily on all those individuals who share responsibility in virtue of benefitting from an unjust institutional environment.

If we could do something to prevent harm and choose not to, this is a failure of moral responsibility: it may well constitute an action worthy of blame. As Chiara Cordelli argues, as individuals we have "prospective duties," that is,

> duties to (i) progressively acquire capacities those agents have never possessed that would enable them to perform beneficent actions in the future and (ii) either preventatively limit the personal costs for themselves of complying with the demands of beneficence in the future or anyway resolve to bear those costs when and if they arise.
>
> *(Cordelli, 2018, p. 275)*

I suggest that as we might well have duties to develop the required capacities at the individual level, so we have duties to develop the shared capacities at the collective level (see Wringe, 2014 for a similar point). Institutions provide the means of making structural changes, and so provide a means of enacting shared capacities. Formalizing these institutions into organizations or political institutions that can be collective agents – and, given the additional criteria noted above, morally responsible collective agents – provides a means of leveraging shared responsibility and institutional control to respond to structural injustice. The ability of the citizenry of Love Canal to organize, to develop an organization capable of collective action, provides a means of making changes in the institutional environment, and to counteract, to some extent, the environmental injustice inflicted upon them. The ability to organize gave them voice, and their organized voice "programmed" change in their institutional environment. Similarly, given our tacit involvement in the institutions that support e-waste traffic and climate change, we have a prospective, forward directed duty, one that may well involve blame if it is not suitably discharged, to develop the organizations and make the requisite changes in our institutional environment (Wringe, 2014). The ubiquity and capacity of institutions to address group-level concerns makes possible responses to injustices in our institutional environment, despite our seeming individual impotence and the lack of collective agents. And failing to so enact responses constitutes a failure to satisfy our collective responsibilities (Gardiner, 2017, p. 30ff).

But even if we cannot reasonably or practically develop collective agents, we might still be able to effect change in our institutional environment. Many of us bear contributory responsibility in cases where harm, or injustice, arises from structural problems in our social world (Shockley, 2016). In this indirect sense, then, we are responsible for environmental injustice. With the focus on contributory responsibility and the mediating role of institutions, there is a way of connecting the agency of individuals with a means of recourse for structural harms and other concerns to collective phenomena that are generally out of the conceptual or practical range of individuals. One way in which moral responsibility for environmental justice arises is through individual responsibilities to engage with those institutions (potential or actual) that provide a means of indirectly affecting the structural injustices at the center of environmental justice concerns. The place for moral responsibility in cases where there is no collective agent to bear moral culpability is with individuals who could contribute to the resolution of a response to those harms. Moreover, failing to have generated an institutional structure, say a political regime capable of responding to climate change, constitutes a shared responsibility, a backward directed shared responsibility. We can hold shared responsibilities for changes to our institutional environment that we should have made.

While we do not have unilateral control over these institutions, they do provide a means of accessing the conditions that generate environmental injustice, and together we can change them, reform them, and use them. If we acknowledge there is some capacity to make change, even if not certain or not under our direct control, we are prospectively responsible for making those changes we can. Indeed, this is one response to Jamieson's thought that we might ruin the world without anyone being morally responsible. *We* are responsible to pursue those options we are able to pursue, and for not having pursued the options that were available to us. And this is a moral responsibility, even if indirect, that complements our more direct moral responsibilities for what we have done and what we do. In many cases, climate change being a clear example, we may not be able to have much of an effect as individuals alone, but, we can have an effect on political institutions and other points of policy leverage.

34.6 Owning Up to our Collective Responsibility for Environmental Justice

In this chapter I have argued that moral responsibility for environmental justice is pressed upon us not merely at the level of the direct responsibilities we have for our individual actions, but also at the level of the contributory responsibilities we have to make changes in our institutional environment. Institutions are the means by which our individual moral responsibilities – spelled out in terms of our capacity to effect change in those structural injustices through our ability to manipulate institutions – are connected to our collective responsibilities – spelled out in terms of the explanatory ineliminability of institutions to resolve group-level, structural injustice. These responsibilities may require that we activate an existing institution or practice, or they may require that we organize or reform institutions that could respond to great environmental injustices. To satisfy forward directed shared responsibilities for responding to structural injustice, we may need to generate collectives, institutions, that are capable of being collectively morally responsible for those changes. If we need moral agency for backward directed responsibility, then we have a shared responsibility to develop those agents in cases where that responsibility is necessary for the prevention of gross injustice. We are responsible not only for failing to use existing institutions to address harms, we are responsible for forming, or failing to have formed, organizations and institutions capable of preventing or mitigating harm and injustice (Wringe, 2014). We need to take ownership of our normative world. We do this by sharing responsibility for our institutions, both those we have made and those we should have made, and using these institutions to program for structural change.

In this limited sense of collective responsibility is it fair to say environmental justice is a matter of collective responsibility? It would seem so. While the moral dimensions of our responsibilities are generally held by individuals, they are only expressed through collective enterprises: the causal connection to effecting change in environmental justice takes place through the capacity of our shared and coordinated activities to program for change in our institutional environment. How does the programming account help us satisfy the responsibility we have (as individuals) to take responsibility (as a group)? By providing a means of channeling our shared responsibilities into the institutions that program for injustice or justice. The causal conduit provided by institutions provides a way of bypassing the seeming causal impotence of individual moral agents in the face of structural injustice. It provides a way of explaining how together we can take control, even if only on occasion. While the moral weight of such responsibilities is held by the individuals who share the responsibility, the focus of the responsibility – what it is a responsibility *for* – is a matter of collective concern. While this should come as no surprise, it does point to the importance of relying on shared efforts and shared responsibilities to generate collective responses, particularly to generate responses that support policy initiatives and effect other changes to practices and cultural norms at the level of groups. As Eckersley reminded us, matters of structural injustice are matters of collective concern; they are group-level phenomena. Even if we do not have full blooded collective moral responsibility, the causal levers for making structural changes are often at the level of collectives, and are best approached through the controlling influence of groups whether loosely coordinated through institutions or more formally orchestrated through organizations. Moral responsibility in such cases falls on individuals not only through their individual actions, but also through their contributory responsibilities, often taking the form of shared responsibilities, to engage with or develop these institutions capable of responding to environmental injustice.

While this might seem just as fraught as claiming that we have individual responsibility for preventing large-scale harms – for it is difficult to see how one person can be obliged to do something that in most cases is beyond their capacity – we have made some progress. We have expanded the scope of responsibility beyond direct individual responsibility in a way that recognizes our role in our institutional environment, and the shared and collective effects of our actions. By focusing on the way aggregate actions might generate institutional change we provide a place for the voice of populations to make a difference in their institutional environment.

Sometimes this takes place through developing formal institutions sufficient to unify disparate voices into a single amplified voice, as in the development of citizens' groups in the case of Love Canal, or through the development of the Basel Convention. Such organizations and institutions provide a means of coordination sufficient to effect change, and the provision of voice sufficient to provide the recognition compromised by environmental injustice. To the extent we assist in these efforts, or provide for similar coordination and amplification of suppressed voices of vulnerable populations affected by climate change, the e-waste trade, and other environmental justice concerns, we have gone toward satisfying our prospective responsibilities for effecting changes in our institutional environment. We have a shared moral responsibility to develop the institutional changes necessary for responding to environmental injustice. As Young might have put it, we have a shared responsibility to take responsibility for the collective harms resulting from our institutions.

As institutions enable our collective response to harms, institutions provide the means by which we might discharge our responsibilities – individual, shared, or collective – for environmental justice. In this chapter we have seen that even in those cases where institutions capable of addressing environmental injustice do not yet exist, but reasonably could be generated, we have a shared responsibility to generate those entities capable of providing a collective response, whether as agents or merely as coordinating institutions. Through a focus on institutional reform, we are more able to focus on the conditions that generate that injustice, and thereby on the victims of injustice. Not only does this put the right focus on matters of environmental justice, it also makes apparent the moral responsibilities we have to make those changes we are able to make, to influence our collectives and take ownership of our collective responsibilities. The problem of environmental justice is not merely political or social or economic. It is moral.

Notes

1 But see List and Pettit, 2011, p. 156, and Neuhauser, 2014, for worries that the forward and backward looking distinction may be a bit misleading.
2 For an excellent summary, see Smiley, 2017.
3 We can see the seeds of one version of this account in List and Pettit (2011). This is anticipated by the programming account of mental causation in Jackson and Pettit (1990).

References

Agyeman, Julian. 2013. *Introducing Just Sustainabilities*. London: Zed Books.

Alternet. 2016. "7 Toxic Assaults on Communities of Color Besides Flint: The Dirty Racial Politics of Pollution" www.alternet.org/environment/7-toxic-assaults-communities-color-besides-flint-dirty-racial-politics-pollution accessed 23 July 2018.

Basel Action Network. 2002. *Exporting Harm: The High-Tech Trashing of Asia*. Seattle, WA: Basel Action Network.

Basel Action Network. 2005. *The Digital Dump: Exporting Re-use and Abuse to Africa*. Seattle, WA: Basel Action Network.

Basel Action Network. 2018. Thailand: Just the First Country to be Hit by the Coming Tidal Wave of Western Waste. http://myemail.constantcontact.com/Thailand--Just-the-First-Country-to-be-Hit-by-the-coming-Tidal-Wave-of-Western-Waste.html?soid=1114999858498&aid=23cw_EKHkN8, accessed 23 July 2018.

Basel Convention. 2018. Overview of the Basel Convention. www.basel.int/TheConvention/Overview/tabid/1271/Default.aspx, accessed 14 October 2018.

Bratman, Michael. 1999. *Faces of Intention: Selected Essays on Intention and Agency*, New York: Cambridge University Press.

Bratman, Michael. 2013. *Shared Agency: A Planning Theory of Acting Together*, Oxford: Oxford University Press.

Bullard, Robert D. 1990/2000. *Dumping in Dixie: Race, Class, and Environmental Quality*. Boulder, CO: Westview Press.

Bullard, Robert D. 1992. "Environmental blackmail in minority communities", in Bryant, Bunyan and Mohai, eds, *Race and the Incidence of Environmental Hazards: A Time For Discourse*. Boulder, CO: Westview Press, pp. 82–95.

Caney, Simon. 2014. "Two Kinds of Climate Justice: Avoiding Harm and Sharing Burdens." *Journal of Political Philosophy*, 22(2), 125–149.

Carmin, JoAnn, and Agyeman, J. (Eds.). 2011. *Environmental Inequalities Beyond Borders: Local Perspectives On Global Injustices*. Cambridge, MA: MIT Press.

Chant, Sara Rachel, Frank Hindriks, and Gerhard Preyer, eds. 2014. *From Individual to Collective Intentionality: New Essays*. New York: Oxford University Press.

Cordelli, Chiara. 2018. "Prospective Duties and the Demands of Beneficence." *Ethics* 128(2): 373–401.

Eckersley, Robyn. 2016. "Responsibility for Climate Change as a Structural Injustice", in Gabrielson, Hall, Meyer, and Schlosberg, eds, *The Oxford Handbook of Environmental Political Theory*, pp. 346–361.

Frasier, Nancy. 1998. "Social Justice in the Age of Identity Politics: Redistribution, Recognition, and Participation," in Peterson, ed, *The Tanner Lectures on Human Values* Vol 19. Salt Lake City, UT: University of Utah Press.

Frasier, Nancy. 2000. "Rethinking Recognition" in *New Left Review* 3 (May-June): 107–120.

Gardiner, Stephen. 2017. "Accepting Collective Responsibility for the Future," *Journal of Practical Ethics* 5 (1): 22–52.

Gilbert, Margaret. 2000. *Sociality and Responsibility*, Lanham, MD: Rowman & Littlefield.

Gilbert, Margaret. 2013. *Joint Commitment*, New York: Oxford University Press.

Guala, Francesco. 2016. *Understanding Institutions: The Science and Philosophy of Living Together*. Princeton, NJ: Princeton University Press.

Hayward, Tim. 2007. "Human Rights Versus Emissions Rights: Climate Justice and the Equitable Distribution of Ecological Space." *Ethics & International Affairs*, 21(4), 431–450.

Hindriks, Frank, and Francesco Guala. "Institutions, rules, and equilibria: a unified theory." *Journal of Institutional Economics* 11.3 (2015): 459–480.

Jackson, Frank, and Philip Pettit. 1990. "Program Explanation: A General Perspective." *Analysis*, 50(2): 107–117.

Jamieson, Dale. 2012. "Ethics, Public Policy, and Global Warming", in Thompson and Bendik-Keymer, eds, *Ethical Adaptation to Climate Change: Human Virtues of the Future*. Cambridge, MA, MIT Press, pp. 187–202.

Lepawsky, Josh. 2018. *Reassembling Rubbish: Worlding Electronic Waste*. Cambridge, MA: MIT Press.

List, Christian and Philip Pettit. 2011. *Group Agency: The Possibility, Design, and Status of Corporate Agents*. New York: Oxford University Press.

May, Larry. 1987. *The Morality of Groups*. Notre Dame, IN: University of Notre Dame Press.

May, Larry. 1992. *Sharing Responsibility*. Chicago: University of Chicago Press.

Neuhäuser, Christian. 2014. "Structural Injustice and the Distribution of Forward-Looking Responsibility." *Midwest Studies in Philosophy*, 38(1), 232–251.

Newman, Richard S. 2016. *Love Canal: A Toxic History from Colonial Times to the Present*. New York: Oxford University Press.

Pacific Standard, 2018. "The Growing Threat of Global Electronic Waste" https://psmag.com/environment/threat-of-global-ewaste, accessed 11 July 2018

Pearce, Fred. 2009. "Greenwash: Weee directive is a dreadful missed opportunity to clean up e- waste." *The Guardian*, www.theguardian.com/environment/2009/jun/25/greenwash-electronic-waste-directive, accessed 11 July 2018.

Pellow, David N. 2006. "Transnational Alliances and Global Politics: New Geographies of Urban Environmental Justice Struggles", in Heynen, Käika, and Swyngedouw, eds, *In the Nature of Cities: Urban Political Ecology and the Politics of Urban Metabolism*. New York, NY, Routledge, pp. 226–244.

Pettit, Philip. 1993. *The Common Mind: An Essay on Psychology, Society and Politics*, New York: Oxford University Press.

Pettit, Philip. 2003 "Groups with Minds of their Own", in Frederick Schmitt, ed., *Socializing Metaphysics*. New York, Rowman & Littlefield, pp. 167–193.

Pettit, Philip. 2007 "Responsibility, Incorporated." *Ethics* 117: 171–201.

Pettit, Philip and Frank Jackson. 1992. "Structural Explanation and Social Theory", in Charles and Lennon, eds, *Reduction, Explanation and Realism*. Oxford, Oxford University Press, pp. 97–131.

Rabinowicz, Wlodek. 2018. "Are Institutions Rules in Equilibrium? Comments on Guala's Understanding Institutions." *Philosophy of the Social Sciences*, DOI: 0048393118798643.
Schlosberg, David. 2007. *Defining Environmental Justice*. New York: Oxford University Press.
Schlosberg, David. 2012. "Climate Justice and Capabilities: A Framework For Adaptation Policy." *Ethics & International Affairs*, 26(4), 445–461.
Searle, John. 1995. *The Construction of Social Reality*. New York: Free Press.
Shockley, Kenneth. 2007. "Programming Collective Control." *Journal of Social Philosophy*, 38(3), 442–455.
Shockley, Kenneth. 2016. "Individual and Contributory Responsibility for Environmental Harm", in Thompson and Gardiner, eds, *The Oxford Handbook of Environmental Ethics*, pp. 265–275.
Shrader-Frechette, Kristin. 2002. *Environmental Justice: Creating Equality, Reclaiming Democracy* 2nd ed. New York: Oxford University Press.
Shue, Henry. 2014. *Climate Justice: Vulnerability and Protection*. New York: Oxford University Press.
Sinnott-Armstrong, Walter. 2005. "It's Not My Fault: Global Warming and Individual Moral Obligations", in Sinnott-Armstrong and Howarth, eds, *Perspectives on Climate Change: Science, Economics, Politics, Ethics*. Amsterdam: Elsevier, pp. 221–253.
Smiley, Marion. 2017. "Collective Responsibility," https://plato.stanford.edu/entries/collective-responsibility/ accessed 23 July 2018.
Tuomela, Raimo. 1989. "Actions By Collectives," *Philosophical Perspectives*, 3: 471–496.
Tuomela, Raimo. 2006. "Joint Intention, We-Mode and I-Mode," *Midwest Studies in Philosophy*, XXX: 35–58.
Tuomela, Raimo. 2013. *Social Ontology*, New York: Oxford University Press.
Velleman, J. David. 1997. "How to Share an Intention," *Philosophy and Phenomenological Research*, 57: 29–50.
Walker, Gordon. 2012. *Environmental Justice: Concepts, Evidence, and Politics*. New York: Routledge.
Wringe, Bill. (2014). "From Global Collective Obligations to Institutional Obligations." *Midwest Studies in Philosophy*, 38(1), 171–186.
Young, Iris Marion. 1990. *Justice and the Politics of Difference*. Princeton: Princeton University Press.
Young, Iris Marion. 2006. "Responsibility and Global Justice: A Social Connection Model," *Social Philosophy and Policy*, 23(1), 102–130.
Young, Iris Marion. 2013. *Responsibility for Justice*. New York: Oxford University Press.
Young, Oran R. 2016. *On Environmental Governance: Sustainability, Efficiency, and Equity*. New York: Routledge.

35
INSTITUTIONAL RACISM AND INDIVIDUAL RESPONSIBILITY

Michael O. Hardimon

35.1 Introduction

Sally Haslanger has suggested that the notion of institutional or structural racism is introduced to account for the possibility of forms of racial oppression (unjust racial hierarchy and inequality), carried out by social institutions, for which no individual is to blame, the underlying idea being that "the structures themselves, not individuals, are the problem" (Haslanger 2004: 107).[1] Surely there is something right about this. But does it entail that individuals are off the hook? Does the very idea of institutional racism require abandonment of the concept of individual responsibility? In what follows, I pursue this question. My primary concern throughout is with the implications of a structural conception of institutional racism for individual responsibility. At the end of this chapter, I will, however, briefly advert to an alternative, non-structural conception of institutional racism of the sort advocated by José Garcia, using it as a foil to sharpen our understanding of the relation between institutional racism generally and individual responsibility.

35.2 Fixing Ideas

Let me start by specifying what I regard as the form of institutional racism with respect to which the no-individual-is-to-blame thesis is most plausible. It is the kind of covert institutional racism that occurs when a social institution E whose policies are officially colorblind,[2] actually has a *covert* racist goal G (for example the perpetuation of racial hierarchy) and is organized in such a way that it promotes G through its normal operation, without any of its office holders having to share G or harbor racially objectionable attitudes.[3]

To clarify: E's policies count as *officially colorblind* in virtue of the fact that they are not overtly discriminatory and make no explicit reference to race. E counts as *intrinsically racist* in virtue of the fact that it has a racist goal and as *racially oppressive* in virtue of the combination of its purpose and effect: it aims at preserving racial inequality and contributes materially to the realization of this goal. E was founded or given its current shape at some point by a group of agents (the "founders") who were themselves racist and intended for E to have a racist goal and organized E so that it would actualize that goal. E's founders were aware of E's racist goal. E's current office holders are not aware that E has a racist goal.

G is *covert* in virtue of the following: (i) the founders did not publicly acknowledge that E has G or any racist goal; (ii) its current office holders do not know that it has a racist goal; (iii) its goals were and are represented as exclusively nonracist and benign. The proximal explanation of how E's officers are able to participate in its structures without admitting its racism is found in the covertness of its goals and the colorblindness of its policies. The underlying explanation can be found in the fact that E's normal operation depends on an ideology, specifically, the ideology of colorblindness.[4] This ideology consists in a normative and descriptive idea. The normative idea is that individuals and institutions *ought* to be colorblind, that is, not "see race" and see "just people" instead. The idea of "not seeing race" is that of not registering the racial categories to which individuals are assigned. The idea of seeing "just people" is that of viewing individuals as individuals rather than members of racial groups. The descriptive idea is that society *is* colorblind in the sense of being free of social structures that maintain racial stratification. The corollary of this idea is the notion that such racial inequalities as there are, are due to the voluntary choices or culture of individuals. It is ultimately because E's officers are in the grip of this ideology that they cannot see E's racism.

Goal G can be attributed to the *institution* E because (a) the institution was specifically founded or given the shape it has by its founders *in order to promote this goal* and because (b) it is organized in such a way as *to actually promote this goal* through its normal operation. E has this goal despite the circumstance that its current office holders fail to recognize this fact. E itself is best understood as a social artifact (something made by human activity as opposed to natural processes), one function of which is to promote the subordination of members of a particular racial group or groups.[5] This function is one that E is *designed* to have: E is intended to serve this function and was specifically made or modified to do so.[6] Just as agents can invest a physical object with a certain physical make-up (for example, a can opener) with a certain end (opening cans) that it continues to have after its manufacturer has left the scene, so too can agents invest a social object (for example, an institution) organized in a particular way with an end that it continues to have after its founders departure from the stage.

The fact that G is *E's* goal can be brought out most clearly by considering the special case in which E promotes G despite the fact that none of its officers share G or hold racist attitudes. Of course, the idea of a racist institution with no racist operatives is an idealization. In the real world, the pervasiveness of racial hostility and contempt is such that at least some of a racist institution's officer holders are virtually bound to harbor racist attitudes. The crucial point for our purposes, however, is that, although E's racist operation may be buttressed and even enhanced by the racist attitudes of its officers, the existence of these attitudes is incidental to the fact that E promotes G, since, by hypothesis, E is organized—structured—in such a way that it will actualize this goal whether or not any of its officers are themselves personally racist.[7] Because this form of institutional racism can promote racial inequality in the absence of personal racism on the part of office holders, it can be called *attitude-independent institutional racism* (*attitude-independent racism* for short). It is "structural" in that it is rooted in the purpose and organization of institutions that exhibit it in the ways we have just seen. It can, accordingly, also be called *structural institutional racism*.[8]

Two clarifications. First, it is not part of the idea of attitude-independent racism that institutions exhibiting it would (continue to) be racist and racially oppressive if all of their officers were anti-racist (Cf. Glasgow 2009: 73). Institutional racism that could survive in the face of officers "wholly committed to eliminating their racist institutions" could be called *attitude-invulnerable institutional racism* (Glasgow 2009: 73). But attitude-independence is not attitude invulnerability. To my knowledge, no theorist who conceives of institutional racism in structural terms thinks of it as attitude-invulnerable. Second, it is not part of the idea of an E-like institution that such an institution could actualize its malefic goal without being supported by racial indifference.[9] By and large, theorists who conceive of institutional racism in structural terms have not attended to the way in which this attitude might figure in the reproduction of racist structures.[10] Now with respect to attitude-independent racism, Haslanger's basic point is well-taken.

When institutions are E-like, the structures themselves *are* the problem. The fundamental explanation of their promotion of racist ends is found in the way in which they are organized, not the "bad attitudes" of their officers (Haslanger 2014). If we want to eliminate the racial inequality to which the institutions contribute, we should focus less on changing their office holders' "bad attitudes" and more on changing their structure. Blaming role occupants is simply a misallocation of political energy. So far so good. But Haslanger goes further. She suggests that, when institutions are racist, no individual is to blame (Haslanger 2004: 103). We are now in a position to examine whether this is true in the case of E-like institutions.

35.3 The Scope of the No-individual-is-to-blame Thesis

If the idea is that no individual is to blame for *establishing* E-like institutions or *first giving them their racist form*, it is quite implausible (Haslanger 2004: 104). It is certainly true that no *single* individual is to blame. Establishing an institution or giving an institution a particular form is invariably a collective act, requiring as it does a number of agents acting together in concert. A group of agents who establish a racist institution or make an already established institution racist richly deserves blame. And to the extent that the individuals belonging to such a group consciously and deliberately seek to establish a racist institution or make an already established institution racist, they are *individually* to blame. It is doubtful, however, that the *genesis* of racist institutions is what Haslanger had in mind in advancing the no-individual-is-to-blame thesis. It seems far more likely that her central concern was the *continuing operation* of already established E-like institutions.

When restricted to established E-like institutions' continuing operation, the no-individual-is-to-blame idea gets traction. It is certainly true that no one individual agent is uniquely responsible for the institution's continuing operation, since that too depends on multiple individuals acting together. Nor is it the case that the racist operation of E-like institutions can be explained by reference to the behavior of a few "bad apples" (a small number of individual office holders who behave in racist ways). By definition, E-like institutions promote racial inequality through their *normal* operation. They actualize their racist goals through the fact that their officers generally act in accord with their "standard operating procedures." Racial oppression is not the result of the violation of their norms; it is the result of observing them.

35.4 Pure Institutional Racism

Let's restrict our attention to the idealized case in which no officer of an established E-like racist institution harbors a racist attitude and in which, owing to ideology, none of its officers recognize that institutions they serve have racist goals or contribute materially to racial inequality. Call this *pure institutional racism*. In this special case, it does seem fair to say that no individual is blameworthy. It should be clear why this is so. The individual officers' racial attitudes do not deserve blame, since, by hypothesis, their attitudes are non-racist. Their ignorance of the goals and material effects of their institutions is due to ideology rather than negligence and hence, plausibly, non-culpable. Non-culpable ignorance is excusing. Since the officers do not aim at the institution's goal, they are not to blame for its material effects. So, in the case of pure institutional racism, it appears that the individual office holders *are* off the hook with respect to *blame*. But the story does not end here.

For one thing, it is not clear that ideology completely exonerates. Even when agents are subject to ideology, they may still be able to see, for example, the harmful effects of their institution's operation. Agents have a responsibility to reflect even when an ideology makes that difficult. And so individual office holders who are subject to ideology may be partly on the hook with respect to blame.

Another point. As Tommie Shelby notes "[t]o say that a person's conduct, an institution, or whole society is shaped by ideology is certainly a type of criticism. It is not however ordinary moral criticism like calling someone a liar, coward, or murderer" (Shelby 2014: 68). The claim that individuals are subject to ideology does not amount to the claim that they are morally at fault. It instead comes to the assertion that they suffer from "false consciousness."[11] False consciousness is a type of (aretaic) impairment. The assertion that individuals are subject to ideology is a type of criticism. To be subject to false consciousness is to be ideologically tainted.

Moreover, individuals who, owing to ideology, support E-like institutions are *on* the hook with respect to *wrongdoing*. Such individuals *enable* the institutions in which they participate *to actualize their malefic goals*. Their participation makes the operation of these institutions possible. Enabling institutions to actualize malefic goals is wrong. More precisely, it is *pro tanto* wrong. That is to say its badness might in principle be outweighed by other good things the officers do, working within their institution. (We are supposing that the institutions have benign as well as malefic goals.) But it is also to say that the wrong they do in participating in these institutions counts as wrong even in circumstances in which its badness is outweighed. Exculpation is not justification. The fact that they are exculpated (wholly or partially) by ideology for participating in E-like institutions does not mean that they are justified in participating in such institutions. Because individuals who carry out their roles within E-like institutions enable these institutions to actualize their malefic goals, they are *implicated* in racial oppression. That is, they are involved *by their own agency* in the malefic activity of the institutions in which they take part.

The fact that individuals who participate in E-like institutions are implicated in the wrongdoing of their institutions is illustrated by the fact that, should they come to understand their involvement in the furtherance of racial oppression, various "reactive" responses on their part may become appropriate.[12] One such response is regret. Guilt would not be appropriate because, for reasons given above, the officers are not morally at fault. The officers might of course "feel" guilty, but just as it would be inappropriate for us to blame them, so it would inappropriate for them to blame themselves. On the other hand, the subjective first-person thought that it would have been much better had she done otherwise, the "constitutive thought" of so-called "agent-regret," *is* fully appropriate for individuals in this position (Williams 1981). Think of it this way: people who together act in such a way as to enable racist institutions' subordination of particular racial groups are not *bystanders* to oppression. They are, quite literally, *agents of oppression*.[13] That is, they are the individual agents who carry out the oppression of the institutions of which they are a part. Note that one can say this *without* going so far as to characterize them as *oppressors* (Haslanger 2004: 102–103, Calhoun 1989). That epithet might be warranted if they acted in such a way as to compound the wrongdoing of intrinsically racist institutions, but we are supposing this is not the case. Other reactive responses might be appropriate, too. One would be to offer a sincere apology, to acknowledge the harm that they had done and the fact that they had wronged others. Still another response would be to atone for their wrongdoing. They might do so by engaging in antiracist activism.

The reflections in this section make clear that the fact that "the structures are the problem," does not entail that we cannot or ought not to ask about the responsibilities of individuals. Even after it has been determined that the structures are the problem, urgent questions remain about the responsibilities of the individuals who occupy them. *Pace* Haslanger (or how she might be read) the moral-political question concerning the responsibilities of individual participants within racist institutions is not nullified by the political question about the oppression wrought by E-like institutions. Nonetheless, Haslanger's claim that in the special case of pure institutional racism, the individuals occupying institutional roles are not to blame is basically right.[14]

35.5 E-like Institutions with Racist Role Occupants

We have been focusing on the special, idealized case of pure institutional racism in which all the individual office holders who participate in E-like institutions are free of racism. Let's take a moment to consider a situation in which the moral ledger of agents who participate in E-like institutions is not so pristine.

Suppose each of the individual officers in an E-like racist institution endorses or would endorse the institution's racist goal were they to become aware of it. Suppose that each of them approves or would approve of the material consequences of the institution's operation if they became aware of it. Suppose further that each is personally hostile to the racial group or groups that are disadvantaged by the institution's operation. Suppose, in other words, that each is personally racist.[15] Now, because the institution in which they participate is E-like, their personal racism does no heavy lifting: its racist operation does not depend upon their racism. Nonetheless, these individuals are blameworthy.[16] One thing for which they are to blame is their personal racism (assuming that agents are responsible for the racial attitudes they hold). Another thing for which they are likely to deserve blame is compounding the harm done by the institutions in which they participate. Their personal racism disposes them to perform actions that make things worse. Racist officers might, for example, augment the harm attaching to an intrinsically racist task by carrying it out enthusiastically, using a derogating tone of voice, or casting a hostile glance, etc. Unlike the nonracist individuals participating in E-like institutions we considered earlier, these individuals *can* be criticized as oppressors. And because each of them endorses or would endorse their institution's racist goal and approve or would approve of the effects of its operation, they can be blamed as individuals for enabling the institution to actualize its malefic goals. This form of institutional racism can be called *agent-supplemented institutional racism*. It consists in agents within E-like institutions supplementing, that is, adding to, the harm the structures of such institutions do.

Upshot. We have been focusing on E-like institutions, that is, social institutions that have a covert racist goal G and are organized in such a way that they actualize G their normal operation, on institutions that are structurally racist. What we have seen is that the fact that an institution is E-like does not entail that its officers are free from blame. The individual officers of such an institution may not be racist and consequently not blameworthy for racism. On the other hand, the individual officers of such an institution may be racist and deserve blame for their racism. The attitude-independent model of institutional racism on which racist institutions can promote racial inequality in the absence of personal racism on the part of office holders, does not absolve individuals of all responsibility.

35.6 Racism Without Racists?

Does the idea of a social institution that has and promotes a racist goal without any of its officers being racist imply that there can be racism without racists?[17] On the face of things, it does. Everything depends, however, upon how (individual) racism is understood.

Let's consider the case in which "racism" is understood to refer exclusively to *overt* racism (Anderson 2010: 47–48). Racism is "overt" when it is conscious and endorsed. To say that an attitude must be *conscious* to count as racist is to say that the person to whom a racist attitude or behavior is attributed must be *aware* of holding the particular attitude or engaging in the particular behavior in question. (It is not, however, to say that the person must be aware *that* her attitude is racist. A person may be aware of holding attitude A without recognizing that A is racist.) To say that that an attitude must be *endorsed* to count as racist is to say that the person to whom the attitude or behavior is attributed must *affirm* or *approve* the attitude or behavior in question. Attitude-independent racism can obtain without overt racists. Racism can exist without there being anyone who is to blame for racism that is overt. Making room for this point is one of the reasons for which the notion of institutional racism is introduced.

Let's now expand our understanding of "racism" to allow that racism consists not only of overt racism but also includes attitudes that are *covert*. Racism counts as "covert" if it is unconscious or unendorsed. This idea can be motivated by starting with the plausible thought that *racial antipathy* (race-based hatred and hostility) and *racial derogation* (treating members of racial groups as unworthy of the respect owed to human beings as such) are properly counted as racist.[18] It is certainly clear that these attitudes are racist when conscious and endorsed. But their content remains the same whether or not they are available to consciousness, whether or not they are endorsed. They appear to be inherently racist. Consequently, there is no reason to think these attitudes cease to be racist when they become unconscious, nor any reason to think they do not become racist until they are endorsed.[19] Unconscious and unendorsed racial antipathy and derogation, then, represent two forms of covert racism. Attitude-independent racism can obtain without there being covert antipathy or derogation racists. Racism can exist without there being anyone who is to blame for covert antipathy or derogation racism.

The understanding of "racism" just presented fixes the usual way in which the adage "racism without racists" is understood. But it is arguable that the term's scope extends beyond racial antipathy and derogation to include racial indifference.[20] To be *racially indifferent* to Rs is to be indifferent to the harm, suffering, or disadvantage Rs experience, simply because they are Rs (members of a particular racial group). It is characterized by the absence of good will toward members of a particular race. Call this *indifference racism*. One specific form of indifference racism is *indifference to racism*. Indifference to racism counts as a species of indifference racism because one cannot be indifferent to racism without being indifferent to the suffering it causes. Like antipathy and derogation racism, racial indifference is inherently racist. It counts as racism regardless of whether it is conscious and endorsed.

Once racial indifference is recognized as a genuine form of racism, the idea of racism without racists loses some of its luster. As indicated above, it is *not* part of the idea of attitude-independent racism that, in the absence of racial antipathy and derogation, such racism can obtain without being supported by some form of racial indifference. "Attitude-independent racism" turns out to be less attitude-independent than at first appeared. It *is* independent of racial antipathy and derogation, the sort of racist attitudes the original defenders of the idea of attitude-independent racism presumably had in mind. But it is not independent of racist attitudes altogether. Racist structures require racist attitudes of some sort: if not racial antipathy or derogation, then at least racial indifference.[21] Correspondingly there can be no rac*ism* without rac*ists* of some sort. Consequently, the scope of the no-one-is-to-blame thesis must be restricted. If attitude-independent racism obtains and no one is to blame for antipathy or derogation racism, someone is to blame for indifference racism.[22] Even when the "structures are the problem," individuals are on the hook for racism of some kind.

These reflections suggest that structures *and* attitudes both play an essential role in the causation and constitution of structural racial oppression. What Haslanger sees clearly is that racial oppression cannot be accounted for without looking at structures. What we have just seen is that racial oppression cannot be accounted for without also looking at attitudes.[23] In racial oppression structures and attitudes work together in tandem.

35.7 Institutional Racism of a Different Kind

We have been focusing on the specific form of institutional racism with respect to which the no-individual-is-to-blame thesis is most plausible, namely attitude-independent racism, and have just touched upon a way in which the thesis needs to be revised. Before closing, I would like to note that there is another conception of institutional racism with respect to which the no-individual-is-to-blame thesis clearly does not hold.

The specific conception I have in mind finds its inspiration in the writing of Jorgé Garcia (1996,1999, 2004). It holds that institutional racism can be exhibited by institutions that are not inherently racist but regularly operate in a racially discriminatory way, owing solely to the personal racism of their members. By hypothesis, the rules and criteria of such institutions are not overtly or covertly racial biased or discriminatory, but are regularly applied in racially biased and discriminatory ways by a significant number of their office holders. Such institutions—call them F-like—count as racist because they generally operate in a racist way.

Since this form of institutional racism is not found in the purpose or organization of the F-like institution but rather in the personal conduct of the individuals who occupy its roles, it might be called *extrinsic institutional racism*. It is wholly due to the personal racism of the occupants of the institution's roles.[24] Since this extrinsic form of institutional racism traces back to the attitudes of individuals, it can be called *attitude-based institutional racism* (*attitude-based racism* for short). It is "non-structural" in that it is not rooted in the organization of the institutions that exhibit it but is instead wholly dependent upon the personal racism of the individuals who inhabit it. And so, it can also be called *non-structural institutional racism*.[25]

A caveat. In calling non-structural institutional racism *non-structural*, I do not mean to suggest that the institutional structures of non-structurally racist institutions do not matter. Obviously, they do. Racist participants in F-like institutions use the institutional structures of those institutions to carry out racist acts. These institutions make it possible for racist individuals to actualize racist ends that individuals could not actualize on their own. "Non-structural institutional racism" should be heard as non-structural *institutional* racism. Institutional structures are essential constituents of racism of this type.

It is clear why the no-individual-is-to-blame thesis fails to hold with respect to attitude-*dependent* racism. By hypothesis, all the racism of an attitude-dependent racist institution traces back to the personal racism of its office holders. Some officers of such an institution may be free of racism, but necessarily a significant number of them are not. Those who are not, can be blamed for their personal racism and for contributing to the racism of the institution of which they are a part. Attitude-dependent racism is thus a kind of institutional racism for which individuals are necessarily on the hook. There can be no attitude-dependent racism without individual racists. Reflection on this case reinforces the point that individual responsibility is not eliminated by the idea of institutional racism as such.

Now the fact that the idea of attitude-dependent racism unambiguously incorporates the idea of individual responsibility might be thought to give it a huge leg up over the idea of attitude-independent racism, in which the place of individual responsibility is more difficult to see. But the clarity of its incorporation of individual responsibility is purchased at a very high price. For it utterly abandons the thought that institutional structures may themselves be a problem. Nor is this an accident. Garcia is hostile to this latter idea. This, indeed, is why Haslanger attributes to him the project of discrediting the idea of institutional racism as such (Haslanger 2004: 98); for, by "institutional racism" (which she prefers to call "structural oppression"), she means structural racism.

Inasmuch as Garcia is perfectly clear about wanting to account for institutional racism and explicitly takes issue with some who deny its possibility, there is some awkwardness in Haslanger's reading.[26] We can sidestep the disconnect by introducing a generic idea of institutional racism as the idea of racism that is perpetrated by institutions, or alternately, racism that can be said to "reside" in institutions. Thinking of institutional racism in this generic way has the advantage of allowing us to say that Haslanger and Garcia have two distinct *conceptions* of the same idea. Haslanger offers an attitude-independent structural conception of institutional racism. Garcia offers a conception of institutional racism that is attitude-dependent and non-structural.

On the face of things, it is theoretically possible that both kinds of institutional racism obtain. Some institutions might conceivably exhibit attitude-dependent racism and others might conceivably exhibit attitude-dependent institutional racism. The US medical system could arguably be said to exemplify attitude-dependent racism (Green et al. 2013) and the US criminal justice system could arguably be said to exemplify attitude-independent racism (Alexander 2010). Addressing the question Which of these two conceptions of institutional racism better accounts for racial oppression generally? would also take us beyond the scope of this chapter. But the hunch which initiated our inquiry is that the structural conception is the better candidate.

35.8 Conclusion

We started with Haslanger's provocative idea that there might be forms of racial oppression with respect to which "the structures themselves, not individuals, are the problem" (Haslanger 2004: 107) and asked whether this meant that individuals acting within racist institutions are always off the hook. The worry was that the very idea of institutional racism might force one to give up the concept of individual responsibility altogether. We have seen that it does not. Nor does the more specific idea of structural racism. Racist officers of attitude-independent E-like institutions can be held to account for their personal racism. Nonracist individuals who, owing to ideology, more or less blamelessly carry out the racist tasks of their roles in E-like institutions are still on the hook for enabling these institutions to actualize their malefic goals—for wrongdoing. Furthermore, if individual office holders of E-like institutions are not to blame for antipathy or derogation racism, it is very likely that they are to blame for indifference racism. The idea that structures are the problem, then, does not entail that individuals are altogether off the hook.

Garcia is certainly right that racist individuals who apply the rules and criteria of otherwise nonracist institutions in racially discriminatory ways deserve blame for doing so. The clarity with which his account brings this out is one of its virtues. But Garcia goes too far in emphasizing individual responsibility. He proceeds from the correct normative idea that individual racists can and ought to be held to account for their racism to the dubious explanatory proposition that the ultimate explanation of racial oppression lies in the "bad attitudes" of individuals.

The main point I have tried to make in this chapter is that one can recognize the role structures play in racial oppression without letting individuals off the hook. A secondary point is that one can recognize the moral or individual dimension of institutional racism without denying the role of structures. A tertiary point is that an adequate account of racial oppression must do justice to the way in which structures *and* attitudes figure in its explanation.

Appendix
A Taxonomy of Institutional Racism

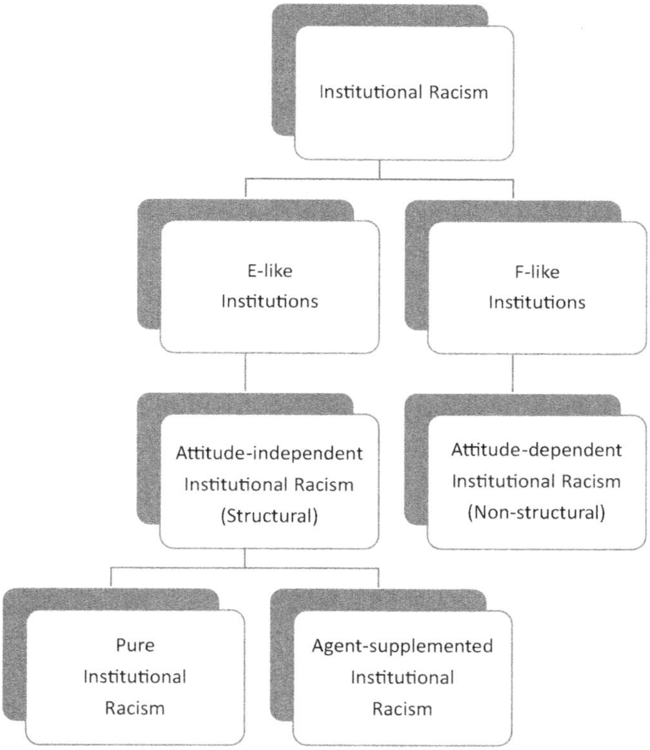

Acknowledgments

Thanks to Mary Devereaux and the editors Saba Bazargan-Forward and Deborah Perron Tollefsen for helpful comments.

Notes

1 There is no agreed-upon understanding of the terms "institutional racism," "structural racism," and "systematic racism." Sometimes they are used interchangeably. Sometimes they are used to pick out different concepts. I do not propose to settle here the question concerning how these terms ought to be used generally. For the purposes of this chapter, I have chosen to take "institutional racism" as my central term, adopting a generic conception of this idea that admits of a structural and non-structural interpretation.

2 I take the term "institution" to refer to both particular organizations (Bellevue) and systems of organizations (the US medical system).

3 This conception of institutional racism satisfies Garcia's requirement that, for an institution to count as racist, its racism must originate in the racism of the agents who first produced the institution or gave it its racist form (Garcia 1996: 12). It breaks with Garcia's apparent view that for an institution to count as racist at t_1, its roles must be occupied by individuals who are racist at t_1. I leave open the possibility that, in an already racist context, an institution might properly be counted as racist in virtue of its negative material consequences for members of a racial group, without having been instituted or given its current form for a racist purpose. In allowing for this possibility, I follow the suggestion of José Jorge Mendoza.

4 For the notion of ideology in general see Raymond Geuss's classic *The Idea of a Critical Theory*. For the idea of *colorblindness* as an ideology see Eduardo Bonilla-Silva's *Racism without Racists* and Michelle Alexander's *The New Jim Crow*.

5 Everything said in this chapter about "racial groups" can be reformulated in terms of "racialized groups" or "socialraces" and consequently should be acceptable to social constructionists about race. For the notion of a "racialized group" see Lawrence Blum *I'm not a Racist But...*. For the notion of a "socialrace" see Michael Hardimon *Rethinking Race*.

6 For a more detailed understanding of how this operation of investing an artifact with a function or purpose works see Kirk Ludwig, *From Plural to Institutional Agency: Collective Action Volume 2*: 104–108.

7 In saying that no E-like institutions' officers will be personally racist, I mean that none of them may exhibit "antipathy" or "derogation" racism, consciously or unconsciously. These forms of racism are discussed in section 35.6.

8 The expression "structural institutional racism" as I understand it is not pleonastic. It contrasts with "non-structural institutional racism" discussed below.

9 This idea is developed in section 35.6.

10 The obvious exception to this is Michelle Alexander (Alexander 2010: 203, 241–242).

11 On the notion of "false consciousness" see Geuss.

12 On the notion of "reactive" attitudes see P.F. Strawson.

13 The fact that institutional oppression is carried out by the agents who occupy institutional roles and the fact that, on Haslanger's view, institutions (structures) operate in agent-like ways, put pressure on her distinction between "structural oppression" and "agent oppression." What she calls "structural oppression" appears to be agent oppression of a kind, namely a form of oppression in which the agent is an institution. It is not part of my view that institutional oppression takes place without agents who carry it out. It can thus accommodate Garcia's correct idea that "oppression is not something that merely exists or happens, but is done and is therefore done by some agents" (Garcia 2004: 39 n.2).

14 I am not sure that there are in fact any cases of pure institutional racism. But I think the idea is interesting and needed for theoretical completeness and making the best possible sense of the no-individual-is-to-blame thesis.

15 I discuss what I mean by characterizing individuals as personally racist in footnote 7 and section 35.6.

16 To say that individuals are blameworthy is to say that they are deserving of blame. But from the fact that an individual is deserving of blame it does not follow that it is actually appropriate to blame him. Still less does it follow that blaming agents is an effective way of combatting structural racism. It may that some individuals who are blameworthy might be better addressed in a non-blaming way. The difficult pragmatic question of how best to address individuals who are racist falls outside the scope of this chapter.

17 The expression "racism without racists" is perhaps most closely associated with Eduardo Bonilla-Silva, owing to his eponymous book (Bonilla-Silva 2010). Garcia suggests that the idea may be originally due to Henry Louis Gates, Jr. (Garcia 1999: 2).

18 I borrow the notion of racial antipathy from Lawrence Blum. The notion of racial derogation derives from his notion of racial "inferiorization" (Blum 2002).

19 These attitudes are of course made morally worse when they are endorsed.

20 Garcia has been tireless in advocating the idea that racial indifference counts as a form of racism (Garcia 1996, 1999, 2004).

21 Racially indifferent individuals who are free of racial antipathy and contempt obviously do not deserve blame for racial antipathy or contempt. They do, however, deserve blame for indifference racism. Racial indifference is arguably less blameworthy than either racial antipathy or contempt but it *is* still morally blameworthy. Being off the hook for racial antipathy and contempt does not imply being off the hook for racism.

22 Michelle Alexander puts the point this way: "[R]acial caste systems do not require racial hostility or overt bigotry to thrive. They need only racial indifference, as Martin Luther King Jr. warned more than forty-five years ago" (Alexander 2010: 14).

23 I don't mean to suggest that Haslanger herself holds the positive view that racial oppression *can* be accounted for without looking at attitudes. But it is not clear that she recognizes that racial oppression *cannot* be accounted for without looking at attitudes. The remark she makes about wanting a "mixed approach" vis à vis what she calls "agent" and "structural" oppression suggests that she might be open to the mixed approach vis à vis structures and attitudes that I am recommending (Haslanger 2014: 107).

24 The idea of a form of institutional racism that is *wholly due* to the personal racism of the occupants of the institution's roles brings us to the threshold of an issue that would take us beyond the scope of the present chapter, namely, the question of the responsibilities that *institutions* may have. Do institutions have a responsibility to prevent their officers from behaving in a racist manner? Might a lack of institutional "will" to block racist behavior indicate the institutional analogue of individual indifference racism? Does this amount to a distinct form of institutional racism?

25 The expression "non-structural institutional oppression" is not an oxymoron. It goes with a generic conception of institutional racism that admits of both a structural and a non-structural subtype. This generic conception of institutional racism is introduced below.

26 Thus, for example, Garcia writes "My account of racism suggests a new understanding of racist behavior and its immorality. This view allows for the existence of both individual and institutional racism" (Garcia 1996: 10). Elsewhere he rebuts D'Souza's rejection of the term "institutional racism" as a "non-sense phrase," saying "If racism is a real element in people's thinking, feelings, and behavior, there is no reason to deny it can become institutionalized" (Garcia 1999: 6).

References

Alexander, M. (2010) *The New Jim Crow: Mass Incarceration in the Age of Colorblindness*, New York: The New Press.

Anderson, E. (2010) *The Imperative of Integration*, Princeton: Princeton University Press.

Blum, L. (2002) *I'm Not a Racist, But... The Moral Quandary of Race*, Ithaca: Cornell University Press.

Bonilla-Silva, E. (2010) *Racism without Racists*, 3rd ed., Plymouth: Rowman & Littlefield.

Calhoun, C. (1989) "Responsibility and Reproach," *Ethics* 99, no. 2: 389–406.

Garcia, J. (1996) "Heart of Racism," *Journal of Social Philosophy*, 27, no. 1: 5–45.

Garcia, J. (1999) "Philosophical Analysis and the Moral Concept of Racism," *Philosophy and Social Criticism*, 25, no. 5: 1–32.

Garcia, J. (2004) "Three Sites for Racism: Social Structures, Valuing, and Vice" in (Levine, M.P and Pataki, Tamas) *Racism in Mind*, Ithaca: Cornell: 35–55.

Geuss, R. (1981) *The Idea of a Critical Theory*, Cambridge: Cambridge University Press.

Glasgow, J. (2009) "Racism as Disrespect," *Ethics*, 120, no. 1: 64–93.

Green, A. et al. (2013) "Implicit Bias among Physicians and its Prediction of Thrombolysis Decisions for Black and White Patients" in (LaVeist, T. and Isaac, L.) *Race, Ethnicity, and Health: A Public Health Reader* 2nd ed. San Francisco: Jossey-Bass.

Hardimon, M. (1994) "Role Obligations," *Journal of Philosophy*, 91, no. 7: 333–363.

Hardimon, M. (2017) *Rethinking Race: The Case for Deflationary Realism*, Cambridge: Harvard University Press.

Hardimon, M. (2019) "Should We Narrow The Scope of 'Racism' to Accommodate White Sensitivities?" *Critical Philosophy of Race*, 7 no. 2: 223–246.

Haslanger, S. (2004) "Oppressions: Racial and Other," in (Levine, M.P. and Pataki, Tamas) *Racism in Mind*, Ithaca: Cornell.

Haslanger, S. (2014) "Social Structure, Narrative, and Implicit Bias" Unpublished handout.

Ludwig, K. (2017) *From Plural to Institutional Agency: Collective Action Volume 2*, Oxford: Oxford University Press.
Shelby, T. (2014) "Racism, Moralism, and Social Criticism," *Du Bois Review* 11, no.1: 57–74.
Strawson, P. (1962) "Freedom and Resentment," *Proceedings of the British Academy*, 48: 1–25.
Williams, B. (1981) *Moral Luck*, Cambridge: Cambridge University Press.

INDEX

Note: Figures and tables are denoted by *italic* and bold text respectively, and notes by "n" and the number of the note after the page number e.g., 270n17 refers to note number 17 on page 270.

Taylor & Francis Group
an informa business

Taylor & Francis eBooks

www.taylorfrancis.com

A single destination for eBooks from Taylor & Francis with increased functionality and an improved user experience to meet the needs of our customers.

90,000+ eBooks of award-winning academic content in Humanities, Social Science, Science, Technology, Engineering, and Medical written by a global network of editors and authors.

TAYLOR & FRANCIS EBOOKS OFFERS:

- A streamlined experience for our library customers
- A single point of discovery for all of our eBook content
- Improved search and discovery of content at both book and chapter level

REQUEST A FREE TRIAL

support@taylorfrancis.com

Routledge
Taylor & Francis Group

CRC Press
Taylor & Francis Group

Printed in Great Britain
by Amazon

80608375R00305